American Military Policy

Its Development Since 1775

AMERICAN MILITARY POLICY

Its Development Since 1775

C. Joseph Bernardo, Major Ordnance Corps

and

Eugene H. Bacon, Ph. D.

THE MILITARY SERVICE DIVISION

THE STACKPOLE COMPANY

HARRISBURG, PENNSYLVANIA

To Lillian and Linda Ann

Preface

AMERICANS have inherited their military policies from their ancestors, and even our Colonial forefathers brought the roots of some of these from Europe. Among the more prominent ideas concerning things military which originated in earliest days are the hatred of standing armies, especially in peacetime, the revulsion against conscription, and the firm resolve to keep the military always subservient to civil authority. These beliefs, which at the very outset crystallized into definite policies, have either persisted through various national vicissitudes or have been revived with each successive emergency.

Some military policies have been modified gradually with the realization that they do not always contribute to the national welfare. Others remain virtually unchanged, even where demonstrably unwise. In their long-range planning today's military leadership has learned to take into account over all national policy. More than ever before, the military have a clear realization that logistics and strategy cannot be separated from political, social, and economic considerations.

This book traces the development of military policy at political level, since the birth of the nation. The treatment is chronological, but there has been no attempt to present a complete and detailed military history of the United States. It has not been our purpose to analyze campaigns, but to point out that results on the battlefield are largely determined by what prior governmental policy has provided in manpower and weapons.

In a one-volume work it is impossible to cover fully all the elements of military policy which constitute the whole, but it is believed that readers who desire further light on these topics will find ample references in the text. Military government, the school system, and other phases of military policy have been treated less fully than the authors would desire. Furthermore the latest developments in military policy cannot yet be discussed exhaustively, for security and other reasons. This must be left for the future.

A work of this nature requires many helping hands and generous friends. Those who have assisted us with aid, encouragement, and advice, but who can in no way be held responsible for any errors or omissions, include the Dean of Georgetown College, Reverend Brian A. McGrath, S. J., Reverend John M. Daley, S. J., Dean of the Graduate School, Georgetown University, Professor Tibor Kerekes, and Professor Charles C. Tansill.

Our grateful thanks are extended also to the Dean of the College of Special and Continuation Studies of Maryland University, Colonel Joseph R. Ambrose, Colonel James Reagan, Jr., and Lieut. Col. Louis J. Ciccoli, the Dean and Assistant Deans of the Military Science Department of the University of Maryland and the staff of the Library of the University of Maryland. The helpful aid of the staff of Riggs Library, Georgetown University, and the Army Library, the National War College Library, the Manuscript Division of the Library of Congress, National Archives, and the Navy Department Library deserve more than just these few words of inadequate thanks.

Special thanks are also due to Miss Mary L. Brown and her staff of the Judge Advocate General's Library, Department of the Army, and Colonel Willard Webb, Library of Congress, Mrs. Emily M. Jahn, Lieutenant Colonel Burdette W. Erickson, Dr. Rocco M. Paone, John Carroll, Anthony Kubeck, Lieutenant Colonel Harold Cone, Lieut. Col. Joseph F. Phillips, and Lieut. Colonel William H. Zierdt, Jr. along with the many other officers and civilians of the Department of Defense whose valuable assistance and encouraging remarks have contributed to the final production of this volume. And finally to our wives, Mildred and Jean, whose abiding devotion and personal sacrifice rendered this arduous task less difficult.

C.J.B.
E.H.B.

Table of Contents

CHAPTER 1

The Revolution: Origins of American Military Policy

Colonial Roots of Military Policy—Fear of Standing Armies—Faulty Manpower Policies—Birth of Naval Policy—Sectional Interests Weaken Military Policy—Martial Spirit Needs Coaxing—Menacing Shadow of Weak Executive—Policy of Voluntary Enlistment Fails—Congress Struggles to Reorganize the Army—National Economy Endangered by Faulty Military Policy—Personnel Policies at End of War—Lessons

Colonial Roots of Military Policy

AMERICAN military policy emerged from the crucible of the Revolution. Some features of it, however, originated even earlier, and may be a heritage of European ancestry. Among the most prominent are an aversion to standing armies, with a consequent effort to rely almost wholly on militia, and a persistent fear that the military might subvert civil authority. Another, and somewhat more obscure facet of American military history, which may have had its beginnings in colonial days and has grown steadily in potency, is the awareness on the part of the Nation's leadership of the latent strength of the country in manpower and other resources. This has induced political leadership to embark in war with surprising confidence.

For example, contrary to the popular belief that the American colonists in 1775 faced an almost hopeless task when they decided to settle the issue in a clash of arms with the might of Britain, there were a number of factors which actually placed the British in the role of the underdog. From a military point of view perhaps the most significant of these was the fact that the colonies possessed a relatively large reservoir of partially trained manpower, a nucleus of experienced officers, and a considerable ability to produce arms, ammunition, and other materials of war. The degree to which this influenced the colonies toward open, organized rebellion cannot

1

be accurately assessed, but it undoubtedly influenced the formulation of early military policy.

In 1775 the British commander at Boston, General Thomas Gage, remained supinely in winter quarters awaiting the arrival of reinforcements and spring to release him from the state of virtual siege in which he had been held by the colonial militiamen. What Gage overlooked was the tremendous resources in manpower that America could count upon; and he, as well as his superiors in London, neglected to attach much significance to Baron De Kalb's report on the militia of the colonies. According to De Kalb's estimate the number was conservatively placed at 200,000 men,[1] and while largely untrained in the art of modern warfare, they did possess a working knowledge of small arms. These men, mostly old soldiers, were known, listed, and assigned to units; and the machinery existed, frequently tested, for calling them out.[2] While their training was defective from the viewpoint of existing European practice, tactical measures against surprise attacks and forest warfare had been perfected since the days of John Smith and Miles Standish.

Although the Americans themselves were generally willing to admit that their militia organizations could not compare with those of their British cousins, Englishmen were prone to exaggerate the proportionate difference. Furthermore it was generally felt in England that American militiamen were no match for British regulars. Few could dispute this claim. But what about the leadership which is a necessary element in any army? Little regard, it seems, was in evidence in Europe for American generalship which had demonstrated itself during the late war with France. Twelve general officers of the Revolutionary War had seen service in the French and Indian War.[3] In addition to all this, individual Americans had proved their mettle under such leadership on more than one occasion. These resources were not easily to be discounted even by proud Britons. And if they were, a healthy respect was soon to be acquired for the pastoral riflemen on Bunker Hill.

Nor could the lack of powder magazines and arsenals be

---

[1] Oliver L. Spaulding, *The United States Army in War and Peace,* New York, G. P. Putnam's Sons, 1937, pp. 24-25.

[2] Spencer Meade, "The First American Soldier," *Journal of American History.* Vol. I, 1907, pp. 122-123.

[3] Spaulding, *op. cit.,* p. 25.

charged as a disadvantage for the patriot cause. Inferiority in artillery weapons was nullified to a large degree by the seizure of many cannon from the weakly garrisoned coast forts, and by the bold exploits of American privateers. Small arms and powder, metals and saltpeter were plentiful; and the numerous navigable rivers and the rich agricultural land provided a reservoir of abundance that could permit the assembling and subsisting of large bodies of troops. Compared with these, British troops were few and widely scattered on the eve of the war; and while England could check the Americans with a naval superiority, she could be checkmated by the tremendous facilities in the hands of the patriots for building and manning ships.[4] If all this were not enough to impress the British with the futility of attempting armed coercion, every problem of logistics, recruiting, and even of strategy that plagued the American commander in chief had to be multiplied (in the British column) by the distance separating the two continents. Britons proved to be poor students of simple arithmetic.

The decision of the British General Gage, to capture the military stores at Concord gave rise to a spontaneous call to arms implemented by dispatch riders throughout New England and to New York spreading the news of the coming of the British. The men who drew up on Lexington Green on April 19, 1775 in answer to this summons were farmers who knew little of military discipline, but they did know how to make the most of the terrain upon which they chose to fight, and when the bloodshed had ended, they had proved their point with callous effectiveness. There was little left for the small British force but to withdraw to Boston for a much needed breather.

When the news of this engagement reached the southern colonies and the western frontier settlements, the cause of America suddenly crystallized into a national crusade. All were now unanimous, the Tories excepted, in the opinion that British tyranny in any form could no longer be tolerated this side of the Atlantic; and although the men beyond the Hudson River felt little compunction for sending their militia immediately to the aid of Boston, there was no dearth of spirit. Arms were quickly collected, outgoing ships were seized, and men organized for the fight.

The swiftness with which an army was gathered around Boston

---

[4] *Ibid.*, pp. 24-25.

was due chiefly to the efforts of Massachusetts. Some weeks before Lexington, her leaders had taken steps to invite the neighboring New England colonies to join in a proposed Army of Observation; and, when Gage struck, chosen delegates were already out on their missions. As early as December, 1774, Rhode Island, acting in accord with the Massachusetts proposal, had made preparations to reorganize her small militia force by amending the old laws to distribute public arms and cannon, seized from Fort George at Newport, and for the dispatch of her militia to the aid of any of the sister colonies. Later in the same month New Hampshire also seized her share of guns and cannon from Fort William and Mary at Portsmouth, and made preparations to qualify her militia for any ordeal. In Connecticut the militia was both well equipped and well trained and stood ready to march to the defense of the Bay State.[5]

Recognizing the necessity for efficient organization and coordination, Massachusetts assumed responsibility for the forces gathering around Boston and selected the general officers to command.[6] On April 23 the provincial legislature proposed raising an army of 30,000 men to be drawn principally from these forces. Of this total, they assigned themselves a quota of 13,400, the rest to be recruited from the other colonies.[7] To encourage recruiting, the Massachusetts Committee of Safety offered the commission of captain to any man who could bring 56 men into camp, and higher grades in similar proportions. While this new army was slowly being recruited to serve for eight months, the men who had held the lines since April 19, and who refused to enlist, began to make their way back home. Thus the minutemen, or irregulars, who had been part of the colonial militia system for over a hundred years, faded out of the picture, giving place to the regular enlisted militia and the Continental Army.[8]

By the middle of May, when the hoped-for enthusiastic enlistment of thousands of men failed to materialize, the Massachusetts

---

[5] Allen French, *The First Year of the American Revolution*, Boston, Houghton, Mifflin Co., 1934, pp. 42-45.

[6] These were Artemas Ward, Jediah Preble, Seth Pomeroy, John Thomas. William Heath, and John Whitcomb.

[7] French, *op. cit.*, p. 61.

[8] The minute man organization was looked upon as the first line of defense to hold the lines until the other civilian components could be brought into the field. This mission passed on to the Regular Army with the adoption of the Continental Army on June 14, 1775.

Provincial Assembly began to grow apprehensive in the face of the tremendous responsibility they had so suddenly inherited. The appeal to a stronger executive power to carry forward the burdens of organizing and supporting this army could no longer be postponed by the Bay State leaders. Traditionally fearful that a powerful military might overshadow the civil authority, reluctant to bear the cause of America alone, and finally admitting the need for a more energetic conduct of military affairs, the Massachusetts Congress on May 16 appealed to the Second Continental Congress which had been assembled in Philadelphia since the 10th.

This appeal was prompted more by the fear that Massachusetts could exert little control over a force recruited from other colonies than by a desire to surrender authority to some national body empowered to do the will of thirteen united colonies. In this narrow outlook, the Bay Colony willingly accepted what was considered a lesser evil rather than gamble on the eventuality of a military force which owed obedience to no other authority than the individual colony each component represented. Haunted by their own petty provincialism, the Massachusetts Congress appealed to the Continental Congress for advice; and, since this army was for the general defense of all the colonies, "we suggest your taking the regulation and general direction of it."[9]

Three days later, May 19, the Continental Congress assumed full responsibility and General Artemas Ward was commissioned to command under this new jurisdiction. On the same day the activation of entire regiments was undertaken;[10] but because recruiting was slow, they were under strength, and the 30,000 man army remained merely a future quantity. Meanwhile, most of the men in the field were wending their way home. Since the British were not fighting, there was no immediate danger, hence no need for them to longer absent themselves from their hearthstones. Furthermore the fields were in need of attention.

This condition gave rise to much apprehension on the part of the leaders who were not slow to realize that, despite an apparent victory over the British, they had no army. Around Boston swarmed an unorganized and undisciplined force, its regiments im-

[9] French, *op. cit.*, p. 66.
[10] Field rank was bestowed on the basis of the number of companies a man could recruit. This unique method of recruiting and commissioning officers was a practice of long duration.

complete and its companies varying in size; but here, they were sure, was the core of a real force. The weeding-out process was deliberate and painful. The militia had to be sent home to be called out again and again as the need arose; and the minutemen as a body disappeared principally because they had no legal standing.[11] Those who remained did so on a voluntary basis, it being difficult to enlist men who already were registered as militiamen in the various colonies, without incurring the displeasure of those colonies.

These legal obstacles in the path of enlisting an army from the militia, together with all the problems of recruiting and supplies, were inherited by George Washington when he arrived on the scene on July 2. But what was very important he assumed the command of a body of troops that had shattered the legend of the invincibility of British regulars.

Fear of Standing Armies

Among the first acts to engage the attention of the Second Continental Congress assembled in Philadelphia was the selection of a commander in chief for the armies to be integrated with the heterogeneous force collected before Boston. After affirming the right of each colony to self-government, the provisional government was named the United Colonies with leadership vested in a President. As the visible head of government, the Congress began to act with the authority of law enforced by the revolutionary committees of the colonies. On June 15, George Washington was selected as commander in chief of the armies largely because of the impression he had made upon John Adams as a delegate to the first Continental Congress in 1774.[12]

That this was a happy choice the episodes of the war bear ade-

---

[11] On December 14, 1775, Connecticut enacted a law setting aside a fourth part of the militia of that state enlisted for one year on a voluntary basis "to stand in readiness as minute men for the defense of this, and the rest of the United Colonies." See Connecticut, *General Assembly Session Laws, December Session,* December 14, 1775. See also Rhode Island, *Journals, Minutes Proceedings of the Upper House, January Sessions,* 1776, January 13, 1776, No. 51; January 15, 1776, No. 88.

[12] Although there were several generals (Philip Schuyler, Horatio Gates, and Charles Lee) with more experience in the command of large bodies of troops, Washington was selected at the instance of John Adams for the effect this would have upon the South in the war effort. See French, *op. cit.,* p. 284. Cf. Thomas G. Frothingham, *Washington, commander-in-chief,* Boston, Houghton Mifflin Co., 1930, *passim.*

quate testimony. That it attests to the wisdom of those who made the selection, the judicious use by Washington of the power thrust into his hands, to uphold and insure American liberties is sufficient evidence. The supremacy of civil authority is the rich heritage Washington bequeathed to posterity; future generations of military heroes were to emulate this example with the inherited wisdom of the patriots who lived and died for freedom. But in spite of these manifestations of sincere devotion to duty, the fiction has continued to grow in the minds of most Americans that a strong military organization constitutes a danger to liberty, and that the only safeguard against such a threat is to render such an entity impotent, even if this means exposing the nation to the mercy of powerful neighbors.

In 1775 this aversion to the military was enhanced by British insistence on quartering large bodies of troops in American cities before the outbreak of the war; and, while New England patriots seized upon such a vivid example of tyranny as material for choice propaganda, the effects upon the public mind lingered long after the war had ended. Congress, in giving expression to the will of the States, insisted upon civil control of the military at all times. This was made clear on October 14, 1774, when the First Continental Congress announced that standing armies within the colonies "in times of peace without the consent of that colony in which such an army is kept, is against the law.[13] This was reaffirmed in June, 1776, when a Board of War comprising six civilians[14] was organized by Congress, and re-emphasized one month later in the Virginia Bill of Rights by the declaration that "standing armies in time of peace should be avoided as dangerous to liberty; and that in all cases the military should be under strict subordination to, and governed by, the civil power."[15] These proclamations of civil supremacy were religiously supported by the Commander in Chief, who made it clear that he would carry out the will of the Congress even if it ran contrary to the dictates of his own reason.

Whatever power the Continental Congress presumed to exercise with reference to military affairs was neutralized by the in-

---

[13] Henry S. Commager, *Documents of American History*, New York, F. S. Croft & Co., 1947, p. 83.

[14] This board assumed the functions of a War Department and continued in that capacity until a Secretary of War was selected.

[15] Commager, *op. cit.*, p. 104.

sistence of the separate states on retaining the right to raise revenue and to levy taxes. In this contingency, resort was had to the emission of bills of credit, the redemption of which was pledged not by the Congress, but by the United Colonies. Not only was the ensuing military legislation seriously handicapped by these restrictions, but it was made to depend largely upon the combined understanding of a body of citizens who in their individual experience were totally ignorant of military affairs. In this limited capacity the Congress was called upon to direct the war effort. On June 14, 1775, it authorized a regiment of 10 companies of riflemen to be recruited from Pennsylvania, Virginia, and Maryland for a period of one year. Thus began the system of short enlistments which was to prolong the war; but this measure also established the Continental Army.[16]

Three days after this momentous decision, the Battle of Bunker Hill occurred, making its imprint indelibly upon the thinking of Americans of that generation and laying the basis for the military philosophy of future generations. This seemed to be the proof necessary to convince Americans that standing armies were unnecesary, for here on that June afternoon untrained men engaged British regulars and won a bloody moral victory. Few were willing to heed warning, however, that the men who fought on Breed's Hill[17] could not have proved their valor without the leadership of trained officers, standing shoulder to shoulder with them, instructing them, encouraging them, and directing their fire for maximum effectiveness. The redoubts, behind which the pastoral militia gained a measure of comfort and safety, were built under the direction of Colonel Richard Gridley, a trained Engineer officer; and while history cannot deny the courage and fortitude of those militamen who fought there, it has failed to accord recognition for the part played in the accomplishments of the day to the ability of the officers who supervised the erection of the defenses on Breed's Hill.

Filled with an overweening confidence in themselves over the outcome of the battle, the patriots gave free rein to their enthusiasm. All signs of discipline soon disappeared while they waited for the British to give battle once more. Added to this was the con-

---

[16] This force, together with the 17,000 men blockading Boston, became known as the Continental Army in contrast to the Ministerial Army.
[17] The Battle was really fought on Breed's Hill.

fusion attending the appearance of increasing numbers of minute-men and militia from up-country and the seacoast towns of the New England colonies who came under the independent orders of those provincial legislatures.[18] When Washington finally arrived on the scene some three weeks later, his trained eyes saw not a military encampment, but an undisciplined mob respecting no other authority than the officers whom they had elected, and who in turn were restrained in their prerogatives by the electors. In the face of such an unmilitary situation, the Virginia farmer assumed formal command of the Army on July 3.

On the following day a general order was issued to the Army which at once placed everything upon a new basis and put an end to the divided command that existed in camp:

> The Continental Congress having now taken all the Troops of the several Colonies, which have been raised, or which may be hereafter raised for the support and defense of the Liberties of America, into their pay and service, they are now the Troops of the United Provinces of North America; and it is hoped that all Distinctions of Colonies will be laid aside; so that one and the same spirit may animate the whole, and the only Contest be, who shall render, on this great and trying occasion, the most essential service to the Great and common cause in which we are all engaged.[19]

This meant a complete reorganization of the armed forces in the face of an enemy who might attack at any moment—a dangerous undertaking even under the most favorable circumstances—but here, with little discipline, order, or even government among the troops, it seemed suicidal. But it had to be done regardless of the hazard.

Washington at once proceeded to organize the Army into three grand divisions with Major General Artemas Ward commanding

---

[18] By this time open criticism of Artemas Ward was rife; although Connecticut agreed to place her troops under his command, Rhode Island refused to surrender her authority until George Washington was selected to command. See French, *op. cit.*, p. 86.

[19] John C. Fitzpatrick, (ed) *The Writings of George Washington*, Washington, Government Printing Office, 1934, Vol. 3, p. 309. Hereafter cited as *W.W.* On August 11, the Massachusetts Assembly reaffirmed its *Resolve to* place its army under Continental authority. See Massachusetts, *Records of the Great and General Court or Assembly for the Colony of Massachusetts Bay, July Session,* 1775, August 11, 1775, p. 77. Rhode Island voted in the same manner on June 29, 1775, See Rhode Island *Journals and Minutes and Proceedings, June Session,* 1775, No. 5.

the right wing at Roxbury, Major General Charles Lee in command of the left, and Major General Israel Putnam in the center. By this, Washington eliminated the separate groupings, while the troops of each colony were held together as much as possible. In the matter of commissions for field officers, however, he was allowed little discretion, and as he was unable to reward officers for meritorious conduct, Congressional appointees often proved more embarrassing than welcome to him. There was little denying that Congress was going to control this army as much as possible.

Although Congress recognized the necessity for assuming control, they failed to make the Army a permanent organization. This oversight was the result of a general feeling that the war would not be of long duration; that a reconciliation with Great Britain could be expected hourly; and a fear that an army of long-term volunteers might be transformed into a standing army which could destroy its progenitors.[20] These reasons were of sufficient moment to limit enlistments to the end of the year. The question could, however, be debated here. It might well be asked whether the conservative element in the Revolution were not more fearful of the patriots who had demonstrated but little regard for the rights and property of their own numbers during the struggle over taxation since 1763. Was it the fear of the conservatives who lived in constant dread of the explosiveness of the more liberal elements that gave wide currency to the fears of a standing army? John Adams gives some evidence of this feeling in declaring that only "the meanest, idlest, most intemperate and worthless . . . would enlist in the army for the duration of the war."

Faulty Manpower Policies

Beginning with Washington, commanders of the Army have been handicapped by faulty policies at national political level, particularly with respect to procurement of manpower for military purposes. In addition to the deep-rooted aversion to a regular army, previously discussed, there has existed at governmental level, from the very beginning, a fondness for instituting short terms of service, even in war time. Although based in part on humanitarian motives, and nearly always on political expediency, this policy has on several occasions brought the nation to the brink of disaster.

---

[20]John C. Miller, *The Triumph of Freedom*, Boston, Little Brown & Co. 1948, p. 81. Hereafter cited as Miller, *Triumph*.

Furthermore it has been in part responsible for excessive war costs in manpower and money.

The open display of prejudice against the Army in 1776 was not lost to the sight of Washington who, hopeful that idealism and patriotism would suffice to induce men to the call of arms, acquiesced in the Congressional policy of short enlistments and opposition to bounties. But, seeing his army melt away as the terms of the men expired on December 31, 1775, the Commander in Chief began to search for means other than patriotism as an inducement to keep men in the ranks.

Unfortunately the soldiers would serve according to the letter of their contract and no more; when their time was up they would go home, leaving it up to others to fill their places. This was the system that would prevail at the termination of each enlistment period unless Congress extended the term of service. But Congress was in no position to reckon with reality. Their power limited by the will of the States, they could do little more than pass resolutions which did not carry the authority of law, while the fluctuating character of the American Army was prolonged indefinitely. Despite the earnest appeals of Washington urging the men to remain at their posts, each expiration period witnessed whole regiments returning home.

With a hostile army only a few miles distant, Washington gloomily observed the first of these ominous episodes on the last day of the year. If it had not been for the New England militia and the few remnants of the minutemen who hastened in to fill the depleted ranks, he would have been left virtually alone; and his disillusionment was not diminished by the sight of the irregular levies who, for the most part, were unaccustomed to the rigors of camp life in the face of an enemy. This transitional period from one army to another gave Washington his most trying moments, and as each succeeding year came to an end, his apprehensions were compounded over and over again. As one authority describes it: "Nations at war have often changed generals in midstream, but it remained for the Americans to change armies." [21] (And late as 1953, Army Chief of Staff J. Lawton Collins was to say, "We are literally rebuilding it [the Eighth Army in Korea] in the face of the enemy for the third time.")

---

[21] Miller, *Triumph*, p. 83.

Nor did Washington's chagrin end here. There was also the problem of supply which, because of the absence of proper organization, would not only become progressively worse, but often would operate to leave whole units without the bare necessities, while elsewhere there was a superfluity.[22] The limited supply of powder was rendered acute by the lack of proper organization, and at critical moments the Army often was forced to withhold its fire for fear of running out of ammunition.[23] Coupled with these was the sensitive question of commissions granted by Congress for the new regiments, an issue which never failed to produce a detrimental effect among those officers of ability who were passed over. These and many other problems continually plagued Washington, dulled the effectiveness of the Army, and dictated the policy to be followed in the prosecution of the war. In this predicament, there was little advantage in preparing plans, the execution of which would be seriously handicapped by the operation of any number of these deficiencies. Strategy, then, was dependent upon the many variations of top level policy which harassed Washington.[24]

The story of the remodelling and reenlisting of the Army is a drama depicting the almost superhuman efforts of Washington to cope with the multitude of difficulties which beset him from every quarter in and out of Congress and in and out of the Army.[25] In a letter to the President of Congress on November 11, 1775, while complaining of the selfish motives exhibited by some of his officers, he described the situation. The personal motive, he was sure, added to the problem of fixing the organization of regiments, especially when manifested even by soldiers who would not "enlist until they know their colonel, lieutenant-colonel, Major, and Captain, so that it was necessary to fix the officers the first thing." [26] Eight days later it had become crystal clear that the men as well as the officers would not reenlist for patriotic reasons alone; and, if the Army was to be kept at respectable strength, it was necessary to provide

---

[22] William Matthews and Dixon Wecter, *Our Soldiers Speak, 1775-1918*, Boston, Little Brown & Co., 1943, p. 54.

[23] For a descriptive analysis of the faulty organization of the services of supply see Miller, *Triumph*, Chapter 8.

[24] For a sweeping review of the complex and interrelated problems handled by Washington as commander in chief, see Douglas S. Freeman, *George Washington*, Charles Scribner's Sons, New York, 1952, Vol. 5, pp. 487-501.

[25] French, *op. cit.*, p. 503.

[26] 4 *WW* 81-84.

stimulus "besides love of Country, to make men fond of the service." [27] The wisdom of these recommendations was borne out by the returns that came in, which, by December 16, were computed at less than 6,000 men, or some 4,000 less than Washington estimated would be needed for defensive purposes. [28]

But added inducements to enlist were viewed with mixed feelings in New England and in the southern colonies. Although Washington now inclined to the side of a bounty for the men as well as officers, sharp differences of opinion were voiced throughout the country. General Nathanael Greene was sure the payment of a bounty would make it possible to pick the best men, fill up the Army, and keep "a proper discipline . . . and good order and government in the camp. . . ." [29] John Adams argued just as strongly against the payment of a bonus which he thought would only impose new hardships upon the New England colonies; [30] and Congress was in no mood to grant any bounty, going so far as to voice disapproval of those already provided by Rhode Island. [31]

But this was December 6, 1775; the Army had not yet disintegrated. Toward the end of that month, when the men began to quit their posts, Congress veered toward the viewpoint expressed by General Greene. By January 19, 1776 each State was advised to encourage enlistments by the grant of a bounty of $6 2-3 to any man who appeared properly clothed and armed for service; and $4 to those men enlisting without such arms and accouterments. [32] By the 26th of June, Congress had resolved to offer a bounty of $10 to each man who would enlist to serve for three years; and on September 16, in reorganizing the Army, raised the bounty to $20 for short term enlistees. To those who agreed to serve for the

---

[27] Washington to President of Congress, November 19, 1775, *ibid.,* p. 101.

[28] French, *op. cit.,* p. 523. This state of affairs was not contemplated by a Committee of Congress appointed to confer with Washington on September 29. After a brief study of the steps to be taken to provide an adequate military policy, they agreed that an army of 20,372 men could be raised with little difficulty; if not, Washington was to be given the power to call upon the militia of the neighboring States to fill the quotas. In order to eliminate the provincial variety of the regiments, the Committee fixed the number for each at 728 men, including officers.

[29] *Ibid.,* p. 517.

[30] Chauncey W. Ford (ed), *The Journals of the Continental Congress, 1774-1789,* Washington, Government Printing Office, 1903, Vol. 3, p. 393. Hereafter cited as JCC.

[31] Emory Upton, *The Military Policy of the United States,* Washington, Government Printing Office, 1907, p. 7.

[32] *Ibid.,* p. 21.

duration of the war (there were few such) an additional gift of 100 acres of land was offered.[33] One month later an annual bounty of $20 was promised to every noncommissioned officer and private enlisting for the duration.[34]

Left to itself, the operation of the Congressional bounty system might have produced the desired effect. But with each state engaging to fill its quota by the grant of similar bounties, and in some cases increasing the amount, it was difficult to secure men for the Continental Army not only for the duration but also for shorter periods. In many instances this competition rendered it impossible to enlist men for longer than three months at a time. In 1777 Maryland offered a bounty of $40 above that of the Continental bounty "to each able bodied recruit who shall enlist for three years, unless sooner discharged, also a pair of shoes and stockings to be furnished them and each of them at a reasonable rate." [35] Bounties were also offered to recruiting officers and any others "who may take up and secure deserters from the continental army in this state [Maryland], agreeable to the resolves of Congress." [36] This method of recruiting was inevitable where there existed a policy implemented by volunteer enlistments; and it placed the Government in the position of suppliant. For when patriotism and popular enthusiasm do not suffice to fill the ranks, resort must always be had to the practice of financial grants or to conscription.

All the best intentions of Congress and the States notwithstanding, the bounty system ·failed to bring much relief to the advocates of a long-term Army, and induced men rather to seek shorter service with the same promise of a bonus which could be repeated over and over again. Despite such experience, this practice has been followed in succeeding wars with little regard for the enormous cost involved. No other solution has seemed possible where national defense is looked upon with suspicion by lawmakers who feel it to be their peculiar calling to safeguard American liberties by beating down the recommendations made by the Army even for defensive purposes.

---

[33] *Ibid.,*

[34] *Ibid.,* p. 22.

[35] Maryland, House of Delegates, *Votes and Proceedings,* 1777, October Session, November 13, 1777, p. 12.

[36] *Ibid.* However undesirable it may have been to induce men to serve by these methods, they were not as distasteful as the attempt to grant bounties to manufacturers for increasing the production of clothing. *Ibid.*

It was under such auspices that the Army was recruited during the winter of 1775, to be kept together only by the indomitable will of George Washington. It was this Army that drove General Howe out of Boston in March, 1776; and, when the account books were balanced, the British "could not claim possession of an acre of ground in the provinces that had joined the revolt. To establish a bridgehead and conquer a hostile continent, this was now the task of the British army and navy."[37] It was a formidable task, and the success which the warriors of the Empire initially enjoyed attests not to their invincibility and prowess, but rather to the weakness of the American military system which suffered from ill-conceived military policies, the torments of provincial jealousies and impotence, and the lack of efficiently centralized control. But, during the first year, Americans still nourished the hope of eventual conciliation with England. After the dismissal of Howe from Boston this became an impossibility, for His Majesty's Government could ill afford to give her other dependencies a vivid object lesson in the proper procedure for achieving independence. Not only national honor, but also respect for recognized law and order were now at stake in the dangerous game of Empire which Britain was playing all over the world. This was the picture in the spring of 1776, and Americans were clear-visioned enough to perceive the signs. It was independence or annihilation, and the patriots chose freedom.

Birth of Naval Policy

Early in the war, it was generally recognized that a navy, regardless of size, was indispensable to the conduct of successful operations. In fact during the first three years most of the powder, ammunition, and guns that were used against the British were captured from them by the unorthodox navy that sprang into existence almost from the very first shot.[38] The faulty administration of the British Admiralty, occasioned by a corrupt officialdom, seriously crippled the efficiency of the Royal Navy.[39] Even more than this, perhaps, Americans were favored with the advantage of an intimate knowledge of their coast line, harbors, and navigable

---

[37] Miller, op. cit., p. 87. See also Freeman, *op. cit,* p. 64.
[38] Freeman, *op. cit.,* Vol. 4, p. 70. See Also Samuel E. Morison, *The Maritime History of Massachusetts,* 1783-1860, Boston, Houghton, Mifflin, Co., 1941, p. 29.
[39] French, *op. cit.,* p. 346.

rivers where light craft could easily put in to lie hidden. These neglected lessons in geography were to prove costly for Britain throughout the course of the war.

In these circumstances, British admirals moved only with the greatest of caution, allowing the Americans plentiful opportunities to exploit their advantages. Unhindered by the enemy, and unfettered by official corruption, the American Navy showed vivid contrast to the British by the vigor of its leaders. By June, 1775, it could boast of superiority on Lake Champlain.[40]

By the summer of 1775 every State had legalized its own navy.[41] On September 2 Washington, acting on his own initiative, created the American Navy by placing a section of the Army aboard ships with the commission to cruise and seize ships of the Ministerial Navy moving to or from Boston laden with soldiers, arms, ammunition, or provisions.[42] The success which attended this experiment pointed the way for additional commissions from Congress to private individuals as well as State authorities, thereby placing upon the sea lanes a formidable fleet of privateers.[43]

But the difficulties which were besetting the Army also posed great problems for the Navy. Each State entered into a spirited competition to fit out ships of every description from brigantines to topsail schooners and small boats, each carrying armament as varied as the number of men who manned them. Privateering, like service in the militia, had a great appeal because of the allurements of increased pay and prizes; but unlike the militia, the term of service was not limited to short periods. While men were plentiful for this militia service, the regular Navy went begging for recruits to fill the ships' complements.[44]

The stimulus for a stronger Navy, like that for a strong Army in 1775, came from New England. After several petitions from

[40] Alfred Thayer Mahan, *The Major Operations of the Navies in the War of Independence*, London, Sampson Low, Marston & Co., Ltd., 1913, p. 16.

[41] See Rhode Island, *Minutes and Proceedings Upper House*, August Session 1775, August 26, 1775, Nos. 38, 46; *Massachusetts Records of the General Court or Assembly*, July Session 1775, January 11, 1776, p. 449; February 4, 1776, p. 539; April 23, 1776, p. 152.

[42] Miller *Triumph*, p. 79. Washington himself directed the operations of the land and sea forces of the United States.

[43] French, *op. cit.*, p. 370. See also Lynn Montross, *Rag Tag and Bobtail*, New York, Harper & Bros., 1952, p. 85.

[44] Matthews and Wecter, *op. cit.*, pp. 27-38. For the exploits of the New England privateers in harassing the British see, Freeman, *op. cit.*, Vol. IV, p. 70; Montross, *op. cit.*, p. 85.

that section, Congress on November 2, 1775 *Resolved* to build, at Continental expense, a fleet of four armed vessels "for the protection of these colonies." [45] This was followed on November 28 by the publication of a set of regulations[46] to govern the new Navy in the same manner as the Articles of War, laid down by Congress in June, governed the Army.[47]

If the patriots could not build a fleet strong enough to check the Royal Navy, they could bring to bear with telling effect what little they had; and if George III and his ministers needed proof of this they had not very long to wait. The value of the small but dauntless American Navy and its contribution to the final outcome would be difficult to determine. But it is certain that without its services vital supplies would not have been obtained; and the British inability or incapacity to cope with these wasps and hornets of the sea paved the way for the French and Spanish intervention. From the former, American received direct and tangible aid in men, arms, and ships; from the latter, the utility of dispersing British seapower from the Mediterranean to the Caribbean.[48] From 1780 on, the pressing need for a strong navy ceased to be a major problem for the Congress. The counterpoise to British maritime supremacy had been established with the Franco-American alliance.[49]

Sectional Interests Weaken Military Policy

Among the warmest advocates of American independence were the staunch supporters of the rights and sovereignty of the individual States. Samuel Adams refused to "subvert" the Revolution by creating a nation. This was a struggle, he thought, for liberty in which individual patriots shared equally. But patriotism "must always be partial to the particular States;" it was an ideal which began at home and never strayed far from one's immediate en-

---

[45] 3 *JCC*, 274, 316, 374-376. In effect these *Resolves* legalized privateering. On March 23, 1776, the clauses referring to legal prizes were redefined. See 4 *JCC*, 230-232.

[46] 3 *JCC* 378-387.

[47] 2 *JCC* 111. The rules for the Army were adopted on June 30, and enlarged on November 7, 1775. See also 3 *JCC* 331-334.

[48] Nicholas J. Spykman, *America's Strategy in World Politics*, New York. Harcourt Brace & Co., 1942, p. 66. See also Mahan, *op. cit.*, pp. 6-7.

[49] The interjection of the French fleet left American sea captains free to flout openly the maritime might of Britain even as close as the coast of Scotland. In 1779 John Paul Jones intercepted the Baltic fleet off that coast and captured two ships of the line. Miller, *Triumph*, p. 172.

vironment.[50] As a result, independence was proclaimed on July 4, 1776, and almost a year later a central governing body was created which followed closely the recommendations of Adams. It was a government which recognized the power of the sovereign states and functioned only as a sort of league of nations. It could make war and peace, but it could not provide the sinews for carrying out the national military policy.[51] Without the authority to tax, no policy could be implemented; and what was executed was done only with the benign affirmation of the States, conducting their affairs as they pleased throughout the war with little regard for the problems which faced the Government.[52]

Instead of uniting and pooling their resources against a common enemy, each State undertook to conduct its own private war with Great Britain; and the States entered into a spirited competition among themselves and against Congress for war material and supplies of all kinds. They engaged in a struggle for survival. To them a strong army and navy at home gave strong assurances at least, that come what may, they could defend themselves without depending upon the others for aid. Each State, except one, boasted of its own navy, with its own admiralty board acting in accord with sovereignty. Whatever aid was rendered to the Continental Army was done in a niggardly fashion that was both dangerous and unwise.

Under these circumstances, the Continental Army came to take on the appearance of an agglomerate of separate armies or "lines," notwithstanding that all were under the command of general officers appointed by the Congress. All vestiges of nationalism or national unity began to wear away. In time, even the controlling influence of the officers was dissipated by the appointments made by the States of all line officers below the grade of brigadier general. In 1778, Congress itself struck a blow for the States by directing them to provide ammunition, arms, and clothing to their

---

[50] Miller, *Triumph*, p. 426.

[51] This was the government under the Articles of Confederation. Although this plan of government was not finally ratified by all the States until 1781, the only authority wielded by the Continental Congress was that permitted under this instrument.

[52] Some idea of the limited authority of Congress may be gleaned from the correspondence between that body and the various States. See Ltr. Pres. of Congress to the Governments of New Hampshire, Massachusetts, Connecticut, New York, New Jersey, Delaware, and Maryland, June 4, 1776, in Peter Force (ed) *American Archives*, 4th Series, Washington, 1846, Vol. 6, pp. 707-708.

own line in the Continental Army, thereby yielding to the States the very powers which made the Army truly national.

But this was not all. While the Government sought financial and material aid in Europe (without which success could hardly be achieved), the States entered into separate negotiations for this aid through their special agents. At the Court of France, Vergennes (the foreign minister) preferred to strengthen the hand of the central government of the United States.[53]

Martial Spirit Needs Coaxing

The anxiety displayed in 1775 by the States to call upon a central authority to supervise the military operations had, by early 1776, sharply subsided. The British had been temporarily driven out of American territory and the prospect of defeat was not seriously regarded by the patriot leaders. But when this feeling of complacency was suddenly displaced by the reappearance of British troops, Americans were constrained to readjust their thinking. The Declaration of Independence had rendered it necessary to erect a system of government embracing the thirteen States. But this Government was at best a nominal entity exercising those functions designed by the separate States. Lacking the proper policy and means to carry it out even for a nation at peace, the Congress struggled to conduct a first class war against a first class power. Powerless to do more than improvise, this body tried to solve the problem of a perennial dissolution of the Army by the adoption of temporary expedients to meet each emergency.

Not long after the Declaration of Independence which in itself was an avowal of free men to fight or die for the preservation of liberty, it became apparent that if the Continental Army was to increase at all, some measure of enlistment encouragement was necessary beyond that which was extended to the militia. In a dual system of military service where the option of lesser periods of enlistment is offered, men instinctively prefer such option, especially when the term of the other is greater by from one to two and three years. How then induce men to serve for long periods?

By the summer of 1776, despite the frank protestations of independence and glib avowals of patriotism on the part of the

---

[53] For a clear picture of these episodes see Samuel F. Bemis, *The Diplomacy of the American Revolution,* New York, D. Appleton-Century Co., Inc., 1935, Chapters 3 and 4 *passim.*

citizenry, this dual system produced only a small increase in the Continental Army. Washington was forced to call the attention of Congress to the inevitable release of the greater part of his Army by the 31st of December. Decrying the reliability of militia troops when pitted against superior numbers of veteran troops, he made an eloquent plea for a standing army which could be relied upon for the duration of the war. The defense of American liberties at this critical period, he was sure, "must of necessity be greatly hazarded, if not entirely lost, if their defense is left to any but a permanent standing Army; I mean one to exist during the War."[54] To accomplish this, he went on, would be difficult if attempted merely by an inducement of a bounty; but, the addition of land "might have a considerable influence on a permanent establishment." [55]

An army such as this, comprising from 50,000 to 100,000 men, would not only assure victory, but also would be less expensive to maintain in terms of bounties and land grants. Washington proposed to solve the problem of shortage of officers by offering good pay or pay equivalent to that enjoyed by British officers for the execution of similar responsibilities. This would "induce Gentlemen and Men of Character to engage;" gentlemen who "are actuated by principles of honor and a spirit of enterprise;" and, with more regard for the *character* of such officers than for "the Number of Men they can Inlist, we should in a little time have an Army able to cope" with any that could be opposed to it.[56]

Moreover, a sizeable standing force would put an end to the horrifying experience of witnessing the dissolution of the Army in the face of the enemy, and would also settle the problem of training created by the appearance of raw recruits at frequent inter-

[54] Washington to President of Congress, September 2, 1776, 6 *WW* 5. It is significant to note that men like Emory Upton have interpreted Washington's critical attitude as showing an abhorrence of the militia. To be sure he made no excuse for their behavior in such battles as Long Island; but it would be to misinterpret Washington to say that he had no faith in the militia system, especially when it is remembered that he expressed high words of praise for those who fought at Bunker Hill. Moreover, he never discounted the use of the militia to augment the regular force.

[55] *Ibid.*, p. 6.

[56] Ltr Washington to President of Congress, September 24, 1776, *ibid.*, pp. 108-110. Cf. Nathanael Greene to Governor Cooke, October 11, 1776, quoted in George Washington Greene, *The Life of Nathanael Greene,* New York, Hurd & Houghton, 1871, Vol. 1, pp. 222-223. Greene blamed Congress for this condition, and blamed the officers for the actions of the militia.

vals. To acquaint men with their military duties and to bring them to an understanding of discipline and subordination was difficult and time consuming. In the Army of 1775 these problems had been compounded by an almost complete absence of distinction between officers and enlisted men. This could only be corrected for the future, observed Washington, by engaging men for the duration even at the expense of a bounty of $30 or more. Not that this was a reasonable assurance of securing the services of the men needed, but something had to be done immediately, for "it will never do to let the matter alone as it was last year, till the time of service was near expiring." [57]

Congress reacted but slowly to Washington's repeated warnings, and on June 26, 1776 voted a bounty of $10 for every non-commissioned officer and soldier who would enlist, not for the war, but for three years. Two weeks earlier, a Board of War and Ordnance was created to carry out the responsibilities of a War Department.[58] This was a necessary reform but a small relief to Washington who required more men. The question was not what shall Congress do, but what can Congress do?

Acting within the limited authority ascribed to it, the Congress tried desperately to follow Washington's recommendations for an adequate force. After many weeks of study and debate, they brought themselves to face the reality of the situation and on September 16 provided for an army of 88 battalions to be pro-rated among the States.[59] The term of service was left to the discretion of the States but was fixed at three years or the duration of the war. Those who chose the former received a bounty of $20 and for the latter an additional 100 acres of land.[60]

Within three weeks Washington again warned Congress that the Army was on the eve of its political dissolution nothwithstanding this legislation. Furthermore, there was a vast difference between voting battalions and raising men, and unless the pay of officers, especially the field officers, was increased, even those

---

[57] Washington to President of Congress, February 9, 1776, 4 *WW* 318.

[58] This was created on June 12, 1776, and made up entirely of civilians, 5 *JCC* 434-435. By the following year representation included military men. 9 *JCC* 818-819.

[59] At this time the term battalion was used synonomously with the term regiment.

[60] 5 *JCC* 762.

worth retaining "will leave the Service at the expiration of the present term." [61]

Meanwhile Congress sought to fill the 88 battalions by authorizing the States to enlist men for three years while softly hinting that enlistments for the duration would be preferable. But the season was getting late, and it was apparent that the full quota of men for the new establishment would not be reached by the end of the year. Fully aware of this condition, Washington urged Congress to increase the number of battalions to 110. This would provide a larger number of officers and although he admitted the impossibility of recruiting a full complement for the original number, the officers of 110 battalions could recruit more men than those of the 88.[62] What was important at this late date was not the size of the establishment, but rather the number of men that could be brought in to fill the void soon to be created by departing soldiers.

In spite of all the entreaties and sundry schemes for enlisting larger numbers for the duration of the war, comparatively few men succumbed to the increased inducements offered by the Congress. Not that the men were wanting in patriotism, but, left to their own devices, and with the individual States offering greater bonuses for shorter periods of service, the men naturally veered away from federal service. The decision of Congress to accept three-year enlistments with the offer of a bounty of $20 minus land was prompted by the policy of the States which offered higher bounties for shorter periods of service. In the competition which ensued, Congress ran second best.

Menacing Shadow of a Weak Executive

Among the many trials and tribulations that were in evidence during 1776, none was more serious nor more evident than the inability of Congress to cope with the new and urgent executive problems which daily came to their attention. This was more embarrassing to Washington who had to refer questions constantly to Congress for authority only to find that Congress had almost no power because of the serious differences of opinion which arose

---

[61] Washington to President of Congress, October 4, 1776, 6 *WW* 152-153. See also Greene, *op. cit.*, p. 222. On the 19th of September, 1776, General Greene warned that calling out large bodies of militia would be "destructive in the end," because the "resources of the country cannot support it.

[62] Washington to President of Congress, December 20, 1776, 6 *WW* 403.

on every important question. Nothing but a catastrophe, it seemed, would bring the delegates to a proper appreciation of the dangers confronting the country.

But Congress merely reflected the general attitude of the country at large. When it became evident that the war was to be waged in earnest, and under some authority where the effort was to be shared by all, the patriotic fever of '75 approached normal in '76, and for the remainder of the war suspicions of executive power ran high in and out of Congress.

For this reason the later Congresses were less able than the earlier ones. Coupled with a feeling of impotence was the degeneracy of the position of delegates into something like a purgatory. Election to that body often meant much labor and great inconvenience which brought little honor or profit. Service in the State governments, on the other hand, afforded special opportunities for usefulness and distinction together with profit. The time was to come when even the position of President of Congress went begging. Complaining of the low regard in which the positions in Congress were held, President Laurens warned: "A most shameful deficiency in this branch is the greatest evil, and is indeed the source of almost all our evils. If there is not speedily a resurrection of able men, and of that virtue which I thought to be genuine in seventy-five, we are gone. We shall undo ourselves." [63]

Prompted by personal motives and provincial jealousies, Congress threw in its lot with private interests to prevent the adoption of measures to create sufficient executive authority to give some substance and efficiency to the management of Army affairs. A War Department with extensive powers should have been established immediately. Instead, Congress retained the military administration in their hands, merely appointing committees for special purposes but granting them no authority to act. This meant that the committees could only study the problems and make reports, after which the Congress engaged in long-winged debates while the Army stood in urgent need of men and supplies.

On January 24, 1776, a Congressional committee was appointed to consider the subject of a war office. After spending five precious months in study and debate, they adopted the plan for a Board of War and Ordnance to consist of five of their own

---

[63] Louis C. Hatch, *The Administration of the American Revolutionary Army*, New York, Longman's Green & Co., 1904, pp. 20-21.

number with a paid secretary.[64] In 1777 this was superseded by a new Board consisting of men who were not members of Congress, allowing membership to military men whose experience was necessary to bring some efficiency to the administration of military affairs. But still there remained the question of divided authority over these questions and finally, in 1781, when Congress became convinced of the advantage of a single-headed Department, the Board was abolished and General Benjamin Lincoln was appointed "Secretary at War."[65] If this belated decision had been made in 1776, there is a strong possibility that many of the problems encountered in raising, equipping, and training the troops for an energetic prosecution of the war might have been eliminated, and Washington might have been spared many trying moments in keeping his Army together.

By December, 1776, the Army was almost completely dissolved, legislation notwithstanding; and to make matters worse, British troops had swept through New Jersey on their way to Philadelphia, the capital of the United Colonies. Alarmed by these events, Congress not only made a vigorous effort to increase the size of the Army, but also vested Washington with extraordinary powers to bring this about. Compelled by that stern and retributive General Necessity, they had been forced to approve that which in any other circumstance they would have shunned as the plague. Placing reliance upon the wisdom and character of the Commanding General, they *Resolved* to grant him full and complete power

> to raise and collect together, in the most speedy and effectual manner, from any or all of these United States, sixteen battalions of infantry, in addition to those already voted by Congress . . . to apply to any of the states for such aid of the militia as he shall judge necessary . . . to displace and appoint all officers under the rank of brigadier general, and to fill up the vacancies in every other department in the American Armies; to take, wherever he may be, whatever he may want for the use of the army; and if the inhabitants will not sell it, allowing reasonable price for the same; to arrest and confine persons who refuse to take the continental currency. . . .[66]

---

[64] This secretary was Richard Peters who remained either in that capacity or as a member during the five years of its existence.

[65] 7 *JCC* 216.

[66] *Resolve* of December 27, 1776, 6 *JCC* 1045-1046. See also Freeman, *op. cit.,* Vol. IV, pp. 336-337. This discretionary power was limited to a period of six months.

Fearful that such a sweeping grant of authority might be misinterpreted by the individual States, Congress on the same day named a committee to prepare a paper explaining "the reasons which induced Congress to enlarge the powers" of the Commander in Chief.[67]

Washington was prepared for this extension of power, for on December 20th he argued that a commander situated at such a great distance from the seat of Government must have some measure of discretion; and perhaps also he was somewhat aware of General Greene's letter of the 21st to Congress along these lines.[68]

However grateful he might have been at this sudden windfall, Washington never let himself forget that he was the servant of a civil authority. He held firmly to the policy that the Army under him was an instrument for safeguarding civil liberties. Instead of regarding himself as being freed from all civil obligation by this mark of confidence, he assured his friends: "I shall constantly bear in mind, that as the Sword was the last Resort for the preservation of our Liberties, so it ought to be the first thing laid aside when those Liberties are firmly established.[69]

Policy of Voluntary Enlistment Fails

Whatever the merits or demerits of the bounty system, the recruitment policy was dependent upon the grant of land and money, and as time wore on, it became progressively more difficult to induce men to serve in the Continental Army. Early in 1777, the New England States provided for an increase of $33 1-3 to the $20 offered by the Government; and within a short time, Massachusetts and New Hampshire increased their allotments to $86 2-3 for each recruit. This tempting increase called a halt to reenlistment in the older regiments whose men naturally went home to take advantage of the larger sums offered.[70] Desertions had become so numerous that Washington on April 6, 1777, was forced to issue a proclamation granting a general pardon to all deserters

[67] 6 *JCC* 1047, 1053.
[68] Greene, *op. cit.*, pp. 290-291.
[69] Washington to Robert Morris, George Clyman & George Walton, January 1, 1777, 6 *WW* 464.
[70] On March 14, 1777, Washington reported to Congress that the Army in New Jersey numbered 3,000. "These, 981 excepted, are militia and stand engaged only till the last of this month." See ltr Washington to president of Congress, March 14, 1777, 7 *WW* 288.

if they would rejoin their regiments by May 15, or surrender to any officer of the Continental Army.[71]

In this contingency each State adopted its own measures to meet the quotas set by Congress. To meet her quota of 2,000 men, Maryland experimented with volunteers who were offered an equitable bounty together with exemption from all taxation during the time they remained on duty, as well as a choice of regiments. And, when even such liberal terms were disregarded by her citizens, Maryland resorted to the dubious practice of granting a free pardon "to all such disaffected persons charged with any crime against the state, who may voluntarily enlist for three years as aforesaid, such persons to be entitled to the bounty and all privileges." [72]

When finally it became evident that voluntary enlistments, even when stimulated by generous offers, failed to procure the Continental quotas, Congress was forced to recommend a draft of the militia.[73] On February 6, 1777, the States were called upon to draft men for nine months to be discharged before that time in proportion to their replacement by the three-year men. Even this brought little assurance of a successful recruitment policy. The States used it as an excuse to enlist criminals, ne'er-do-wells, and vagabonds of every description. In Maryland, every idle person who was able-bodied and with neither fixed domicile nor family, was made eligible for service with a choice of enlisting for nine months or for three years.[74]

In administering these draft calls the States demonstrated a laxity which emphasized the apprehensions of the general officers especially in the northern theater where it was reported that Massachusetts was drafting men lately deserted from Burgoyne's army. Fearful of the consequences of such a procedure, Washington memorialized the Massachusetts Council of Safety on "the danger of substituting, as Soldiers, men who have given glaring proof of a treacherous disposition, and who are bound to us by no motives of attachment."[75] In the South, Congress recommended raising

[71] Washington's proclamation, April 6, 1777, *ibid.,* p. 364.
[72] Maryland, *Votes and Proceedings, op. cit.,* p. 12. Tax exemption was extended to include all bounty lands offered by the Congress since September 16, 1776. *ibid.,* July Session, 1779, p. 137 (August 5, 1779).
[73] Freeman. *op. cit.,* Vol. IV, p. 387.
[74] Maryland, *Votes and Proceedings,* March Session, 1778. p. 86.
[75] Washington to James Bowdoin, March 17, 1778, 11 *WW* 98-99.

battalions of regular troops to be engaged for one year for the defense of the Southern States, but not to be compelled to serve in any enterprise or in any State north of Virginia.[76]

Meanwhile the British Government had dispatched a commission to America to discuss the possibility of settling the difficulties by conciliation. But by this time, all hope of settling the issue upon peaceful grounds had vanished. Burgoyne's magnificent army had been defeated and captured, and the French had made last-minute preparations to intervene by force of arms in America's behalf. Having tasted the fruits of partial victory, and encouraged by the prospect of French and Spanish aid, the patriot leaders were in no mood to talk of peace. Complete independence was the only solution. Any concessions made now by the British, Washington was sure, were merely "specious allurements of Peace" and the only manner in which to counter whatever sympathies Americans would entertain for ending the war on this note was to strengthen the Army, and place it upon a substantial footing. This would "conduce to inspire the Country with confidence, [and] enable those at the head of affairs to consult the public honour and interest." [77]

In answer to those who taunted him with the familiar bogey of militarism, Washington wisely called attention to the illogical reasoning which prompted such fears. The jealousy which Congress unhappily felt for the Army was based upon the prejudices of Europeans for armies of mercenaries who possessed none of the ties "or interests of Citizens or any other dependence, than what flowed from their Military employ;" and, while Europeans were so disposed against standing armies in peacetime,

> it is our policy to be prejudiced against them in time of war; and they are Citizens having all the ties, and interests of Citizens, and in most cases property totally unconnected with the Military Line. If we pursue a right System of policy, in my Opinion, there should be none of these distinctions. We should all be considered, Congress Army, &c. as one people, embarked in one cause, in one interest; acting on the same principle and the same End.[78]

Furthermore, this jealousy demonstrated a weak tendency to disregard the terrible suffering endured by the men thus far. No

---

[76] Congress also authorized the payment of a bounty not to exceed $200 for these recruits. See *Resolve*, March 29, 1779, 13 *JCC* 388.
[77] Washington to John Bannister, April 21, 1778, 11 *WW* 287.
[78] *Ibid.*, pp. 290-291.

history, he concluded, "now extant, can furnish an instance of an Army's suffering such uncommon hardships as ours have done, and bearing them with the same patience and fortitude."[79]

Because of the legislative body's policy, already firmly rooted, against a strong army threatened to undermine all his plans as well as to alienate the support of "our recent" allies, Washington poured forth a veritable flood of letters upon Congress, his friends, and the various governors in a desperate effort to bring the armed forces to some respectable size.[80] With the defeat of Burgoyne and the expected intervention of France and Spain, it was idle fancy to think the British would not step up the crescendo of the war. Against this possibility Washington laid his plans; to meet the ominous situation more men, not less, were needed. And, if it proved difficult to recruit men for the Continental Army, regardless of the increased bounty, then stronger measures were in order.

Mounting problems together with the failure of the recruitment policy, led Congress to grant Washington another measure of increased power for procurement and supplies. Each State was asked to meet the quota set up by the Commander in Chief,[81] who again administered his authority with wisdom and justice. While it was necessary to fill the quotas, it was also equally important to avoid any disturbance of the economic equilibrium of the various States. Food was an essential item of war material, just as were munitions and clothing. Therefore the farmer, as well as the artisan and the soldier, played equally significant parts in the war effort.[82] Washington had to study this, with the weak aid of a Congressional committee, for the purpose of coordinating the various parts of the young nation's economy; but it was a task he

---

[79] *Ibid.*, See also Miller, *Triumph*, p. 483. The suffering of the men at Valley Forge was well known in the country and in Congress; and it contributed in no small degree to deter others from enlisting lest they share the same fate. On the other hand, these "ragged continentals" served to inspire their countrymen by their fortitude. John Laurens cherished "those dear ragged Continentals, whose patience will be the envy of future ages;" and Von Steuben recognized in them a soldierly talent superior to any he had ever seen. See John McAuley Palmer, *General Von Steuben*, New Haven Yale University Press, 1937, p. 137.

[80] Washington to Thomas Wharton, Jr., April 11, 1778, 11 *WW* 248; Washington to Thomas Johnson, May 17, *ibid.*, pp. 404-405; Washington to R. H. Lee, May 25, *ibid.*, p. 452; Washington to Patrick Henry, May 23, *ibid.*, p. 438; Washington to General Charles Scott, May 22, *ibid.*, pp. 433-434.

[81] See Upton, *op. cit.*, p. 30.

[82] Washington to President Thomas Wharton, Jr., April 11, 1778, 11 *WW* 369-370.

had to perform alone, and all major decisions had to be made by him.

Left to his own devices, Washington made the most of the opportunities thrust into his hands. As the new recruits came into the ranks, time began to play an important role in the strategy to come. With little time to train large bodies of militia in the ways of war, he boldly distributed them among the regular troops, who, "being divided in this manner to the militia, will serve to give them confidence and probably make them act better than they would alone." [83] After three years of war, the Commander in Chief had learned to make the most of his inferior resources. This experiment served him well and paid large dividends two years later when General Daniel Morgan at Cowpens with his Carolina militia routed the superior Tory cavalry under Colonel Tarleton.

This increased effectiveness of the militia troops, however, did not tempt them to remain in the service beyond their terms of service; by the end of 1778 the perennial problem of personnel turnover reappeared to plague Washington. By this time he had made up his mind conclusively that the only salvation lay in a vigorous prosecution of the draft by State quotas. This, together with the voluntary enlistments in the Continental Army, he felt, would yield a larger return, although, he admitted, "both modes in all probability will not produce near as many as may be found necessary." [84] In Maryland a spirited effort was made to meet the assigned quotas, but the men thus drafted were permitted to choose service for nine months, three years, or for the duration.[85] Moreover, the draftees were not to be turned into companies with regular troops, and for every 25 men there was to be at least one commissioned officer chosen from among their own number.[86] Similar experiments were conducted by the other States. Each granted large bounties, and left to the soldier's own discretion the alternative of service in the Continental or State organizations. This active competition between the local and central authorities had by now become so keen that it was difficult to guarantee any enlistment in the Continental Army.

Again Washington called the attention of Congress to the

[83] Washington to Lafayette, July 27, 1778, 12 *WW* 237.
[84] Maryland, *Votes and Proceedings,* 1778, March Session, pp. 87-91.
[85] *Ibid.*
[86] *Ibid.*, p. 97.

necessity for improving this condition, with special emphasis upon the coming campaign of 1779. While urging that body to either enlist the men already in the Army for the duration of the war or to adopt some similar plan, he made it clear that recruitment would be contingent upon the plan of operations to be determined by the Board of War with reference to offense or defense. Since offensive operations required a larger force, the requirements of the Army would naturally hinge upon the decision of Congress; but in any event something had to be done to correct the inequality resulting from the desire of the States to recruit for their own purposes first. Moreover, the enormous bounties granted by them made it difficult to stimulate interest in the Continental Army; and it was almost impossible for the Congress to grant equal sums. But if the State bounties were to be abolished by act of Congress, then it would be wise to raise the Continental bounty as high as a hundred and fifty dollars or perhaps higher.[87]

Acting upon this recommendation, Congress on January 23, 1779, authorized Washington to take the most effectual methods to reenlist for the continuation of the war, all such of the Continental troops as were not expressly engaged for that period, as well as raising new recruits for completing the battalions to their proper complement.[88] Whatever Washington might have achieved by the promise of these resolves was negated by the failure of Congress to abolish the State bounties. Instead of limiting the bounty system, the States proceeded to increase them to excessively high figures. By the summer of 1779 New Jersey offered $250 to each recruit in addition to the clothing, land, and the $200 offered by Congress. Virginia, on May 3, offered $750, a suit of clothes once a year, and 100 acres of land to each recruit enlisting for the duration.[89] But despite these manifestations of generosity, the Virginia battalions were only one third complete and little hope could be held out for bringing them up to strength.[90] Other States followed suit, placing the Congress at a serious disadvantage; and while the States interfered in this manner, no general system for regulating the bounty could be adopted.[91] This was not to mention

---

[87] Washington to Committee of Congress, January 13, 1779, 14 *WW* 4.
[88] 13 *JCC* 108; 298-299.
[89] Upton, *op. cit.*, p. 41. See also Montross, *op. cit.*, p. 331.
[90] Palmer, *op. cit.*, p. 209.
[91] By this time the Continental currency was in such a sad state of depreciation that money values had spiraled downward.

the grumbling that arose among those who had volunteered for smaller sums. Alarmed over the growing discontent among the veteran soldiers because of this iniquitous system, Washington urged the Board of War to make some adjustment for those men who had undergone a long service, and who engaged for the duration of the war in the first instance, on a very moderate bounty. A gratuity at this time, in recognition of the services rendered by the older men, would serve a dual purpose. It would put an end to desertions, and while operating as a reward might have a good effect and quiet their discontent.[92] Within two weeks, Congress resolved to grant the $100 gratuity as a reward for the "services of those faithful and zealous soldiers who at an early period engaged in the armies of the States during the war." [93]

Even all these lucrative gifts failed to inspire men to volunteer their services for the duration of the war, and by the end of this year Washington again repeated his remonstrances for an adequate military force to achieve success. For five years the system of recruitment had failed miserably, and because he could not count with any degree of certainty upon the number of men needed for any campaign, Washington was forced to go on the defensive, resorting to the offensive only when the enemy would leave an opening. This condition was well known, but little regard was expressed among politicians for the dangers to which such a system exposed the nation. And, while the men were not forthcoming as they were needed to fill the battalions, each unit remained understrength although the number of officers remained fairly constant.

Congress Struggles to Reorganize the Army

By January, 1778 Washington could count 87 battalions in the field, all understrength, but all with the required complement of officers. This could be corrected, he was sure, by temporarily reducing the number of battalions and sending the supernumerary officers "back to the State, to collect such men, as on various pretenses were left behind, and deserters; and aided by the whole efficiency of the State . . . to exert all their endeavors towards

---

[92] Washington to Board of War, June 9, 1779, 15 *WW* 252-253.
[93] 14 *JCC* 758.

completing the other regiments or such of them as Congress should direct." [94]

Voluntary enlistments being what they were, Washington re-affirmed the necessity for an annual draft of the militia,[95] a pro-posal he had made early in 1777. This, he felt, was more practical than a draft for the duration or for a number of years, either of which might be looked upon as disgusting and dangerous; and although even this might not be desirable, it was

> the best our circumstances will allow; and we shall always have an established corps of experienced officers. . . . It is the only mode, I can think of, for completing our battalions in time . . . and it has this advantage, that the minds of the people being once reconciled to the experiment, it would prove a source of con-tinual supplies hereafter.[96]

Within a month Congress resolved to instruct the States accord-ing to the letter of Washington's recommendations, to fill up by drafts from their militia their respective battalions of Continental troops. The men so drafted were to serve for a period of nine months, and under no circumstances were prisoners of war or deserters from the enemy to be counted among the draftees.[97]

As the troops recruited in this manner made their way to Washington's headquarters at Valley Forge, without arms, ac-couterments, and clothing, he began to grow apprehensive, not only for himself, but also for his generals because of the difficulties of properly arming and clothing these men. Even the genius of Von Steuben for turning raw recruits into disciplined soldiers did not suffice to arm and clothe these men. While making final preparations for the campaign of 1778, Washington was con-strained to urge upon the States the necessity for drawing supplies and arms from their own magazines.[98]

Notwithstanding the earnest efforts of Congress to follow the advice of the Commander in Chief, the personnel procurement problem remained as acute as it had been. And now that France had definitely undertaken to dispatch troops as well as supplies in

---

[94] Washington to Committee of Congress with the Army, January 29, 1778, 10 *WWW* 371.

[95] Washington urged the draft of enlisted men only, there being a sufficient number of officers on duty.

[96] Washington to the Committee of Congress with the Army, January 28, 1778, 10 *WW* 366-367.

[97] *Resolve* of February 26, 1778, 10 *JCC* 199-203.

[98] Washington to Board of War, March 6, 1778, 11 *WW* 33-34; Washington to Governor William Livingston, April 26, 1778, *ibid.*, p. 310.

support of the Cause, the situation became embarrassing as well as dangerous. As the year drew to a close, Washington went into winter quarters perhaps with some misgivings and a longing for his own hearthstone. But there was little time to dwell upon such thoughts; the job was yet to be done. The Army was under strength, few men were enlisting for long periods, and it was almost certain that the British effort would be stepped up in the spring.

Something had to be done to counteract the cause of these conditions. It was necessary to offset the effect of the increased State bounties; the only solution seemed to be an increase in the Continental bounty. After much debate and more dissension, Congress on January 23, 1779 gave Washington the added authority to offer a bounty of $200 to all enlistees for the duration of the war.[99] But within five weeks of this decision, he was relieved of this responsibility when Congress decided, in the interest of economy, to reduce the number of State battalions to 80, and requested each State to complete their quotas by drafts upon the militia or in any other manner they should think proper.[100]

In November, anticipating the need for the campaign of the coming year, Washington pushed this plan a little further by recommending the adoption of a proposal whereby each State be informed of the *"real deficiency"* of its troops and called upon to make it up by a draft; that the men drafted join the Army by the 1st of January in the succeeding year." The advantage to Washington of such a system, whereby the levies would be brought to the Army at a particular time, to serve for a fixed period, was obvious. With this system he could make plans of operation with some degree of certainty.[101]

In Congress this latest appeal for fixing the military establishment made but a small impression;[102] in fact it was bitterly criticized. Many felt that "the Number of Men inlisted for the War is already sufficient and that reinforcements are not necessary." This feeling was brought to the attention of Washington by Elbridge Gerry who implored him to renew his recommendations

---

[99] 13 *JCC* 108.
[100] *Ibid.*, pp. 298-299. The bounty of $200 was continued.
[101] Washington to President of Congress, November 18, 1779, 17 *WW* 128-130.
[102] One authority shows that Congress sometimes spent as much as three months in framing a recommendation to the States; and they, in turn, might take six months in approving or rejecting the proposal. See Miller, *Triumph*, p. 434.

in order to set the matter straight, and also because of the un-
easiness this Congressional apathy was creating in the French
Court, "who last year remonstrated in very friendly, but *expressive*
Terms, against the Delays of our military preparations for that
Campaign." [103]

But no number of letters or remonstrances from the Commander in Chief could change the situation in Congress. Being
powerless to do more than recommend a policy procedure, and
prone to reflect upon the tendencies of their constituencies, the
Congress spent a great deal of time in debate and examination,
while the States were disposed to find every excuse for evading
the issues brought to their attention. Washington could assign ten
thousand reasons why this condition was dangerous even to the
last extreme, and unless Congress could be vested "with the con-
troulling power in matters of common concern, and for the great
purposes of War," he gave it as his honest opinion "that it will
be impossible to prosecute it to any *good effect.*"[104]

This Congressional debility was sharply emphasized on
February 9, 1780, when it was resolved to raise the number of
men in the service to 35,211, leaving to the States the discretion
as to the manner in which the men would be enlisted as well as
the period of such enlistments. Furthermore, in following the
dictates of the States, Congress neutralized any hope of expediency
by directing Washington to furnish the States with accurate returns of the troops belonging or accredited to their respective
quotas. In effect, this meant that the States could refuse to meet
any quota until they were informed of the exact number of men
they had in service.[105] As a result, the State authorities made little
effort to meet the quotas set for them, and by June, Washington
in despair penned a letter to James Bowdoin describing the consequences the country would face if the men were not recruited
immediately. If this were not done "we cannot cooperate with our

---

[103] Gerry to Washington, January 12, 1780, quoted in Edmund C. Burnett (ed.)
Letters of Members of the Continental Congress, Washington, Carnegie Institute
of Washington, 1931, Vol. 5, p. 7. For the attitude of Congress in this regard
see 16 *JCC* 81 ff. On February 9, 1780, Congress fixed the size of the Army
at 35,211 men and urged the States to fill their respective deficiencies for the
service of the present year. In other words, these deficiencies were to be filled
by men who would serve only to the end of the year. *Ibid.,* pp. 150-151.
[104] Washington to John Armstrong, March 26, 1781, 21 *WW* 379.
[105] 16 *JCC* 150-151. This was an almost impossible task for Washington had
no way ascertaining the exact number of men from each State in the service
especially when it is understood that the Army was scattered over the country.

Ally on any large scale, and may easily become a ruined and un-done people.[106]

While the States were ill-disposed to support the idea of a large army recruited for the duration of the war, under the control of Congress, the only alternative was to rely upon whatever new levies could be brought in for shorter terms. This meant a continued fluctuation in manpower which made it impossible to consider offensive operations, and which threatened to reduce Americans to the humiliating condition of seeing the cause of America, in America, upheld by foreign arms.[107] Worse than this, perhaps, was the financial condition of the nation which was aggravated by each successive attempt to engage men for the service. Short-term enlistments gave the Army two sets of men to feed and pay, the discharged men going home, and the new levies coming in. This situation doubled the consumption of provisions, arms, accouterments, and military stores of every description despite every precaution taken by the Commander in Chief to avoid such a financial burden.[108]

While this policy accelerated the inflationary spiral by forcing the Congress to increase their paper emissions, it also undermined the economic structure of the country. The frequent calls upon the militia interrupted cultivation, decreased the quantity of production, and occasioned a scarcity in food commodities with an attendant increase in prices. In an Army "so unstable as ours," wrote Washington,

> order and economy have been impracticable. No person who has been a close observer of the progress of our Affairs can doubt that our currency has depreciated without comparison more rapidly from the system of short inlistments, than it would have done otherwise.[109]

Furthermore, he continued, there was every reason to believe the war had been protracted on this account, for "had we kept a permanent Army on foot, the enemy would have had nothing to hope for, and would in all probability, have listened to terms long since." Military, political, and economic considerations dictated the need for a more permanent army, and after five years of experimentation, even the people could see the wisdom of such

---

[106] Washington to Bowdoin, June 14, 1780, 19 *WW* 10.
[107] Washington to President of Congress, August 20, 1780, 19 *WW* 404.
[108] *Ibid.,* p. 409.
[109] *Ibid.,* p. 410.

a move. Many incentives of immediate interest could be held up to them as an inducement to submit to a draft for three years or for the duration, among which were the repeated bounties they had to pay and the frequent economic interruptions occasioned by the necessity for calling out the militia periodically.[110]

The advantage of a long-term army, or at least one sufficiently strong to serve for the duration, had already been brought to the attention of the several governors by Washington and his close friends. Few could doubt that it would be less costly to make every exertion for a more permanent military establishment, and many in and out of Congress began to display a sympathetic regard for the advice so often tendered but so sadly neglected. After a close examination of the status of the organizations in being, Congress concluded that what was needed was not more men, but rather a regrouping and consolidation of the units in existence. This would correct the ratio of officers to men with a resultant efficiency of organization as well as order and economy.[111]

Guided by these objectives, Congress on October 3, 1780 resolved to reorganize the Army and at the same time strongly recommended that the length of service be for the duration of the war. The Regular Army was fixed, as of January 1, 1781, at 4 regiments of cavalry, 4 regiments of artillery, 49 regiments of infantry, Moses Hazen's regiment, and 1 regiment of artificers; or approximately 36,000 men. These were apportioned among the States, who were to furnish not men, but regiments in full strength enlisted for the war.[112] If the quotas could not be filled with recruits for the duration, then the States were urged to

> supply the deficiency with men engaged to serve for not less than one year, unless sooner relieved by recruits inlisted for the war, which they are requested to exert their utmost endeavours to

---

[110] *Ibid.,* p. 411. Nathanael Greene called the attention of Congress to the dangers of any plan for calling out large bodies of militia: "the resources of the country cannot support it." See Greene to Reed, September 19, 1780, Greene, *op. cit.,* Vol. 2, p. 222.

[111] Congress tried to correct this situation as early as December, 1777, when the number of officers was out of proportion to that of the privates, by urging the States to suspend "Filling up any vacancies in their respective regiments until they shall hear further from Congress on the Subject." Resolve of December 31, 1777, 9 *JCC* 1037.

[112] On October 11, Washington objected to the incorporation of 4 regiments of cavalry, urging instead 4 legionary corps each consisting of four troops of mounted dragoons and two of dismounted dragoons. In addition to this he recommended also 2 partisan corps consisting of mounted and dismounted dragoons. These were approved by Congress on October 11. 18 *JCC* 960.

obtain, as speedily as possible; and in order thereto, it is further recommended that the officers at camp be empowered and directed to use every prudent measure, and improve every favourable opportunity, to inlist, for the continuance of the war such of the men belonging to their respective states, as are not engaged for that period.[113]

By this act, Congress lopped off many of the regiments which were understrength and consolidated those remaining for added efficiency and economy; and it gave Congress the opportunity of separating the wheat from the chaff in the selection and retention of officers, many of whom now faced the prospect of immediate separation as surplus officers. To avoid giving offense to those who became jobless, and also to soothe the feelings of those who remained on duty, the supernumeraries were granted, beginning January 1, "half pay for seven years, in specie, or other current money equivalent, and also to grants of land at the close of the war, agreeably to the resolution of the 16 September 1778.[114]

In general the merits of this reform met with genuine approval. But the summary dismissal of the supernumerary officers, a policy unfortunately to be put in effect after each war, left something to be desired. Looking beyond the existing state of emergency, Washington warned Congress that this method of solving the problem of excess officers was filled with the most mischievious consequences. The solution lay not in separating them in such a manner, but rather in providing a policy which would lay the foundation of a sound preparedness program for future contingencies. The half-pay provision as envisioned in the Congressional plan would leave those separated dissatisfied and unwilling to commit their services at any future date; and would leave those remaining in the service suspicious of the intention of Congress toward them. On the other hand, half-pay for life would provide the prospect of a permanent financial security and keep many such officers closely associated with the Army, in return for which they would unhesitatingly "submit to many privations and to the inconveniences which the situation of public affairs makes unavoidable."[115]

With reference to the 49 regiments of infantry, Washington ex-

---

[113] *Ibid.,* pp. 893-895.

[114] *Ibid.,* pp. 896-897. On October 21, the rank and file of the infantry regiments was fixed at 612 men each.

[115] Washington to President of Congress, October 11, 1780 20 *WW* 158-159. In this regard, Washington no doubt had in mind a reserve officer system wherein the members could be called to duty in any emergency.

pressed some misgivings. Even if the regiments could be completely enrolled, the aggregate number of men, after deductions for casualties, sick, and absent, would still remain too small. Fully aware of the temper of the States with reference to recruitment, his goal of 30,000 effectives could not possibly be attained. For this reason, he deplored the conduct of Congress in proposing an alternative term of service and in leaving the reduction and incorporation of the regiments to the discretion of the States. Reliance upon them to fill the quotas of men and supplies was contrary to his sentiments and policy because it was an adherence to the State system, and also because it would be productive of great confusion and discontent.[116] "In the present humours of the States," he continued,

> I should entertain the most flattering hopes that they would enter upon vigorous measures to raise an army for the War, if Congress appeared decided on the point; but if they hold up a different idea as admissible, it would again be concluded [by the States] that they [Congress] do not consider an Army for the War as essential.[117]

Congress translated these observations into a set of resolutions ten days later.[118] Washington, gratified by this turn of heart, unburdened himself to a friend: "Congress, at length, have resolved to do that, which an adoption of four years ago, would 'ere this have put an end to the war. I mean the raising of an Army for the War."[119]

More than resolutions, however, were necessary to arouse the States from their habitual laxity in filling their quotas of men. During the first three months of 1781 Washington exhorted his friends and the various governors to fill the requisitions for men, but by the first of April the Adjutant General could only make a partial report on the total number of men in the Army at that time.[120] By mid-July, the rank and file of the Continental Army, computed by

---

[116] *Ibid.*, p. 165.

[117] *Ibid.*, p. 164.

[118] 18 *JCC* 958-960.

[119] Washington to Edmund Randolph, November 7, 1780, 20 *WW* 317. The Congressional Resolves of October 21, were executed into General Orders by Washington and published for the Army on November 1. See *ibid.*, pp. 277-281.

[120] For the four States of Connecticut, Rhode Island, Massachusetts, and New York, General Hand could report a total of only 527 men.

brigades, regiments, and detachments, totaled 5,835.[121] Meanwhile the campaign against Cornwallis in Virginia had begun. With such meager resources, and with small prospect of improvement, the campaign was carried on to a successful conclusion. For this victory the American people are indebted not so much to the valuable material aid of the French as to the militia organizations[122] which sprang to the defense of that State, and to a benevolent Providence, Who, despite all their shortcomings, approvingly guided their destinies.

Thus, on the eve of the Battle of Yorktown, with Congress exerting its authority to an unprecedented degree, with the Army organized on an efficient basis, and with the States inclined to be more sympathetic to the resolutions of Congress for recruiting men, the Army dwindled to less than 6,000 men. The conclusion cannot be avoided that the delegates to Congress, after six years of service in that deliberative body, must have influenced their States to a degree sufficient to permit the grant of larger discretionary powers for Congress. Some evidence of this may be ascertained from a cursory glance over the *Journals*. More specifically, some time in the latter part of 1780 a committee selected to study the increase of powers for Congress made its report. The prosecution of war, said the report, "renders it highly important to the interests of these United States that at this crisis the common council of America [Congress] should be vested with sufficient power to call forth from time to time the military resources of the said States."[123]

What was responsible for this situation? The answer was six years in the making. While the interests of the States dictated the policy of the Government, the central authority was rendered impotent to deal with the many problems created by the war, which the States individually could not solve, and not the least among which was the depreciation of the currency and its attendant evils.

---

[121] Washington to Benjamin Lincoln, February 21, 1781, 21 *WW* 264-265; Washington to John Armstrong, March 26, *ibid.*, p. 379; Report of T.A.G. on Recruitment, April 1, *The Manuscript Collection of George Washington*, Washington, Library of Congress, Vol. 169, No. 93; Memo Tench Tilghman, July 15, 1781, 22 *WW* 388 note.

[122] Washington was fearful that the resort to short enlistments, despite the *Resolves* of October 21, 1780, would weaken the campaign. See Washington to Col. Fitzhugh, August 8, 1781, *ibid.*, p. 481.

[123] 18 *JCC* 897.

National Economy Endangered By Faulty Military Policy

To raise and equip the armies necessary to combat the mother country, the Continental Congress began as early as 1775 to print paper money backed only by the promise to redeem it at some future date. The States also retained a free hand to issue their own currency, making a total of fourteen different media of exchange in a country where one third of the population, indifferent or even hostile to the cause of independence, refused to accept any of it as legal tender. The consequences of this whole system of questionable finance brought with it the inevitable forces of inflation, profiteering, price raising, stockjobbing, and the host of other evils connected with a spiraling and uncontrolled economy.[124]

Skyrocketing prices and diminishing dollar values prompted Washington to increase the bounties for recruits. By the end of 1780, conditions had grown so bad that even essential supplies of food and clothing, as well as arms and ammunition, had disappeared from the market because of unscrupulous speculators who hoarded these items only to sell them for all that the traffic would bear. Fearing the consequences inherent in the continuation of this state of affairs, Washington tried to interest Congress in some sort of solution. Although the enlistment program of 1780 was essential, Washington was sure this could not be successful because "there are wanting many concomitants to bring about this event; among which, placing our finances upon a proper footing is not the least difficult." [125] On December 10, 1780 he reechoed this note of pessimism to Gouverneur Morris, confessing that although the Army was small, and recruits were needed badly, added levies would not provide a remedy unless provisions and supplies were also made available.[126]

The frightful portents of the debilitated structure of American economy, and the growing distrust of the people in the financial system, were matters of grave concern to the Commander in Chief. When even the genius of Gouverneur Morris was insufficient to

---

[124] Miller, *Triumph*, pp. 433-451.

[125] Washington to Edmund Randolph, November 7, 1780, 20 *WW* 317.

[126] Washington to Morris, December 10, 1780, *ibid.*, pp. 457-458. The States were called upon to supply clothes to their own recruits, Congress being unable to procure them at this time. As the theater of war shifted southward, Virginia passed a series of acts to recruit her quota of troops fully clothed and supplied to sustain them in combat. See John Dunlap and James Hayes, *Acts Passed at the General Assembly of the Commonwealth of Virginia*, 1781, pp. 1-20.

draw blood from a stone, Washington looked to France for a solution. By mid-January of the new year, John Laurens was ready to go to the Court of Louis XVI armed with Washington's observations on the causes of America's weakened condition. Considering the diffused population of the land, Laurens was advised, together with

> the consequent difficulty of drawing together its resources; the composition and temper of a part of its inhabitants; the want of a sufficient stock of national wealth as a foundation for Revenue and the almost total extinction of commerce; the efforts we have been compelled to make for carrying on the war, have exceeded the national abilities of this country and by degrees brought it to a crisis, which renders immediate and efficacious succors from abroad indispensable to its safety.[127]

Reliance upon allies for financial aid did not, however, deter some of the patriot leaders in their efforts to stabilize the currency. Towards the end of the summer of 1781 the campaign in the South was turning against Cornwallis; with the prospect of an early end to hostilities, financial stability became not only desirable but urgently necessary if the credit of the nation was to be established in Europe. While strongly recommending measures to give "proper stamina" to the country's finances, Washington also lamented the wasteful method by which the war was waged in the absence of a strong central government: If the resources which have been drawn forth had been applied to great objects by one common head, American independence would have been secured and rendered as unshaken as Mount Atlas.[128]

The surrender of Lord Cornwallis at Yorktown on October 19 was met with mixed emotions among the people. There were those who felt that the war was over, hence there was no need for continued military preparations; there were others who insisted that preparedness should be continued. Sensing the dangerous implications of this divided opinion, Washington hastened to Philadelphia in an attempt to restrain Congress from falling "into a State of Languor and Relaxation," and to stimulate them "to the best Improvement of our Late Success by takg. the most vigorous and effectual Measures, to be ready for an early and decisive Campaign the next year." [129] By January 4, 1782, amid the gaiety and

---

[127] Washington to Laurens, January 15, 1781, 21 *WW* 105.
[128] Washington to Col. Fitzhugh, August 8, 1781, 22 *WW* 481.
[129] Washington to Greene, November 16, 1781, 23 *WW* 347.

patriotic exuberance everywhere to be evidenced in the city of brotherly love, Washington was happy to note that Congress had displayed the best disposition imaginable to prepare vigorously for another campaign.[130]

Personnel Policies At End of War

After the surrender of Cornwallis the war deteriorated into a series of savage raids on both sides which did little more than to increase the restlessness of the American soldiery who were nursing an accumulating list of grievances against the Congress. Poor food and lack of clothing and shelter coupled with an absence of pay for months at a time were strong motives for dissension within the ranks of the American Army; and now that the war, for all intents and purposes, had ended, the men began to insist upon a more equitable solution for their problems.

Although the soldiers had endured their privations and suffering with more than extraordinary fortitude, they now looked with some misgivings upon the apparent intention of the States and Congress to neglect their well-being. For many there was the matter of pay to be settled and for others, especially the officers, there was the prospect of returning to their homes laden with debt much of which had been incurred while in service.[131] All were reluctant to go home until these problems were agreeably settled.

With little or no fighting to occupy the Army, it was logical that the men would readily lend themselves to speculation over their fate and eagerly listen to the exhortations of some of the more outspoken malcontents. Congress therefore had more than ample warning of the ominous portents of a soldiery whose every want and need had been neglected whether wilfully or not. The lesson of the uprising of the Pennsylvania and New Jersey Lines in January, 1781 [132] should have been sufficient to move Congress and the States to arrive at a just solution of such lingering difficulties. But neither this nor the special pleas made by Washington [133] in behalf of the troops were sufficient to stimulate Congress to a more respectable plan for settling the grievances of the Army.

[130] Washington to Lafayette, January 4, 1782, *ibid.*, p. 429.
[131] Freeman, *op. cit.*, V, pp. 430-431.
[132] Miller, *Triumph*, pp. 542-545; Freeman, *op. cit.*, V., chap. 15; Carl Van Doren, *Mutiny in January*, New York, Viking Press, 1943, *passim*.
[133] Frothingham, *op. cit.*, p. 375.

The plain fact was that Congress was powerless to do anything about it and the States individually refused to assume the financial burden involved. This was a strange dilemma. Congress had found it difficult to recruit an Army during the course of the war, and now they found it even more difficult to disband it.

By March, 1783, the troops at Newburg had grown more dissatisfied by the failure of Congress to arrive at a suitable formula for settling the question of pay, and listened attentively to the solutions offered by some of their own numbers. On March 10, a general meeting was called to make vigorous demands upon Congress for compensation and redress of just grievances. To Washington, the strong tenor of these anonymous addresses posed a danger not only to the war effort, but also to the civil liberties for which so many had sacrificed their lives.

The General met this new threat head on by going before the men themselves as spokesman for Congress as well as defender of the just rights of the soldiers. He reminded them of the honor and glory their arms had won for the country, and urged them to turn from those who sought "to open the flood Gates of Civil discord, and deluge our rising Empire in Blood.[134] By a show of humility, firmness, and tact, Washington succeeded in quelling the disturbance in the main Army but there soon developed an equally disquieting circumstance among the Maryland line.[135]

By June, 1783, these troops were in garrison in Philadelphia. Most of them were foreigners and almost all were short-term recruits who had experienced few of the hardships of battle. Raising the same cry as their brethren at Newburg, these men grew more intolerable and under the influence of their loosely held liquor they marched upon the State House, forced the Congress to flee, and caroused around the city in a drunken melee. In this case Washington ordered Continental troops to Philadelphia whereupon the insurgents quickly laid down their arms. Menacing as this situation was, Congress by its precipitate action sacrificed what little prestige and dignity it possessed. Unable to solve the great problems of war, this august body fled the city, sharply emphasiz-

---

[134] 26 *WW* 227.
[135] On April 11, 1783, Congress issued a proclamation for the cessation of hostilities but offered no method by which the Army was to be disbanded. See 24 *JCC* 238-240. This was put into effect by Washington eight days later See GO April 18, 1783, 26 *WW* 334-336. This merely ordered the cessation of hostilities and did not refer to a general peace.

ing the degree of its debility when its collective courage deserted it.

But despite all the shortcomings of Congress, and notwithstanding the action of a handful of foreigners in the Maryland Line, few men in the Army were willing to transfer Congressional authority to thirteen States. In fact most of the soldiers were for the maintenance of one continental body, looking up to one sovereign authority, and one of their favorite toasts was: "A hoop to the barrel and cement to the Union." Leading nationalists like John Adams called attention to the need of a strong union to frustrate the evil designs of European monarchies. A strong union, supported by a sizeable Army and a strong Navy, together with an adequate diplomatic corps, they argued, would compel respect for America. But American statesmanship was to ignore all three elements of the national strategy.

The strong nationalistic bent of the Army was no small consideration in the decision to reduce the Army. The States were in no mood to sanction the permanency of an Army which showed signs of allegiance to a central authority rather than to the individual States. This Army, which would enforce the laws of the Union to the detriment of States rights, was a "menace"; and, when all was said and done, the States had not gone to war to transfer authority from London to Philadelphia.

It is a tribute to the men under arms, who had endured all manner of privation and suffering, and who had a just right to make strong demands for redress, that they refused to subvert the authority of the Government. Though tempted and even partially swayed, they remained steadfast in their loyalty and devotion to the cause of liberty and freedom. Few armies in history had ever suffered so much as the American Army and yet had made so little representation for a just recognition of the rights of the men who fought and bled, starved and grew lean, and froze and died to bequeath to a greater posterity the fruits of their sacrifices. What transpired in the mutinies of 1781, and at Newburg and Philadelphia in 1783, was simply the final culmination of the enduring hardships that faced the men. The cup of forebearance had overflowed. That the great majority remained loyal to the very end attests to their patriotism and loyalty. *At no time was there a serious military threat against the civil authority*. Whatever the lessons of the Revolution, none should stand out more glaringly than the Army in America, under the distinguished leadership of George Washington, was the guardian of the liberties of the people. This was the rich heritage the Commander in Chief willed to the unborn millions of Americans who under similar circumstances would emulate the examples set forth by the heroes of the Revolution. But because of a traditional hatred and fear of European military systems, the American Army has never been separated in the public mind from those systems, and the fiction has endured that an American Army can be a threat to democratic institutions. The story of the Revolution disproves this thesis and the subsequent military history of the United States further refutes it.

Lessons

Of the many important lessons derived from this war, one of the most significant was the danger to which inexperienced statesmen exposed the cause of independence by ignorance of military affairs and an unsound military policy as expressed in legislation. By the end of the conflict, some 400,000 men had been mustered into the service at a cost of some 370 millions of dollars,[136] when only 25% of this number would have been sufficient to achieve victory in considerably less time and at considerably less cost. Despite the host of men called to the colors, Washington never had at any one time more than 17,000, and at Trenton and Princeton, when his needs were greatest, he had an effective force of less than 4,000.

Competition between the Congress and the individual States for the services of men made it difficult to place an Army in the field for any length of time. This problem was accentuated by the general lack of resources which developed as the war dragged on until it was no longer a question of how to procure men but of how to equip, feed, and shelter them once they were enlisted. All the problems which beset the Commander in Chief for eight years might have been solved if a determined effort had been made in the beginning by a sufficiently strong executive, to "bring thousands into the field, push the enemy with vigor, drive them from our towns, storm their strongholds, and never pause until they were forced from our shores." [137] Instead, we pursued a

---

[136] *American State Papers, Military Affairs,* Vol. I, pp. 15-20.
[137] Article in New Jersey Gazette, March 18, 1788, quoted in Montross, *op. cit.,* pp. 274-275.

policy which suffered the enemy to conduct an almost unmolested military occupation of our cities for eight years. With these costly lessons fresh in mind, not more than a year after the cessation of hostilities, Americans, weary of war and its consequences, relaxed their guard. The valuable military experience of the men who fought was allowed to slip into eternity.

The narrative thus far has brought out that the Revolutionary War was the genesis of several basic features of US military policy. The most prominent of these is the manpower procurement policy. This stemmed from a traditional and deep-seated aversion to standing armies and long terms of service. It led to too-complete reliance on the militia system, and too rapid a personnel turn-over. Its faults showed up glaringly almost at once, forcing the adoption of such expedients as an enlistment bounty or bonus, and finally a modified form of draft. Other strong features of our military policy, born during this period, were the firm resolve to keep the military always responsible to civil authority, and the determination to dissolve the military forces as soon as danger subsided.

CHAPTER 2

Postwar Policies

Washington Lays the Foundation For a Sound Military
Policy—Need For a Peacetime Military Policy—The Un-
guarded Ramparts—Opponents of National Defense Pre-
vail—Von Steuben and Knox Attempt to Remodel the
Militia—Military Requirement For Preserving Domestic
Tranquility—Comments

THE VOLUMINOUS testimony of George Washington and
of the officers under his command urging the adoption of a
firm military policy, together with the costly experience of the war,
unmistakably pointed the way toward a sound military posture.
But the emotional imbalance that was prevalent toward the end
of the war took hold of the American mind; local prejudices were
permitted to sway the judgment of thinking men and the United
States embarked upon a wavering and hesitant course chartered
by a negative military policy. Surrounded by enemies or potential
enemies, and forced to assume the responsibility for protecting the
wide frontiers, shortsighted Americans could not escape the need
for an adequate military force arranged, organized, and projected
on a long-range plan. But instead of accepting this responsibility,
they succumbed to the long-standing fear of European military
systems and turned their backs upon those who were clear-visioned
enough to perceive that the only insurance for peace is to be prepared for war.

Washington Lays the Foundation for a Sound Military Policy

With the episodes of Newburg and Philadelphia fresh in mind,
Congress began to study the question of disbanding the Army.
Hostilities had ceased; therefore there was no need, they felt, for
keeping a large army in the field. Also it was expensive to keep
men under arms, argued some who wished to economize at all
costs. But there were others in Congress who feared the consequences of letting down the country's guard too precipitately; consequently a lively debate ensued over the relative merits of partial
or complete disarmament. On the one side were those who urged
caution, with the argument that it was impolitic to disband the

47

army while the British remained in the United States.[1] The opposite view was expressed by those who considered the war to be at an end and consequently "not a moment ought to be lost in disburdening the public of needless expence *(sic)*." [2] As a compromise it was agreed on April 23, 1783 to offer the soldiers who had enlisted for the duration the option of a furlough or a discharge.[3]

Meanwhile, Congress had appointed a committee, with Alexander Hamilton as chairman, to inquire into and report upon the measures necessary for the arrangement of a general peacetime military establishment. On April 9 Hamilton informed Washington of these plans and asked for his sentiments upon "such institutions of every kind for the interior defence of these States as may be best adapted to their circumstances and conciliate security with economy."[4] Acting with deliberate dispatch, Washington summoned the views of his most trusted officers and within two weeks he had before him their opinions.[5]

After a brief but thorough study of these remarkable papers, Washington outlined his plan for a peacetime establishment and on May 2, 1783 addressed it to Hamilton. In it he grouped his ideas under four main headings: First, a regular army for garrison purposes on the frontiers "to awe the Indians, protect our trade, prevent the encroachment of our Neighbours of Canada and the Florida's, and guard us at least from surprizes; Also for security of our Magazines." [6] Second, a well-organized militia "upon a Plan that will pervade all the States, and introduce similarity in their Establishments." Third, establishing arsenals of all kinds of military stores, and fourth, the introduction of one or more academies "for the Instruction of the Art Military; particularly those

---

[1] 25 *JCC*, 963, James Madison, "Notes of Debates in the Continental Congress."

[2] *Ibid.*, p. 965.

[3] *Ibid.*, p. 963.

[4] Hamilton to Washington, April 9, 1783, 219 *GWMSS,* No. 19.

[5] See ltr Von Steuben to Washington, April 15, 1783, *Ibid.*, No. 52, April 21, Nos. 119-122; Samuel Huntington to Washington, April 16, *Ibid.*, No. 71; Henry Knox to Washington, April 17, *Ibid.*, Nos. 85-86; William Heath to Washington, April 17, *Ibid.*, No. 84; Geo. Clinton to Washington, April 17, *Ibid.*, Nos. 82-83; Timothy Pickering to Washington, April 22, *Ibid.*, Nos. 130-137; Rufus Putman to Washington, April 25, *Ibid.*, Vol. 220, Nos. 21-23. Washington drew heavily upon the recommendations of these experts, recommendations which may be applicable even today. See also John McAuley Palmer, *Washington, Lincoln, Wilson, Three American Statesmen*, New York, Doubleday Doran & Co., Inc., 1930, Chap. V.

[6] See Palmer, *Washington, Lincoln, Wilson,* pp. 70-71.

Branches of it which respect Engineering and Artillery, the knowledge of which, is most difficult to obtain. Also Manufactories of
some kinds of Military Stores."

With reference to a standing army, Washington reaffirmed his
earlier admonitions that large standing armies "hath ever been considered dangerous to the liberties of a Country"; and fortunately
for the United States their isolated position from Europe freed
them of the necessity of maintaining, in peacetime, a large regular
force. And, because of the tremendous debt incurred in waging
war against England, a standing army, adequate for defense, could
not be maintained without great oppression of the people. What
was more necessary, he was sure, after the discharge of those debts,
was a well-equipped Navy, without which, in case of war, "we
could neither protect our Commerce, nor yield that Assistance to
each other, which, on such an extent of Sea-Coast, our mutual
Safety would require." [7]

The requisite number of troops to maintain a respectable
position before the Indians and the British in Canada, as well as
our neighbors to the south, Washington estimated at 2631 officers
and men. These would be distributed among the posts in the northwest and in those forts to be erected along the entire frontier from
north to south. If this number proved to be too large, it could be
reduced by degrees. This solution was preferable to one where the
initial force might be smaller only to find it necessary to increase
"after some unfortunate disasters may have happened to the
Garrisons; discouraging to us, and an inducement to the Enemy to
attempt a repitition [sic] of them." [8]

This force of 2,631 Washington would consider as Continental
troops looking to Congress for their orders, their pay, and supplies
of every kind. He proposed to divide them into four regiments of
infantry, 1,908 men, and one regiment of artillery, 723 men.
Looking to the future, he refused to reduce the number of units
and insisted upon eliminating instead one sergeant and 18 enlisted
men from each company, but keeping the number of officers constant. The importance of this proposal could not be overestimated
because the situation on the frontiers made it imperative to detach
men from those regiments and "in the detached State in which

---

[7] "Sentiments on Peace Establishment," 26 *WW* 375-376.
[8] *Ibid.*, p. 380.

these Regiments must be employed, they cannot consistently with the good of the Service be reduced."

In case of a war this force could easily be brought up to strength simply by the addition of 18 men to each company; and if additional men had to be recruited, there would be a number of officers sufficiently trained and experienced who could "mix and diffuse their knowledge . . . to other Corps, without the lapse of Time, which, without such Provision, would be necessary to bring intire [sic] new Corps acquainted with the principles of it." [9]

The officers necessary to command the proposed establishment Washington would select from among those who declared an intention to remain in the service. This should be done in such a manner "that they might be so blended together from the Several Lines, as to remove, as much as possible, all Ideas of State distinctions." Enlisted men could be drawn from among those still in service who had engaged for three years. Subsequent enlistments were not to be for less than three years. [10]

By staggering the enlistment of the soldiers for the Regular Army, the country would be assured of the services of experienced men in any emergency. And, by basing the system upon a small nucleus of adequately trained and disciplined men, Washington offered an inexpensive form of national peace insurance which would pay large dividends to the stockholders. Around this well-knit and highly trained body could be built a system through which the legions of citizen soldiers of the future could benefit from the experience of the professional soldier. [11]

In his reference to the militia as the great bulwark of liberty and independence, Washington alluded to a well-trained and well-established organization. The future tranquility of the United States, he wrote, was dependent in a great measure upon the contemplated peacetime military establishment. The only insurance against insult, hostility, and the calamities of War "is to put the National Militia in such a condition as that they may appear truly respectable in the Eyes of our Friends and formidable to those

---

[9] *Ibid.*, 380-381. There is no doubt that Washington had in mind the expansible army idea proposed by Secretary of War John Calhoun in 1820. *Cf.* John McAuley Palmer, *America in Arms,* Washington, The Infantry Journal Press, 1943, p. 72.

[10] *Ibid.*, 384-385.

[11] Although Washington did not spell this out in his recommendations on the standing army, it is difficult to escape the inference.

who would otherwise become our enemies." [12] Calling upon the lessons of the historical past to demonstrate the utility of a well-organized militia, the Commander in Chief drew attention to the military greatness of Rome and Greece and the example of Switzerland. And after assuring himself that the American people were too well acquainted with the merits of a strong militia to dwell at length upon the subject, he proceeded to the heart of the problem.

Citizenship in a free government, he said, implied an obligation to defend its freedom. For that reason, Americans from 18 to 50 years of age should be

> borne on the Militia Rolls, provided with uniform Arms and so far accustomed to the use of them, that the total strength of the Country might be called forth at a Short Notice on any very interesting Emergency.[13]

From the vast body of the militia, Washington recommended the organization of something like an elite corps or minuteman organization under federal control which he would term the Continental Militia. These ranks were to be filled by specially selected groups of young men between 18 and 25, and while they would be viewed as

> the Van and flower of the American Forces, ever ready for Action and zealous to be employed whenever it may become necessary in the service of their Country; they should meet with such exemptions, privileges or distinctions, as might tend to keep alive a true Military pride, a nice sense of honour, and a patriotic regard for the public. Such sentiments, indeed, ought to be instilled into our Youths, with their earliest years, to be cherished and inculcated as frequently and forcibly as possible.[14]

In order to prove effective in the scheme of things, this portion of the militia should be exercised at least from 12 to 25 days in a year. Thus by calling on the best men and bringing them before the public as often as practicable, a just sense of pride could be easily instilled in the people that would make it universally reputable to bear arms and disgraceful to decline. In short, "by keeping up in Peace a well regulated and disciplined Militia, we shall take

---

[12] 26 *WW* 388.
[13] *Ibid.,* 388-389.
[14] *Ibid.,* 390.

the fairest and best method to preserve, for a long time to come, the happiness, dignity, and Independence of our Country." [15]

On the proposition relating to arsenals of all kinds of military stores, Washington deferred to the superior judgment of his expert, General Knox, who had worked up an elaborate plan of execution in this regard.[16] However, since West Point had been designated as the main depository for all military stores, and since this post was vulnerable to surprise attack, Washington preferred to store there only an adequate supply for its defence in almost any extremity. The important arsenals he would establish in the interior, one in the south, one in the middle States, and one for the eastern States;[17] each to be equipped with arms, ammunition, and implements of war to accommodate 30,000 men.[18]

With reference to the subject of military academies and manufactories, Washington again made few observations, leaving the details to Von Steuben who was making a thorough study of the subject.[19] There was little doubt in the Commander's mind as to the need for these institutions, but how far the United States was able at this time to go into great and expensive arrangements was still another matter. Nevertheless he was sure that some such undertaking should be initiated to free the Government from dependence upon outside sources for war materiel. It was his opinion that

> if we should not be able to go largely into the business [of manufacturing] at present, we should nevertheless have a reference to such establishments hereafter, and in the means *(sic)* time that we ought to have such works carried on, wherever our principle Arsenals may be fixed, as will not only be sufficient to repair and keep in good order the Arms, Artillery, Stores &c of the Post, but shall also extend to Founderies and some other essential matters.[20]

Until a system of military education could be adopted which would meet the needs of the service, Washington would provide

---

[15] *Ibid.,* 393-394. It is interesting to note the similarity between this plan and the proposals made by Secretary of War Henry L. Stimson in 1912 with reference to the land forces of the United States.

[16] See ltr Knox to Washington, April 17, 1783, 219 *GW MSS* 85-86.

[17] General Knox proposed the erection of five arsenals.

[18] 26 *WW* 395-396.

[19] See Von Steuben, *"A Letter on the Subject of an Established Militia and Military Arrangements Addressed to the Inhabitants of the United States,* New York, J. McLean & Co., 1784. Hereafter cited as Von Steuben, "A Letter." See also Washington to Von Steuben, March 15, 1785, 26 *WW* 359-360.

[20] *Ibid.,* 397-398.

instruction for a select few at those posts where the "principle Engineers and Artillerists shall be stationed." This would "render
them much more accomplished and capable of performing the
duties of Officers, even in the Infantry or any other Corps whatsoever." Preserving the talents of this specialized group by means
of an institution calculated to keep alive and diffuse the knowledge
of the military art was indispensable

> unless we intend to let the Science become extinct, and to depend
> entirely upon the Foreigners for their friendly aid, if ever we
> should again be involved in Hostility. For it must be understood,
> that a Corps of able Engineers and expert Artillerists cannot be
> raised in a day, nor made such by any exertions, in the same time,
> which it would take to form an excellent body of infantry from
> a well regulated Militia.[21]

On the whole Washington was convinced that his proposals
for a small standing army would not be seriously challenged. But
with reference to the "well-regulated Militia," the experience of
the war coupled with the attitude of the States was sufficient reason
for sober reflection. Recognizing the possibility that the States
might turn deaf ears to any proposition for regulating the militia
on a national scale, he drew their attention to the importance of
placing the "Militia of the Union" upon a regular and respectable
footing. "The Militia of the Country," he wrote,

> must be considered the Palladium of our security, and the first
> effectual resort in case of hostility; It is essential therefore, that
> the same system should pervade the whole; that the formation
> and discipline of the Militia of the Continent should be abso-
> lutely uniform, and that the same species of Arms, Accoutre-
> ments and Military Apparatus, should be introduced in every
> part of the United States; No one, who has not learned it from
> experience, can conceive the difficulty, expense, and confusion
> which result from a contrary system, or the vague Arrange-
> ments which have hitherto prevailed.[22]

Need for a Peacetime Military Policy

After five months of careful study and analysis of Washington's "Sentiments on the Peace Establishment," Alexander

---

[21] *Ibid.*, 396-397. Over a period of years this system would give to the Regular
Army a body of highly expert technicians who could take their places wherever
they might be needed "in the Infantry or any other Corps whatsoever. . . ."
Whether Washington intended it or not, this fell in with the general scheme of
things in the expansible army idea.
[22] Circular to the States, June 8, 1783, 26 *WW* 494.

Hamilton submitted a comprehensive report to the Congress. Drawing upon the legal authority implied and expressed in the Articles of Confederation for supporting a standing army in peace and war, he went on to prove that it was not the intention of the framers of this document to deprive the Government of the right of taking such precautions as should appear to them essential to the general security. A distinction that the general security would be provided for in time of war by the forces of the Union, and in time of peace by those of each State, was illogical and dangerous to the Nation. For if this distinction be admitted, then the Government could prepare for an emergency only after an open attack had occurred. Then, and then only, would they be authorized to prepare for defense, to raise a single regiment, or to build a single ship. Considering the length of time required to raise and organize an army and still more to build and equip a navy, it would presume an intention in the Confederation of obliging the United States to suspend all provision for the common defense until after a declaration of war, or an invasion.[23]

There were many factors which inclined the opinion of this committee report toward a preference for a federal establishment over individual State organizations. From the viewpoint of economy and efficiency, the construction and maintenance of fortifications, the organization and subsistence of standing forces, and the establishment of founderies and "manufactories of arms, powder &c.," calculated to provide a systematic defense of each section of the country, dictated the need for centralized federal control. Moreover, such objects as jurisdiction over the territory not included with in the original claim of any of the States, free navigation of the Mississippi as well as the Great Lakes, unhampered foreign commerce, and the rights to the fisheries, all dependent upon the laws of nations and on treaty, "demand the joint protection of the Union, and cannot with propriety be trusted to separate establishments."[24]

The federal establishment proposed by the Committee was somewhat similar to that advocated by Washington. It was to consist of four regiments of infantry and one of artillery.[25] Each regi-

---

[23] Report of the Committee, October 23, 1783, 25 *JCC* 723.
[24] *Ibid.,* 724.
[25] The artillery regiment was to be incorporated with the engineers and the whole called the Corps of Engineers.

ment of infantry was to consist of two battalions, each battalion of four companies, and each company of sixty-four rank and file which in time of war was to be recruited to one hundred and twenty-eight.[26] The number of troops requisite to fill these regiments would be raised by the States in proportion to their respective populations. But since no State would be required to furnish a complete regiment, the appointment of officers posed a difficult problem. This could be solved, however, if the States "could be induced to transfer this right to Congress and indeed, without it there can never be regularity in the Military system."[27]

Washington's proposal to erect and maintain fortifications also met with the approval of the Committee, but they recommended two types: Those for internal security (the forts) and those for the protection of the fleets of the United States. Along the line of these fortifications were selected several sites for the arsenals and magazines necessary to completely equip 30,000 men for the field or for a siege calculated on a three years' supply.[28]

Because it was considered that military academies rarely compensate for the expense, and because it was felt that military knowledge is best acquired in service, it was decided to defer judgment upon this point until some future date.[29] The establishment of ordnance factories, however, was a matter of immediate concern. There were two reasons for this:

> The first that every country ought to endeavour to have within itself all the means essential to its own preservation, as to depend on the casualties of foreign supplies is to render its own security precarious; the second, that as it will be indispensable to keep up a Corps of Artillery and some other troops, the labor of a part of these, bestowed upon the manufactories will enable the public to supply itself on better and cheaper terms than by importation.[30]

For these purposes the Committee recommended that the "Secretary at War" be directed by Congress to draw up a detailed plan designating the places where those founderies and manu-

---

[26] 25 *JCC* 725.
[27] *Ibid.*, 736-737.
[28] *Ibid.*, 738. Five locations were selected: Springfield, Massachusetts; West Point; Carlisle, Pennsylvania; some convenient point on the James River, Virginia; and Camden, South Carolina. Each was to maintain stockage sufficient for 6,000 men.
[29] *Ibid.*, 738.
[30] *Ibid.*, 739.

factories could be erected with advantage, considering the means to be employed and the expense to be incurred in the execution.[31]

After carefully outlining the plan of a standing army, the Committee then proceeded to the item of next importance, the militia. In considering all the means of national defense, Congress could not overlook that of a well-regulated militia. Admitting the necessity of federal supervision and control of the arsenals and magazines, and recognizing the advantages flowing from a uniform militia similar in all details to the regular forces, the conclusion could easily be drawn that it would be proper for Congress to adopt and recommend a plan for this purpose.[32]

This plan classified all able-bodied free male inhabitants, between the ages of 20 and 50, of each State into two general classes: the married and the single men. Each class to be formed into corps of infantry and dragoons, organized in the same manner as proposed for the regular troops. The single class was required to serve nine days a year and the married men only six, each category to be subject to the proper penalties in case of absence from duty. In addition to these, a third class was to be organized and called "fencibles, fusileers, train bands, or whatever else may be thought proper," with the same organization as the infantry of the other classes. These were to be recruited from the first two classes on a voluntary basis engaged for a term of eight years, provided they should not exceed the proportion of one to fifty of all the enrolled militia of the State, and provided that if a war broke out, they would be obliged to serve three years after they took the field, and to march wherever the service might require.[33] The expenses for this organization were reckoned at $60,000 per year, a sum which could be nearly defrayed from "the militia fines if properly managed," or be small burden to the people as a whole.[34]

Immediately after this report was read to the delegates as-

---

[31] *Ibid.*

[32] *Ibid.*, 741.

[33] *Ibid.*, 741-742. It is significant to note that this latter provision was intended to correct the error made during the War in recruiting for short terms. Moreover, it was also intended to abolish any restriction which the individual States might choose to impose upon these men as members of the State militia. Based upon the population of the time, some 8,000 were eligible for this class, all under Federal control. If this plan was accepted an immediate force of some 12,000 would have been created.

[34] Although it was looked upon as an equitable solution for defraying the expense, it was filled with abuses and inequalities. See Lena London, "The Militia Fine," *Military Affairs*, Vol. 15, pp. 133-134.

sembled in Congress, the Committee of the Whole [of Congress] concluded: "that some garrisons ought to be maintained in time of peace at the expence *(sic)* of the United States for their security and defense, under their present circumstance." [35]

Within two weeks, Elbridge Gerry made an attempt to leave to the discretion of the Commander in Chief the size of the Army necessary for security. A motion was made to direct Washington to discharge the Army, after the British evacuated New York, except 500 men, with proper officers, or such number as he might judge necessary for garrisoning the posts, and guarding the public magazines of the United States.[36] However, the delegates were not ready to grant such discretionary power, and the question was lost. The vote against this important measure did not represent the attitude of the thirteen States, but rather that of seven. With only seven of the States represented, it required the unanimous approval of the whole of Congress for the passage of any measure. But this was nothing new. It had been the practice since the early days of the war for members, for one reason or another, to absent themselves. Now that peace had returned, the necessity for a full representation could no longer be ignored by those present nor those absent. There was the question of the definitive peace treaty to be voted upon as well as the peacetime military establishment and other matters of national concern. On November 1 a committee was created to bring these important questions before the attention of the recalcitrant States and to urge them to make full representation.[37]

It was not until December 23 that a resolution was passed notifying those States that their conduct was not only delaying public business, but also dangerous to the national welfare.[38] Earlier that year Washington had tried to warn against the menacing implications of a weak executive branch of the government,[39] but this was heeded only by a few. Now, in December, governmental debility made it even difficult to bring to a halt the accumulating train of events occasioned by the cessation of hostilities. Little had been done to adjust the problem of back

---

[35] 25 *JCC* 745.
[36] *Ibid.,* 806.
[37] *Ibid.,* 790-791.
[38] *Ibid.,* 836.
[39] 26 *WW* 486.

pay for the troops,[40] the British retained possession of the north-west posts, and no decision could be reached with reference to Hamilton's report on the peacetime military establishment. In this atmosphere of indecision, the Army was demobilized and the ships of the Navy were offered for sale.

After the British had evacuated New York,[41] Washington on his own initiative ordered the discharge of all troops in that State except one battalion of infantry "of 500 Rank and file, and about 100 artillery and these to be of the Men who had the longest to serve." [42] Two days later, after he had informed Congress of this step, the Commander in Chief took formal leave of the Army at Annapolis, Maryland.[43] The question of national defense with reference to the whole frontier was left to await the deliberate judgment of an impotent Congress.

The Unguarded Ramparts

The strategic importance of the northwestern posts to the se-curity of the United States was not overlooked by Washington, nor did he fail to bring it to the attention of Congress. Whatever were the intentions of Congress in this connection, he wrote on May 3, 1783, that the posts should certainly be occupied by United States troops the moment they were evacuated by the British.[44] But neither Congress nor Washington had any means for ascertaining the intentions of the British. As the weeks dragged on, the Com-mander in Chief made preparations to place the troops and every-thing destined for the posts on the western frontiers in a situation to move the moment that it was learned when the British would evacuate them.[45]

In these preparations Washington was forced to act with de-liberate hesitation, first because the British made no pretense at withdrawing, and secondly, Congress had not agreed upon a peacetime military establishment. While His Majesty's troops re-mained in that quarter there was little Americans could do to put

---

[40] Several attempts had been made to raise money for this object by the levy of an impost tax, but the States refused to surrender this privilege to Congress. See Miller, *Triumph*, pp. 666-669.
[41] American troops marched into New York City on November 26, 1783.
[42] 27 *WW* 278-279. General Henry Knox was selected to command. See also Washington to Knox, December 3, 1783, *ibid.*, 256-257.
[43] *Ibid.*, 284-285; 27 *JCC* 518.
[44] Washington to President of Congress, May 3, 1783, 26 *WW* 399.
[45] Washington to Major General Robert Howe, August 13, 1783, 27 *WW* 100.

an end to the Indian menace;[46] and, while Congress could make no decision on the size of the Army to be retained, it was difficult for Washington to estimate the number of troops which might be retained, or raised for this garrison duty on the frontier.[47]

As the year drew to a close the only positive action taken on this subject was the selection of a committee to look into the security of the military stores at Albany, Fort Schuyler, West Point, and Springfield. On January 29, 1784 the report of this committee verified the recommendations made by Washington on December 3 for 500 rank and file, but expressed some doubt as to the necessity for continuing a major general "in Command of the department of West-Point, with pay annexed to a separate department." [48]

Pending the findings of still another committee selected to study the measures proper to take possession of the frontier posts, Congress, on April 1, 1784, placed upon New York the responsibility for the security of the northwestern part of that State.[49] Five days later the committee report was read before Congress predicating the military policy for frontier defense upon the inevitable expansion westward. If and when the British evacuated the frontier posts, the defense of the western territory could only be guaranteed by American occupation of those sites in addition to the creation of such other forts "as may be necessary for the defense of the Western Territory proposed to be purchased of the Indian inhabitants of the United States." [50]

Some doubt was cast over the desirability of extending the garrisons west of Detroit because of the considerable expense involved, the size of the force required, the inconveniences arising from the great distance of the forts, and their exposed condition despite all efforts to secure them from attack. On the other hand, the strategic location of Niagara, Oswego, Fort Erie, and Detroit demanded immediate occupation by American forces. For

[46] The Indians on the frontiers of Virginia and Pennsylvania, encouraged by debility of Congress, were murdering and scalping many settlers. See Washington to Lafayette, May 10, 1783, 26 *WW* 421.

[47] Washington to Robert Howe, August 31, 1783, 27 *WW* 124-125. In response to General Nathanael Greene's query on the number of troops to be retained in the South, Washington could make no explicit recommendation while Congress remained indecisive. See Washington to Greene, May 18, 1783, 26 *WW* 442.

[48] 26 *JCC* 54.

[49] *Ibid.*, 180.

[50] *Ibid.*, 201-202.

these purposes the committee recommended the enlistment, as soon as possible, of 896 men to serve the term of three years. These were to be furnished from quotas assigned to the different States. These troops were to be formed into three battalions of infantry and one of artillery.[51]

All this, however, was contingent upon the good intentions of Great Britain to relinquish the forts under the treaty stipulations; and this was in turn contingent upon the American fulfillment of their obligations under the same stipulations. This meant that the British would remain in the northwest until the problem of the loyalist and his property rights was settled and until all outstanding debts due English merchants were satisfied.[52]

If Congress had been powerless to enforce their will upon the States during the war when they were calling for a united effort against a powerful antagonist, how much more impotent were they when asking the States to make restitution to the hated loyalist and the despised London merchant? Reluctant to recede from this position, and egged on by Canada who insisted that surrender of the posts would dislocate an immensely profitable fur trade,[53] England took advantage of the American violations of the peace treaty, and retained control of the frontier posts for ten years.[54]

Opponents of National Defense Prevail

Americans had no way of determining, except by inference, the intentions of the British to remain in American territory, but it should have been obvious that without a respectable show of force, national objectives would remain subject to the whims of chance. It had been argued that in their bankrupt condition the United States could not afford to maintain a sufficiently strong force to impress the British or anyone else. But a nation that had carried on a great war for eight years and had prepared to go still further, could have found the means within itself to provide the sinews to safeguard those liberties so hard won. It would be to oversimplify the problem to ascribe the neglect of American security to bankruptcy. It should be remembered that there were

---

[51] *Ibid.*, 205.
[52] Great Britain had announced that she would retain the posts until these were satisfied. See Bailey, *op. cit.*, pp. 41-43.
[53] *Ibid.*, p. 42.
[54] The forts were turned over to the United States by the terms of the Jay Treaty, November 19, 1794.

many who viewed with suspicion the Continental Army which had demonstrated such a friendly regard for a strong national government. This nationalistic bent of the Army was unpalatable to those who feared any system of government which relegated the States to an inferior position, and which might make use of the military arm to awe the States. This group subscribed to the provincial insistence upon a weak central government with the military establishment under the exclusive control of the individual States.

After a full year of deliberate and careful scrutiny of the measures considered adequate to maintain a proper military balance, and notwithstanding even the recommendations made by Washington, Congress on June 2, 1784 voted the Continental Army out of existence, except 80 men,[55] on the premise that "standing armies in time of peace are inconsistent with the principles of republican governments, dangerous to the liberties of a free people, and generally converted into destructive engines for establishing despotism." [56] On the following day a resolution was passed to raise an army of 700 men organized as one regiment of eight companies of infantry and two companies of artillery.[57] This was considerably less than the figure recommended by the military experts in 1783.

National defense was measured in direct proportion to the geographic relation between Europe and America. Any warlike move against the United States would be considerably modified by this equation; and in the process, the militia could be brought to combat efficiency. But when this formula was applied to the national strategy and national objectives, expansion westward, its curative powers became less efficacious.

In the southwest, Spain had made it clear by 1781 that American expansion westward would be limited to a line far to the east of the Mississippi.[58] This was punctuated by the Spanish occupation of West Florida in 1781, and by the detachment of the Indian tribes east of the Mississippi River to serve as a barrier

---

[55] 27 *JCC* 524.
[56] *Ibid.*, 433, 518-519.
[57] *Ibid.*, 530-531.
[58] Lawrence Kinnaird (ed.), "Spain in the Mississippi Valley, 1765-1794," *Annual Report of the American Historical Association,* 1945, Vol. 3, Washington, Government Printing Office, 1946, p. xiii.

against the advancing American frontier.[59] In the lower Mississippi region, Spanish-American relations became complicated over the debts contracted by Oliver Pollock on behalf of Virginia and the Continental Congress,[60] and by the summer of 1784 led to the proclamation against the American right of free navigation of that river.[61] To the northwest, the British and their Indian allies posed a similar bar to American expansion. Against this double-barreled threat of containment which could be turned into a threat of invasion of United States' territory, American statesmen preferred to rely upon a system of passive defense. The army of 700 men was conceived for defense of the northwestern frontier; Spain was still considered a great friend and noble ally.

This small force of 700 men was to be recruited for one year, unless sooner discharged, from the militia of four States in the following proportions: Connecticut 165, New York 165, New Jersey 110, and Pennsylvania 260. The last two acted upon this by mid-August, 1784;[62] while in New York, because the legislature had adjourned, no action was taken until mid-October.[63] That this force of 700 men was not sufficient to assume the responsibilities that were carried, on the other side, by several regiments of British Regulars, only time would tell. But it was certain that within one year the perennial recruiting problem of the war days would be present again.

These important considerations were overshadowed by the disinclination of the States to yield competent powers to Congress so as to avoid the disintegration of the Union through internal as well as external influences. But for the tireless efforts of those delegates to Congress who championed the idea of a stronger central government, the final chapter in the history of the United States might have been written early in 1784. These men aroused their constituents to a recognition of the dire necessity for increasing the powers

---

[59] *Ibid.*, p. xi.
[60] *Ibid.*, pp. xiv-xv.
[61] *Ibid.*, p. xviii.
[62] See New Jersey, *Votes and Proceedings of the General Assembly,* August 6, 1784, pp. 95-96, 109; New Jersey, *Journal of the Proceedings of the Legislative Council,* August 13, 1784, pp. 5-7; New Jersey, *Minutes and Proceedings of the Joint Meeting,* August 18, 1784; Pennsylvania, *Minutes of Third Session of the Eighth General Assembly of the Commonwealth,* August 6, 10, 11, 1784, pp. 265, 271, 274.
[63] New York, *Votes and Proceedings of the Senate,* October 18, 1784, p. 4: New York, *Votes and Proceedings of the Assembly,* October 18, 1784, p. 6. The files for the State of Connecticut revealed no information in this regard.

of Congress, and they made a determined bid to save the government from its crippling defects.

The resultant increased support which the States rendered the Congress, though not very large, made it possible to effect an important change in the military policy. On April 1, 1785, it was *Resolved* to continue the Army of 700 men, but this time the length of service was increased from one to three years. Although the number remained insignificant in terms of population and extent of territorial domain, this was a noteworthy achievement—a Regular Army was thus created. As far as the militia organizations were concerned, the individual States modified their laws to bring the militia up to date according to State needs and desires.

Von Steuben and Knox Attempt to Remodel the Militia

After submitting to Washington his views on a peacetime national defense policy, Von Steuben continued to study this problem and in early 1784 published his findings. For the protection of the western frontiers he recommended a small regular army. To employ the militia for such duty "would be extremely embarrassing and expensive and fall infinitely short of both the wishes and expectations of Government." [64] To meet the needs of the country he placed his estimate for the military establishment at one complete legion of 3,000 men, a corps of artillery of 1,000 men, and seven legions of well-disciplined militia of 3,000 men each, subject to the call of their country at a moment's notice.[65]

Since the militia of the United States in 1784 was computed at some 400,000 men,[66] any plan to arm and train all of them according to the existing laws, was not only impracticable, Von Steuben thought, but also burdensome and intolerable from a social, economic, and industrial viewpoint. His plan therefore contemplated the training, for 31 days each year, of the younger men only. As the peace force was estimated at 21,000 men (7 legions) expansible to 42,000 in an emergency, this meant that only one-twentieth part of the militia would be subject to military training. This was less expensive to maintain than the whole. And, perhaps

---

[64] Von Steuben, "A Letter," p. 3.
[65] *Ibid.*, p. 7.
[66] *Ibid.*, p. 11.

more significantly, such a number could easily be raised on a voluntary basis without recourse to the distasteful draft.[67]

Because of the sparsely settled condition of the United States, and in order to facilitate nation-wide training, Von Steuben proposed the legion organization of 3,000 men comprising two battalions of artillery, a squadron of two troops of cavalry, and two small brigades of infantry.[68] This organization, multiplied seven times, was to be decentralized administratively in a manner consistent with the division of the country into three geographical departments. To the Northern Department, which encompassed New England, he assigned two militia legions; three were allocated to the Middle Department which comprised New York, New Jersey, Pennsylvania, Delaware, and Maryland; and the remaining two to the Southern Department which included Virginia, the Carolinas, and Georgia. Each department was to include the necessary arsenals, ordnance manufactures, and a system of military education.[69] This very realistic and intelligent plan went unheeded.

Two years later, General Henry Knox, as Secretary at War, offered his plan on the organization of the national defense. Unlike Von Steuben who would train only a volunteer militia, Knox insisted upon military training for all able-bodied men on the principle of the military obligation of all citizens. Accordingly, he divided the militia into three classes. Those between the ages of 18 and 20 he placed in the "advanced corps;" those between 21 and 45 in the "main corps;" and the remainder up to age 60 in the

---

[67] Von Steuben proposed to engage the men at the outset for three different periods. The first class to consist of one-third for two years, one-third for three years, and one-third for four years. After the expiration of the time of the two-year men, their places would be filled by another enlistment of the same number for three years. In operation this system would add every three years 7,000 well-disciplined and equipped men to the effective force of the United States. *Ibid.,* pp. 13-14.

[68] John McAuley Palmer, *Washington, Lincoln, Wilson,* p. 80. In a further breakdown, the triangular concept was maintained, i.e., one brigade of infantry, one troop of cavalry, and one battery of artillery complete with a field train. This resembles the present-day regimental combat team.

[69] *Ibid.,* pp. 80-81; Von Steuben, "A Letter," pp. 11-12. Palmer states that this departmental organization was the forerunner of the corps areas of pre-World War II days. With some minor alterations, George Washington approved Von Steuben's plan. See Washington to Von Steuben, March 15, 1784, 26 *WW* 359-360. It is to be noted that Von Steuben made no secret of the fact that his plan, in practice, really stood for a standing army; but, he added, "it is a Standing Army . . . composed of your brothers and sons. . . . Be assured you reflect upon yourselves by nourishing the suspicion, and wound the feelings of men who at least are entitled to your gratitude and esteem." Von Steuben, "A Letter," p. 16.

"reserve corps." [70] By this plan, Knox concentrated the system of military training in the advanced corps, which was to be trained for six weeks each year. After three years, this group would pass on to the main corps, which made up the largest reservoir of the manpower, thence to the reserve corps. Within due time, the organized militia of the United States would have been graduated from the first class.

Knox estimated the potential militia strength at 450,000, giving the three classes a strength of 45,000, 292,500, and 112,500, respectively. [71] By concentrating military training upon the first class, the total cost per year was computed at $750,000, which could be drawn from the exemption taxes in all three classes. [72] More important than this, the advanced corps, in any emergency could be mobilized immediately to serve, if need be, for three years. This mobilized force would constitute a Continental Army organized upon the legional or small division basis. For lesser emergencies Knox estimated that the required number could be obtained on a voluntary basis from each of the local units also for a period of three years. Mobilization for any emergency, according to this plan, would be systematic. All men were required to assemble fully armed at a designated rendezvous thence proceeding to other points until they arrived at the final rendezvous of the legion. Thus by bringing the men through successive stages of mobilization, they would arrive at legion headquarters fully equipped, officered, and organized into companies, brigades, and regiments. [73]

With reference to the Navy, Knox's plan made provision for the registration of all actual mariners or seamen in the several States, and divided them into two classes. The first was to comprise all seamen between 16 and 30, and the second those between 31

---

[70] Henry Knox, "A Plan for the General Arrangement of the Militia of the United States," March 18, 1786, p. 8; hereafter cited as Knox, "A Plan."

[71] *Ibid.*, p. 25.

[72] Palmer, *Washington, Lincoln, Wilson*, p. 90. *Cf.* Knox, "A Plan," pp. 26-27. Knox estimated the triennial expense of a legion at $146,356.

[73] Palmer, *Washington, Lincoln, Wilson*, pp. 91-93. Palmer says that Knox proposed to dispense entirely with the professional regular army. It is interesting to note that Knox left to the discretion of each State the responsibility for providing the necessary arms, accouterments, and equipment for the annual encampments. In order to provide some uniformity in these items, "specimens of the several articles shall be forwarded to the respective States from the war-office of the United States." This implied at least a supervision of training and equipment by professional army men. See Knox, "A Plan," p. 19.

and 45 inclusive. The first class would serve three years on board some public armed vessel or ship of war, as a commissioned officer, warrant officer, or private seaman. Should no demand be made upon men in this class after age 30, they would be exempt entirely from service.[74]

However feasible this plan may have been, like Von Steuben's proposal it was not acted upon. Not so much that it was impossible to finance the organizations (as we have seen, they could have been financed from funds derived from the militia itself), but Congress was powerless to place the stamp of approval upon such sweeping proposals. By this time it was evident that if the Nation was to survive, some constructive measures for strengthening the hand of the Government were imperative. But the fear of things military overshadowed necessities and by 1787 the military establishment was fixed at 700 men for three years.[75]

Military Requirements for Preserving Domestic Tranquility

By 1786 the economic and financial condition of the Nation led to a series of incidents in New England posing a challenge to government. The change in business incident to the war, in the absence of governmental controls created a maladjustment in the economic structure of the land; flooded the country with paper money; and increased the load of debt both private and public. This development, coupled with the burden of unequal taxation upon a people who had recently experienced an agonizing struggle to win liberty of political action, was pregnant with extreme danger.[76]

Throughout the country, and especially in New England, the distress of the poor was aggravated by the operation of laws which permitted a man to be jailed for debt; and which allowed the creditor, in cases of distraint, to seize the debtor's tangible property as well as his person. It was in Massachusetts where the fuse to this potential powder keg was ignited in the summer of 1786.[77] Up to that time, demonstrations by the people against the courts

[74] *Ibid.*
[75] October 3, 1787, 33 *JCC* 602-604.
[76] See James T. Adams, *New England in the Republic, 1778-1850*, Boston, Little Brown & Co., 1927, p. 144. See also Irving Brant, *James Madison, the Nationalist, 1780-1787*, New York, Bobbs-Merrill Co., 1948, p. 391.
[77] John Fiske, *The Critical Period of American History, 1783-1789*, Boston, Houghton Mifflin Co., 1916, pp. 172-186.

of law, and against the lawyers, had been peaceable enough. But by August, with no relief in sight, the opposition grew more audible. On August 29 a band of armed men surrounded the Court of Common Pleas in Northampton and forced its adjournment.[78] A week later 300 armed men assembled in front of the court house at Worcester for the same purpose.[79] On September 12 the court at Great Barrington[80] was invested by 800 men and here the insurgents broke open the jail, set the prisoners free, and committed other acts of violence.[81]

General Henry Knox who had been ordered by Congress to personally investigate the disturbances in the Bay State (because of the threat to the military stores collected at Springfield Arsenal) reported on the 28th that the Arsenal was in danger of attack. He could not ascertain with any degree of precision the danger which threatened the stores, but he was sure this would depend upon the vigor with which the government might proceed in punishing the ring leaders of the insurrection.[82] A feeble attempt to raise a guard for the protection of the Arsenal might precipitate its loss, as the malcontents might regard it as the first step towards their destruction.[83] Even if it were practicable to send out a large force to preserve law and order, "the expense of subsisting them would be considerable, and must be defrayed by the United States, which . . . would greatly embarrass the Treasury." In view of these circumstances, Knox advised Congress to let the local authorities handle the situation in their own way,[84] with their own militia. The appearance of a federally organized militia in Massachusetts could very well operate to force the "well affected" into the ranks of the disaffected.

---

[78] Adams, *op. cit.*, pp. 151-152.
[79] *Ibid.*, p. 152.
[80] *Ibid.*, p. 153.
[81] *Ibid.*
[82] Knox to President of Congress, September 28, 1786, 31 *JCC* 698.
[83] *Ibid.*, 699.
[84] On September 20, Knox informed Congress that he had made arrangements with Governor Bowdoin requesting him to "take such measures for the security of the stores as the state of the case might require." Knox to President of Congress, September 20, 1786; *ibid.*, 676. Among the military stores collected in the arsenal at Springfield were: 7,000 stand of arms complete with new bayonets, 1,300 barrels of powder of excellent quality, and 200 tons of shot and shell; *ibid.*, 675.

General Knox also called attention to the grave dangers aris-
ing from the very weakness of the Government in these exigencies.
"Were there a respectable body of troops in the service of the
United States," he remarked,

> so situated as to be ordered immediately to Springfield, the
> propriety of the measure could not be doubted. Or were the
> finances of the United States in such order, as to enable Con-
> gress to raise an additional body of four or five hundred men
> and station them at the respective arsenals the spirit of the times
> would highly justify the measure. For it may be observed that
> if one of the arsenals which was conceived to be perfectly secure
> from its situation, is suddenly endangered from strange circum-
> stances, the others are liable to the same evil, and in an instant
> the nation may be deprived of its valuable apparatus of war,
> which may be converted to the subversion of all government.[85]

At this point Daniel Shays, a former Revolutionary War officer, made his appearance in Springfield at the head of a mob of
1,000 men. Thus an insurrectionary leader had been found. Within a short time the number under his command swelled to 2,000.
Flouting the law; threatening, beating, and even firing officials;
emptying jails of men imprisoned for debt; the insurrectionists
demonstrated vividly the dangers of mob tyranny. Law-abiding
men looked upon these demonstrations with growing concern and
the Providence *United States Chronicle* scored the challenge to the
law as a dishonest attempt to encourage villainy. If a constitutional
legislature "cannot redress a grievance a mob never can. Laws are
the security of life and property—nay, what is more, of liberty." [86]

Prompted by the insidious implications of the increasing dis-
respect for law, Congress, on October 20, took a hand in the matter. Using actual Indian uprisings on the frontier as a veil, it was
Resolved to augment the standing Army by 1,340 men.[87] These
additional troops were to be raised for a term of three years unless
sooner discharged, distributed among the States in the proportion:
New Hampshire 260, Massachusetts 660, Rhode Island 120,
Connecticut 180, Virginia and Maryland each 60 cavalry. Each
was requested to "use their utmost exertions to raise, with all pos-

---

[85] *Ibid.*, 699.
[86] Quoted in Connecticut *Journal,* November 6, 1786. See also Novermber 27,
1786.
[87] 31 *JCC* 891-892. Note that only New England States were given quotas.

sible expedition, the quota of troops respectively assigned to them." [88]

As the insurgents in New England grew bolder in their demands, little could be done until the local legislative bodies concerned acted upon the Congressional recommendations. Military preparations were predicated upon the celerity with which the State legislatures could act upon the requisitions for additional men. Washington's admonitions in this regard had now come to haunt those who had refused to listen. If the Congress had been vested with sufficient authority for raising troops in such emergencies, the Nation would not have been exposed to such dangers. The weakness of the Government, and the procrastinating antics of the States, posed a far greater menace to the security of the people than a strong standing army could under any circumstances.

On November 5, 1786 Washington reiterated his warnings against the lack of Governmental authority. What stronger evidence, he asked of James Madison, "can be given of the want of energy in our governments than these disorders? If there exists not a power to check them, what security has a man for life, liberty or property?" [89] Worse still, the refusal of the States to work out a system of government that could insure the pursuit of liberty and happiness "will soon bring ruin on the whole." [90]

Looking upon the situation from such a safe distance as Paris, Thomas Jefferson was more complacent: These "commotions . . . offer nothing threatening." The American people had liberty

---

[88] The machinery of local government moved slowly, and precious months were wasted before the decisions were reached to recruit the men. See New Hampshire, *Journal of the Proceedings of the Honorable House of Representatives,* December 26, 1786, p. 132; New Hampshire *Spy,* December 22, 1786, Vol. 1, No. 18, p. 70; Massachusetts, *Journal of the House of Representatives,* October 27, 1786, pp. 298-300; November 13, p. 342. By the end of October, a group of men in Massachusetts volunteered their services at their own expense. See New Hampshire *Spy,* October 31, 1786, Vol. 1, No. 3, p. 11. Rhode Island *Journals of the House of Delegates,* November 4, 1786, pp. 1-5. By November 6 this State had resolved to raise its quota and a few days later appointed a major to command. See New Hampshire *Spy,* November 21, 1786, Vol. 1, No. 9, pp. 35-36; Virginia, *Journal of the House of Delegates,* November 20-24, 1786, pp. 51-58; January 11, 1787, pp. 156-157. By November 21, Connecticut had selected a colonel to command the troops raised under this quota. See New Hampshire *Spy,* November 21, 1786, Vol. 1, No. 9, p. 35. From the available evidence it is fair to assume that the quotas were filled by the States; *cf.* Upton, *op. cit.,* p. 70. This author says: "It does not appear that any of these troops were raised save two companies of artillery."

[89] Washington to Madison, November 5, 1786, 29 *WW* 52.

[90] *Ibid.* See also Washington to Knox, December 26, 1786, *ibid.,* 121-124.

enough; and, if the happiness of the majority of the people could be secured "at the expense of a little tempest now and then, or even of a little blood, it will be a precious purchase." [91] But on December 26 he addressed his friend Carmichael in a different tone. Commending the action of the vast body of citizens in their refusal to take up arms against their local governments, he assured his friend that such loyalty "will strengthen our government." [92]

Meanwhile, Governor Bowdoin of Massachusetts was taking active measures against the rebels. On January 1, 1787, General Benjamin Lincoln was appointed to lead an expedition to crush the insurrection, and by February 16 had carried out his mission. Daniel Shays had fled to Vermont. [93] The rebellion was at an end. Conservatives breathed with more comfort. But this might prove to be a temporary respite unless some vigorous measures were undertaken to provide for a more stable form of government and to adopt a more realistic military policy. [94] On February 21, 1787, Congress, acting upon the recommendations of such men as Washington, Hamilton, and Madison fixed the date for the meeting of a convention to revise the existing Government. [95]

Comments

Thus it has been shown that the infant Nation, pursuant to its first military policies, demobilized its armed forces too completely at the conclusion of the war. Then, still bemused with the theory that security could be attained through the exclusive use of militia, it suffered a series of embarrassments on its frontiers and at home, which compelled the Congress to provide for a small standing army. There began to evolve—albeit slowly, reluctantly, and with procrastination—a policy of maintaining a small regular force to cope with internal disorder and to act as a nucleus for larger military forces to be levied in the event of external threat.

---

[91] Jefferson to Mr. Stiles, December 24, 1786, *The Writing of Thomas Jefferson* (Memorial Edition), Washington, 1903, Vol. 6, p. 25. Hereafter cited as *T. J. Writings.*

[92] Jefferson to Carmichael, December 26, 1786, *ibid.,* 30.

[93] Adams, *op. cit.,* p. 162. See also Newport *Mercury,* March 17, 1787.

[94] This was strongly recommended by the Congressional delegation from Massachusetts. See 32 *JCC* 98-99.

[95] See Madison to Edmund Pendleton, February 24, 1787, *The Writings of James Madison,* (Gaillard Hunt ed.), New York, G. P. Putnam's Sons, 1901, Vol. 2, p. 317. The date for the meeting of the convention was set for the second Monday in May, 1787.

CHAPTER 3

Modest Beginnings
Under the Constitution

The Constitution Replaces the Confederation—The New Policy Meets a Stern Test—Military Obligation of Citizenship—US Military Policy is Influenced by the War in Europe—The Navy As the First Line of Defense—Marine Corps Established—Effect of Quasi War With France

WEAK AT HOME and discredited abroad, the Government under the Articles of Confederation was at best a meaningless entity, at worst, an invitation to riot, insurrection, and anarchy. This was the inevitable result of a stubborn resolve on the part of each State to uphold and preserve its own political freedom. Steeped in traditional provincialism, the States in 1787 were not altogether willing to surrender any part of their sovereignty even to a general government of their own choosing.[1] It was not until this hard core of settled conviction was broken by a series of compromises that an agreement was reached upon a system of government which could be accepted by States jealous of their rights and prerogatives.

The caution with which the delegates approached vital questions was nowhere so strongly manifested as in the deliberation over the nature of the military establishment [2] to be erected for the joint protection of the thirteen States.[3] In an atmosphere of jealousy and suspicion, the founding fathers finally concluded that although standing armies did not conform to the spirit of liberty, some force of professional soldiers was necessary to guard the

---

[1] Ltr George Washington to David Stuart, July 1, 1787, 29 *WW* 238.

[2] Max Farrand, ed, *The Records of the Federal Convention of 1787,* New Haven, Yale University Press, 1911, Vol. 2, pp. 616-617. See also William R. Tansill, "The Concept of Civil Supremacy over the Military in the United States," *Public Affairs Bulletin* No. 94, February, 1951, Washington, Library of Congress Legislative Reference Service, pp. 6-7.

[3] Rhode Island sent no representatives to the Convention. New Hampshire elected but did not send delegates until August, 1787.

71

frontiers against the British and the Spaniards, and against Indians incited to action by both. Furthermore, a standing force was necessary as a deterrent to sudden attack from abroad. Such a probability was not entirely remote, because improvements in the science of navigation had "rendered distant nations, in a great measure, neighbors." [4]

The Regular Army was accepted as a necessary evil because the militia, especially in times of peace, "would not long, if at all, submit to be dragged from their occupations and families," to do service on the frontier. Even if they could be prevailed upon or even compelled to do it, "the increased expense of a frequent rotation of service, and the loss of labor . . . would form conclusive objections to the scheme." [5] The only recourse was to a permanent corps in the pay of the government which amounted "to a standing army in time of peace; a small one, indeed, but not the less real for being small." [6] In the event of war, the main reliance for the defense of the nation remained the responsibility of the militia organizations in each State.

The instrument of government which the Convention presented to the people was a radical departure from the weak and inefficient Articles of Confederation. The authority so sadly lacking during the Revolution to raise and support armies, to provide and maintain a navy, to levy and collect taxes, to regulate commerce, and to borrow on the credit of the United States was finally vested in a central governing body.

Full responsibility for the national welfare and for the national defense was now to be assumed by the people's elected representatives in Congress, and by the Presidency. Henceforth, military unpreparedness and the incidence of military failure could no longer be conveniently excused as a consequence of insufficient authority. But at that time it was difficult to foresee the submergence of this authority in the rise and division of American political parties. As a result the military establishment, the implementing instrument of national policy, became a highly controversial issue in the perennial party struggles for power. Debating halls echoed with the always popular references to economy in

---

[4] J. C. Hamilton, ed. *The Federalist,* Hallowell, Glazier, Masters & Smith, 1837, Paper No. XXIV, pp. 112-113.
[5] *Ibid.,* p. 113.
[6] *Ibid.*

government; and as it suited the political conscience, measures of economy could always begin within an agency which in times of peace might become "a destructive engine of the people's liberties." Parsimonious appropriations, tardy legislation, and general lack of sympathy for essential military needs, so vividly manifest during the dawning days of the Republic, intensified as the Nation grew in political and economic stature.

On August 7, 1789, after the new instrument of government had gone into operation, the Department of War was established under a Secretary, General Henry Knox, who was responsible not to Congress but to the President.[7] Seven weeks later, on September 29, the Army as established by the Act of October 3, 1787 was recognized "to be the establishment for the troops in the service of the United States." [8] All personnel were required to take the oath of allegiance to support the Constitution, and the President was authorized to call forth the militia of the States when necessary for the purpose of protecting the inhabitants of the frontiers of the United States from the hostile incursion of the Indians.[9] Thus by legal definition the Army would remain small. In any emergency, the bulk of the forces would be drawn from the militia. But even this small establishment caused some observers to reflect that "a standing army in the hands of a government so independent of the people, may be made a fatal instrument to overturn the public liberties." [10]

The New Policy Meets a Stern Test

Meanwhile the relentless westward expansion brought larger numbers of Americans into contact with the Indians, who were reluctant to yield their lands to the white men. Reports of Indian atrocities kept pace with the increasing number of settlements. As the momentum intensified, the Indian tribes began to show signs of uniting against their common enemy. To meet this increasing menace, the Congress on April 30, 1790 voted to increase the

---

[7] I *Stat.* 49-50. The War Department included naval and military affairs.

[8] *Ibid.,* p. 95

[9] *Ibid.* The oath of allegiance was altered on April 30, 1790. Thereafter, allegiance was sworn to "the United States of America, and to serve them honestly and faithfully against all their enemies or opposers whatsoever."

[10] The Philadelphia *Independent Gazeteer,* September 4, 1789. Reliance upon the militia to meet current emergencies on the frontier soon proved to be a shortsighted and mistaken policy which placed "the lives and property of our hardy settlers on the frontier" in constant jeopardy. See Upton, *op. cit.,* p. 75.

Army to 1,216 men with the term of service fixed at three years. The authority of the President to call out the militia was reaffirmed.[11]

Within six months the strength and wisdom of this new policy received its first test. On October 22, 1790, Brevet Brigadier General Josiah Harmar, in command of the Army, encountered the Miami Indians at what is now Fort Wayne, Indiana, with a force of 320 regulars and 1,133 militiamen. Of this number only sixty regulars and 340 militia were committed. In a short engagement the Americans were driven back with a loss of 183 killed and 31 wounded.[12] In the Congressional investigation which followed this catastrophe, General Harmar's conduct was vindicated[13] but nothing was done to rectify the weak legislation which had paved the way for his defeat. The Army was too small to provide garrison troops in the various posts and at the same time organize for a fight against a superior force of savage Indians. The militia, as in the past, could not be counted upon to do that which should have been entrusted to a highly trained and disciplined professional organization. The test of strength lay in quality as well as quantity.

Reluctant to do more than provide for bare essentials, Congress on March 3, 1791, voted to raise an additional regiment of infantry of 912 noncommissioned officers and privates organized upon the same basis as the existing establishment. The President was again vested with authority to call out the militia, but in addition, he could now call into service, at his discretion, "a corps, not exceeding two thousand noncommissioned officers, privates, and musicians, with a suitable number of commissioned officers." Furthermore, if the two regiments now authorized could not be brought up to strength in time "to prosecute such military operations as exigencies may require," the Executive could substitute the levies or "such a body of militia as shall be equal thereto."[14]

---

[11] I Stat. 119-121. The organization was established at one regiment of three battalions of infantry and one of artillery with command vested in a lieutenant colonel.

[12] Upton, op. cit., pp. 77-78.

[13] Harmar's defeat was bitterly criticized in the press. See Philadelphia General Advertiser, February 4, 1791, p. 28.

[14] I Stat. 222-223. The levies referred to in this Act were volunteers authorized under the plenary power of Congress to raise and support armies. The right to appoint officers in this "corps" was vested in the President "to whom it obviously belonged, as the levies were wholly distinct from the militia or state troops." See Upton, op. cit., p. 79.

With this increased strength, it was thought possible to remove the obstreperous Indians from their vantage point on the frontier. On November 4, 1791, Major General Arthur St. Clair with another mixed force of regulars and militia, 1,400 effective, while seeking out the Indians was attacked and repulsed.[15] This time the losses were much heavier, 632 killed and 264 wounded. Again Congress undertook to investigate the conduct of military operations, and again were compelled to vindicate the commanding officers. The failure was not one of commission but rather of omission, and had been created by the Government through faulty and half-hearted support of the War Department.[16]

In their investigation, both Hamilton and Knox directed the attention of Congress to the real reasons for the failure. The powder furnished the troops was not worthless as had been alleged; it was ruined by being stored in worthless tents. Pack saddles were not defective, they were so big that few could be used; and, guns were ruined by inexperienced soldiers, while contractors failed miserably in furnishing supplies. All this was part of the system made possible by the policy of Congress to restrain the development of the War Department.[17]

By overstressing the principle of military subserviency to civil authority, the Government had paved the way for two disastrous military campaigns endangering the security of the nation while weakening its prestige abroad.

But this would be only a prelude to even more serious difficulties unless something were done to improve the national policy. To the enemies of a standing army, the military reversals served to strengthen the conviction that a military establishment was unnecessary. They pointed to the futility and uselessness of a war against the Indians which merely reflected a wanton expenditure

---

[15] One source computed St. Clair's force at 8,000 effectives. See the *Massachusetts Magazine*, November 1791, p. 719.

[16] Upton, *op. cit.,* p. 79. See also *Freeman's Journal*, February 9, 1791, p 2, col. 3. This source placed militia of Massachusetts at 75,000 men "all armed for war . . ." See also *Gazette of the United States*, November 20, 1790, p, 3, col. 1, for reference to the Connecticut militia which was computed at 30,000 effectives. Cf. Virginia, *Acts Passed at a General Assembly of the Commonwealth of Virginia,* 1785, pp. 3-6; New York, *Journal of the House of Assembly of the State of New York,* 1789-1798, (Lower House) *passim;* Pennsylvania, *Minutes, Journals and Proceedings,* 1793, pp. 67-299.

[17] Irving Brant, *James Madison: Father of the Constitution, 1787-1800,* New York, Bobbs-Merrill Co., Inc., p. 367.

of "the revenues of the States . . . in disgraceful campaigns." [18]
Any land, they said, requiring "a standing body of troops to settle,
is not worth, at this time, our acceptance;" for, the expense of
maintaining the Army was considerably greater than the benefits
arising from "the culture." [19]

In truth, however, it was ill-advised to continue a policy which
was undermined by parsimony.

On March 5, 1792, Congress finally undertook to create a
force of sufficient strength to cope not only with the Indians in
Ohio, but also to impress the British who still retained the posts
in Northwest Territory and who found it convenient to embarass
the United States by inciting the Indians.[20] Provision was made to
bring the two existing regiments up to strength, 960 enlisted men
each, and to augment those by three additional regiments of the
same strength, all to be enlisted for three years unless sooner discharged.[21] This would bring the total up to 5,000 rank and file.

For the purpose of efficient administration, discipline, and
training this force was organized upon a legional basis and became known as the Legion of the United States.[22] Such a plan had
already been introduced by Von Steuben on a small scale into the
American Army during the Revolution. It was favorably considered by Secretary Knox who even worked its details out in his
militia recommendations. Now, in 1792, it was the most plausible
and economical organization for satisfying the needs of frontier
fighting on a distended line.[23]

Subdivided into four sub-legions of 1,280 men each,[24] the

---

[16] Boston *Independent Chronicle,* December 22, 1791, p. 3, col. 2.
[19] *Ibid.,* December 29, 1791, p. 2, col. 4-5. Even the War Department came
in for its share of criticism for "mismanaging" the war effort. See *Ibid.,* June 7,
1792, p. 2, col. 1-2.
[20] See letter Washington to S/W, August 22, 1792, 32 *WW* 125-126.
[21] One of the regiments was to comprise 2 battalions of infantry and one
squadron of dragoons. Discretionary power was allowed the President to enlist
a certain number of Indians. 1 *Stat.* 241-243. Three weeks later Congress authorized the President to appoint four brigadier generals. *Ibid.,* 246. This law
dealt exclusively with the Army. A subsequent law enacted on May 2, 1792,
took up the details for calling upon the militia in emergencies. See *Ibid.,* 264.
[22] The term Legion was adopted to avoid using "the horrid term, regular
army." See William A. Ganoe, *The History of the U. S. Army,* New York, D.
Appleton-Century Co. Inc., 1942, p. 100. In 1796, the Legion was abolished.
[23] Ltr Washington to S/W, August 13, 1792, 32 *WW* 113.
[24] Each sub-legion was commanded by a brigadier general. Each of these units
represented a whole army in miniature comprising mixed elements of all arms;
2 battalions of infantry, 1 battalion of rifles, 1 troop of dragoons, 1 company of
artillery.

Legion provided the added punch that was necessary to meet the challenge of the Indians.

In June 1792, Major General Anthony Wayne was selected to command the Legion. Following Washington's recommendations, he drilled the men intensively in preparation for war: By May of the following year, Wayne made his way with 2,643 men to the land of the Miami tribes. On August 20, 1794, at Fallen Timbers, the two previous defeats were courageously avenged,[25] and in the very sight of a British fort, Wayne destroyed the Indian villages in the vicinity.

This display of force coupled with the manner in which the State militias came to the aid of the Federal Government in suppressing the Whiskey Rebellion in Pennsylvania[26] convinced the British that they were risking war with a government whose authority within its own borders could no longer be disregarded. By the middle of November 1794, England saw the wisdom of negotiating a treaty for the withdrawal of British troops.

The militia organizations had justified their existence in support of the Federal Government in suppressing a domestic upheaval. How effective they would be in the face of an organized foreign aggression was a matter which remained to be tested.

Military Obligation of Citizenship

As early as 1783 Washington 'had called for a well-organized militia within the United States as being the only force appropriate to a bankrupt economy. The hostility of the Indians together with the dubious attitude of the British and Spaniards on the frontiers, strengthened his convictions that either a regular force or a well-regulated militia was necessary if only to warn aggressors that the United States Government was sufficiently strong to demand respect at least within its own borders. On August 7, 1789, while urging Congress to deal vigorously with the Indian menace in the west, and while recognizing that any proposal for a large standing army would find small acceptance in the prevailing climate of opinion, he stressed the need for some uniform and

---

[25] Of this number, 2500 were regulars supported by 1000 mounted Kentuckians.

[26] This incident grew out of the reluctance of the farmers in Western Pennsylvania to pay the excise on distilled spirits. It reached its climax during the summer of 1794, when President Washington, spurred on by Alexander Hamilton, called out 15,000 militiamen from four neighboring states to restore order and to instill a proper respect for the laws of the United States.

effective system for the organization of the militia of the United States. It required no great amount of argument to prove that the time for such a reform was *now*, because it was:

in our power to avail ourselves of the military knowledge disseminated throughout the several States by means of the many well-instructed officers and soldiers of the late Army.[27]

In opposition to the notions prevailing in many quarters that the constitutional right to bear arms constituted the best definition of an organized militia, Washington argued that "A free people ought not only to be armed but disciplined; to which end a uniform and well digested plan is requisite." This would be a form of peace insurance, for, in the final analysis, "to be prepared for War is one of the most effectual means of preserving Peace."[28]

On January 21, 1790, after he had interpolated these remarks into his earlier study on the militia, Secretary Knox laid before the Congress his plan of militia organization. By insisting upon the principle of universal obligation to military service, Knox was in the best American tradition, notwithstanding a natural reluctance on the part of some citizens to be obliged to shoulder arms in peacetime. As an argument against the solicitation of this group, he sought to prove that any attempt to exonerate the members of the community from all personal service, was to render them unworthy of the character of free men.[29]

But by an unhappy choice of subsequent words he gave offense to the most articulate groups in the various States as well as in Congress. In a republican form of government, he pointed out, where great decisions "must be the result of multiplied deliberations . . . [the Government] ought to possess such energetic establishments as should enable it, by the vigor of its own citizens, to control events as they arise, instead of being convulsed or subverted by them."[30] For this reason the Government should possess a "strong corrective arm."[31] However praiseworthy the plan might

---

[27] James D. Richardson, *A Compilation of the Messages and Papers of the Presidents*, 1789-1897, Washington, Government Printing Office, 1896, vol. I, p. 60. Hereafter cited as Richardson, *M&P*.
[28] Richardson, M&P, Vol. I, p. 65.
[29] *American State Papers*, Military Affairs, Vol. I, p. 13. Hereafter cited as *ASP, MA*. It should be noted that Knox also referred to a naval militia, by implication at least, when he said that sailors of the Merchant Marine could easily man the ships of war.
[30] *ASP, MA*, Vol. I, pp. 6-7.
[31] *Ibid.*, The convulsive events referred to here were associated with Shay's Rebellion and similar disturbances.

have been in the considered judgment of thinking men, "a strong corrective arm" in the United States of that day could only be viewed as obnoxious; and such a declaration by a Secretary of War did not lessen the existing prejudice against the military establishment. Although in principle the plan was agreeable to those who were opposed to a standing army, and in spite of the conclusive manner in which it seemed to prove that a well-trained and well-organized militia could dispense entirely with a standing army, the people made no distinction between State militia and Federal forces when confronted with the reference to a "strong corrective arm." The plan, therefore, was doomed to defeat.

In Boston the people were fed extracts from the New York press accusing the Secretary of War of perpetrating a deliberate, barefaced, and ridiculous scheme for generating business for his office.[32] In Philadelphia the *Packet and Advertiser* took Knox to task for advocating universal military service. Compelling all able bodied male citizens to serve their country in peace was thought to be pregnant with mischief both to the agricultural and mining interests as well as having a tendency to debauch the morals of the rising generation.[33] On April 26, 1790, the plan was withdrawn from the Committee of the Whole House and referred to a committee appointed to prepare and bring in a bill providing for National Defense.[34] It was apparent that Congressmen, torn between their obligation as members of a Federal governing body and their inclination to lean toward the best interests of their individual States, would yield only with the greatest reluctance to any military reorganization proposed by the military themselves. It seemed to make little difference that perhaps the outline of a system of national defense to meet all emergencies might best be conceived by those whose professional abilities qualified them to do so.[35]

On July 1 this new committee, headed by Elias Boudinot, one

---

[32] Boston *Gazette and Country Journal*, February 22, 1790, p. 3, col. 2.
[33] Quoted in Palmer, *America in Arms*, p. 45. It should be noted that if accepted, this plan would have cost the American people $384,440 per year to support a militia force of 325,000 men, or ⅛ of a dollar per person in a population of three million. See *ASP, MA,* Vol. 1, p. 12.
[34] U. S. *Annals of Congress,* 1st Congress, 2nd Session, April 26, 1790, vol. 2, p. 1544.
[35] This congressional attitude is reflected in the military legislation and appropriations for the War Department throughout the entire course of American history. In the absence of adequate legislation, the War Department has not even been able to meet the needs of the Nation in peace.

of Washington's close friends, reported a bill [36] which substantially included the President's *Sentiments on a Peace Establishment.* The Militia of the United States was to include all able-bodied men between the ages of 18 and 50, but emphasis was to be placed upon the training of those younger men between 18 and 25, who would be separately enrolled, officered by the States, and formed into companies.[37] For training purpose, these separate groups would rendezvous four times a year as companies and twice a year as a regiment.[38] This plan, while not as vigorous as that given in Washington's *Sentiments,* replaced thirteen separate systems by one uniform Federal system.[39]

Still refusing to underwrite any system which might not meet with the universal approval of the States, Congress lost little time in killing this new bill. The will of the sovereign States was not to be denied. Undisputed authority over the militia was a fundamental right of the States not to be violated even for the common good. Consequently, on December 10, 1790, the question was again taken up in committee,[40] and four days later a new bill was laid before the Congress. Under the consideration of a Committee of the Whole, the bill struck many snags involving the prerogatives of the States with reference to all its provisions.[41] Hung up in this manner, Congress on January 4, 1791 appointed Jeremiah Wadsworth to prepare an amendatory bill and on the following day this was ready for printing.[42]

Meanwhile the suspended animation of the Congress in considering the whole question of the militia elicited a mixture of emotions in the press. The Providence *Gazette and Country Journal* grew suspicious of the whole intent and purpose of the Militia bill,[43] while the New York *Journal and Patriotic Register* drew the attention of its readers to the fact that Congress had been organized for fifteen months and during that time had taken no effectual measures to regulate the militia, by one general plan, notwithstanding it had been repeatedly and earnestly impressed

---

[36] New Haven, Connecticut, *Journal,* July 7, 1790, p. 2, col. 1.
[37] Palmer, *America in Arms,* p. 47.
[38] See 26 WW 389-390, 393.
[39] Palmer, *American in Arms,* p. 47.
[40] Annals of Congress, 1st Congress, 2nd Session, Vol. 2, p. 1791.
[41] See Providence *Gazette & Country Journal,* January 1, 1791; New Jersey *Journal,* January 5, 1791, p. 1, col. 1.
[42] New Haven, Connecticut, *Journal,* January 19, 1791, p. 2, col. 3.
[43] January 15, 1791.

upon them by the President.[44] In a similar vein, the Connecticut *Journal* emphasized the observations of the President that "the present time affords the most favorable opportunity to lay the foundation of an efficient and competent militia," the wisdom of which should "have a due influence on the minds of our civil fathers in expediting the militia establishment of the union." [45] The Philadelphia *Gazette of the United States* sharply criticized the prolonged debates over the whole question of exemptions from military service, a practice, if adopted, which would mean that apprentices and miners should be debarred from the privilege of bearing arms in defense of their country.[46]

Bombarded by the criticism of the press, and restrained by the inertia of the Congress itself, the new committee under Wadsworth struggled with the measure until March 5, 1792, at which time the bill was placed before the House.[47] Two months later this bill, containing provisions which were far removed from the original ideas of Washington, Von Steuben, and Knox, became the organic law governing the Militia of the United States. Under it the whole idea of a well-disciplined and well-organized militia became fiction. Lip service was paid to the truly democratic principle of the military obligation of citizenship by the pious declaration that "every free and able-bodied white male citizen of the respective states" between the ages of 18 and 45 would be enrolled in the local militia organizations. But within six months of such enrollment, every enrollee was required to provide himself with arms, ammunition, and equipment.[48]

In this manner, the responsibility for arming and equipping the militia, a responsibility which unquestionably rested with the Government itself, was shifted upon the individual. Many, though willing, could not afford to purchase a rifle; and with Congress powerless to enforce the law, the entire edifice depended upon the manner in which the individual States administered the law. The

[44] August 20, 1791, p. 3, col. 2.
[45] January 5, 1791, p. 3, col. 2.
[46] January 19, 1791, p. 3, col. 4. See also New York *Journal and Patriotic Register*, June 1, 1791, p. 172, Connecticut *Journal*, February 9, 1791, p. 2, col. 1.
[47] Some of the delay in the preparation of this bill was due to the removal of the seat of the National Government from New York to Philadelphia. See Van Wyck Brooks, *Henry Knox, Soldier of the Revolution*, New York, G. P. Putnam's Sons, 1900, p. 224.
[48] I *Stat*, pp. 271-274.

means of defense[49] in a future war with a major power were thus dependent upon the good will of the States rather than on the firm resolve of the general government constitutionally responsible for the national welfare. The lessons, so indelibly written in blood, sweat, and tears during the Revolutionary War, had been conveniently and quickly forgotten.

Instead of abolishing the thirteen armies that operated during that War, the law of 1792, gave them federal sanction. Instead of placing the power to appoint officers in the hands of the President, it remained with the States, where the appointments were based upon political expediency rather than individual ability. In addition, the strictures against the employment of militia organizations beyond the territorial limits of the Nation circumscribed the ability of the Government to define a national policy in peace and war.

U. S. Military Policy is Influenced By the War in Europe

When the news arrived that France had declared war against England on February 1, 1793, America became divided in its opinion in favor of either belligerent. Many were convinced that the future destiny of the new Republic was dependent upon the policy adopted by the Government, a policy which some interpreted as aid to our late ally, while others were inclined to aid the British. But the President of the United States, again demonstrating his great genius, wisely decided to guide the people along the more fruitful paths of neutrality and on April 22 issued a proclamation urging Americans to be friendly and impartial toward the belligerent powers.[50] Nevertheless, on December 3 he warned the people that it was idle to contemplate any measure of security in a determination to remain neutral while a great war was being waged between nations whose trade we cherished. The United States, he said,

> ought not to indulge a persuasion that, contrary to the order of human events, they will forever keep at a distance those painful

---

[49] The law also provided that within one year after the passage of this Act, the militia of the respective States "shall be arranged into divisions, brigades, regiments, battalions, and companies." Each division was officered by one major general and two aides-de-camp with rank of major; one brigadier general for each brigade, and to each regiment one lieutenant colonel. The omission of the grade of full colonel was a matter of grave disappointment to the colonels of the late war. This rank was not re-instituted until April 20, 1816. Upton, *op. cit.*, p. 84.

[50] The Philadelphia *Ladies Magazine,* April, 1793, p. 252.

appeals to arms with which the history of every other nation abounds. . . . If we desire to avoid insult, we must be able to repel it; if we desire to secure peace, one of the most powerful instruments of our rising prosperity, it must be known that we are at all times ready for war.[51]

Unfortunately American unpreparedness for these responsibilities was painfully evident in the operation of the Militia Law within the States.[52] However, by this time, the European war had awakened a lively interest within several States with reference to their militia organizations. Massachusetts, New Jersey, Pennsylvania, Maryland, and North Carolina passed laws inflicting penalties by fines against those militiamen who failed to equip themselves at their own expense, and who failed to appear for musters.[53] These ordinances failed to produce the desired result, first because of a widespread financial disability on the part of the militiamen, and secondly, because the war created a scarcity of arms.[54]

In his next annual message, on November 19, 1794, Washington again called attention to the striking defects in the Militia Law, an enforcement of which would be extraordinarily wasteful and expensive.[55] The responsibility of the Government for arming the militia as well as organizing and disciplining it could no longer be ignored. On December 29 a special committee of Congress vainly attempted to make provisions by law for arming the militia of the United States, and for enforcing the execution of the existing militia laws, by adequate and uniform penalties.[56] But with the burden of a huge war debt still upon them, Congress preferred to look toward economy. National defense was considered too expensive a luxury even for those who witnessed almost daily Indian depredations and massacres on the frontier; and without an army of respectable size, the British still could not be forced to leave American territory. American national policies were implemented by piecemeal legislation enacted in the face of constantly recurring emergencies, legislation which was limited to meet current needs only.

On May 9, 1794, Congress provided for the enlistment, for

[51] Richardson, *M&P*, Vol. I, p. 140.
[52] *Ibid.*
[53] *ASP, MA*, Vol. I, p. 70.
[54] *Ibid.*
[55] *ASP, MA*, Vol. I, p. 107.
[56] Richardson, *M&P*, I, pp. 184, 204.

three years, of 764 noncommissioned officers and men to be designated as the "Corps of Artillerists and Engineers," and incorporated them with the four companies of artillery then comprising a part of the Legion of the United States.[57] To augment these forces, this law authorized the President to direct the States to organize, arm, and equip, according to law, their assigned quotas of 80,000 men. These were to be held in readiness to march at a moment's notice and when called to duty would serve for three months.[58] One month later, the Legion, as the regular establishment was designated, numbered 3,578 or 1,542 less than the authorized 5,120; and it was estimated that this number would continue to fall off. These diminishing numbers, coupled with a weak militia organization and short-sighted legislation bearing upon the military establishment, was evidence of a dangerously complacent attitude when the threat of danger became obscured by the specious allurements of security resulting from the geographical isolation of the United States. This attitude was to become so fixed as to assume the nature of a policy.

Such complacency was reflected even in the military legislation where each law was limited in duration to one year. Because of this, it became necessary on March 3, 1795 to enact another law to continue the Legion and the Corps of Artillerists and Engineers subject to the amazing proviso that the President could, if he deemed it expedient, discharge the whole or any part of the troops.[59] The strength of the Legion was reduced to 4,800 men while the "Corps" was increased to 992.[60] But with the return of temporary peace on the frontier together with the general feeling that the European war no longer posed an immediate threat to the country, a congressional investigation went far to "prove" that the total of 5,792 men was some 2,788 in excess of the actual needs.[61] Therefore on May 20, 1796 the strength of the Army was fixed at the Corps of Artillerists and Engineers as established in

---

[57] I *Stat*, p. 367.
[58] *Ibid.*
[59] I *Stat*, p. 430.
[60] *Ibid.*
[61] *ASP, MA,* I, p. 112. Report of the Committee to Study the Organization of the Army.

1794, together with the two companies of light dragoons and four regiments of infantry of eight companies each.[62]

Then the uneasy world situation created by the French Revolution and the rise of Napoleon threatened to clear the oceans of American shipping with a consequent loss of income as well as prestige. Alarmed over the seriousness of this new situation, President Adams, in his message of May 16, 1797, warned against the dangers of inadequate defense; and, while stressing the necessity of a moderate navy to protect our commerce on the high seas, he underlined also the desirability of protecting it along the coast.[63]

In addition, attention was drawn to the general condition of the military establishment, which could be improved by an addition to the regular artillery and cavalry, and by arrangements for forming a provisional Army.[64]

Aroused by the tenor of this message, the Federalist controlled Senate assured the President of their support. Peace and harmony with all nations had always been sought for,

> but such being the lot of humanity that nations will not always reciprocate peaceful dispositions, it is our firm belief that effectual measures of defense will tend to inspire that national self-respect and confidence at *home* which is the unfailing source of respectability *abroad,* to check aggression and prevent war.[65]

In a similar vein, the New Hampshire General Court sounded the keynote of Federalist opinion against violations of American rights on the high seas: "We wish to live in peace, upon equal and honorable terms, with all the nations of the earth. We should be just to all—but we will be dictated by none." [66] On June 24, Congress, under the impulse of such outbursts of opinion, redefined the Act of 1794 with reference to the militia force of 80,000 men. But no troops were to be raised under this new law unless the circumstances of the United States should, in the opinion of the President, render it absolutely necessary.[67]

---

[62] I *Stat,* p. 483. This law fixed the General Staff at 1 Major General with two Aides-de-camp; 1 Brigadier General with 1 Brigade Major; 1 Quartermaster General; 1 Inspector to do duty also as Adjutant General; 1 Paymaster General. On March 3, 1797, this was changed to 1 Brigade General; 1 Quartermaster General; and 1 Judge Advocate General. See I *Stat,* p. 597.

[63] Richardson, *M&P,* I, p. 237.

[64] *Ibid.,* p. 238.

[65] *Ibid.,* p. 240.

[66] Quoted in New Hampshire *New Star,* June 13, 1797, p. 987.

[67] I *Stat,* p. 522. This law was limited to one year.

Such tepid legislation failed to impress Napoleon, who continued to disregard American grievances. Armed attacks against the seacoasts of America became a strong possibility; on April 27, 1798 the Corps of Artillerists and Engineers was increased by an additional regiment of three battalions with enlistments fixed at five years.[68] One week later, two acts were passed appropriating some $1,150,000 for the construction of coastal fortifications and for the purchase of arms and munitions of war.[69]

These were followed on May 28 by an act establishing a provisional 'force of 10,000 men enlisted for three years to be raised under the authority of the President in the event of a declaration of war against the United States or of actual invasion. Furthermore, the President was empowered at any time within three years after the passing of the act to accept any company of volunteers either of artillery, cavalry, or infantry, who might offer themselves for the service.[70] Washington was appointed Commander in chief with rank of lieutenant general. Although this law was never implemented, it was evident that in this instance, at least, the mistake of short enlistments was not to be repeated.

On July 16, 1798, still another law was enacted which added two companies to the four existing eight company regiments of infantry, and made provision for raising twelve additional regiments of ten companies each, and six troops of light dragoons "to be enlisted for and during the continuance of the existing differences between the United States and the French Republic, unless sooner discharged." [71] Meanwhile the undeclared war between the United States and France grew in intensity. Ships on both sides were seized or sunk, and apprehensive of the intentions of Napoleon in possession of strategically located islands off the Atlantic coast, Congress felt the need for even more extensive defensive preparations.

On March 2, 1799, the Chief Executive was authorized, in the event of war between the United States and any European

---

[68] *Ibid.*, pp. 554-556.
[69] Act of May 3, 1798, *Ibid.*, pp. 554-555; Act of May 4, 1798, *Ibid.*, pp. 555-556. The last Act vested the President with the authority to establish foundries and armories for the manufacture of cannon and small arms. This was imperative because these implements were not available in the foreign market at this time. Washington's admonitions against such a possibility now became established facts.
[70] *Ibid.*, p. 558. A bounty of ten dollars was offered for each recruit.
[71] *Ibid.*, p. 604. The eight troops of dragoons were to be formed into a regiment. This law increased the bounty to twelve dollars.

Power or of threatened invasion, to raise the military forces of the Nation by twenty-four regiments of infantry, one regiment and one battalion of riflemen, one battalion of artillerists and engineers, and three regiments of cavalry.[72] Had this force been raised, the regular Army would have been increased to 40,000 which together with the 75,000 volunteers provided for in this same law would have given the country a mixed force of regulars and volunteers instead of placing reliance upon the State militia to augment the standing army. For all practical purposes, however, the utility of these volunteers was severely handicapped by the limitation of the law which prohibited their employment, beyond the States in which they resided, for longer than three months after their arrival at the place of rendezvous.[73]

With the imminence of a situation which called for an all-out preparation for war, regard was had first for the individual enlistees and the States they represented and secondly for the well-being of the Nation. The framers of this policy of piecemeal legislation therefore breathed more easily when America's outstanding differences with France were settled amicably; and, while Americans and Frenchmen joined their voices in the refrains of national anthems, Congress took immediate steps to lighten the economic burden of the taxpayer.[74] On May 14, 1800, Congress reduced the Army to the General Staff, four regiments of infantry, two regiments of artillerists and engineers, and two troops of light dragoons—293 officers, 106 cadets, and 5,038 enlisted men—a total of 5,437. By the 19th of December, 1801, the Republican administration under Thomas Jefferson further reduced this to 248 officers, 9 cadets, and 3,794 enlisted men—a total of 4,051. During this year the war in Europe had been temporarily halted by the Treaty of Amiens. The counsels of State in America shifted United States policy according to the apparently peaceful intentions of Napoleon and his British adversaries.

The Navy As the First Line of Defense

America avoided war during this period, not because of the

---

[72] *Ibid.*, pp. 725-726. Time of service was fixed at three years with a bounty of ten dollars.

[73] *Ibid.*

[74] The peace was not finally promulgated until September 30, 1800. See Bailey, *op. cit.*, p. 88.

military legislation hastily put together and sorely handicapped by many limitations; but because of a small but growing fleet of ships whose daring exploits excited the admiration even of its enemies. The fabrication of these ships, always an expensive item, met with the approval of an economy-minded Congress because they had grown weary of paying tribute to the Barbary pirates who controlled the rich sea lanes of the Mediterranean; and because without a protective fleet, American merchantmen were fair prize for any power strong enough to challenge the right of free navigation. To secure the respect due a neutral flag, observed Washington, "requires a naval force organized and ready to vindicate it from insult or aggression." Furthermore, such a force, far from involving us in continuous wars, would, in effect, prevent the necessity of going to war by discouraging belligerent powers from committing such violations of the rights of the neutral party as may, first or last, leave no other option.[75] Two months after his inauguration, President Adams reechoed these sentiments in evaluating the utility of a navy. "A naval power," he said, "next to the militia is the natural defense of the United States." Moreover, the experiences of the Revolutionary War were sufficient proof that a "moderate naval force" was indispensable.[76]

In 1789, when the Executive Departments of the Government were denominated, the United States had no navy.[77] "There was no need for one." Hence a separate Navy Department, in the minds of many, would have been an unnecessary and costly piece of administrative machinery. This general feeling was in consonance with the poverty of the treasury and the fixed popular prejudice against anything resembling extensive military preparations and operations.

It was not until Washington's second administration that a situation arose which would even permit some talk about a fleet. American relations with the Barbary Powers were reaching the breaking point over what Morocco and Algeria claimed as their right to prey upon American commerce and to demand large ransoms for the release of prisoners. But economy-minded statesmen

---

[75] Richardson, *M&P*, I, p. 201.
[76] Richardson, *M&P*, I, p. 201.
[77] The last ships of the Revolutionary Navy were sold in 1786.

still preferred to submit to extortion, and no constructive measures were taken to right this wrong.[78]

By late 1793 the commerce of the United States was also threatened in the Atlantic by the belligerent powers (England and France) who with impunity seized American ships.[79] The young Republic, so dependent upon trade to improve her economic condition, was finally brought to a realization that a protective naval force was necessary for survival. The first step in this direction was taken on March 27, 1794, when the President signed a bill providing for the construction of four ships each of 44 guns and two of 36 guns, with a personnel of some 2,060 men.[80] Significantly the President was vested with the authority to appoint and commission officers for the ships. In the event of peace with the Algerian corsairs, however, the provisions of this act were to terminate immediately.[81]

With his fingers alertly on the public pulse, and careful to avoid giving offense to certain groups, President Washington shrewdly distributed the benefits deriving from the construction of these ships. The 44-gun vessels were to be built at Boston, New York, Philadelphia, and Norfolk; while the 36-gun ships would be built at Portsmouth, New Hampshire, and Baltimore.

Work on these ships[82] was pushed rapidly forward until a treaty of peace signed early in 1796 with the Barbary States threatened the suspension of this work.[83] Washington delayed executing the provisions of the Act of March 27, 1794, citing as his reasons the great loss which the public would incur from the sudden termination of these projects.[84] The Federalists, led by Alexander Hamilton and John Adams, narrowly defeated an attempt by the

---

[78] Secretary Knox tried in 1790 and again in 1791, to procure an armed fleet. See Charles O. Paullin, "Early Naval Administration under the Constitution," *Proceedings of the United States Naval Institute*, Vol. 32, p. 1002. Hereafter cited as Paullin, "Early Naval Administration." It may be noted that while Congress could not find the financial means to provide for national defense during this period, they did see fit to appropriate large sums for paying the tributes levied against America by the Barbary chieftains. Such policy finds an echo in more recent times in the "ransoming" of U. S. citizens held by Communist authorities.

[79] Richardson, *M&P*, I, p. 146.

[80] I *Stat.* 350-351.

[81] *Ibid.*, 351.

[82] These were the *Constitution, President, United States, Chesapeake, Congress,* and *Constellation.*

[83] Richardson, *M&P*, I, p. 192.

[84] *Ibid.*, p. 193.

Republicans to abolish the Navy and dispose of the ships as well as all the materiel gathered at the various shipyards. The President advised against such a proposal and invited attention to the necessity for at least the gradual creation of a navy. Neither maritime trade nor national self-respect, he said, could long endure without an armed fleet; and in the light of British, French, and Algerian ,insults inflicted upon the American flag, it seemed advisable to begin without delay to provide the materials for the building and equipping ships of war, and to proceed in the work by degrees, in proportion as U. S. resources should permit.[85] By compromise, three ships were allowed to go on to completion, and commencement of work on the other three was postponed.[86] In the summer of 1797, when American relations with France were all but severed, construction of these three ships was resumed and pushed rapidly to completion. On July 1, Congress authorized President Adams to man and employ the three frigates and laid down the rules and regulations governing the Navy.[87] Provision was also made to employ these warships as convoys for merchantmen and for arming those merchantmen which plied the Mediterranean Sea.[88]

By this time it had become apparent that the administration of naval affairs had grown to such proportions that immediate steps were necessary to meet the consequent growing demands made upon the Secretary of War. A separate Department was the only solution. A project to accomplish this was set in motion by the President in his annual message of November 22, 1797, vigorously stressing the necessity for protection, on the high seas, of the commerce of the United States.[89] The question was taken up by a committee of Congress on March 8, 1798, and after some study it was concluded that enormous expenditures and unaccountable delays attended the administration of naval affairs within the War De-

---

[85] *Ibid.*, p. 201.

[86] Paullin, "Early Naval Administration," p. 1009. The *Constitution, United States,* and *Constellation* were completed.

[87] I Stat. 525. These regulations were similar to those which governed the Continental Navy of November 28, 1775. The wary manner in which Congress approached military preparations is best reflected in the provisions of this law. For example, this Act was to continue for just one year. On March 2, 1799, the regulations were redefined in another Act which was repealed by the Act of April 23, 1800. *Ibid.* 709 fn.

[88] See New Hampshire *New Star,* July 18, 1797, p. 120.

[89] Richardson, *M&P,* I, p. 251.

partment. Secretary of War John McHenry suggested that the only alternative lay in the separation of the Navy entirely from the War Department.[90] After several weeks of heated debates on McHenry's proposition, the Department of the Navy was created on April 30, 1798.[91]

Marine Corps Established

Ten weeks later, on July 11, the Marine Corps was established. In defining their duties, the law provided that these troops of the Navy in addition to sea duty, were liable at any time to do duty in the forts and garrisons of the United States, on the seacoast, or any other duty on shore as the President at his discretion, should direct.[92]

Effect of Quasi War with France

The quasi war with France stimulated an increased interest in naval affairs, so that by the close of the year 1798, twenty ships were in service as compared to three for the preceding year. In 1799, thirty-three ships were in commission in addition to nine galleys built for the protection of southern ports,[93] and eight revenue cutters were procured from the Treasury Department. On February 25, 1799, three acts were passed which defined the needs of the new Navy.[94] One provided for the construction of six 74-gun vessels,[95] a second made provision for the establishment of two docks for the purpose of repairing naval vessels, and a third appropriated $200,000 for the purchase of timber or land upon which timber was growing. Secretary of the Navy Benjamin Stoddert, displaying rare wisdom and foresight, stimulated production of raw materials needed for the construction and repair of ships by

---

[90] Paulin, "Early Naval Administration," pp. 1010-1011.
[91] I *Stat.* 553-554. At this point it might not be amiss to speculate with an opinion that agreement to create a Navy Department, in a climate of hostility toward military expenditures, might not have been reached if the Capital of the United States remained in Philadelphia or closer to New England. A strong navy meant protection for the maritime interests and prosperity of New England. The location of the Capital at Washington placed it closer to the South which voted against the creation of this Department, and sufficiently distant to prevent constant lobbying by the New England interests.
[92] I *Stat.* 594-596.
[93] These were built under the provisions of the Act of May 4, 1798, which authorized the construction of 10 galleys for the protection of the United States. *Ibid.* 556.
[94] *Ibid.* 621-622.
[95] These were the "Battleships."

offering subsidies to the growers of hemp and to the manufacturers of copper and canvas materials.[96].

No phase of this early naval development was so important nor as far-reaching as the initiation of the program to establish Navy yards. These were the "manufactories" which Washington referred to in 1783, and without which little progress could be made in building ships, or in repairing and improving naval materiel. The first yards were rented and proved to be too small for the construction of large ships such as the 74-gun frigates. Improving these facilities to meet the demands of a growing Navy did not appear to be economical for the Government. For this reason Secretary Stoddert, by resorting to a liberal interpretation of the existing laws, found authority to purchase sites for yards. By April, 1801, the Government had secured title to six localities at a total cost of $135,848.[97]

This auspicious start ended abruptly early in 1801 when peace with France dictated a return to the ways and policies of peace. In making provision for a peacetime naval establishment, Congress on March 3, 1801 authorized the sale of all vessels of the Navy except thirteen, six of which were to be kept in commission and the remainder laid up in "moth balls." This measure represented sound economy since the vessels to be sold were constructed of inferior materials and were too small to meet the needs of national defense. Peace brought also the painful task of releasing outright large numbers of officers despite the recommendations of Secretary Stoddert to retire all higher officers on half pay, subject to recall to duty in emergencies.[98]

---

[96] Paullin, "Early Naval Administration," p. 1029.
[97] *Ibid.*, pp. 1026-1028.
[98] II *Stat.* 110-111.

CHAPTER 4

Economy Before Preparedness

Jeffersonian Policy—Military Establishment Is Reduced
—War With Tripoli—Military Weakness Invites War—
Neutral Rights Versus National Defense—Jefferson Seeks
Peace Through Economic Coercion and Passive Defense

O N MARCH 4, 1801, Thomas Jefferson was inaugurated
President of the United States in an atmosphere of domestic
tranquility and diminishing world tensions. His election dispelled
the fears of those staunch defenders of states' rights who had
viewed with alarm the growing tendency toward increased Federal
authority. Every Federalist measure which strengthened the hand
of the central government now was challenged, but not all of them
were discarded. Even Jefferson himself, the arch foe of a strong
federal government, refused to scrap Alexander Hamilton's financial structure. But he was not reluctant to attack the Federalist
created Army and Navy; and, being a practical politician, he was
firmly convinced that reductions in military expenditures would
create small opposition among the people. Reducing such expenditures meant the abolition of internal taxes. This simple lesson in
economics was understood by all. Few were eager to remember
the ponderous theorems of national defense as expressed by Washington, Hamilton, and Knox.

Though consistency was never one of Jefferson's characteristics,
and although he departed from his dedicated principles of states'
rights, he did remain consistent in his outlook on the military and
naval establishment. In his first inaugural address he coupled
economy in Government with disarmament, he repeated the conviction held by Washington and his generals of the supremacy of
the civil over the military authority, and he pleaded for a well-
disciplined militia as our best reliance in peace and for the first
months of war, until the regulars might relieve them.[1] But he failed

[1] Richardson, *M&P*, I, p. 323. This was impractical if not impossible, owing
to the fact that the small Army was scattered over the whole frontier and in
certain garrisons along the coast.

to add that in the event of a war, those regulars he expected to relieve the militia could not do so for the simple though illuminating reason that they would have been dispensed with in the economy program.

On December 8, 1801, in his first annual message to Congress, he observed that a regular establishment (the very backbone of America's defenses) was not only unnecessary but also a burden upon the laboring classes. Based upon a report of the Secretary of War, the number of men necessary for garrison purposes was considerably less than the existing military establishment.[2] According to the law of May 14, 1800, the military establishment totalled 5,437 officers and men. On December 19, 1801, the total was at 4,051 officers and men. In such a state, then, it was inadequate for defense against invasion but remained a threat, in times of peace, against civil authority. This force, then, which was unnecessary, dangerous, and inadequate, and which Jefferson would abolish, was the imaginary force which he would call upon to relieve the militia in an emergency.[3]

In his discussion on the militia, however, the President was on a sound footing. The extended coast line and the vast hinterland made it difficult to determine, beforehand, where an enemy might choose to invade. The only practical force which could cope with such uncertainties was "the body of neighboring citizens as formed into a militia," to be relieved by the Regulars.[4] Jefferson was aware of the existing deficiencies in the militia organization, but he could not go any further, in improving them, than recommend reforms to Congress, who in turn were restrained by the States, who were reluctant to regulate the militia in the interest of the Federal Government.

With reference to the Navy, although Jefferson was anxious to lay up in the Navy Yard in Washington under the protective eye of the Executive, all the larger ships[5], circumstances forced him to refrain from reducing it. He had not been in office three months when war with Tripoli compelled him to dispatch a portion of the fleet to the Mediterranean, and because it was probable that the hostilities might include Algeria, Tunis, and Morocco as well, he

[2] William A. Ganoe, *History of the United States Army*, New York, Appleton Century Co., 1942, p. 108.
[3] Richardson, *M&P*, I, p. 329.
[4] *Ibid.*
[5] *Ibid.*, p. 330.

urged the continuation of a small naval force for actual service in the Mediterranean. Beyond this, however, he refused to go. Continued construction on the Navy yards was ordered to be studied with a view to discontinuing some of these projects, and the whole program of coast defenses, which had fallen into a sad state of repair, was temporarily set aside. If it had not been for the war with the Barbary Pirates the whole Navy would have been laid up; and but for the presence of Indians on the frontier, even the Regular Army might have been abolished.[6]

Under Jefferson's republican theory of government, the States were individually required to provide for defense against invasion and to enforce order within their own jurisdictions. If each State met its own responsibilities, then (according to the Jeffersonian Democrats) it naturally followed that the national defense would be assured. However, in this case, the corollary disproved the theory; for it also naturally followed that the States "were not competent to act in matters which concerned the Nation." The public domain, the Great Lakes, boundary adjustments with Canada in the North and Spain in the South, the Mississippi River, and the coastal waters were all objects which belonged within the exclusive sphere of the national government.[7] Failure of the Government to assume these responsibilities did not represent sound economy, and in fact might prove more costly in the long run.[8]

But America was at peace with Europe, and the times seemed propitious to devote more attention to the development of the interior. The Government, and the people as well, were insensitive to the many undercurrents which threatened the serenity of the times. The population was small (about 1½ millions, white), scattered, and surrounded by potential if not active enemies. The Mississippi River, the Gulf Region, and the southern part of the Atlantic coast were in the hands of Spain, which was still a powerful nation. The British had begun anew the practice of naval impressment, and it was suspected that Napoleon was bargaining for Louisiana, a negotiation which boded ill for the prospect of American westward expansion. But the country was not prone to analyze this threatening condition in the face of a promise to reduce tax-

---

[6] It was Jefferson, not Washington, who would make use of the Regular Army as a police force to maintain law and order on the frontier.

[7] Henry Adams, *History of the United States of America*, New York, Charles Scribner's Sons, 1889, Vol. I, p. 240.

[8] See New York *Evening Post*, November 27, 1801.

ation. The pocketbook was a concern of every household while the frontier was distant and impersonal; and as long as taxes were eliminated, it mattered little to the average man how these tax reductions were brought about. It mattered still less if they were brought about by limiting military expenditures.

It could even be admitted as a general principle that reduction in the armed forces, at this time, was a radical departure from sane counsel. To some authorities, depletion of the military resources was acceptable, but only because some positive measures were taken for providing adequate safeguards in an emergency. According to this premise, there was no need for a large standing army; what was needed was the machinery for creating an army to meet whatever exigency might arise. This machinery—providing an establishment capable of ready expansion to fulfill the demands of war—had been provided by the Act of March 2, 1799, which gave the nation a body of national volunteers who could bring the skeletonized force in being up to the required emergency strength.[9] But this very real reform, which should have been adopted as the only practicable solution to the problem of national expenditures and conjectured militia organizations, was quickly tossed into the political discard.

Military Establishment Is Reduced

On March 16, 1802, Congress reduced the Army to two regiments of infantry, one regiment of artillery; a total of 156 officers, 40 cadets, and 2,846 enlisted men.[10] Three military agents were designated to carry out the duties of a Quartermaster's Department with full authority to purchase all military stores and other articles for the troops in their respective departments. This was a function which could only be performed by specially trained military men in a highly skilled organization. Instead it became a political plum to be doled out to deserving cronies whose only qualification for the office was the ability to post bonds or "sufficient sureties, in such sums as the President of the United States shall direct . . . and shall take an oath faithfully to perform the duties . . ."[11] The only redeeming feature of this law was the provision establishing the military academy under the guise of a corps

---

[9] See Upton, *op. cit.*, p. 88. See also Justin Winsor *Narrative and Critical History of America*, Boston, Houghton Mifflin Co., 1888, Vol. VII, p. 358.
[10] II *Stat.*, 132-137.
[11] *Ibid.*, p. 136.

of engineers of seven officers and ten cadets to be stationed at West Point.[12]

Well might the economy minded Republicans rejoice over the Administration's policy of retrenchment, for by this time the Navy as well as the Army had felt the axe. In July, 1801 the strength of the Marine Corps was reduced to 31 commissioned officers and 400 men, while the naval personnel scarcely numbered more than 1,000 officers and men.[13] Ships had been laid up "preserved against the elements" to be recommissioned when needed. Little thought was spent upon the very important consideration that warships would have little effect in giving substance to the nation's foreign policy without men experienced in the science of naval warfare. Progress in naval affairs, as well as in military affairs, was dependent upon a continuous policy of training and education. This could not be administered in periodical doses. To be effective, as well as economical, it had to be continuous. The Sunday driver is not the safest driver, especially in a situation where conditions are incessantly altered by foreign influences.

In 1784 these influences had been perfectly clear to Jefferson, the diplomat. At that time he deplored the conduct of the Government in acceding to the demands of the Barbary pirates for ransom and inquired into the feasibility of building a strong navy which "cannot begin in a better cause nor against a weaker foe." [14] In 1785 he again urged the necessity of a naval force while drawing attention to the obvious fact that weakness provokes insult and injury, while a condition to punish it often prevents it. Furthermore, he said, it was to our interest to punish the first insult, because an insult unpunished is the parent of many others.[15] In 1786 while Von Steuben and Knox were presenting their views on military policy, Jefferson reasoned that the "coercive instrument"

[12] *Ibid.*, p. 137. The permanent school was opened on July 4, 1802. See Spaulding, *op. cit.*, p. 122. The New York *Albany Register,* on April 16, 1802, warmly praised the Government for the reduction of the Army and Navy, which had been raised "to enforce by the bayonet, submission to a sedition law aiming its deadly blow at the freedom of speech and the liberty of the press."

[13] Charles O. Paullin, "Naval Administration under Secretaries of the Navy Smith, Hamilton, and Jones, 1801-1814," *Proccedings of the U. S. Naval Institute,* Vol. 32, p. 1302. Hereafter cited as Paullin, *Naval Administration, 1801-1814.*

[14] Jefferson to Horatio Gates, December 13, 1784, Paul Leicester Ford (ed.), *The Writings of Thomas Jefferson,* Vol. 4, pp. 23-24, hereafter cited as Ford, *T. J.*

[15] Jefferson to John Jay, August 23, 1785, *ibid.,* pp. 89-90.

should be established as a navy to protect national honor. "A naval force can never endanger our liberties, nor occasion bloodshed; a land force would do both." [16] It was evident that Jefferson the President had considerably altered his views on the Navy as an instrument of national policy.

War With Tripoli

The war with Tripoli, which lasted until 1805, stayed the hand of Jefferson in reducing the Navy to the status of a police force. Hardly had he taken office when the Pasha of Tripoli declared war against the United States. Instead of following the example of his predecessors, who paid hundreds of thousands of dollars to the Barbary States to avoid such a war, Jefferson wisely calculated that the use of force in the long run would be more economical and judicious. The honor of the American flag and the safety of American citizens forced Jefferson to violate his principles of peace and economy in government. This bold positive course of action was not seriously challenged, although disapproving mutterings were to be heard among the die-hard Federalists who eagerly sought every occasion to embarrass the Administration. Their vindictiveness, however, was dulled by reports of American victories against the malignant pirates and when the war had ended on a successful note, the Navy had justified its existence.

The lessons of this episode should have been indelibly written. If America wished to trade with the world, her best interests dictated the need for a protective naval force. Furthermore, in the future, this trade might be challenged by a powerful nation. To be prepared for such a development, a stronger navy was urgent. No nation can claim its rights under international law unless it can meet the challenge to its rights. This does not imply involvement in continuous war; it is simply the best insurance that a nation's peaceful intentions will not be disturbed. Thomas Jefferson and his party preferred to shout about rights without making preparation to protect them.[17] Fortunately, the distressed condition of the world, America's geographical position, and the benign blessing of Divine Providence were all America's allies.

---

[16] Jefferson to James Monroe, August 11, 1786, *ibid.*, p. 265.
[17] New York *Evening Post,* July 1, 1801.

Military Weakness Invites War

Late in 1801 rumors had already reached America that Spain was making ready to transfer the Louisiana Territory to France.[18] In the hands of so powerful, enterprising, and adroit a nation as the latter this domain would become a retaining wall against American westward expansion, and the very livelihood of our citizens could be throttled by cutting off travel on the Mississippi River. On October 15, 1801 the transfer was made by the terms of the Treaty of San Ildefonso, and on the following day the Spanish Intendant at New Orleans suspended the right of deposit at that city.[19] To the men of the western country, this was but a preliminary step toward closing off the entire river. War fever spread like wildfire[20] throughout the affected areas presenting Jefferson with a dilemma. If he failed to heed the demands of his countrymen in the west, the Union might be rent apart; if he chose to challenge the Spanish order, a disastrous foreign war might be provoked.[21]

Military weakness created by the Administration's economy program brought Jefferson and his party close to war. The worst of it was that the Government was unable to do anything about it, and in this condition ran the imminent risk of being insulted by other nations.[22] Against this predicament, Jefferson, in almost complete disregard of his principle of no entangling alliances, had already wedded himself to the idea of calling upon the British fleet for assistance.[23] Besides this there was also another solution available to the sage of Monticello—the purchase of the territory in question.

Negotiations were quickly opened for this transaction;[24] and in anticipation of a breakdown in these plans, Congress on March

---

[18] *Ibid.,* November 30, 1801.

[19] Bailey, *op. cit.,* pp. 95-96.

[20] Charleston *Courier,* January 11, 1803. In the Senate, resolutions were made for immediately raising 50,000 militia and appropriating $5,000,000. *Ibid.,* March 5, 1803.

[21] The Government was in no position to take advantage of a well-circulated rumor that Spain had shut down the port "in order to induce the Western people to take possession of it," preferring this to its getting into the hands of the French. See Charleston *Courier,* March 10, 1803.

[22] Bailey, *op. cit.,* p. 96.

[23] See letter, Jefferson to Livingston, April 18, 1802, A. A. Lipscomb (ed). *The Writings of Thomas Jefferson,* Vol. 10, pp. 312-315.

[24] The American commissioners were instructed to offer $10,000,000 for the city of New Orleans. Napoleon offered them instead 828,000 square miles of territory for $15,000,000.

3, 1803, passed the old familiar act providing for a detachment of 80,000 militiamen and authorizing the President to require the Governors to hold their quotas in readiness to march at a moment's notice. It also made provision for an appropriation of $25,000 "for erecting . . . on the western waters [the Mississippi River] . . . one or more arsenals, and that the President cause the same to be furnished with such arms, ammunition and military stores as he may deem necessary." [25]

Fortunately, Napoleon fell upon hard days and with the loss of Santo Domingo his dream of resurrecting the old French Empire in America was shattered. Louisiana became a liability in the Little Corporal's estimate of the situation; with his plans ready for renewing hostilities with England, a transfer by sale of the entire Louisiana territory for $15,000,000 was more of an asset than spending precious divisions of men to defend the area. From the American viewpoint, the acquisition of the territory would save them from the embarrassment of being forced to refuse the British permission to cross their country to get at the French in the west. All things considered, the purchase of Louisiana was a master-stroke of diplomacy. On October 20, 1803 the Senate approved the sale, and one month later formal transfer of sovereignty was accomplished.

Neutral Rights Versus National Defense

On May 18, 1803, Napoleon declared war on Great Britain, a war that was to last for twelve years and which eventually would involve peaceful America. It is difficult to avoid being sucked into a whirlpool when preparations against such a contingency are wilfully or carelessly neglected. That the United States was able to keep clear of war until 1812 was due not to a respect on the part of the belligerents for American rights nor even to the ability of the Government to defend those rights, but rather to the subservience of the Administration to a spurious peace policy which invited humiliation and insult.

Instead of taking measures to build formidable sea-going vessels, Congress, on February 26, 1803, authorized the building of four 16-gun ships for the Mediterranean service in addition to fifteen gunboats.[26] This was in line with Jefferson's military policy

---
[25] II *Stat.* 241. This Act was repealed by the Act of April 18, 1806, to be referred to below.
[26] *Ibid.*, p. 206.

of reliance upon the militia. By distributing the gunboats among the seaport towns, they could, with promptness, "be manned by the seamen and militia of the place in which they are wanting." [27] And, because of the facility of assembling smaller vessels where they were needed, coupled with the low cost of maintaining and servicing them, Jefferson urged Congress to increase their number "until all° our important harbors, by these and auxiliary means, shall be secured against insult and opposition to the laws." [28] No circumstance, he assured Congress, had arisen which called for any augmentation of our regular military force. [29]

By February 4, 1805, the annual returns on the strength of the Army showed it to consist of 2,579 officers and men, morale low, and the officers generally ignorant of their duties. The Navy consisted of two 44's and five small vessels all out in the Mediterranean; [30] and when one of the 44's was captured by the Tripolitan pirates, she was replaced by two 18-gun brigs, the *Hornet* and the *Wasp*, the last sea-going vessels to be built under Jefferson's administration. [31] In June, 1805, the war with Tripoli ended, but the Navy which Jefferson and his party tried to avoid had won a firm hold on the popular sympathy. The brilliant exploits of young naval officers in chastising the lawless pirates were popularized throughout the countryside; they had matched the magnificent achievements of John Paul Jones.

While these accomplishments were developing, the European war had made the United States heir to the carrying trade of the world. The people grew anxious to continue "business as usual, unrestricted trade with all nations and interference from none." It was not long before England challenged this newly found prosperity. On July 23, 1805 the British Court of Appeals in Prize Causes handed down a decision in the celebrated *Essex* case. Invoking the Rule of 1756, and examining the intent of the American shipper, trade between the French West Indies and the United States (which was held to be direct trade between France and her colonies carried on by neutral America) was not permissible. Under this ruling, Yankee shipping became fair prey for any

[27] Richardson, *M&P*, I, p. 372.
[28] *Ibid.*
[29] *Ibid.* None except the added responsibility of providing security to the increased frontier line due to the purchase of Louisiana.
[30] Henry Adams, *History of the United States*, Vol. 2, p. 136.
[31] *Ibid.*, p. 140.

British warship. In effect, a virtual blockade of the United States was initiated, the right of visit and search was justified, and the impressment of American seamen was multiplied.[32] To meet this flagrant challenge to neutrality, the President applied the language of diplomacy, which in any exigency could only be as effective as the ability to defend,[33] and punctuated his opposition by economic retaliation.

On her side, France committed similar outrages upon the American flag, but these foul deeds were committed thousands of miles distant from home. French impunity was characterized by the disdain they held of a Government which made "no concealment of its military weakness" and which "will avoid every serious difference which might lead to aggression and will constantly show itself an enemy to war." [34]

But by December, 1805, even Jefferson had perceived the wisdom of a more forceful policy. He could no longer abstain from recommending "such preparations as circumstances call for." This he would bring about by improving the seacoast defenses with additional heavy cannon, and to supplement these he felt that we should have a competent number of gunboats, and the number to be competent, must be considerable.[35] There was some doubt about increasing the Regular Army but expediency dictated the organization and classification of the militia according to age (18-26) which would give a return of some 300,000 able-bodied young men. By thus separating the younger men, "we may draw from it when necessary an efficient corps fit for real and active service, and to be called to it in regular rotation." [36] With reference to the "regulars" Jefferson preferred to rely upon this select "corps" of men, calling upon regulars only when "necessity of them shall be-

---

[32] Actually only few Americans were pressed into the British service. In effect, the United States made little effort to deport British deserters, which left English sea captains no other recourse.

[33] On December 21, 1806 William Pinckney and James Monroe drew up a treaty with England over the question of impressment and the *Chesapeake* affair, but it was so distasteful that the President refused to submit it to the consideration of the Senate. See Bailey, *op. cit.,* pp. 113-114.

[34] Henry Adams, *History of the United States,* Vol. 3, pp. 84, 111.

[35] Richardson, *M&P,* I, pp. 385, 386. After the *Leander* incident in April, 1806, Jefferson recommended the construction of some 74's. See Adams, *History of the United States,* III, p. 201.

[36] *Ibid.,* p. 385. The military returns for April 4, 1806, showed approximately 470,000 privates of infantry and riflemen. See *ASP, MA,* I, p. 202. Only 250,000. however, were said to possess firearms. *Ibid.,* p. 193.

come certain." Jefferson's scheme for organizing the militia was similar to Washington's.

Despite these manifestations of a tougher policy, Great Britain continued her blockade of the American coast in search for deserters. Angry citizens protested against the wilful violations of neutral rights by both belligerents and pledged their support in favor of all measures adopted to vindicate and secure the just rights of the country.[37] The Administration's positive measures were neutralized in the House by John Randolph, who was instrumental in defeating a proposal to build larger ships. As a result, no more was done for naval defense than was allowed for the land defenses.[38]

At a time when Jefferson pressed for a settlement of our eastern and western boundaries with France and Spain, Congress began to block the President's course.

Congress, on January 2, 1806, rejected the proposal to reclassify the militia, asserting that as presently constituted, it "was sufficient for the protection of the United States." The political implications in this decision were clear. Young men refused to be picked out for special duty; mill owners refused to allow their factory workers time off for drill; schools and universities were reluctant to excuse students. These elements exercised a powerful influence over the Government. In Massachusetts, the existing militia organization was the object of just pride.[39]

Realizing that the crisis in Europe gave America a precious advantage in settling these questions, Jefferson urged the use of force at least to a moderate degree. While such a policy could lead to war, it was more than probable that it would advance the object of peace.[40] The President might have precipitated war merely by dispatching small forces to the Mississippi and Florida frontiers, but he refused to violate the constitutional prerogatives of Congress to declare war.

Congress listened attentively to Jefferson's proposals for a determined policy, but refused to follow in his footsteps. Instead

[37] Charleston *Courier*, January 10, 1806, Memorial of the Merchants of New York City to the President, Senate and House. See also January 18, 1806.

[38] Adams, *History of the United States*, III, pp. 178-180. One year later, Randolph took the administration to task for not taking a decisive attitude against Spain. See Boston *New England Palladium*, January 30, 1807.

[39] *ASP, MA, I*, p. 189. See also Boston, *New England Palladium*, March 21, 1806.

[40] Richardson, *M&P*, I, p. 390.

they gave him authority to require the Governors to take measures to organize, arm, and equip, according to law, 100,000 militia, and to accept the services, for not longer than six months, of any corps of volunteers. In the event of hostilities, the whole body of militia and volunteers were to serve for six months.[41] Three days later, another law authorized the President to employ in time of peace as many of the frigates and other public armed vessels of the United States, as his judgment might require, and to cause the residue to be laid up "in ordinary" in convenient ports.[42]

In the following year, on February 24, 1807, after it had become more evident that the belligerent powers would continue to disregard American rights, the President was authorized to raise 30,000 volunteers either of artillery, cavalry, or infantry, committed for two years, but required to serve only 12 months.[43] Eight days later, $150,000 were appropriated for coast defenses,[44] and within a week, Jefferson reported that experience in the·Mediterranean proved that gunboats could be used to augment the coast fortifications. To do this efficiently, he estimated that some 200 of these craft were necessary; 73 were already built or building, leaving 127 to be provided at a cost of some $500,000.[45] The military policy, thus defined, placed reliance for national defense upon a very small regular army, the militia, and a navy consisting primarily of gunboats to patrol the seacoast. This was purely a defensive policy embracing (1) land batteries furnished with heavy cannon and mortars at several points; (2) movable artillery which could be carried to points with no fixed batteries; (3) floating batteries; and (4) gunboats which could cooperate with the land batteries.

While America was subjected to this weak military policy, France and England had begun to carry out the codes of international law according to their own interpretations. British orders in council were met with French edicts in an effort to bring one another to submission by restricting neutral trade. American in-

[41] II *Stat*. 383-384, April 18, 1806.
[42] *Ibid*., 390, April 21, 1806. The President's recommendations for building some 74's were refused.
[43] II *Stat*. 419.
[44] *Ibid*. 443. On March 3, Congress authorized the President to augment the naval establishment by 500 men. *Ibid*.
[45] Richardson, *M&P*, I, pp. 419-420. On December 18, 1807, Congress provided for the construction of 188 gunboats and appropriated $852,500 for this purpose. II *Stat*. 451.

terest in this war of economic strangulation ran high but it did not
stir the heart-strings until June 22, 1807 when the frigate *Chesapeake* was roughly treated by His Majesty's frigate *Leopard*.[46]
The badly crippled *Chesapeake* made her way back to Norfolk
where a wave of public indignation spread throughout the country
almost instantaneously.

The New York *Republican Watch-Tower* studiously observed
that a war but little short of extermination should be preferred to
unatoned submission;[47] while the Boston *Repertory* in a similar
tone concluded that the conduct of the *Leopard* was WAR.[48] This
outrage "has no parallel," shouted the Boston *Independent
Chronicle*,[49] and the Philadelphia *Aurora* referred to "the deceitful
character" of the British.[50] But the Norfolk *Gazette and Public
Ledger* preferred to vent its spleen upon the wilful neglect of what
it called the system of defense commenced by Washington and
continued by Adams.[51]

Unmoved by the wave of popular opinion in favor of strong
retaliatory measures, Jefferson issued a proclamation demanding
British vessels in American waters immediately and without delay
to depart from the same. Failure of His Majesty's officers to obey
the order would be followed by a prohibition of all intercourse
with them, or any of them.[52] The nation wanted war, Jefferson
preferred peace, and the British remained in American waters. In
view of the menacing aspects of this contingency, the President,
on July 30, called Congress into special session.

Three months later, British war vessels were still in American
waters. The aggression begun with the *Chesapeake* affair continued
on the part of British commanders "by remaining within our
waters in defiance of the authority of the country, by habitual
violations of its jurisdiction." [53] To cope with this situation, Jefferson sought the extremes of his dilemma. He could force a just
recognition of the nation's sovereignty either by never admitting

---

[46] The British commander was seeking four deserters alleged to be on board
the ill-fated *Chesapeake*. When Commodore Barron refused to give them up,
the attack took place.
[47] January 7, 1807.
[48] July 7, 1807. One week later this paper criticized Jefferson's military policy
of defense behind gunboats. July 14, 1807.
[49] September 10, 1807.
[50] July 15, 1807.
[51] May 13, 1808.
[52] July 2, 1807, Richardson, *M&P*, I, p. 423.
[53] *Ibid.*, October 27, 1807, p. 426.

an armed vessel into our harbors, or by maintaining in every harbor such an armed force as might constrain obedience to the laws. The first could prove embarrassing in the absence of a formidable array of force and the second was unthinkable because the expense of such a standing force and its inconsistence with our principles forbade it.[54] It was evident that the President of the United States recoiled from meeting the challenge head-on and preferred to resort to a policy of expediency.

Jefferson Seeks Peace Through Economic Coercion and Passive Defense

After ordering all British warships out of American ports,[55] Jefferson, with a passion for peace, resorted to economic coercion of Great Britain, and on December 22, 1807, forced through Congress his embargo.[56] Although this policy did serve to embarrass England in her struggle with France, it also served to stifle American commerce and threatened to divide the country in two. Maritime New England turned thumbs down on Jefferson's terrapin policy and shipowners began to smuggle goods out of the country.[57] While the opposition predicted that the embargo would suspend peace by a thread and bring misery and ruin to the United States,[58] supporters of the measure looked upon it as the surest means for avoiding war.[59]

Meanwhile a Congressional Committee on November 24 brought in a report supporting the President's policy of passive resistance. Protection against aggression, it was declared, could "be best and most expeditiously afforded by means of land batteries and gun boats . . . against ships of any size." [60] Three weeks and three days later, Congress approved the construction of 188 gunboats and appropriated $852,500 for this purpose.[61] On

---

[54] *Ibid.*, 426-427.

[55] Republican reaction to this act was best illustrated in the *National Intelligencer*, July 15, 1807.

[56] II *Stat.* 451.

[57] See Morrison, *op. cit.*, pp. 187-193.

[58] See letter, Timothy Pickering to Governor of Massachusetts in Baltimore, *North American and Mercantile Daily Advertiser*, March 18, 1808. See also Charleston *Courier*, January 27, 1808.

[59] Boston *Independent Chronicle*, April 4, 1808. See also Albany *Register*, January 1, 1808, Richmond *Enquirer*, May 3, 1808, *National Intelligencer*, July 31, 1807.

[60] *ASP, MA*, I, 217-218.

[61] II *Stat.* 451.

January 8, 1808 Congress authorized the repair and completion of the coast fortifications already in existence and such other fortifications and works to be erected as would afford more effectual protection to our ports and harbors. For these purposes $1,000,000 was appropriated.[62] As an added precaution against the possibility of war, Secretary of War Dearborn recommended a force of 24,-000 volunteer militia under federal supervision and increasing the Regular Army to 6,000 men.[63] Two days later the President urged Congress to act upon these recommendations without delay.[64]

But Congress, reluctant to raise a volunteer force under Federal control, fell back upon the familiar reference to a militia detachment apportioned among the States with the proviso that volunteers might be accepted.[65] With reference to augmenting the Regular Army, however, they voted in the affirmative by providing for an increase of five regiments of infantry, one regiment of riflemen, one regiment of light artillery, and one regiment of light dragoons, enlisted for the term of five years, unless sooner discharged.[66] Ten days later the most important military legislation of this period was passed: The law of April 22, 1808, which provided for an annual appropriation of $200,000 for arming the militia.[67] Although this was a feeble beginning, it did bring the Government to a realization of their responsibility for arming the militia of the States.

Another attempt was made to raise a volunteer force late in 1808 when a select committee of Congress reported in favor of raising an army of 50,000 volunteers, to be engaged for two years and to serve, if required for actual service, any proportion of the term, not exceeding twelve months.[68] While no action was taken upon this report, a law was passed on January 31, 1809, providing that there be fitted out, officered and manned, as soon as may be the four following frigates; *United States, Essex, John Adams,* and *President.* In addition, the President was also authorized to recommission "as many of the armed vessels as the service might

---

[62] *Ibid.,* 453.
[63] *ASP, MA,* I, 228, February 24, 1808.
[64] Jefferson to Congress, February 26, 1808, *ibid.,* 227.
[65] II *Stat.* 478-479, March 30, 1808.
[66] *Ibid.,* 481-482.
[67] *Ibid.,* 490. No increase was made in this amount until 1887 when it was raised to $400,000. When compared with the population increase over this period the increase pales into insignificance.
[68] *ASP, MA,* I, 235, December 26, 1808.

require." [69] This law also increased the personnel of the Navy by 300 midshipmen, 3,600 seamen to serve two years unless sooner discharged; and appropriated $400,000 for its implementation.

Jefferson's make-haste policy of national defense, intended to discourage aggression against American territory, was but a small guarantee of security. Aimed primarily at relying upon militia and volunteers, with the aid of a very small Regular Army, this policy was both ineffective and futile. The militia was in no condition to test the strength of a strong invading force.[70] Jefferson regarded militiamen as civilians who would be drawn from their farms and homes only to do service in local emergencies. They were not to be sent "to a distance, they shall not—they could not—be kept in armies very long."

Volunteers, because of the reluctance to build a strong federal force, were few; and the Regular Army was too small and too widely scattered to be effective. In the face of this feeble defensive apparatus, the experiment in economic warfare was displeasing to the British and encouraging to the French, who seized American shipping with increased vigor.[71] In the year following the proclamation of the embargo, the French, under one pretext or another, seized some $10,000,000 worth of American shipping. This, coupled with the increased crescendo of opposition at home which threatened civil strife and disunion, forced Jefferson to terminate the embargo. On March 1, 1809, just three days before James Madison was inaugurated, the most unpopular law since the Intolerable Acts was repealed.[72]

With honest intention, Jefferson sought to promote peace by discouraging adequate military preparations, but he succeeded only in bringing the country to the verge of economic stagnation. With the same intention, his reluctance to defend American rights on the seas provoked a general feeling of contempt among Europeans for America's claims to those rights. If nothing else, Jefferson's efforts should have served notice upon his successor that the nation's destiny could not best be served by philosophical resignation and resort to expediency. No better example than this could be offered to support Washington's oft-repeated advice: the best insurance for peace is to be adequately prepared for war.

---

[69] II *Stat.* 514.

[70] Dumas Malone, *Jefferson the Virginian*, Boston, Little Brown & Co., 1948, p. 344.

[71] Bailey, *op. cit.*, p. 122.   [72] II *Stat.* 533.

CHAPTER 5

The War of 1812

Manpower Resources—War Hawks Lead the Way—
Militia System Still Inadequate—Congress Dictates to
the President—On to Canada—Still More Legislation—
William Henry Harrison Retrieves Some American
Prestige—The Specter of Mediocre Leadership Stalks the
American Army—A Sound Military Policy Is Not Yet
Attained—Andrew Jackson Writes the Final Chapter—
Monroe Defines Federal Authority Over Manpower—
Prelude to Peace

Manpower Resources

UPON JAMES MADISON fell the responsibility for steering
the Nation clear of war in an atmosphere which was heated
at home and abroad by the program of commercial retaliation.
He inherited also the weak military edifice which since 1802 had
leaned upon the militia and volunteers to the almost total exclusion
of the Regular Army. Surprisingly this deterioration was permitted
despite all the warnings of past experience including twenty years
of desultory Indian warfare and a growing conviction that the
Indians, united and supported by British intrigue, posed a real
threat to American westward expansion. In the face of a constantly
growing danger of war with either England or France, this vitia-
tion was inexcusable.

In 1809, the strength of the Army was less than 3,000 men
notwithstanding the legislation of 1808 which authorized 9,921
men. This small force was required to do duty in twenty-four forts
and thirty-two inclosed batteries with an armament of some 750
guns of various calibers, all of which required the services of 12,-
610 men. The Navy fared little better. In that same year its
strength was some 200 officers and 2,104 men, attached for the
most part to the small gunboats which were scattered from
Maine to New Orleans.[1]

[1] See Ganoe, *op. cit.*, p. 113; Spaulding, *op. cit.*, p. 126; Paullin, "Naval Administration—1801-1814," p. 1303, 1318; Francis Beirne, *The War of 1812*,
New York, E. P. Dutton & Co., Inc., 1949, p. 126. By January 30, 1810, the
total strength of the Army was computed at 6,954 men or 3,000 under the
authorized total of 9,921. See *ASP MA*, I, 249.

As long as the judgment of Congress and the President, from 1800 to 1808, was in opposition to an efficient regular army and navy, leadership in the former rested upon generals · who had grown too old and infirm to assume the burdens and responsibilities of active campaigns. Furthermore, as long as the Army was tolerated only as a necessary evil, the service was not likely to attract men of ability, all the more since promotions, especially to the higher ranks, were considerably dependent upon political considerations. In the Navy the opposite was true. This was due to Jefferson's policy of reducing officer strength in the Navy; only the more capable survived.

While the country drifted toward war, the only school of command for the Army, the school of experience, was limited to but few officers. True, West Point had existed since 1802, but there were too few graduates to make its worth felt at this time. Failure in this most important aspect of military affairs meant also a failure in war plans, logistics, and leadership. This meant that war would bring the same painful experiences as had the Revolutionary War.

It meant even more. Americans had forgotten the value of a single commander in chief for the successful prosecution of war.[2] As a result, command was divided among men who were old, those whose talents bordered upon mediocrity, those who had influential political friends, and, in the case of James Wilkinson, it meant a traitor at the head of an army.[3]

The decayed condition of the Army, however, was partially offset by the administration of the War Department under men of ability and experience. With the exception of one, Knox's successors up to 1812 were men who had seen active service in the Revolution.[4] Their shortcomings, whenever they became apparent,

---

[2] General Armstrong as Secretary of War attempted to assume the responsibilities of a commander-in-chief and in so doing paved the way for the disasters on the Canadian frontier and the burning of the capital of the United States.

[3] Marquis James, *Andrew Jackson, The Border Captain,* Indianapolis, Bobbs-Merrill Co., 1933, p. 141. Henry Adams, *op. cit.,* Vol. VI, p. 292. See also Royal O. Shreve, *The Finished Scoundrel,* Indianapolis, Bobbs-Merrill Co., 1933, pp. 12; 133. After the failures of the northern campaigns, Madison was inclined to place the blame not only upon the inexperience of the commanders but also upon the policy of reliance in time of peace upon a small military establishment. See Madison to William Wirt, September 30, 1813, *Letters and Writings of James Madison,* Philadelphia, J. P. Lippincott & Co., 1865, Vol. II, p. 575. Hereafter cited as Madison *L & W.* See also Philadelphia *Aurora,* January 1, 1813, p. 1.

[4] Justin Winsor, *Narrative and Critical History of America,* New York, Houghton, Mifflin & Co., 1888, Vol. 7, p. 358.

were due to the limitations imposed upon the military establishment by existing legislation. This was especially true with reference to the militia. Although the militia was viewed as the bulwark of defense, the laws rendered it impossible to effect any well-digested scheme of national defense or even to coordinate the activities of the state and federal forces. With the exception of the law of 1808, which provided for an annual expenditure of $200,-000 for the support of the militia, Congress and the President did nothing to permit coordination from the War Department. Thus the manpower resources of the Nation on the eve of the war, were out of the reach of the Government, and ensuing legislation accentuated this separation. Nor did the loud talk of the young war hawks improve this languid condition. In fact, their militant phrases were uttered in almost complete disregard of America's military debility.

War Hawks Lead the Way

The Congressional elections of 1810 swept out of office the majority of those who were opposed to war and brought into power a group of young men whose boasting of American destiny and prowess accelerated the trend toward war.[5] They were more than a match for James Madison who tried to find a peaceful formula but succeeded only in committing a series of blunders offensive to the British and heartening to the French. This left the President no alternative but to follow the lead of the War Hawks who were bent on war with England.[6]

The surge of ultra nationalism leavened by the War Hawks led the west and south into a political alliance in a determined effort to rid the continent once and for all of British influence. The west anxiously entered into this marriage to secure the lucrative fur trade and to destroy the barriers to further westward expansion. The south pledged its troth because Spain, in the Florida's, was now in league with Great Britain thus rendering the southern frontier insecure. Both west and south championed the cause of war in the interest of freedom of the seas while the maritime states

---

[5] Everywhere but in New England, men who temporized were turned out of office and their places given to younger men who stood for war. See Charles M. Wiltse, *John Calhoun, Nationalist, 1782-1828*, Indianapolis, Bobbs-Merrill Co., Inc., 1944, p. 53. See also, Glyndon G. Van Deusen, *The Life of Henry Clay*, Boston, Little Brown & Co., 1937, pp. 78-79.

[6] Adams, *op. cit.*, Vol. VI, p. 122. This is vividly described in Bailey, *op. cit.*, pp. 136-144.

of New England for the most part remained steadfastly opposed to any war against England.

While the "War Hawk" Congress was in the democratic process of organizing, the western Indians under the leadership of the Shawnee Tecumseh and his brother The Prophet, encouraged by the British, formed a confederation. A systematic destruction of frontier settlements commenced. The terror that was foreseen by George Washington—unification of the Indians—again threatened to become a reality. The challenge was quickly answered, not from the seat of Government, but from the Indian territory. Under the inspired leadership of William Henry Harrison, a mixed force of 800 men met and defeated the Indians at Tippecanoe and completely destroyed the confederation.[7] Thoroughly aroused, westerners issued a sharp indictment of England for fomenting this latest aggression and asked for an immediate declaration of war. Secretary of State James Monroe sustained the Administration against the western charge that it was lacking in patriotic spirit and promised that if existing grievances were not satisfied by the following May, Congress would declare war against Britain. [8]

Less than six months remained for America to prepare for war in a climate of opinion which found the country divided, where the military forces were below even authorized strength, and where the President of the United States was completely ignorant of the problems entailed in preparation for war. This catalog of weakness and indecision was overlooked by the War Hawks who relied upon their own audacity to win a war, and whose favorite expression, reechoed by Jefferson from his retreat at Monticello, was the empty boast that Canada could be conquered simply by marching into it. But Canadian militia, commanded by one able general, coupled with a series of blunders committed by mediocre and "decayed" American generals were to provide bitter evidence against the military sagacity of Jefferson and his young western contemporaries.

Militia System Still Inadequate

What was the condition of the militia which the militant congressional newcomers would employ to march into Canada? Each State had preserved its own system of organization and all had

---

[7] Spaulding, *op. cit.*, p. 126. The battle took place on November 7, 1811.
[8] Wiltse, *op. cit.*, p. 57.

placed different construction upon the law of May 8, 1792.[9] Objections were made by many that no effective service could be expected until Congress fulfilled its constitutional responsibility for arming the militia. Until such time as this was done, reasoned the more sober-minded, it was ill-advised to call out any portion of the militia for field duty each year.[10] Without proper arms and equipment, the assemblage of the militia was little more than a festive occasion where neighbors met to exchange witticisms. But even if Congress had been willing to assume these responsibilities, the limits they would be permitted by the people to reach "will be just so far as to make them [the militia] food for powder in the day of battle; and death, or what is worse, loss of honor."[11] In these circumstances Congress balked, and the militia became more deficient in those skills which would make them the palladium of our security.

While the Senate was stating its position with reference to the militia, the President, on January 3, 1810, urged Congress to consider the expediency of such a classification and organization of the militia as would best insure prompt and successive aids from that source adequate to the emergencies which might call for them.[12] Furthermore, since the act authorizing a militia detachment of 100,000 was to expire within ninety days, Madison recommended the enlistment, for a short period of service, of 20,000 men, and at the same time he cautiously hinted at the need for some additional naval armament.[13]

The only significant response to all this clattering about military necessities was a radical change in uniforms to single breasted coats with silver lace along the buttonholes.[14] Congress having refused to acknowledge the wisdom of George Washingtons' recommendations to create a federal force of militia, the nation had now to witness all over again a series of experiments on how best to bring a fighting force on the field, not only for offensive warfare, but even for defense against invasion by a handful of British soldiers. Having discounted the value of professional military train-

[9] See ltr Benjamin Tallmadge to General E. Huntington, December 18, 1809, *ASPMA* I 263.
[10] Ltr Joseph Bloomfield to Col. Benj Tallmadge, December 29, 1809, *ibid.* 266.
[11] Ltr General E. Huntington to Benj Tallmadge, January 5, 1810, *ibid.* 263.
[12] Richardson, *M&P*, I, p. 478.
[13] *Ibid.* The language of this message was toned to political expediency.
[14] Ganoe, *op. cit.*, p. 112.

ing in peacetime, the people, and the men who served, were forced to accept mediocrity. Having failed to keep in naval service twenty ships of the line, the nation was forced into war by the machinations and intrigues of British agents on the frontiers.[15] Consistency in neglect, a peculiar American virtue, led the nation into war and forced the Government to embark upon a haphazard, hasty, and piecemeal policy of national defense under the difficult conditions of war.

Congress Dictates to the President

On November 5, 1811 President Madison recommended that adequate provision be made for

> filling the ranks and prolonging the enlistments of regular troops; for an auxiliary force to be engaged for a more limited term; for the acceptance of volunteer corps, whose patriotic ardor may court a participation in urgent services; for detachments as they may be wanted of other portions of the militia, and for such a preparation of the great body as will proportion its usefulness to its intrinsic capacities.[16]

To this Congress responded with more than was asked, and this was done not so much to take every possible precaution to prepare for war as to embarrass the Administration. Assuming the role of a schoolmaster, Senator William B. Giles, the new chairman of the committee on foreign relations, chided the President and the Secretary of War for recommending less than was competent for the conquest of Canada. Ten thousand men, he was sure, could not successfully wrest the northern domain from England, but 25,000 could. Under the guise of patriotism, Giles vented his spleen upon the President and his Secretary of War and forced acceptance of an army which would not, under the existing scheme of things, be enlisted.[17]

The debates in Congress, pro and con, demonstrated the danger to which the Republic was exposed by neglecting in peacetime to take adequate measures of security. There were those who supported Giles (this included Federalists and Republicans alike)

---

[15] Gouverneur Morris, quoted in George Fielding Eliot, *The Ramparts We Watch,* New York, Reynal & Hitchcock, 1938, pp. 15-16. Cf. Alfred Thayer Mahan, *Seapower In Its Relations to the War of 1812,* London, Sampson Low, Marston & Co., Ltd., Vol. I, p. 261.

[16] Richardson, M&P I, p. 494. For the Regular establishment Madison recommended raising 10,000 men. See Henry Adams, *History of the United States,* Vol. VI, p. 147.

[17] *Ibid.* Van Deusen, *op. cit.,* p. 79.

only to embarrass the unpopular President. There were those who feared the financial consequence of raising such a large force, and there were those who feared that an army as large as this might easily be used to destroy the liberties of the people. And there was John Randolph, whose poignant shafts of abuse never wavered in their aim at the Army which he asserted "was filled with depravity and dissoluteness."[18] Outraged at his inability to defeat Giles' measure, Randolph advocated authorizing the employment of the Army, when not in active service, in constructing roads and canals.[19]

On January 11, 1812 the Regular Army was increased by ten regiments of infantry, two of artillery, and one regiment of cavalry, enlisted for a term of five years. This, together with the existing force of 10,000 men, gave a nominal total of 35,000 men. To encourage enlistments in these regiments a bounty of sixteen dollars was offered in addition to three months pay and 160 acres of land after satisfactory completion of service. Nine days earlier the President was authorized to raise not to exceed six companies of rangers by voluntary enlistment for one year to augment the forces defending the frontiers against Indian incursions.[20]

Without allowing a fair amount of time in which to enlist the regular regiments, Congress proceeded to make it even more difficult to do so by enacting a law providing for a volunteer force of 50,000 committed for two years but required to serve twelve months. To these men and their heirs was allowed a bounty in land of 160 acres. On April 10, the detachment of 100,000 militia proportioned among the States to serve not longer than six months was again authorized.[21] On paper the fighting strength of the United States was now colossal; a Regular Army of 35,000, a volunteer force of 50,000, and a militia detachment of 100,000. But voting the battalions and enlisting the men again proved to be

---

[18] *Annals of Congress,* 12th Congress, 1st Session, January 10, 1812, p. 719, in this regard, Randolph singled out James Wilkinson. See Shreve, *op. cit.,* pp. 233-235.
[19] *Ibid.,* pp. 719-720. See also Van Deusen, *op. cit.,* p. 81.
[20] II *Stat.* 670, 671. The number of companies was limited probably to avoid competition with the enlistment of regulars for five years service. On July 1, 1812, an additional ranger company was authorized bringing the total to seven or 492 men. *Ibid.* 774-775.
[21] *Ibid.* February 6, 1812, pp. 676-677. The officers for these troops were to be selected according to the State laws. On July 6, the President was vested with the authority to commission new officers without regard for the State laws. *Ibid.,* 705-706; 785.

different. In fact, by April, 1812, it was evident that few men would seek service in the Regular Army for a five-year tour under officers who were strangers. In recognition of this fact, Congress on April 8 reduced the term of service in the regular units to eighteen months but limited the number recruited under this law to 15,000.[22]

Thus within a period of three months Congress enacted legislation which was contradictory and which crippled any serious attempt to bring the Regular Army up to strength. In dealing with volunteers little regard was had for those who must have volunteered in the first instance to serve for five years in the regular units. By creating the option of lesser periods of service and preference for local units, morale in the Regular Army was weakened as it had been during the Revolutionary War. Under these acts, the whole military edifice was a hodge-podge of under-strength units. No regularity existed with reference to company strength nor with reference to the number of companies in a regiment. It was not until June 26, 1812, eight days after the declaration of war, that the military establishment was placed on something of an efficient basis.[23]

Thus Congress, after forcing the hand of the President in the direction of war, deliberately defeated the purpose of national defense. Legislation served as ample proof of the inability and unwillingness of the Congress to adjust democratic process to the needs of a democratic apparatus designed to defend and protect democratic principles. The very fact that six different laws were enacted in six months[24] to bring men to a proper recognition of their military obligation as citizens (on their own terms) was evidence enough to indict the lawmakers as not equal to their responsibilities.

On the side of the Navy, the war advocates in Congress refused to be stampeded into what was considered an extravagant expendi-

---

[22] *Ibid.*, 704. A bounty of sixteen dollars was offered.

[23] *Ibid.*, 764. The infantry of the Army of the United States was fixed at twenty-five regiments of ten companies each. Company strength was set at 90 privates. In the cavalry each troop was fixed at 64 privates.

[24] Interspersed among these laws, in addition to those pertaining to the Navy, were three others. On March 28, a Quartermaster's Department was established under a Quartermaster General. This eliminated the "evils" attendant upon the system of military agents to perform these duties. *Ibid.*, 696-699. On April 29, the number of cadets at West Point was fixed at 250, and a small increase was made in the Corps of Engineers. *Ibid.*, 720-721. On May 14, the Ordnance Department was established. *Ibid.*, 732-733.

ture of money. On January 17, 1812, the chairman of the House Naval Committee recommended the appropriation of $7,500,000 to build twelve 74's and twenty frigates as a war necessity. But although the Republicans felt no compunction at breaking tradition by allowing a large Army, they refused to give one hundred percent support to the Navy. The western War Hawks argued against the proposal and some even referred to the Navy as both expensive and dangerous. Despite Henry Clay's reference to the Navy as a "bond of connection between the states, concentrating their hopes, their interests, and their affections,"[25] the House refused to build the large ships asked for.

On the eve of war the Navy consisted of eighteen ships, ten frigates, and eight brigs, together with 165 gunboats, sixty-three in commission and the rest in ordinary or undergoing repairs, and all of them scattered from Maine to New Orleans. The Navy Department itself was deficient in every essential:

> It had no dry docks. It had few ships. With the exception of the naval establishment at Washington, the navy-yards were in a state of neglect and decay. The navy had few conveniences for building, repairing, and laying up ships. . . .[26]

There were no 74's (battleships), and considering the intention of the War Hawks to march into Canada, a task which would involve naval operations on the Great Lakes, no effort was made to build yards and naval depots on these waterways until after war had been declared.

No one in the Government, observed one authority, gave much thought to the military dangers created by the war. The entire seacoast was defenseless, the Lakes unguarded, and the whole frontier country subject to the wanton depredations of an Indian uprising incited by the British. In the vast northwestern territory, the defenses were left to several petty garrisons whose combined total numbered 296 men. The situation in the south and southwest was little better. Here the Indians relied upon the support of British forces at New Orleans or Mobile to expel every American garrison from the territory. This was the defense effort of the Government

---

[25] *Annals of Congress,* 12th Congress, 1st Session, January 22, 1812, 910-919; *ASPMA* I 247-252. See also Van Deusen, *op. cit.,* pp. 81-82.

[26] Paullin, "Naval Administration—1801-1814," p. 1318. When the war ended, the naval strength was computed at approximately seventy-five armed vessels of from ten to seventy-four guns each, and about 240 gunboats, barges, and other small craft. These additions were made by purchase, construction, or capture. *Ibid.,* pp. 1317, 1319.

to protect a rich hinterland which once lost could only be regained through another and perhaps more costly war.[27]

America declared war against the mistress of the seas with a military and naval establishment whose puniness startled even the British. A paper Army, a dispersed Navy, and mediocre leadership in the former, was the extent of the military might that could be thrown against England in June 1812. And, if Americans could not find the means of uniting for a common purpose and against a common enemy, England could find an invaluable ally in the disaffection of New England towards the war.[28] Only the most profound believers in metaphysics could see an American victory under this strange set of circumstances, yet the nation plunged headlong into war.

The declaration of war was met with mixed emotions throughout the country. After categorically listing the high patriotic motives which prompted the Revolutionary War, the Boston *Repertory and General Advertiser* condemned the Southern men who voted a war which would "impoverish and weaken the force of the commercial States." The Hartford *Courant* regretted the decision made by "the government of a country, without armies, navies, fortifications, money or credit, and in direct contradiction to the voice of the people to declare war." In Philadelphia, the *Aurora* advertised a book purporting to make a dispassionate inquiry into the reasons for "declaring an offensive and runious (sic) war against Great Britain."[29] But in Savannah, Georgia, the news of the war was met by demonstrations of pleasure and satisfaction which reached out into the west.

On To Canada

Before the end of the first year of the war, all the errors of judgment and indecision as well as the obstructionist tactics of men like Randolph and Giles were to manifest themselves in the disgraceful defeat of American arms all along the northern frontier. In spite of the advantage growing out of the declaration of war (selection of time and place of attack) the plan to invest Canada

---

[27] Adams, *op. cit.,* Vol. VI, pp. 293-294.
[28] Charles M. Fuess, *Daniel Webster,* Little Brown & Co., 1930, Vol. I, pp. 136-138. President Madison himself was a little annoyed at the decision of the War Hawks, and hoped that peace with England or even with France might take him off the horns of his dilemma. See ltr Madison to Jefferson, May 25, 1812, Madison *L&W.* II 535.
[29] September 11, 1812; June 23, 1812, p. 3; August 31, 1812, p. 1, col. 1.

failed miserably first because no consideration was given to General Hull's advice to secure control of the Great Lakes; secondly because of the selection of poor commanders by the inexperienced President; thirdly because the forces moving northward did not act in concert; and fourthly because the plans were based upon manpower which was not in being as a military force.

To command the armies created by the recent legislation, Congress authorized the selection of two major generals, nine brigadiers, one quartermaster general, one inspector general and adjutant general, and four colonels. As senior officer, Secretary of War Eustis nominated the President's close friend Henry Dearborn, aged sixty-two, whose New England antecedents seemed to make him a happy choice. To fill the other positions in these grades, Eustis selected three more men who like Dearborn were over sixty, and one (James Wilkinson) who was suspected of accepting bribes from the Spaniards.[30] Into such infirm and slippery hands were entrusted the plans to carry the war into Canada.

The campaign opened as a three-pronged offensive stretching from Detroit to Lake Champlain. The venerable Hull was on the left, General Van Rensselaer in the center, and Dearborn on the right. With some misgiving General Hull pushed on into Canada only to be driven back to Detroit where he was duped by his adversary, General Isaac Brock, into surrendering his entire command. Of the many factors contributing to the failure of Hull's expedition, none stand out so glaringly as the utter incompetence of General Dearborn, who had been selected to act as commander in chief of the entire northern front except Detroit.[31] Ordered to create a diversion in the center, Dearborn hesitated and later confessed that he was unaware that the troops on the Niagara were a part of his command.[32]

But even if Dearborn had been disposed and able to act vigorously in the exercise of his authority as generalissimo, the force collected in the center under Van Rensselaer proved to be a liability. In July and August its strength was well under 700 men

---

[30] Beirne, *op cit.,* p. 90.

[31] John Armstrong, *Notices of the War of 1812,* New York, George Dearborn, 1836, Vol. I, p. 49. Cf. Beirne, *op. cit.,* p. 104.

[32] James Monroe, who acted more like the Secretary of War than did Eustis was sharply critical of the surrender at Detroit. See ltr Monroe to Dearborn August 28, 1812, *The Writings of James Monroe,* S. M. Hamilton, New York, G. P. Putnam's Sons, 1901, Vol. V, pp. 218-219. Hereafter cited as Monroe, *Writings.* See also ltr Monroe to Dearborn September 17, 1812, *ibid.* 223-226.

most of whom were ill-equipped, ill-fed, without shoes, and all of them clamoring for pay. By October, the number grew to 6,000 regulars and militia as opposed to 1,500 of the enemy which included some British regulars. However, this superiority was dissipated by the rivalry which grew up between General Alexander Smyth, a regular officer, and Van Rensselaer the militiaman, and by the enterprise of General Brock who was quick to take advantage of the disagreeing American generals. On October 13, American arms suffered a second stinging defeat whereupon Van Rensselaer resigned his commission. General Smyth succeeded to the command but by November 30th his bombastic declarations had frightened few of the enemy and had encouraged few Americans to stand and fight. Unable to do much more, Smyth ordered his men to withdraw.[33]

The dangers to which the militia, in the absence of Federal control, would expose the nation in time of war, became dangerously manifest in the East where General Dearborn was in command. It was to offset the disaffection of the New England States that he, a New Englander, was selected as generalissimo. He might have succeeded if he had been twenty years younger. But the infirmities of age were too great a handicap where an army had to be recruited in an atmosphere of hostility against "Mr. Madison's war."

Fair warning had been given, as early as April, that the militia could not by law be marched out of the territory of the United States. On May 9, 1812, the New York *Evening Post* reminded the Government of the limitations imposed upon them by the Constitution in cases where it became legal to order the militia out. If the militia could be drafted "in any other case than those specified by the Constitution, there is an end to our liberties as soon as we have a President daring enough to make an attack upon them."[34]

By the time war was declared, the military legislation enacted to meet the emergency had succeeded only in raising a loud furor throughout the East. Instead of the large numbers of volunteers expected during the first flush of patriotic zeal, in New York nothing was heard but lamentation and dissatisfaction from those militiamen who were called to make up the quota of 13,000 men for

---

[33] Beirne, *op. cit.*, pp. 109-111, 118, 120.
[34] New York *Evening Post*, April 30, 1812; May 9, 1812.

that State.[35] In Massachusetts, opposition to the war was so strong that by July that State had done nothing to meet its quota. When apprised of the effect such an attitude would have on operations against Canada, Governor Caleb Strong informed the Secretary of War that the militia of his State had no desire to leave their garrisons to the protection of others; and, furthermore, they preferred to defend their firesides, in company with their friends, under their own officers, rather than be marched to some distant place.[36]

Reechoing the opposition to the Federal requisition for a quota of State troops, the Boston *Repertory and General Advertiser* refused to concede that the laws regulating the militia even intended that they be ordered into the service of the United States, to assist in carrying on an offensive war.[37] Any attempt on the part of the Government to place an interpretation upon the Constitution which would authorize the employment of the militia in any case other than actual invasion was constitutionally illegal in the Bay State.

The Massachusetts legislature counseled their constituents to express sentiments against the war; while the New York *Evening Post* raised the question: "Why is it that a standing army should be raised under the name of militia?" Furthermore, observed this journal, when the militia "are degraded into regular troops they would become terrible."[38]

New Hampshire, however, refused to be swayed by the critical attitude of Massachusetts and Connecticut, and Governor William Plumer assailed those who argued against the President's authority to call out the militia. To contend, he said, that the Governors could refuse to honor the President's request for militiamen would establish a principle of insubordination incompatible with all military principles, and would in fact, nullify the authority vested in the President as Commander in Chief of the militia. Moreover, the contention that militia could not constitutionally be employed until an actual invasion, "is a construction favorable indeed to the enemy, but fatal to the security of our own country." The Concord *Patriot* indicted the Boston *Repertory* for its "treasonable" utter-

[35] *Ibid.*, May 12, 1812.
[36] See correspondence between S/W Eustis and Caleb Strong, July-August, 1812, *ASPMA* I 321-326.
[37] September 14, 1812. A similar viewpoint was entertained by Rhode Island and Connecticut.
[38] Hartford *Courant,* July 7, 9, 12, 1812.

ings and quoted from the Philadelphia *Aurora* to support the charge.[39]

Meanwhile the seditious opposition of Massachusetts and Connecticut, aided by intrigues elsewhere, had so clogged the wheels of war that Madison became convinced the northern campaign could not accomplish its objectives.[40] The regular enlistments were far below expectations, and volunteers could not be attracted even for one years' service. The militia from some States were not forthcoming because of the distorted constitutional interpretation. If the mistakes of the Revolutionary War were to be avoided, something had to be done to keep a regular force of sufficient numbers in the field. Madison tried to stimulate his general (Dearborn) to make increased efforts to bring this about in the north,[41] but enlistments continued to fall off.[42]

By comparison with the failures of the Army, the small Navy achieved a remarkable success. The loss of territory occasioned by misapplied manpower on land was more than compensated for in the humiliation once again visited upon His Majesty's naval might by the brilliant exploits of American seamen in the regular and auxiliary Navy.

In addition to the tiny flotilla of ships authorized by law, Congress on June 26, 1812 made provisions for a fleet of privateers.[43] Within a few weeks, these ships plied the seas in search of prizes[44] and, but for the small inducements held out by the Government, many more might have been commissioned.[45] In their willingness to keep costs down, Congress preferred to rely upon this auxiliary Navy which occasioned no large outlays of money and which, in effect, was a source of revenue. With the exception of those ships of the line launched on the Great Lakes, by the following summer

---

[39] Concord *Patriot*, November 24, 1812. After the war Congress inquired into the constitutionality of the right of the Government to call upon the militia in times of national emergency, and sought also to settle the relations between militia and regular officers where acting together in war. See ASPMA I, 604 ff. Cf. Carl Brent Swisher, *American Constitutional Development*, New York, Houghton Mifflin Co., 1943, pp. 141-142.

[40] Madison to Jefferson, August 17, 1812, Madison *L&W* II 542-544.

[41] Madison to Dearborn, October 7, 1812, *Ibid.* 545-547.

[42] During the year 1812, 49,187 militiamen were called into service. When to this was added 15,000 regulars and volunteers the total swelled to 65,000. But these were so widely distributed that not more than a few thousand were ever brought together on a single field. See Beirne, *op. cit.*, p. 123.

[43] II *Stat.* 759-764.

[44] Boston *Patriot*, July 11, 1812, p. 3, col. 1; July 1, 1812, p. 2, col. 6.

[45] Philadelphia *Aurora*, July 2, 1813.

"not a single vessel of war has the government launched"; nor had they taken any measures to stimulate privateering by which .means the enemy could be more vitally affected.[46]

When the results of the first year of naval operations were tabulated, the Navy, which the President's cabinet twice tried to convert into floating batteries for harbor defense,[47] had stung the British war effort to the tune of 4,330 tons captured or destroyed. This was exclusive of the innumerable prizes taken by the privateers.[48] These significant results might have been more impressive had the Congress, as well as the Administration, provided the necessary means for equipping, fitting, repairing and building a larger number of heavier ships.[49] If this had been done, the failures in the northern theater might not have occurred. If the American strategy had envisioned the importance of securing command of the Great Lakes and the St. Lawrence River as the key to the successful invasion of Canada, a different story would have been recorded for the campaign of 1812. Control of the Great Lakes would have crushed British military power in the northwest, and guaranteed the conquest which for frontier Americans was one of the main objects of the war.[50]

Taken all in all, the end of the first six months of fighting conclusively showed that all the shortcomings of the Revolutionary War were being repeated and in some instances the errors compounded. Militia companies refused to serve under other than commanders of their own choosing,[51] the democratic practice of electing officers was continued,[52] the vicious system of procuring substitutes was again permitted,[53] and costly bounties again threatened

[46] *Ibid.,* July 3, 1813.
[47] Upton, *op. cit.,* p. 106.
[48] Beirne, *op. cit.,* pp. 136-137. The loss to the American Navy in these operations was 820 tons.
[49] If a fleet of capital ships had been authorized, the defense of the coasts would have been secured against invasion and predatory raids made by British commerce raiders and privateers. See Harold & Margaret Sprout, *The Rise of American Naval Power, 1776-1918,* Princeton, Princeton University Press, 1942, p. 84.
[50] *Ibid.,* p. 75.
[51] Philadelphia *Aurora,* June 25, 1812, p. 1, col. 4.
[52] Savannah *Republican and Evening Ledger,* September 25, 1812; Charleston *Courier,* March 1, 1813.
[53] New York *Evening Post,* July 9, 1812; May 19, 1812. During the campaign of 1814 on Lake Champlain, soldiers were enlisted in the Navy as substitutes, a practice which was threatening to deplete the field forces. See ltr S/W to Major General Izard, May 25, 1814, Military Book No. 7, Letters Sent, S/W, July 11, 1813-December 20, 1814, National Archives.

to drain the treasury.[54] More amusing than embarrassing perhaps, was the spectacle of private entrepreneurs advertising for sale such items of military need as cannon balls and grapeshot,[55] gunpowder, pistol holsters and uniform buttons, patent guns which would be "discharged four times, in the same space in which one of the old construction can be loaded and discharged once," muskets and cutlasses "Suitable for Privateers or Armed Merchantmen,"[56] "1 half-worn Main Sail," and maps "of the Seat of the War on the Borders of Canada and North-West Territory."[57]

Still More Legislation

In an effort to find a solution for the successful prosecution of the war in the coming campaigns, Secretary Eustis preferred to rely upon the Secretary of State, James Monroe, who was a staunch supporter of the Regular Army. Realistically approaching the problem Monroe drew up a study on the military requirements for the chairman of the Senate military committee. After making provision for defensive operations by dividing the country into military districts, he went on to show that the conquest of Canada could only be accomplished with a regular force of 20,000 men supported by a reserve of 10,000. This total could be reached by enlisting 20,000 in addition to the existing force, not for five years, but for twelve months with provision for reenlistment if necessary.[58]

On January 20, 1813, Congress enacted legislation designed to complete the existing military establishment by offering twenty-four dollars in advance pay to every soldier who would enlist for five years or the duration.[59] Nine days later, another law was passed adding twenty regiments of infantry to the Regular Army.[60]

---

[54] Boston *Patriot*, June 24, 1812, p. 3. Philadelphia *Aurora*, August 10, 1813, p. 1. *Ibid.*, May 17, 1813, p. 1, col. 1. Charleston *Courier*, March 23, 1813.

[55] Boston *Patriot*, July 11, 1812, p. 4; July 1, p. 3; p. 4, col. 3.

[56] Philadelphia *Aurora*, July 3, 1812, p. 1, col. 1. *Ibid.*, September 15, 1812, p. 1, col. 3; September 16, 1812, p. 1, col. 5.

[57] Charleston *Courier*, June 2, 1813. *Ibid.*, March 18, 1813.

[58] *ASPMA* I 608-609. For defensive purposes, Monroe proposed a force of 9,350. By reducing the term of service to one year, he hoped to stimulate enlistments.

[59] II *Stat.* 792.

[60] *Ibid.*, 794-796, January 29, 1813. The authorized strength of the Regular Army, as a result of this Act was increased to forty-four regiments of infantry, four of artillery, two of dragoons, one of rifles, and a corps of engineers—nominally 60,000 men. The law also replaced the Act of February 6 and July 6, 1812 relating to the volunteers. See also Upton, *op. cit.*, p. 107; Spaulding, *op. cit.*, p. 131.

Under this new dispensation, the period of enlistment was short-ened to one year, thereby providing for two categories of regulars, the five-year men and the one-year enlistees. This increased the problems of recruiting and defeated any semblance of uniformity. During the following month six major generals and six brigadier generals were added to the list of general officers; and to strengthen the defenses of the frontiers, ten additional ranger companies were authorized.[61]

Under the shock of the first six months of war, coupled with the pressure of military necessity, public opinion, and the patriotic sentiment aroused by the glorious single-ship victories at sea,[62] po-litical opposition toward a stronger Navy sharply subsided. Al-though conservatives continued their objections to energetic meas-ures of naval defense, they were unable to muster enough strength to prevent the passage, on January 2, 1813, of a law appropriat-ing $2,500,000 to build four 74's and six frigates.[63] This was fol-lowed on March 3, by an act authorizing six sloops and as many others of such design as would be required for duty on the Great Lakes, in addition to the appropriation of $100,000 for the con-struction of a dockyard for the purpose of repairing vessels of war.[64]

In the meanwhile, the President himself, in a determined bid to stiffen the American effort, was induced to take steps to correct some of the errors of the preceding year. On January 8, 1813 he nominated William Jones of Philadelphia as Secretary of the Navy;[65] and one month later, John Armstrong, another Pennsyl-vanian and author of the notorious Newburg Letters, was made Secretary of War.[66] Both nominations were made to give assurance to the people that every effort was being made to introduce a new measure of vigor into both departments.

[61] II *Stat*. 801, February 24, 1813. *Ibid.*, 804, February 25, 1813. These ten companies were to be recruited in lieu of one infantry regiment.

[62] Sprout, *op. cit.*, p. 78.

[63] II *Stat*. 789. See also Paullin, "Naval Administration—1801-1814," p. 1318. Naval expenditures rose from $1,970,000 in 1811 to $3,960,000 in 1812; to $6,450,000 in 1813; to $7,310,000 in 1814; to $8,660,000 in 1815. In 1816, the expenditures fell to $3,910,000. *Ibid.*, Sprout, op. cit., p. 87.

[64] II *Stat*. 821. Steps were also taken to encourage private citizens to engage in a systematic destruction, by sabotage or other means, of British war vessels hovering off the coasts. *Ibid.*, 816, March 3, 1813.

[65] Paullin, "Early Naval Administration," pp. 1308-1309. Jones was not un-friendly to gunboats. See Madison to Jefferson, June 6, 1813, Madison *L&W* II, 564.

[66] Charleston *Courier*, January 18, 1813, p. 3.

Despite these strong manifestations of an increased awareness of the requirements of the coming campaigns, the lesson was again to be learned that legislated armies alone would bring few men into the field. Moreover, the conflicting legislation which offered the option of lesser periods of service would still leave the manpower problem largely unsolved. On April 2, 1813, Madison confessed to his friend John Nicholas that his calculations to raise a strong force were defeated "by mixing and substituting preparations necessarily producing fatal delays.[67] To ease this difficulty, Madison finally accepted Monroe's proposal to divide the country into nine military districts. This reduced the recruiting difficulty and at the same time organized a system of defense which, under the coordination of the War Department, was intended to simplify the problems of the individual commanders of those districts with reference to supplies, munitions of war, defenses, and recruiting. Each district became a supply depot as well as a recruiting center for the area it encompassed.[68]

But the defects in the laws which created the option of service still had to be overcome. To Madison this could be accomplished by establishing more favorably for the private soldier the proportion between his recompense and the terms of his enlistment.[69] This meant a proportional adjustment of bounties which could only be altered upwards. As a result, these financial inducements were increased from sixteen dollars and 160 acres of land at the beginning of the war to $125 and 320 acres of land at the close of the war, to say nothing of the additional payments made by local communities and recruiting officers throughout the land.

The President, in a special session called on May 25, 1813, urged upon Congress a better appreciation of the necessity for filling the ranks by making additional provisions to improve the military establishment and the means of defense.[70] Six weeks later Con-

---

[67] Madison to John Nicholas, April 2, 1813, Madison, *L&W* II 562-563. Even the measures designed to improve coast defenses fell far short of expectations. On May 8, 1813, the Mayor of Philadelphia was forced to borrow $30,000 from private individuals "to aid in the defense of the bay and river Delaware . . ." Philadelphia *Aurora*, May 17, 1813, p. 1, col. 2.

[68] May 1, 1813. *ASPMA* I 432; 385-388. See also ltr W. D. to Gov. Strong (Mass.) September 17, 1814, Military Book No. 7, Ltrs Sent, S/W, pp. 314-315, National Archives. Each district was placed under command of a Regular Army officer. Ltr Madison to General Assembly of the State of North Carolina, December 11, 1813, Madison *L&W*, II pp. 577-578.

[69] Annual Message, November 4, 1812, Richardson *M&P* I 518.

[70] Richardson, *M&P* I 528.

gress responded by raising the term of service from one year to the duration of the war for those enlisting under the terms of the Act of January 29, 1813, and limiting their services, or such part of them as the President might determine, to the defense of the sea coasts.[71] On the same day, and to augment this act, authority was granted to build without delay a number of barges "to be armed, equipped, and manned . . . of a size not less than forty feet long, and capable of carrying heavy guns." In further pursuance of the determination to defend more adequately the coasts, on July 26, a corps (10 companies) of sea fencibles was authorized to be "employed as well on land as on water, for the defence of the ports and harbours of the United States." [72] With these forces and supplemental measures of defense, the campaigns of 1813 were carried out but with small success. The military equation was still out of balance.

William Henry Harrison Retrieves Some American Prestige

After the surrender of General Hull, General William Henry Harrison became the sole military leader in the northwest. With a small force of some 2,000 regulars and militia he was assigned the mission of reoccupying Detroit. The campaign, like that of 1812, opened with disaster for the Americans and brought increased encouragement to the Canadians under General Proctor. Fearful of repeating the mistakes made by Hull, Harrison urged that Lake Erie be wrested from British control and that a large mixed force be placed at his disposal for the successful prosecution of operations into Canada. But the Secretary of War, interpreting the law of January 29th as an indication that Congress refused to prosecute the war with militia, was not disposed to allow more than 7,000 men for the western campaign. During the interim in which the new regiments were being recruited, however, Harrison was allowed a measure of discretion in employing militia.[73]

With his small force of 2,000 the American commander was forced to wait on the east bank of the Miami River until reinforcements arrived. On May 5, 1813, 1,200 Kentucky militia were moving toward Harrison's headquarters. But major operations

---

[71] July 5, 1813, II *Stat.* 3. The bounty in money and land was fixed at the same amount as that allowed for five year enlistees.

[72] *Ibid.*, 47.

[73] *ASPMA* I 453.

against Canada could not be opened until Lake Erie was secured. From May to September activities were limited to raiding sorties along the frontier. On the 10th of September Commodore Oliver H. Perry in a notable engagement won Lake Erie from the British, giving the American Army under Harrison direct water communication with the enemy's stronghold.[74]

By this time Harrison's force had swelled to 7,000 men, mostly from Kentucky and Ohio. It was quickly transported into Canada, and on September 27th he overtook General Proctor at the Thames River. Within eight days he forced the British to surrender. This victory restored to American control the entire northwestern territory.[75] But instead of seeking further victories, Harrison was obliged to discharge his militia and twelve-month men. With the remainder of his force (1,300 regulars) he set out for Buffalo. Not long after, he resigned his commission because of a difference of opinion with Secretary Armstrong concerning the proper exercise of the Secretary's powers. This arose over insistence of the Secretary of War, with the "ill-advised" sanction of the President, in issuing orders direct to subordinates in the military districts without regard for the proper channels of command. Harrison tendered his resignation hoping that his popularity would induce the President to coax him to remain on duty. However, when his letter arrived in Washington, the President was absent and Secretary Armstrong, without the authority, accepted the resignation. This assumption of power was never intended in the Constitution.

The Specter of Mediocre Leadership Stalks the American Army

Secretary of War John Armstrong assumed his duties with a fixed notion that the direction of the armies in the field fell within his proper sphere of jurisdiction. Convinced that he possessed a broader view of the situation than the individual commanders, he tried to direct all military operations, notwithstanding the open hostility of many generals.[76] By thus going beyond his sphere of

---

[74] Sprout, *op. cit.,* p. 75. Upton, *op. cit.,* p. 110. A year later, Commodore Thomas Macdonough's equally important victory over the British flotilla on Lake Champlain checked the southward advance of the British from Canada and paved the way for an American counter-attack. See also Beirne, *op. cit.,* pp. 205-211. Soon after Hull's defeat, Madison perceived the wisdom of securing the Lakes. See Madison & Dearborn, Oct. 7, 1812, Madison *L&W,* Vol. II, p. 547.
[75] Spaulding, *op. cit.,* p. 131.
[76] Beirne, *op. cit.,* p. 292.

responsibility, which was the administration of the War Department, and which should have occupied all his time, Armstrong left the Department without proper supervision. Turning his attention toward the armies in the field, Armstrong was forced to find a replacement for General Dearborn who resigned his command in July. For this very important post, the ambulating Secretary had to make a choice between tainted James Wilkinson and the able Tennessee border captain Andrew Jackson. Resentful of the verbal attacks hurled by Jackson upon the Administration in the past, Armstrong chose Wilkinson and thus placed the northern campaign in the hands of a man who had achieved a remarkable success in evading conviction for malfeasance, complicity, and dereliction of duty.[77] By turning away from Jackson, Armstrong refused to recognize the ability of the frontier warrior to wage successful war.[78]

Selection of incapable officers, however, was not the limit of Armstrong's errors in judgment. His insistent demand to run the whole show found him in the field issuing orders to the troops outside the normal channels of authority. These channels alone could insure the proper subordination to authority necessary in any army. He failed also to estimate correctly the intentions of the British and in so doing he left the defenses of the City of Washington to the whims of chance.[79] To the irritating problems of recruiting, militia, and paper armies, was thus added the exasperation of a blundering Secretary of War.

Against this background the campaigns in the north were opened under the leadership of Wilkinson and Wade Hampton, influenced by meddling antics on the part of the Secretary. With a force of 13,000 men, mostly regulars, the two generals through lack of cooperation and want of vigor were thrown back by a force of less than 2,000 British regulars, militia, and Indians. This spineless effort led to the collapse of the American endeavor along the frontier east of the Niagara River and encouraged the enemy, on December 19, to cross over and plant the Union Jack on American soil a second time. It was perhaps with not a little regret that

[77] James R. Jacobs, *Tarnished Warrior*, New York, the Macmillan Co., 1938, pp. 243-244; pp. 265-275; pp. 309-314. See also Shreve, *op. cit.* Chapters 17 & 18.
[78] James, *op. cit.*, pp. 155-158. Beirne, *op. cit.*, p. 222. Benson J. Lossing, *Pictorial Field Book of the War of 1812*, New York, Harper & Bros., 1868, p. 742.
[79] Beirne, *op. cit.*, pp. 268-271.

the Secretary of War received news from the southern theater that General Jackson had defeated the Creek Indians who, incited and aided by the British, had threatened to overrun the frontier in that area.[80] Jackson's victory was a painful salve for the Secretary's wounded pride.

To conduct the ill-conceived plans of campaign which met with disaster in every theater save the south and on the seas, the United States was forced to employ in 1813 a total of 149,000 men, 19,036 of whom were regulars. And, at the end of it all, the only satisfaction remaining for the people was the tardy resignation of those incompetents whom the Secretary of War preferred over men of proved ability. The ironical part of it was that the two men whom Armstrong rebuked, Harrison and Jackson, would both bring their untarnished reputations to the White House.

A Sound Military Policy is Not Yet Attained

If the necessary materials for waging war, observed one authority as early as October 1811, would be carefully and ably organized, the energy, enterprise, and perseverance of the American character would render them irresistible.[81] This meant that military preparations and operations could succeed only as the result of careful and systematic supervision by competent leaders of the war effort. There was nothing novel about this observation. George Washington's experiences with the Continental Congress, with the States, and even with the men who served under him had underscored the profundity of this fundamental requirement. Furthermore, American statesmen responsible for the conduct of the war could find some guidance in the revealing and incontrovertible evidence of Washington's recommendations of 1783 for the salient features of a proper military posture.

Obviously, in accord with the democratic principles of the Constitution, the backbone of American ability to wage war was a national militia; but this still remained under the control of the State authorities. In this condition, any reliance upon the militia to carry on sustained military operations was nothing more than wishful thinking. In the condition of American politics during this

---

[80] Upton, *op. cit.*, pp. 113, 115, 117-120; Lossing, *op. cit.*, pp. 630-637, 780-782; James, *op. cit.*, pp. 170-173.

[81] See article by Wallace in Boston *Chronicle* reproduced in New Hampshire *Patriot*, October 22, 1811.

period few States were in accord with Governor John Langdon of New Hampshire who urgently counseled Congress to effect "a general arrangement of the Militia throughout the States . . . for the better support and encouragement of this body of our citizens, who are the natural defence of our country." [82]

However, the war Congress of 1812, like its predecessors, remained reluctant to interfere in what was considered the proper sphere of the State governments, with the result that the militia of the United States remained the weak instrument of defense it had proved to be in the past. For this reason, Congress was forced to meet the emergencies of the war as they arose, by the expedient of temporary legislation which disrupted not only the war effort but the economy of the nation as well. Frequent calls on the militia meant frequent interruptions in mills, in factories, and in other business establishments which were hard-pressed to meet the needs of the Government for war material. Two years of war under these conditions which were aggravated by the ineptitude of the commanders, and the seditious attitude of some States brought the people farther from victory and enlarged the drain upon the public treasury.

The financial strain was intensified by the lack of a well-defined policy or system for the procurement of supplies. Government armories, because of the Jeffersonian program, were not adequate to meet the demands for war, nor were the civilian establishments capable of meeting these needs. There was a deficiency in all other military stores which it had been hoped could be supplied by private enterprise. To meet this condition resort was had to the foreign market—an uncertain resource because of the blockade. And finally, the ration supply, which was decentralized to the nine military districts, could not be funneled to the armies in the field. As the fighting areas expanded, this situation became more acute and the questionable practice of employing civilian contractors was again initiated. Not only was this expensive, but it was also militarily unsound. In time of war these contractors were a liability. Not being confidential and responsible agents of the Government, they could betray an army, force commanders to their will, and yet remain outside the jurisdiction of military courts.

Because there was no systematic planning on a long-term basis,

---

[82] *Ibid.*, June 11, 1811.

additional legislation was necessary to conduct the campaign of 1814, and each law increased the burdens of the taxpayers. To encourage men to take the field, bounties in land and money were increased but still the regiments remained understrength. In January and February 1814, no less than five acts were passed to fill the ranks.[83] In the final analysis, resort was had to the militia which should have been the great reservoir of manpower from the very beginning of the war. When enlistments for long periods of service fell off, the Government fell back upon militia companies enlisted for short periods.

Recourse to a large reservoir of militia was a luxury not to be enjoyed by the Navy. Hence the personnel procurement problem in the naval service was more pronounced. Enlistments in this service were exclusively upon a voluntary basis except when by special agreement the Army could loan men for temporary duty.[84] Neither could any measure of relief be expected from legislation, for, despite increased inducements, the option of service with privateers made service in the Regular Navy less alluring. Consequently, Naval legislation multiplied the financial burdens but failed to procure sufficient men. From March to November 1814, four laws were enacted for the Navy and the privateer service.[85]

When these practices threatened to bankrupt the Government, regard was had first for the financial condition and secondly for the defense of American cities. The urgent necessity for bringing the militia into service became dangerously manifest when the de-

---

[83] Act of January 27, 1814 to fill the ranks of the Regular Army. A bounty of $124 was offered. III *Stat*, 94-95. Act of January 28, 1814, authorizing the President to raise additional regiments. III *Stat*. 96. Act of February 10, 1814 to raise three additional regiments of riflemen. III *Stat*. 96. Act of February 24, 1814, to continue in force the Act to raise ten additional companies of rangers. III *Stat*. 98. Act of February 24, 1814, authorizing the President to receive the service of volunteers. III *Stat*. 98. Each act made provision for the bounty of $124. On December 10, 1814, the land bounty was doubled to 320 acres. III *Stat*. 146. On March 30, 1814, an act was passed to improve the organization and system of supply and pay in the Army. III Stat. 113-116.

[84] This was done on Lake Champlain in the campaign of 1814. See ltr S/W to Major Gen. Izard, May 25, 1814, Military Book No. 8, Ltrs Sent, S/W, p. 205, National Archives.

[85] Act of March 9, 1814, for one or more floating batteries, III *Stat*. 104; Act of April 16, 1814, appointing officers in the flotilla service, III *Stat*. 125; Act of November 15, 1814 to build and man no less than twenty vessels of war carrying not less than eight nor more than sixteen guns, III *Stat*. 144; on March 9, 1814, a bounty of $100 was offered for each prisoner taken by "the owners, officers, and crews of private armed vessels of the United States;" III *Stat*. 105. On April 16, 1814, an act was passed increasing the Marine Corps by 846 officers and men, III *Stat*. 124.

feat of Napoleon released large numbers of trained British veterans for duty in America. Notwithstanding even the presence of a large enemy force on the coasts, the President was prompted to implore the Governors to avoid the employment of large numbers of militiamen for fear of exhausting the public monies. What could not escape the most serious reflection, he observed, was "the employment of bodies of militia sufficient to give security and tranquility everywhere would rapidly exhaust our pecuniary means, and soon put everything at hazard." [86] As a result, this resource in manpower could not be tapped until the enemy made his appearance, for then only could it be ascertained what numbers would be required for defense and where they would be employed. The States were reluctant to employ their militia at their own expense while the Federal Government refused to assume the financial burden. This difference of opinion laid American cities open to invasion and depredation.

The policy of the Government in this regard was clearly outlined to the Governors of Connecticut and Massachusetts on September 17, 1814, one month after the capital of the United States was laid to the torch by the British invaders. The military districts, they were informed, were created for the purpose of laying the foundation, in each district, for a small army to be supplemented by calls on the local militia. The State Governments could take any measures they wished for their defense but the expenses attending them were chargeable to the State and not to the United States. [87]

It was this interpretation of the relation between the State militia and the military districts which led to the surrender of the city of Washington to the torch bearers of His Majesty's Government. On the 26th of June 1814, official information was received in the capital of a large enemy force presumably bound for the Potomac River. Five days later the President called his cabinet together to discuss defensive preparations and on July 2nd a tenth military district was created embracing Maryland, Washington City, and part of Virginia. Two days later a requisition was made for a force of 93,500 men to be placed under the command of Brigadier General William H. Winder of that District. Of this

---

[86] Ltr Madison to James Barbour, June 16, 1814, Madison *L&W* II 583.

[87] Ltr WD to Governors of Connecticut and Massachusetts, September 17, 1814. Ltrs Sent S/W Vol 7, pp. 314-315.

force, 15,000 plus 1,000 regulars were placed at the disposition of the Commanding General for the defense of Washington. But General Winder, recognizing the policy of the Government with reference to the employment of large bodies of militia, interpreted the call to mean that this force would only be held in readiness. As such, no part of it would be called into actual service until it was probable that a serious attack was contemplated by the enemy.[88]

On August 1, 1814, Winder reported that he had in camp his 1,000 regulars and less than 4,000 militia. But the British had not landed as yet and the Secretary of War was quite certain that there was no cause for alarm. Not until the enemy was enroute to Washington did Armstrong finally become convinced that they intended an attack on the capital.[89] Meanwhile, on August 16, the British squadron in the Chesapeake was reinforced by two powerful fleets carrying several thousand seasoned troops and made ready to overpower the small American flotilla under Commodore Barney in the Patuxent River. Eight days later an enemy force of 5,000 men was in Washington destroying the public buildings. On the 25th they moved out of the city unmolested.[90] The estimated damage of $2,000,000 was small compared to the national humiliation for which the military policy of the Government was responsible.

On September 4 the British force still remained undisturbed on board ships at the mouth of the Patuxent. It now became apparent that the whole eastern seaboard was subject to the same wanton acts of desolation that had been perpetrated in Washington. It also became apparent that the naval policy of passive defense offered little security against a vigorous assault by ships of the line. Worse still, the initiative rested with the enemy who might attack at any point along the coast leaving Americans no other option than to await the decision of British commanders.

Because of Jefferson's naval policy, no system for recruiting seamen to man additional ships had been effected. Even if it were feasible and possible to build additional ships, it was impossible to man them. This was brought out by a survey of the proposal to increase the Navy. As a solution for the naval recruiting problem, Congress on December 15, 1814 enacted a law directing the staff

---

[88] *ASPMA* I 524. See also Lossing, *op. cit.*, pp. 917-919.
[89] Lossing, *op. cit.*, p. 923 fn.
[90] *Ibid.*, pp. 922-938. Cf. Armstrong, *op. cit.*, II, p. 231; Ingersoll, *op. cit.*, II, p. 170; Paullin, "Naval Administration—1801-1814", pp. 1325-1328.

of the Army to comply with the personnel requisitions of the Navy when it became necessary for seamen to cooperate with land forces on shore.[91]

The struggle for supremacy on Lake Champlain had been under way since May 13. In this action the British hoped to succeed where Burgoyne had failed in 1777. On July 31, the British force of 15,000 outnumbered the Americans in northern New York by three to one, and there was every indication that they planned to invade that State. Notwithstanding these indications and the numerical inferiority of the American force, the Secretary of War further weakened it by ordering General Izard with his command to the Niagara frontier.

On September 11, the enemy in a combined land and naval movement began their invasion at Plattsburg. With 14,000 men Sir George Prevost moved toward this town while his fleet under Commodore Downie simultaneously moved against Macdonough's squadron in the bay. The American naval force consisted of 1 ship, 1 brig, 1 schooner, 1 sloop, and 10 gunboats—86 guns and 882 men. The British had 1 frigate, 1 brig, 2 sloops, 12 gunboats —95 guns and over 1,000 men. By superior skill and daring, the American commander outmaneuvered his adversary and won a complete victory.[92] News of this setback forced Prevost, despite his numerical superiority, to withdraw on the 12th. Ten days later the British Army retired to Montreal. This victory over a superior force made it less painful to reckon the loss of the national capital.[93]

Andrew Jackson Writes the Final Chapter

In the southern theater Andrew Jackson's victories over the Creek Indians pointed him up as the most outstanding commander in the field. But the War Department was still disinclined to solicit his advice on the military policy to be followed in that theater. With one eye on Jackson's popularity and the other on economy, Armstrong, as early as May 24, 1814, urged Jackson to dismiss his militia troops. The 1,000 regulars of the 3rd and 39th infantry were considered sufficient to cover the peace negotiations with the Creeks at Fort Jackson whence they could "be carried

---

[91] III *Stat.* 151-152, ASP Naval Affairs, Vol. I, pp. 275-276, 305-307
[92] Lossing, *op. cit.*, p. 866 fn.
[93] *Ibid.*, p. 875.

promptly to New Orleans, where their services may be wanted."[94]

Rumors, fragmentary information, and official notices reached Jackson almost daily purporting to show that the British, in league with the Spaniards, were making East Florida a base for operations to be launched against New Orleans. Furthermore, it was an open secret that the refugee Creek Indians found succor in Florida where they were fed, armed, and incited to fresh hostilities against the west. To Jackson this was the dangerpoint to American security in the south. He ridiculed the fiction of Spanish neutrality and made repeated requests for permission to reduce the fortifications under their control. The Secretary of War, however, was not disposed to accede to Jackson's advice which would deprive the British of a supply depot and secure to America a convenient harbor for the operation of her privateers.[95]

Instead, the British were permitted to strengthen Florida without molestation whence they could make frequent appeals through their agents to the people of Louisiana to forswear allegiance to the United States. The pernicious effects of this propaganda spread throughout the territory and even into the militia organizations which began to show a spirit of disaffection and reluctance to take the field.[96]

Six days after the fall of Washington, Jackson informed the Secretary of War of his plans to defend Mobile and expressed his regret that some action was not permitted against Pensacola where the British had established their base of operations. The strategic location of that point gave the enemy a vantage point from which to assail, at will, any point along the coast. In this contingency, every weak point would have to be strengthened as soon as practicable, an undertaking which would seriously cripple the Treasury. For these very real reasons the Border Captain continued to assail the War Department with requests to move against Florida.[97]

Diplomatic considerations, however, prompted the Secretary of

[94] James, *op. cit.*, pp. 164-184; 186-187. On May 22, 1814, Jackson was promoted to Brigadier General in the Regular Army and six days later he was elevated to Major General. See also ltr Armstrong to Jackson, May 24, 1814, Ltrs Sent, S/W Vol 7, p. 203.

[95] Jackson to Armstrong, June 27, 1814, J. S. Bassett (ed) *Correspondence of Andrew Jackson*, Washington, Carnegie Institute, 1927, Vol. 2, p. 12. Hereafter cited as Bassett, *Correspondence*. Jackson to Armstrong, July 30, 1814, *ibid.*, p. 22.

[96] Jackson to Armstrong, August 5, 1814, *ibid.*, p. 31.

[97] Jackson to S/W August 30, 1814, *Ibid.*, p. 37.

War to recommend a different plan. On September 5, Jackson was instructed to organize the friendly Indians in his district and to hasten to New Orleans.[98] Twenty days later, Governor William Blount of Tennessee was importuned by the War Department to dispatch 5,000 men, in addition to those already requisitioned, to aid Jackson in Louisiana. These troops were to be supplied and equipped, in the first instance, at local expense because "it is impossible at this time to furnish the funds for this object."[99]

In the meanwhile, new life was breathed into the whole war effort. Armstrong had been forced to resign from the cabinet and the reins were turned over to the vigorous Secretary of State.[100] With immediate dispatch, Monroe made every resource available to Jackson and called upon the Governors of Kentucky, Georgia, and Tennessee to fill the requisitions for the troops required.[101] Old Hickory himself moved with equal alacrity and on October 5, marched out of Mobile toward Pensacola. By November 6, with a mixed force of 3,000, he was before that city and on the next morning he began the attack.[102] But by this time the British had returned to their ships and were on their way toward New Orleans.

Moving back to Mobile, Jackson made preparations to meet an attack on Fort Bowyer between Mobile and New Orleans where it was understood the enemy would attack. On December 1 he arrived at New Orleans and made ready to meet the British force of 10,000 seamen, 1,500 marines, and 9,600 troops who were accompanied by their wives. Twenty-two days later this force landed on American soil and began the battle which would end on January 18, 1815, with the retreat of the enemy carrying with them the body of their commander, Sir Edward Pakenham, preserved in a

---

[98] WD to Jackson, September 5, 1814, Ltrs Sent, S/W, Vol 7, pp. 300-301.

[99] WD to Blount, September 25, 1814, *Ibid.*, p. 317.

[100] On September 3, after the militia in the environs of Washington refused to obey his orders any longer, Armstrong quit the field, went to Baltimore where he officially resigned. See John B. McMaster, *History of the People of the United States,* New York, D. Appleton & Co., 1908, Vol 4, p. 147.

[101] WD to Governor of Tennessee, October 3, 1814, Bassett, *Correspondence,* II, 337. See also ltrs WD to Governors of Kentucky, Georgia and Tennessee, October 10, 1814, *ibid.*

[102] Acting Secretary of War Monroe on October 21, 1814 advised Jackson to take no steps which might involve the United States in a contest with Spain, but he congratulated him for his conduct against Florida. Monroe to Jackson, October 21, 1814, *ibid.*, p. 79. Jackson apparently did not receive this letter in time, for on October 28 he wrote Monroe informing the Acting Secretary of his intention to move toward Pensacola. See Jackson to Monroe, October 26, 1814, *ibid.*, p. 82.

cask of rum. "What a sight for his wife who is aboard and who had hoped to be Governess of Louisiana." [103]

By a display of military genius, Jackson won a victory in a situation where hundreds of militiamen were placed under arrest for mutiny, and where the mixture of population coupled with the presence of Lafitte's pirates were less than assuring signs of security. After the departure of the British, Jackson continued the restrictions of martial law and he refused to allow the militia to disband. But when news reached the city that an official treaty had been signed to terminate hostilities, the militia commands began to disappear. Jackson fumed but the men went home. [104]

Monroe Defines Federal Authority Over Manpower

Despite all the legislation from 1812 to 1814, and notwithstanding all the increased inducements in land and money to fill the regular regiments, the military establishment continued to remain understrength. The authorized strength of the Army on October 17, 1814 was 62,448. Monroe recommended that this number be preserved and made complete, and he would add another permanent force (for the duration) of 40,000 men for defensive purposes. [105] When men were offered such options as shorter periods of service, only the more unsophisticated could believe that the laws with their provisional bounties would attract men to longer periods. The failure to maintain the establishment authorized by law was due to the dual system of recruiting—long periods in the Regular Army and shorter periods in militia units. Added to this were the special dispensations made to attract volunteer organizations for one or two years service. This was a problem which could not be overlooked by the Secretary of War when he was directed by the Committee on Military Affairs to study the defects of the system.

Borrowing from Washington, Von Steuben, and Knox, Secretary Monroe embodied their ideas in a novel proposition to draft the young and unmarried men under a selective service plan. This envisaged a grouping of the free male population between 18 and 45 into classes of 100 men based upon an equal distribution of property. Each class was required to furnish four men for the

---

[103] James, *op. cit.*, pp, 213 269.
[104] *Ibid.*, pp. 278-279.
[105] *ASPMA*, I, 514.

duration with provisions for replacements of casualties. Failure of any class to meet the requirements would be met by a draft. All bounties would be defrayed by a tax levied against the local inhabitants.

Such a plan, if carried into effect, would establish a direct relationship between the Federal Government and the individual concerned to the exclusion of the States. It meant that the Government, according to Monroe, would exercise its constitutional prerogatives to provide for national defense against all enemies, foreign and domestic. It meant further that the law would operate on all with no exceptions but the President and the Governors. In addition, this plan would operate "to engage in the defense of the State the unmarried and youthful, who can best defend it, and best be spared," and the expenses attending this draft would be carried from the voluntary contributions of the more wealthy in every class. This would spare those militiamen who because of family and other responsibilities were forced to pay huge sums to procure substitutes under the detached militia plan.[106]

As alternates, Monroe proposed three other plans for raising men. A second proposition would classify the militia into three age groups—18-25, 25-32, and 32-45, giving the President authority to call any portion of them as the exigencies might require.[107] The third plan provided for the exemption of any five men who could enlist one for the duration. As a last resort, in the event Congress could not be brought to accept the first three, the existing system would be continued, with provisions to increase the bounty in land as an inducement to attract larger numbers.[108] But Congress remained adverse to any schemes for increasing the authority of the Government over the citizens of the States, and voted to accept the last resort.[109]

Opposition to Monroe's proposal for Federal conscription became vehement in New England. His measure provided the climax to a growing list of grievances held out by Massachusetts and her

---

[106] *Ibid.*, 514-521. The law providing for a detachment of 100,000 militia to be held in readiness.

[107] Substitutes were not acceptable in this plan.

[108] *ASPMA* I, 515-518.

[109] The opponents of the bill found a strong ally in Daniel Webster who predicted that its passage would lead to the surrender of liberty and the rise of despotism. He described conscription as an infamous expedient, unconstitutional as well as illegal, and a transgression upon the rights of the individual States. See Fuess, *op. cit.*, Vol. I, p. 168.

neighbors against the war in the first instance and against the military policy of the Government for the prosecution of the war [110]
Especially displeasing was the clause in the detached militia plan
which forced the States to keep their militia organization in readiness at their own expense.[111] Keeping the militia in readiness to
defend against the common enemy was an expensive luxury which
New Englanders felt should be shared by the Government. The
refusal of the Administration to accept this responsibility except
in those cases where the militia was under Federal requisition was
viewed as an attempt to force part of the country to assume obligations which were the duty of the entire Union. This being the
case, Massachusetts petitioned Connecticut, Rhode Island, New
Hampshire, and Vermont to meet in convention "to deliberate
upon the dangers to which the states in the eastern section of the
Union are exposed by the course of the war," and to devise a system "of security and defense which may be consistent with the
preservation of their resources. . . ." [112]

On December 15, 1814 the convention got under way at Hartford. In secret session the delegates voiced a series of objections
against the war policy. These included opposition to the authority
of the President to order the State militia into Federal service; the
division of the country into military districts under the command
of Regular officers;[113] the refusal of the Executive to supply or pay
the militia called out under the authority of the United States;
Monroe's plan for conscription; the expenditure of revenue in
offensive operations against Canada; and the "failure of the government of the United States to provide for the common defense. . ." [114]

The work of this deliberative body terminated on January 4,
1815, the results of their labors being presented in the form of
resolutions to be laid before the Government at Washington. But
before the commissioners could reach that city, news of Jackson's
victory vitiated their bold demands; and when only a few days later

---

[110] As late as 1814, and even when Sir George Prevost planned his invasion
of New York, the enemy on the Canadian border received subsistence from
New England. See Adams, *op. cit.*, Vol. III, p. 146.
[111] See ltr S/W to Governors of Massachusetts and Connecticut, September
17, 1814, Military Book No. 7, Ltrs Sent, S/W, pp. 315-316. National Archives.
[112] Lossing, *op. cit.*, p. 1012.
[113] Placing these districts under the command of Regular officers with discretionary authority to call out the militia was bitterly opposed.
[114] Lossing, *op. cit.*, p. 1013.

rumors of peace began to trickle out, the entire episode came to an inglorious end.[115]

Prelude To Peace

While Jackson was making preparations for the defense of American territory in the southern theater, an American peace commission had arrived at Ghent in anticipation of an early end to hostilities. Meanwhile, however, Monroe had taken every precaution to meet another British threat from Canada. Confirmed reports had reached Washington that the enemy was collecting a large force at Halifax and strengthening his position in the district of Maine. Although the Secretary would prefer to make use of a strong offense as the best defense, the refusal of Massachusetts to support an expedition toward the Maine frontier rendered it impractical to execute the plan.[116]

Congressional failure to accept the conscription bill forced the Government to fall back upon temporary as well as expensive expedients to recruit sufficient numbers to guarantee any measure of success against the threat of the enemy to the north and south. Anxious hopes were expressed throughout the country for some solution to the recruitment problem. But all that could be promised was the sanguine hope that enough money could be accumulated to meet the increased bounties offered recruits. The failure of the conscription bill and the reluctance to employ the militia left only the alternative of raising local corps of volunteers for different terms of service to be employed where they might be required.[117] Until this was authorized, however, militia companies would be continued in service despite the economic burdens involved. For with the enemy poised on the north and south, and without authority to receive these local corps it was ill-advised to allow the militia to retire to their homes.[118]

On January 27, 1815 Congress responded to the growing pressure from the War Department and the President by authorizing

---

[115] Wiltse, *op. cit.*, p. 100.

[116] Monroe to Maj. Gen. King, January 2, 1815, Military Book No. 8, Ltrs Sent S/W, p. 7. Monroe to Maj. Generals Brown and Macomb, January 25, 1815, *ibid.*, pp. 28-29. See also *ASPMA* I, 514.

[117] Monroe to William C. Nicholas, Governor of Virginia, January 4, 1815, Military Book No. 8, Ltrs Sent, S/W, p. 10.

[118] *Ibid.* Similar recommendations were sent to the Governor of Ohio with reference to the western frontier. See Monroe to Thomas Worthington, January 5, 1815, *ibid.*, pp. 13-14.

the President to accept the services of 40,000 men to be employed within the States where recruited for local defense only. This act also authorized the President to receive into the service a similar number of volunteers.[119] The method by which these men would be enlisted, and the quota assigned to each State and Territory was quickly transmitted to the respective Governors.[120] At the same time a board of officers was convened at Baltimore to determine the number of general officers to command the military establishment which by February 6, had reached an authorized strength of 64,000 men.[121]

But before these measures could be acted upon, news reached the Capital that a treaty of peace had been concluded on December 24, 1814, bringing to an end the second war with England. Notice of this exciting news was immediately relayed to the various Governors and to the commanders of the ten military districts.[122] In this manner was terminated a war in which the United States, for lack of a well-defined military policy was forced to employ a total of 527,654 men,[123] and for which the American taxpayers continued to pay until 1940.[124] On March 3, 1815, the peacetime military establishment was set at 10,000 men, while arrangements had already been made to provide a general system for the gradual and permanent increase of the Navy.[125]

---

[119] III *Stat.* 193. Time of service was twelve months.

[120] Circular ltr S/W, January 31, 1815, Military Book No. 8, Ltrs Sent, S/W, pp. 31-32; February 6, 1815, pp. 36-37. See also Ltr Monroe to Jackson, February 13, 1815; Monroe to Brigadier General McArthur, February 13, 1815, *ibid.,* pp. 42-44.

[121] Monroe to Winfield Scott, February 6, 1815, *ibid.,* p. 35.

[122] Circular ltr, February 14, 1815, *ibid.,* p. 45. Circular ltr, February 16, 1815, *ibid.,* pp. 47-48.

[123] Upton, *op. cit.,* p. 137.

[124] Beirne, *op. cit.,* p. 391.

[125] III *Stat.* 224-225. *Ibid.,* p. 226.

CHAPTER 6

Development of Military Policy, 1816-1845

A New Naval Policy—The Militia Policy Is Restudied—
Retrenchment—Unity of Command Is Challenged—Ten
Years of Indian Warfare—The Military Policy Is Defined
—Fortifications, The Periphery of Defense—Morale and
Desertions—Developing Naval Concepts, 1820-1844

"NO PEOPLE," declared President Madison on March 4, 1815, "ought to feel greater obligations to celebrate the goodness of the Great Disposer of Events and of the Destiny of Nations than the people of the United States." [1] Although this remark was prompted by the return of peace, the President was closer to reality than even he suspected. For, while the policy of the Nation would be to continue to neglect national defense, the only recourse left to the people for guidance in security and peace was the benevolence of a patient, protecting, and kind Divine Providence.

By 1815, however, it seemed that the people were going to be reluctant to repeat the mistakes made in 1784 when the Army was completely demobilized and plans had been made to place the Navy upon the auctioneer's block. The Act of March 3, 1815 emphasized the people's determination to continue the Army as a permanent organization. From the experiences of the war it was learned that the division of the country into military districts solved many of the problems of logistics, recruitment, and even of training. To continue this system the law divided the country into two divisions with Major General Jacob Brown in command of the North and Major General Andrew Jackson commanding the South. [2] On May 17, 1815, for purposes of efficient administration the divisions were subdivided into departments, five in the north and four in the south, thereby preserving the old divisions under the District plan. [3]

---

[1] Richardson, *M&P*, I, 561.
[2] Wiltse, *op. cit.*, pp. 151-152. See also III *Stat.* 426-427.
[3] *ASPMA* I, 635.

143

The law provided for four brigadiers to command the subdivisions. A General Staff was also provided for, but because its personnel "was drawn indiscriminately from the line and from civil life," a change was necessary. After careful study under tutelage of John Calhoun, Monroe's Secretary, a new law was passed on April 14, 1818 adding a Judge Advocate General and a Surgeon General to the Staff which then comprised an Adjutant and Inspector General, a Quartermaster General, and a Commissary General.

The only flaw in the Act was the failure to create the office of Commanding General for the entire Army. It was apparent that Congress did not appreciate the urgent necessity of a single commander in chief in peace and war. In so doing, command in the field remained divided, paving the way for the assumption of authority, concerning the entire Army, by anyone who might be successful in gaining the ear of the Secretary of War. Worse still, it could as in the past lead to the practice of the Secretary of War issuing orders to men in the field outside the normal channels of command.[4] By overstressing the principle of civilian control of the Army, Congress by indirection sanctioned a process which threatened to undermine discipline and subordination to military authority, dangerous in peacetime and suicidal in war. But for this error, Congress had come a long way in their understanding of the needs for an effective national policy.

A New Naval Policy

To serve the best interests of the United States abroad as well as at home, Congress as early as January enjoined the Secretary of the Navy to study and report upon the steps necessary for the gradual and permanent increase of the Navy.[5] In the meanwhile, and in order to simplify the problems within the Navy Department, Congress on February 7, 1815 created the board of Navy Commissioners consisting of three naval captains attached to the Secretary's Office. This brought experienced men into the focus of policy planning which heretofore remained the exclusive function of a civilian clerical force. Without relinquishing the civilian control over the Navy, this measure cleared the way for a more efficient handling of complicated technical and administrative details

---

[4] Upton, *op. cit.*, pp. 129, 145-147; Spaulding, *op. cit.*, pp. 148-149.
[5] ASP Naval Affairs I, 363-365.

by professional men.[6] The creation of such a board had been advocated among naval officers even before the war had begun. It was recommended by Benjamin Stoddert, the first Secretary of the Navy and agitated by many until the Senate became interested. Not until the war was almost ended, however, and when the work of the Secretary of the Navy had grown to huge proportions, did the idea receive general acceptance. The law attached the board to the Office of the Secretary of the Navy but specifically stated that it would not relieve the Secretary of his control and direction of the naval forces of the United States.

On December 4, Secretary of the Navy Benjamin Crowinshield made his report on a permanent naval establishment, reciting the great importance attached to such a program. A permanent naval force would free the nation of a dependence upon foreign sources of supply, the dangers of which were all too apparent and because of which steps had already been initiated to place the cannon foundries and "manufactories of sheet copper, cordage, canvass . . . in a state to furnish the several supplies which may be required." Furthermore, a strong naval force became axiomatic in the existing situation where the commerce of the United States and growing population would bring Americans into closer contact with foreign countries. For this reason, Crowninshield recommended an annual increase in the Navy of one ship of 74 guns, two frigates of 44 guns and two sloops of war; and he directed the attention of Congress to the importance of evolving a balanced program of ship-building, navy yards, drydocks, and naval ordnance to fit the growing needs of the Navy.[7]

These proposals found immediate favor in Congress and on April 29, 1816 an act was passed providing for the gradual increase proposed by Crowninshield. An annual appropriation of one million dollars for eight years was authorized for the building of nine line of battle ships and twelve 44's, together with appropriate measures for harbor defenses.[8] This act specifically committed the country to the policy of building, in peace, a fleet of

---

[6] III *Stat.* 202-203, 231. See also Charles O. Paullin, Naval Administration Under the Navy Commissioners, 1815-1842, *Proceedings of the U.S. Naval Institute,* Vol. 33, pp. 602-606. Hereafter cited as *Paullin,* "Naval Administration 1815-1842."
[7] ASP *Naval Affairs* I, 365.
[8] III *Stat.* 321. "Naval Administration 1815-1842," p. 614; Sprout *op. cit.,* pp. 88-89.

heavy ships comparable to the fleets of European powers.[9] In 1816 the Navy consisted of five 74's and four 44's in a total of forty-one vessels excluding those craft below ten guns. By 1842 the total was increased to 56 vessels which included one 120-gun, ten 74's and fourteen 44's. Although only about one half of the authorized vessels were placed in commission, the far-reaching implications of the law could not be minimized.

Of immediate consequence was the effect the new naval policy exercised upon American foreign relations. It prompted the British to agree to a demilitarization of the Canadian boundary[10] and brought the American flag to every corner of the earth. American trading vessels began to ply the sea lanes practically unmolested under the protective wings of Yankee sea eagles. The new policy strengthened American interest in the Caribbean Sea as well as in South America where Spain and Portugal were being dispossessed of their colonies by revolution; and regardless of the peace settlements to be made by European statesmen, the American naval policy served fair warning that this Government would not tolerate any infringement of its declared intentions and interests in this hemisphere. Within a few years, President James Monroe would outline these intentions in a fundamental pronouncement of policy for the benefit of those foreign powers who might seek to raise the standards of royalty once again over the independent provinces to the south. But in so doing, America was placing all the eggs in one basket—security behind a Navy supported by British intentions of good will.[11]

The Militia Policy Is Restudied

When Monroe launched his first administration the nationalism of the war period had begun to wear away under the severe shocks of selfish interests, personal ambitions, and political bickering in and out of Congress. The attention of the national legislature was too much taken up with domestic and political issues to be interested in augmenting the Army whose responsibilities grew apace with the expansion westward. Furthermore, little could be

[9] Paullin "Naval Administration 1815-1842," pp. 614-616. See also George T. Davis, *A Navy Second to None*, New York, Harcourt Brace & Co., 1940, p. 5.
[10] *ASP Foreign Rel* Vol. IV, 205-6. See also Sprout, *op. cit.*, p. 90.
[11] The Monroe Doctrine was promulgated with the friendly assurance that Great Britain at least was not indisposed toward a proclamation which would keep the rest of Europe out of the Western Hemisphere. See Bailey, *op. cit.*, pp. 188-189; Richardson, *M&P*, II, 218.

expected to improve the condition of the military establishment until such items as, the unsettled financial accounts of the War Department were satisfied.[12]

It was under these circumstances that Congress ordered the subject of the militia to be studied with a view to its improvement. As early as December 13, 1816, Acting Secretary of War George Graham in compliance with a House Resolution of the preceding April submitted a plan for the better organization and discipline of the militia. This included a classification of the militia into three classes, similar to the Knox Plan, with provisions for an annual encampment of the first two classes, periodic drills, the establishment of depots in each state to facilitate equipping the men, and the reaffirmation of the President's authority to call them out in emergencies.[13]

This was taken up by the House, with the result that a committee report on January 17, 1817, made by William Henry Harrison, recommended the organization of the state militias into regiments, brigades, and divisions as better adapted to tactics of the day. After reciting the advantages of placing the main stress upon the training of the younger men, and the importance of diffusing a knowledge of the military art among a greater portion of the male population, the report went on to show that recent improvements in military tactics and strategy dictated the need for increased instruction among the militia. To accomplish this, the art of war would be taught in all "the higher seminaries." Since it was evident that the required military duty could not be conveniently satisfied without great inconvenience to the individual and his employer after the men "have arrived at the age of manhood, the only alternative is to devise a system of military instruction, which shall be engrafted on, and form a part of, the ordinary education of our youth." [14] But Congress here merely resolved to shift responsibility to the Secretary of War, who was asked to prepare a plan for the following session of Congress. The whole episode began and ended with a resolution of Congress asking the Secretary of War to study the issue.

---

[12] Wiltse, *op. cit.*, p. 149.
[13] *ASPMA* I, 642-643.
[14] *Ibid.*, 663-665. On January 22, 1819, Congress was still studying the question. See *ibid.*, 824-833.

Retrenchment

By late 1817, murmurs for retrenchment were growing louder while the military policy was grounded upon a division of command in the Army, an unsettled Indian policy, inadequate coast defenses, and a system of supply in the hands of irresponsible private contractors. In addition to these deficiencies which called for immediate attention, there still remained the unsettled financial accounts of the War Department to the tune of 45 millions which had to be liquidated before any increase would be made in military appropriations.

In view of this staggering sum, coupled with the prevalent notion that a strong Navy constituted a sufficient safeguard to American liberties, Congress on April 17, 1818 directed Secretary of War Calhoun to report, at an early period, what reduction might be made in the military peace establishment, with safety to the public service.[15]

By December 11, Calhoun was ready to make his report. After carefully considering the size and extent of the American frontier lines as compared with those of 1802 and 1808, and the size of the Army authorized during those periods, the Secretary justly concluded that the increase of territory, population, and prosperity, together with a concurrent rise in foreign relations offered little justification for a reduction of the expense of the present establishment. Taking advantage of the opportunity to express himself fully on the subject, he went even further by pointing to the need for an efficient general staff. This branch of the service, he showed, could not, consistent with the public safety, be neglected in peace. "It is in peace," he continued, "that it should receive a perfect organization, and that the officers should be trained so that, at the commencement of a war, instead of creating anew, nothing more should be necessary than to give it the necessary enlargement." [16]

With so many and such distant small posts as the service required, a greater staff organization was necessary. This not only increased the expenses of the Army but raised the price of every article of supply as well. In an establishment thus situated, even under the most efficient management, "our army must be more expensive than European armies collected in large bodies, in the

---

[15]*Ibid.*, 779.
[16] *Ibid.*, 780.

midst of populous and wealthy communities." Hence expenses could not be kept down by shifting a military responsibility upon civilians for subsisting the Army. The defects of a contract system were so universally acknowledged that nothing "can appear more absurd than that the success of the most important military operations, on which the very fate of the country may depend, should ultimately rest on men who are subject to no military responsibility, and on whom there is no other hold than the penalty of a bond." [17] The soundness of these arguments could not with logic and consistency to the public safety be refuted. But the temptation to dole out political favors as a *quid pro quo* for remaining in office was too much for the politicians of that day. The contract system, with all its inherent evils, was continued.

Notwithstanding the validity of the position taken by the Secretary of War to maintain and to improve the existing establishment, Congress on May 11, 1820 directed that the Army be reduced to 6,000 noncommissioned officers, musicians, and privates[18] and be rearranged in a manner to reduce the public expenditures. Realizing the futility of pressing his point to keep the strength at 10,000 men, and moved by the seeming danger of eliminating complete units within the Army, Calhoun on December 12, 1820 placed before Congress one of his greatest state papers. Drawing attention to the fact that in the light of past experience little reliance could be placed upon the militia when pitched against regular troops in open battle, he quickly concluded that the future safety of the nation depended upon the manner in which the Regular Army could function to bring enough men, within a reasonable time, to a proper understanding of their duties as soldiers. This meant that the militia, in an emergency, would be utilized to garrison the forts, and to act in the field as light troops. Actual operations against an enemy in the field became the responsibility of the Regular Army which, according to this plan, could be expanded without too much administrative difficulty from the proposed 6,000 to 19,000 officers, noncommissioned officers, and privates.[19]

To arrive at this figure of 19,035 for the war organization Calhoun proposed to begin with the figure of 6,316 men. The organization of the staff would be complete in every detail and each

---

[17] *Ibid.*, 781-782.
[18] *ASPMA* II, 188.
[19] *Ibid.*, 189, 190.

branch "should terminate in a chief, to be stationed, at least in peace, near the seat of the Government, and to be made responsible for its condition." In advocating the expansible army, Calhoun borrowed from Washington but he went further in that he would dispose of the services of the militia except for garrison duty in emergencies. No consideration was given to training the militia for these peculiar duties, nor for providing for the training of the whole body of the militia.

By such a design, where the number of companies instead of being reduced would be doubled by simply doubling the number of battalions, the officer strength would in effect be increased. At the commencement of a war, then, with the organization intact, there would be nothing either to model anew or create, and the change from a peace to a war establishment could be effected merely by implementing the plan. This would eliminate the costly necessity of bringing into service new units, in which every phase of military duty would have to be learned by the officers as well as men.

Furthermore, the Secretary measured the validity of his arguments in terms of the great evolutions that had taken place in military and nautical science. He refused to accept the theory that distance and pacific intentions were equivalent to security. On the contrary, in spite of these, the efforts of the Congress of Vienna coupled with the machinations of the Holy Alliance, went a long way to prove that the United States had become more liable to be involved in war. In such a contingency then, peace could only be secured by keeping up a well-trained body of men who could diffuse their knowledge to larger bodies in times of national crisis. "War," he said, "is an art, to attain perfection in which, much time and experience, particularly for the officers, are necessary. Those qualities which essentially distinguish an army from an equal assemblage of untrained individuals, can only be acquired by the instruction of experienced officers." [20]

This plan represented a radical departure from precedent and relegated to the militia organizations the less alluring duty in garrisons. Congress as the weathervane of public opinion also reflected the general attitude of the States; and after discarding the

[20] *Ibid.*, 188. One year earlier, Calhoun proposed the creation of an additional military academy to prepare a larger number of officers. See *ASPMA* I, pp. 834-836.

vital features of Calhoun's plan, they voted on March 2, 1821 to reduce the Army to 6,183 men.[21] As a further measure of economy, the law reduced the major generals from two to one and the brigadiers from four to two. This in effect provided the Army with a General in Chief known as the Major General Commanding the Army, with two subordinates who commanded the new geographical divisions, Eastern and Western Departments.

Unity of Command is Challenged

Within a few years, and again as an economy measure, the office of the Major General came under the careful scrutiny of Congress. In response to the resolutions of Congress for abolishing that office, the Senate Committee on Military Affairs under the chairmanship of William Henry Harrison advised against such a course of action because it would place the Army under divided command and imperil its efficiency, discipline, and administration.[22] Secretary of War Peter B. Porter reasserted the recommendations of the Committee by showing that in the absence of a general in chief, unity of command would have to be placed in the hands of the Adjutant General or some other subordinate officer stationed at the seat of the Government, under the Secretary of War, and who would, in fact, perform the appropriate duties of the chief of the Army.[23] Hence no economy could be effected.

Congress agreed with these logical deductions and voted to retain the office. But in failing to define the authority of the Major General over the personnel of the Army, the path was paved for the staff chieftains to sidestep the General and to strengthen their political bond with the Secretary of War to the injury of the Army. Sharply critical of this remissness, General Emory Upton says:

> Instead of acknowledging the general in chief, under the President as the military head of the Army, the chiefs of staff corps have magnified the duties of the Secretary of War and have preferred to look to him, not only as the chief of administration, but as their sole and legitimate military superior.[24]

Whatever the reasons for this policy, whether from oversight or for political motives to diminish the authority of the Command-

---

[21] II *Stat.* 615-616. For the organization of the Army see *ASPMA* II, 452.
[22] *ASMPA* III, 820-822, March 19, 1822.
[23] *Ibid.*, IV, 91. Cf. Upton, *op. cit.*, 155-158.
[24] Upton, *op. cit.*, pp. 158-159.

ing General, this failure would permit the intrusion of political favor in the staff which would continue, to the detriment of the military establishment, until 1912 when the final issue was settled by the forced resignation of the Adjutant General.

Ten Years of Indian Warfare

American interest in Florida, from a military viewpoint, became acute in 1811, when under the impulse of the bombastic utterings of the War Hawks, Congress began to toy with the idea of occupation lest the territory pass into the hands of a foreign power.[25] Throughout the course of the War of 1812, the wisdom of this bold assertion came to be felt with increasing solicitude. There were misgivings that Andrew Jackson, because of the national policy, did not receive a free hand in dealing with Florida.

When the war ended, the British withdrew from Florida but left in the Appalachicola River fort some 3,000 stand of arms and a large stock of powder.[26] This soon came into the possession of a colony of renegade Indians and fugitive slaves who used it as a base of operations in a series of sporadic raids into lower Georgia. After each foray they would retreat to the sanctuary of the Spanish flag. Spain by the treaty of 1795 was bound to restrain the Indians from committing these acts of hostility, and their continuance only emphasized the Spaniard's inability to fulfil these obligations. As a measure of self-defense, the United States was justified in pursuing the Indians into Spanish territory to perform what Spain was bound to have performed herself.[27]

In disregard of War Department orders to refrain from attacking the Spanish forts in which the Indians found refuge, and upon his own initiative enlisting large bodies of troops, Andrew Jackson made ready to seek out the enemy with little regard for the sensitivity of diplomatic relations. After seizing the fortress of St. Marks, he pushed on towards Fort Barrancas at the mouth of Pensacola Bay and by June 2, 1818 he reported to Secretary Calhoun that "the Seminole War may now be considered at a close." [28] By such a vigorous display of force, Jackson brought the struggle to a speedy termination, but in the process he disturbed the equi-

---

[25] II *Stat.* 666.
[26] Spaulding, *op. cit.*, p. 149.
[27] *ASPMA* I, 681, Message of the President to Congress, March 25, 1818.
[28] Jackson to Calhoun, June 2, 1818, Bassett, *Correspondence* of *Andrew Jackson*, Vol. II, p. 379.

librium of American relations with England as well as Spain; and in the absence of a strong force of regulars, Jackson had assumed authority to enlist an army. While his action was illegal constitutionally, it was the logical result of the policy because of which, in the existing situation, with communications slow, the commanding general was forced to assume authority not otherwise intended by law.[29]

The Black Hawk War, which began in March, 1832 and ended in September, 1833, created a series of problems that were not solved until 1845. This war grew out of American relations with the Winnebago and Sac and Fox Indians who occupied the old Northwest. It aggravated these relations to such an extent that the Government was forced to keep a large expense account current until 1845 when, with peace assured, the forts on this frontier were abandoned.

During the War of 1812, the Sac and Fox tribe allied with the British, and after the peace they continued their struggle until May, 1816 when by treaty they agreed to cede a strip of land in western Illinois to the white men.[30] The terms of this treaty were distasteful to their chief, Black Hawk, who denied the legality of the cession, and encouraged by British donations of provisions and firearms brought matters to a head in 1823. The Indians refused to move out of the territory in dispute and finally the Governor of Illinois began to recommend the use of force.[31]

It was not long before the unstable frontier became the scene of inter-tribal wars involving the Sac and Fox, Sioux, Chippewas, and Winnebagoes. These inter-tribal difficulties increased the hostility of the Indians towards the whites and threatened, as a consequence, all the frontier settlements. After repeated attempts to put an end to these hostilities,[32] the Governor of Illinois, in the spring

---

[29] Jackson was sustained in his action by Congress. For a full presentation of the inquiry into the matter and Jackson's defense of his action see *ASPMA* I, 681-767.

[30] Reuben G. Thwaites, *The Story of the Black Hawk War*, State Historical Society of Wisconsin, 1892, (Reprinted from Vol. XII, *Wisconsin Historical Collection*, p. 7.

[31] Clarence W. Alvord and E. B. Greene (ed) *Governors Letter Books, 1818-1834*, Collections of the Illinois State Historical Library, 1909, Vol. IV, pp. 129-130.

[32] Henry R. Schoolcraft, *Personal Memoirs of a Residence of Thirty Years With the Indian Tribes on the American Frontiers*, Philadelphia, Lippincott, Grambo & Co., 1851, p. 315ff; Grant Foreman, *Advancing the Frontier, 1830-1860*, Norman, Okla., University of Oklahoma Press, 1933, p. 111.

of 1831, decided to call out 700 militia. He asked General Edmund P. Gaines, commanding general of the Western Department, who was at St. Louis, for military aid.[33] Gaines acted with dispatch and called out 1500 mounted volunteers from the Illinois militia. By June 30 he succeeded in signing a treaty which committed the Indians to remain west of the Mississippi River. That being accomplished, the volunteers were disbanded and the general headed south for Baton Rouge. Unrestrained, the Sac and Fox turned their warlike talents on neighboring tribes and by the end of the following month the frontier was aflame once more.[34]

Towards the end of the year, elements of the 6th Infantry from Fort Leavenworth were ordered up to the scene of hostilities. On April 8, 1832 General Henry Atkinson moved with these troops against the Sac and Fox. Within a month 1300 mounted volunteers from Illinois joined Atkinson to track down the warlike tribes. Shortly after an initial brush with the Indians the militia elements became war-weary, and early in June they were mustered out.[35] Two weeks later another force was ready for the field and from the Great Lakes region came the regulars of the 2nd Infantry together with an additional 3,000 militia from Illinois. With this overpowering force the pursuit of Black Hawk commenced in earnest.

On August 2 the Indians met disaster. The campaign was now over but General Atkinson was bitterly criticized for not having won a decisive victory sooner. Upon him was heaped the blame for some two hundred deaths and the expenditure of some three millions of dollars.[36] By searching their consciences, Congress might have arrived at a different conclusion and thereby have vindicated those generals, who, under the most unfavorable conditions were keeping the peace on the frontiers. The reluctance of the militia to remain in the field after they had become "war-weary" was not a shortcoming attributable to the commanding general. The liability resided with Congress who because of its reluctance to provide for an adequate standing force made it

[33] *ASPMA* IV, 717.
[34] Alvord & Greene, *op. cit.*, p. 169, 188-189, 198; *ASPMA* IV, 716, 717.
[35] *ASPMA* V, 29; Frank E. Stevens, *The Black Hawk War*, Chicago, F. E. Stevens, 1903, pp. 110 ff, 159; Thwaites, *op. cit.*, p. 27.
[36] *ASPMA* VI, 811. It is interesting to note that Governor Reynolds of Illinois who was commanding troops in the campaign, became discouraged and went home in the midst of operations. See Thwaites *op. cit.*, p. 35.

necessary to depend upon the militia who would serve only for short periods of time. If General Gaines had had a sufficient force of regulars in June, 1831 the frontier would have been secured against further Indian depredations. The language of the tomahawk remained the law of the frontier despite the specious promises made by the Indians to keep peace.

On September 21, 1832 a treaty was concluded with the Sac and Fox tribe which completely scattered them along the frontier among friendly bands.[37] But the attempt to remove the Indians from their reservations according to the terms of this treaty failed because of the absence of a strong permanent military force. A series of treaties negotiated with the various tribes brought small relief. The Indians remained reluctant to leave their hunting grounds.[38] It now became evident that the military legislation of 1821 left something to be desired. To patrol the line of the frontier settlements, mounted soldiers were necessary. This was brought before the attention of Congress by the War Department between 1829 and 1832, and finally on June 15, 1832 a law was passed authorizing 600 mounted rangers.[39] With these forces the frontier was kept peaceful during the winter of 1832-1833.[40]

From 1832 to 1842, the various Indian tribes in the old Northwest were escorted out under the incessant vigil of the Army aided by volunteers and militia. While in most instances this was met with the violent opposition of the Redmen, by 1841 most of them had been moved out. Some opposition was offered by the Winnebagoes who feared that removal to neutral territory would leave them open to attack from the Sioux and Sacs and Foxes, but by adroit management they were moved out of the disputed territory. With their departure was concluded one of the most colorful adventures of the United States Army.[41]

By the terms of the Treaty of Payne's Landing of May 9, 1832

---

[37] Winfield Scott, *Memoirs*, N. Y., Sheldon & Co., 1864, Vol. I, pp. 226-228. See also 4 *Stat.*, 637.
[38] William Salter, "Henry Dodge," *Iowa Historical Record*, Iowa City, 1890, Vol. VI, pp. 453-454.
[39] See *IV Stat.*, 154, 585, 716, *V* 18-19; *IV* 533.
[40] Slater, *op. cit.*, pp. 453-454.
[41] For a vivid account of the removal of the Indians see Daniel McDonald, *Removal of the Pottawatomie Indians from Northern Indiana*, Plymouth, Ind., D. McDonald & Co., 1899, *passim*. Army and Navy Chronicle, January 7, 1836, Vol. II, p. 13; March 21, 1840, Vol. X, p. 202; *ASPMA VII*, 785-786; Cornelia S. Hulst, *Indian Sketches Pere Marquette and the Last of the Pottawatomie Chiefs*, New York, Longman's, Green & Co., 1912, pp. 66-68.

and the additional treaty of Fort Gibson of May 28, 1833, the Seminole Indians were committed to move out of Florida. However, by 1833, the War Department had received notice that these Indians had positively refused to move west under those treaty stipulations.[42] At that time, and in the face of hostilities with these bands, the military strength of the United States in Florida, an area of some 52,000 square miles, totaled a mere 536 men. This show of weakness prompted the Governor of Florida to appeal to the Secretary of War on March 8, 1835 to employ his utmost endeavors to avoid war, but if it should come then "let not by any means the militia be appealed to; they will breed mischief." Success could be achieved, the Governor pointed out, only by sending a strong, imposing regular force. "But send only a handful of men and difficulties will come upon you." [43]

This sage advice went unheeded. Under the existing military establishment no show of force could be made, and in fact, the war was conducted, at least for the last four years, by the limited operations of small detachments of from fifty to one hundred men.[44]

On March 14, 1836 the commanding officer in Florida was authorized to employ the services of any five hundred Creek warriors, to be employed as auxiliaries,[45] in addition to the militia force which were to be called out periodically for short terms for the remainder of the war. On May 23, the President was authorized to raise 10,000 volunteer infantry and cavalry to serve no longer than twelve months,[46] but no authority was granted for increasing the Regular Army. Added to this handicap was the frequent change made in the command of the forces operating in Florida and the inclination to conduct the campaign only during the winter months. All things considered, there was little likelihood of success until the war could be conducted on a twelve-month basis and a substantial increase made in the military establishment.

On July 5, 1838 the Army was increased by one regiment of infantry, and to each regiment of artillery was added another company, giving a total of 12,577 officers and men. It was not until

---

[42] John T. Sprague, *The Origin, Progress & Conclusion of the Florida War*, New York, D. Appleton & Co., 1848, pp. 74-76, 80.
[43] *ASPMA* VI, 493.
[44] Upton, *op. cit.*, p. 185.
[45] *ASPMA* VII, 520.
[46] V *Stat.*, 32.

the summer of 1841 that the war went on a yearly basis, when the command devolved upon Colonel William S. Worth. The inauguration of summer campaigns prevented the Indians from harvesting their crops; without this subsistence they were forced to capitulate.[47] On August 14, 1842 it was announced from the War Department that the war in Florida was at an end.

The unhappy policy of the Government which made it necessary to rely upon levies for short terms of service greatly protracted the struggle. This cost the taxpayers (Army and Navy expenditures) $115,032,335.88, and required the services of 60,691 men.[48] The extravagance of this episode was emphatically underscored by the simple fact that a nation of 17,000,000 people had to contend for seven years against an enemy whose total strength was 1,200 warriors.[49] Just nine days after the official termination of the war, Congress reduced the strength of the Army from 12,-539 to 8,613.[50]

The Military Policy is Defined

Increasing difficulties with the Indians on the frontiers and in Florida focused the attention of President Jackson and the War Department on the weak and inefficient militia system in the States. But Jackson, on August 12, 1829 did little more than utter a passing remark on the need for training and equipping the militia.[51] Two years later, when relations with the Indians had become sorely strained, the Secretary of War reminded the President of the continuing defects in the organization, system, and administration of the State forces, all of which had impaired the public confidence in this component. The time had long since arrived for Congress to exercise the powers granted in the Constitution for "organizing, arming, and disciplining the militia, and if the laws upon this subject are inadequate or inadequately executed, it is for the wisdom of that body to apply the remedy." [52] Jackson brought this to the

---

[47] *National Intelligencer*, January 17, 1842, p. 4, col. 3. Sprague *op. cit.*, ch. V-XIII.
[48] Upton, *op. cit.*, pp. 190, 192. The financial figure includes a total of $45,-280,724.35 expended by the Navy in transporting men and supplies. See also Report S/W, December 2, 1837, *Congressional Globe*, 25th Congress, 2nd Session, Appendix p. 3.
[49] *Ibid.*, p. 194.
[50] V *Stat.*, 512-513.
[51] Richardson *M&P*, August 12, 1829.
[52] Rpt S/W November 21, 1831, (Duff Green Pub), p. 26.

attention of Congress on more than one occasion but he neglected to exercise the leadership which that august body, on occasion, demands.[53]

In his annual reports from 1837 to 1841, Secretary of War Joel R. Poinsett sought to bring the military needs of the nation into consonance with the expanding frontier, the Indian problems, difficulties with England concerning Canada, the growth in population, and the domestic and political as well as economic situation. Consistent with these developments, Poinsett set the minimum defensive force at 15,000 regulars, and recommended the construction of a chain of forts along the western frontier. These together with a competent organization of the militia of the frontier states would secure that area against any threat.[54]

However, in order to receive the maximum benefits from the disposable manpower resources (an army of 15,000 and a potential militia of slightly less than one and one-half millions) the Secretary of War proposed to revolutionize the existing concepts regarding the mission and function of the militia and the Army. To render the Army efficient and to effect a policy which would give the greatest return during national emergencies, the bulk of the Army "must be kept together in masses, and the garrison duty be performed by small detachments, aided, in case of need, by the neighboring militia." [55] If this not be done, warned the Secretary, and the policy continued of relying on the militia to march to the aid of the Army in garrison, "we fail to avail ourselves of the advantages that may be derived from the different qualities of these troops." [56] Experience had proved that militia, covered by works and fortifications, were superior to European troops. But in the field, because of lack of instruction and military organization, the militia could not stand against seasoned troops.

---

[53] In his annual and special messages to Congress, Jackson preferred to impress his readers with his awareness of the dangers of a large standing army, for which he received the plaudits of the press. See Richmond *Enquirer*, March 6, 1829. See also messages March 4, 1829; December 4, 1832; December 7, 1835; December 6, 1836, Richardson *M&P*, II, 437; 603; III, 170; 254-255. Cf. Rpt S/W December 3, 1833, (Duff Green Pub), pp. 17-18; Rpt S/W November 30, 1835, (Gales & Seaton Pub), pp. 48-51.

[54] Rpt S/W December 2, 1837, *Congressional Globe*, 25th Cong. 2nd Sess., Appendix, p. 5.

[55] Rpt S/W November 30, 1839, *ibid.*, 26th Congress, 1st Session, Appendix, p. 23. At this time the Navy constituted the first line of defense against attack from the seaboard or the lakes.

[56] Rpt S/W November 28, 1838, *ibid.*, 25th Congress, 3rd Session, Appendix, p. 1.

These novel ideas would be implemented by dividing the country into eight military districts and organizing the militia in each so as to have a body of twelve thousand five hundred in active service; and another of equal number as a reserve. This would give an armed militia force of 200,000 men properly drilled and stationed as to be ready to take their places in the ranks in defense of the country, whenever called upon to oppose the enemy or repel the invader.[57]

Essentially this plan envisaged keeping the Army so situated as to render it an effective striking force supported by an auxiliary force of militia organized, trained, and disciplined to take its place in the forts. Centrally organized in this manner, the regular troops could, in any emergency, move to relieve the militia. The futility and wastefulness of dividing the Army into small detachments widely scattered over the land could not be too strongly urged by the Secretary of War. Furthermore, any plan other than a concentration of force at strategically located posts would render the northern and maritime frontiers insecure.[58]

But Congress turned a deaf ear to the Secretary of War. Considerations of military policy which involved additional expenditures were prone to meet with small favor where Congress was deliberating on such items as internal improvements, the tariff, the extension of slavery, negotiations with Texas and Mexico, and conversations with Great Britain over the northeastern boundaries.

Opposition to such a general and sweeping reform of the military resources was championed by Henry Clay whose political aspirations had been undermined by the party of Andrew Jackson. Motivated by his personal animosity for the Administration, the Speaker of the House called Poinsett's plan a "monstrous project." Forgetting his previous nationalistic principles, he warned against such a proposal which would expunge the boundaries of states, melting them up into a confluent mass. Moreover, by dividing the country into military districts the militia, in effect, would be withdrawn from "the authority and command and sympathy of its constitutional officers . . . [This plan] puts it [the militia] under the command of the President and subjects it to be called out on occasions not warranted by the Constitution." [59]

---

[57] *Rpt S/W* November 30, 1839, *ibid.*, 26th Cong., 1st Sess., Appendix, pp 23-24.
[58] *Rpt S/W* December 5, 1840, *ibid.*, 26th Cong., 2nd Sess., Appendix, p. 10
[59] *Niles Weekly Register*, July 25, 1840, p. 324.

Under the impulse of the Speaker's whip hand, the congressional committee charged with reorganization of the militia, for the present at least, was not prepared to adopt the plan recommended by the Secretary of War, nor to make any other material change in the organization and discipline of the militia. In more direct terms the *National Intelligencer* cited the reasons for the opposition by inquiring:

> Is not the militia force, as the Secretary chooses to call it . . . recruited for eight years—stationed wherever the Secretary of War shall direct—armed and paid by the United States—to all intents and purposes a standing army, and denominated a militia force only to avoid the instinctive jealousies which the name of a standing army calls up in the mind of every freeman? [60]

In citing his arguments for the plan, Secretary Poinsett was sure that his proposals would insure an adequate defense while relieving the country of "the necessity of maintaining at any period a large standing army."

When measured against the weakened defenses of the nation, the strong prejudices against a sound form of peace insurance are not only revealing but startling.

Fortifications, the Periphery of Defense

The unsettled condition of American foreign policy immediately following the Treaty of Ghent with special reference to the northern and southern frontiers, coupled with the inevitable expansion westward, prompted the War Department to carefully scrutinize the defensive apparatus of the United States.

To render the northwestern frontier completely secure, General Jacob Brown, the commander of the Northern Department, was instructed on October 17, 1818 to take steps to advance U. S. posts on the Mississippi and Missouri farther westward in positions which would compel the awe of the Indians, insure navigation of those rivers, and command the country in that vicinity in a manner to prevent any intrusion from foreign traders. No effort was to be spared to conciliate the Indians, particularly the powerful bands of Sioux; to extend these gestures of peace, an Indian agency would be created north of Prairie du Chien at the St. Peters River.[61]

On the northeastern boundary General Brown's strategy was

---

[60] September 15, 1840. See also October 26, 1840.
[61] S/W to Brown, October 17, 1818, Military Book No. 10, Ltrs Sent, S/W, p. 108.

based upon a recommendation for building a series of roads joining Plattsburg with Montreal which would facilitate an invasion of Canada in the event of a future war. But President Monroe, with his keen sense of strategy, advised against such a network of roads because they could be employed just as easily by the Canadians to invade this country. Indeed, the President pointed to the advantages which could be derived from a direct communication between Lake Champlain and the St. Lawrence River through Plattsburg thence to Sacketts Harbor. This would operate to the exclusive advantage of the United States and minimize the dangers of invasion from the north. Another military road was contemplated by General Brown to join the Niagara River with Lake Erie. But the possibility that this road, strictly speaking, would not be of a military nature, prompted Secretary Calhoun to advise against the employment of troops in its construction.[62]

These ambitious undertakings in the northwest could not fail to arouse the anxiety of the Indians whose lands were coveted by the intrepid white man in his trek westward. In recognition of the Redman's penchant for taking up the tomahawk in defense of his rights, two expeditions were ordered west under the respective army commanders (Brown and Jackson) to expedite the security of the frontier and to extend and improve trade relations with the Indians. Plans involving the employment of regulars acting in concert with Michigan militia were drawn up to meet any danger of war in that area.[63]

While these expeditions were in progress, an examination of available Quartermaster funds to conduct the operations revealed that the current appropriations were almost exhausted. Although the importance of these movements could not be minimized, it was apparent that Congress would not respond to any proposal for augmenting those funds. This was borne out in Calhoun's urgent request to both generals for strict economy in all transactions. By confining expenses to the bare necessities, the meager unexpended balances could be stretched to meet the needs, and this would make a good impression on the next session of Congress which, it was known, would insist upon retrenchment.[64]

---

[62] S/W to Brown, January 10, 1819, *ibid.*, p. 218; September 2, 1819, *ibid.*, p. 366; September 22, 1819, *ibid.*, p. 384.

[63] S/W to Brown, March 11, 1819, *ibid.*, p. 272; S/W to Brown July 26, 1819, *ibid.*, p. 325.

[64] Circular ltr, S/W July 19, 1819, *ibid.*, p. 316; S/W to Brown, August 15, 1819, *ibid.*, p. 343.

Calhoun's desperate determination to disarm the Army's critics by keeping expenses down went for naught. Congress, remaining insensitive to positive needs, cut the Army in half on March 2, 1821. And this was done despite the recommendations for adequate fortifications along the line of frontier settlements from north to south. While Congress was willing to appropriate about a million dollars a year for coast and harbor defenses, the fringes of civilization[65] were left to the protective devices of frontiersmen who, it was hoped, had lost none of their ability to make the most of the rifle, and to the efforts of the Army which erected posts and garrisons in the west as necessity dictated.

Based upon the program initiated in 1816 to complete the seaboard defenses, it was estimated that most of the works would be completed by 1832. But the limited appropriations made for ordinance manufactures placed armament production eighteen years behind the construction of the forts.[66] To correct this amazing discrepancy President Jackson in 1830 urged Congress to increase the ordinary ordnance appropriations to adjust this discrepancy between requirements and procurement.[67] In 1839 Secretary Poinsett reported that the maritime defenses were still unfinished, unarmed, and totally inadequate to protect the harbors they were intended to guard.[68] Moreover, the disturbed state of the Canadian frontier dictated an augmentation of defensive works along the northern border.[69]

Meanwhile the whole concept of coast defenses had become revolutionized by the improvements in steam navigation and the increased destructiveness of projectiles. These innovations rendered obsolete the principles of defense which had been evolved after the War of 1812. Now, after some thirty years of struggle, with small success, to bring the defensive apparatus up-to-date, a new set

[65] See ltr S/W to General Simon Bernard, May 6, 1816, and S/W to General Joseph G. Swift, May 2, 1816, *ibid.*, No. 9, p. 6; p. 2. S/W to Andrew Jackson, May 20, 1816, *ibid.*, p. 23.
[66] Rpt of the Commanding General, November 30, 1831, in rpt S/W 1830, p. 81.
[67] Richardson M&P II, 526, Annual Message, December 7, 1830.
[68] Sen Doc No. 1, 26th Cong., 1st Sess., rpt S/W November 30, 1839, p. 42. See also rpt S/W December 5, 1840, *Congressional Globe*, 26th Cong., 2d Sess., appendix, pp. 10-11. To expedite the production of ordnance, Poinsett proposed the establishment of a national foundry. This, he felt, would solve future problems of requirements. Rpt S/W November 30, 1839, *ibid.*, appendix, p. 24; rpt S/W November 30, 1835, *ibid.*, 24th Congress, 1st Sess., Appendix, p. 2.
[69] Rpt S/W November 30, 1839, *Congressional Globe*, 26th Cong. 1st Sess., Appendix, P. 23.

of principles were beginning to develop with reference to national defense in terms of fortifications around the whole periphery of the United States.[70] This involved a change from sail to steam vessels, battery emplacements made of concrete instead of wood, and the modification of guns to improve and increase their fire power. Opponents of a strong military establishment and a well-defined military policy could now point with a measure of conviction to the futility of spending the taxpayers' dollar for defensive instruments which became obsolete even before they could be tested in war. The proponents, however, cou'd point with equal vigor to the fundamental maxim that defensive preparations, efficiently and adequately administered, progressed in a proportion to innovations in technology. The safeguards of today insure the peace of tomorrow; and in the final analysis these safeguards could only be as effective as the men who would administer them. The individual soldier still remained the first requirement, but his well-being was consistently overlooked.

Morale and Desertions

While Congress looked with disfavor on any plan to strengthen the Army or to improve the defenses along the wide extent of frontiers, the unsung hero in the Army was required to exert almost super-human efforts in the exercise of his routine duties. Almost completely forgotten while in campaign against the Indians or while in the performance of garrison duties, the soldier displayed his dissatisfaction with his lot by absenting himself without leave. The lot of the soldier was vividly portrayed by Co'onel Zachary Taylor while in command of a frontier post in 1820:

> . . . such unfortunately is the passion in our country for making roads, fortifications, and building barracks . . . under the head of internal improvements, with soldiers a number of which will never be of any utility . . . the axe, pick, saw and trowel has become more the implement of the American soldier, than the cannon, musket or sword.[71]

And after completing one road (some of them ran over a hundred

---

[70] Rpt S/W May 31, 1841, *ibid.*, 27th Cong. 1st Sess., appendix, pp. 6-7. See also rpt S/W December 1, 1841, *ibid.*, 27th Cong. 2nd Sess., appendix, p. 12. In 1838, Secretary Poinsett recommended the adoption of a rocket brigade because these "projectiles have lately been brought to great perfection in Europe. . . ." See rpt S/W November 28, 1838, *ibid.*, 25th Cong. 3rd Sess., appendix, p. 3.

[71] See Ltr Taylor to Brig. Gen. Thomas S. Jessup, QMG, September 18, 1820, *The Manuscript Collection of Zachary Taylor*, Library of Congress. Hereafter cited as Taylor *MSS*.

miles) or project, the soldiers were almost immediately placed upon another project without regard to military training. As such, the men were not soldiers in the strict sense; they were laborers under military supervision which was tantamount to penal servitude.

Underpaid, forced to live under the Spartan conditions imposed upon him by those in the Government, and subjected to the perils of Indian warfare, the soldier did his duty uncomplainingly. And when these severe conditions became unbearable, he took refuge where he could find it. As a result, desertions multiplied from year to year, until in 1830 the Secretary of War reported over one thousand deserters. Many efforts had been made and theories tested "to arrest an evil so injurious to the operations and character of an Army," but to no avail. The only alternative, still untried, was an offer of reasonable compensation to those who obtained an honorable discharge. This might operate as a strong incentive to good conduct, and would correct the existing standard where the soldier retired from the service as dependent and poor as when he entered.[72]

To correct this demoralizing condition, Congress on March 2, 1833 passed an Act "for the improvement of the condition of the noncommissioned officers and privates of the Army, and for the prevention of desertion." The added inducements provided by this Act attracted a large group of a more respectable class, and the number of desertions fell to one-third less than reported for corresponding periods in the past. Furthermore, the soldiers who now were honorably discharged more readily re-enlisted, which was considered a decided advantage to the public both with regard to economy and efficiency.[73]

The salutary effects of the law to improve the morale and efficiency of the Army were clearly enunciated by President Jackson in his annual message of December 7, 1835. Under such laws, he pointed out, the Army had become more useful and efficient, while at the same time it preserved that knowledge which education and experience alone can give, and which, if not acquired in time of peace, must be sought under great disadvantages in time of war.[74]

---

[72] Rpt S/W December 1, 1830, ASPMA IV 585. See also rpt of November 21, 1831, *ibid.*, 708.

[73] See rpt Maj. Gen. of the Army in *Rpt S/W 1833*, (Duff Green Pub.), November 23, 1833, p. 51.

[74] Richardson *M&P* III, 168.

In 1836 the Secretary of War pointed to the propriety, while promoting morale in the Army, of granting a large land bounty to those soldiers completing enlistment tours. This was preferable to a bounty in money since most of the men in service, being on the western frontiers, when discharged in those regions would probably find it for their interest to become actual settlers. By so doing, the Government would solve two problems—that concerning the disposition of public lands, and that concerning the procurement of settlers in the new western regions. Furthermore, this would, in effect, improve the efficiency of the Army while providing for the frontier a hardy settler trained in the ways of the wilderness.[75]

The Secretary of War and the Commanding General were also solicitous of the insufficiency of personnel to adequately man the posts and garrisons throughout the country. If the object of legislation was to guard against the evils of war, argued the Secretary in 1836, then it could hardly be denied that prevention of Indian hostilities should command the immediate attention of Congress. But hostile Indians could not be contained under the existing military establishment, and since neither volunteers nor militia would be acceptable or even capable of permanent garrison duty, then "the object can only be effected by the increase of the regular army without delay." [76] It was not until July 5, 1838 that Congress proceeded to grant an increase. Four years later, the men who had built an empire out of the wilderness, and who had suffered every measure of privation in campaigns against hostile Indians, were once more forgotten and the Army was reduced. The auspicious start in defensive preparations, which had begun in 1815, was allowed to pale into insignificance under the impact of political differences. This affected not only the Army but the Navy as well.

Developing Naval Concepts, 1820-1844

Immediately following the war with Great Britain the principal duty of the Navy was the protection of American commerce throughout the world. This involved the Navy in operations against piratical bands in the Caribbean Sea area, the suppression of the slave trade, protection of American interests in revolution-

---

[75] Rpt S/W December 3, 1836, pp. 113.
[76] *Ibid.*, pp. 110-111; rpt Major General of the Army, November, 1836, *ibid.*, p. 130.

torn South America, protection of American fishing rights in the North Atlantic and North Pacific, American adventures in eastern Asia, and Algerian difficulties in the Mediterranean.[77] In addition, the small American Navy entered into a series of harbor and river surveys to meet the growing demands of an accelerating industrial and agrarian economy. These duties so increased the administrative burden of the Secretary of the Navy that a Board of Naval Commissioners, as we have seen, was created in 1815.

For the Navy afloat, this increasing crescendo of activities brought about a new concept of defense. To fulfill the obligations imposed upon the few ships in existence, the Navy was divided, during the period, into seven squadrons. Beginning in 1815 with the Mediterranean Squadron, through the years in succession were created the West India Squadron, the Pacific Squadron, the Brazil or South Atlantic Squadron, the East India Squadron, the Home Squadron, and the African Squadron.[78] Thus tactically organized, the Navy not only defended American commerce abroad, but also promoted these interests. This exhibition of force secured the respect of nations, who, "though they may be jealous of our power, yet will not readily violate our rights."

There were those, however, who questioned the constitutionality of spending public funds for the protection of trade in distant lands notwithstanding the fact that a conspicuous absence of force would threaten not only American commerce but also the vital interests of the United States as outlined in the Monroe Doctrine.[79] Moreover, and perhaps what was more important, "wars often arise from rivalry in trade, and from the conflicts of interests which belong to it." The only safeguard against such contingencies was

---

[77] For a description of these varied activities see Dudley W. Knox, *A History of the United States Navy*, New York, G. P. Putnam's Sons, 1948, pp. 139ff; Davis, *op. cit.*, pp. 5-6; Paullin, "Naval Administration, 1815-1842," p. 623. By 1827, our commerce with Hawaii had grown to such proportions that it was necessary to order war vessels to visit the area periodically. See rpt S/N, December 1, 1827, (Vol. 1826-1829), Doc. No. 1, pp. 206-207; *ibid.*, (Vol. 1830-1839), p. 4.

[78] Sprout, *op. cit.*, pp. 94-95; Paullin, "Naval Administration, 1815-1842," pp. 623-625. See also Connecticut *Courant*, December 11, 1821; rpt S/N December 21, 1825, (Vol. 1823-1825), p. 97.

[79] In 1835, following a rupture in Franco-American relations over French claims dating back to the French Revolution, rumors were allowed to circulate that France was sending a fleet to awe the United States. See Sprout, *op. cit.*, p. 106. In 1836, France established a blockade against Mexico. See rpt S/N, November 30, 1838, (Vol. 1830-1839), p. 5. In 1829, Spain led an expedition into Mexico. See *ASP Naval Affairs* III, 348.

the presence of a naval force as the "Best means of preventing those disputes and collisions which are so apt to interrupt the peace and harmony of nations." With an annual trade of some 150 million dollars, conducted over the oceans and the Great Lakes,[80] only the less informed could quarrel with the need for an adequate floating navy.

General considerations of policy based upon the experience of the War of 1812 prompted such men as John Adams, the former president, to alter their views on the Navy. With the world in ferment, Adams observed, we "shall interfere everywhere [because of maritime interests]. Nothing but a strong Navy under Heaven can secure, protect or defend us." [81] In his first inaugural address, President Monroe referred to the necessity for protecting American commerce abroad which, in the existing situation, was exposed to invasion in the wars between other powers. He would protect these interests, but he would do so only with moderate forces. He would place the main stress upon coast defenses and inland fortifications.[82]

By 1825 the alignment of political parties, the Whigs and Democrats, influenced and even retarded the progress in naval development which had been presaged by the Act of 1816. Debates over the tariff brought forth the argument that a "Chinese policy" (the tariff) obviated the need for a navy. Of what use, it was asked, was the Navy under the tariff? The Navy was created "to defend your maritime rights. If you have no commerce, of what use can be your navy?" In this atmosphere of political opinion, it was not long before motions were made looking toward a possible reduction of naval expenditures.[83]

By 1824 American interests abroad, supported by the Monroe Doctrine, had grown to such proportions that President Monroe forthrightly directed the attention of Congress toward a stronger

---

[80] Rpt S/N, December 4, 1841, Doc. No. 2, pp. 357, 358.
[81] Ltr of John Adams, January 5, 1813, quoted in *Niles Weekly Register*, March 14, 1818, p. 33.
[82] Richardson *M&P* II, 7.
[83] Congressional Debates, quoted in New Hampshire *Gazette*, May 9, 1820. These arguments were heard as early as 1820. See *ibid.*, May 23, 1820, December 5, 1820. On March 3, 1821, the appropriation of $1,000,000 under the act of April 29, 1816 was cut in half, but this smaller amount was spread over a longer period of time, from $1,000,000 per year for three years to $500,000 per year for six years. See Paullin, "Naval Administration, 1815-1842," pp. 615-616.

naval force. But the strategic concept in war, as far as the Navy was concerned, was that of defending the coasts and raiding the commerce of the enemy. The object was to stop the enemy at the coasts and for the accomplishment of this, Monroe thought coastal fortifications to be sufficient.[84]

Viewed in the light of historical experience, and with the knowledge that technological improvements would completely revolutionize the whole concept of warfare, Monroe was in error. But analyzed in the climate of the times, this doctrine of defense was plausible.

When it came to legislating for more ships, navy yards, dry docks, and naval hospitals, Congress demonstrated an eager willingness to pander to the pressures of local political interests. But when it came to legislating for personnel, increased rank, and professional training for young officers, the National Legislature became unduly adamant. These recommendations did not appeal to local interests.[85]

The general attitude of Congress toward the personnel problem was best reflected in the fluctuating strength of the Navy from 1816 to 1842. In 1816 the total strength was at 5,540 men. From 1822 to 1823 this fell to 4,000 and remained close to that figure for the next fourteen years. From 1837 to 1842, it rose rapidly from 6,250 to 11,250 men. The low water mark of the 1820's was a source of grave concern to the advocates of a strong navy because of the large number of foreigners enlisted in that service. With one-third of all the seamen foreigners, the New Hampshire *Gazette* warned the people of the serious implications such a practice would have in the event of war.[86]

As a solution for this depressing problem, the Secretary of the Navy and the President, as late as 1835, urged the adoption of a system to enlist boys between 13 and 18 to serve until they became 21. This would, within a few years, afford a sufficient corps of able seamen to man our Navy, and would operate also to offer opportunities to these boys who otherwise would be leading "lives of

---

[84] Richardson *M&P* II, 224-225.

[85] Paullin, "Naval Administration 1815-1842," pp. 612-613.

[86] January 18, 1831. American seamen were seeking service in the navies of foreign Governments and in the merchant service which were holding out inducements of higher wages. See rpt S/N December 2, 1825, (Vol. 1823-1825), p. 100; *ibid.*, May 28, 1828, (Vol. 1826-1829), p. 207; Paullin, "Naval Administration 1815-1842," p. 636.

idleness and vice."[87] On March 2, 1837 Congress responded by enacting a law providing for the enlistment of boys between 13 and 18 to serve until 21.[88] Under this apprentice system, the young men were offered the advantages of an education in reading, writing, arithmetic, navigation, seamanship, and the Navy received the services of native born seamen.

For officers, however, few incentives were held out for a naval career. In their relations with foreign governments, American naval officers were always inferior in rank to their foreign counterparts. This operated to the detriment of the service, impaired morale, and in general stifled initiative among subordinate officers.[89] Succeeding Secretaries of the Navy, from 1815 to 1842, continuously advocated, without success, the creation of the rank of admiral. Too often the charge was made that the term "admiral" savored of royalty and had no place in the democratic American Navy. Those who made these charges, however, refused to acknowledge the inconvenience and even embarrassment lower rank bestowed upon American officers when acting in concert with foreign navies.[90]

Indisposed to create at least a commensurate rank with that of general in the Army, Congress was even more reluctant to permit the establishment of a naval academy. Nautical experience, it was felt, could only be achieved by actual service on the seas. Furthermore all this clamor for an academy of this sort was nothing more than a desire, on the part of few, to "foster a military class whose members would monopolize all the higher positions in the Navy, contrary to the spirit of democracy."[91] And, since the emphasis was placed upon seamanship rather than tactics and strategy, enough officers in emergencies could be procured from the merchant fleet.

Despite this powerful opposition, Secretaries of the Navy, some members of Congress, and many others in and out of Government urged the adoption of a professional school similar to that at West Point. As early as February, 1815 resolutions were heard

---

[87] Rpt S/N December 5, 1835, (Vol. 1830-1839), Doc. 2, p. 332; Richardson *M&P* III, 173. See also Savannah *Republican,* February 19, 1838.

[88] V *Stat,* 153.

[89] Paullin, "Naval Administration, 1815-1842," p. 628.

[90] Rpt S/N January 24, 1824 (Vol. 1823-1825), pp. 10-11.

[91] Sprout, *op. cit.,* p. 103. cf Rpt S/N December 4, 1841, *Congressional Globe,* 27th Cong., 2nd Sess., appendix, p. 21.

in the House for the creation of an academy, repeated the following year,[92] and agitated for the next twenty-seven years. In 1827
a measure providing for an academy narrowly missed adoption
and its rejection was applauded in many circles. Nevertheless, the
agitation in favor of the measure was vigorously pursued by the
Navy Department in a determined effort to fix upon the nation a
proper understanding of the need for professional training to improve the efficiency and morale of officers. In 1835, a proposal
was made to provide this instruction for midshipmen at West
Point but even this was defeated.[93] It was not until eight years
later, and only after the reorganization of the Navy Department
which created the bureaus, that the Naval School which was established at Philadelphia and, transferred to Annapolis, Maryland,
became the Naval Academy.[94]

During the Jacksonian era, 1829-1841, the controversy over
the Naval Academy involved the entire question of the Navy. Not
until Jackson was ready to retire from office, however, did he
finally accept the views of professional naval men that the best
way to avoid invasion was to be possessed of a navy strong enough
not only to ward off attack but also to meet the danger at a distance from home.[95] The concepts of passive defenses with the Navy
acting as a first line in the echelons of fortifications along the seaboard and interior had become obsolete with the development of
steam-driven craft and of explosive shells which in their turn made
the massive wooden craft obsolete.

For twenty-five years after the War of 1812, the steamship did
not produce any revolutionary concept of national defense. Successive Secretaries of the Navy viewed it as the means for alleviat-
ing the need for fixed coastal fortifications. These "steam batteries"
were to be employed from place to place where they might be
needed in an emergency. But by 1841, with the rapid strides made
in developing the steamship as a ship of the line, the Secretary of
the Navy entertained few doubts about their utility in the American Navy. Recent experience had definitely proved the adaptabil-

---

[92] *Niles Weekly Register*, February 25, 1815, p. 415; March 30, 1816, p. 77.
[93] Rpt S/N December 5, 1835, (Vol. 1830-1839), Doc. No. 2, p. 132.
[94] Charles O. Paullin, "Naval Administration, 1842-1861," *Proceedings of the United States Naval Institute*, Vol. 33, p. 1456. The school was named the Naval Academy in 1850.
[95] Richardson *M&P* III, 306-307.

ity of these new ships to the purposes of war, and their rapid increase in other countries served notice of their importance to national objectives.[96]

With the gradual improvement of the Navy went a parallel though slower improvement in ordnance research and development; and although explosive shells as late as 1842 remained a rarity in the Navy, a series of experiments had been conducted by American naval officers. In the matter of improving the yards and docks to accommodate the larger ships rapid strides were made during this period. The smaller yards were improved and the number of yards was increased. By March 3, 1827 Congress authorized the construction of two docks, one at Boston and one at Norfolk.[97]

When Anglo-American relations reached a low ebb in 1841 and 1842, Congress provided for the Navy with less hesitancy. But when these international differences were amicably adjusted in the Webster-Ashburton Treaty of August 20, 1842,[98] the axe fell upon the service. Congress was unwilling to remember the motto: "in time of peace prepare for war," and on June 17, 1844 the number of seamen was reduced from some 12,000 to 7,500.[99] The situation was becoming normal.

[96] Rpt S/N December 5, 1840, Miscellaneous Documents, p. 411; rpt S/N December 4, 1841, Doc. No. 2, p. 360. In their operations against Syria during this period, the British employed steamships to transport troops over a distance of 2,000 miles. *Ibid.* In 1839, provisions had been made for the construction of three steamers for the Navy. See rpt S/N November 30, 1839, (Vol. 1839-1845), p. 553.
[97] Paullin, "Naval Administration, 1815-1842," pp. 618-621.
[98] Bailey, *op. cit.*, pp. 215-225.
[99] V *Stat*, 699.

CHAPTER 7

From Manifest Destiny To Disunion

The War Department Evaluates The Policy—Texas Introduces Manifest Destiny—War Mobilization—Public Opinion—On To Mexico City—Improving The Wooden Navy—Military Policy, 1850-1860

The War Department Evaluates the Policy

TOWARD the latter part of 1842 and for the next three years, the Secretary of War and the Major General of the Army complained about the weakness of the military establishment as fixed by the law of August 23, 1842. In their reports they pointed to the dangers arising from this legislation with reference to the Northwest where the Indians were still exposed to unfriendly influences, and to the undue proportion of foreigners in the Army who owed no allegiance to the United States. They urged a reform of the militia policy of the Government with a view to effectively arming and equipping the whole body of the militia, and they viewed with alarm the prospect that, in the absence of sufficient inducements to encourage enlistments as well as reenlistments, the Army would very soon fall below its authorized strength of 8,613 men.[1]

In evaluating America's military weakness, the War Department was directing the attention of Congress toward a dereliction of responsibility for the safety and well-being of the Nation. The decision to reduce the Army in 1842 was made by Congress over the strong protests of the Secretary of War and prominent military men, and in the face of mounting difficulties with England over the Oregon boundary and a growing problem in the southwest where Americans were contending with Mexico for independence. Moreover, the reduction in force meant fewer patrols along the whole line of the frontier, thus tempting the Indians to take up arms against the intruding settlers. With conditions in such a deli-

---

[1] Rpt S/W, November 26, 1842, *Congressional Globe*, 27th Cong., 3rd Sess., appendix, p. 33, 34. November 30, 1843, *ibid.*, 28th Cong., 1st Sess., appendix, p. 10. On May 21, 1843, authority was granted through General Orders to officers in the field to recruit as vacancies occurred. See *National Intelligencer*, May 29, 1843, p. 3.

cate state of equilibrium, what was needed was a sufficient military force to command respect. The law of 1842 so weakened the country that it was even difficult to defend the neutrality of the United States in the conflict between Texas and Mexico.

Texas Introduces Manifest Destiny

By 1835 the peaceful settlement of Americans in Texas had turned into a conflict of ideas and interests between the Republic of Mexico and the hardy settlers which threatened to disrupt American relations with that country. In 1835 the Texans revolted against the Mexican edicts which threatened their well-being. With the Indian wars at their height, the United States cast a watchful eye over developments in the southwest first to prevent a repetition of events in Florida, and secondly to preserve at least an outward sign of neutrality. For these purposes the Commander of the Western Department, General Gaines, was on January 23, 1836 ordered to the western frontier of Louisiana. By mid-summer, Gaines was allowed the discretion of crossing the boundary line into Texas to pursue the hostile Indians and to call upon the militia of neighboring territories for aid.[2] Thus, while professing neutrality, the United States became an interested party in the conflict, with a large portion of the Army operating in the hostile theater. The massacre at the Alamo on March 6, 1836 and Sam Houston's exploits at San Jacinto six weeks later made the Texas question more critical. On the last day of his administration, Jackson recognized the independence of the Lone Star State. It is significant to note that Jackson refused to make these decisions until they could not embarrass him politically.

During the next eight years the question of Texas annexation loomed large in the American political arena but divisions of opinion over slavery coupled with a weak military establishment obviated any bold positive course in that direction. Moreover, Mexico had served notice that such a course would mean war. The continued presence of American forces in Texas was looked upon with suspicion from Mexico City; and the tenor of American public opinion increased these suspicions.

On April 17, 1844 Brigadier General Zachary Taylor was or-

---

[2] Ltr S/W to Gaines, January 23, 1836, Military Book No. 15, Ltrs Sent, S/W, p. 37, also May 11, 1836, *ibid.*, p. 421; July 11, 1836, *ibid.*, No. 16, p. 214. Circular ltr W.D., July 22, 1836, *ibid.*, p. 261.

dered to Natchitoches to establish a "corps of observation" with seven companies of dragoons and 16 companies of infantry, to be held in readiness for services at any moment. He was instructed to determine from the President of Texas whether any external dangers threatened that Government and if any such danger was found to exist, and appeared to be imminent, he was to collect and march his force to the Sabine river, but would not proceed beyond the frontier without further instructions.[3] The external danger was apprehended from Great Britain who was reported to have made advances toward Texas in order to keep that territory detached from American interests.[4] Finally on March 1, 1845[5] the annexation of Texas was consummated in answer to the popular clamor of manifest destiny, the re-annexation of Texas, and the re-occupation of Oregon. The British bogey disappeared and it remained a matter of time before this act would be challenged by the Mexican authorities.

By the end of June, Taylor at Fort Jessup had collected 25 companies of infantry and was ordered to displace closer to Mexico with his Army of Observation. Making his headquarters at Corpus Christi, Taylor soon had gathered some 4,000 regulars and prepared to move toward the Rio Grande. Authority was granted him for calling upon the neighboring militia.[6] General Gaines, commanding the Western Department, upon his own initiative and responsibility raised a body of volunteers to join Taylor's expedition.

Gaines' action was quickly challenged by the Secretary of War, William Learned Marcy, who knew of the general's habit for raising troops without authority. He felt that the appearance of large bodies of volunteers might adversely affect Taylor's plans which were evolved according to confidential instructions from the War Department. The United States was not at war with Mexico and the hope was still entertained that Mexico might accept a peaceable solution to the question of the annexation of Texas. More-

---

[3] See *National Intelligencer*, May 18, 1844. These instructions had been given by the War Department under the most strict injunction of confidence. This was either good news reporting or weak security.
[4] Bailey, *op. cit.*, pp. 253-255.
[5] Texas accepted the offer on July 4 and the American flag replaced the Lone Star twenty-two days later. See New Orleans *Picayune*, August 3, 1845.
[6] Ltr S/W to Taylor, August 23, 1845, Military Book No. 26, Ltrs Sent, S/W, pp. 62-63, 66. After American recognition of Texas independence, Taylor's army was referred to as the "Army of Occupation."

over, these volunteers had to be paid, equipped, and fed, an obligation which was embarrassing to a Government which had not authorized the action, and dangerous to Taylor who remembered only too well the habit of short-term volunteers to consume supplies and then go home when needed most. When Gaines sought to defend his procedure, he was directed to abstain from all interference with Taylor's command.[7]

When the prospect of a peaceful settlement with Mexico faded, the President ordered Taylor to advance to the Rio Grande, but cautioned him to avoid giving the impression that this was a hostile move. Polk wanted Mexico to commit the overt act. On April 24, 1846 the Mexicans obliged by attacking a detachment of dragoons on the north side of the Rio Grande and war had begun by "Act of Mexico."

War Mobilization

As Taylor made preparations to move toward the Rio Grande, General Winfield Scott recommended enlargement of the Regular Army to 15,843 men by increasing the number in each company rather than creating new units made up of raw recruits. This mode of strengthening the forces in existence would generally improve their comparative efficiency, he said, and would be preferable to that of effecting the same object by raising new regiments at that time. Because of the imminence of war in a theater where bridge construction was a prime necessity, a recommendation was made for the organization of a corps of engineer troops to be known as miners, sappers, and pontoniers.[8] Attention was also directed toward a modification of the laws governing the militia which in its present state was not capable of resisting foreign aggression and preserving internal order and tranquility. For these reasons, it was suggested that militia duty be required only of those over 21 and under 30. This change, it was felt, would remove many complaints against the militia, and would aid in restoring the confidence and consideration justly due to it as an auxiliary of a free government and a safeguard to public liberty.[9]

---

[7] S.W. to Gaines, August 28, 1845, *ibid.*, pp. 68-69; September 13, 1845, p. 80. See also Baltimore *Sun*, September 2, 1845.
[8] Rept S/W November 29, 1845, *Congressional Globe*, 29th Cong., 1st Sess., appendix, p. 14.
[9] *Ibid.*, p. 16. In 1841 only 15,000 muskets were apportioned among 1,673,415 militia. See *Niles Weekly Register,* January 7, 1843, p. 302.

No action was taken upon these recommendations, nor even to provide legislation to support an active engagement until news reached Washington of the exchange of fire on the Rio Grande. On May 11, 1846 President Polk delivered his war message to Congress in which he asked authority to raise a body of volunteers to serve at least six and not more than twelve months.[10] Two days later Congress authorized 50,000 volunteers to serve twelve months or the duration of the war, and appropriated $10,000,000 to carry the law into effect. The insistence on volunteers was evidence that the mistakes of the War of 1812 would not be repeated. This was to be a war which would involve invasion of a foreign country, a responsibility which the militia was not bound to assume. However, if the militia would be called, this law extended their term of service from three months to six. On the same day another law made provision to double the authorized enlisted strength with the proviso of five years' service.[11]

As the senior general in the Army, Scott made detailed plans for calling out the men and to provide a period of intensive training before embarking for the theater of hostilities. But President Polk and his Secretary of War had little patience with any proposal which called for a delay in operations. Scott was left on the side lines[12] while Taylor moved through a succession of quick victories with his small force of regulars aided by some 12,000 short-term volunteers.[13]

With some exceptions in New England, the people throughout the country were quick to respond to the call for volunteers. Although in some instances, as in Illinois, more regiments were raised than were requested.[14] Few men could be induced to enter the Regular Army for a long period of service.[15] In Louisiana, close to the scene of hostilities, however, there was a noticeable lack of enthusiasm for even volunteer service. These volunteer troops

---

[10] Richardson M&P IV, 443.

[11] VI Stat, 9-14. Because the War Department was unable to prepare in advance (because of lack of funds), the volunteers were required to furnish their own equipment for which they would be reimbursed at a later date. The system of logistics was faulty only because Congress refused to prepare in peace for future emergencies.

[12] Smith, op. cit., I, p. 478, 190-200.

[13] Of these, 12,000 were called out illegally by General Gaines. To stop him from recruiting any more, he was relieved of command. See Upton, op. cit., p. 201.

[14] Smith, op. cit., Vol. I, pp. 194-195.

[15] Spaulding, op. cit., p. 183.

lacked training for sustained field operations against a well-disciplined enemy; but against Mexico, despite the repeated boasts of her leaders, there was little doubt that the volunteer regiments of the United States would attain the end which the American government was pursuing.

Public Opinion

In his campaign speeches Polk gave wide circulation to the popular appeal of "54-40 or fight" and to the doctrine of manifest destiny which served notice that Texas and the lands to the west belonged within the American orbit. Orators throughout the country gleefully grasped the opportunity to twist the British Lion's tail and vehemently denounced the "bandits" of Mexico. This threatened to give Polk, upon election, a war on two fronts while we were ill-prepared for one. Notwithstanding the obvious implications of these rhetorical exercises, and the consequent danger to the nation, there was little lack of press support for Mr. Polk's stand.[16] But there were those who looked upon the War with Mexico as a monstrous scheme to despoil the "peaceful" Mexicans of their territory.

And there were many well-intentioned pacifists who accepted the fact that America must expand but they preferred to acquire the territory "by the schoolmaster than the cannon, by peddling cloth, tin, anything rather than bullets." [17] Daniel Webster in a speech at Faneuil Hall, Boston, vaguely threatened to impeach the President by showing that he was guilty of an impeachable offense for bringing on the war without the consent of Congress.[18] Many others looked upon the war as an attempt by the South to bring about the subjugation of the North.

On to Mexico City

Taylor's successful advance to Monterey gave some assurance that Mexico would accept terms of peace. But the stubborn resistance of Santa Anna in command of Mexican forces opposed to Taylor, coupled with the failure of that Government to make peaceful overtures, prompted the Administration to open a new

---

[16] Bernard DeVoto, *The Year of Decision,* Boston, Little Brown & Co., 1943, p. 23. See also Vermont *Gazette,* February 16, 1847; May 19, 1847.

[17] DeVoto, *op. cit.,* p. 205.

[18] Fuess, *op. cit.,* pp. 167, 169.

campaign toward Mexico City via Vera Cruz. The command of this new force devolved upon General Winfield Scott who estimated he would need 10,000 men to make the initial assault, supported by an additional 20,000 to act as reinforcements.[19]

In January, 1847 Taylor was notified that some three thousand of his regulars would be detached from his command and sent to Scott. After some delay Scott was ready to move. By March 7 he was on the way to Vera Cruz with a considerably smaller force than he had requested. With these he invested that city on the 9th and within twenty days effected its capitulation.[20] One month later he was ready to move on Mexico City which lay open before him. But before he could go any further he was forced to discharge his volunteers whose term of service had expired. In the midst of a hostile people Scott then lay in wait for reinforcements from April to August.[21]

Finally on August 7, with his army reinforced to some 14,000 regulars and volunteers, Scott resumed the offensive against an enemy force estimated by the Mexicans themselves at 36,000 men and 100 pieces of cannon. With the aid of additional reinforcements who were raised under the legislation of February 11, 1847 as well as the law of May 13, 1846, the campaign was carried on to a successful conclusion, and on February 2, 1848, the Treaty of Guadalupe Hidalgo officially terminated the war. These laws provided for an addition of nine regiments of infantry and one of dragoons to be enlisted for the duration. Providing for an additional major in each authorized regiment, the way was paved to at least by-pass the field officers who were too old for duty, but who were kept on because of faulty legislation. This handicap in field grade officers was keenly felt in Taylor's operations. On March 3, 1847, Congress authorized the appointment of three brigadier generals and two major generals to fill out the complement of the additional ten regiments. It should not be forgotten that each of these laws made provision for bounties.[22]

If the Mexican campaigns had been undertaken against a people whose government was more stable, a landing at Vera Cruz would have been difficult. Any show of determined resistance at that place would, perhaps, have saved Scott the embarrassment

---

[19] Upton, *op. cit.*, p. 210.
[20] Vera Cruz was taken with the cooperation of the Navy.
[21] Upton, *op. cit.*, p. 211, Spaulding; *op. cit.*, p. 211.
[22] VI *Stat*, 123-126; 184-186.

and even the danger of discharging his short timers in hostile territory. The policy of the American Government was at best courting disaster.

At the onset of the war, no plans had been evolved for the procurement and distribution of supplies to the combat areas. Even worse than this, little information existed with reference to what was needed in the terrain to be traversed by the troops. This was borne out in the correspondence between Taylor and the War Department. From Corpus Christi, and as he advanced toward the Rio Grande and later into Mexico itself, Taylor made numerous appeals for wagons, camp equipage, and supplies of every description.[23] In the southern theater, Scott's campaign was handicapped by lack of transportation as well as supplies.[24]

There existed also a conspicuous deficiency in uniforms. Governed by the appropriations of the preceding years, no effort could be made to procure enough uniforms to meet the needs of any significant increase in the armed forces. Hence the volunteers were requested to furnish their own uniforms and equipment, with a promise of reimbursement; finally the awkward conditions thus imposed had to be corrected but not until the war was almost over.[25]

These and a multitude of other problems dealing with training, morale, and hygiene had to be overcome as the war followed its course, all of which should have been efficiently dealt with at the very beginning. With the experience of two major wars together with more than a decade of Indian warfare there was little excuse for the helter-skelter mode of preparations which marked the Mexican War. But there seemed to be an unwillingness to learn these hard lessons. In fact, they would be repeated over and over again throughout the whole course of American history. Considerations of political advancement coupled with the political, economic, and social development of the nation would command the attention of the Government. Military policy would remain a secondary determinant in the evolution of national destiny.

---

[23] See House Exec. Doc. No. 60, 30th Cong., 1st Sess., pp. 638 ff; Smith, *op. cit.*, Vol. I, pp. 490-491.

[24] Spaulding, *op. cit.*, pp. 207-208.

[25] January 26, 1848, VI *Stat*, 210.

Improving the Wooden Navy

The revolutionary developments in nautical science, ship construction, naval ordnance, and steam vessels, dictated a need for a greater distribution of labor within the Navy Department. Increasing demands for specialized activities brought about the reorganization of the Department on August 31, 1842 by abolishing the Board of Navy Commissioners and establishing the bureaus.[26] While the change was intended to meet with and solve the mounting problems of procurement and distribution of naval materiel, ship-building programs and facilities, ship repairs, storage, warehousing, and associated activities, it deprived the Navy of a board of experts which under the preceding program was of great importance in the evolution of naval policy. Acting independently of each other and individually responsible to the Secretary of the Navy, the bureau chiefs did not, nor were they required to coordinate their activities. Hence the evolution of naval policy during the period 1842-1861 was dependent upon the independent opinions and judgment of five bureau chiefs. Professional analysis rested with the civilian Secretary of the Navy.

·   Under this organization, the Navy during this period began to change from sail to steam; but, in the absence of professional guidance, the change failed to keep pace with developments abroad. Stubborn resistance within many circles and even in the Navy itself defeated any attempt to build armored vessels. Instead, the great advantage of steam power was applied to wooden vessels with no apparent regard for the destructiveness of newly developed naval ordnance. American taxpayers were asked to support a dissipated system which was foisted upon the nation by selfish shipping interests. Lacking foresight, the Navy Department, the Secretary of the Navy, and special interests in and out of the Government accepted a naval building program that would become obsolete during the Civil War.

In the meanwhile, however, there was no lack of energy in the agitation for a stronger navy to coincide with America's growing interests at home and abroad. This agitation was stirred up by Polk's slogan of 54-40 or fight and continued unabated, but

---

[26] V *Stat,* 579-581. See also Paullin, "Naval Administration 1842-1861," pp. 1435-1440. The five bureaus were: Bureau of Navy Yards and Docks; Bureau of Construction, Equipment and Repairs; Bureau of Provisions and Clothing; Bureau of Ordnance and Hydrography; Bureau of Medicine and Surgery.

along more conservative lines, even after the outstanding difficulties with England over the Oregon boundary were settled amicably in 1846.[27]

The opponents of a large navy subscribed to "the more democratic practice" of subsidizing commercial steamers as the cheapest means for providing a sufficient naval force to meet the needs of war. By compromise, the large navy men in Congress secured approval for four steam warships in return for the grant of a large subsidy to private shipping interests for vessels that could be converted into ships of the line.[28] This was a recognition of the dangerous fallacy that an effective naval force could be quickly improvised in an emergency from the country's merchant marine.[29] These differences were momentarily set aside to fight the Mexican War.

As early as March 29, 1845, the Secretary of the Navy took steps to offer naval protection to American interests in the Gulf of Mexico but placed the naval commander under the same vague instructions as those received by General Taylor. "The policy of this government is the preservation of peace, if possible." [30] Once war broke out, however, Navy operations in the Gulf of Mexico and on the California coast were in concert with the Army. While Taylor advanced across the Rio Grande, the principal Mexican ports in the Gulf of Mexico had been placed under blockade by Commodore David Conner.[31] On the West coast, Commodore Robert F. Stockton effectively cooperated with General Philip Kearney by opening a line of communications from California to the general's advancing columns, and subjected to blockade all the ports, harbors, bays, outlets, and inlets, on the west coast of Mexico south of San Diego.[32]

In the campaign against Vera Cruz, the Navy played a large part in the subsequent victory of General Scott. With the small squadron situated in the Gulf of Mexico, the herculean feat of

[27] Not until a wild flurry of press opinion on the relative merits of this question had run its course, however. See *National Intelligencer*, January 12, 1846, Hartford *Courant*, June 5, 1846, Philadelphia *North American*, April 16, 1846. The Oregon Treaty was concluded June 15, 1846.
[28] IX *Stat*, 187.
[29] Sprout, *op. cit.*, p. 134.
[30] Rpt S/N December 5, 1846, p. 380.
[31] *Ibid.*, pp. 380-382. On November 14, Commodore Conner captured Tampico.
[32] Rpt S/N December 4, 1848, pp. 1048-1054; December 6, 1847, pp. 359-360.

transporting an army into hostile territory was effected without loss by

the capture of Tampico, by protecting the transportation and the landing of the troops at Vera Cruz, by its gallant cooperation in the siege, bombardment and capture of that city and its defenses, by its successful operations against Tabasco, Tuspan, Laguna, and other points in the interior and on the coast, but especially by holding a constant command of the sea, and by its vigilance and activity.[33]

In addition to the activities conducted during the war period, the Navy continued to offer protection to American interests throughout the world. So effective had the performance of this duty been that our increasing commerce in the most distant seas felt no check and met no interruption.[34] But the war had pointed up some definite deficiencies. The ships of the Navy were not constructed to do duty in the shoal waters of the southern areas. Moreover, there became apparent a decided opinion that the future naval policy would parallel that of the pre-war days unmindful of the fact that this war was waged against a power that had no navy.

Growing commercial interests in the Caribbean and in South America, accentuated by the discovery of gold in California, renewed the arguments for a transisthmian canal but British interest in such a project forestalled American plans.[35] This sharply pointed up the need for a stronger navy.

Increased trade in Europe and in Asia strengthened the appeals for a stronger naval force to protect these commercial interests.[36] Succeeding secretaries of the Navy carried this message to Congress each year.[37] But not until 1853 did Administration

---

[33] Rpt S/N, December 4, 1848, p. 609. This was one of the first American experiences in amphibious warfare. A battalion of Marines joined the main army under Scott at Puebla on August 6, 1847 and played a conspicuous part in the Battle of Chapultepec. See Rpt S/N December 6, 1847, pp. 13-14.

[34] Rpt S/N December 4, 1848, pp. 606-610.

[35] The Clayton-Bulwer Treaty of April 19, 1850 pledged the United States and Great Britain to recognize their mutual interests in any canal project through the Isthmus.

[36] See Rpt S/N December 1, 1849, p. 438; rpt S/N 1853, S. Doc. No. 1, p. 307; rpt S/N 1854, pp. 390-392. *Ibid.*, rpt S/N 1850, Doc. No. 1, pp. 204, 205, protection was asked for American commerce in the South Pacific and Eastern Asia; rpt S/N 1852, H. Doc. No. 1, pp. 295-297; rpt S/N 1854, pp. 387-388. There was a great deal of loose talk about the Sandwich Islands at this time. See rpt S/N 1851, Doc. No. 2, p. 5. See also Dudley Knox, *A History of the United States Navy*, ch. 17.

[37] See *National Intelligencer*, September 9, 1853; rpt S/N December 3, 1855,

spokesmen take their cue from the Navy Department to outline naval policy in accord with that of European nations with whom this country might become involved over the maritime trade.[38] The time had come to modernize in keeping with developments in technology if aggression, at home and abroad, was to be checked.

But America moved slowly in modern improvements. Although the young Republic had shown unmistakable signs of greatness, and its people were not lacking in the courage to span a mighty continent, there existed a peculiar backwardness to make a quick change in established patterns of behavior. America was ready to respond to the clamor for a stronger navy, but she remained conservative in her reaction. The naval policy of the decade preceding the Civil War envisaged an increase in ships[39] and also encompassed an improved personnel policy,[40] but it fell far short of the great developments demonstrated by the Crimean War (1854-1856). Despite the proved vulnerability of unarmored wooden vessels against shell-fire, American shipbuilders continued their construction and even improved their designs. In response to the pressures of interested constituencies,[41] Congress neglected to lead the way, while the President of the United States, James Buchanan, during the four years preceding 1861 preferred the path of least resistance; and when the tabulations were made, the Navy could boast of 44 sailing ships and 38 steam vessels.[42]

Senate Exec. Documents, 34th Cong., 1st Sess., Vol. 3, p. 14; rpt S/N December 1, 1856, ibid., 34th Cong., 3d Sess., Vol. 3, p. 408; rpt S/N December 6, 1858, ibid., 35th Cong., 2d Sess., Vol. 4, p. 7; rpt S/N December 2, 1859, ibid., 36th Cong., 1st Sess., Vol. 3, p. 1140.

[38] Rpt S/N 1851, Doc. No. 2, p. 9; rpt S/N 1852, H. Doc. No. 1, p. 319. The general condition of Europe in 1848 prompted some lively discussion in the press. See Boston *Courier*, May 5, 1848; New York *Herald*, May 7, 1848; Boston *Advertiser*, October 2, 1848.

[39] By the Act of April 6, 1854 six first class steam frigates were added to the Navy. See X *Stat*. 273; Sprout, op. cit., pp. 140-150. On August 31, 1852, a navy yard and depot was authorized to the built at San Francisco, California, ibid., 104, 223. See also rpt S/N December 6, 1858, p. 6.

[40] On February 28, 1855 an Act, made provision for removing inefficient officers kept on the active lists for various reasons. See X *Stat* 616. To promote efficiency within the enlisted ranks, an Act was passed on March 2, 1855 giving seamen who served honorably an honorable discharge upon completion of service and the offer of a bounty for re-enlistment. See ibid., 627. The apprentice system was extended to the Marine Corps on June 12, 1858. See XI *Stat* 318. On June 1, 1860 the pay of the Navy was increased. See XII *Stat* 23-27.

[41] See Sprout, op. cit., 143ff. See also rpt S/N 1850, Doc. 1, p. 198.

[42] See rpt S/N 1853, S. Doc. No. 1, p. 302; Paullin, "Naval Administration, 1842-1861," p. 1449; Alfred T. Mahan, *From Sail to Steam*, New York, Harper & Bros., 1907, pp. 34-35.

The fluctuating strength of the Navy was nowhere more sharply reflected than in the policy governing personnel. Ever since the return of friendly relations with France in 1801, no statute for more than forty years ever limited the sum total of persons to be employed in the Navy or in its several ranks and offices. By 1853 the enlisted strength reached 7,500 men though for the next seven years repeated requests were made to increase the total to 10,000.[48] The difficulty of retaining even the former number under existing conditions prompted the Secretary of the Navy to ask [44] for, and the Congress to pass, a law to improve the efficiency of the Navy in addition to offering inducements for reenlistments.[45] During this decade various recommendations were also made to bring the enlisted strength of the Marine Corps to a figure at least proportionate with that of the British Navy. Considering that a large percentage of the seamen were foreigners, a sufficient number of marines was urgently necessary to provide adequate guards on the war vessels.[46] This hue and cry for a salutary personnel policy was also heard from the War Department whose responsibilities grew apace with expansion westward.

Military Policy, 1850-1860

After the War with Mexico, America looked westward toward the newly acquired provinces and the long Pacific coastline. The stream of settlers toward the land of promise had swelled to a torrent with the discovery of gold in California, increasing the demand for military protection. The difficulties which this mass movement imposed upon the Army were partially solved on June 17, 1850 when Congress provided for an increase in the company strengths of existing units.[47] This raised the size of the military establishment to 12,927 men but because of the lure of greater promise in the west as well as in the east, the actual strength

[44] Rpt S/N 1850, Doc. No. 1, p. 199. Rpt S/N 1853, S. Doc. No. 1, p. 311; rpt S/N December 3, 1855, p. 17. The apprentice system was still in operation. See rpt S/N December 3, 1855, p. 16; rpt S/N December 1, 1856, pp. 422-423.
[44] Rpt SN December 1, 1856, p. 422. The length of cruise time was reduced from three years to two.
[45] See Act of March 2, 1855, X *Stat* 627. On February 28, 1855, Congress passed a law providing for dismissal of inefficient officers. *Ibid.*, 616.
[46] Rpt S/N 1850, Doc. No. 1, pp. 370-371. Rpt S/N 1852, H. Doc. No. 1, p. 592; rpt S/N December 3, 1857, pp. 580-581; rpt S/N December 6, 1858, p. 11; rpt S/N December 2, 1859, p. 1141.
[47] IX *Stat* 438.

reached only 10,763 men distributed among some 100 stations.[48]

To execute the arduous duties of frontier patrols this small force was organized without a regular cavalry. The apparent expenses of maintaining a cavalry regiment prompted the government to dispense with it and substitute mounted infantry which in effect could only result in "disorganizing them as infantry, and converting them into extremely indifferent horsemen." The great expanse of frontier, warned the General in Chief in 1850, rendered indispensable two additional regiments of horse (dragoons or mounted riflemen).[49]

With the Indians to challenge the white man's progress,[50] the lack of regular cavalry made less desirable the doubtful policy of increasing the number of small posts. Not only was this system expensive but it was also conducive of bad discipline, injurious to instruction and efficiency, and invited aggression by that exhibition of weakness which must inevitably attend the great dispersion of any force. Deficiency in numbers pointed to the feasibility of posting the troops in large bodies at commanding positions among the Indians. This would restrain aggression by the exhibition of powers adequate to punish.[51]

In 1853 a temporary lull in Indian warfare was sufficient to permit the War Department to direct its energies toward the more fruitful development of the west. Numerous surveys were undertaken in the interior for railway projects, military roads, river and harbor surveys.[52] By 1855, the results of these surveys called attention toward the military necessity of joining the Pacific Coast with the East. The remote situation of American holdings on that coast and the impossibility of affording adequate defense with a small navy were strong arguments for such a railroad.

Open to attack in this manner, the advantages lay with an enemy [England] "possessing a considerable military marine and

---

[48] Spaulding, *op. cit.*, p. 230.
[49] Rpt General-in-Chief, November 30, 1850, *ibid.*, pp. 116-117.
[50] There were twenty-two Indian Wars during the 50's. See Spaulding, *op. cit.*, pp. 230-231.
[51] Rpt S/W, December 1, 1853, Senate Documents, 33d Cong., 1st Sess., Vol. I, pp. 5-6.
[52] Especially in the Oregon Territory. See X *Stat* 35, 150, 151, 303, 304, 306, 603, 610, 634, 641; XI *Stat* 108, 252, 337, 371; XII *Stat* 19, 208. See also ltr William T. Sherman to John Sherman, March 20, 1856, quoted in Rachel S. Thorndike, *The Sherman Letters*, New York, Charles Scribner's Sons, 1894, pp. 56-57. See X *Stat* 56, 307, 608; XI *Stat* 24, 25, 44, 144.

subject us to enormous expense." Considering the dangers, the cost, and the final return to the people, together with the military necessity, the War Department carefully examined the prospect of railroad communication between the navigable waters of the Mississippi and those of the Pacific Ocean. Railway transportation had already improved the means of defending our Atlantic and inland frontiers, so that it became imperative to extend these benefits to the Pacific. This would relieve us of

> the necessity of accumulating large supplies on that coast, to waste, perhaps, through long years of peace; and we could feel entire confidence that, let war come when and with whom it may, before a hostile expedition could reach that exposed frontier, an ample force could be placed there to repel any attempt at invasion.[53]

The remarkable increase in railroad mileage strengthened the defensive condition of the United States and eased the necessity for large standing armies. This was affirmed by no less an authority than the Secretary of War as early as 1857 [54] and it served to confirm the position of the advocates of a small army and navy. But there was no substitute for an army and the standing force was not large. Despite the addition of four regiments of cavalry (two on foot)[55] the Army remained understrength and the governmental responsibility "to afford perfect protection to its citizens against outrage and personal violence is not performed by the government of the United States." [56]

Other military experts such as Captain George B. McClellan, who was destined to create one of the most formidable armies of modern times, were in accord with the belief that our regular army never could be large enough to provide for all the contingencies

---

[53] Rpt S/W December 3, 1855, Senate Exec. Documents, No. 78, 33rd Cong., 1st Sess., Vol. 7, pp. 8-10. Jefferson Davis also experimented with the use of camels to solve some of the problems of transportation. See *ibid.*, 35th Cong., 2nd Sess., Vol. 2, p. 14; 36th Cong., 1st Sess., Vol. 2, p. 6.

[54] Rpt S/W December 5, 1857, Senate Exec. Documents, 35th Cong., 1st Sess., Vol. 3, p. 17.

[55] X *Stat* 639, March 3, 1855.

[56] Rpt S/W December 5, 1857, Senate Exec. Documents, 35th Cong., 1st Sess., Vol. 3, p. 4. The authorized strength of the Army in 1855 was 17,867 while the actual strength was 15,752. This discrepancy continued from year to year and in 1859 the authorized figure was 18,165 and actual strength was 17,498. However, of this last figure only 11,000 men were available for actual service in the field. See Rpt S/W December 3, 1855, *ibid.*, 34th Cong., 1st & 2nd Sess., Vol. 2, p. 1; December 1, 1856, *ibid.*, 34th Cong., 3rd Sess., Vol. 3, p. 3; December 1, 1859, *ibid.*, 36th Cong., 1st Sess., Vol. 2, p. 3.

that might arise.[57] McClellan, recently returned from observing the Crimean War, pointed out that the Army should be as large as its ordinary avocations in the defense of the frontier would justify. To meet emergencies as they might arise, the militia and the volunteer system should, he said, be placed upon some tangible and effective basis, instructors furnished them from the Regular Army, and all possible means taken to spread sound military information among them.[58] But, like Calhoun, McClellan was ahead of his time. Sound instructional doctrine necessarily depended upon a well-organized Army school system without which a continuing program was impossible.

Aside from the ordinary objections of lack of facilities to conduct a proper program of instruction, there was the other and more distressing problem of detached service which would necessarily become more aggravated by this system. This problem had grown out of the failure or lack of appreciation for the need of a separate staff corps. The practice of detail from the line to the staff operated to place the detailed officer upon an independent basis from the commander he served while at the same time it reduced his sphere of observation and experience, and thus unfitted him for change or advancement.[59]

The Secretary of War scored this practice and recommended a solution which would be reluctantly adopted forty-five years later. To place the staff in a proper relationship with the rest of the Army all officers performing staff duty would be organized into one corps, and each officer

> assigned by authority of the President to such duties as each may seem to be best fitted for. . . . A general provision dispensing with the staff bureaus and giving the President authority to regulate the duties on principles above stated, and to transfer, when necessary, officers to and from the line and staff, would restore the institution to its proper effectiveness.[60]

Neither the Bureau Chiefs nor Congress were ready to accept these revolutionary ideas and the detail system remained to hamper the effectiveness and efficiency of the Army.

---

[57] Peter S. Michie, *General McClellan*, New York, D. Appleton & Co., 1901, pp. 46-47.
[58] Michie, *op. cit.*, p. 47.
[59] Rpt S/W December 5, 1857, Senate Exec. Documents, 35th Cong., 1st Sess., Vol. 3, p. 9.
[60] *Ibid.*, p. 10. See also Rpt S/W December 6, 1858, *ibid.*, 35th Cong., 2nd Sess., Vol. 2, p. 16.

Based upon their observations in the Crimea, McClellan and his colleagues made strong recommendations for improving the seacoast fortifications. The siege of Sebastopol proved the superiority of steam vessels against a weak defensive system. This new combination of force placed the American coast line under a serious handicap which could only be overcome by fortified "cities and harbors . . . and those fortifications must be provided with guns, ammunition, and instructed artillerists." [61] These observations were communicated to Congress in an urgent plea for liberal and regular grants from Congress for the completion of the works [seacoast defenses] already under construction, and for the commencement of such new ones as it was proposed to erect. But Congress undermined an effective coast defense by limiting ordnance appropriations.[62]

The effects of limited appropriations were also felt in the organization of the militia. Although the population had increased some eight-fold since 1808, and with it came a relative increase in the militia force throughout the country. The annual appropriation of $200,000 for arming this component remained the same. For this reason it became increasingly difficult to meet the State requisitions made upon the Government for armament of every description;[63] it was impossible also to furnish gratuitously the existing training literature.[64] Furthermore, this lack of interest from the Federal Government was reflected in the States themselves who, according to law, were required to make annual returns to the War Department in order to qualify for financial aid. The lackadaisical attitude in making these returns and their incompleteness evoked strong criticism from the Secretary of War in 1856. "It is to be feared," he warned, "judging from the irregular and very defective returns received at this department, that the militia system is falling into disuse." This seemed to indicate the necessity for further legislation to improve the condition and render more perfect the instruction of the militia force of the United States.[65]

[61]Michie, *op. cit.*, p. 46.
[62] Rpt S/W December 1, 1856, Senate Exec. Documents, 34th Cong., 3rd Sess., Vol. 3, p. 15; Rpt December 5, 1857, *ibid.*, 35th Cong., 1st Sess., Vol. 3, p. 17; Rpt S/W December 1, 1859, *ibid.*, 36th Cong., 1st Sess., Vol. 2, p. 10.
[63] Rpt S/W December 1, 1859, Senate Exec. Documents, 36th Cong., 1st Sess., Vol. 2, p. 11.
[64] See rpt General-in-Chief, November 29, 1851, Senate Documents, 32nd Cong., 1st Sess., Vol. I, p. 163.
[65] Rpt S/W December 1, 1856, Senate Exec. Documents, 34th Cong., 3rd Sess., Vol. 3, p. 25.

While these were considerations of great national importance, the continuous turmoil with the Indians on the frontiers, with the Mormons in Utah, and in Congress over the slave issue overshadowed all. With the exception of an act authorizing three regiments of mounted volunteers for duty in Texas and Utah,[66] the national defense policy remained unsettled. Faced with a multitude of problems which even included military intervention in the political disputes in Kansas and Nebraska, the War Department was asked to reduce expenditures. In response the Secretary of War on December 6, 1858 reduced his estimates by over 9 million dollars. He further entertained a strong hope that expenses might be still further reduced in the course of another year. Secretary John B. Floyd continued his search for economy while the South prepared for war; and President Buchanan, who had been disturbed about the "dangers of a Mormon invasion," allowed his term of office to expire without exercising his constitutional right to provide an adequate defensive arrangement against the imminence of civil war.

Abraham Lincoln's election in 1860 fanned the sparks of rebellion into a raging inferno but with the military establishment understrength and distributed over 198 posts, camps, and stations, the concentration of force urged by Poinsett and by Jefferson Davis became conspicuously impossible. As a result, the bold and audacious plans of the South were allowed to materialize. The absence of a strong concentrated force permitted Southern leaders to challenge the authority of the Federal Government; and the failure to force a just respect for this authority precipitated the attack on Fort Sumter on April 12, 1861. The Civil War, which so many had predicted, was upon the Nation. The Government, despite all warnings, found itself without the necessary force even to defend against attack.[67]

---

[66] See XI *Stat* 262, April 7, 1858. On December 3, 1860, the Secretary of War urged that breach-loading fire arms be provided for the Army. See rpt S/W, Senate Exec. Documents, 36th Cong., 2nd Sess., Vol. 2, p. 11.

[67] The regular force which was not in garrison numbered a little over 11,000. But these were employed in prosecuting the Indian Wars which extended "from the British possessions on the Pacific to the border settlements of Texas . . ." See Rpt S/W December 6, 1858, Senate Exec. Documents, 35th Cong., 2nd Sess., Vol. 2, p. 3.

CHAPTER 8

The Civil War—
Manpower Policies

Political Restraints on the Nation at War—The Call to Arms—Bull Run Brings Out the Shortcomings—Recruiting Under States Rights—Compulsory Military Service—The Regular Army—Selecting the Officers—The Bounty

Political Restraints On the Nation at War

FROM THE ELECTION of Abraham Lincoln on November 6, 1860, to his inauguration on March 4, 1861, the South organized the movement toward secession which had been growing stronger during the latter part of the decade 1850-1860. What kind of a situation he would find as President, Lincoln had already known even before his election. He had watched with intense interest the feeble determination of Congress to protect Government property in the Southern States[1] but the responsibility for leading the Congress out of this wilderness of confusion remained with President Buchanan until March 4, 1861. By this time there was little to prevent Southern leaders in their determination to oppose the new Administration and to secede from the Union in protest against a man who had once said *A house divided against itself cannot stand.*

But after March 4, this responsibility for protecting Government property became Lincoln's. Despite the vast amount of information which was in his possession, he had no carefully outlined plan of action to meet the challenge against Federal authority. Weeks of inaction followed until news was received in Washington that Fort Sumter had been attacked. There now could be no doubt of the position to be taken nor the steps to be followed with reference to the all-important question of the preservation of the Union.

With Congress adjourned, the President gathered his Cabinet and military advisers about him and laid the plans for immediate action. These plans necessarily were based upon the weak military

---

[1] A. Howard Meneely, *The War Department, 1861,* New York, Columbia University Press, 1928, pp. 60-62.

edifice in existence (regulars and militia) which made it difficult to determine the extent of the force necessary and the length of time required to bring the South to a proper recognition of Federal authority. There remained to be settled also the whole question of the manner in which mobilization would be conducted; the position of the States with reference to their militia organizations in the service of the Government; the procurement of supplies and materiel; the selection of commanders for the newly organized forces; and the myriads of other associated problems which follow in the wake of a violent transition from peace to war.

Because of the diversity of interests in New England, the Middle Atlantic States, the West, the doctrine of States Rights remained more pronounced in the North than it was in the South. This rendered effective centralized control difficult if not impossible. The whole question of the relationship between the Government and the States was not effectively settled even by the war's end. While the Northern governors' influence penetrated the councils of the Federal Government, the principles of States Rights became applied to the organization of the Army.[2] And, although the Administration succeeded by 1863 in enacting legislation affirming the supremacy of the Government over the States with reference to the recruitment of manpower, the President remained reluctant to exercise this right.[3] Against this background of political power, which would affect every Army activity, the President of the United States strove for four years to bring some order and efficiency to the conduct of military affairs. In the end, the States still remained decisive factors in the organization, training, and equipping of the Army.

One authority says that Lincoln assumed the control and direction of the Army as early as May 3, 1861 when he called not for militia but for volunteers. According to this, the soldiers now would be subject to the laws and regulations of the Army, and although the Governors would continue to commission officers, "the President would control and direct the Army."[4] In effect, while the Enrollment Act provided for conscription, the procure-

---

[2] See Fred A. Shannon, *The Organization and Administration of the Union Army*, 1861-1865, Cleveland, Arthur H. Clark Co., 1928, Vol. I, pp. 16-17.

[3] The Enrollment Act, passed March 3, 1863.

[4] See William B. Hesseltine, *Lincoln and the War Governors*, New York, Alfred A. Knopf, 1948, p. 165. See also *ibid.*, chapter 14.

ment of personnel continued on a voluntary basis with the Governors encouraging volunteer enlistments. Lincoln might cajole the State Executives but he preferred not to do so.

The Call to Arms

Concern over the safety of the Capital led Lincoln to inquire into the legal means for augmenting the meager forces at the disposal of the Government. He might have convened Congress but instead he effected a hasty review of existing statutés for this authority and fell upon the Militia Act of February 28, 1795 which vested the Chief Executive with the power to call out the militia to enforce the laws of the United States against the obstructions of any State.[5] Employing the authority of this old law, Lincoln proceeded to make hasty preparations for the defense of Washington. Between April 9 and April 16, he issued three calls for twenty-three companies of militia from the District of Columbia.[6] The reluctance of these militia contingents to take the oath, for fear that they would thereby surrender their rights under the Constitution, was to warn the Administration of the opposition to be encountered against any attempt at Federal control over the military forces of the States.[7]

While the defenses of Washington were being prepared, a state of war was created by the Southern action against Fort Sumter, South Carolina. Trusting to the patriotic sentiments of the northern people, Lincoln was willing to overlook some manifestations of hostility against Presidential authority to muster an army, and, on April 15, 1861, he issued a call for 75,000 militia to serve for ninety days, "to cause the laws to be duly executed." [8]

Some authorities considered this call a little weak especially in view of the fact that such states as New York and Indiana had indicated a willingness to raise more than half that amount not for ninety days but for two years.[9] If this was an experiment to deter-

---

[5] This authority was granted to President Washington during the height of the Whiskey Rebellion in western Pennsylvania. I *Stat* 424-425.

[6] See *War of the Rebellion: A Compilation of Official Records of the Union and Confederate Armies*, Washington, 1880-1901, Series I, Vol. 51, Pt. I, pp. 321-325; Series III, Vol. 1, p. 75. Hereafter cited as *O.R.*

[7] *Ibid.*, Series I, Vol. 51, Pt. I, pp. 322-323. See also Shannon *op. cit.*, Vol. 1, p. 31.

[8] Richardson *M&P*, VI, 13-14. Accompanying this proclamation was a call for a special session of Congress, but the date of convening was postponed until July 4.

[9] Shannon, *op. cit.*, Vol. 1, p. 32.

mine how far the States would go in support of the decision to force the South to obey the laws, Lincoln did not have long to wait. Governor Curtin of Pennsylvania assured the Secretary of War of a prompt response to the call of duty, and the Philadelphia *Inquirer* punctuated the Governor's remarks by saying, "Money is forthcoming in any amount, and men in any numbers."[10] Similar responses were issued from other northern States.[11] But from the border and Southern States the reaction went from a desire to abstain from commitment to violent opposition. Maryland and Delaware insisted upon the constitutional restrictions against employing their militia while Governor John Letcher of Virginia challenged the right of the Government to subjugate the southern states.[12]

This experiment with the militia not only went far to prove that the traditional militia problems still existed but also served notice of the extent to which the South was capable of going. Simultaneously with the call for the 75,000 militiamen, four more States seceded from the Union. It was now apparent this was not a mild insurrection but rather a full-scale war where the force of the North would have to be more than equal to what the South could place in the field. The Confederate Government was not toying with any ninety-day militia organizations; their forces were made up of volunteers. Fortunately for the North, Jefferson Davis limited the term of service, in the beginning at least, to one year. In recognition of these hard facts, the President was made to see the need for a more permanent force of volunteers.

On May 3, 1861 the new call, again in the absence of Congress, was made for 42,034 volunteers to serve three years. Going still further in the exercise of presidential prerogatives, the Chief Executive ordered an increase of 22,714 officers and men in the Regular Army, together with the enlistment of 18,000 seamen to serve from one to three years.[13]

The response to these two calls for volunteer duty exceeded the expectations of the Administration and the War Department. Instead of the 75,000 under the first call almost 100,000 men

---

[10] See Philadelphia *Inquirer*, April 15 and 17, 1861.
[11] Shannon, *op. cit.*, Vol. 1, p. 32.
[12] *O.R.*, Series III, Vol. 1, pp. 70, 79-80, 114, 210.
[13] See General Orders No. 15, May 4, 1861, *O.R.* Series III, Vol. 1, pp. 151-154. Company and field officers of the new regiments were to be appointed by the Governors.

came up for service. Within a few days of the second call it became evident that more men would volunteer than had been asked for. But because the War Department was not prepared to meet the needs even of the smaller numbers called up, it became necessary to bring a halt to the zealous desires of the northern Governors to recruit more regiments than were requested. The intense desires of the northern Governors to keep on recruiting was the natural result of the increased patronage that would flow from the authority to recruit new regiments. With each new regiment went the right to appoint officers. Hence, during the war the Governors would be reluctant to fill old regiments while they insisted upon recruiting completely new regiments.[14]

This flush of patriotic zeal, which seemed to indicate a willingness to follow the President's lead, had been accomplished while Congress patiently waited to be called into special session. It now remained for the President to convene the legislators and to ask for legal sanction to his actions, a request that could hardly be answered in the negative. On July 4, Congress assembled and the President laid before them the accomplished fact.[15]

Accompanying the message was the report of the Secretary of War which placed the strength of the land forces at 310,000 men. While this seemed to be large, deductions of 80,000 representing the three-month men, and 50,000 which were still in the process of recruiting, left a total of 230,000 or 188,000 volunteers and 42,000 regulars.[16] There was little doubt that Congress would approve these figures, but by this time the War Department was convinced that a larger force would be required to restore the Union. For this purpose, and also to settle the issue as quickly and economically as possible, the Secretary of War urged Congress to grant at least 400,000 men and $400,000,000.[17] But Congress was not convinced that the existing forces were insufficient to bring the struggle to a speedy and successful conclusion.

Bull Run Brings Out the Shortcomings

In July 1861, the defenses of Washington were placed in the hands of General Irvin McDowell and his army of civilians in uni-

---

[14] Rappaport, *op. cit.*, p. 98. See also rpt S/W, July 1861, Senate Exec. Document No. 1, 37th Cong., 1st Sess., pp. 22-23.

[15] Richardson, *M&P*, VI, 20-31.

[16] Rpt S/W, July, 1861, Senate Exec. Document No. 1, 37th Cong., 1st Sess., pp. 21-22.

[17] *Ibid.*, p. 10.

form. Under pressure from the people, this untrained and undisciplined mob was hurled against the Confederate forces at Bull Run on July 21, and was driven back in disorder. Consternation gripped the northern mind and a reappraisal of the war effort called for immediate remedial action. Indiscriminate charges of inefficiency were hurled at the Union commanders (McDowell and Robert Patterson) for the behavior of their troops.

On July 14, General Patterson reported from Martinsburg, Virginia that his three month men showed signs of restlessness at the prospect of being retained over their time. Next day General Benjamin Butler warned the War Department that within fifteen days he would lose 750 men. On the 17th Patterson at Charlestown, Virginia reported that his Pennsylvania troops would depart within seven days, and on the following day he remonstrated against the failure of the Government to pay his men and to furnish them with shoes. Under these circumstances Patterson felt that he could not ask nor expect the three months' volunteers to stay longer than one week.[18]

One day before Bull Run, General McDowell confessed his embarrassment over the inability of the troops to take care enough of their rations to make them last the time they should, and over the expiration of the term of service of many of them. On the 21st while McDowell was engaged at Manassas, General Patterson tried in vain to keep General Joseph Johnston from operating against the Federal right wing but could not pursue the fleet Johnston with barefooted troops whose time expired in a few days. At Beverly, Virginia, General George B. McClellan was forced to abandon a plan to march on Staunton, Virginia because his three-month men were homesick and discontented.[19]

Recruiting Under States Rights

Under these discouraging circumstances, the first concern was for procuring additional numbers without regard for any system of replacement. The best interests of the nation would have been served if a system of replacement had been inaugurated. But such a system would not serve the best interests of the Governors whose appetite for doling out patronage had only been whetted. To make matters worse, Congress turned its back upon the ex-

---

[18] *O.R.*, Series I, Vol. 2, pp. 166-168, 741.
[19] *O.R.*, Series I, Vol. 2, pp. 172, 308, 745, 752.

perience of the past which warned against short term enlistments.

On July 22 the President was given authority to call up 500,-000 men to serve from six months to three years. The Governors were allowed to appoint the company and field officers for the new regiments growing out of this call. General officer selection remained with the President who was also authorized to create military boards to examine into the qualifications of officers.[20] Although this was a healthy proposal, it was vitiated by the democratic practice by which officers were elected to their posts by the men. Recruiting and processing of these volunteers was conducted by the States who were reluctant to fill up existing units and eager to create new regiments.

McClellan, selected to replace McDowell on July 22, 1861, viewed with concern the tendency of the State Governments to create new regiments before filling even the newer units.[21] No one was more aware of the dangers of such a system of recruiting than McClellan especially as it concerned his command of the Army of the Potomac. Acting upon his recommendations, the Secretary of War published an order effective January 1, 1862 terminating enlistments by State authorities except on special requisition. At once, this act placed the recruiting service in the hands of the Federal Government. It initiated a system of regimental recruiting by creating a recruiting superintendent and general depot in each State where the recruits would be received, clothed, equipped, and trained before joining their regiments.[22]

However, Federal control of these activities was short-lived. Secretary of War Cameron was replaced by Edwin M. Stanton who was not in sympathy with the policies of his predecessor. On April 3, 1863 employing as his excuse the size of the Army already in existence,[23] Stanton abolished the volunteer recruiting service and placed the responsibility again in the hands of the State Executives.[24]

The plan now was for field commanders to requisition the War Department for troops to fill their units. In turn, the War Department placed the call upon the Governors who would recruit the

---

[20] XII *Stat*, 268-271. See also *O.R.* Series III, Vol. 1, pp. 380-383.
[21] Rappaport, *op. cit.* pp. 96-97.
[22] *O.R.* Series III, Vol. 1, pp. 722-723. Cf. Hesseltine, *op. cit.*, p. 192.
[23] The Army totaled some 661,000 men. See Rpt S/W, December 1, 1861, *Ibid.*, p. 699. See also Shannon, *op. cit.*, pp. 266-267.
[24] *O.R.* Series, III, Vol. 2, p. 2.

necessary numbers.[25] It was evident that Stanton was resolved to keep the Army at the existing figure. But within a month military operations were to bite into the Army, and, as figures fell off, the Secretary urgently exhorted the Governors to speed up enlistments for any length of service. Fewer men were now heeding the calls to duty. Bull Run had served as a vivid example of the personal danger in war.[26]

On June 6, 1862 the recruiting system abolished in April was re-established but it was now difficult to stimulate enlistments. News of the heavy losses sustained in the Peninsula Campaign and the Battle of Shiloh further discouraged volunteering. To save the situation, the Governors were inveigled into a scheme for saving the Administration the embarrassment of calling for more men. A petition from the States urging the President to accept 300,000 more volunteers could be graciously honored. Fully prepared for this overture, the President sent out the answers on July 1, and on the following day the quotas were issued. These called for 334,835 volunteers for three years with the provision of a bounty of $100.[27]

While the immediate response to the call was slow, the need for additional men became more acute and the only solution seemed to be in a draft. Men like Oliver P. Morton of Indiana and Governor E. D. Morgan of New York warned the President to force upon Congress the passage of a law by which men could be drafted in the Army.[28]

President Lincoln called this to the attention of Congress who responded on July 17, 1862 with "a halting and poorly devised measure which stands condemned because of its inefficiency." The law merely amended the Militia Act of 1795 which contained no provision for a draft of the militia. As such, the enforcing authority was lacking and the people remonstrated against the attempt to force an enrollment.[29]

On August 4th and 9th, two War Department general orders notified the States of the proposal to draft 300,000 militia to serve

[25] Shannon, *op. cit.*, p. 270.
[26] *O.R.* Series III, Vol. 2, pp. 29, 76-86, 201.
[27] Shannon, *op. cit.*, p. 270. *O.R.* Series III, Vol. 2, pp. 180, 187-188, 198-205, 225-226.
[28] *O.R.* Series III, Vol. 2, pp. 212, 223.
[29] James G. Randall, *Constitutional Problems Under Lincoln*, New York, D. Appleton & Co., 1926, pp. 244-246. See also XII *Stat* 597.

for nine months unless sooner discharged. August 15th was established as the deadline for meeting the quotas set up on July 1 for 334,835 volunteers. In those cases where the quotas fell short, the deficiency of volunteers in that State was made up by special draft from the militia. This proviso was made to insure against the preference for lesser terms of service; but it aroused the ill-feelings of the people whom it affected.[30] Regardless of added inducements, men leaned toward the lesser period of service and when the Government created the option to operate on the basis of first come first served, disaffection was sure to set in. With all the experience with such a practice, it is a little surprising that the mistakes of earlier wars would be repeated at this time.

Under the regulations of August 9, for enrolling the militia for draft, the States were, in effect, bringing their militia laws to some degree of uniformity. Full authority, however, for carrying out the measure rested with State officials. The discretion allowed for conferring exemptions from such a draft was carried so far as to relieve large numbers of the responsibility to serve their country. These lists extended from government workers to mill hands, "habitual drunkards, and paupers." [31]

But despite the concessions to State prerogatives as well as to the individuals concerned, the enrollment procedure bogged down. In Madison, Wisconsin, more time was spent apprehending shirkers than in enrolling the militia. Soon this became a matter of serious concern. "What shall be done with the men arrested? It will take too many to guard them." Some States objected to the use of the draft to fill up old regiments because it interfered with the right of the men to elect their own officers.[32]

Fearful of arousing the further opposition of the people, the States preferred to postpone the experiment. Draft riots and threats of armed violence convinced the Governors of the futility at this time of trying to enforce such a measure.[33] Furthermore, there was no need to draft since the increased bounties and the threat of a draft had produced the desired effect. Under the calls of July 1 and August 4, some 431,958 volunteers and 87,558 militiamen were brought into the service.[34] If nothing else, the draft act stimu-

[30] O.R. Series III, Vol. 2, pp. 291, 333.
[31] Shannon, op. cit., Vol. 1, p. 285. ff.
[32] O.R. Series III, Vol. 2, pp. 714, 761, 765.
[33] Ibid., pp. 201, 212-213, 289, 401.
[34] Hesseltine, op. cit., p. 202.

lated enlistments, but the problem of securing manpower without the offer of large inducements still remained to be solved.

Compulsory Military Service

The need for adequate Federal control over the manpower resources of the nation could no longer be disregarded especially after Robert Lee served notice at Antietam of the ability of Confederate Armies to penetrate Union territory. With little difficulty, on March 3, 1863, Congress created the administrative machinery for control of manpower by the passage of an act for enrolling and calling out the national forces.[35] All male citizens and declarant aliens between the ages of 20 and 45 with certain exceptions were liable for draft; and all those enrolled were subject to call for two years after enrollment. Once drafted they would serve for three years or the duration. Thus after two years of war and experimentation, a federal law provided for raising the armies without regard for States Rights.[36] But its significance lay in the numbers who could claim exemption under the law.

Of the many defects in this law, the privilege of substitution in return for the payment of $300 was the worst. The principle of obligatory service in citizenship was seriously weakened by deferring to those who could afford the luxury of a paid substitute. Conscientious objectors also were permitted to discharge their obligations by the payment of the stipulated sum. The whole general scheme of exemptions as provided in the law was subject to criticism because of the drain it made upon the manpower pool, and the popular disapproval which was sure to follow.

Shortly after the first enrollment got under way on May 25, 1863 resistance to the draft grew violent throughout the country and in New York City the riots grew to such proportions that the local police, the militia, and elements of the Regular Army restored order only after four days of demonstration.[37]

The successful application of the law required the services of

---

[35] XII *Stat.* 731-737. See also *O.R.* Series III, Vol. 4, pp. 128-133. It also provided for the enrollment of Negroes and extended the draft to the Naval service and the Marine Corps.

[36] The Administration of this Act was placed under the new Provost Marshal General's office which it created. See L. D. Ingersoll, *A History of the War Department of the United States,* Washington, Francis B. Mohun, 1880, pp. 348-349.

[37] Randall, *Civil War and Reconstruction,* pp. 412 and ff. See also Hesseltine, *op. cit.,* p. 306.

a large military force which vitiated the measure to such an extent that the Provost Marshal General was forced to admit that the law was impractical.[38] After tabulating the figures it was found that only about six percent of the forces were actually conscripted.[39] Viewed in the light of the serious disturbances created in enforcing the law, it was quickly concluded that the measure was a failure and that some other means had to be devised for tapping the manpower pool.

While the enforcement of the law continued through the summer of 1863, the armies in the field which had largely been recruited under the coercive stimulant of conscription began to disintegrate under the influence of the elements which created them. Patriotism and the will to fight was lacking also because of the discriminating features of the Conscription Act. The Government was forced to abandon this plan for raising a national army; it employed the threat of a draft only to coerce the governors into redoubled efforts to enlist troops.[40]

It is significant to note that although the Negroes, by an Act of July 17, 1862 could be received into the service of the United States[41] as laborers or on any military or naval service for which they might be qualified, it was not until after the law of March 3, 1863 that the general employment of colored troops was authorized. Although the President in the beginning had shown a pronounced reluctance to employ colored troops, by March, 1863, (two months after the Emancipation Proclamation) he had shifted his position,[42] and before the end of March the War Department had taken steps to implement the law.[43] By December, 1863 it became the settled policy of the Government to recruit colored troops. On February 24, 1864, the position of the Negro with ref-

---

[38] *Hesseltine*, op. cit., p. 306. Randall, *Civil War and Reconstruction*, pp. 412-413.

[39] According to the report of the Provost Marshal General in 1918, it was shown that the draft actually accounted for 46,347 conscripts and 117,986 substitutes. See *Second Report of the Provost Marshall General*, December 20, 1918. Washington, Government Printing Office, pp. 376-377.

[40] Hesseltine, *op. cit.*, pp. 306-307.

[41] See Rpt PMG, *O.R.* Series III, Vol. 5, pp. 654-660.

[42] See ltr O. M. Hatch, Secretary of State, Illinois, to Lincoln, February 27, 1863, *Lincoln Mss*, Vol. 104, p. 22020; Lincoln to Banks, March 29, 1863, *ibid.*, Vol. 107, p. 22703; Lincoln to Hunter, April 1, 1863, *ibid.;* p. 22767. The Emancipation Proclamation was issued on January 1, 1863.

[43] See ltr Stanton to William A. Adair, March 21, 1863, *O.R.* Series III, Vol. 3, p. 82; G.O. No. 46, Hq. 18th Army Corps, December 5, 1863, *ibid.*, p. 1139.

erence to length of service and bounty gifts was carefully defined.[44] This additional source of manpower eased the recruitment problem.[45]

Under the coercive influence of the draft, the President issued four more calls for procuring sufficient manpower to fill up the depleted field forces.[46] Although the Governors met these calls as promptly as possible, in some instances recourse was had to the draft. The net result was that the States oversubscribed the requisitions and no further difficulties were encountered in mustering the men into the service. The success attending the answers to these last calls was due in part to the threat of draft and also to the increased bounties which were offered; and the gratifying response seemed to indicate that the North had an almost inexhaustible resource in manpower. The war weariness of the Confederate soldiers was accelerated by the appearance of large bodies of fresh Northern troops who were well-equipped and well-fed. As time wore on it became more apparent to Southern leadership that a continued contest was futile.

The Regular Army

At the outbreak of the war, the Regular Army was dispersed along the frontier in garrisons or engaged in combat with the Indians. Fifteen of the 198 companies of Regulars were distributed along the Canadian border and the Atlantic coast. Congressional attitude toward the bone and sinew of American defense is described by Upton who showed that Army appropriations for 1860 were the lowest since 1855.[47] Viewed in the perspective of time, some authorities have felt that perhaps a large standing army would have been useless unless it was large enough to do the job of winning a war. But it is well to bear in mind that a sufficiently strong force might have tempted Southern leaders to reflect upon the odds against them. Sober reflection in the perspective of time would give the lie to those who insist that a larger standing army would proportionately have increased the strength of the South. Although some 313 officers resigned their commissions to go south,

---

[44] XIII *Stat.* 11.
[45] The largest number of colored troops in the Army at any time was 123,156. See Ingersoll, *op. cit.*, p. 353. See also Rpt Bureau for Colored Troops, October 20, 1864, Rpt S/W, 1864-1865, p. 27.
[46] See *O.R.* Series III, Vol. 5, pp. 635, 717-719.
[47] Upton, *op. cit.*, p. 224.

the loyalty of the enlisted men remained steadfast. Therefore, while South Carolina was making preparations for armed conflict, the North would have had a sufficient striking force to compel at least a less bellicose attitude. It is sufficient to reflect also that a good-sized Army might have served to discourage the attempt at secession and consequently there would have been no call to arms. The impending crisis was irrepressible only because the Government lacked the vigor to insist upon peace.

With the exception of the law of May 3, 1861 which authorized the increase of 22,714 for the Regular Army, no significant steps were taken for increasing the regular force. The general attitude of the press reflected the opinion of the State governments against the expediency of making a large addition to the line of the Regular Army. Grounded upon this attitude and the policy of enlisting volunteers and militia for shorter periods of service, any plan for increasing the Regular Army became utterly hopeless.

The difficulty of recruiting regulars for five years in competition with volunteers for shorter periods was suggestive of the feasibility, according to Upton, of reducing "the line of the Army to a cadre, and the dispersion of its officers as commanders and instructors among the new troops." [48] But Scott was opposed to detaching the regulars and was insistent in his demand to keep the Army intact. Deterioration at this time, he felt, would have brought irreparable harm to the regular service.

On June 21, 1862 Congress by joint resolution offered to increase the inducements to encourage enlistments in the Regular Army and volunteer forces.[49] But as the bounty offers were similar for both components, men naturally inclined toward the volunteers where they could at least serve with neighbors and elect their own officers. The dual system was sharply criticized by the Executive Committee of the United States Sanitary Commission. If anything beneficial had been learned during the first year of the war it was the recognition of the mistake

> to keep the Regular Army and the Volunteer Army separate. Had the regulars been from the first intermingled with the volunteers they would have leavened the whole lump with their experience of camp police, discipline, subordination, and the sanitary conditions of military life. We should have no Bull

---

[48] Upton, *op. cit.*, p. 235. See also Randall, *Civil War and Reconstruction*, p. 426.

[49] *O.R.* Series III, Vol. 2, p. 171. See also XII *Stat.* 620.

Run panic to blush for. Our little Regular Army, diffused among the volunteers of last year, would within three months have brought them up to its own standard of discipline and efficiency.[50]

By October, 1862, it had become apparent that some measure of relief was necessary. General Halleck ordered the transfer of volunteers, with their own consent, to the regulars. Not more than ten volunteers were to be recruited to any one company, and, to make the offer more appealing, commissions were open to enlisted men for meritorious service.[51] Although few volunteers would filter into the regular ranks, State officials expressed alarm over this practice and urged the Secretary of War to put an end to it. However, their fears were unfounded for on June 25, 1863 in order to encourage enlistments, the bounty was set at $402.[52] Despite even these measures to stimulate regular recruitment, it remained difficult to compete with the volunteer service and the Regular Army maintained its authorized strength only with the greatest difficulty.

Selecting the Officers

The rapid mobilization of manpower, in the absence of carefully prepared plans, created among other problems that of selecting officers. Because this was a delicate task, it was felt that as far as the company officers were concerned, at least, there was no better method than to let the enlisted men elect their own.[53] While this had a salutary effect within the companies, the mode of electing field officers proved detrimental. Whatever the effects of such a system, it was made permanent on July 22, 1861 by an Act of Congress.[54]

Although such a practice clearly overlooked certain fundamentals in leadership, it was unavoidable at the onset. As of January 1, 1861 there were 1098 commissioned officers but, of these, 313 resigned their commissions to fight on the side of the Confederacy.[55] The small residue then was hardly sufficient for keeping the Regular Army intact according to the policy of General Scott.

---

[50] *O.R.* Series III, Vol. 2, p. 237.
[51] *Ibid.,* pp. 653, 654, 676.
[53] Rappaport, *op. cit.,* p. 103.
[53] Jacob D. Cox "War Preparations in the North," *Battles and Leaders of the Civil War,* (ed) Robert U. Johnson and Clarence C. Ruel, New York, The Century Co., 1884-1887, Vol. I, pp. 91-93. Hereafter cited as *Battles & Leaders.*
[54] XII *Stat.* 270.
[55] *O.R.* Series III, Vol. 5, p. 605.

Guided by this principle, the General in Chief refused permission to those young regulars who asked leave to accept commissions in State regiments.[56] As a result, many of these experienced young men were forced through circumstances to serve in subordinate capacities throughout the war. What effects a mass transfer of officers from the Regular Army would have had upon the Army remains a matter of conjecture. But there were many who felt that true policy would have been to encourage the whole of this younger class to enter at once the volunteer service.[57]

A look beyond the Regular Army, however, would have revealed a large source of trained and experienced officers who like McClellan and Grant were willing to come out of retirement to serve their country. The number that did so was sufficient to have staffed all of the responsible positions in the Union Army. Instead of making a judicious disposition of this available pool of trained officers, the selection of field officers was conducted as it had been during the Revolutionary War. And, while the shortcomings of such a policy were clearly apparent to the war Governors, the great need for field officers (as well as company officers) coupled with the limited resource of competent men in civil life, was sufficient inducement to appoint the ones who would produce the most agreeable consequences in the next election.[58] The importance attached to elections outweighed all other considerations to such an extent that the Governors succeeded in forcing the Government to grant furloughs from active service to enable the men to get back home to vote. Absentee ballots were unheard of, nor could they be as reliable as having Johnny back home to show his gratitude by voting right.[59]

Since willingness to lead is not the equivalent of ability, many of the selections made in this manner and by elections "ranged in ability from technical ignorance to gross incompetence and total incapacity to learn." [60] McClellan in later years was wont to speak of some selected in this manner as unfitted from their education, moral character, or mental deficiencies for ever acquiring the

---

[56] See Upton, *op. cit.*, pp. 242-243.

[57] *Battles & Leaders* I, p. 94. According to this viewpoint the South profited by the lack of a Regular Army because their experienced officers were distributed among the volunteer forces.

[58] Shannon, *op. cit.*, Vol. I, p. 156, 158.

[59] Hesseltine, *op. cit.*, pp. 341, 357. Emory Upton labelled this practice a subsidy to the Governors. See Upton, *op. cit.*, p. 438.

[60] Shannon *op. cit.*, Vol. I, p. 160.

requisite efficiency.[61] Two days before the first battle of Bull Run, the victor of Antietam begged the War Department to give him some general officers who understood their profession.[62] Later in that year General Robert Anderson informed the President: "You will confer a favor on me by not appointing any more civilians brigadiers. I would rather let the colonels compete by gallant deeds for these positions." [63]

However well-intentioned the President and his Secretary of War may have been, the determination of the Governors to promote their own interests, coupled with the onslaught of office seekers and political cronies, rendered it difficult if not impossible to do otherwise than give at least tacit assent to such a system. But by allowing it to continue, it became progressively worse. This was not due to the officers themselves; on the contrary, many were to distinguish themselves in battle before the war ended. It was rather due to the pernicious practice of appointing new officers who were still at home and could exert political influence, rather than promote those who were still in the field. "Worse than denying them promotion," says Upton, "those who remained faithfully at their posts had the mortification of seeing many worthless officers, who had been dismissed or compelled to resign, come back to the field with increased rank and command." [64]

After seventy-five years of experience as a nation which witnessed three wars with foreign governments together with the incessant Indian wars, Americans came to realize the wisdom of Washington, Alexander Hamilton, Calhoun, and also Poinsett with reference to additional military academies[65] or "seminaries"

---

[61] George B. McClellan, *McClellan's Own Story*, New York, Charles L. Webster & Co., 1887, p. 97.

[62] *O.R.* Series I, Vol. 2, p. 288. McClellan also sought the assistance of the President in this matter. See ltr, McClellan to Lincoln, July 17, 1861, *Lincoln Mss, The Manuscript Collection of Abraham Lincoln*, Library of Congress, Vol. 50, p. 10779. Hereafter cited as *Lincoln Mss*. General William T. Sherman was plagued with the same problem. See ltr Sherman to Lincoln, October 9, 1861, *ibid.*, Vol. 58, p. 12385. The appearance of civilians in higher grades in some cases brought forth insubordination from subordinate regular officers. See ltr R. D. Goodwin to Lincoln, August 22, 1861, *ibid.*, Vol., 53, p. 11325.

[63] Anderson to Lincoln, September 28, 1861, *ibid.*, Vol. 56, p. 12097.

[64] Upton, *op. cit.*, p. 437. Beginning with the Act of July 22, 1861, Boards of Officers were created to determine the ability and efficiency of the newly appointed officers. Many of those who were declared by these boards as unfit to command were re-appointed by the State authorities to command in new units. See XII *Stat.* 270. See also XIII *Stat.* 181; Rpt Surgeon General, October 20, 1864 in War Department Annual Reports, 1864-1865, p. 99.

[65] For the year 1864 twenty-seven cadets graduated from West Point. See Rpt S/W, *W.D. Ann Rept*, 1864-1865, p. 7.

wherein the curriculum would prepare men for their duties as officers and leaders. The ROTC system was advocated as early as 1781 when Washington's lieutenants were giving their views on a "Peacetime Military Establishment." Washington's pleadings for peacetime preparations for war emergencies envisaged the preparation of citizens not only to follow but also to lead.

The Bounty

The offer of monetary inducement as a stimulant to bring forth a proper appreciation of the obligations of citizenship in a national crisis, though deplorable in previous wars, reached scandalous proportions during the Civil War. During the first few months of the war no bounty was offered simply because Congress was not in session. But within the States themselves, widespread patriotic exhuberance brought forth a generous offer of bounties as an expression of gratitude. After the first Battle of Bull Run the local bounties were multiplied quickly in the effort to fill the ranks with volunteers. Before very long this practice became so unwieldy that the States, in trying to keep their own individual manpower pools filled, began to offer inducements to citizens of other States and in the ensuing *melee* the recruit often sold his services to the highest bidder.[66]

By July 22, 1861 the Federal Government was awarding a bounty of $100 to all volunteers or regulars enlisting for three years and serving at least two years or for the duration.

> Better results could undoubtedly have been obtained by simply adding four dollars a month to the pay of the soldiers. This would have made the immediate prospect of army service more attractive, would have been more easily administered, would have avoided later complications in the distribution of the payments, and would have put the pay of the soldiers on a strictly business basis.[67]

Under the Act of July 17, 1862 the States, reluctant to experiment with a draft of the militia, began to increase the offer in the effort to get volunteers rather than draftees. In the competition that followed between the States and the Government, the former could offer larger cash payments than the War Department. Therefore

---

[66] Shannon, *op. cit.*, Vol. II, p. 53. This authority refers to the bounty as "The Mercenary Factor." See also Randall, *Constitutional Problems Under Lincoln*, pp. 249-250.
[67] Shannon, *op. cit.*, Vol. II, pp. 53-54.

candidates leaned toward the State system of recruiting. Although the Government bounty was larger, it was not paid until the termination of service. On the other hand, the States offered less but it was cash, tempting to the recruit and to the bounty broker.[68]

The system of substitution had also been in vogue in previous wars. But by this time it had become a vicious scheme on the part of the individual offering his services and on the part of the "substitute broker" who engaged in bringing seller and buyer together while the Government gave assent. It was simply another recruiting device which began as a "democratic" gesture of substitution where a man could offer his services for his brother, his father, or even his neighbor. It became pernicious when it served the purpose of those who could afford to buy such services. When the monetary consideration was turned to serve the interests of the "seller" it became scandalous in the eyes of those who had to pay. Before very long this commodity sold at prices which made even the rich balk. Congress stepped in and halted the spiral by the law of March 3, 1863.

In a sense the Enrollment Act operated as a price control device by limiting the price of a substitute to 300 dollars. Thereafter anyone seeking immunity from military service paid the Government the stipulated sum whereupon a substitute was enrolled.[69] This sum was then paid to the person offering his services. The injustices of this system led to a loud clamor which Congress could not disregard. On July 4, 1864 the commutation clause was repealed, but the privilege of procuring substitutes was continued.[70]

The effect of all this was to raise the bounty from one hundred dollars to four hundred. At this time, losses through normal attrition, desertion, and battle casualties exceeded the rate of enlistment in the Regular Army. Fearful of the consequences in allowing this condition to continue, a bounty of 402 dollars was offered to all men enlisting, within a ninety-day period, in the Regular Army. Similar advantages were allowed to the three-year volunteers already serving who would within a limited period reenlist for an additional three years.[71] While this was gradually offered

---

[68] *Ibid.*, p. 54-55. Rhode Island at this time was offering $350 over and above any other bounties the soldier might receive. *Ibid.*, p. 59.
[69] See Rpt PMG, November 15, 1864, Rpt S/W, 1864-1865, p. 56.
[70] XIII *Stat.* 379.
[71] *O.R.* Series III, Vol. 3, p. 414. This increased bounty brought about a levelling off in the system of substitution and subsequent legislation began to define more accurately the status of the substitute. See XIII *Stat.* 6, 10, 379, 380.

to all volunteers, within a short time Congress decided to terminate this huge expenditure.

On December 23, 1863, by joint resolution Congress declared that after January 5, 1864, "no bounties, except such as are now provided by law, shall be paid to any persons enlisted after the fifth day of January next." [72] This meant that resort must be had to the draft without compensation in the form of a gratuity. In recognition of this fact, the War Department opened the doors on enlistments and the current bounties to encourage recruits.

Meanwhile Secretary Stanton and the Provost Marshal General prevailed upon the President to review the new law in its effects upon the veteran soldiers. Based upon information received in the War Department prior to the enactment of the resolution, it was indicated that a very large proportion of the forces then in service would have cheerfully reenlisted for three years under the terms authorized. But a careful check revealed that such enlistments would be stopped by the restrictions imposed by the action of Congress.[73]

Convinced that veteran soldiers, even when paid the bounty, constitute a cheaper force than raw recruits or drafted men without bounty, the President urged Congress to extend the payment of bounties at least until February 1, 1864.[74] Those recommendations and the Congressional response was dictated by the necessity for party unity in the coming Presidential election. On March 3 the joint resolution of Congress extended the bounty to April 1, and on July 4, a new law made provision to pay a bounty of 100, 200, and 300 dollars to volunteers enlisted for one, two, or three years respectively.[75] With this arrangement, the nation moved toward Appomattox.

---

[72] XIII *Stat.* 400.
[73] *O.R.* Series III, Vol. 4, p. 5.
[74] *Ibid.*, Richardson M&P. 195.
[75] XIII *Stat.* 403, 379.

CHAPTER 9

The Civil War—Strategy

The War Cabinet—Logistical Problems—Civil-Military
Relationship—McClellan Assumes Command—The Navy
—Disunion and the Confederacy

The War Cabinet

IT WAS in the selection of the Cabinet that President Lincoln
made perhaps his greatest mistake of the war. Forced by political necessity and promises made for him at the nominating convention, the War Office portfolio was tendered to Simon Cameron
of Pennsylvania. At a time when the country was threatened by
the wilful acts of South Carolina, the War Department became the
most important single office in the nation. Upon it was thrust the
responsibility for immediately initiating steps to give stamina to the
national administration by creating the military force which had
been sadly neglected through the years. Here rested the responsibility for organizing, regulating, and directing the multifarious activities concerned with the disruptive transition from peace to war.

Wisdom and sagacity demanded an honest, efficient, courage-
ous, and indefatigable director of the War Department. But the
discipline of party and the discharge of a political bargain brought
to the War Department a man who would use his office as a dis-
pensary for political favors. The catalog of shady deals and manipulations of which he is accused is well known.[1] The effect of this
loose conduct upon the war effort goes beyond the mere tabula-
tion of errors. According to one authority on this subject, if examples were sought on how not to run a war department in a
national crisis, no better demonstration could be found than the
activities of Simon Cameron in the first six months of the war.[2]

Equally significant in the detrimental effect upon the war effort was the strained relationships existing within the Cabinet.

---

[1] For a vivid description of these deals and manipulations see Burton J. Hendrick, *Lincoln's War Cabinet*, Boston, Little Brown & Co., 1946, pp. 219-227.
See also Shannon, *op. cit.*, Vol. I, pp. 57, 59, 61-62; Meneely, *op. cit.*, pp. 264-
267; Fletcher Pratt, *Stanton: Lincoln's Secretary of War*, New York, W. W.
Norton & Co., 1953, pp. 131-132.
[2] Hendrick, *op. cit.*, p. 223.

Secretary of State Seward reportedly refused to serve on the same Cabinet with Salmon P. Chase,[3] and he loathed Gideon Welles the Secretary of the Navy. Secretary Cameron did not have a single friend in the President's official family except Seward.[4] Hence, while the Cabinet should have been of assistance to the President, it was wracked by petty jealousies; and at its first meeting on March 6, 1861, while events were rapidly moving toward war, nothing was accomplished.[5] Against this backdrop of political indecision, dissension, and jealousy, the grand design of war was to be outlined. Upon this Cabinet and the President rested the responsibility for gearing peaceful America to a war economy, for the conduct of the large scale operations on land and sea, for preserving intact the principles of the Monroe Doctrine, and for the maintenance of international equilibrium with reference to the question of blockading the southern coastline.

Logistical Problems

It was upon the War Department that the most important responsibilities would be placed initially. With but a small and widely scattered Army on hand, and with no plans in existence for conducting a war, the immediate question of supply and equipment for the vast armies that would soon be summoned to duty could not effectively be answered. Existing plans envisaged the equipping of only the small peacetime force but it was not until after the first calls were made that serious reflection was made upon the Federal incapacity to meet the needs of a vastly increased military establishment. When finally it became apparent that much ordnance equipment and other essential items of supply had to be secured in the foreign markets, Federal agents discovered that the Confederates had made first inroads on this source.

With no reserves of food, clothing, and equipment, and lacking a proper staff organization to undertake the huge task of initial supply and equipment, the War Department was forced to rely upon the States. In the pattern of the methods employed during the Revolutionary War, the States were asked to supply and equip the men with the promise of financial reimbursement at a later

---

[3] See James G. Randall, *Lincoln The President,* New York, Dodd Mead & Co., 1945, Vol. I, p. 291.

[4] Hendrick, *op. cit.,* pp. 72, 128.

[5] Randall, *Lincoln The President,* Vol. I, p. 313.

date.[6] This relieved some pressure but the still larger problem of transportation was to be solved as the war progressed.

In the disorganized state of the War Department during the early period of the war, the decentralized procurement activities created havoc and gave rise to all the vicious practices employed during previous wars. Frauds of every description went unchecked and even reached the War Department itself. Until Cameron was replaced on January 13, 1862, the vicious practices which grew out of the competition between State and Federal authorities created huge profits for many but gave to the Army an ill assortment of inferior supplies.[7] Despite the large numbers of people engaged in procurement, the troops in many instances did not receive their supplies when needed.

To effect a system of procurement and disbursement of supplies and materiel, the initial burdens fell upon the Quartermaster, Ordnance, Commissary, Medical, and Adjutant General's Bureaus. Whatever efficiency could be commanded here was to rest with the "old men" who headed up these offices, whose staffs were small and incapable of expansion under existing laws.[8] After Lincoln's first call, the stocks of supplies were either quickly exhausted or were not distributed properly. Furthermore Cameron did not improve this condition when, on April 23, he relieved Colonel Craig as Chief of the Ordnance Bureau.

Ordnance supplies became critical almost immediately. Although reportedly there were 475,000 muskets and rifles in the United States, complaints were registered everywhere for want of them. The Governors were loud in their protests against the failure of the Government to furnish arms.[9] Few of these executives, however, were willing to acquaint themselves with the history of the preceding seventy-five years which was replete with instances of Governmental indifference and neglect of the military establishment. In their haste to forget these lessons, the statesmen neglected to reason that even under more favorable conditions than those existing, supplies and equipment could not be written into existence where they were most needed. Once again the mistakes of the past were cropping up to annoy and distress Americans.

[6] See *O.R.* Series III, Vol. 1, p. 132. This system accelerated the inflationary spiral during the Revolutionary War.
[7] See Shannon, *up. cit.*, Vol. I, pp. 56-57.
[8] Meneely, *op. cit.*, pp. 110-111.
[9] *O.R.* Series III, Vol. 1, p. 89; Series I, Vol. 2, pp. 730-731.

On April 19, 1861, one week after the attack upon Fort Sumter, Major General Patterson, who was in the vicinity of the main Quartermaster Depot in Philadelphia[10] with a force he had collected there, was unable to march to Washington because many of the men were without muskets, and all were without ammunition, service clothing, greatcoats, and blankets. Although there was an abundance of these items at Frankfort and Gray's Ferry arsenals, it was impossible to procure them without an order from the War Department.[11] This attitude on the part of civil officials in Philadelphia surprised General Patterson but what was even more astonishing was the palpable neglect of the Secretary of War to see to this problem initially. Three weeks later Major General George Cadwalader, commanding the Department of Pennsylvania, reported that some of his regiments were issued muskets entirely unfit for use. "Most of the springs of the locks are broken," he said. "And those that are not will not explode a cap." [12]

As the armies advanced into Virginia and the west in July, 1861, the commanding officers repeatedly complained about the lack of supplies and clothing. General J. M. Schofield on July 15 was forced to abandon any further advancement in the west, and confessed he could not hold for very long. He stated that his troops were badly clothed, poorly fed, and improperly supplied with tents, and that the three months' volunteers had become disheartened to such an extent that very few of them were willing to renew their enlistment.[13]

When Congress met on July 4, the report of the Secretary of War recited the difficulties visited upon the Quartermaster Bureau by the press of war. Because of this it was urged that every facility should be afforded its chief for meeting with promptness all requisitions.[14] But because of the shortage of personnel and management, recourse was necessarily had to State contracts; this system of local

[10] Three other depots were located at New York, Chicago, and St. Louis.

[11] Patterson to Scott, April 19, 1861, *O.R.* Series I, Vol. 2, p. 579.

[12] Cadwalader to Major F. J. Porter, May 6, 1861, *ibid.*, p. 626. See also ltr of May 9, 1861, *ibid.*, pp. 631-632. Much of this was the result of the forced reliance upon foreign supply. See H. A. DeWeerd, "American Adoption of French Artillery, 1917-1918," *Military Affairs*, Vol. 3, p. 104.

[13] *O.R.* Series I, Vol. 3, p. 395. During the winter of 1863-1864, the transportation system in the vicinity of Alabama was all but suspended. This left the troops without badly needed items of issue. See Frank Moore, *The Civil War in Song and Story, 1860-1865*, New York, P. F. Collier, 1889, pp. 370-371.

[14] Rpt S/W, July 1, 1861, pp. 25-27.

supply was continued throughout the war despite repeated admonitions from the Quartermaster General himself.[15]

With reference to the procurement of arms, the private contract system was also continued although some steps were taken by the Government to check the increased price-fixing combinations set up among manufacturers, importers, and agents.[16] By 1864 the capacity of American arsenals for the manufacture of munitions began to approach a maximum. A survey showed among other things that Springfield Arsenal could turn out 300,000 muskets annually. However, even at this late date breech-loading arms were still not in use in this country.[17]

Although graft and fraud were widespread under the contract system for supplying the Army with needed supplies and materiel, the development of the railroad as a strategic concept in warfare limited the scope of these wrongdoings. Once the supplies had been accumulated, the railroads transported them to the armies in the field or to convenient concentration points. On February 11, 1862 the operation of the railroads as well as the telegraph system was placed under the control of the War Department and thereafter these operations ceased to pose any difficulty in the over-all strategy.[18]

But the railroad did not solve all the problems of transportation. There were some areas where wagon trains could not be replaced. In mid-July, 1861 while Patterson was operating around Martinsburg, Virginia, he was prevented from joining the main Union force because of a dire need for ample transportation for supplies and baggage.[19] This was the result of the response to the popular clamor for a quick march on Richmond. Few understood or had any conception of the time and labor required to bring this host of almost 50,000 men to a condition of readiness for such a venture. To meet these requirements it was necessary to procure

> seven hundred and fifty wagons, three thousand horses, and almost a thousand teamsters, to carry provisions, tents, intrench-

---

[15] Shannon, *op. cit.*, Vol. I, p, 100.
[16] Rpt S/W, December 1, 1861, pp. 7-8.
[17] Rpt S/W, 1864-1865, pp. 5-6. It is significant to note that at the outbreak of the war, the Government had in its possession, machinery, shops, and power to make 40,000 stand of arms a year but appropriations limited the output to 18,000. This was sufficient for the Regular Army in peacetime but not for the militia. See Meneely, *op. cit.*, p. 49.
[18] From the very beginning of the war, however, the railroad and telegraph officials heartily cooperated with the Government.
[19] *O.R.* Series I, Vol. 2, p. 166.

ing tools for an army of fifty thousand men, such as was ordered to engage in the business of going forward to Richmond. These wagons had to be made, and the horses purchased, and the teamsters engaged. Only about ten weeks had been allowed for these preparations to be made, when *"Forward to Richmond!"* was the war-cry of the people.[20]

Toward the end of the war the faulty policies for procurement and distribution of supplies became more sharply defined by the threats emanating from Mexico directly, and indirectly from France and England. Earlier in the war, France, in open violation of the Monroe Doctrine, placed Archduke Maximilian of Austria-Hungary in power in Mexico.[21] Furthermore, while France and England remained sympathetic to the South, the exposed nature of California drew more than passing notice from the State, War, and Navy Departments. On February 17, 1864 the precariousness of this situation was outlined by the Commander of the Department of the Pacific in a request for 10,000 rifles, 8,000 pistols, 40,000 rifled muskets, and 9,000 sabers.[22]

Civil-Military Relationship

It is generally agreed in the United States that the control and direction of a war is the function primarily of the statesman. Only a government can begin a war and decide upon the measures necessary to bring it to a successful conclusion. That being the case, policy is the master and strategy the servant. The responsibility of the military commander who is chosen to implement the decisions of government is to crush the main armed forces of the enemy. To this end,

> all military efforts must be concentrated against the center of gravity of the enemy's main armed forces and action must be swift and resolute. It follows that the secret of success in war lies in maintaining harmony between policy and strategy; and this in turn depends upon both statesmen and military commanders seeing things as they really are. They must understand war.[23]

---

[20] Benson J. Lossing, *Pictorial History of the Civil War,* Philadelphia, George W. Childs, 1866, Vol. I, p. 580, fn 2. See also Meneely, *op. cit.,* p. 188. The correspondence in the *Lincoln Mss* is also illuminating with reference to deficiencies of every sort. See Vol. 75, pp. 15964, 15973, 15983; Vol. 76, pp. 16016, 16138, 16159, 16201; Vol. 80, pp. 16852, 16988.
[21] See Frank Owsley, *King Cotton Diplomacy,* Chicago, Univ. of Chicago, 1931, pp. 533-539.
[22] *O.R.* Series I, Vol. 50, pt II, p. 756.
[23] J. M. Scammel, "Spencer Wilkinson and the Defense of Britain," *Military Affairs,* Vol. 4, p. 134.

Working out a proper balance between the civil and military requires statesmanship of a high order, on the part both of the civil executive and military commander. This formula was lacking during the first three years of the war.

It has already been noted that within the President's own official family the undercurrents of discord threatened to upset the Administration. And, if this were not enough to drive the President to distraction, the disaster at Ball's Bluff coupled with the Radical suspicion of Lincoln's war aims[24] incited the Radicals to create an investigating committee whose assigned mission was to observe closely every military movement or plan of operation and to hold military commanders to strict accountability for defeat. Therefore before the end of the first year, the President, the Secretaries of State, War, Navy, and the Treasury, together with the Congressional Committee each claimed special powers over the conduct of the war. All of this meant constant interference with the plans of military commanders by civil authorities who were uninitiated in military affairs. It was clearly demonstrated in the Civil War that these authorities are on dangerous ground when they undertake the direction of military operations in the field.

Invading the province of the Presidential Office, the Committee went far in its investigations of the fitness of appointed officers and established a peculiar norm for military ability and stupidity. Military genius was measured in terms of political allegiance. Hence only the Republicans of the "Radical" breed could be capable. Democrats like McClellan and Don Carlos Buell had no right, in their estimation, to lead the armies of freedom; and, if these generals did not move as swiftly as the Committee and other Radicals wished, they were branded as pro-Southern traitors. But during the first three years of war, Lincoln, in no position to challenge the legality of the Congressional Committee, bore it as a painful thorn in his side.[25]

Interference in military operations was not limited to the Congressional Committee. Lincoln himself on frequent occasions interposed his will upon military commanders. Untutored in the art of

---

[24] The Committee to investigate the Conduct of the War was created in December 1861. It constantly interfered with the conduct of the war. See Hendrick, *op. cit.*, pp. 280-281.

[25] Professor Randall held the view that Lincoln saw the Constitution, in time of war, as restraining Congress more than the President. Randall, *Civil War and Reconstruction*, p. 385.

warfare, and without the benefit of a modern staff organization to aid him with professional skill and advice, the President sought these wherever he could find them. Without regard for the office of General in Chief, he was in constant communication with officers in the field. Suspicion, among the leading politicians, of Winfield Scott's ability had brushed off on the President. It was difficult, Lincoln thought, to place much reliance upon a man who was older than the capital, and who had to be helped into his carriage.[26]

McClellan Assumes Command

The immediate problems growing out of the attack on Fort Sumter were just as puzzling to the aged Scott as they were to the President and the Secretary of War. But viewing the situation as a soldier, it was obvious that the war could not be won by a handful of ninety-day militiamen. Success could only be achieved by creating an army of 300,000 men. This would require time and patience. Scott regarded the call for 75,000 militia as a stop-gap measure until Congress could be assembled. Meanwhile he urged his views upon the President. However, influential congressmen were not inclined to be patient with the plan of a gout-ridden general to "waste" four or five months on the meticulous training of Americans.

The plain fact was that in the frenzied condition of the North, the immediate aim was revenge for the wanton attack upon the flag. Sober reflection and considered judgment, however, would have made clear that some time was necessary to gear the peace structure to a war psychology; and that the war had to be planned in all essentials if the submission of the South was to be secured. While all this was apparent, the very fact that it required time, and because it was recommended by Scott who was considered too old to make a clear decision, the plan ran against the wishes of those who clamored for revenge. "On to Richmond" was the slogan, and few were willing to acknowledge the wretched condition of America's preparedness for such a venture.

When it was finally proved on the battlefield of Bull Run that Scott was correct, sanity replaced emotion. The country was ready to settle down to an orderly pursuit of objectives. General Mc-

---

[26] Margaret Leech, *Reveille in Washington,* New York, Garden City Pub. Co., 1945, pp. 1-13, 62. See Charles C. Tansill, "A Secret Chapter in Civil War History," *Thought,* June, 1940, Vol. 15, pp. 215 ff.

Clellan had displayed a tendency to win victories while McDowell with the same kind of troops was humiliated by defeat. McClellan's name suddenly became a household word. Conscious of this public sentiment, President Lincoln summoned him to command the troops around Washington.

On July 25, the Division of the Potomac was created, with "Little Mac" in command. The following day he reached the city. What he found there was an ill-assortment of soldiers many of whom were drunk and under no discipline, a situation which was "fraught with great danger." [27] Less than two weeks later, McClellan had replaced chaos with order. He then pursued his job with greater vigor and the full support of the President, Congress, and the War Department.[28] In his relations with Scott, McClellan found the aged general to be a handicap, so that soon (November 1, 1861) McClellan became General in Chief as well as commander of the Army of the Potomac.[29]

Every manifestation of confidence had been directed toward the new "Napoleon," but even the Little Emperor would have acknowledged the impossible situation into which McClellan was thrown by the dual command status thrust upon him. This meant that while the work of training and preparing the Army of the Potomac for the invasion of Virginia continued unabated, his attention was also drawn towards the other Military Departments and theaters of operations. The over-all plans became his responsibility. Recruitment, supply, training and equipment, as well as troop movements in every quarter had to be dovetailed into his master plan. But here he ran into the same difficulties that had plagued Scott. The President had not overcome his habit of by-passing his military experts; his frequent communications with generals in the field, outside the normal channel of military command, even brought a mild warning from his private secretary John Nicolay.[30]

Under ordinary circumstances, there was a fair chance of

---

[27] *McClellan's Own Story*, pp. 68-69. Leech *op. cit.*, pp. 108-109. The country hailed him as another Napoleon. See Philadelphia *Inquirer*, August 26, 1861.
[28] Meneely, *op. cit.*, p. 194.
[29] See ltr McClellan to Lincoln August 2, 1861, *Lincoln Mss*, Vol. 51, 10983-10984; August 10, 1861, *ibid.*, Vol. 52, pp. 11143-11144.
[30] Nicolay to Lincoln, October 17, 1861, *ibid.*, Vol. 58, p. 12518. This practice was common at this time. Scott complained bitterly that McClellan went over his head in dealing with the President. See ltr Scott to Cameron, October 4, 1861, *ibid.*, Vol. 57, pp. 12291 ff; August 12, 1861 *ibid.*, Vol. 52, pp. 11187-88.

success. In these extraordinary times, however, the prospect of success was sharply modified by many factors over which Mc-Clellan had no control. There was the selection of officers conducted by the President and the Congressional Investigating Committee, which chagrined every successor to General Scott.[31] There was also the question of espionage which was carried out by such enticing creatures as the notorious double-spy, Mrs. Rose Greenhow, who succeeded in penetrating the shield of military security.[32] And there was the attitude of the Committee toward McClellan because he was a Democrat.

One month after McClellan was elevated to supreme command of the armies in the field, he was besieged by demands to advance into Virginia. The tremendous task of shaping into an army the disorderly mob which thronged the city of Washington had been four months under way, the system of supplies was not working smoothly, transportation to equip and supply an army of 100,000 men was still inadequate, the movement of the forces in the west had to be coordinated with the advance of the Army of the Potomac, and the Confederates had effected a blockade of the Potomac River. These and hundreds of other problems which become the lot of any supreme commander were of small consequence to the press and itinerant politicians who howled against the delay.

Then on December 2, 1861 the experiment in civil control over the Army in wartime was launched as an investigation to determine future war policies. The Senate made it clear that military failures would not be tolerated. The Committee proceeded to usurp Executive powers. And although none of the members of the Committee had any military experience except as interested spectators at parades, they felt qualified to examine into every aspect of military affairs. Filled with profound contempt for professional military men, especially Democrats, they ridiculed the idea that military science was a specialized technical subject, and

---

[31] Hendricks, *op. cit.*, p. 281. In 1862, General Henry W. Halleck as General in Chief complained excitedly about the part politics played in the Army. George Fort Milton, *Abraham Lincoln and the Fifth Column*, New York, Vanguard Press, 1942, p. 73.

[32] She entertained such guests as Secretary Seward, Senator Wilson of Massachusetts, and many aides and clerks in the Government service. Leech, *op. cit.*, p. 95. See also Ben Perley Poore, *Perley's Reminiscences*, Philadelphia, Hubbard Bros., 1886, Vol. II, pp. 111-112; Louis A. Siguad "Mrs. Greenhow and the Rebel Spy Ring," *Maryland Historical Magazine*, September 1946, Vol. 41.

could find no reason why the average American could not "make himself a master of military science in a short time." [33]

Precautionary measures advanced by commanders to insure a safe retreat were bitterly criticized by the Committee as indicating a lack of resolve to win battles. On this point Benjamin Wade censured McClellan's plan to construct a bridge over the Potomac to provide the means for withdrawal in safety. With 150,000 of the best troops in the world, Wade declared, there was no need of a bridge. McClellan's plain duty, as Wade saw it, was to take the men over to fight, and if they could not defeat the enemy, "let them come back in their coffins." [34]

After more delay occasioned by McClellan's illness and the President's reluctance to accede to his general's plan for crushing Richmond, the Army was ready to move. But on the eve of the operation, Lincoln fell in with the Committee's plan to limit McClellan's authority and from that time on Little Mac was restricted in the use of his army. On March 8, 1862, the Army of the Potomac was divided into five corps, four of whose commanders had refused to support McClellan in the councils of war. In addition to limiting his authority over the Army, the Presidential order stripped McClellan of his title as General in Chief [35] and it was not until July 11 that another general was selected to fill this post.[36]

The story of McClellan's dilatory tactics, occasioned to a large extent by the constant interference of the Radical politicians who by now had even Secretary Stanton on their side, is too well known to be treated at length here. The correspondence between Lincoln and McClellan is filled with requests from the latter for reinforcements and more supplies, and with the President's replies in the negative.[37] Presidential patience soon gave out, with the aid of the

---

[33] See T. Harry Williams, "The Committee on the Conduct of War," *Military Affairs*, Vol. 3, p. 141. Also William Whatley Pierson, Jr., "The Committee on the Conduct of War," *American Historical Review*, Vol. 23, pp. 555-556, 144-145.

[34] Pierson, *op. cit.*, p. 567.

[35] See Pierson, *op. cit.*, p. 568; Williams, *op. cit.*, pp. 151-152, Randall, *Lincoln the President*, Vol. II, pp. 82-83; also Philadelphia *Inquirer*, March 10, 1862; also *O.R.* Series I, Vol. 50, pt. I, p. 938.

[36] *O.R.* Series III, Vol. 2, p. 217. Henry W. Halleck. In the meantime, the practice of direct communication from the generals in the field to the Secretary of War was carried on.

[37] McClellan to Lincoln, April 6, 1862, *Lincoln Mss*, Vol. 73, pp. 15404-15405; McClellan to Lincoln, April 6, 1862, *ibid.*, pp. 15407-15408; McClellan

Committee's constant clamor for McClellan's scalp, and early in July McClellan was relieved in favor of John Pope.

This was one of those instances, remarked an outstanding authority on President Lincoln,

> when the confused machinery of central military control played readily into the hands of scheming politicians and subjected the appointment and removal of generals to political interference. Though McClellan had not attained his object, he had by no means failed. The President, however, having withheld from his chief general the full use of the Union armies in the East, now submitted to the Radical clamor for his removal.[38]

The promotion of Pope was one of those amateurish experiments so often tried by the authorities in Washington.[39] Within a short time Pope would prove how wrong the Committee could be in preferring none but generals of their own political stripe.

While the Army of the Potomac straggled back toward Washington after the defeat at the second Manassas, Lincoln, fearful for the safety of the Capital hastily restored McClellan to command. Defeat was soon changed to victory on September 17 at bloody Antietam, where Lee was defeated. The desperate Confederate bid for a victory which would have meant the intervention of England and France in favor of the South was checked. Despite even the long procession of mediocre generals that was paraded at the head of the Union Armies until the coming of Grant, from then on the South could only hope for a possible mediation on agreeable terms. Antietam and not Gettysburg was the turning point of the war. It was only the Confederate failure in this campaign which persuaded the British Government not to intervene.[40]

But when McClellan failed to destroy or capture Lee's Army, the President could no longer ignore the urgings of such men as Governor Morton of Indiana who was convinced that "we will never succeed until the leadership in our armies is placed in the hands of men who are greatly in earnest and who are profoundly

---

to Lincoln, April 7, 1862, *ibid.*, pp. 15415-15416; Lincoln to McClellan, April 9, 1862, *ibid.*, pp. 15431-15433; Lincoln to McClellan, May 9, 1862, *ibid.*, Vol. 75, pp. 15856; Lincoln to McClellan, July 2, 1862, *ibid.*, pp. 16744-16745.
[38] Randall, *Civil War and Reconstruction*, p. 303. See Bernard A. Weisberger, *Reporters for the Union*, Boston, Little Brown & Co., 1953, p. 140.
[39] Randall, *Civil War and Reconstruction*, p. 303.
[40] Owsley, *op. cit.*, p. 360. See also Randall, *Lincoln the President*, Vol. 11, pp. 285-286. The dangers of foreign intervention were clearly foreseen by Governor Morton of Indiana. See Morton to Lincoln, October 7, 1862, *Lincoln Mss*, Vol. 89, p. 18925.

convinced of the Justice of our cause."[41] Having lost confidence in his general, the President relieved him for the second and last time.[42]

As successor to the command of the Army of the Potomac, Lincoln elevated General Ambrose E. Burnside whose incapacity soon led to the disaster at Fredericksburg on December 13, 1862.[43] Dissension among the officers in Burnside's command soon led to his dismissal and he was relieved by General Joseph Hooker on January 26, 1863.[44] Hooker soon found himself plagued with the same intrigues that besieged his predecessors,[45] a malady which remained unavoidable as long as the Congressional Committee interposed its will upon the conduct of the war.

With the victory over Lee at Gettysburg and the final elevation of Ulysses S. Grant to Lieutenant General [46] the problems gradually diminished and the war was at last brought to an end. Taken all in all, most of these perplexing difficulties of command and direction of the war effort could have been avoided if the politicians had remembered Madison's lamenting remarks as he viewed the ruins of the Capital in 1814: "Leave to the military functionaries the discharge of their own duties." Much of the difficulty also could have been eliminated if Lincoln had not left the office of General in Chief vacant from March 11 to July 11, 1862. It was during this three month period that the Secretary of War became one of the important advisers to the President on the conduct of the war; and when finally Halleck was appointed General in Chief, the pattern of civil control reduced that office to an advisory

---

[41] Morton to Lincoln, October 7, 1862, *Lincoln Mss,* Vol. 89, p. 18925. See also Lincoln to Carl Schurz, November 24, 1861, *ibid.,* Vol. 93, pp. 19731-19732.

[42] *O.R.* Series III, Vol. 2, p. 869. See also *O.R.* Series I, Vol. 19, pt. I, pp 10 ff.

[43] See Kendrick, *op. cit.,* p. 324. Burnside asked Lincoln to dismiss and relieve eight generals, one of whom was Joseph Hooker, and also eight colonels. See Ganoe, *op. cit.,* p. 286. Also ltr Burnside to Lincoln, January 5, 1863, *Lincoln Mss,* Vol. 99, p. 20971, 20973.

[44] See New York *Tribune,* January 27, 1863.

[45] See ltr Lincoln to Carl Schurz, April 11, 1863, *Lincoln Mss,* Vol. 108, p. 22920; Lincoln to Hooker, May 14, 1863, *ibid.,* Vol. 110, p. 23458; Lincoln to Hooker, June 16, 1863, *ibid.,* Vol. 114, p. 24160. By this time Lincoln had come to the conclusion that the objective of the Army of the Potomac was Lee's army and not Richmond. See Lincoln to Hooker, June 10, 1863, *ibid.,* Vol. 113, p. 23962.

[46] Poore, *op. cit.,* pp. 149-150. Grant was promoted on March 1, 1864. See Bruce Caton, *U. S. Grant and the American Military Tradition,* Boston, Little Brown & Co., 1954, pp. 116-119.

capacity.[47] In the quest for a formula to bring quick victory, the President permitted the experiments in military affairs conducted by Congress and the Secretary of War which could not but result in failure because of the inexperience of the experimenters.

The Navy

Although the Navy on the eve of the Civil War was stronger than at any previous period in American history, in the light of modern improvements in armored vessels, shell and shot, and steam navigation, it remained relatively weak. There were no iron-clads, and most of the vessels were of the smaller type and of light draft. However, this element of weakness became an advantage in the operations against the southern coasts and inlets whose shallow waters could easily be navigated by these lighter ships.[48]

The small fleet was so dispersed among the foreign stations that of twenty-six steamers only one was on the northern coast ready to operate against the enemy.[49] President Lincoln's proclamations of April 17 and 27, 1861 on the blockade emphasized the nation's naval weakness and hurried dispatches were issued ordering fifteen steamers back to home waters.[50] Ships laid up in ordinary were hastily prepared for sea duty and the Navy Department under Gideon Welles and his able assistant Gustavus V. Fox took further measures, before Congress assembled, to increase the size of the Navy.

Authorizing a number of naval officers, together with a group of civilians, to purchase or charter vessels from whatever source, a large fleet of vessels was hastily gathered together and distributed among four blockading squadrons. By the end of the first year of the war these numbered some three hundred vessels (blockaders) of varying design from hoary frigates and converted merchant

---

[47] Although the office was thus shorn of authority, the responsibility for military disaster rested with the General in Chief. The President could plan campaigns and order his generals to carry out his mandates, but under this system the people could never blame the President "for a reverse, if any shall come." See ltr James W. White to Lincoln, *Lincoln Mss*, Vol. 105, pp. 22206-22207. See also Upton, *op. cit.*, p. 320.

[48] See Paullin, "Naval Administration, 1842-1861," pp. 1448-1455. Sprout, *op. cit.*, pp. 151-152; Alfred T. Mahan, *From Sail to Steam*, pp. 31-32.

[49] Charles B. Boynton, *History of the Navy*, New York, D. Appleton & Co., 1867, Vol. I, p. 107.

[50] Dudley W. Knox, *A History of the United States Navy*, p. 195. This left only three vessels for duty abroad.

steamers to Ericsson's *Monitor*.[51] The magnitude of these purchasing and chartering activities naturally gave rise to cries of fraud and in some instances there was evidence of palpable collusion.[52] But such was the price to be paid when in the stress and strain of a national crisis resort had to be made to these dubious modes of providing for national defense.

Lifting a page from the episodes of the Revolutionary War, Massachusetts demanded the right to equip and man a navy of her own. Tactfully though firmly Welles reminded the Bay State leaders that State navies would not be tolerated. In answer to those Governors who wanted to raise a volunteer navy in the same manner as the volunteer regiments were being raised, and who insisted upon fitting out privateers to counter Jefferson Davis' privateers, the Secretary drew attention to the Treaty of Paris which outlawed that practice.[53] There would be one Navy, one code of laws, and one system of regulation to carry out the principal aims of naval strategy, blockade of the South, and cooperation with the land forces.

The strategy of the Federal Government called for a tight blockade of the southern coastline and command of the Mississippi River and Gulf of Mexico to split the Confederacy in two. Surrounded in this manner, the South would soon be forced to capitulate for want of foreign supplies. Although during the first year of the war the Federal blockade was merely a paper proclamation, during the remainder of the conflict the pinch of deprivation grew more intolerable. The Confederacy, unable to break through the cordon of ships, saw her resources rapidly being depleted. Surrender became inevitable.[54]

At the outset, however, the Southern challenge to domination of the coastal waters by the introduction of the ironclad *Merrimac* caused fear and consternation in the North. The epic of the *Monitor* and its victory over the Confederate "iron monster" presaged

[51] Richard S. West, Jr., *Gideon Welles: Lincoln's Navy Department,* Indianapolis, Bobbs-Merrill Co., 1943, p. 182.
[52] *Ibid.,* p. 125; Boynton, *op. cit.,* Vol. I, pp. 35-36; Meneely, *op. cit.,* pp. 266-267; Hendrick, *op. cit.,* p. 221. Welles' conduct in these purchases was beyond reproach.
[53] West, *op. cit.,* pp. 145-146.
[54] One authority called the blockade "hopelessly deficient and ineffective." Meneely, *op. cit.,* pp. 301-302. The Secretary of the Navy in his report for 1864 referred to the blockade as an undertaking without precedent in history. See Rpt S/N, December 5, 1864, pt. V.

the passing of the wooden ships as well as of the sailing vessels. Bolstered by such hard facts, Welles on March 25, 1862 outlined for Congress a bold plan for expanding the Navy according to the concepts developed from this naval engagement.

That titanic duel at Hampton Roads proved that steam was indispensable in naval warfare, but also that steam vessels without proper armament were useless against ironclads. Since the Navy as then constituted could not successfully contend against armored vessels, Welles recommended' the construction of ironclads on a scale commensurate with the great interests involved. To meet these needs the Secretary had placed orders for heavier guns of increased caliber, but because of the limited facilities for manufacturing these he urged the appropriation of $500,000 to improve the capacities at the Washington Naval Yard. Congress approved these measures and Welles immediately instituted the largest naval expansion the Nation had ever seen.[55] This was an open challenge to England and France, who lightly regarded, but refused to violate the blockade.

The chief threat to the blockade, however, came from the South whose primary objective was to bend every effort at breaking through. Realizing that a shortage of cotton would deter England and France from intervening in their behalf, Southern leaders made a desperate bid to break the blockade. The experiment with the clumsy *Merrimac* having failed, new weapons were sought in Europe. This brought about the introduction of the rams which threatened to sweep the oceans clear of Federal merchantmen. In turn, Welles admonished the naval captains to redouble their efforts to seize or destroy these destructive vessels. But as the summer of 1863 wore on and the defeat of Lee's Army at Gettysburg failed to bring an end to the war, the need for ironclad warships became more pronounced.[56]

As early as August 3, 1861 Congress authorized the Secretary of the Navy to appoint a board of naval officers to investigate the

---

[55] Quoted in West, *op. cit.*, pp. 185-187. The Navy grew from forty-two ships in March, 1861 to eighty-two July 4, 1861; to 264 in December 1861; to 427 in December 1862; to 588 in December 1863 to 671 in December 1864. See Randall, *Civil War and Reconstruction*, p. 574. cf. Davis, *A Navy Second to None*, p. 11.

[56] On July 4, 1863, almost simultaneously with Lee's defeat, Vicksburg surrendered. This battle set a brilliant record of naval cooperation with the Army. West, *op. cit.*, pp. 214-215; Knox, *op. cit.*, chapter 23.

possibilities of ironclads.[57] But so little had been done to collect and evaluate information on the value of such vessels that much time was spent in looking for bits of available data.[58] What Mr. Welles sought, however, was an ironclad of shallow draft to operate in the narrow harbors and inlets of the Southern coastline; but even after accepting Ericsson's model, no large scale production of the monitors was undertaken.

After the victories of Vicksburg and Gettysburg Welles rushed the construction of twenty light-draft monitors. By this time, however, it was seen that the effectiveness of monitors against well-defended fortifications left something to be desired; and their extreme vulnerability "to sinking from impairment of their water-tight integrity" [59] should have prompted the Secretary of the Navy to re-evaluate the merits of the monitors. Instead, these ships, which proved to be unseaworthy, were pushed to completion. Their effectiveness against the South, who had no modern striking naval force, was erroneously accepted as sound policy. Against a strong naval force they could do no better than augment the coast fortifications. It was apparent that America, even during the trying ordeal of Civil War, was still wedded to the strategic policy of passive defense. While statesmen continued to criticize and replace generals for adopting such a procedure, they could see no error in their acceptance of it.

Notwithstanding the handicaps of the monitors, the need for ironclads of shallow draft was extremely urgent. Because they were not in existence in sufficient numbers, operations in the Gulf areas had to be suspended, and smuggling operations on the Rio Grande arising from Napoleon's invasion of Mexico could not be checked.[60] These embarrassing conditions were the inevitable result of the failure to create the facilities adequate to the construction of ironclads.

Little could be done, however, while the national policy was modified by the political equation. In his annual report for 1862, Welles recommended the establishment of an "iron navy yard" at Philadelphia. This was challenged by New London. The result was that Congress, "confused by the conflicting opinions of experts,

---

[57] XII *Stat.* 286.
[58] West, *op. cit.,* p. 149.
[59] Knox, *op. cit.,* pp. 266, 267. See also Walter B. Wood and J. E. Edmonds, *The Civil War in the United States,* London, Methuen & Co., 1905, pp. 491-493.
[60] West, *op. cit.,* p. 240.

and sensitive to political considerations, indefinitely postponed the important matter of a government-operated iron yard." [61] In his report for 1864 the Secretary of the Navy, in measured phrases, directed the attention of Congress toward their consistent neglect in the matter of "iron yards." When hostilities commenced, he declared:

> our government had provided no suitable navy yard with machine shops and foundries to manufacture the necessary machinery for our rapidly increasing and expanding navy; but the department was compelled to rely on the few private establishments, which it could divert from other engagements, for the immense work that was calling out the resources of the nation.
>
> Great embarrassment was experienced in consequence of this neglect . . . and although the naval service and the country are suffering constantly from this neglect, measures for the establishment of a suitable navy yard for the construction and repair of iron vessels, their armature and steam machinery are still delayed. [62]

Intertwined with the problem of sufficient ships and facilities for their repair there was the question of personnel. At the outbreak of war the number of seamen remained under 9,000. [63] Of the 1,563 officers on the Navy list, 321 resigned to "go south." [64] On May 3, 1861 the President called for 18,000 seamen for the Navy. Recruiting progressed as the number of ships was increased.

But while monetary inducements for volunteers and substitutes for Army service were increased, they were withheld from the sailors. Hence the men leaned toward the more profitable Army service with the result that the ships remained short-handed. This was not corrected until February 24, 1864 when Congress by Joint Resolution made provision for the transfer of landsmen to the Navy. [65] Under the stimulus of this law and the resolve to diminish bounty payments, 22,930 enlistments were made in the naval serv-

---

[61] *Ibid.*, p. 223.

[62] Rpt S/N December 5, 1864, p. xxx. Welles also showed that experiments had been conducted on all types of coal and even of petroleum as a substitute for coal. *Ibid.*, p. xxix. He also urged the purchase of additional waterfront at Boston and Philadelphia to accommodate iron ships and recommended that thereafter every vessel-of-war be a steam vessel. *Ibid.*, pp. xliv-xlv; xxxvi.

[63] Paullin, "Naval Administration, 1842-1861," pp. 1457-1458.

[64] Milton, *Conflict, The American Civil War*, pp. 136-137. These officers did not all resign at the same time. From March 4, to July 4, 1861, some 259 either resigned or were dismissed. See Boynton, *op. cit.*, Vol. I, p. 104.

[65] XIII *Stat* 402-403. This law provided for an advance of three months' pay as a bounty "to be refunded to the treasury from any prize money to which such enlisted man may be entitled."

ice[66] together with a total of 3,568 transfers from the various military departments.[67] Although such large numbers were being enlisted during these late stages, the Secretary of the Navy reported that the want of seamen was still felt. The total strength of the Navy by the end of 1864 was placed at 45,000 men and 6,000 officers.[68]

Morale among the Navy officers remained weak because of the failure to provide rank relative with that held in the Army. The highest naval commission in 1861 was still captain. There was little satisfaction to be found in the awkward title of "flag officer" created by Congress in 1857 for a commander of a squadron.[69] Such an officer still remained, on the lists, a captain. Finally under the prodding of the Secretary of the Navy, Congress on July 16, 1862 passed a law creating the new grades of Commodore and Rear Admiral. To avoid promoting "aged" officers, the law was so constructed as to provide for the retirement of those who were too old for active service.[70]

The rapid increase in personnel, brought about by the law of February 24, 1864 made it necessary to make provisions for increasing the officer strength. From April 21 to July 4, 1864 four laws were enacted which created the machinery for selecting these men.[71] With an establishment of more than 50,000 officers and men, the Secretary of the Navy urged the creation of a rank commensurate with that of lieutenant general.[72] On December 21, 1864 the rank of Vice Admiral was created.[73]

At the war's end, the United States emerged with "the strongest Navy in the World," [74] despite tremendous losses in merchant tonnage. With this force, American foreign policy grew more vigorous and the resultant international overtones brought a

---

[66] Rpt PMG November 15, 1864, *Ann. Rpt S/W 1864-1865*, pp. 54-55.
[67] Rpt of the Adjutant General, October 31, 1864, *ibid.*, p. 20.
[68] Rpt S/N, December 5, 1864, pp. xxxiv-xxxv, xlv.
[69] XI *Stat* 442. See also Paullin, "Naval Administration, 1842-1861," p. 1466.
[70] XII *Stat* 583-587. See also West, *op. cit.*, p. 190.
[71] Act of April 21, 1864, XIII *Stat*, 53; Act of May 17, 1864, *ibid.*, p. 79; Act of June 25, 1864, *ibid.*, p. 183; Act of July 4, 1864, *ibid.*, p. 393. The last law made provision for the training of naval cadets in steam engineering.
[72] Rpt S/N, December 5, 1864, p. xxxiv. On March 1, 1864, Congress approved the rank of lieutenant general for the Army which was conferred upon Grant the next day.
[73] XIII *Stat* 420.
[74] Knox, *op. cit.*, p. 317. According to this authority the size of the Navy reached 626 vessels, sixty-five of which were ironclads. The enlisted strength stood at 51,500 men. Officer strength was between six and seven thousand.

healthy respect for the American eagle. With this show of force coupled with a huge reservoir of trained manpower (three million Federal and two million Confederate veterans) the peaceful attitude of the rest of the world toward the United States grew more pronounced. Although the thesis that might makes right is subject to severe criticism, in the case in point it became rather difficult to seriously challenge America's decisions. That the United States refused to exercise her power in the troubled international arena is strong testimony of the peaceful intentions of the American people. The great development of war potential insured the peace of the land and in so doing gave the lie to those who feared that a strong nation would always look for trouble.

Disunion and Confederacy

The decision of Southern leaders to settle by a clash of arms their differences with the Federal Government was made with their full knowledge that all the advantages lay with the North. In the South the white population numbered about 5,500,000 while for the rest of the United States it was 21,000,000. Although the South was making strides toward adjusting to an industrial economy,[75] the gigantic industries of the North completely dwarfed their Southern contemporaries. The North's 19,000 miles of railroad track was double that of the South, and in real wealth the North again was twice as rich. In addition, there was the tremendous potential of the industrial North to meet any emergency. The agrarian South could not match this. And, without a navy, the South was forced to improvise with each passing day of the war. Why, then, it may be asked, did the South, handicapped in this manner, elect to go to war rather than rely upon the genius of her statesmen to settle the outstanding differences through the orderly process of government?

To attempt an enumeration of the various reasons that have been advanced would be beyond the scope of this work. The answers, however, are to be found in the unity of purpose and the strong patriotic impulse of the Southern people. This was a war to defend their homes and their property against the aggression of the enemy, and there was a will to win.

From the very beginning, the strategy of the Confederacy was

---

[75] Textile mills, iron mines, coal mines, and blast furnaces though few in numbers were to be found scattered throughout the South.

aimed at securing foreign intervention in her behalf. Failing in this she hoped to be able to rely upon outside sources to make up the deficiencies in war materiel and supplies of every description. The large purpose of this strategy was a resolve first to fight defensively, secondly to bring about foreign intervention, and thirdly to maintain a continuous foreign supply market.

Defensive war and the will to win are somewhat incongruous, yet this was the policy adopted by Jefferson Davis and which ultimately led to the downfall of the Confederacy. In the first few months of the war, beyond making a strong concentration of force in Virginia, Davis had no positive military plan.[76] Despite his previous experiences as war Secretary under President Pierce and his broad grasp of military science and strategy, Davis committed the South to a policy of defensive warfare which at best could only create a stalemate.

Schooled in the hard facts of the Mexican War, where he had learned under Zachary Taylor that the best defense is a good offense, his policy for the conduct of the war should have been vigorous and decisive. At a time (during the first year) when the Federal Government was recruiting men for 90-day terms Davis had an army of 100,000 men enlisted for one year under competent leadership and equipped and disciplined to win a quick victory. But the golden opportunity slipped by. For the remainder of the war the Confederacy was plagued by the same problems which beset the North but which would materially lead to the collapse of the South while the North improved its position and solved those problems toward the end.

Without a Navy,[77] the Confederate Government settled down to a policy of passive defense, a policy which had been tested during the War of 1812 and which had led to the burning of the Capital. Strongly fortified coast defenses were successful in warding off an invasion at the point of contact but when the Mississippi River passed into Federal hands and the Union Armies closed in, like a giant pincer, on the heart of the Confederacy, the coast fortifications became useless. Similarly, the campaign to attack Richmond from the East, devised by McClellan and implemented

[76] Allen Tate, *Jefferson Davis: His Rise and Fall;* New York, Minton Balch & Co., 1929, p. 106.
[77] See Clifford Dowdey, *Experiment in Rebellion*, New York, Doubleday & Co. Inc., 1946, p. 72.

by Grant, neutralized the strongly defended positions along the coast. The defense of Richmond became the paramount objective.[78]

Accepting the limitations in resources, the Secretary of the Confederate Navy, Stephen Mallory, sought to improvise a fleet of some kind. The failure of the *Merrimac* emphasized the need for a fleet of raiders first to operate against the blockade and secondly to protect the South's own navy yards.[79] The commerce destroyers soon plied the ocean, wreaking havoc on Northern shipping; but from 1863 on, the attempt to break the blockade weakened. The South improvised to the utmost of its abilities but failed because of the preponderant resources of the North and because neither England nor France could be enlisted in a cause which could not win a signal strategic victory.

But even without a Navy, the South would have been more formidable if her manpower resources could have been mobilized adequately. Like the North, she had to refuse large numbers of volunteers during the first flush of patriotic rushing to the colors. But after the first year, the policy of the State Governments in their refusal to pool these resources for the common purpose of war dictated a need for a more forceful government policy. On April 16, 1862, one year before the Federal Government, the South enacted a conscription law.[80] In addition to laying down the procedure for conducting the draft, this law extended the term of service from twelve months to three years, and provision was also made for the employment of substitutes.

Since there was no provision for exempting certain classes this law threatened to disrupt the economy of the South. As it stood, workers in essential industries such as iron mines, foundries, and furnaces, in telegraph offices and the railroads, and ministers, educators, and hospital employees, were all subject to draft. To correct the maladjustments that were sure to arise from the operations of the draft, another law was passed on April 21. In application, this method of exempting essential personnel approached the

---

[78] Lincoln always remained fearful that a strong forward movement toward Richmond would be countered ·by a Southern movement toward Washington. For this reason he disagreed with McClellan's plan to go South by water. He preferred the land route by which all danger of an attack on the Capital would be eliminated.

[79] Dowdey, *op. cit.*, pp. 70-75.

[80] *O.R.* Series IV, Vol. I, pp. 1095-1097.

selective service system used by the United States in World War I and II.[81] Subsequent legislation overhauled the whole[82] system and on December 28, 1863 the obnoxious principle of substitution was repealed. [83]

However, despite the long strides taken toward bringing the manpower resources within the reach of the Government, the prolongation of the war made it increasingly difficult to meet the needs of the armies in the field.[84] Although it was even necessary to draft boys under eighteen and men over forty-five, the Confederate Secretary of War by April, 1864 was forced to remind his President that

> fresh material for the armies can no longer be estimated as an element of future calculation for their increase, and necessity demands the invention of devices for keeping in the ranks the men now borne on the rolls. . . . For conscription from the general population, the functions of this Bureau [Bureau of Conscription] may cease with the termination of the year 1864.[85]

Not only that the manpower was insufficient to keep the armies up to strength, but by 1864 even those in the ranks were ill fed, poorly clothed, and without even the medicinal facilities to fight off malaria and typhoid. The Confederate soldier looked like anything but a soldier. Dirty, ragged, and barefooted, he recalled to mind the heroes of Valley Forge. All that was left by 1865 was the will to carry on.

Although there were many contributing factors to the downfall of the Confederacy, the most important single element was the insistence upon States Rights. The South repeated the mistakes that were made in the Revolutionary War and the War of 1812. The States insisted upon, and succeeded in maintaining, strong

[81] cf. E. Merton Coulter, *The Confederate States of America, 1861-1865,* Louisiana State Univ. Press, 1950, pp. 315 ff; *O.R.* Series IV, Vol. 2, pp. 401-402. ary 17, 1864, *ibid.,* Series IV, Vol. 3, p. 178. On the same day a law authorized

[82] Act of September 27, 1862 *ibid.,* Series IV, Vol. 2, p. 160; Act of February the use of Negroes as laborers, *ibid.,* pp. 208-209. On March 30, 1865, provision was made to employ slaves as soldiers. One authority, however, says that not a single colored soldier reached the firing line. See Tate, *op. cit.,* p. 277.

[83] *O.R.* Series IV, Vol. 3, p. 11; Vol. 2, pp. 648, 808.

[84] There was widespread opposition to the law, and its operation contributed to widespread desertion. Robert S. Henry, *The Story of the Confederacy,* Indianapolis, Bobbs Merrill Co., 1931, p. 125. A. B. Moore, *Conscription and Conflict in the Confederacy,* New York, The Macmillan Co., 1924, *passim* cf. Richmond *Dispatch,* April 4, 1862.

[85] *O.R.* Series III, Vol. 5, p. 695.

forces within their own boundaries[86] thereby defeating the larger purpose of the Confederacy. Because of this no general strategy for the whole war could be evolved, and the divided counsels within the Government, and between the States and the Government, focused the war through the narrow lens of localism. Instead of strong concentration of forces at several strategic points, the narrow views of the States forced a dispersion of strength which was no small factor in the loss of the Mississippi and the final collapse.[87]

However, before Lee was to surrender to Grant at Appomattox Court House, the South was to lay down some broad concepts for future wars. Handicapped by meager resources, the Confederacy exploited every available weapon and tactic to the utmost of its adaptability. Unable to float a large number of fighting ships, the Confederates took to such defensive tactics as marine mines and torpedoes. In land warfare, they laid belts of land mines that should have prepared tacticians for the experiences of World War II. Experiments were also conducted to improve upon the destructive capacity of artillery shells and there was even talk of filling the skies with flying machines "each loaded with fifty pounds of bombs" which could be "dropped on the enemy armies and navies and terminate the war immediately." [88] A small beginning was also made in aerial observation by means of balloons though McClellan's use of balloons for these purposes outstripped the Confederate attempt.[89]

Many other valuable lessons could be derived from a close study of the war on both sides. Many of them served as a basis for future studies although full implementation of these early concepts was to be delayed until the United States would again become involved in war. The science of tactical and strategical operations was completely revolutionized by the railroad, the telegraph, and captive balloons for observation, as well as by the final acceptance in this war of the cavalry as a tactical weapon.

---

[86] In imitation of the Confederate Government, the States passed conscription laws of their own. It was the operation of these local laws that kept Lee from receiving the quotas assigned. See Tate, *op. cit.*, p. 264.

[87] See Coulter, *op. cit.*, pp. 342 ff. For a general view of the many problems encountered in the Confederacy, see Clement Eaton, *A History of the Southern Confederacy*, New York, the Macmillan Co., 1954.

[88] *Ibid.*, pp. 333-334.

[89] See Charles DeF. Chandler and Frank P. Lahm, *How Our Army Grew Wings*, New York, Ronald Press Co., 1943, pp. 31-39.

Despite these advances in the art of warfare, the struggle was prolonged for four years. And when finally the rifle was replaced by the ploughshare, the people on both sides emerged a little wiser and much saddened. On the Northern side there were about 360,000 deaths (military) due to the war and the South could count some 260,000.[90] This was a huge price to pay for the settlement of an issue that the statesmen could have achieved by a little give and take. The war ended, but in its train came the sordid chapter of reconstruction which the "Radicals" forced upon the South in order to perpetuate their stay at the helm of government.[91]

---

[90] Samuel E. Morrison & Henry S. Commager, *The Growth of the American Republic,* New York, Oxford Univ. Press, 1942, Vol. 2, p. 4.

[91] Lincoln's magnanimous policy of restoring the South to its former position in the councils of Government threatened to short-circuit the "Radical" hold on power. Restoration of the South would have meant a strong Democratic opposition in Congress. Stripping the South of their power meant a strong Republican majority because the carpet-bag governments were Republican.

CHAPTER 10

Thirty Years of
Restrained Progress

Demobilization—The Army and Reconstruction—The Military Establishment is Reduced—Law Enforcement—Morale—The Indians Create New Problems For the Army—Concentration of Forces—Weapons and Defenses—The War Department Strives To Strengthen the Militia—Who Shall Command the Military Establishment?

AFTER THE Civil War had ended, America could look forward to a long period of peace because of her large reservoir of trained manpower together with an impressive Navy afloat. Four years of war had made the United States the most formidable power in the world.[1] Yet such was the genius of the American people that they would exploit this resource for the maintenance of peace, not for aggression on their neighbors. They did not even display a warlike spirit. The inclination of the United States toward peaceful pursuits, while they were thus so powerful, gives abounding evidence that the best insurance for peace is to be ready to repel insult and aggression.

In recognition of this tremendous American defensive potential, Louis Napoleon lost little time in divesting himself of the notion that he could, by force of arms, continue to disregard the Monroe Doctrine in his Mexican venture. Equally impressed were the British, who began to lay the foundations for a lasting Anglo-American friendship by agreeing to arbitrate their differences with the victorious Yankees. When Her Majesty's emissaries agreed to arbitration they did so with not a little sober reflection that the United States was in a position to give the British lion's tail a severe twist. It is to the enduring credit of British statesmanship that having recognized the tremendous latent power of our country, they lost no opportunity in cultivating her friendship. Anglo-American cordiality was perhaps the most important single result of the Civil War.

---

[1] This was emphasized by the Secretary of War in his report for 1865, Vol. I, p. 22.

Assured of the absence of danger from without, America could look with positive intent toward the development of the vast interior domain. But in the relentless movement westward, the Indian problem grew more acute and there was no prospect of peace in that direction. America's show of strength might impress the French and the British, but it failed to awe the ill-informed Indians who became more stubborn in their refusal to yield to the white man. The Indian Wars would continue to hamper westward progress because of the failure of the Nation to demonstrate a show of physical strength. This shortsighted policy was the result of the firm resolve in Congress to keep the Army below a safe minimum. Furthermore, the attention of Congress would be too much taken up with other problems which were daily developing during this eventful period.

Among other things the Government would be concerned with the claims made against England for supplying the Confederacy with commerce raiders, the reconstruction of the South, the Alaskan venture, the delicate question of revolutionary activity in Cuba, the Isthmian Canal, the threat to Anglo-American relations growing out of the Fenian movement, the Franco-Prussian War, and the more immediate problem created by the French in Mexico. In addition, there was the legislative program dealing with industry, foreign trade, and the veterans. In this busy atmosphere it was difficult to give more than a passing glance toward the improvement of the Army. Moreover, it was more convenient, politically, to reduce it and forget it.

Demobilization

With the return of peace, there arose a clamor in various parts of the country for the immediate discharge of volunteers. On May 1, 1865 the total strength of the Army was 1,000,516; by the end of the year 800,963 men were mustered out. The remainder were dispersed among nineteen military departments embraced in five military divisions,[2] the Divisions of the Atlantic, the Mississippi, the Gulf, the Tennessee, and the Pacific. One year later the volunteer force was reduced to 11,043 men of whom 10,000 were Negroes.

Meanwhile serious concern was expressed over the condition

---

[2] Rpt, S/W 1865, Vol. I, pp. 1, 19, 21.

of the Regular Army, whose regiments, because of the exigencies of the war, had been widely scattered and most of them reduced to mere skeletons. An attempt was made to bring these units up to strength by opening recruiting stations at especially designated points, and offering a handsome bounty to all who would re-enlist within ten days after discharge.[3] But realizing that even these plans would not bring the standing Army to a strength commensurate with the responsibilities of military government in the South, Grant, as commander of the Army, urgently recommended a permanent force of 80,000 men. But the Secretary of War was more responsive to the demands of conservatives for an Army of 50,-000,[4] and steps were taken to reorganize the Regular Army around this smaller number.

On July 28, 1866 Congress enacted legislation which completely reorganized the Army by abolishing the three-battalion infantry regiments and established the peacetime strength at 54,302 expansible to a maximum of 75,382 men.[5] By the end of September enlistments had brought the strength of the Army to 38,545 and there was a fair prospect that the authorized strength would soon be reached.[6]

In New York the decision to reduce the Army to 50,000 was hailed as a boon to the people. The difference was one of "tens of millions of dollars in our annual taxation; and the greater burden, though it can be borne, is one which nobody is willing to bear." [7] But in the far west where Americans were in close proximity to the wild Indians, reduction in force would subject white settlers to a wanton cruelty. Despite various warnings, the reduction of the Army continued unabated and by the end of 1866, corresponding cuts were made in materiel and expenditures.[8]

The Army and Reconstruction

Differences of opinion concerning the future status of the seceded States led to an open break between the President, An-

[3] Halleck to Grant, May 1, 1865, *O.R.* Series I, Vol. 46, pt III, pp. 1055, 1227-1228.
[4] See ltr Grant to Stanton, October 20, 1865, *Ibid.,* Series III, Vol. 5, pp. 126-127.
[5] XIV *Stat* 332. Ganoe, *op. cit.,* pp. 306-309; Spaulding, *op. cit.,* p. 340. The law also abolished the office of sutler and made the term of service five years for the cavalry and three years for the infantry and artillery.
[6] Rpt, S/W, 1866, House Exec Documents, No. 1, 39th Cong. 2nd Sess., p. 3.
[7] New York *Times,* January 12, 1866. See also January 11.
[8] Rpt S/W, 1866, pp. 4-6.

drew Johnson, and the Radical Congressional leaders. The President's policy, which followed closely Lincoln's design to affect the reconstruction quickly and painlessly was sharply challenged by the vindictives and steps were quickly undertaken to divest the Chief Executive of all authority in this regard. After asserting that no State would be readmitted until Congress should have declared each State entitled to such consideration,[9] the Radicals sought additional means to enhance their position. Seizing the opportunity afforded in their appropriating authority, on March 2, 1867 they attached to the Army Appropriation Act a provision aimed at curtailing the President's constitutional authority. Specifically, it provided that all orders issued to the Army would be made through the General in Chief, whose headquarters would be placed in Washington, and who could not be removed nor assigned to duty outside the Capital without the consent of the Senate.[10] Because it was an appropriation bill, Johnson could not withhold his signature but he did call attention to the fact that Congress overstepped their legal prerogatives by depriving the President of his constitutional functions as Commander in Chief of the Army.[11]

Under questionable interpretation of the law, the reconstruction of the South was conducted as a military occupation over a conquered province; and by this means, the Radicals perpetuated themselves in office for the next fourteen years. In three successive Acts, Congress abolished all legal government in the South and divided it into five military districts each under a military governor[12] until such time as Congress was satisfied that all conditions for readmission were complied with. Thus the Congressional policy of military occupation of the South made the Army an instrument for carrying out the law as politicians saw it. Thus did the Army serve its masters, the sovereign people.

The Military Establishment is Reduced

The threat of involvement in Mexico to oust Emperor Maximilian and his French bayonets, coupled with the military occupation of the South, forced the people to accept an Army of from 50,000 to 75,000 men. But with the withdrawal of French troops

---

[9] Randall, *Civil War and Reconstruction*, p. 750.
[10] XIV *Stat* 486-487.
[11] Richardson, *M&P*, Vol. VI, p. 472.
[12] Acts of March 2, 23 and July 19, 1867. See Spaulding, *op. cit.*, p. 339; also *Army and Navy Journal*, March 9, 1867.

and the knowledge that the Southern States would soon be reconstituted, it was reasonable to assume that even the minimum force of 50,000 would be pruned down. It was also generally accepted that the Regular Army could no longer be kept at its prewar level.

During this long period of peace numerous proposals were made to bring about a workable plan designed to meet the needs of the nation in peace and war. Although there were some differences of opinion, the expansible theory found general acceptance among the majority in the Army.[13] Some interest was generated in the adoption of a reserve officers program,[14] but this was a radical departure from the accepted principles in vogue during that period. However, the operation of an effective reserve system would have solved many of the problems of military policy, and when finally America went to war again in 1898, it would have been less difficult to meet the requirements of expanding from 30,000 to 250,000.[15]

While the military experts were seeking the best formulas for national defense, the country began to insist upon further military reductions. Although it was shown that the actual strength of the Army was below that authorized,[16] and as constituted it was insufficient to afford protection on the Indian frontiers, in 1868 Congress reduced the appropriations by $20,000,000. The next step in retrenchment was taken on March 3, 1869 when a provision of the Army appropriations act reduced the authorized strength to 45,000.[17] This was done despite the urgent pleas from the West and the need to garrison the newly purchased Territory of Alaska.[18]

On July 15, 1870 the authorized strength of the Army was

---

[13] See Rpt S/W, 1877, Vol. 1, pp. 47-49; House Misc., Doc. No. 56, 45th Cong. 2nd Sess., *Report of a Subcommittee of the Committee on Military Affairs relating to the Reorganization of the Army,* Washington, 1878. Hereafter cited as *Maish Report.*

[14] *Maish Report,* pp. 125-127; 150-151. The reserve program referred to closely approximated the present National Guard organization.

[15] A beginning had been made to create a pool of trained reserve officers by the operation of the Morrill Act of July 2, 1862. This law required land grant colleges to give instruction in military tactics. By 1888 there were some fifty officers detailed as instructors at these colleges.

[16] Rpt S/W 1867, p. 6.

[17] XV *Stat* 318. Also Ganoe, *op. cit.,* pp. 324-325; Rpt S/W, 1869. The term of service was for all arms fixed at five years.

[18] See Spaulding, *op. cit.,* pp. 369, 372.

further reduced to 30,000 enlisted men[19] and this force was scattered throughout 203 military posts and stations in forty-two States and territories.[20] While the soldier was striving to make the wilderness safe for settlement, the Congress unconcernedly lowered service attractiveness by reducing the number of major generals to 3 and brigadiers to 6.[21]

For the next three years, the annual Army appropriations were consistently below the War Department estimates. Economy-minded Congressmen could not even be made to see the wisdom of providing a fireproof building in which to house the Department's valuable papers which were scattered here and there.[22] In 1874, while the country was busy seeking the way out of an economic depression, the House Military Affairs Committee stated that there were too many soldiers engaged in the ordinary duties connected with periods of "profound peace." The handful of troops fighting the Indians was considered ample to do this duty. Furthermore, the number of troops

> in the Department of the Lakes and on the Atlantic and Pacific seaboard is about 5,000, constituting a reserve which heretofore could be drawn upon in case of emergency, and is deemed now of little use, as the policy of reconciling and pacifying the Indians progresses to a successful completion. Beside these there is a large number of troops stationed in the interior, having no special duty to perform.[23]

Based upon these questionable findings, this Committee deemed it "not to be unsafe to reduce the Army to twenty-five thousand men of all arms."[24] On June 16, 1874, two months after the report was read, Congress pared the Army down to that figure.[25]

For the next twenty-four years the Army would number some 25,000 officers and men notwithstanding the recommendations of the Secretary of War, the General in Chief, and commanders in the field to bring it up to 30,000. A due regard for the safety of the settlers on the frontiers, the serious domestic disturbances occurring in the East and the interior region, and the necessity

[19] XVI *Stat* 317.
[20] Rpt S/W 1870, p. 3.
[21] Ganoe, *op. cit.*, p. 330.
[22] See Rpt S/W 1871, Vol. I, pp. 3-4, 17; Rpt S/W 1872, Vol. I, p. 3.
[23] *Report of the Committee on Military Affairs of the House of Representatives Upon the Reduction of the Military Establishment*, April 16, 1874, 43d Cong., 1st Sess., pp. III-IV.
[24] *Ibid.*
[25] XVIII *Stat* 72.

for protecting our vast and valuable military stores and property, imperatively required a large increase. But Congress remained insensitive to the real needs of the Army and once even failed to pass an annual military appropriation bill.[26]

In 1879, the Secretary of War reminded Congress that the policy of keeping the Army in such a weak condition was responsible for the disasters attending Indian hostilities. In the preceding year the Secretary's report showed that because of the smallness of the Army, its efficiency was seriously impaired.[27] Military instruction and drill

> has been much interrupted during the year owing to the reduced state of the companies, the exceedingly small garrisons, and the large amount of labor necessarily imposed upon the men in building, repairs, care of public property, etc.[28]

Congressional plans for reorganizing the Army so seriously crippled its effectiveness that it was only with the greatest difficulty and by a strenuous exhibition of heroism and patriotic devotion that the officers and their men fulfilled their obligations to the people.

Law Enforcement

Dissipated in strength, the Army, which the House Military Affairs Committee in 1874 declared was bogged down with routine duties of "profound peace" when not engaged in fighting Indians, was called upon by the civil authorities to put down disorders all over the country. From 1877 to 1880 the soldiers were busily engaged in restoring order in New Mexico which was in a virtual state of anarchy. In 1885, it was called upon to enforce the suppression of polygamy in Utah, and during the same period was actively engaged in restoring order in the anti-Chinese demonstrations on the west coast.[29] From 1877 on the great labor strikes forced the Government to call on Federal troops to protect public property and to prevent bloodshed.[30] The "coercive arm" of the

---

[26] In 1877. See Spaulding, *op. cit.*, p. 369. To meet living expenses, officers had to borrow money at interest.
[27] Rpt S/W, 1879, Vol. I, p. III. See also Rpt S/W 1880, Vol. I, p. V; Rpt S/W 1881, p. 4.
[28] Rpt S/W, 1878, Vol. I, p. XIX.
[29] Spaulding, *op. cit.*, pp. 370, 371.
[30] Matthew Josephson, *The Politicos 1865-1896*, New York, Harcourt Brace & Co., 1938, pp. 254-255, 563, 566, 567, 574, 579-581, 584-587; Ida M. Tarbell, *The Nationalizing of Business*, New York, Macmillan Co., 1946; pp. 232-243; Ganoe, *op. cit.*, p. 368.

Government, which had frightened Congress in 1790, was now engaged in the preservation of law and order without threatening civil liberties. Under the parsimonius Congressional policy, the pay and subsistence in the Army attracted few but the mediocre including numerous human derelicts, many of whom were illiterate.[31] When the tour of duty became distressing, desertions multiplied.

Morale

The effect of Congressional economy upon the Army was to lower morale among the troops. In 1870 the Army was reduced to 30,000, which necessitated a re-distribution and curtailment of units. In 1871 the increased workload of the individual soldier, coupled with the fact that he had to face the Indians with fewer companions, brought the number of desertions up to 8,800 or thirty percent of the total authorized strength.[32]

The heavy desertion rate diminished gradually until 1876 when it was reported at 1,844. This sharp decline was due to an improvement in the system of enlistment whereby greater care was exercised in the selection of men and greater effort made to reject unworthy characters.[33] But by 1882 the number of desertions increased to 3,721. This time the Secretary of War analyzed the situation as one in which recruits enlisted in the larger cities, were transported at government expense to the West, where by desertion they obtained positions at the highest wages. As a corrective measure it was recommended that the pay of enlisted men be raised to what it was in 1865, and the punishment for desertion be more clearly defined by law and increased in severity.[34]

The problem ceased to be critical after 1893. The economic depression in that year brought an increasing number of men into the Army. As a result, the enlistment process grew more selective and on August 1, 1894, Congress limited enlistments to those who were citizens or declarant aliens under thirty years of age with an ability to read, write, and speak English.[35] In his annual report

---

[31] Ganoe, *op. cit.*, p. 334.
[32] Rpt S/W, 1876, Vol. I. p. 7.
[33] Rpt S/W, 1877, Vol. I, p. VII. In 1883, 3,578 desertions cost the Government $322,356. See 1tr A.G. to Lt. Gen. of the Army, December 19, 1883, Document File Hq. Army, 1883, Vol. I ltrs sent, ltr No. 380, National Archives.
[34] Rpt S/W, 1882, "Report of the General of the Army," pp. 6, 7. The current pay for an enlisted man was $13 a month. In 1865 it was $16.
[35] XXVIII 216. The term for enlistment was three years, and restrictions as to citizenship were not applicable to Indians.

for that year, the Secretary of War attributed a reduction of 609 in the rate of desertions to the improvement in the character of the men enlisted.[36]

The Indians Create New Problems for the Army

When Congress decided to reduce the Army, they did so in complete disregard of the harmful effect scattered bands of Indians, whose combined total was 300,000, would have upon the efficiency of the military establishment. Reduction in force meant a greater distribution of progressively smaller units to meet the needs of the distressing frontier situation.[37] This in turn meant that the Army could not concentrate its units.

Concentration of force in the face of retrenchment is an indisputable military axiom. Yet the policy of the Government in the expansion westward, inconsistent as it was with the military policy of Congress, rendered a concentration impossible. As a result, the frequent and numerous incidents on the frontier forced the military authorities to spread the small Army thinly in order to keep everyone satisfied.[38] It was because the Army was so dispersed that adequate preparations for future contingencies could not be made. And, when finally the United States went to war with Spain, there were a large number of well-trained Indian fighters but it was difficult to translate their experience into an ability to conduct modern warfare against a civilized power.

In 1866, Congress sought to alleviate the difficulties that would be encountered in the west through the reduction in force, by enacting a law giving the President authority to enlist 1,000 Indians to act as scouts.[39] While this was designed to assist in the work of scattered units of regulars, the divided responsibility over the Indians between the Army and the Interior Department often made it difficult to enlist them. At Fort Leavenworth, the agent for the Delaware Indians refused to permit the enlistment of the braves

---

[36] Rpt S/W 1894, Vol. I, p. 13.

[37] General Sherman estimated that he received hundreds of calls for protection from a hundred places hundreds of miles from each other. *Ibid.* See also June 22, 29, 1867; *Rocky Mountain Herald,* April 5, 1868, Ganoe, *op. cit., p.* 318.

[38] Ganoe, *op. cit.,* p. 317. In 1878, General Sheridan while berating Congress for its niggardly policy said: "No other nation in the world would have attempted the reduction of these wild tribes and occupation of their country with less than 60,000 or 70,000 men." Rpt S/W 1878, Vol. I, p. 36.

[39] July 28, 1866, XIV *Stat* 333.

under his charge.[40] Of this divided authority, General William T. Sherman said:

> These Indians are universally, by the people of our frontier regarded as hostile, and we, the military, charged with a general protection of the infant settlements have to dispose our troops and act as though they were hostile; while by the laws of Congress, and the acts of our executive authorities, these Indians are construed as under the guardianship and protection of the general government, through civilian agencies. Indians do not read, and they always look to the man who commands soldiers as the representative of our government.[41]

Hence, the Indian was fighting the soldiers while at the same time he was under the protection of the civilian agents. He would draw supplies, arms, and ammunition which he used against the Army all summer long and then could find security during the winter on the agency-controlled reservations.

By 1876, measures had already been undertaken to disarm and dismount the agency Indians.[42] But despite even these precautionary measures, divided authority coupled with dispersion of force rendered it difficult to put a quick end to Indian warfare. Nevertheless the gradual conquest of the hostile tribesmen continued;[43] and with the rapid growth of the railroads, the concentration of military force so often recommended began to take place.

Concentration of Forces

The great forward strides made in transportation as a result of the extension of the railroads, coupled with the gradual subjugation of the Indians, finally made it possible to concentrate the widely scattered units of the Army. As early as 1880, the Secretary of War began to outline War Department policy by insisting upon the abandonment of the numerous small frontier posts. This, as well as a concentration of force at strategic points near the frontier

---

[40] See ltr S/W to Dept of Interior, October 15, 1866, Military Book No. 58A. Ltrs Sent, S/W, p. 15. See ltr Frederic Remington to S/W, June 4, 1893, the *Manuscript Collection of Daniel S. Lamont,* Library of Congress, Vol. 13, pp. 2485-2489. Hereafter cited at *Lamont Mss.*

[41] Quoted in Spaulding, *op. cit.,* p. 351. See also Richard O'Connor, *Sheridan The Inevitable,* Indianapolis, Bobbs-Merrill Co. Inc., 1953, pp. 337, 345.

[42] Rpt S/W, 1876, Vol. I. p. 6.

[43] By 1883, the General in Chief regarded the Indian problem as substantially solved from the viewpoint of the Army. See Rpt S/W, 1883, Vol. I, "Rpt of General of the Army," p. 45.

or at points of railroad intersection, was expected to facilitate more thorough drill and discipline of the Army, by bringing together full regiments and fostering a proper *esprit de corps*.[44]

This policy was energetically pursued. But Indian disturbances, while not on a large scale, continued to demand the presence of small detachments of soldiers. In 1892 the Secretary of War's report encouraged the belief that although the concentration of regiments had not been accomplished to the extent desired, "our Army, small as it is, and distributed in little bunches here and there over the country, is nevertheless a well-ordered and well-trained organization."

The difficulty experienced in trying to achieve the desired goals of *esprit de corps,* efficiency in maneuver, evolution of doctrine to coincide with modern concepts, ability to bring to bear, in time of national emergency, a well-trained and concentrated force, was due not only to the continued Indian problem, but also to the reluctance of the Government to provide a larger force. While the population had been increasing and the exodus to the west accelerated in pace, the Army had been progressively diminished.

Phillip Sheridan when General in Chief strongly reiterated his predecessor's recommendations for concentrating the troops in large garrisons near important cities as a measure of economy. When and if the troops were required on the frontier, the present railroad facilities would be ample to transport them speedily.[45] Furthermore, centrally located troops could readily be dispatched in any direction threatened by danger.

Others who perceived the dangers of scattered forces urged the creation of an Indian scout corps. These would, in effect, make concentration possible, by doing the work of scattered troops in the Indian country.[46] The time had come for the country to be ready for any emergency. Growing as the United States was

> in population, wealth and military power, we may become the envy of nations which led in all these particulars only a few years ago; and unless we are prepared for it we may be in danger of a combined movement being some day made to crush us out.[47]

---

[44] Rpt S/W, 1880, Vol. I, p. vi; Ganoe, *op. cit.,* p. 369. See also "Editorial Notes," *United Service,* November, 1884, Vol. xi, pp. 567, 568, 569.
[45] Rpt S/W, 1885, Vol. I, p. 7.
[46] Ltr Frederic Remington to S/W, June 4, 1893, *Lamont Mss,* Vol. 13, pp. 2485-2489. Remington was opposed to the use of Indians as regulars however.
[47] U. S. Grant, *Personal Memoirs of U. S. Grant,* New York, World Publish-Co., 1952, p. 587.

Weapons and Defenses

Although substantial progress had been made before the Civil War on the repeater rifle as well as the revolver, the Union forces fought the Civil War with a modified form of the musket used in the Revolutionary War.[48] It was idle to suppose that the same Congress which refused to experiment with a weapon which would have increased the firepower of the Federal soldier, would adopt a more modern weapon in peacetime.

Nevertheless Secretary Stanton, convinced of the superior qualities of the breech-loaders, had continued to recommend their use in the Army. This was taken up by a joint committee of Congress who soon decided against any further modifications of the service muskets into breechloaders because such modification would render useless existing stocks of ammunition.[49] However, some 50,000 Springfields had been so modified and used extensively during the 1866-1867 Indian campaigns.[50] The success attendant upon their use prompted the War Department to continue experimentation with the result that the Springfield Model 1869, a single-shot breech-loader, was adopted. This was a dependable weapon but, as one authority put it, the repeaters were better, and officers and men who could afford to, purchased them. Consequently the soldier had purchased out of his own pocket a weapon that the nation should have furnished him.[51]

Worse than the failure to encourage improvements in modern arms, was the failure to supply adequate reserve stocks of those weapons. By the end of fiscal year 1875 it was estimated these would reach a total of 40,000 stand, "about enough, in case of war, to arm one Army corps." [52] Two years later, because Congress failed to appropriate for the Army, the manufacture of arms was halted at the Springfield Armory.[53] The reserve stocks now stood at 8,552 rifles and 5,983 carbines of the latest model.[54]

At this slow tempo, ordnance items were manufactured for the three branches of the service at six Government arsenals or by

[48] I. B. Holley, *Ideas and Weapons,* New Haven, Yale Univ. Press, 1953, p. 10.
[49] Rpt S/W, 1866, pp. 9-10. It is interesting to note the parallel with the situation just prior to World War II. Because there was on hand a large amount of unexpended 75 mm ammunition, a newer weapon was not then adopted.
[50] Rpt S/W, 1867, pp. 17-18.
[51] Ganoe, *op. cit.,* pp. 334, 316.
[52] Rpt S/W, 1875, Vol. I, p. 18.
[53] Rpt S/W, 1877, Vol. I. p. xxiv.
[54] *Ibid.* See also Rpt S/W, 1878, Vol. I, p. xvii.

contract with private manufacturers.[55] Continued experiments at Springfield Armory for a magazine rifle of reduced caliber brought about the adoption, in September, 1892, of a 30 caliber carbine.[56] This improved weapon was initially intended for use by the regulars, but its success was so impressive that the General in Chief urged an increased production of these arms so that not only all the regular troops and organized militia might be fully armed with them, but that there might be an adequate reserve for any additional force that should be called into service.[57] But despite even the Secretary's proposals for supplying the new weapon to the militia at small cost to the Government, Congress, during this period of industrial strife (1893-1895), remained reluctant to grant the authority.[58]

At first glance this Congressional attitude toward national defense would seem to indicate that the past policy of passive defense was still being scrupulously adhered to. Closer examination, however, reveals that even this method of defense was dangerously neglected during this period.

Since the governmental policy of passive defense necessarily depended upon an efficient system of coast defenses, it naturally followed that greater attention would be paid to improving the coast fortifications. But while the War Department remained alert to the demands made upon it to carry out this policy, Congress remained reluctant to supply the funds and even reacted slowly to the great changes that were evolving in the science of modern warfare.

Within a few years after the Civil War, the weak coast defenses that had been established began to show signs of obsolescence and as early as 1879 the Chief of Engineers warned against these conditions.[59] One year later the Secretary of War made a special effort to prove that

> our fortifications are not in a condition for the defense of important cities and depots of military and naval supplies, in case of war with any of the maritime powers. These powers have been rapidly and steadily increasing their means for offensive warfare,

---

[55] The arsenals were: Watervliet, Springfield, Frankford, Rock Island, Benicia, the Proving Ground at Sandy Hook, New Jersey. Rpt S/W 1893, Vol. I, pp. 19-20.
[56] *Ibid.*, p. 12. Manufacture of the 45 caliber rifle was discontinued.
[57] Rpt S/W, 1894, Vol. I, p. 14.
[58] *Ibid.*, pp. 16-17.
[59] Rpt S/W, 1879, Vol. I, pp. xv-xvi.

while the United States has been for years retrograding in its means for carrying on such a war.[60]

Again and again the War Department issued repeated warnings against the niggardly policy of Congress with reference to these defenses. Rebuilding such defenses could no longer be postponed, the Secretary urged, because modern seacoast defenses require many years for their construction.[61]

Finally after years of assurances by leading authorities that America's smooth-bore cannon could not compete against the modern rifled cannon in use abroad, Congress authorized the creation of a board to study the problem.[62] This Board, which came to be known as the Endicott Board, within a few months drew up a comprehensive scheme of coast defenses which contemplated the placement of 2,362 pieces of artillery at specially designated sites. It was estimated that the work could be completed within thirteen years at a cost of one million dollars. In 1893, eight years after the Board met, the Secretary of War applauded the progress made thus far which, he thought, was sufficient to warrant the belief that with adequate appropriations the essential features of the plan could be carried to completion within the specified time.[63] But by April 1, 1898, five days before the declaration of war against Spain, only 151 of the contemplated 2,362 cannon were in position.[64] Congress had refused to heed the timely warnings from the War Department that the time had long since arrived when the future possible or probable military necessities should dictate military policy.[65]

The War Department Strives to Strengthen the Militia

To illustrate further that the Congressional policy of passive defense was indicative of a lack of policy, the militia, which by law constituted the great reservoir of manpower, was also feebly supported.

During the period between the wars, the term "National

---

[60] Rpt S/W, 1880, Vol. I, pp. xviii, xix-xx.
[61] Rpt S/W, 1882, Vol. I, p. xv.
[62] March 3, 1885, XXIII *Stat* 434.
[63] Rpt S/W, 1893, Vol. I, p. 14.
[64] R. A. Alger, The Spanish-American War (New York, Harper and Bros., 1901), p. 10. This notwithstanding the fact that the Ordnance Department had invented disappearing gun carriages for 8- and 10-inch guns of a type "unequalled for rapidity and simplicity of action by any carriage elsewhere in use." Rpt S/W, 1894, Vol. I, p. 15.
[65] See Rpt S/W, 1890, Vol. I, pp. 44-45.

Guard" began to be applied to the militia of the various states in an effort to more closely identify the State forces with the National Government. While the need for such a close relationship was felt in the War Department and also by some members of Congress, the necessary legislation to bring this about failed to materialize.

Laboring under the provisions of the law of 1792 which made it an individual State responsibility for arming the militia, and the law of 1808 in which Congress appropriated the meager sum of $200,000 annually for its support, the militia organizations drifted further and further away from the supervision of the Government. And, as the westward expansion accelerated in pace, the militia organizations of the eastern regions, where the dangers of Indian hostilities were more remote, grew less effective. The growth of industry and the concomitant rise of large cities rendered the "organized" militia a useless appendage of society, especially in times of peace. Not altogether useless, however, for the local Governors looked upon their militia organizations as strong political assets.[66]

Year after year the War Department emphasized the necessity for strengthening the militia and increasing the annual appropriations.[67] In 1875 the Secretary of War underlined the need for increasing appropriations by showing that

> the annual appropriation of $200,000 was made in 1808, when the population was about eight millions. At the present time, with a population of over forty millions, the amount is the same, and it is impossible for this Department to meet all the demands made upon it by the States and Territories.[68]

Congress perceived the need for a general reformation of the existing militia system but unfortunately the attempt to work out an equitable formula led to a general strengthening of political control over the organizations. Debates in Congress concerned the manner in which the "active militia" would be raised. In 1879 a

---

[66] New York was "supporting a powerful machine patronage [militia] with more generals than good regiments." See Brig Gen Theodore F. Rodenbough, "The Militia of the United States," *United Service*, April, 1879, Vol. I, p. 284.

[67] See Rpt S/W 1870, Vol. I, p. 289; Rpt S/W 1872, Vol. I, pp. 13, 315. Rpt S/W 1873, Vol. I, p. 16, Vol. III, p. 5. The Chief of Ordnance in 1873 recommended an increase to $1,000,000.

[68] Rpt S/W 1875, Vol. I, p. 16. At this time the organized militia numbered 84,724 and the unorganized 3,701,977. *Ibid.* Two years later the organized militia had increased to over 90,000 men. See Rpt S/W 1877, Vol. I, p. xxiv.

bill under consideration in the House proposed to create an active force of militia by raising 700 men in each Congressional district. This would give the country 200,000 men; and while the Secretary of War was sure these would be soldiers in fact, in organization, in discipline, in the use of arms,[69] there were others who felt the measure would increase the independence of the States and grant them new privileges.[70]

Meanwhile the stimulus for placing the militia upon the same footing, with reference to rules and regulations, as the regular forces continued to be generated in the War Department. In 1880 the Adjutant General opened correspondence with the adjutant generals of the States offering to be of service to them in the hope that these efforts would end in the production of a trained force, so officered and disciplined as to be ready at once to be added to the Regular Army in time of need.[71] The response to these overtures was so warm that shortly afterward numerous requests were made upon the War Department for the detail of regular officers to inspect the state encampments of militia.[72]

On May 19, 1882, Congress made a small though positive contribution to this effort to create a strong second line of defense. Provision was made to authorize the Secretary of War to issue upon request of the Governor of any State bordering on the sea or gulf coast, two heavy guns and four mortars if such could be spared, for the proper instruction and practice of the militia in heavy artillery drill.[73] By the end of that year only one State, Massachusetts, availed itself of this opportunity to prepare its citizens for what might be a most important duty.[74]

However, most of the States demonstrated an eager desire to closely associate their National Guard units with the Regular Army. Larger numbers of Regular officers were detailed on inspection trips among these units and finally in 1886 the Secretary of War recommended an annual inspection in all the States.[75] Reports of these inspecting officers, while demonstrating the great

[69] Rpt S/W 1880, Vol. I, p. vii.
[70] Rodenbough, "The Militia of the United States," p. 285.
[71] Rpt S/W 1880, Vol. I, p. vii.
[72] Rpt S/W 1882, Vol. I, pp. v-vi.
[73] XXII *Stat* 93.
[74] Rpt S/W 1882, Vol. I, pp. xiii-xiv.
[75] Rpt S/W 1886, Vol. I, p. 20. See also Rpt S/W 1883, Vol. I, p. 22; Rpt S/W 1884, Vol. I, pp. 6, 48; Rpt S/W 1887, Vol. I, pp. 10-12.

value of such contacts, also indicated a growing need for arming and equipping the State forces.

Typical of the many recommendations emanating from the War Department to arm and equip the militia were the Adjutant General's views of 1885:

> At present nearly the entire militia of the country is armed with a rifled musket different in caliber and less effective than that in use in the army, and for which no ammunition is now manufactured.[76]

The response made to these repeated reminders came from Congress on February 12, 1887 in the form of a feeble increase in the annual appropriations from $200,000 to $400,000 for the purpose of providing arms, ordnance stores, quartermaster's stores, and camp equippage for issue to the militia.[77]

Although this law stimulated a lively interest in militia activities among the people,[78] there was no escaping the obvious fact that the appropriation was pitifully small. In analyzing these figures, the Secretary of War showed the regularly organized and uniformed "reserve army" to be 106,500 men against which the application of $400,000 meant $3.75 per man. In addition, while the population had increased sevenfold since 1808, the amount of money for militia purposes was only doubled.[79]

Despite this, the State organizations continued to demonstrate an unexampled eagerness to become closely associated with the Regular Army, and the War Department, in turn recognizing the importance of the militia as the second or reserve line of national defense,[80] gave unstinting support, within its meager resources, to the men who in most cases had to go down in their pockets to serve their States.[81]

Not only were the number of officers on detail to militia duty increased, but the practice of sending small detachments of regulars to participate in the State encampments was begun.[82] This was so successful that by 1895, the "efforts of recent years to bring the Army into closer relations with the National Guard of the States

[76] Rpt S/W, 1885, Vol. I, p. 11.
[77] XXIV *Stat* 401-402.
[78] Rpt S/W, 1888, Vol. I, pp. 14-15.
[79] Rpt S/W 1889, Vol. I, p. 14.
[80] Rpt S/W 1893, Vol. I, pp. 27-29.
[81] Rpt S/W 1894, Vol. I, p. 183.
[82] Rpt S/W 1889, Vol. I, pp. 68-69.

may now be regarded as having established a permanent union between the two forces, advantageous to both." [83]

But while conditions were favorable to the development of a strong force of more than 100,000 militia,[84] existing legislation proved to be a stumbling block. Without sufficient arms, the State organizations did not form an effective second line, and because of the limiting features of the laws, it was impossible to arm them uniformly. As a result, a wide variety of arms were distributed among the militia units to such an extent

> as to preclude the employment of considerable bodies of the militia of different States in cooperation, and the longer the Federal Government delays action the greater the possibility that different States will select different models of rifles, requiring different forms of ammunition, thus rendering almost impossible the employment in joint action of the troops of the different States.[85]

The wisdom of these observations would become vividly apparent three years later when war was declared against Spain and the arsenals were stripped of reserve arms. The result was that instead of issuing one rifle, the 30 caliber, it was necessary to issue the Springfield 45 caliber in order to get rifles in the hands of the fighting men. Two rifles of different caliber added to the acute problem of ammunition at a time when efficiency meant the difference between victory and defeat. But while Congress overlooked these fundamentals in peacetime, once war was declared, it inspired the nation by its unanimous vote for the war fund.[86]

Who Shall Command the Military Establishment?

Under the Constitution the President of the United States is designated Commander in Chief, a function he exercises through the Secretary of War. But because both the President and Secretary of War are civilians, the claim to command the armed forces is titular; this responsibility naturally devolves upon the military who by professional training and outlook alone could be capable of exercising military command. However, control over the mili-

[83] Rpt S/W 1895, Vol. I, pp. 15-18.
[84] *Ibid.* In 1893 the total organized militia numbered 112,597 officers and men. In 1894, the number increased to 117,533. See Rpt S/W 1893, Vol. I, pp. 27-29; Rpt S/W, 1894, Vol. I, pp. 23-24. In 1896 the States were appropriating $3,-000,000 annually for the support of a force that would be called upon to defend the Federal Government. See Rpt S/W 1896, Vol. I, pp. 17-18.
[85] Rpt S/W 1895, Vol. I, pp. 16-18.
[86] Alger, *op. cit.,* p. 6.

tary establishment remained, as it should be, in the hands of the constitutional commander in chief promulgated through the Secretary of War.

When the civilian authorities undertook to effect command, as in the War of 1812, without regard for the professional soldier who should have exercised command untrammelled and unburdened, chaos soon followed.[87] This unfortunate mistake was repeated during the first three years of the Civil War and the prospects bade fair for a continuation of this dangerous and costly system as long as the relationship between civilian control and military command was not clearly defined.

It is universally recognized that the President delegates his authority over the military establishment to tested military commanders, and this does not mean the Secretary of War. This cabinet officer, burdened with the routine administrative and financial responsibilities of his office, could find little time for anything except his own duties. Hence a third office, the office of command, had to be created, and this was done as early or as late as 1821. But because the office of General in Chief grew out of expediency and was not defined by law, a natural difference of opinion soon developed. Because transportation was slow in those early days, and communications were modified by the absence of modern inventions, the Secretary of War often issued orders direct to individuals in the Army, outside the normal channels of command. Although this assumption of authority was challenged by men like Andrew Jackson, and sustained by men like John C. Calhoun, little effort was made to correct the abuse.

The failure to delimit authority between the Secretary of War and the Commanding General led Winfield Scott to leave Washington and set up his headquarters in New York.[88] Similar circumstances forced General William T. Sherman to remove to St. Louis.[89] In the latter case, the "conflict" between Gen. Sherman and the Secretary of War cast an ominous shadow over President Grant who, as an outstanding military expert, might have been expected to find the solution to this perplexing problem. But

---

[87] See Upton, *op. cit.*, pp. 129-133; 145-147; 155-159.

[88] "The National Defense," *Hearings Before the Committee on Military Affairs, House of Representatives,* 69th Cong, 2nd Sess, March 3, 1927, pt. I, p.. 79. Hereafter cited as "National Defense, 1927."

[89] William T. Sherman, *Memoirs,* New York, D. Appleton & Co., 1931, Vol. II, pp. 453-454.

while Grant insisted upon, and received, a proper recognition of his prerogatives as General in Chief, he steadfastly refused to intervene in Sherman's behalf.

When General Sherman in May, 1869 succeeded Grant as Commanding General, the position of the staff chiefs in their relation with the Secretary of War and with the Army came into sharp focus. Through the years these staff departments functioned independently of the General in Chief by reporting directly to the Secretary of War. By law and custom, these bureau chiefs held their office for life; before the Civil War the Adjutant General held his office for 27 years, the Quartermaster General for 42 years; the Commissary General 43 years; the Paymaster General for 32 years, and the Surgeon General for 25 years.[90] With permanent tenure of office and a tendency to be jealous of their authority even at the expense of one another, these chiefs were prone to court the favor of the Secretary of War and Congress as well. With such a powerful political influence, it was not difficult to overlook the authority of the Commanding General which was viewed as more theoretical than actual.

In 1867 a board of officers consisting of Lt. Gen. William T. Sherman, Maj. Gen. Philip H. Sheridan, and Brevet Maj. Gen. C. C. Auger prepared a system of Army Regulations which in addition to placing the military establishment, "in all that regards its discipline and military control," under the orders of the Commanding General, also stipulated that the staff corps "act under the general in chief, in his name and by his authority." These regulations were approved by General Grant but were not promulgated by the Executive, and General Orders No. 28, 1869 redefined the duties of the General:

> 126. All orders and instructions relating to the military operations, or affecting the military control and discipline of the Army, issued by the President or the Secretary of War will be promulgated through the General of the Army.[91]

No clearer and saner statement in this regard could have been made than the utterance of General J. M. Schofield in 1869: "In time of peace, and when not in the field with a separate army, the

---

[90] See Ganoe, op. cit., pp. 534-538; Ralph P. Thian, *Legislative History of the General Staff of the Army of the United States,* Washington, G.P.O., 1901, pp. 52, 86, 148, 238, 362, 443, 483.
[91] James G. Harbord, *The Expeditionary Forces, Its Organization and Accomplishments,* Scranton, Pa., Scranton Pub. Co., 1929, pp. 35-36, 50-53.

general should command the whole Army, staff as well as line." [92]

On March 5, 1869 Schofield, as Secretary of War, placed the chiefs of staff corps, departments, and bureaus under the immediate orders of General Sherman.[93] Before that month had expired General John A. Rawlins became Secretary of War and the provisions relating to the staff corps departments and bureaus were rescinded. By way of explanation for the rescission of the Orders of March 5, Sherman explained:

> I was soon made aware that the heads of several of the staff corps were restive under this new order of things, for by long usage they had grown to believe themselves not officers of the army in a technical sense, but a part of the War Department, the civil branch of the Government which connects the army with the President and Congress.[94]

Appeals to President Grant, whose experiences as General in Chief qualified him to disabuse the bureau chiefs of their peculiar contentions, availed Sherman little.[95] General Rawlins fell in with the pattern of the politically influential chiefs and on many occasions issued orders to individuals in the Army without notifying the General.[96] Things went from bad to worse when the Army Appropriations Act of July 15, 1870[97] stripped the office of Commanding General of all influence and prestige.[98] In vain Sherman appealed to the President. After returning from a European tour only to find the Secretary of War exercising all the functions of commander-in-chief he decided to move his headquarters to St. Louis. On September 3, 1874 permission granted, accompanied by two aides and their newly married daughter Minnie, the Shermans moved to St. Louis where they could, at least, escape "the mortification of being slighted by men in Washington who were using their temporary power for selfish ends." [99]

---

[92] *Ibid.*, p. 37. Schofield reiterated his contention in 1876. *Ibid.*
[93] General Orders No. 11, March 5, 1869, quoted in Sherman *Memoirs,* Vol. II, p. 441.
[94] General Orders No. 28, March 27, 1869, quoted in *ibid.,* pp. 441, 442.
[95] See ltr Wm. T. Sherman to John Sherman, July 8, 1871, quoted in Thorndike, *Sherman Letters,* p. 331.
[96] Sherman, *Memoirs,* Vol. II, pp. 442-443.
[97] XVI *Stat* 318-320. This law was brought about by the intrigues of the politically corrupt Secretary of War W. W. Belknap who sided with the bureaucrats to curtail Sherman's influence. See Lloyd Lewis, *Sherman Fighting Prophet,* New York, Harcourt Brace & Co., 1932, p. 608.
[98] See ltr Wm T. Sherman to John Sherman, July 8, 1871, quoted in Thorndike, *Sherman Letters,* pp. 331-332.
[99] Sherman, *Memoirs,* Vol. II, pp. 450-454, 463. Sherman resumed his headquarters in Washington on April 6, 1876 after Secretary of War Belknap was forced to resign in disgrace because of fraud.

On November 1, 1883, Phil Sheridan succeeded to the command of the Army and to the same problems encountered by his predecessor. Within a year, Sheridan fell upon hard days in his relation with the Quartermaster General who quickly sought the intercession of Secretary of War Robert Todd Lincoln. On January 17, 1885, in a long letter to Sheridan, Mr. Lincoln agreed that there were not "two channels of command to a staff officer serving with troops, the one through the line of General officers, and the other through the chief of their staff Department." [100] However, Sheridan was reminded, orders from the line did not affect the Quartermaster General nor his subordinate officers not detailed to the line. Furthermore, it was obvious to Mr. Lincoln that Sheridan did not fully understand the limits of his office as Commanding General. To emphasize these limitations, the Secretary pointed to established procedure and custom which was

> to assign the ranking general officer of the Army to a command superior to all commanding generals, at the Headquarters of the Army, and to express his assignment as the "command of the Army" leaving the interpretation of that convenient and conventional phrase to be limited by the Acts of Congress, Regulations, and established usage.[101]

Subsequent interpretation of the "convenient and conventional phrase," however, brought out an increased disregard for the proper channels of command. The staff departments continued to issue orders to their officers on detail with the troops which in effect vetoed the authority of commanding officers in general and the General in Chief in particular.[102] Sheridan's insistence upon a proper recognition of the prerogatives of his office made his tenure as much of a purgatory as that of Sherman's. In 1887 he called attention to the dangers attending the theory of military administration in the United States. This theory,

> of which the extreme is the multiple representation of the Commander-in-Chief in the persons of the several chiefs of Bureaus of the War Department has been steadily opposed by all the eminent generals who have commanded armies in this country; and it is . . . self evident that military operations cannot possibly

---

[100] Ltr. Lincoln to Sheridan, January 17, 1885, Ltrs Sent, S/W, 1885, National Archives.
[101] *Ibid.*
[102] Rpt Lt Gen of the Army in Rpt S/W, 1887, Vol. I, pp. 117-118. See ltr Martin T. McMahon to Daniel Lamont, September 11, 1893, *Lamont Mss* Vol. 20, pp. 3832-3834.

be conducted with success under such a system of administration.[103]

General John M. Schofield, Sheridan's successor, learned to live with his problem by abandoning "all pretense of being the commanding general and to content myself with acting as the Chief of Staff of the Army under the Secretary of War and the President." [104] But this did not solve the problem of the relationship of the bureau chiefs to the line of the Army. Reform was necessary if disaster in war was to be avoided, and General Sheridan admitted that "Congress alone has the power to remedy an evil which all military men in this country have uniformly regarded as very serious." [105] The wisdom of Sheridan's utterances would be tested in the Spanish American War, episodes of which dictated an immediate reappraisal of the military establishment.

---

[103] *Ibid.*
[104] "National Defense, 1927" p. 165.
[105] Rpt Lt Gen of the Army in Rpt S/W 1887, Vol. I, p. 117.

CHAPTER 11

The Emergence of
The Modern Navy

Naval Deterioration After the Civil War—Old Concepts
Prevail—A Fresh Approach—Increasing Naval Con-
sciousness—The Merchant Marine—The Naval Militia—
Personnel—Higher Education in the Navy

Naval Deterioration After the Civil War

WHEN THE Civil War ended, the American Navy was the strongest in the world.[1] Clearly, all indications pointed toward a vigorous resumption of America's world-wide maritime interests. The industrial and agricultural capacity of the nation had fairly been tested throughout four years of warfare yet these great resources had not been tapped deeply. America's destiny seemed to lie not only in fulfilling Jefferson's dream of westward expansion, but also in extending her economic and commercial supremacy in world trade. It was a great challenge to the young and vigorous republic, whose fiat could have been made law on the high seas. But instead of taking up the challenge, the nation turned its attention toward the vast interior.

There were many reasons why the young American Eagle was not permitted to spread his wings at this time; these are too well-known to permit of detailed treatment in this narrative. But it would not be amiss to venture the observation that Americans were weary of martial activities in an atmosphere where the evidence of war's cruel experiences was to be found in nearly every household, both in the North and in the South. Congress, keenly aware of this traditional post war attitude, geared their legislative programs accordingly. The champion of retrenchment was looked upon as the highest exponent of peace, and the feeling was gradually generated that wars, or at least foreign wars, should no longer be the lot of Americans.

By 1866 the number of ships in the Navy was reduced to 278,

---

[1] In 1865 there were 626 serviceable vessels of which sixty-five were powerful ironclads and 160 others were steam men-of-war. See Knox, *op. cit.*, p. 317.

only 115 of which were in commission, and the total number of seamen had shrunk to 13,600.[2] This rapid deterioration of the Navy was permitted despite the fact that the French were still in Mexico, two wars were raging in South America, and revolutionary disturbances in Haiti and Santo Domingo were threatening the lives and property of American residents.[3] Despite the weakened state of the Navy, American warships patrolled the affected areas and at the same time our foreign squadrons had been reestablished in the hope that pre-war commercial prestige could be restored.

While the United States had made rapid strides in the evolution of modern naval warfare, and had improved monitors to such a degree that two of them journeyed with great success to Europe, the ironclad warship remained a thing of the future. Although it was generally conceded that iron men-of-war would supersede wooden ships, Secretary Welles and many of his contemporaries were also convinced that steam could not, nor should it replace sails. "Ships for cruising and offensive operations must be such as can use sails, for no vessel can long keep the sea under steam alone." [4]

Because the United States lacked coaling stations it was more prudent to insist upon a combination of sail and steam for the vessels of the Navy; and this policy was rigidly adhered to. Thus in 1870 every ship in active service, with the exception of four or five ironclads and a few side-wheel steamers, were equipped with full sail power.[5] Meanwhile, and up to the end of the Reconstruction period, the whole number of vessels in commission and laid up or under construction gradually diminished to 146.[6] The monitors, because of insufficient appropriations, received little care, and even as early as 1869 they were in a state of rapid deterioration.[7]

The depths to which the Navy had sunk became painfully apparent late in 1873, during the Cuban insurrection. A Cuban-owned ship, the *Virginius*, engaged in smuggling arms into that island, was seized by Spanish authorities while flying the Ameri-

---

[2] Rpt S/N, 1866, p. 11. See also New York *Tribune*, December 5, 1866.
[3] Brazil, Uruguay, and Argentina united to make war on Paraguay; and Spain was at war with Peru and Chile. Rpt S/N, 1866, pp. 19, 21. *Ibid.*, pp. 17-18.
[4] *Ibid.*, pp. 15-25.
[5] Rpt S/N, 1870, p. 159.
[6] See Rpt S/N, 1867, p. 1; 1868, pp. VII-VIII; 1869, p. 6; 1870, p. 3; 1872, p. 3; 1874, pp. 5-6; 1876, pp. 3-6.
[7] Rpt S/N, 1869, p. 6.

can flag. This insult to the Stars and Stripes evoked a loud protest, and a fleet of antiquated and half-rotted ships was hastily gathered.[8] Sensational newspapers loudly proclaimed America's ability to avenge the insult. but sober analysis revealed that the country was not prepared for such an emergency.[9] The inability to redress a wrong was due to "the hesitancy of Congress to make those appropriations without which no secretary can keep the Navy in proper condition." Furthermore, Congress was in duty bound "to stop short in its dangerous and fatal policy of degrading our Navy beyond the point of usefulness, and to take measures to give it the strength which is absolutely necessary to it as an integral part of our national power." [10]

Old Concepts Prevail

But naval weakness was not due so much to insufficient appropriations as it was to the political graft and corruption which went with the policy of keeping old and decrepit ships in repair. Congress voted millions for material and labor to keep old hulks in operation and in the end had little to show save a collection of obsolete vessels and some enriched patronage.[11]

A contributing factor was the attitude of the senior line officers toward the staff. Men like Admirals D. D. Porter and Daniel Ammen steadfastly refused to acknowledge the need for a complete transition from sail to steam because such a change would place ships in the hands of engineers who as mere members of the staff were not considered capable of commanding men-of-war. Because of this narrow notion, sail power remained a prevailing official concept, and, come what may, the resurrection of ancient windjammers kept command in the hands of old-time line officers.

There is justification for disagreeing with the elaborate reports of Secretary George M. Robeson, who held his office eight years, purporting to show that the condition of the Navy was far superior to what it was when he entered upon his duties.[12] The *Army and*

---

[8] Sprout, *op. cit.,* p. 175; Bailey, *op. cit.,* pp. 423-424.
[9] *Army and Navy Journal,* November 22, 1873, Vol. II, p. 232.
[10] November 22, 1873, Vol. II, p. 232. Naval appropriations were not too small, but they were voted with a view to maintain the Navy yards which were equipped to service wooden vessels and which employed some four or five thousand men. The political significance of these yards was not lost sight of by the National Legislature.
[11] Sprout, *op. cit.,* p. 180.
[12] Rpt S/N 1876, pp. 3-6.

Navy Gazette on January 8, 1876 described the condition of the Navy as a "fraud," [13] and the British *Broad Arrow* concluded that there "never was such a hapless, broken-down, tattered, forlorn apology for a navy as that possessed by the United States." [14] The Portland *Morning Oregonian* cynically remarked: "Perhaps it would be more accurate to say our alleged Navy." After showing that Mr. Robeson's figures presented a distorted picture of the naval strength, this organ concluded that nothing more could be expected in a system where "mere politicians who know nothing whatever of the affairs to which they are called" are placed at the head of the important departments. [15]

This open criticism coupled with the Congressional investigation of 1876 brought to light a huge amount of information on naval policy. Ensuing discussion went far to prove that continental isolation in the absence of a strong navy was not a sufficient guarantee of peace. It also became apparent that Americans had devoted most of their attention to the development of the West, with little regard for foreign interests. To Admiral Porter, Americans had demonstrated an unusual ability to increase their material interests but they had not acquired the sense to protect them. [16] Admiral Ammen, while still reluctant to depart from his fixed notions on sail power, agreed that it was time to design and test whatever seems calculated to make naval warfare formidable, destructive, and economic, remembering that nothing is economic that is not effective. [17]

Nevertheless the United States was still not prepared to sanction huge expenditures for naval vessels that had not been fairly tested and proved effective. It was preferable and less expensive to adopt a wait-and-see attitude while Europe experimented with modern ship building. This would afford the nation the benefit of the perfected models without the necessity for experimentation. Discerning Americans, however, clearly understood that perfection in naval architecture and ship building was a continuous evolution and perfection was at best only temporary. Invention, the hand-

---

[13] Quoted in *Army and Navy Journal*, January 22, 1876, Vol. XIII, p. 282.
[14] *Ibid.* Widespread criticism of Secretary Robeson led to a Congressional investigation of the activities of the Navy Department. See *Army and Navy Journal*, July 15, 1876, Vol. XIII, p. 787; July 29, 1876, Vol. XIII, p. 820.
[15] Portland *Morning Oregonian*, August 20, 1878.
[16] D. D. Porter, "Our Navy," *United Service*, January 1879, Vol. I, p. 4.
[17] Daniel Ammen, "The Purposes of A Navy," *Ibid*, April, 1879 Vol. I, pp. 245-255.

maiden of the great industrial revolution, quickly rendered obsolete even the most perfect war machinery.

This waiting policy was annoying to the ultra-nationalists in the United States, and perplexing to the British who held firm to the belief that there could be only one naval policy, "That of keeping the Navy up to its highest possible pitch of perfection, in ships, guns, and men. All else is mere child's talk, and unworthy of a great nation." [18] Pronouncements from the U. S. Navy Department that the new submarine torpedo strengthened America's defensive position[19] drew forth another retort from Englishmen who, it seemed, were more interested in a strong American Navy than were Americans themselves. While the British critics agreed with the U. S. Navy Secretary that torpedo warfare was a powerful development, they saw no excuse for a great commercial country like the United States to sink into the position of a third-rate naval power.[20]

A Fresh Approach

By 1880 the attention of the whole country had been focused upon the Navy and it had become evident that some change in policy was necessary. The elevation of James A. Garfield to the Presidency ushered in a new era of nationalism which was punctuated by a vigorous foreign policy. This made a new navy an indispensable necessity and toward this end a Naval Advisory Board was created in 1881. Headed by Admiral John Rodgers, this board, made up of naval officers representing all branches of the service, was instructed to study every phase of naval policy.[21] The responsibility for policy planning and procedure was lifted from the bureaus and placed in the hands of this Advisory Board.

On November 7, 1881 the board strongly recommended that all new ships be built of steel. After nine months of deliberation, Congress, on August 5, 1882, authorized the construction of two steel cruisers with full sail power but failed to appropriate the

---

[18] *Broad Arrow,* quoted in *Army and Navy Journal,* October 11, 1873, Vol. XI, p. 135.
[19] See Rpt S/N 1870, p. 11; 1871, p. 39; 1872, pp. 19-20. However, the torpedo was still in the experimental stage. See Rpt S/N 1882, Vol. I, p. 21, Vol. III, p. 7.
[20] London *Engineer* quoted in *Army and Navy Journal,* March 22, 1873, Vol. X, p. 503.
[21] Leon B. Richardson, *William E. Chandler,* New York, Dodd Mead & Co., 1940, pp. 289-290.

money therefor.[22] Nevertheless, it was clearly recognized that the wooden vessels in being would have to be eliminated, but here Congress was forced to move slowly because of the patronage attached to ship yards equipped to handle and repair these old ships. Despite the protests of representatives of these interests, however, Congress injected a clause in that law by which expenses to keep wooden ships in repair were not to exceed 30% of their original cost.[23]

When William E. Chandler became Secretary he found nine naval yards in operation "maintaining," at great expense, the phantom fleet.[24] The continuous recommendations since the end of the Civil War to bring some of these yards and at least one depot to a state of efficiency for the needs of ironclads went unheeded because of the political influence wielded by the thousands who found employment in the old yards.[25] As a result, the Government was without the facilities to build the new steel ships authorized or to be authorized by Congress. Even private contractors were reluctant to enter upon the business of building steel ships, which meant a large investment for new machines and tools with little guarantee that the Government would continue to place orders. While the Government jealously guarded infant industries by the protective tariff, they refused to subsidize shipbuilding in the manner that the railroads were subsidized or as the British had encouraged their shipbuilders. As a result invitations to builders to submit plans for cruisers were not accepted.

While the foundations for the modern Navy may be said to have been laid during the administration of Secretary Chandler, the inevitable political antagonisms growing out of the attempt to revamp the whole structure of the Navy Department retarded whatever progress might have been made. Under the Appropriation Act of March 3, 1883,[26] the first four steel vessels were authorized and two years later two additional small cruisers and two small gunboats were authorized. These eight ships were but a small beginning toward achieving the total of forty-three un-

---

[22] XXII *Stat* 291. Cf. Rpt S/N 1881, pp. 3, 5; Richardson *op. cit.*, p. 290.
[23] Richardson, *op. cit.*, pp. 290-291, Sprout, *op. cit.*, p. 188. In the following year this was reduced to 20%; Rpt S/N 1884, Vol. I, p. 15.
[24] Richardson, *op. cit.*, p. 287; Rpt S/N 1882, Vol. I, pp. 9-11.
[25] See Rpt S/N 1866, pp. 24-25, 28; 1869, pp. 16-17; 1870, p. 13.
[26] XXII *Stat* 472. The Office of Naval Intelligence had also been created. See *United Service*, December 1883, Vol. IX, pp. 668-670.

armored cruising vessels recommended by the Naval Advisory Board on November 7, 1881.[27] But it is significant that the new naval policy was geared to the pre-Civil War concept of commerce raiders and not to the battleship concept. Rear Admiral Ammen, one of the strongest advocates of this procedure of "hit-and-run," recommended the construction of five fast and handy marine rams for auxiliary defense, a position which found favor with Secretary Chandler.

The transition wrought in the Navy Department by Chandler was continued by Secretary William C. Whitney. under the first Democratic administration since 1861. He did not veer from the then current concept of commerce raiding but he did insist upon faster ships. Although in 1886 the country still had a rump fleet of antiquated wooden vessels,[28] before the end of his term of office Congress had authorized thirty naval vessels of different classes;[29] and where Chandler failed to encourage American steel industry, Whitney succeeded. Before the Democrats left office in 1889, the United States was no longer completely dependent upon England for rolled iron and for rifled cannon. The Bethlehem steel interests had erected a special mill which Whitney predicted would furnish armor and gun-steel second to none in the world.[30]

Increasing Naval Consciousness

The prospects of still greater progress in naval projects appeared extremely favorable under the administration of Benjamin Harrison who had been elected on a protective tariff platform. In line with this platform, subsidies were promised American steamship companies and a stronger Navy was encouraged. The rapid progress that had been made during the eighties was tested on November 18, 1889 when a squadron of four of the new steel vessels began a cruise that took them to the principal ports of Europe. The point emphasized was that these ships were the first we had built of steel of our own manufacture, as well as their engines and a large portion of their ordnance. The only point of weakness in this display of power was the absence of battleships.

[27] See Rpt S/N 1883, pp. 89-90; See also Philadelphia *Inquirer,* July 4, 1884.
[28] Mark D. Hirsch, *William C. Whitney: Modern Warwick,* New York, Dodd Mead & Co., 1948, pp. 298-299.
[29] Sprout, *op. cit.,* p. 189.
[30] Allan Nevins, *Grover Cleveland: A Study in Courage,* New York, Dodd Mead & Co., 1947, p. 222.

The battleship and its place in the Navy had been a subject of wide discussion in naval circles while the President and his Secretary of the Navy were basing naval policy upon the theory of purely passive defense. Commenting upon the absence of these heavy ships, Rear Admiral S. B. Luce remarked "In the absence of anything and everything that might resemble naval policy, we have reversed the usual order of naval development." Since the battleship was the very foundation of a navy, it was plain that, in a military sense, the United States "has no navy." If there was any one fact clear to the Admiral it was the true function of a navy: "The role of a navy is essentially offensive," and since the United States was not possessed of the offensive weapon it naturally followed this nation could not take rank as a naval power.[31]

But even more important and notwithstanding the remarkable progress made in building the Navy, by 1889 its real strength stood at eleven armored vessels only three of which were battleships and thirty-one unarmored vessels, making a total of forty-two.[32] When this was considered in the light of the weak coast defenses of the nation, the security of the entire coast line was dangerously low.

Public interest in the Navy grew stronger toward the latter part of the eighties because of the startling stories of naval activities throughout the world. News accounts of the imminence of danger arising from the dispute between the United States, Britain, and Germany over Samoa in 1888, coupled with French interest in an isthmian canal which might establish the commercial supremacy of Europe in South America called attention to the need for an increased awareness of America's naval position. With the final conquest of the West, American energies were now directed toward the maritime frontier and the necessity for the revival of the merchant marine.

The attitude of the proponents for a stronger navy was reflected by the Secretary of the Navy who urged the policy of building first class battleships[33] and the response of Congress in authorizing the construction of three such vessels.[34] But Congress did

---

[31] S. B. Luce, "Our Future Navy," *Proceedings of the United States Naval Institute,* Vol. XV, pp. 544-546. See also Rpt S/N 1889, Pt. I, p. 3. See *Proceedings of the United States Naval Institute* in 1888, especially Vol. XIV, pp. 200, 206, 218, 220, 222, 224.

[32] Rpt S/N, 1889, Pt. I, p. 3.

[33] Rpt S/N, 1890, pp. 11-14.

[34] XXVI *Stat* 205. The Secretary of the Navy had advised the construction of twenty battleships for the protection of both coasts. See Rpt S/N 1890, p. 37. The first three were the *Maine, Texas* and the *Monterey.*

not move rapidly enough for the advocates of a large navy; by 1892 the House Naval Affairs Committee was bitterly assailed for failing to adopt the Secretary's proposal to increase the number of ships and the total tonnage of those ships.[35]

Increase in naval tonnage, while continuous, went slowly. In 1882 an inventory of the ships built or building showed only a total of forty-two vessels of which one was a battleship of the first class and three were battleships of the second class.[36] Within five years during which Japan demonstrated her naval might in war against China, and the Cuban insurrection again threatened the peaceful relations of the United States and Spain, the Navy showed the following strength:

    4 battleships of the first class
    2 battleships of the second class
    2 armored cruisers
   16 cruisers
   15 gunboats
    6 double-turreted monitors
    1 ram
    1 dynamite gunboat
    1 dispatch boat
    1 transport steamer
    5 torpedo boats

In addition there were under construction five battleships of the first class, sixteen torpedo boats, and one submarine boat. These together with sixty-four other naval vessels and an auxiliary fleet of twenty subsidized steamers[37] seemed to indicate a mighty naval armada for both defensive and offensive purposes. These bright prospects prompted the Secretary of the Navy to remark: "Nothing will so surely make for peace and give us weight abroad and security at home as a substantial navy constructed of the best materials and manned by the highest intelligence and skill." [38]

The country was committed to a strong navy by the declarations of our people and the action of their representatives. The very fact that

> we are capable of manufacturing armor and guns, powder and projectiles, and to construct ships which are the equals of those

---

[35] See New Orleans *Times* Democrat March 13, 18, April 18, 19, May 1, 1892; Galveston *Daily News,* January 27, 1892.
[36] Rpt S/N 1892, p. 4.
[37] Rpt S/N 1897, pp. 3-6.
[38] Rpt S/N 1896, p. 9.

built anywhere else, is in itself a source of great naval power, and our present resources in this respect should not be impaired.[39]

Along these lines, the Assistant Secretary of the Navy, William McAdoo, warned that in the procurement of materiel we were still far behind the needs of the nation; and although the ships were unexcelled and the ordnance was superior, there were not enough of them. Mr. McAdoo could not find language strong enough to condemn what he termed the criminal folly which leaves this nation practically unarmed.[40] On June 2, 1897 Theodore Roosevelt, the new Assistant Secretary of the Navy, emphasized the needs of the nation not for war but to *avert* fighting. Preparedness, he insisted, deters the foe and peace, like freedom, "is not a gift that tarries long in the hands of cowards," despite the utterances of "the timid doctrinaire who preaches timid peace from his cloistered study."[41]

The Merchant Marine

The decline of the Merchant Marine Service after the Civil War deprived the country of the reservoir of manpower trained in seafaring upon which it had, in past wars, depended to supplement the naval establishment. The importance of a merchant fleet was seen by the Secretary of the Navy in 1869 when he urged the Government to provide and protect the great means of commercial intercourse, both domestic and international.[42] In the interest of the naval establishment, and because so much of the national defense was dependent upon foreign trade, it was earnestly recommended that immediate steps be taken to induce our own merchants and shipbuilders to enter into this field of enterprise. But American capital found it more profitable to invest in domestic enterprises

---

[39] Rpt S/N 1897, pp. 40-41.

[40] "Address by Hon. William McAdoo, Asst Secy of the Navy before the Naval War College, June 2, 1896," *Proceedings of the United States Naval Institute*, Vol. XVII, p. 442. Also Lt. John M. Ellicott USN, "The Composition of the Fleet," *ibid*, pp. 539-543. H. A. Herbert, "The Sea and Sea Power as a Factor in the History of the United States," *ibid*, p. 573. For a full discussion of the progress in naval armament and the dependence of the United States upon foreign sources of supply see *ibid.*, Vol. X, pp. 568-573; *United Service,* May 1882, Vol. VI, p. 512; Rpt S/N 1867, p. 28; 1868, pp. 72-75; 1882, Vol. I, p. 7; 1887, pp. iii-iv, x-xi; 1884, Vol. I, pp. 8-9, 30. "Report of the Gun Foundry Board approved by act of Congress March 3, 1883," *ibid.*, p. 259, also *ibid.*, pp. 323, 349; Philadelphia *Inquirer*, August 9, 1884; New York *Herald*, September 21, 1887; Omaha *Herald*, January 21, 1888.

[41] "Washington's Forgotten Maxim," *Proceedings of the United States Naval Institute*, Vol. XXIII, pp. 459-461.

[42] Rpt S/N 1869, pp. 15-16.

where at least it did not have to compete with cheaper costs and operations abroad. Furthermore, it was more economical to export goods in foreign bottoms because they could operate at less cost.

Two years after Southern reconstruction officially terminated, the Secretary of the Navy published an alarming report of the state of the merchant service. Of a total freightage of imports and exports excluding passenger service, amounting to $1,137,105,438, foreign shipping carried 70.1%, leaving American shippers only 29.9%. These important facts clearly proved that every facet of American economic life would soon be at the mercy of foreign shippers who because of the absence of competition would impose upon our people even heavier and more oppressive burdens.[43]

Aside from these commercial and financial considerations, an enlarged merchant fleet would establish a naval reserve similar to that of Great Britain, composed of officers and seamen who, having served a limited number of years in the regular or volunteer navy were then allowed to go upon the reserve list.[44] This could easily be accomplished by the adoption of a ship-subsidy policy which had always been sponsored by England.

The close connection between the improvement of the Navy and the development of the merchant marine,[45] while always recognized continued to be woefully disregarded. The United States was at peace with the world but that could at any moment have been violently disturbed in an era when nations like Germany threatened the political equilibrium of international relations in their tardy quest for colonial domain. Where these interests would run counter to those of the United States, the absence of a large fleet of merchantmen left this country with little in the shape of a navy; and if war came under such conditions, the country would be helpless upon the sea.

Agitation for the resurrection of the American mercantile fleet continued unabated under the slogans of the protective tariff

[43] Rpt S/N 1878, pp. 11-16. See also ltr Aaron Vanderbilt to Grover Cleveland, December 3, 1887, *Cleveland Mss*, Vol. 185, p. 9597. Nearly every nation of any consequence was outstripping the States in this service. See Rpt S/N 1871, pp. 46-47; also D. J. Kelley, "Free Ships and Subsidies," *United Service*, May 1881, Vol. IV, pp. 520-533.

[44] Lt. R. M. G. Browns, "The Commercial and Naval Policy of the United States," *United Service*, May 1881, Vol. IV, pp. 603-610.

[45] See W. I. Chambers, "The Reconstruction and Increase of the Navy," *Proceedings of the United States Naval Institute*, Vol. XI, pp. 7, 40.

and free trade party pledges,[46] and before the war with Spain the United States was paying subsidies to a number of fine, swift-sailing vessels which were capable of being promptly converted into useful men of war.[47] The merchant marine was returning to its traditional role as the "militia of the sea."

The Naval Militia

While the makers of American military policy had given much thought and time to the militia concept in national defense, for the most part it was concerned with the land forces. The naval militia in United States history played a less conspicuous part than its land counterpart. During the Revolutionary War, reliance was placed upon the Continental Navy and privateers as well as the State navies. But after this war State navies as well as the Continental Navy disappeared.

Wedded to the concept of militia forces as the only efficient and economical means for protecting the liberties of the people, Thomas Jefferson recommended the establishment of a naval militia but legislation toward that end failed of enactment.[48] Naval defense was left to the responsibility of the Regular Navy with the merchant marine acting as an auxiliary force as well as a reservoir of trained personnel in case of war. But trained merchant mariners could not quickly be transformed into trained sea fighters, with the result that much difficulty was encountered in securing the necessary manpower for the heterogeneous fleet that fought the Civil War. While the experiences of this war had forcefully demonstrated the need for citizen forces for naval defense, no significant attempt was made to maintain personnel released from active duty in a trained reserve status.

Because of the rapid decline of the merchant marine after the Civil War, even the traditional dependence upon that service as a reserve force, ready at a short notice to be incorporated into our Regular Navy,[49] was discarded. The time had arrived to bring into being a naval militia to augment the dwindling personnel of the Regular Navy.

---

[46] See ltr Daniel Barnes to Grover Cleveland, December 5, 1887, *Cleveland Mss*, Vol. 185, pp. 9604-9605.

[47] Rpt S/N 1896, p. 18.

[48] See Lt. J. C. Soley, "Naval Reserve and Naval Militia," *Proceedings of the United States Naval Institute*, Vol. XVII, pp. 473-474.

[49] John A. Grier, "Should We Buy or Build our First Class Merchant Steamers," *United Service*, June 1881, Vol. IV, pp. 759-762.

Interest in a naval militia was generated by private citizens who possessed a knowledge of seafaring and who wished to associate themselves with the service. If the military volunteer had received recognition from both the State and Federal authorities, why "should not the same encouragement be extended to the naval volunteer?" This public feeling in favor of a naval reserve reached the Navy Department in the form of inquiries from Chambers of Commerce in leading cities along the coasts;[50] and the Secretary of the Navy called these to the attention of Congress.

In response to this great wave of public spirit, Senator Washington C. Whitthorne on June 26, 1888[51] introduced a bill which, while it failed to become a law, served as the basis for the independent action of several States and generated a lively discussion in favor of the measure in the leading service periodicals.[52] Massachusetts was the first State to pass an act in 1888 creating a naval militia by providing for an organization appropriately named the Naval Battalion of the Volunteer Militia. This was followed by similar legislation in other States during the next few years.[53]

On March 2, 1891 the first Federal appropriation of $25,000 for arms and equipment of the Naval Militia was made. This was the beginning of annual grants, but it was not until just prior to the Spanish-American War that this amount was increased to $50,000 despite the rapid growth of the militia.[54] During this war, the naval militiamen were employed both in the United States Auxiliary Naval Force and in the Regular fleet thus neglecting to

---

[50] Rpt S/N, 1887, pp. xv-xvi.
[51] *Proceedings of the United States Naval Institute,* Vol. XIV, p. 189.
[52] Capt A. P. Cooke, USN, "Our Naval Reserve and the Necessity for its Organization," *ibid.,* Vol. XIV, pp. 170-185; J. W. Miller, "Remarks," *ibid.,* p. 188; Lt J. C. Soley, USN (ret), "Remarks," *ibid.,* pp. 189-192; Lt R. P. Rodgers USN, "Remarks," *ibid.,* pp. 193-195; Frederic Tams, "Remarks," *ibid.,* p. 206; Park Benjamin, "Remarks," *ibid.,* pp. 209-210; Capt A. R. Yates USN, "Written Remarks," *ibid.,* pp. 215-219; Prof. R. H. Thurston, "Written Remarks," *ibid.,* p. 222.
[53] Harold T. Wieand, *The History of the Development of the United States Naval Reserve, 1889-1941,* University of Pittsburg Doctoral Dissertation, 1951, pp. 11-16. See also New York *Herald,* November 30, 1889. New Orleans *Times Democrat,* March 1, 1892; Philadelphia *North American,* August 3, 1891; Rpt S/N, 1889, p. 25; J. C. Soley, "Naval Reserve and Naval Militia," pp. 475-476.
[54] Wieand, *op. cit.,* pp. 45-46. In 1892, the number of naval militiamen was 1,794 dispersed among the States of Rhode Island, Maryland, South Carolina, North Carolina, Massachusetts, California, and New York. In 1896 they numbered 3,339 with the States of Pennsylvania, Illinois, Connecticut, Michigan, New Jersey, Georgia, and Louisiana now also having militia units. See Rpt S/N 1896, pp. 19-20, 87-90; 1895, pp. xliii, 48-49, 1894, pp. 31-32, 87-90.

define their status either as a second line of defense or as reserves. A total of 24,123 enlisted men served of whom 4,224 were mustered in from the militia organizations. Of this number 2,600 served in the Regular Navy and the remainder in the Naval Auxiliary and Coast Signal Service. In addition, 267 naval militia officers were commissioned in the Navy.[55]

After the war the Navy Department began to draft plans for the organization of a Federal naval reserve, a step which had been recommended through the years of agitation. But the exact relationship between such a force and the existing militia organizations remained unsettled. The State organizations were not adverse to the creation of a Federal reserve, but they did insist upon the preservation of their own organizations. In the continued development of the Navy, the question of a naval militia occupied a prominent position and like its land counterpart it became increasingly federalized.

Personnel

By 1869, the total strength of enlisted personnel in the Navy was fixed at 8,500 men.[56] The great inconvenience this rapid contraction visited upon the Navy Department was a source of continued irritation not only to the Secretary[57] but also to the ships' commanders who either sailed without full complement or were compelled to reject former sailors who sought to re-enlist.[58]

Although the Secretary insisted upon at least 12,000 men, and was even willing to accept the lower figure of 10,000, by 1877 the total sank to 7,012. Five years later the number reached 8,018 with 1,817 officers to man thirty-one vessels in commission.[59] This large number of officers was considered disproportionate to the small number of ships; hence Congress, on August 5, 1882, took steps to prohibit any further increase and even directed a slight gradual reduction in officer strength. This Congressional action was sharply criticized by the line as a great mistake. The personnel of the Navy "should be fixed on a permanent basis" and not

---

[55] Wieand, *op. cit.,* pp. 60-61.
[56] XV *Stat* 68-72, Sec. 2. After the war the apprentice system initiated on March 2, 1837 was revived. See rpt S/N, 1866, pp. 33-34; 1867, pp. 21-22.
[57] Rpt S/N, 1869, pp, 23-24.
[58] Rpt S/N, 1870, pp. 157-158.
[59] Rpt S/N 1877, pp. 6-10. The number fluctuated because of attrition and enlistment.

changed simply because the ships were too few to give all the officers active employment. But Secretary Chandler looked upon the proposed reduction as a healthy program by which a promotion policy could be evolved offering opportunities heretofore closed because "old men" held down the rank. Furthermore, he recommended the enforced retirement of all officers at age 62,[60] and the adoption of a promotion policy based upon merit.[61]

Meanwhile enlisted personnel remained at a low figure. If this was not enough to chagrin the Secretary of the Navy, then a study of types who made up the rosters soon gave him cause for pained alarm. In his report for 1888 he deplored the large number of enlisted men who could not speak English. When the Trenton, "our best ship, lately went into commission, as fine a body of Germans, Huns, Norsemen, Gauls, Chinese, and other outside barbarians as one could wish to see were on board." [62] In 1897 the pay table showed an active list of 1,508 officers, 11,000 petty officers, seamen and other enlisted men and 1,200 apprentice boys.[63]

The strength of the Marine Corps paralleled that of the Navy. In 1868 it was fixed at 2,500[64] and four years later it fell to 2,293 enlisted men.[65] When Congress in 1874 was debating the Naval Appropriations Bill, the Boston *Transcript* was sure that amendments "will be offered to merge it [the Marine Corps] into the Army, and others for its total abolition, on the ground that it is a useless and unnecessary organization, rendered so by the modern style of land and naval warfare." [66]

Although the authorized strength was placed at 2,500 enlisted men, Congress rarely appropriated enough money, and the number enlisted was well under the authorization.[67] In 1893, the figure was given as 2,093 or seven short of the total number appropriated[68] for and in 1896, Congress voted an increase of 500 additional marines.[69] The Corps was not abolished, nor was it merged

---

[60] See Rpt S/N, 1882, Vol. I, p. 8; 1883, Vol. I, pp. 10-11, 393-394.
[61] Rpt S/N 1884, Vol. I, pp. 43-46.
[62] Rpt S/N 1888, p. 10, appendix, also 1899, Pt. I, p. 22.
[63] Rpt S/N 1897, pp. 36-37. See also **XXIX** *Stat* 648-649.
[64] Rpt S/N 1868, p. 33.
[65] Rpt S/N 1872, p. 164.
[66] January 9, 1874.
[67] See Rpt S/N 1889, Pt. I, p. 46; 1883, Vol. I, pp. 366-367.
[68] Rpt S/N 1893, p. 579.
[69] Rpt S/N 1896, pp. 34-35.

with the Army. Subsequent Marine Corps history would beat a path of glory from Chateau Thierry to Iwo Jima to Korea.

Higher Education in the Navy

In the renaissance of the Navy, the establishment of the Naval War College deservedly holds a high place. The need for the establishment of a postgraduate school for naval officers grew out of a spirited discussion in the pages of the *Proceedings of the United States Naval Institute* and was the genesis for the formation of the Naval Board which was commissioned on May 3, 1884 by Secretary Chandler to study the subject. The Board, under the direction of Commodore S. B. Luce, emphatically recommended the creation of such an establishment and on October 6, 1884 Chandler issued the orders establishing the college at Newport, Rhode Island.[70] In his letter of February 11, 1885 to the Senate, the Secretary said, "This college is intended to complete the curriculum by adding, to an extent never herebefore undertaken, the study of naval warfare and international law in their cognate branches." [71]

At its inception, the institution suffered "from the indifference, if not enmity, of the bureau chiefs," [72] and Congress was indisposed to favor an institution founded without its consent by executive decree.[73] Therefore the first years of the Naval War College were marked with neglect and even open criticism.[74]

In 1886 when Luce was transferred to command the North Atlantic Squadron, Alfred Thayer Mahan succeeded to the presidency of the college. Since 1885 Mahan as staff member of the college was delivering his memorable lectures which subsequently would revolutionize naval doctrine when they were published under the title: *The Influence of Seapower Upon History, 1660-1783*. Although he would be relieved as president in 1888 because

---

[70] See Charles O. Paullin, "A Half Century of Naval Administration in America, 1861-1911," *Proceedings of the United States Naval Institute,* Vol. XXXIX, p. 1496. Hereafter cited as Paullin, "Naval Administration, 1861-1911," also Richardson, *op. cit.,* p. 307.

[71] *Proceedings of the United States Naval Institute,* Vol. XXXVI, pp. 561-562.

[72] *Ibid.,* p. 559; see also Richardson *op. cit.,* pp. 307-308.

[73] Paullin, "Naval Administration, 1861-1911," p. 1497.

[74] There is a wide difference of opinion among the biographers of leading personalities as to who was critical and who was friendly. See Chandler, *op. cit.,* pp. 307-308; Hirsch, *op. cit.,* p. 388. See also Paullin, "Naval Administration, 1861-1911," p. 1497.

of a difference of opinion with Secretary Whitney,[75] Mahan left his impress upon the Naval War College.

Within a short time of Mahan's ascendancy to the president's chair, the permanent, instead of temporary, assignment of faculty members was inaugurated. Emphasis was placed upon the solution of war problems, and the War College soon began to operate like a general staff.[76] Thus the Naval War College developed into something much more than simply a postgraduate course, for not only were the theory and art of war studied and developed, "but knowledge is being acquired and practical information is being amassed without which the Navy Department cannot possibly in the event of war, utilize the naval resources of our country." [77]

The Navy had come a long way as an effective instrument of national policy and because of the intense interest generated by a widespread discussion of the new manifest destiny it was prepared for the war that was in the making against Spain. The United States still was not a first class naval power nor was it necessary to be so against a Spain weakened by internal dissension. The quick and highly popularized victories of Dewey and Sampson helped to create a more favorable climate of opinion for the construction of a powerful fleet. The Spanish-American War would give an impetus to every naval activity, and in the period following, large sums were freely granted for naval purposes.

---

[75] Hirsch, *op. cit.,* pp. 349-350.

[76] Paullin, "Naval Administration, 1861-1911," p. 1498. The experience of Tasker H. Bliss as a staff member of the College would serve him well when the Army opened its War College in 1901.

[77] Address delivered by H. A. Herbert, August, 1893, *Proceedings of the United States Naval Institute,* Vol. XXXVI, p. 575. There is little doubt that Elihu Root in 1900 and 1901 found much in the scope of the Naval War College to sustain his plan to inaugurate the Army War College.

CHAPTER 12

The Spanish-American War

Imperialism and Righteousness Unite In a Marriage of
Convenience—A Vigorous Foreign Policy—Diplomacy
Relies Upon a Weak Reed—The Results of Grudging
and Dilatory Legislation—The Press Highlights Defi-
ciencies of the Army—Difficulties in the War Point the
Way for Necessary Reforms—Elihu Root is Appointed
Secretary of War—The Responsibilities of Imperialism

THE CLOSING YEARS of the 19th Century found the United
States ready to assume new importance upon the stage of
world affairs. America had been transformed from an agrarian
nation into a young industrial giant that had tamed the vast continental domain and was now seeking new fields to exercise its
restless and latent powers. Throughout a large part of their history
the American people had shown little interest in nor developed
any definite concept concerning their nation's destiny in the world.
Until the 1890's, a dominant American desire was to build a
domestic civilization with more abundant life for all within the
growing continental domain.[1]

Imperialism and Righteousness Unite in a Marriage of Convenience

However, by the 1890's the idea that national destiny extended
even beyond the seas had triumphed. It was argued that America
must expand in order to spread its republican institutions and give
the benefits of Anglo-Saxon civilization to "backward peoples."
Josiah Strong, a Congregational minister, gave currency to these
ideas in *Our Country*[2] in which he stressed the mission of the
American people to carry to the far reaches of the globe the great
benefits of civil liberty and Christianity. Other able apostles of
imperialism included Theodore Roosevelt, Alfred Thayer Mahan,
Joshua Fiske, Henry Cabot Lodge, Professor Burgess and many

---

[1] Merle Curti, *The Growth of American Thought*, New York, Harper & Bros.,
1943, pp. 659, 664.
[2] Josiah Strong, *Our Country*, New York, Baker & Taylor, 1885, pp. 159-179.

others in important sections of American intellectual and political life.[3]

Americans were told, seemingly with the scientific sanction of Darwinism, that all Anglo-Saxons[4] possessed innate and superior governing talents, hence were destined to extend their rule over those less fortunately endowed.[5] Mahan, in addition to preaching the doctrine of naval supremacy, as essential to national greatness, also supported the thesis of America's mission to spread Christianity and democracy over backward regions, thus linking war and imperialism with moral righteousness and idealism. The moral nation, the powerful nation, he argued, must assume responsibility for the triumph of morality on earth.[6] Captain Mahan's experience at the Naval War College admirably fitted him for this crusade. By 1890, he was stoutly preaching the doctrine of the new manifest destiny which was already shaping the role of the United States in modern imperialism.[7]

Grasping the full implications of an isthmian canal under American auspices, Mahan began to develop the tenets of the "large policy" in the Caribbean, a policy which was to be translated into action by Theodore Roosevelt by "seizing" Panama and in the enunciation of the Corollary to the Monroe Doctrine. Mahan stressed the importance of an isthmian canal built under American supervision, and its effect upon the security of two widely separated and extensive coasts.[8]

Mahan's ideas had an early influence on Theodore Roosevelt who combined an interesting blend of idealism and vigor with a conviction that "the man who fears death more than dishonor, more than failure to perform duty, is a poor citizen; and the na-

---

[3] Julius W. Pratt, *The Expansionist of 1898*, Baltimore, John's Hopkins, 1936, pp. 3ff.
[4] *Congressional Record*, 56th Congress, 1st Session, p. 711.
[5] Curti, *op. cit.*, p. 671. It might also be added that Kipling's "white man's burden" to manage "backward" people had its share in shaping the American mind to accept this new "Manifest Destiny."
[6] Alfred T. Mahan, "The United States Looking Outward," *Atlantic Monthly*, December, 1890, Vol. LXVI, pp. 817-822.
[7] For a lively and interesting treatment of America's venture in imperialism see Julius W. Pratt, *America's Colonial Experiment*, New York, Prentice-Hall Inc., 1951.
[8] Mahan, "The United States Looking Outward," pp. 819-823; "The Isthmus and Sea Power," October, 1893, Vol. LXXII, pp. 467-472. The whole subject of an isthmian canal was frequently discussed by the Secretaries of the Navy. See rpt S/N, 1869, p. 24; 1872, pp. 9-10; 1873, pp. 9-10; 1875, pp. 12-14. See also William P. Livesey, *Mahan on Sea Power*, Univ. of Oklahoma, 1947, pp. 82, 93, 104.

tion that regards war as the worst of all evils and the avoidance of war as the highest good is a wretched and contemptible nation, and it is well that. it should vanish from the face of the earth." [9]

A Vigorous Foreign Policy

These tenets of imperialism, aided and abetted by an inaccurate but sensational press, produced a forceful attitude in the conduct of American diplomacy. America was at a turning point in her history, and a strong foreign policy seemed to be popular even if it did nothing more than divert attention from embarrassing domestic questions. The frontier was gone and the industrial revolution was remorselessly marching toward its final and complete acceptance. Passions and emotions had largely lain dormant since the great tragedy of the Civil War, and the nation's leaders had carefully ignored or tried to smother the basic principles and issues in their unceasing quest for office and power. But now a new national self-consciousness stirred, and the pulse of the nation beat in a more rapid tempo. The Navy, which had been allowed to dwindle, was rising from its impotence. In May of 1892, the U.S.S. *New York* was given her trials and it was felt that the humiliation of the past quarter century was eradicated.[10] Interest in an inter-oceanic canal was revived and platform oratory became more vociferous and grandiloquent.

Expressions. of the new manifest destiny began to take root during the administration of Benjamin Harrison. His Secretary of State, James G. Blaine, as the outstanding exponent of a vigorous foreign policy, tried to purchase the Danish West Indies and to secure naval bases in Haiti and Santo Domingo. In Samoa,[11] he sought to prevent exclusive control of the British and Germans, and he became anxious to pick the "ripe pear" of Hawaii.

In 1889, the American public awoke to an appreciation of the Samoan affair which for a time presented the sensational possibility of war with Germany. There was no war, but there was the glamorous Congress of Berlin in which American diplomats strutted across the world stage. Then in 1891 there was more excitement in South America when a liberty party from the U.S.S. *Baltimore* was

[9] Curti, *op. cit.*, p. 672.
[10] Walter Millis, *The Martial Spirit*, New York, Houghton Mifflin Co., 1931, p. 6.
[11] See Portland *Oregonian*, December 5, 1878; *Army and Navy Journal*, January 22, 1881, p. 506.

set upon by a mob in the streets of Valparaiso. This insult to the American flag evoked such a wave of belligerence that for a time there was a distinct possibility of war between Chile and the United States. The Chilean crisis passed, but in 1892 there was the proposal to buy the Danish West Indies as a naval base; and while this failed, it did serve to whet imperialistic appetites for a bite of the Hawaiian pear. Revolution in Hawaii would have meant annexation except for Grover Cleveland. Although the plans of the imperialists had been checked, the Hawaiian venture unfolded a renewed vitality in the doctrine of manifest destiny.

America's forceful foreign policy reached its peak when Secretary of State Olney, in 1895, delivered his "twenty-one gun salute" to Britain with reference to the Venezuelan boundary dispute:

> The United States is practically sovereign on this continent, its fiat is law upon the subjects to which it confines its interposition. Why? It is not because of the pure friendship or good-will felt for it. It is not simply by reason of its high character as a civilized state, nor because wisdom and equity are the invariable characteristics of the dealings of the United States. It is because in addition to all other grounds its infinite resources combined with its isolated position render it master of the situation and practically invulnerable against any and all other powers.[12]

This open display of vigorous diplomacy served notice that American fundamental policies were not to be dismissed by a casual nod from Downing Street. The Monroe Doctrine meant hands off. It also meant that even the pacific and anti-imperialist Cleveland was being swept along by the spirit of the day. It was to be only a matter of time until sharp phrases would be aimed at the Spanish Government whose last vestiges of empire in the New World were obstructing the Caribbean policy of the United States

Diplomacy Relies Upon a Weak Reed

If there had been no Cuban question there would have been no war with Spain, but behind the Cuban question there was the larger problem of the Isthmian question—what power would control the future waterway between the two oceans? Annexation or control of Cuba and Puerto Rico would be of immense importance in the protection of vital American interests in the Caribbean.

Led by the yellow journals, the American public forced a

---

[12] *Foreign Relations of the United States*, 1895, Vol. I, p. 558.

reluctant President to war in April, 1898. This was the culmination of jingoism, frenzy, and imperialism as exemplified in the forceful foreign policy since 1889. America had been talking in a high key during these years, but did America possess strong enough arms to provide the necessary orchestration for this symphony of imperialism?

The United States had a pitifully small army to support its belligerent foreign policy. In the reorganization of the Army in 1866, the available strength was 51,606; in 1869, 35,036; in 1870, 32,788; and in 1874 it was reduced to 25,000.[13] Upon the outbreak of the Spanish-American War the Army numbered 28,-183 officers and men who manned the coast defenses and the many military posts scattered throughout the country. Upon the conclusion of the Civil War, this country had been one of the most formidable military powers in the world. However, by the 1890's this was no longer true. Although the nation had increased greatly in population and immensely in wealth, it had become "by far the feeblest in a military sense of all the nations called great." [14] Population and wealth alone do not constitute military strength. They are only the elements from which military strength may be developed in time and by appropriate means.

The War Department would annually storm the heights of Capitol Hill in an endeavor to increase its appropriation and strength. However, the guardians of the Nation's safety and purse were easily able to ward off these forays. The War Department had as its allies only logic and necessity while Congress could always call upon apathy and, at times, hostility and prejudice against the military.

In addition to stressing the need to be prepared against foreign aggression, the War Department asked for larger funds and more men on a variety of grounds. Continental isolation, it was argued, was no longer any security against attack. The recent vast increase in the means of rapid ocean transportation had changed the Atlantic from its former character of a barrier to the operations of a great army, into a secure, easy, and cheap line of operation, of communication, and of supply for any nation having the necessary naval supremacy.[15]

---

[13] Rpt S/W, 1895, Vol. I, p. 69.
[14] Rpt S/W, 1887, Vol. I, pp. 115-116.
[15] Rpt S/W, 1894, Vol. I, pp. 62-63

Another argument of the War Department was to the effect that a larger army was needed to preserve order and that the local militia could not be relied upon to suppress civil disorder. In the light of the labor strife and unrest of the period this argument might have been expected to be listened to with sympathetic interest. But even this appeal to propertied interests fell upon barren ground.[16] Finally, it was argued that in a country as prosperous as the United States reasonable annual expenditures in preparation for the nation's defense would not diminish the annual increase of national wealth. On the other hand, if war came, to the unprepared nation the loss would amount to thousands of millions of dollars, beside the great loss of life and other evils which could not be estimated.[17]

When war was declared against Spain, public opinion was soon to be thoroughly aroused by the press reports of the war. Previous to the Spanish-American War, the faults of the military establishment had largely been heaped upon the commander in the field; consequently, public opinion was directed not at the system, but at the hapless general who had to conduct his campaigns without the benefit of staff planning. The War Department was not only starved for money and men it was also badly in need of internal reorganization. It required a debacle like that at Tampa, involving the logistical problems of an overseas movement,[18] and an influential and active press to shift the criticism from the line to the staff.

Our incompetent conduct of the Spanish-American War was unbecoming a nation on the eve of becoming a major world power. We began and fought the war with Spain with a staff untrained for its mission except that of maintaining the peacetime military force. National policy was imperialistic, yet to support this reliance was placed upon an Army organization not only lacking in quantity but quality as well.[19] The lack of quantity might be ex-

---

[16] Rpt S/W, 1877, Vol. I, p. 5; 1894, Vol. I, pp. 58-59.

[17] Rpt S/W, 1887, Vol. I, p. 116.

[18] Alger, *op. cit.,* pp. 62-82. *Report of the Commission Appointed by the President to Investigate the Conduct of the War Department in the War with Spain,* Washington G.P.O., 1899, Vol. I, pp. 214-215, 222-231. Hereafter cited as *Dodge Commission.*

[19] Henry Pringle, *Theodore Roosevelt,* New York, Harcourt Brace & Co., 1931, p. 187.

cused by the traditional aversion to a strong peacetime military establishment, but the lack of quality was inexcusable.[20]

Such considerations did not move the political masters of the Army. In the middle 1890's, authorities seemed to believe that America's wars were over.[21] Therefore the military reducing diet had been a steady one. The Secretary of War, Daniel L. Lamont, was quite complacent about the structure of the staff organization in 1896:

> In previous reports attention has been called to what are believed to be defects in the organization of the Army staff—a redundancy of staff corps, more officers in some corps than can be usefully employed and an excessive number of staff officers of high rank.
> Notwithstanding the reductions that have been recently made, the public interests have in no manner suffered as a consequence, the work is not in arrears or lacking in thoroughness, there has been no complaint to the War Department that any officer is overworked. On the contrary it is believed that some further reductions can be made without detriment to the service.[22]

The structure of the Army was considered sound (as indeed, individual scattered units were sound) due to experience in the Indian Wars. Officers' thinking, however, became geared to small units and slow promotions. All details of decision were handled by the War Department bureaus in Washington. It was an army which lacked both the men and the organization to carry on an overseas campaign.

Upon the outbreak of war the Army numbered 28,183 officers and men,[23] but "there was no mobilization plan, no organization of major units, no training in the use of combined arms or in joint operations, no provisions for the assembly or movement overseas or for the command and supply of large bodies of troops."[24] During the war with Spain, military policy was almost wholly subordinated to the dictates of day-to-day expediency. With the administration of the War Department as then existing it was almost impossible to formulate or carry to a legitimate conclusion any

---

[20] William G. H. Carter, *The American Army*, New York, Bobbs Merrill, 1905, p. 27.
[21] Spaulding, *op. cit.*, p. 148.
[22] Rpt S/W, 1896, Vol. I, p. 8.
[23] Alger, *op. cit.*, p. 7. The total was distributed among seventy-seven military posts. Rpt S/W, Vol. I, p. 5.
[24] Millis, *op. cit.*, p. 152.

military policy which attempted to make provision beyond a few months in the future.[25] But, of course, even the most efficient organization attempting to formulate policy without the necessary funds to implement its plans, would find it difficult to achieve objectives.

The Results of Grudging and Dilatory Legislation

War was declared on Spain on April 21, 1898. Secretary of War Russell A. Alger noted that "The governmental machinery was altogether inadequate to meet the emergency. For the preceding thirty years it had been called upon to plan for the needs of the regular army in time of peace, and naturally enough had become quite fixed in the narrow grooves of peace."[26] The attitude of Congress during those thirty years certainly contributed to the disorder and maladministration which followed. Although the war was brief, and the Spanish resistance crumbled quickly, the problems confronting the War Department were gigantic. This was enough to try a most effective staff. Mr. Alger's War Department struggled valiantly to bring order out of chaos, but the handicaps were too great.

From the moment it became apparent that a volunteer army was to be raised and that there was to be an increase in the Regular Army, the office of the Secretary of War and the Adjutant General and the corridors of the War Department were uncomfortably crowded with applicants for appointments, or with members of Congress presenting the claims of constituents for appointment to office. The Secretary of War and the Adjutant General could only attend to the proper functions of their offices in guiding organization, equipment, and mobilization of the volunteer army by secreting themselves for a few moments at a time, or during the night, when most of the real business of the Department had to be conducted, to avoid the pressure from office seekers.[27]

This political pressure even served to emphasize the lack of military intelligence and suitable staff planning. A division of military information had been in operation since 1889 as an adjunct of the Adjutant General's Office, but it had been so dwarfed and

---

[25] Memorandum of Brig. Gen. Wm. H. Carter for Secretary Root, October 30, 1903. AGO 2639296, National Archives.
[26] Alger, *op. cit.*, p. 17.
[27] Carter Memorandum for Secretary Root, 1902, AGO 2639296, National Archives.

subordinated to the routine work of the Department that the outbreak of the war with Spain found it without accurate maps of the enemy's territory and with but meager information of his defenses and military resources.[28]

Lack of planning was reflected also in the sombre picture presented in all of the Army's improvised camps which had to care for 270,000 hastily mobilized men, and especially in the selection and operation of Tampa as the port of embarkation. Colonel Theodore Roosevelt, in his biting phrases, vividly described the confusion and lack of system and the general mismanagement of affairs there.[29] General Shafter, in command of the expeditionary force at Tampa, also poured out a tale of woe into the sympathetic ear of General Henry C. Corbin.[30]

It was apparent that the organization of the War Department left much to be desired, and the lack of coordinated staff planning was vividly underscored. Yet many critics of the War Department's performance in the war are blinded by the blunders and fail to grasp the real significance of the War Department's problems. Keeping in mind the difficulties and handicaps already cited, an objective evaluation of the episodes of the war can only be made in the light of the overwhelming task that suddenly was thrust upon the overburdened War Department.

The Regular Army numbered only 28,183 men and this was the nucleus around which to muster in, equip, organize, and mobilize approximately 250,000 men. After thirty-three years of peace, during a great part of which the Army did not exceed 26,000 men, it suddenly became necessary to arm, clothe, feed, and equip more than a quarter of million men. Even with the best of preparation and equipment this was a tremendous job, as indicated by a later Chief of Staff who was opposed to plunging into a sudden expansion of personnel, and who intimated that no large addition could be readily digested by an Army short in both the personnel and material facilities for training recruits.[31]

---

[28] Charles D. Rhodes, "Experience of our Army," *Journal of the Military Services Institute of the United States*, March-April, 1905, pp. 199-200.
[29] Roosevelt to Lodge, June 10, 1898. Elting E. Morison (ed.) *The Letters of Theodore Roosevelt*, (Cambridge, Harvard U. Press, 1951), Vol. I, p. 837.
[30] Shafter to Corbin, June 7, 1898. *Corbin Mss.* (Library of Congress).
[31] Testimony of General George C. Marshall, February 23, 1940, on the *Military Establishment Appropriation Bill for 1941*, as cited by Mark S. Watson, *The War Department Chief of Staff: Prewar Plans and Preparations*, Washington, GPO, 1950, p. 158.

Lack of equipment is a point often raised in criticism of the War Department. Here again, however, the finger of blame should be aimed at the Congress and not the War Department. On March 9, 1898 Congress appropriated $50,000,000 for national defense. However, none of this was to be used for offensive preparation, it was to be used only for coast defenses and the Navy.[32] On the eve of conflict the War Department was not permitted to make offensive preparations. The War Department could make no purchases or even contract for any of the material so soon to be needed for the new Army. None of the bureaus had on hand reserve supplies. Being unable to increase its stock, each had produced only enough for the immediate everyday needs of the regular establishment on a peace basis.[33] The economy of previous years, by reason of which nearly every article of equipment not immediately needed by the Army was disposed of and no provision made for emergencies, rendered immediate effective expansion of the Army impossible.[34]

The Press Highlights Deficiencies of the Army

The popularity of the war with Spain was almost entirely due to the press, which had apparently convinced even the Chairman of the Senate Foreign Relations Committee that the Spanish Government, through its commander in Cuba, General Weyler, was guilty of atrocities.[35] Senator John Sherman was not alone in his desire to drive the hated dons out of Cuba. Volunteers and militia units swamped the camps and they in turn were swamped by newspaper correspondents.[36]

Embarrassing to the Army and often hindering its operations, this army of newspaper correspondents proved to be a blessing to

---

[32] *Dodge Commission*, Vol. I, p. 113.
[33] Alger, *op. cit.*, pp. 8-9.
[34] *Dodge Commission*, Vol. I, p. 119. The National Guard units quickly revealed their weaknesses and lack of equipment. As far as equipment was concerned they were little better off than recruits, and not a single regiment was fully ready for the field.
[35] "The sensational press had finally triumphed. Led by the *World* and *Journal*, partisan newspapers, after carefully arranging the stage for the final act in the drama of war propaganda 'played up' the *Maine* explosion without restraint and left the American public reeling from a bombardment of half-truths, misstatements of facts, errors, and faked dispatches. Sensing the popular tide, a hesitant administration, egged on by a 'jingo' Congress, proposed war with a nation already on the verge of collapse from internal strife and rebellion." Marcus M. Wilkerson, *Public Opinion of the Spanish-American War*, Baton Rouge Louisiana State Univ., 1932, p. 132.
[36] *Review of Reviews*, July, 1898.

the future military establishment, because it brought to the attention of the public the difficulty encountered in the past in securing consideration of any comprehensive policy concerning preparation for national defense.[37]

The same press which had done so much to bring about the war by its attacks on the Spanish regime in Cuba, now turned its guns on the War Department. This criticism was not based upon misinformation or lack of coverage, rather it stemmed from a first-hand observation of the chaos the war had wrought within the War Department. Among the crowds which filled the rooms and corridors

> was a host of newspaper reporters, who listened to almost all the business which was carried on between the Adjutant General and his assistants. It was next to impossible to keep anything from the press under those conditions. Almost all the orders given appeared in the newspapers about the time, or before, they were received by those for whom they were intended.[38]

Indictments and abuse flowed from the pens of the war correspondents, whose style had been sharpened by their vitriolic attacks upon Spain.

And who was at fault? The *Review of Reviews*[39] felt that it was the inevitable consequence of "the policy that we adopted after the Civil War, which was to do without an army altogether, except as we needed it for detached garrison and guard service, chiefly in the Indian Country." While the national policy had not been conducive to military preparation, the fact still remained that "the Cuban campaign had been foreseen by intelligent officers for more than a year, but the department which clothes the army had taken no steps toward providing a suitable uniform for campaigning in the tropics until war was declared." [40] Even Theodore Roosevelt, who as much as anyone else had wanted this "nice little war," in biting phrases complained that "there is no head, no management in the War Department. Against a good nation we should be helpless." [41] Partially the fault was in the system, the system under

---

[37] Carter, *op. cit.,* p. 14. John D. Miley, *In Cuba with Schafter,* New York, Charles Scribner, 1911, p. 44.
[38] Carter Memorandum for Secretary Root, 1902, AGO 2639296, National Archives.
[39] *July,* 1898.
[40] *Review of Reviews,* December, 1898.
[41] Millis, *op. cit.,* p. 217. The New York *Times* on October 14, 1898, strongly berated Alger for his alleged failure to protect the staff from political interference.

which a bureau chief could "work along his own lines in ignorance of, and on a different basis from, what other bureaus were doing —a course contrary to every economic and business principle." [42]

Difficulties in the War Point the Way for Necessary Reforms

The war with Spain brought forth, in a very marked degree, dissatisfaction with the method of Army administration. So widespread was this feeling in the country that the President assembled a board to investigate the conduct of the war. This commission, headed by General Dodge, sustained almost all the charges of incompetence made by the press. The report of this body focused attention upon the need for reform and reorganization within the Army. For many years, it pointed out, "the divided authority and responsibility in the War Department has produced friction, for which, in the interest of the service, a remedy, if possible, should be applied." [43]

Thus the Spanish-American War drew attention to two grave deficiencies: (1) The relationship between the Secretary of War and the Commanding General with reference to command responsibility in the Army, and the relationship between the bureau chiefs and the Secretary of War to the almost complete disregard of the interests of the Army and the prerogatives of the General of the Army. (2) The lack of preparation by the War Department for a war with a foreign power to be conducted on foreign soil.

With reference to the first, the issue was one of house cleaning which should have been done by the head of the household or his chief servant—the President or Secretary of War. But the unique situation in which the staff departments had been operating for a hundred years, and with the sanction of law, made it unlikely that any agreement could be reached by a voluntary surrender of their strong prestige in the interest of the office of the Commanding General. In this case, a reform was necessary in order to define the proper relationship, in the interest of the Army, between the staff and the line.

In the second instance the issue was one of the culpability with reference to the unpreparedness for war. Although many have said that the War Department knew some four months in advance that the war was coming, few of them put the blame where it belonged.

---

[42] Carter, *op. cit.*, p. 212.
[43] Dodge Commission, Vol. I, p. 115.

In fact, official Washington knew that trouble had been brewing since 1873 (the *Virginius* Affair). The Cuban revolution quieted down and smoldered until 1895 when it broke out again. During the entire period the Cuban Junta had been operating in New York and it is only reasonable to assume that they were giving somebody in official U.S. circles all the information that was needed to conduct war on Cuban soil.

If the War Department knew some four months before the outbreak that war was inevitable, a reasonable assumption would be that officials in the State Department knew much more through unofficial contact with the Junta. Therefore, one may assume that somebody in Congress also knew what was transpiring. Why then, it may be asked, did not the stimulus for war preparations come from Congress which had to appropriate the money before anything could be done?

The War Department did not entirely neglect its responsibilities. They were operating on a minimum and not maximum peacetime basis. There were many who could detect the signs but they were unable to plan anything which involved the expenditure of large sums of money. But they should have had some plan in readiness to solve the maze of logistical problems involved in overseas operations. However they could only do as much as finances permitted them to do and no more.

Elihu Root is Appointed Secretary of War

In order to obtain a clear picture of the chaotic situation in the War Department one should differentiate between the War Department proper and the staff departments. To say that Alger's War Department was inefficient is not altogether just. Alger could do nothing at all to change the situation as far as the staff departments were concerned. This was a canker of long duration and even his successor, Elihu Root, could have done little in 1898. The remedy lay only in the process of law and that remedy might never have been applied if Elihu Root had not been appointed Secretary of War.

President McKinley was not looking for a remedy when he appointed Root. McKinley was not looking for "anyone who knows anything about war or for anyone who knows anything about the army; he has got to have a lawyer to direct the government of these Spanish islands and you are the lawyer he wants." [44] Perhaps it was fortunate that Mr. Root had no knowledge of military affairs for, because of this, he took office with the criticism of the Spanish War fresh in mind. Unfettered by any previous connections with the military he could view the problem objectively. He began to study the background methodically by reading volumes of material on the subject and talking with Army officers and other men of experience. As a result of his research, the Army seemed to him very much like a corporation run without a general manager or board of directors by the superintendents of the various departments of the business. [45] The difficulty was not what to do but how to accomplish it. As Senator Lodge pointed out:

> Today the system stands guilty of the blunders, delays, and needless sufferings and deaths of the war, and the war being over, reforms are resented by patriots who have so little faith in the republic that they think that a properly organized army of 100,000 men puts it in danger, and by bureau chiefs and their friends in Congress who want no change, for reasons obvious if not public spirited. [46]

Root realized that any attempt to provide a "general manager" for these "superintendents" must be cautiously made. Therefore, prior to the issuance of his first annual report, he tried to carefully prepare the groundwork for its favorable reception. [47] He knew that the plans he was maturing would meet stubborn, bitter resistance, and he also grasped the fundamental importance of the reforms that he contemplated. However, he also knew that reorganization must take place while the lessons drawn from the experience of the recent war were still fresh in the public mind. [48] Here Elihu Root was in the best American tradition, in reflecting George Washington's observations of 1783.

The Responsibilities of Imperialism

The war with Spain not only established American mastery of the Caribbean area but also extended American influence into the turbulent waters of the Far East. Here America was forced to

---

[44] Phillip C. Jessup, *Elihu Root,* New York, Dodd, Mead & Co., 1938, Vol. I, p. 215.

[45] *Ibid.,* p. 254.

[46] Henry C. Lodge, *The War With Spain,* New York, the Macmillan Co., 1899, p. 281.

[47] Jessup, *op. cit.,* Vol. I, p. 242.

[48] Rpt S/W, 1899, Vol. I, p. 45.

crush the Philippine Insurrection, thus invoking a larger military operation than the Cuban campaign. Also of great significance was the establishment of a new base of American diplomacy as exemplified by the Open Door Notes of 1899 and 1900. The emergence of the United States as an active participant in Far Eastern diplomacy was marked not only by the notes of Secretary John Hay, but also by the Boxer Rebellion of 1900. America's participation in the joint expedition to crush this uprising was the first military operation undertaken in conjunction with allies since the Revolutionary War.

When it became evident to the Filipinos, after the signing of the Treaty of Paris, December 10, 1898, that they were merely exchanging Spanish for American masters, they rose in revolt on February 4, 1899. Insufficient manpower was to be one of the most pressing problems of the campaigns. Before the end of the insurrection, the total number of troops in the Philippines reached 75,000, and during the course of hostilities the American commander was plagued by a traditional American malady, "the relief and replacement of an army in the face of the enemy."[49] Wartime legislation had authorized the raising of volunteers for the duration of the war only; consequently the end of hostilities with Spain meant a hasty mustering out of the volunteers. In August, 1898 the War Department announced the demobilization of half the total number, or 100,000 men.[50] But the volunteers in the Philippines were not affected by this order. With the passage of legislation on March 2, 1899 the authorized strength of the Regular Army was increased from 27,000 to 65,000, supplemented by 35,000 volunteers for service in the Philippines.[51] This law further provided for the discharge of the volunteers by June 30, 1901; therefore General Arthur MacArthur was faced with the traditional task of reorganization in the face of the enemy.[52]

Legislation of February 2, 1901 increased the size of the Regular Army to meet the immediate demands in the Islands only after months of delay. Perhaps one reason why Congress was tardy in meeting the military requirements of the Army was the military successes gained in the early months of 1900. After this there was

---

[49] Spaulding, *op. cit.*, p. 387.
[50] Rpt S/W, 1898, Vol. I, p. 7.
[51] XXX *Stat* 977.
[52] Spaulding, *op. cit.*, p. 393.

but little resistance except guerrilla warfare which finally collapsed with the capture of Emilio Aguinaldo in January, 1901.[53]

American ventures in the Philippines were sharply criticized by some of the press which compared McKinley with Simon Legree and declared "our soldiers and sailors who so bravely enlisted for the war with Spain should not be engaged in a long war with the Filipinos."[54]

---

[53] XXXI *Stat* 748-758.
[54] See Baltimore *Sun* as quoted in the *Literary Digest*, April 8, 1899.

CHAPTER 13

The General Staff Concept:
A Decade of Controversy

Elihu Root Displays His Talents—The Bureau Chiefs Object—The General Staff Is Adopted—The Adjutant
General Defines His Position—The Chief of Staff Defines
His Position—The President Calls a Halt to the Controversy

Elihu Root Displays His Talents

I N LOOKING over the situation which he had inherited from
Alger, Secretary of War Root was convinced that a thorough
reorganization was needed to remedy the manifold ills of the War
Department. The only cure lay in the establishment of a general
staff system based upon that of Germany. But to do this he first
had to break through the hard core of established military precedent and to cultivate a favorable opinion for such a system in the
Army, in Congress, and in the country.

To a person with Root's logical and orderly mind the chaos
inherent in the divided authority of the War Department was intolerable. A Commanding General, with responsibilities but little
authority, struggled with the Secretary of War for authority and
prestige. The uncoordinated bureau chiefs operated in their almost
impenetrable compartments, largely ignoring the Commanding
General, but bowing to the power of the Secretary's control of the
purse strings, while strengthening their positions by currying favor
with Congress. Root, who was greatly influenced by the writings
of General Emory Upton in his whole program of reorganization,
agreed with Upton that this situation had made possible the
estrangement of the Commanding General and Secretary of War:

> Instead of acknowledging the general in chief, under the Presi-
> dent, as the military head of the army, the chiefs of staff corps
> have magnified the duties of the Secretary of War and have pre-
> ferred to look to him, not only as the chief of administration, but
> as their sole and legitimate military superior. Under his protection,
> they have to a large degree withdrawn the operation of their de-

partments from the control and even inspection of the general in chief and other military commanders. The Ordnance, for example, manufactures our guns and carriages; the Engineers build the fortifications on which the guns are mounted, and both are turned over to the Army to be tested in war without an opportunity for the general in chief, or the officers who may die in their defense, to make the slightest suggestion.[1]

With deliberate purpose, Root broke the ground for his General Staff in an address before the Marquette Club in Chicago on October 7, 1899. He told his audience that it rested with them, through the senators and representatives in Congress whom they should elect, to determine whether the lesson of the Spanish war should be learned, and the military reorganization of America be put in the front of American progress.[2] In his first Annual Report for 1899 Root outlined two fundamental propositions: That the real object of having an Army was to prepare for war (which was not being done); and that the Regular Army would probably never be the whole machine with which any war will be fought. While he did not recommend a General Staff as such, he did lay the groundwork for it in a general outline for the reorganization of the War Department. He called for a systematic study of plans of action under all contingencies of possible conflict; the preparation of material of war; a method of officer promotion by selection instead of on a rigid basis of seniority; and the introduction of field maneuvers with large bodies of troops. To implement his plans Root recommended: (1) the establishment of an Army War College; (2) instruction at the College for every officer below the rank of field officer at some fixed period during his service; (3) the inauguration of a short detail plan (four or five years) for service on the staff with a return to the line.[3]

---

[1] Emory Upton: *The Military Policy of the United States*, Senate Document 379m 64th Congress, 1st Session, 1916, 4th ed; p. 159. Root unearthed this unpublished manuscript and had it published as an official document to which he contributed a foreword. John Dickinson: *The Building of an Army*, (New York: The Century Co., 1922), p. 255 lists the following defects in the War Department when Root took office. "(1) The absence of connection between the staff bureaus and the army proper. (2) The absence of any central agency for the formulation of any general military policy for working out the details of a military program and for the accumulation of military information. (3) As one of the causes for the foregoing, the permanent assignment of officers to staff duties. (4) The lack of coordination between the various staff bureaus. (5) As an incident of the foregoing, the wastefulness of a decentralized system of purchase and supply."

[2] Robert Bacon and James B. Scott: *The Military and Colonial Policy of the United States, Addresses and Reports by Elihu Root*, (Cambridge: Harvard University Press, 1924), p. 4.

[3] *Annual Report, Secretary of War*, p. 44 *passim*.

The idea of an Army War College was a natural growth and development of the Army's educational system which already included schools for the basic branches. However, there was a lack of a general system of military education under the inspection and supervision of a single coordinating and supervisory body. In line with these recommendations for the creation of an Army War College, and with the approval of the President, the Secretary of War appointed on February 19, 1900 a board of officers to draft a plan for an Army War College which would bring the service schools and the Division of Military Information (this was the Military Intelligence Division) under one control, and which would supplement and perfect the course of instruction. The letter of instructions to the board included such items for consideration as cooperation in instruction, the formulation of plans, procurement of information, and the extension of military instruction to men in civil life in such a way as to build up a reserve list of officers remaining in civil life, but instructed and competent for volunteer commissions whenever necessary.[4]

The first appropriation for the establishment of such a college was made in the Army bill approved on May 26, 1900. Other appropriations for the War College were made in the Army appropriation bill for fiscal 1902, making possible the formal establishment of the War College under General Order No. 155, of November 27, 1901.[5] The creation of the Army War College and the duties imposed upon it was probably as near an approach to the establishment of a general staff as was possible under existing laws.[6]

The first fruits of the Army War College, under the presidency of Brigadier General Tasker H. Bliss, were impressive. In addition, the School at Fort Leavenworth was reorganized as a General Service and Staff College and the special service schools were also reorganized. A system of schools was established at the principal posts under which a compulsory course was required of all junior officers.

It was the aim of the Army War College that the best men from the post schools should be sent to Leavenworth and the spe-

---

[4] Root to Church, February 20, 1900. *Church Mss.,* Library of Congress. Unless otherwise noted, the Mss. collections are in the Library of Congress.
[5] Bacon and Scott, *op. cit.,* p. 390.
[6] *Annual Report, Secretary of War, 1901,* p. 25.

cial service schools and from there to the Army War College where they would study and confer upon the great problems of national defense, of military science, and of responsible command.[7] Some confusion seems to have existed as to whether the primary aim of the Army War College was educational or as an adjunct of the General Staff. The instructions to General Bliss, the first president of the War College, under date of October 27, 1903 ordered him to report a detailed scheme of lectures and practical work. General Bliss interpreted this to mean that emphasis should be placed on the practical. He pointed out that Mr. Root's first idea of the institution, as given in his *Report of 1899*, was that the word "college" was used in its old Latin sense of collegium, that is, a body of men associated together with the object of doing something rather than to learn how to do it, or, at the most, the learning how is subordinated to the doing.[8] Under this concept, the Army War College began its career primarily as an adjunct of the General Staff rather than an institution of learning. The establishment of the new system of military education was to prove to be not only of immense benefit to the Army, but also as an important step in the final victory of creating a General Staff.

The Bureau Chiefs Object

Root moved slowly and cautiously to implement his program, for he realized that in order to overcome "the diversity of opinions and personal interests desirous of being left undisturbed" and to help create "a sufficient strong conviction of the importance of good organization," it was necessary to gain the backing of public opinion. He asked for support of the Army Reorganization Bill which was "but one of a series of measures included in the general plan which I outlined in my Annual Report. It is designed to secure some reasonable opportunity for selection in line promotions, to secure flexibility in the staff, and break up the excessive bureaucratic tendency and to reorganize the Artillery on modern lines." [9] This legislation was framed to meet the immediate requirements of the Army, including troop strength in the Philippines, and to include only such new matter as was acceptable to the Congress.[10]

[7] Bacon and Scott, *op. cit.,* p. 122.
[8] George P. Ahern, *A Chronicle of the Army War College, 1899-1919,* (Washington: G.P.O., 1919), pp. 25-26, 97.
[9] Root to Church, February 20, 1900. *Church Mss.*
[10] William H. Carter: *Creation of the American General Staff,* (Senate Document 119, 68th Congress, 1st Session, 1924), p. 4,

Though this was an organization bill trimmed down to the narrowest range of subjects[11] it required much tact and persistence to persuade a reluctant Congress to enact it. The Act of February 2, 1901 provided for an increase of line organizations from twenty-five regiments of infantry to thirty, from ten regiments of cavalry to fifteen, from seven regiments of artillery, including sixteen field batteries, to a Corps of Artillery, practically equivalent to thirteen regiments under the old organization, and from one battalion of engineers to three. Minimum and maximum numbers of enlisted men for the different organizations were established by the same statute, so that the total number of enlisted men might be varied by the President, according to the exigencies of the time, from a minimum of 59,131 to a maximum of 100,000, without any change of commissioned officers or in the number of organizations. "Had this wise provision obtained in 1898," General Corbin wrote, "it would have resulted in the saving of many lives to the nation and many millions of dollars to the Treasury." [12] The Act also provided for the permanent appointment in the Regular Army of 1135 selected volunteer officers and enlisted men as well as the establishment of the office of Chief of Artillery. As far as fundamental reorganization went the only serious change of system was that embraced in the abolition of permanent appointments in many of the staff and supply departments, and the substitution of detailed officers.

Early in 1902 Root directed Col. William H. Carter to prepare a bill, embodying his ideas on the General Staff, for presentation to Congress. The measure was introduced on February 14, 1902 by Mr. James Howley. Sections one to three of the bill provided for the consolidation of the Quartermaster's Department, Subsistence Department, and Pay Department into a Department of Supply. Sections four to ten related to the creation of a General Staff.[13]

Root's efforts to bring about reform aroused strong and bitter opposition among many high ranking officers. That opposition was personified by General Nelson Miles, the Commanding General of the Army, who wielded a large measure of influence in Con-

---

[11] Root to Wood, January 19, 1901. *Root Mss.*

[12] *The Army and Navy Journal*, May 21, 1901. Hereafter cited as *ANJ*.

[13] Otto L. Nelson Jr., *National Security and the General Staff*, (Washington, Infantry Journal Press, 1946), pp. 86-87.

gressional circles. Perhaps the chief motive in Miles' opposition to the proposed bill was not so much an aversion to reform on grounds of administrative efficiency, but rather an ingrained distaste to a change in the *status quo*. According to Miles, the proposed bill would

> revolutionize our system of administration and take out of the hands of the commanders of the Army and of the Departments, Divisions and Brigades, as well as the Corps of Inspectors, the proper control of military affairs and transfer it to a corps of detailed officers of junior rank. You will notice by the bill that out of 37 officers who are to compose the General Staff, 24 are Majors and Captains. There is now only one Captain in the Army who is a veteran of the Civil War, and only 31 Majors. The veterans of the Civil War are mostly Colonels, and the experience acquired by them in the great Civil War is invaluable to the nation. They are today giving tone and character to the Army, and this is so much needed in view of the fact that so many new men have been pushed into the Army during the last few years, many of whom have been given unusual rank and station.[14]

In the hearings on the bill, the testimony of General Miles was responsible for defeating any prospects of success at that session of Congress. Colonel Carter was advised that favorable action on the bill could not be expected at this time, and to prepare for a reintroduction of it at the next session of Congress. Within the War Department itself it was generally understood that the combination of General Miles and the influential bureau chiefs could easily obstruct such legislation as proposed in the original bill. To overcome these obstacles, Root decided to inaugurate a publicity campaign to win support throughout the country and in Congress itself. Every effort was made to concentrate attention upon the creation of the General Staff. This was accomplished by the preparation of a separate bill, couched in simple language, in support of a General Staff organization which was to have combined with it the duties of the Inspector General's Department.[15]

The General Staff is Adopted

On December 1, 1902, in his Annual Report, Root re-emphasized the need for a General Staff. The report was given wide publicity, for Root very much desired public understanding and public interest[16] in his proposed reforms. To one familiar with verbose

---

[14] Miles to Church, March 26, 1902. *Church Mss.*
[15] Carter, *op. cit.*, p. 43.
[16] Root to Church, November 26, 1902. *Church Mss.*

and tedious state papers it is hard to imagine that a Report of the Secretary of War would have wide influence. Yet such was the case with Root's Report of 1902. Certainly it had influence in Army circles, for Major General Theodore Schwan called it "the ablest document of the kind that has ever emanated from the War Department. The Secretary exhibits in this exceedingly valuable paper a knowledge of Army conditions that would do credit to one who has devoted his life to the solution of difficult military problems." [17] The report was widely read by members of Congress and doubtless was influential in reducing opposition to the General Staff Bill pending before Congress. [18]

Finally, on February 14, 1903, exactly one year after its first presentation to Congress, the General Staff Act, as it was known, was enacted. This act abolished the separate office of a General Commanding the Army, provided for a military Chief of Staff to the President, who, acting under the directions of the President, or of the Secretary of War, should have supervision not only of all troops of the line but of the special staff and supply departments which had formerly reported directly to the Secretary of War. It created, for the assistance of the Chief of Staff, a corps of forty-four officers who were relieved from all other duties. The terms of the act provided that it was not to take effect until August 15, 1903 (Miles would be retired by then). [19] During the period from February to August the General Staff was selected and new regulations were issued to implement the provisions of the act.

The law as finally approved differed in many particulars from the original bill, but Root, like Theodore Roosevelt, was a firm believer in "a half loaf is better than none." Most important among these changes was that the powerful Inspector General's Department was retained, and it was not made a part of the General Staff. This was due to the political adeptness of the Inspector General himself, General Breckenridge. Likewise, the Chief of the Bureau of Pensions and Records was able to preserve his position. This was General Frederick C. Ainsworth's first oppositional contact with the General Staff idea. But it was by no means his last.

---

[17] Schwan to Corbin, December 18, 1902. *Corbin Mss.*
[18] Nelson, *op. cit.*, p. 99.
[19] William H. Carter, *Creation of the American General Staff*, pp. 47-50.

The Adjutant General Defines His Position

In some quarters the general staff idea was received with reserve if not outright hostility.[20] Even the most enthusiastic supporters of the General Staff were aware of the difficulties in store for this latest addition to the War Department's already large family of organizational entities. General Adna R. Chaffee, who was appointed Chief of Staff in 1904, reached the conclusion that "some in authority, who had not agreed entirely with the retiring Secretary of War, Elihu Root, in the reforms introduced during his administration were determined upon a reactionary campaign." [21] This was to be expected in a situation where the independence of action heretofore exercised by the bureau chiefs would be curtailed. The greatest difficulty, General Carter implicitly warned, was forthcoming from the Adjutant General "who has in the past performed many duties of the Chief of Staff to the Secretary of War." [22]

Realizing that in the old days the Adjutant General often gained the inside track when in rivalry with the Commanding General, simply because his office adjoined the office of the Secretary of War, the Chief of Staff decided that his office should occupy this location.

This slight change in internal office arrangements had no appreciable effect on the rising star of General Ainsworth, who still had free and easy access to the halls of Congress where he had already built up the legend that the Adjutant General was, in military matters, the Congressman's best friend. To strengthen his position against the authority of the Chief of Staff, General Ainsworth set out to improve his own claim to authority. Seizing upon the waste prevalent in the overlapping duties with respect to the maintenance of records in the Adjutant General's Office and in the Bureau of Records and Pension Office, he set out in December 1903 to persuade the Secretary of War to effect a consolidation. Ignoring the General Staff, which was the proper agency for the consideration of the proposal, a board of officers, with Ainsworth as a member, recommended that in the interests of greater efficiency and economy, the Bureau of Records and Pensions and

---

[20] *ANJ*, April 15, 1905.

[21] William H. Carter, *The Life of Lieutenant General Chaffee*, (Chicago: U. of Chicago Press, 1917), p. 268.

[22] Nelson, *op. cit.*, p. 73.

the Office of the Adjutant General should be consolidated under the name of the Office of the Military Secretary.[23]

The manner in which the board's recommendations were enacted into law is of prime interest because it provides the background necessary to understand the coming controversy between Ainsworth and General Leonard Wood. The measure to consolidate the duties of the Adjutant General's Department and those of the Records and Pension Office was strongly defended by Secretary Root in a letter and memorandum by which he transmitted his recommendations to Congress.[24]

Prior to his departure from office on August 19, 1903 Secretary Root thought that it would be a wise move to change the name of the Adjutant General's office to that of the Office of the Military Secretary, since during the many years that the Army had been without a General Staff, the Adjutant General's office had been performing many of the duties now assigned to the Chief of Staff. He felt that the name "Adjutant General's Department" held connotations of power that were inconsistent with the new role that the chief of the bureau was to perform as Military Secretary.

Secretary Root pointed out in his memorandum, citing the historical background of the Adjutant General's department, that

> Before the creation of the General Staff, the Adjutant General's Department was the most important of the Staff Departments of the Army, because the Adjutant General and his assistants then discharged many of the important duties that are now discharged by the Chief of Staff and his assistants. In default of officers specially authorized for the purpose they became the principal advisors of the Secretary of War and the higher military commanders with respect to the administration and command of the Army and in respect to military matters in general. But the establishment of the General Staff has relieved the Adjutant General's Office of substantially all of its advisory and discretionary functions, and the Adjutant General's Office is a bureau of records and correspondence. The head of that bureau is virtually a corresponding secretary for the Secretary of War and the Chief of Staff, his principal duties being to conduct and record their correspondence, the transmission or publication of orders being a part of such correspondence and to furnish information for their use from the records in his custody.[25]

---

[23] *Ibid.*, p. 83.
[24] *ANJ*, January 16, 1904.
[25] *Ibid.*

Secretary Root's recommendations appeared quite acceptable until the measure to consolidate the Adjutant General's Office and the Records and Pension Office into the Office of the Military Secretary was made public through an amendment to the Army Appropriation Bill for the ensuing year, in which appeared two provisos that brought the bill under the fire of sharp criticism. The bill provided "that the officers of said consolidated department shall be subject to the supervision of the Chief of Staff *in all matters pertaining to the command, discipline or administration of the existing military establishment.*" The words underlined had been added. "The bill was better as it originally stood," commented the *Army and Navy Journal*, "the amendment is fruitful of suggestion between the Chief of Staff and the Military Secretary, of a conflict of authority, which should never be permitted in a military establishment." The bill was also amended to provide that the Military Secretary "shall hereafter have the rank of major general," but that proviso was to apply only to Ainsworth for in the future the post would carry the rank of Brigadier General.[26]

The *Army and Navy Journal* was staggered by the amendment and reported that the Army felt this was a "most radical piece of legislation" particularly as it affected Ainsworth.[27]

The *Journal* also lamented that those who had supported Root in his plans of reform "have been betrayed in the house of their friends" and their confidence in Root "has not been justified." Root answered this attack of the *Army and Navy Journal* in a personal letter to its editor, William C. Church, scoring the author of the editorial for having failed to appreciate the effect of the General Staff legislation upon the Adjutant General's Department; for the act creating the General Staff had transferred to that body all of the functions of advice and control which for a century had been vested in the Adjutant General. The proposed change, Root continued, would

> merely effect a much needed reform in the clerical work of the business establishment in the War Department building which is quite distinct from the Army. The change of name from Adjutant General to Military Secretary was specially intended to emphasize the fact which the writer of this article has lost sight of, that the old office of Adjutant General no longer really exists. . . . The provision making the Military Secretary a Major General was a

---

[26] *ANJ*, January 30, 1904.
[27] *Ibid.*

change made in Committee, and was not in the bill as it went from the War Department.[28]

Root was quite capable of taking care of himself, but it soon became evident that Ainsworth would not suffer from lack of support. Senator Cockerell of Missouri recounted the epochal success of Ainsworth in his organizational streamlining and the efficiency he had brought to the Record and Pension Office. "General Ainsworth has done a work which has never been equalled by any executive officer of this Government from 1789 to date and I challenge any comparison with his record." [29]

General Ainsworth had not only been an able administrator but an astute politician, for he had been preeminently successful in establishing smooth relations with Congress. As an indication of his strength in Congress he felt bold enough to warn Root that the consolidation measure would not pass without the amendments under attack.[30] The measure passed in the form that Ainsworth desired and once again the general had won an important victory.

Ainsworth was not disposed to remain and function as the Military Secretary in the sense that Root had intended. Indeed, it would have been strange had an administrator as brilliant and energetic as Ainsworth been content with the stenographic role which it was intended that the Military Secretary should play. He knew that he was on sound ground by urging the Chief of Staff, Major General Franklin Bell, to divest the General Staff of routine tasks many of which had been taken over by it as a means of justifying its existence in its youthful eagerness; these tasks which should never have been disturbed and should have remained with the proper bureau. In correspondence with former Secretary Root,[31] his views in this regard found sanction and support which prompted General Bell to lean more and more upon his capable Military Secretary. Bell found particular justification in a letter of Root which strongly supported the position of Ainsworth.

> I consider it important to avoid imposing on the General Staff duties of an administrative character. . . . Of course experience may show that in specific matters there is occasion for reassignment of particular duties in accordance with this principle; but I am not now aware of any occasion which were left to the

---

[28] Root to Church, January 30, 1904. *Church Mss.*
[29] Nelson, *op. cit.*, p. 86.
[30] Ainsworth to Root, March 9, 1904. *Root Mss.*
[31] Ainsworth to Root, May 5, 1904. *Root Mss.*

Adjutant General's Department should be imposed upon the General Staff. On the contrary, I think that constant watchfulness should be exercised to avoid loading the Staff down with matters which are really administrative.[32]

By the time that General Bell's detail as Chief of Staff expired on April 22, 1910 and he was succeeded by Major General Leonard Wood, Ainsworth had done much to recoup the former position of the Adjutant General's office. Very quietly and apparently without any reference to the General Staff, Congress had by an Act of March 2, 1907 changed the name of the Military Secretary's Office back to its former designation, The Adjutant General's Department.[33]

The Chief of Staff Defines His Position

Like his predecessor, General Bell, Wood arrived in Washington with very definite ideas about the War Department and what should be done to further such ideas. His appointment as Chief of Staff was generally accorded favorable reaction,[34] although the New York *Evening Post* was inclined to be critical and wondered if professional army training was worth the effort, especially when appointment to the most influential position in the Army was tendered to one

who attended neither West Point, nor any other military school in or outside of the Army; who was until eleven years ago in the active practice of medicine and surgery; who never drilled a company in his life; whose experience as a regimental commander lasted about two months in 1898. Many officers will not fail to say, with a good deal of force that if a man of this education and experience is entitled to practically the leadership of the Army, all the laborious studying of the modern officer is needless.[35]

When Wood arrived in Washington he was met by Ainsworth, with whom he stayed a few days. They dined frequently and spent evenings talking shop. But such amenities were soon to cease and relationships were to become more and more strained as it became increasingly evident to Wood that Ainsworth was completely out of sympathy with progressive ideas of War Department reform. Ainsworth looked upon the whole General Staff concept with disdain, and he had not been alone among the bureau chiefs in hop-

[32] Jessup, *op. cit.,* I, p. 262.
[33] *General Order 46, War Department,* March 7, 1907.
[34] *ANJ,* December 18, 1909.
[35] New York *Evening Post,* December 16, 1909.

ing that one of their own kind, a man in sympathy with the *status quo,* would be appointed to the office of Chief of Staff. In the upheaval following the break between the two men, the General Staff was to receive a large amount of unfavorable publicity. General Wood eventually won his point, General Ainsworth was retired, but acceptance of the General Staff concept was retarded.

The struggle was precipitated by General Wood's efforts to secure a large increase in appropriations. Unsuccessful, he began to look for means to make the allotted funds go further. In the reforms that followed, the ire of many of the bureau chiefs was aroused and the conflict with Ainsworth was brought to a head. To Wood it seemed apparent that no appreciable administrative economies could be effected unless the office of the Adjutant General could be invaded. Therefore in December of 1910 he appointed a board of officers to investigate the immense amount of paper work and the cumbersome methods of making returns.

This invasion of the domain of the Adjutant General ruptured the already strained relationship. The move brought on an ominous rumbling from the office of the Adjutant General and within six weeks, the first explosion was heard:

> . . . Ainsworth lost his temper, telling Wood that his office was not having "its proper influence in the Department." Wood answered that, while recognizing Ainsworth's office, he proposed to treat it precisely like any other bureau of the War Department, having no intention either to deprive Ainsworth of any privileges he had rightfully enjoyed or of turning over to him any of the duties of the chief of staff.[36]

Thereafter it was open and declared warfare. When the Chief of Staff in December, 1911 moved to reduce the period of enlistment from three to two years, in order to provide what he termed a more adequate national defense program,[37] General Ainsworth appeared before the Committee on Military Affairs of the House with his heaviest artillery. The committee indulged his gift for brilliant irony, and by skillful questions, encouraged the Adjutant General to pour his scorn upon the Chief of Staff. Representative James Hay, Chairman of the Committee and intimate friend of Ainsworth, adopted the democratic procedure of circularizing four

---

[36] Hermann Hagedorn, *Leonard Wood: A Biography,* New York, Harper & Bros., 1931, 2 Vols., Vol. II, p. 99.

[37] Another aim of Wood was to discourage re-enlistments and thus make the Army not an establishment of veterans, but a school for youth and thus help create a trained reserve.

hundred officers of the Army. The replies from the officers then in command of troops were indicative of a disposition toward the three-year enlistment by a two to one margin.[38]

This apparent victory for the Adjutant General, however, was short-lived, for the search for economies had brought forth the recommendation for abolishing the muster roll system of Army records. This was approved by the Secretary of War, and on December 15, 1911 General Ainsworth was asked for his comments. Not until February 3, 1912 and after repeated efforts to secure his comments, did he submit his reply. Impugning the whole theory behind the proposals for the abolition of the muster roll system, he referred to this move as both illegal and impractical.

When General Wood read Ainsworth's further charges that the proposed plan was "a subterfuge" such as "would be scorned by honorable men," and scoring the folly of entrusting to "incompetent amateurs" the management of important business,[39] he knew that the time was ripe for a show down. Here was a good case for the purpose. He took the memorandum to Secretary of War Henry Stimson who had interpreted the Adjutant General's dissent as an attack upon himself and

> under date of February 14, 1912, the Secretary of War addressed a letter to Maj. Gen. F. C. Ainsworth, The Adjutant General of the Army, charging him with insubordination and other improper official conduct, quoting in said letter extracts from various official and personal communications in support of that charge and relieving him from the discharging the duties of his office and directing him to await further orders.[40]

From the accounts in the public press it appears that news of the suspension of General Ainsworth was received at the Capitol sometimes during the day of February 15, and a copy of the letter was read on the floor of the House while the Army Appropriation Bill was under consideration. There was a lively exchange in the House just when the amendment extending the enlistment from

---

[38] Army Appropriation Bill Hearings, December 15, 1911, p. 719 as quoted in Nelson, *op. cit.*, p. 138. It was the long run versus the short run point of view. The actions of the Congressional Committees sharply emphasized the divergent tendencies within the War Department. The hearings also clearly showed that Ainsworth did not exhibit the loyalty that Wood had a right to expect.

[39] House of Representatives Report, 508: "Relief of the Adjutant General of the Army from the duties of his Office," 62d Congress, 2d Session, p. 13. Hereafter cited as *House Report 508.*

[40] *Ibid.*, p. 2.

three to five years was being debated. The amendment was endorsed by General Ainsworth but was strongly opposed by the General Staff.[41]

The Secretary of War's letter charged General Ainsworth with impugning the fairness and intelligence of the Secretary of War; with criticizing and questioning the military capacity, experience, intelligence, fairmindedness, honor, and good faith of the officers of the General Staff and the War College; with insubordination and impropriety of official conduct. All this was looked upon by the House Committee on Military Affairs as unjustified and without support.[42] The views of the Committee were also held by some few who had intimate knowledge of both sides of the question.[43]

Many facts in the background of the controversy leading up to General Ainsworth's relief were before the people. Public opinion was based almost entirely on the statements made by Stimson in his letter to Ainsworth. In earnest support of the Secretary's action the New York *Evening Post*[44] declared: "all who have the good and honor of the Army at heart will rejoice at this decisive way of dealing with an officer who has long borne himself as if he were a privileged character, beyond the possibility of criticism or of discipline."

Secretary Stimson, amid the intense excitement, quietly pursued the course he had elected to follow and prepared for the court-martial. The day following Ainsworth's suspension, Senator Warren of Wyoming, Chairman of the Senate Committee on Appropriations, but formerly Chairman of the Senate Military Committee, carried to the President a request from Ainsworth, asking that he be allowed to retire. The request was approved by President Taft.

> For Wood it was a notable victory not only because it assured his personal supremacy, but because it assured in the War Department the supremacy of the law over the willful despotism of any individual, and established the conception of the government of the Army which was the heart of Root's plan of reorganization. The chorus of relief and satisfaction was practically unanimous. From the officers of the army no dissenting voice reached Wood's ears. But the House took its revenge, the very day Ainsworth

---

[41] *ANJ*, February 17, 1912.
[42] House Report 508, p. 3.
[43] *ANJ*, February 17, 1912.
[44] New York *Evening Post*, February 16, 1912.

retired, by passing all the legislation Wood had opposed and Ainsworth had defended.[45]

The *Army and Navy Journal* expressed hope that the case of General Ainsworth would restore harmony among the counsels of the War Department, and was ready to bring to a close the final chapter of the controversy by placing the blame squarely on Ainsworth, for "there should be no place in the Army for a man who is not disposed to subordinate to his own ambition or to his own pride of opinion the interest of a service whose very instinct should be that of patriotism, duty and self-sacrifice." [46] General Wood had his victory, but for the General Staff it meant running the gamut of political red tape, indecision, and suspicion. The General Staff was plunged into the murky waters of partisan political strife.

The President Calls a Halt to the Controversy

Secretary of War Stimson and General Wood formulated an extensive plan of Army reorganization, including the abandonment of certain Army posts as soon as adequate facilities could be provided in localities for which there existed military justification for the presence of troops. Among those listed for eventual disposal was Fort Russell, Wyoming, a pet project of Senator Warren on which over four million dollars had been spent. Such a move naturally rankled in the senatorial breast and Warren, backed by Hay, went hunting for Wood's scalp. In a conference between the House and the Senate on the Army Appropriation Bill they forced through two amendments to embarrass the Chief of Staff.

> The first created a commission of five retired Army officers, named in the bill, and two members from each House of Congress, to report upon the location and distribution of Army posts and forbade the President meanwhile to make any changes whatsoever in the existing posts. The second provided that after March 5, 1913, no officer should be permitted to serve as Chief of Staff unless he should have served at least ten years as commissioned officer of the line of the Army in grades below that of brigadier general. As Root pointed out in the Senate, this provision "could not better accomplish its purpose if it read that after the 5th of March no man whose initials were L. W. shall be Chief of Staff.[47]

[45] Hagedorn, *op. cit.*, Vol. II, p. 123.
[46] *ANJ*, February 17, 1912.
[47] Hagedorn, *op. cit.*, Vol. II, p. 123.

The press was of one accord that the President should veto the bill on the grounds of the principle involved. The New York *Times* voiced the opinion that "obviously this sort of legislation cannot be countenanced by the people of the United States unless they are willing to have their army demoralized altogether . . . the proposed legislation should be set aside because of the personal motive that characterizes it." [48]

Wood was attacked from all sides: Ainsworth's friends, led by Hay; the men with Army posts to defend; the Progressive Republicans who attacked him because he had the Administration's support; the Taft men who fought him because he was conspicuously Roosevelt's friend. But he also had some staunch support:

> Root and Lodge fought for Wood in the Senate. In the House, Representative Martin of Colorado commented sharply on Senator Warren's personal interest in a vacancy in the office of the chief of staff, since his son-in-law, General Pershing, stood close in line of succession. Representative Cooper, of Wisconsin, charged that Wood was the victim of a Conspiracy, hatched by Mark Hanna when Wood exposed Rathbone.[49]

As the time for his action on the bill approached, Taft expressed strong dissatisfaction at the manner in which Congress, particularly the Democratic House, was trying to coerce him by including objectionable legislation in an appropriation bill.[50] He had conferred with Stimson on the matter, and with Senator Root, who agreed to "fight the army conference report" which included the objectionable sections upon the adoption of which the House of Representatives was insisting. Taft was sure that the Democrats had put in the bill a restriction in regard to the reappointment of the chief of staff, in order to "get even with Gen. Wood for the part he is supposed to have played in the relief of General Ainsworth." [51]

In his veto message on the bill, Taft noted that the danger of attaching substantive legislation to appropriation bills had been pointed out by former Presidents. He objected to the provision limiting the eligibility of officers to be Chief of Staff, thereby narrowing the choice of the President in selecting incumbents for the most important position of the Army. If it had been in effect in

⁴⁸ New York *Times*, May 31, 1912.
⁴⁹ New York *Press*, June 13, 1912.
⁵⁰ Taft to Henry A. DuPont, June 15, 1912. *Taft Mss.*
⁵¹ Taft to Francis E. Warren, June 5, 1912. *Taft Mss.*

former years, a majority of the most brilliant officers would have been disqualified, including the present Chief of Staff. The contemplated reduction in the number of the General Staff, Taft continued, would tend to cripple the most important corps of the Army, and it, as it appeared, the work of the War College would have to be curtailed, well-nigh incalculable damage would be done to the military establishment. Taft's further objections included the provision limiting the time during which an officer could remain upon detached service or staff duty, the lengthening of the term of enlistment from three to four years, and, the alleged savings in expenditures by the bill was "arrived at by a failure to appropriate over $3,000,000," which would actually become necessary for the support of the Army, before the end of the coming year.[52]

After the message was read, the matter was referred to the House Military Affairs Committee, and a bill without most of the objectionable features was passed and approved.[53] The New York *Times* reflected a general feeling of approval for the President's veto and made no attempt to veil its feelings for the individuals involved: "The rebuke to the promoters of personal legislation, who have used their personal power as law makers to inflict insult upon an officer who has fairly won the respect and esteem of the Army and of the people will be cordially approved by fair-minded men of all parties.".[54]

This had been a decade of controversy, but out of the years fundamental reforms had taken place, and of these reforms the creation of the General Staff was the most important. The General Staff was not yet a smooth running machine, but it had a firm foundation and it was soon to demonstrate its worth. And with the question of the authority of the Chief of Staff finally settled, the General Staff was free to concentrate upon the formulation of a much-needed military policy for the United States.

[52] *Congressional Record*, June 17, 1912, pp. 8282-8284.
[53] H.R. 25531; approved August 24, 1912.
[54] New York *Times*, May 31, 1912.

CHAPTER 14

Reform and Apathy

The Military Go to School—The Militia Receives Some
Needed Reforms—The Navy Continues To Improve—
Secretary Root Points Out the Advantages of an Ade-
quate Reserve—The Impact of General Leonard Wood
—The Shaping of a Military Policy in 1912—The Reserve
Program Bogs Down—The War Department Casts Hope-
ful Eyes at the Volunteers—The Administration is Lack-
ing in Military Policy

THE SPANISH-AMERICAN WAR projected America into
the ranks of the great powers and gave the United States the
responsibility of defending its newly acquired overseas empire.
One of the objectives of Theodore Roosevelt's administration was
to consolidate and defend this empire. In order to add a bulwark
to our Caribbean and Pacific defenses, he promoted the acquisition of the Panama Canal Zone. Roosevelt materially aided in
bringing the Navy to a pinnacle of strength and efficiency which
was spectacularly advertised when he sent the fleet on a cruise
around the world. The President was also interested in the reorganization of the Army and he tried to make sure that the lessons
of the Spanish-American War and the Philippine Insurrection
would not be forgotten. A General Staff was created to work out
plans for the proper defense of the United States and its territories.
The Army War College and other Service Schools attempted to
carry on the military education of the Army. The size of the Army
was not greatly increased, but new militia laws, designed to make
the National Guard a more dependable second line of defense,
were enacted in 1903 and 1908. Thus the new world position of
America led to an expansion of American arms and served warning to the world that in the troubled years of the 20th century the
United States was not to be ignored.

The Military Go to School

The founding of the Army War College was not the first manifestation of the Army's awareness of the need for continuing the
education of its officer and enlisted personnel. Early instruction in

the Army had been given solely at the unit level. This was obviously unsatisfactory from the point of view of standardization, but it was not until after the War of 1812 that the Army's school system was established.

The artillery was organized, under the Act of March 2, 1821, into four regiments, each with eight foot companies and one battery of light artillery. These units were not mounted, so virtually the entire organization was assigned to garrison duty. To give some training to these troops it became necessary to institute a school for artillery training.[1]

Orders were issued in April, 1824 for the establishment of an Artillery School of Practice at Fort Monroe, Virginia, and this became the first of the Army graduate schools.[2] An administrative and instructional staff were formed, which included departments of mathematics, engineering, drawing, and chemistry.[3] It is significant to note that orders from the Adjutant General in December 2, 1824 put the Artillery School under the exclusive control of the War Department which was a clear indication of the intention of the Staff to keep authority in its own hands and not allow the Line to exercise command authority over the Service Schools.[4]

Graduates of West Point [5] who had been assigned to the Artillery were sent to Fort Monroe for one year of practical and theoretical training before joining their regiments. Except for periods of national emergency, such as the Civil War the artillery school was in continuous existence until 1907, when the Artillery split into the Field Artillery and the Coast Artillery. The school at Fort Monroe thereafter taught only coast artillery subjects. In 1911 a Field Artillery School was established at Fort Sill, Oklahoma. At the outbreak of World War II the Coast Artillery went out of existence, to be replaced by the Antiaircraft Artillery. In 1950 the artilleries were reunited into one arm. At present, 1955, the Artillery School is continuing to function at Fort Sill, with an antiaircraft and guided missiles branch at Fort Bliss, Texas.

---

[1] Spaulding, *op. cit.,* p. 154.
[2] Ganoe, *op. cit.,* p. 164.
[3] Spaulding, *op. cit.,* p. 154.
[4] Ltr. Adjutant General, December 2, 1824, Military Book, No. 18, S/W, Ltrs. Received, Letter 133A, National Archives.
[5] Limiting the student body to cadets was soon abandoned, and students were selected from officers of some experience which made it possible to raise the standard of instruction. Spaulding, *op. cit.,* p. 154.

During this period of the founding of the Artillery School, two regiments of infantry, the 3rd and 6th, were ordered to Jefferson Barracks, Missouri, for the purpose of founding an Infantry School of Practice. The site was chosen by Generals Gains and Atkinson in the early summer of 1826 and it was first occupied on July 10. The school was short lived, being abandoned in 1828.[6]

The Infantry School was not reconstituted until 1881 when there was established at Fort Leavenworth a School for Application for Cavalry and Infantry. On January 25, 1882, War Department General Order No. 8 provided the program for the practical instruction "in everything which pertains to army organization, tactics, discipline, equipment, drill, care of men, care of horses, public property, accountability, etc., and generally of everything which is provided for in Army Regulations." Attention was also to be directed toward elementary subjects "which ought to precede a commission, but is not always the case," and the science and practice of war.[7] On June 22, 1886 the name of the school was changed to the United States Infantry and Cavalry School, and in the following year a board of officers was appointed to study the curriculum and make recommendations as to needed changes in the school. The board's recommendations formed the basis for new orders issued on March 27, 1888 which called for a two-year course with a program of instruction under the Departments of Military Art; Law; Engineering; Cavalry; Infantry; Artillery, and Military Hygiene.[8]

The value and prestige of the school was enhanced when the War Department directed in 1890 that honor graduates of the institution would be so designated on the Army Register. In the following year, graduates were ordered exempt for five years from the examination in professional subjects for promotion.[9] The outbreak of the war with Spain caused the suspension of the school

---

[6] Henry Shindler: *History of the Army Service Schools* (Fort Leavenworth, Kansas: Staff College Press, 1908), p. 5.

Brigadier General H. H. Fuller: "The Development of the Command and General Staff School, Fort Leavenworth, Kansas," *Military Review*, Vol. 21, January, 1942, p. 5.

[7] *Ibid.*, pp 5-6.

[8] Fuller, *op. cit.*, pp. 7-8. A preliminary volunteer course in mathematics was added in 1892 and in 1897 the Departments of Infantry, Cavalry, and Artillery were consolidated with the Department of Military Art. Their places were taken by the new Departments of Tactics and Strategy.

[9] *Ibid.*, pp. 7-8.

for four years and upon its reopening a new period of military education was to begin.

In 1890 the War Department directed that graduates of the Infantry and Cavalry School be given preference for the detail as professors of military science and tactics at selected colleges and universities. This order was related to the Act to Fix the Peace Establishment of July 28, 1866, which also provided for promoting knowledge of military science, for it gave the President authority "upon the application of an established college or university . . . to detail an officer of the army to act as president, superintendent, or professor of such college or university." The legislation also called for the establishment of schools at all posts, garrisons, and camps "where all enlisted men may be provided with instruction in the Common English branches of education." [10] The present Infantry School was established, during World War I, at Fort Benning, Georgia.

The detailing of Army officers as professors of military science and tactics to civilian institutions proved to be extremely successful. In 1895 a total of one hundred and four officers were giving instruction at over one hundred institutions of higher learning. Nearly all the military instructors earned the approbation of the college authorities. The importance of their duty was recognized and the effort to bring it to the highest practicable standard was evident upon all sides.[11] As early as 1893 the Secretary of War had recommended the extension of military instruction to the high schools of the large cities. "The introduction of military training into the free school systems of the States should stimulate patriotism, of which that system is one of the best products, and should in time become a most potent factor in making the United States a nation capable of bearing arms intelligently and victoriously under all conditions." [12]

Other service schools established after the Civil War included the Cavalry School, the Signal Corps School, the Engineer School, and the Army Medical School. The Cavalry School, authorized by the Act of January 29, 1887, was established in 1891 at Fort Riley, Kansas, as a permanent school of instruction for drill and practice for the cavalry and light artillery service of the Army of

---

[10] XIV *Stat* 336.
[11] *Annual rpt S/W, 1895, Report of Inspector-General,* Vol. I, pp. 204-205.
[12] Kansas City *Star,* December 11, 1893.

the United States.[13] Coincident with the establishment of the Cavalry School, a School for the Instruction of the Signal Corps was begun the same year.[14] The Engineer School of Application was founded in 1867 and in 1890 its official title was changed to United States Engineer School. In 1901 the name of the school was again changed to the Engineer School of Application, United States Army, and its facilities were moved to Washington, D. C. Shortly after the founding of the Cavalry School, a school for the Hospital Corps was organized at Fort Riley, Kansas. The school was ultimately renamed the Army Medical School, being located in the nation's capital. Its first session, in November, 1893 was for the purpose of instructing approved candidates for admission to the Medical Corps of the Army in their duties as medical officers.[15]

The Spanish-American War forced the closing down of most of the Army's schools, but their reopening after the war marked a new and more vigorous chapter in military education. Under the able direction of Elihu Root the entire school system was reorganized, and capped by the establishment of the Army War College.

Using the service schools as stepping stones to the Command and General Staff College which in turn led to the Army War College, the Army established a firm and enduring basis for its educational system. While the Army was setting up its postgraduate courses the other services were following suit and after the close of World War II the process of evolution had created a comprehensive and elaborate educational system not only in the several services but also for the benefit of the Joint Forces.

On the top level in the Army system in 1955 were the Army War College at Carlisle Barracks, Pennsylvania, the Command and General Staff College at Fort Leavenworth, Kansas, and the various branch service schools. The Navy, of course, had its Naval War College at Newport, Rhode Island, while the Marine Corps had responsibility for joint amphibious training at the Amphibious Warfare School, Senior Course, at Quantico, Virginia. The youngest of the services, the U.S. Air Force, established its Air University at Maxwell Air Force Base, Montgomery, Alabama.

---

[13] Ira L. Reeves: *Military Education in the United States,* (New York: Free Press Printing Co., 1914), p. 266.
[14] *Ibid.,* p. 267.
[15] Reeves, *op. cit.,* pp. 255-261, 282.

Among the first steps taken after the unification of the Armed Forces were provisions to supply joint study and training programs by the establishment of the Armed Forces Staff College at Norfolk, Virginia. Graduation from this institution or from a service war college became a prerequisite for further advanced training at the National War College or the Industrial College of the Armed Forces, both being located at Fort McNair, Washington, D.C.

There is no doubt that the educational system of the armed forces have been one of the great assets of our military establishment in the 20th century. The magnificent accomplishments of our officers in the wars of this century can to a large measure be attributed to the training and education they received during the course of their professional careers. As General John J. Pershing remarked:

> During the World War the graduates of Leavenworth and the War College held the most responsible positions in our armies, and I should like to make it of record that in my opinion, had it not been for the able and loyal assistance of the officers trained at these schools, the tremendous problems of combat, supply and transportation could not have been solved.[16]

The Militia Receives Some Needed Reforms

The power position of the United States in the 20th century was hardly enhanced by the fact that its militia organization and laws went back into the dim mists of the 18th century. Removed from the clamor and bitterness of the struggle raging over the establishment of the General Staff, important legislative reforms were made in the fundamental framework of the National Guard. The first of these legislative reforms was the passage of the Dick Act on January 21, 1903. This act to promote the efficiency of the militia[17] was another of Secretary Elihu Root's contributions to the fundamental organization of our land forces. Behind this reorganization of the militia was the growing realization of the need for a strong National Guard, for if the United States became involved in war, "the Regular Army will form but a small part

---

[16] Fuller, *op. cit.*, p. 9.
[17] XXXII *Stat* 775. Among the basic weaknesses of the Militia Act of 1792 mav be listed the rqeuirement that members had to supply their own equipment which meant a total lack of uniformity. An even more basic criticism was the lack of federal control which some authorities feel is inherent in the Militia clause of the Constitution.

of its armed forces; and the country must also rely, for immediate and special exigencies, upon militia." [18] A meritorious provision of the Dick Act was the separation of the militia into two classes. The organized militia, or National Guard, formed one class, and the other was composed of the rest of the able-bodied male citizens between eighteen and forty-five years of age. The militia act was also designed to accomplish, within five years, the reorganization of the National Guard so as to make it conform as far as practicable to the organization, armament, and discipline of the Regular Army. The Dick Act also provided for federal inspections of National Guard units, joint maneuvers, fixed pay and allowances, and some other less important details. It also presaged future federal volunteer service and prescribed age-in-grade limits and examinations for officers in that future volunteer force. The Dick Act was the first legislation dealing with the militia since the organic militia act of 1792.

The principal defects of this legislation were the omission of the compulsory service feature of the law of 1792; the retention of the practice of calling the militia only through State Governors, thus risking their refusal;[19] the repetition of past error in restricting the use of the National Guard when called by the President to service in the United States and the service to be limited to a period of nine months; and finally, the failure to provide adequate machinery for enforcement. In spite of these criticisms the Dick Act is believed to mark an important forward movement in the formulation of an adequate military policy. This was the first reform in the militia since 1792, and fortunately the primary defects in the legislation of 1903 did not have to wait another hundred years for their remedy.

Basic weaknesses in the whole concept of the National Guard were again ignored. The place of the National Guard in the military establishment was not likely to be effective until it came under more complete federal control.[20] The financial resources necessary for the creation of a strong Guard were left to the efforts of the individual states. The annual Federal allotment for the militia was set at $1,000,000 and it was not until June 27,

---

[18] *Annual rpt S/W, 1904*, Vol. I, p. 28.
[19] It was estimated in 1904 that 75% of the militia would volunteer. *Ibid.*, p. 72.
[20] This viewpoint is also reflected by James B. Scott: *The Militia*, Washington: G.P.O., 1917), and Samuel T. Ansell: "Legal and Historical Aspects of the Militia," *Yale Law Review*, Vol. XXVI, pp. 471-480.

1906 that it was increased to $2,000,000, while at the same time the militia averaged over 100,000 men. With such meager financial resources even the best efforts of the Army and National Guard could not transform the militia into an efficient military organization.[21] Neither can it be said that the Army was half-hearted in its approach to the militia or to the Dick Act, for in his first Annual Report after the enactment of the militia legislation the Secretary of War was eloquent in his praise regarding the attitude of the States and the beneficial effects of the Act. According to the report, the new militia act has "aroused the interest of the young men of the country in military affairs," increased their inclination for military service, improved the personnel of the organized militia, raised the standard of its discipline, and increased the efficiency of the militia.[22] Nevertheless, within the limits of the Dick Act, much remained to be accomplished in the line of supply, discipline, and training before the National Guard could be brought to a high state of efficiency.

Two of the weaknesses of the Dick Act were eliminated in the Militia Act of May 27, 1908. The Dick Act, as previously noted, restricted the use of the National Guard when called forth by the President to service in the United States and for a period of nine months. The Act of 1908 removed these restrictions and also called for conformity in organization, armament, and discipline with the Regular Army by January 21, 1910.[23] This legislation also authorized the Secretary of War to appoint a board of five officers from the active ranks of the National Guard for consultation with the Secretary of War respecting the condition, status, and needs of the whole body of the organized militia.[24] Thus was created the Division of Militia Affairs which in turn was succeeded by the National Guard Bureau.

Despite these advances the National Guard was still essentially an institution of the individual States to which it belonged, and its use by the Federal Government was limited to the comparatively narrow functions of executing the laws of the Union, suppressing insurrection, and repelling invasion. The use of the National Guard outside of the United States was declared un-

---

[21] *Annual rpt S/W, 1904*, Vol. I, p. 28, *1905*, p. 35, *1906*, pp. 136-137.
[22] *Annual rpt S/W, 1904*, Vol. I, pp. 71-72.
[23] *Annual rpt S/W, 1908*, Vol. I, pp. 33-36.
[24] XXXV *Stat* 399-403.

constitutional by the Attorney General in 1912.[25] Still, the National Guard was the only force of men, outside of the Regular Army, with any military training. Improvements had been made under the legislation cited, but the problem of Federal control, inadequate appropriations, and insufficient Regular Army officers for instruction and inspection made the National Guard an unreliable instrument of national defense.

The first step, since the enactment of the Dick Act, looking to the organization of the National Guard into higher tactical units, was taken in 1910 in the organization of The First Field Army, as set forth in War Department General Orders No. 35, 1910. The First Field Army comprised the militia organizations of New York and the New England States together with the Regular Army regiments stationed in those states. However, when it became apparent that this organization contained serious deficiencies, as it included elements of different degrees of training and efficiency, the project of combining Regular troops and National Guard units was abandoned. Instead, the plan to develop the National Guard into a completely independent and organized force was adopted. This plan was formulated in 1912 after study by the General Staff and the Division of Militia Affairs. It contemplated the formation of 12 tactical divisions corresponding to 12 groups of contiguous states.[26] The division plan, while a noteworthy effort to obtain maximum results from the National Guard, pointed up the basic weaknesses of our second line of defense as was vividly illustrated by the mobilization of the National Guard on the Mexican border in 1916.

The National Guard mobilized with an alarming slowness and inefficiency, and both the War Department and the nation were enabled to take a long careful look at this instrument of national defense. Major General Tasker H. Bliss, Assistant Chief of Staff, on his tour of inspection found the physical condition of the troops was not all that could be desired. Equipment was lacking and the men appeared almost entirely ignorant of the duties of soldiers and were poor even in the simple evolutions of company drill. The mobilization further revealed that the National

---

[25] *Annual rpt S/W, 1912*, Vol. I, p. 24.
[26] *Report on Mobilization of the Organized Militia and National Guard of the United States, 1916*, (Washington: G.P.O., 1916), p. 48. Hereafter cited as *Report of Mobilization.*

Guard was considerably understrength for it was only able to furnish 59.2% of its required war strength.[27] Also disturbing were the large number of physically unfit and those who failed to respond to the call for mobilization. These unfit and the unheroic seriously depleted the strength of the National Guard, and justified the prediction of General John J. Pershing that when an emergency arises "it will be no time to muster raw recruits to fill the partially organized militia companies. It [the National Guard] could not be counted on, after the beginning of war, until it could be thoroughly organized and equipped, and that will take time." [28] It was quite clear that the militia, in its present state, was not the answer to the problem of defense in the perilous days that lay ahead.

The Navy Continues to Improve

Theodore Roosevelt, advocate of preparedness, also turned his attention to the Navy and no President thus far had had such abiding interest in the Navy or such a grasp of its functions and value in foreign affairs.[29] It was a propitious time for naval expansion, for public attention was focused sympathetically on the Navy as the result of its exploits in the Spanish-American War. It was clear to Congress and public alike that what would have been an adequate Navy in previous years was totally inadequate for the performance of duties growing out of our new possessions in the Atlantic and Pacific.[30] Among the most important lessons learned in the war with Spain was that a modern navy can not be improvised during a war or upon the threshold of war. During the war vast sums of money were expended upon the purchase of ships. Many of them served useful auxiliary purposes, but it may well be doubted whether they added materially to the fighting efficiency of our fleet.[31] In sympathy with the maxim "in time of peace be prepared for war" Roosevelt moved vigorously to make the Navy a strong bulwark of our defenses.

[27] *Ibid.*, pp. 62, 154.
[28] Pershing to the Adjutant General, May 1, 1915. AGO 2287322, Records of the War Department, National Archives.
[29] Carroll S. Alden and Allen Westcott: *The United States Navy*, (New York: J. B. Lippincott Co., 1943), p. 328.
[30] Alden and Westcott, *op. cit.*, p. 327, suggest that the concentration of the British fleet in home waters as a check on the rising German navy and the consequent lessening of British naval influence made America look more to her own defenses.
[31] *Annual rpt S/N, 1902*, p. 13.

In his first annual message to Congress, the Chief Executive called the attention of the nation to the need for a strong naval program. No single policy, he contended, "is more important than this to the honor and material welfare, and above all to the peace of our nation in the future." Under his proddings Congress moved to implement this program. During the next four years the Navy added fifty-four ships (of which fifty-one were combat vessels) and had under construction or authorized thirty-seven more (only six of which were not combat vessels). Naval enlisted strength increased by more than one-half and the Marine Corps, in this same period, increased its strength from 7,032 to 9,049.[82] Operationally, the Navy made long forward strides toward the crystallization of modern doctrine and concepts. Fleet organization changed from dispersion by single ships and small groups of miscellaneous composition to a concentration of force in a fleet of component parts. During these years the several scattered shore stations and numerous individual ships were gradually organized into homogeneous groupings and combined into two great fleets in the Atlantic and Pacific.

This program of expansion with few exceptions was applauded by the press of the country.

But within the Navy the same problem that had so bedeviled the Army had to be solved. The naval situation was similar to that of the Army in that there was no clear-cut demarcation of authority and responsibility in the higher echelons of command At the head of the Department was the Secretary and under him were eight bureau chiefs appointed by the President for a term of four years. The bureaus, independent of and unrelated to each other, created conditions out of which grew conflicts of jurisdiction and a tendency to consider the interests of the bureau rather than the interests of the Navy.[83]

Advocates of preparedness and efficiency within the Department stressed the need for a General Staff to prepare plans for war, the study of strategic problems, the collection of military information, the coordination of the work of the bureaus, and the advising of the Secretary of the Navy.[84] Instead of adopting these

---

[82] Cf. Annual rpts S/N, 1903, 1904, 1905, 1906. The Navy's strength of 21,-433 on June 30, 1902 rose to 32,163 on June 30, 1906.
[83] Annual rpt S/N, 1903, p. 3.
[84] Charles Paullin: "A Half Century of Naval Administration in America, 1861-1911," Proceedings of the U. S. Naval Institute, Vol. XL, pp. 111-128.

sweeping proposals a General Board was organized in 1900 and its functions and authority were further outlined in subsequent legislation in 1901 and 1905.

On July 17, 1903 the Joint Army and Navy Board was established under the impact of the experience of the Spanish-American War. The operations at Santiago had provided an example which it was desired to avoid in later years. According to Admiral Chadwick, the Army finally did by brute force and much loss that which might have been accomplished with little loss had the operation been carried on with the assistance of a trained staff and the co-operation which the Navy was only too anxious to give. The difficulty was the lack of a general staff system in both the War and Navy Departments which prevented intimate understanding and mutual study of conditions as they arose.[35] The Board consisted of four officers of the Army and four of the Navy, designated by name, and the key phrases defining its objectives were:

> . . . to hold such stated sessions and such extraordinary sessions as shall appear advisable for the purpose of conferring upon, discussing and reaching common conclusions regarding all matters calling for the cooperation of the two services. Any matters which seem to either Department to call for such consideration may be referred by that Department to the board thus formed.[36]

This new organization did not distinguish itself by its activities until its reorganization in 1919. The Annual Reports of the Secretaries of War through these years do not even mention it and the War Department General Orders which were published to appoint or relieve Army members by name did not appear after 1911. Here, however, was the faint and unappreciated appearance of the concept of unification.

Secretary Root Points Out the Advantages of an Adequate Reserve

General Leonard Wood was to write in 1911 that unless we had a reserve of instructed men the strength of our regiments could not be increased for war more than fifteen percent without causing more or less demoralization, unless we had three or four

---

[35] Alden and Westcott, *op. cit.*, p. 318.
[36] It is difficult to credit any single individual for originating the Joint Board, although various claims have been advanced. Lawrence J. Legare, Jr.: *Unification of the Armed Forces*, Harvard University Doctoral Mss., 1951, p. 57.

months to get the men in shape.[37] In substantial agreement with Wood, Secretary Root proposed the idea which became the underlying principle of the future American Army, the peacetime, nonprofessional exclusively federal, and essentially citizen Army.

Root's first mention of the reserve concept in his Annual Report of 1899 was quite modest, for he merely mentioned the value and importance of securing, during peacetime, information with reference to the capacity and fitness of civilians who had had previous military training. In 1902, Root outlined the Army educational system to meet the needs of the civilian components. "The course," he wrote, "both of the officers schools at the posts and the General Service and Staff College, will be arranged so that the young men wishing to fit themselves for volunteer commissions may spend their vacation in military study." The year before he had urged the President to convene boards of officers for the examination of citizens to determine their qualifications for volunteer commissions.[38] These commissions would only be granted when volunteers were called to service. In a memorandum of January 2, 1908, General Franklin Bell, Chief of Staff, very clearly pointed out that it was the traditional custom of this nation to rely largely upon volunteer soldiers to fight its wars. "However, when sudden expansions of the Army are necessary, trained officers are needed to organize, muster, and instruct volunteers. Because we have never had extra officers in peacetime we have been compelled to appoint as officers many persons from civil life who were without any military training or experience. Our history is not without well known illustrations that this necessity has resulted in very inefficient service." [39]

The reserve program as envisaged by Root was not implemented by the recommended legal provisions and actually there appear to have been no concrete results. Perhaps one reason for the failure of the program was the widely held belief that in the case of a national emergency commissions could be obtained with relative ease. Perhaps our historically minded young men in reviewing our military policy had ample grounds for this belief. If the young men could look to the past, perhaps the Regular Army was looking to the future in viewing these proposals unfavorably,

---

[37] Wood to William C. Church, June 26, 1911. *Church Mss.*
[38] *Annual rpt S/W, 1899*, p. 44; 1902, p. 25; 1901, p. 20.
[39] WCD 1979. Records of W.D.G.S., National Archives.

for many officers could understandably not be enthusiastic about certifying persons as qualified for rank in a future expanded establishment to which the Regulars might themselves aspire. A third and very important factor was the lack of sufficient instructional staff members and facilities to provide an opportunity for training civilians.[40]

There was one harmful result of Root's concept. The group which did take advantage of the opportunity to qualify for volunteer commissions were persons who already held National Guard officer status. These officers established their right, by means of examinations, to receive commissions in future national volunteer forces, usually at grades higher than those they held in the National Guard. This was the beginning of the pernicious practice of permitting officers of the National Guard to hold a dual rank status simultaneously in different components of the Army.

The Impact of General Leonard Wood

General Leonard Wood, who was to exert a very considerable influence upon the nature of our military policy and upon the basic structure which it supported, was appointed Chief of Staff of the Army on July 19, 1910. Wood's biographer, Hermann Hagedorn, states that Wood believed in short enlistments and a reserve with brief periods of training, "making the Army not an establishment of elderly veterans, but a school for youth, . . . ready to come to the colors when the emergency arose, not as raw volunteers, but as men already trained." He was to emphasize this theme in a letter of January 17, 1911, stressing the importance of an effective reserve while belaboring Army and National Guard opposition to its creation. Five months later he became more specific in his conceptions of a reserve force and how it was to be created. Although General Wood insisted upon a year of instruction, he was willing to accept the alternative of six months training for young men fresh from high schools and colleges.[41]

General Wood was to have a tremendous impact on the preparedness question and the way was paved for him by a series of magazine articles[42] which caused Congress to speculate about the state of the nation's defenses. On June 23, 1910 Congress re-

[40] *Annual rpt S/W, 1903*, p. 13.
[41] Hagedorn, *op. cit.*, Vol. II, p. 109.
[42] *Everybody's Magazine*, Vol. XVIII, (1908), p. 301.

quested the Secretary of War to submit a report on the state of preparedness of the Army. The Army War College's analysis of the lack of preparedness was frank and supported by an imposing array of facts. It stressed the weakness of the Regular Army which included inadequate manpower, lack of munitions and ordnance, and the lack of combat balance of the Army's organization. The conclusion of the report aptly expressed the situation: "It is apparent that we are almost wholly unprepared for war . . . that the things we need most will take the longest to supply." [43]

Such a situation was a stimulating challenge to a person of the ability and ambition of Leonard Wood. One of the first tasks to which he turned his attention was the reorganization of the General Staff. He quickly learned that it was bogged down with many matters not properly its concern. He discovered, for example, that out of one hundred staff studies submitted to the Office of the Chief of Staff, not one that bore any relation to war, and only three were of any consequence in matters of peace _or_ war. His staff was quickly directed to prepare more pertinent and shorter studies. In 1911, the General Staff was reorganized into four divisions which included the Mobile Army, Coast Artillery, Militia, and War College. [44]

The War College Division was now firmly established as the central planning agency of the Army, and it gradually developed a high level of efficiency as is reflected in its "Statement of a Proper Military Policy for the United States," presented in 1915. The importance of the War College Division lay in the fact that for the first time in our history the Army had an organization to plan and prepare for future emergencies.

Wood's reform program, however, was headed straight toward the accumulating opposition of the War Department bureau chiefs who began to threaten the General Staff itself. The problem of command authority [45] had established the principle that the Chief of Staff was the principle officer of the Army, deriving his power from the President, but his functions were advisory rather than operational. This limitation of authority was in the nature of a concession to the powerful groups in the Army establishment at the time who, through their influence in Congress, continued effec-

---

[43] _Annual rpt S/W, 1911_, pp. 7-10.
[44] Hagedorn, _op. cit._, Vol. II, pp. 99-100.
[45] _Cf._ Chapter 13.

tively to oppose necessary military reforms and succeeded in evolving the fiction that a General Staff was a sinister militaristic apparatus which had no place in a democratic America. As a result, Congress began to view· with alarm the growth of a "militaristic entity" which might endanger the very foundations of our free institutions.

Fuel was added to the fires of the growing congressional antipathy when the growing friction over the proper exercise of authority by the Adjutant General came to a head in 1912.[46] As a result of the notoriety attached to the Ainsworth case, Congress authorized the reduction of the General Staff from forty-five officers to thirty-six. Although this was not a singular triumph for the advocates of the old order, the effectiveness of the General Staff was severely handicapped and on the eve of America's entrance into World War I the War Department was possessed of a General Staff of only nineteen officers as compared with Germany's six hundred and fifty.

The Shaping of a Military Policy in 1912

In midsummer of 1911, John McAuley Palmer was directed by General Wood to prepare a plan for the organization of all of the land forces of the United States. The policy underlying the plan which Palmer prepared was to mobilize a pre-existing citizen army instead of expanding a standing army. He realized, however, that in the event of a great war a volunteer system on so vast a scale would certainly fail.[47] That this was nothing new or particularly concealed by the Army was evidenced by such public statements as "our whole military establishment on its present lines is useless for any real military purpose. It is altogether useless and foolish to gloss over the matter." [48]

Despite the clear-cut need for reform no logical policy was formulated. Instead, Secretary of War Henry L. Stimson, in his annual report of 1911, proposed shortening the term of enlistment to three years on the ground that the theory of the modern state is that it is the duty of the citizen to train himself as promptly as possible to perform his function as a soldier in case of possible war

---

[46] *Cf. Chapter* 13 and also Nelson, *op. cit.*, p. 217.
[47] John McA. Palmer, *America in Arms*, pp. 135-137.
[48] *Infantry Journal*, Vol. VIII, (1911), p. 918.

and to return as quickly as possible to his normal civil life.[49] He then proposed the formation of a reserve to be used to maintain first line units at fighting strength. This reserve was to be composed of soldiers who had received training in the Regular Army.

Other ideas as to what was lacking and what was needed in the Army appeared in a series of magazine articles in the spring of 1912. These articles were later collected and printed as a House document entitled "What is the Matter with our Army?" Secretary Stimson attempted a partial answer in the last article when he wrote that the trouble with the Army was due to our own lack of an intelligent military policy in dealing with it.[50] With this groundwork carefully laid, Stimson ordered the General Staff to prepare a report on the organization of the land forces of the United States.[51]

This report, prepared by the General Staff and subsequently to be known as the Stimson plan, was a comprehensive statement of a military policy for the United States. It included consideration of such problems as cooperation between land and naval forces, the administration of the land forces, tactical organization of mobile troops, raising and organizing volunteers, the militia, and other aspects of military strength with the exception of economic mobilization. The report pointed out that it was the traditional military policy of America to have a small Regular Army which in wartime was augmented by a great body of citizen soldiers. Reliance upon such a source of manpower, however, was subject to the limitation "that they cannot be expected to meet a trained enemy until they, too, have been trained. Our history is full of the success of the volunteer soldier after he has been trained for war, but it contains no record of the successful employment of raw levies for general military purposes." The most important problem, therefore, was to devise means of preparing great armies of citizen soldiers to meet the emergency of modern war. Its solution, the report concluded, involves the provision of a sufficient peace nucleus, the partial organization and training of citizen soldiers in peace, and provisions for prompt and orderly expansion on the outbreak of war.[52]

---

[49] *Annual rpt S/W, 1911*, pp. 13-15.
[50] *House Document No. 621*, 62d Congress, 2d Session.
[51] *Annual rpt S/W, 1912*, pp. 69-128.
[52] *Annual rpt S/W, 1912*, p. 76.

The report recommended a six-year enlistment period for the Regular Army, three years on active duty and three in the reserves, with some of these reserves being used to bring Regular Army companies to full strength during emergencies to prevent a dilution of their strength with untrained recruits. The remainder of the reserves would form a replacement pool. A reserve officers program would be instituted, West Point would be expanded, and the national militia program would be improved. The entire land forces would include the following components:

1. A Regular Army organized in divisions and cavalry brigades and ready for immediate use as an expeditionary force or for any other purposes for which the citizen soldiery is not available, or for employment in the first stages of war while the citizen soldiery is mobilizing and concentrating.

2. An army of national citizen soldiers organized in peace in complete divisions and prepared to reenforce the Regular Army in time of war.

3. An army of volunteers to be organized under prearranged plans when greater forces are required than can be furnished by the Regular Army and the organized citizen soldiery. The peace establishment of the Regular Army with the organized division districts of the National Guard should include the machinery for the recruiting, organization, and mobilization of this third great line of the national defense.[53]

The Reserve Program Bogs Down

The elections of 1912 returned the Democratic party to power and thus a new administration had to deal with the pressing problems of defense. The new President was a sincere pacifist whose campaign had reflected no burning desire to grapple with military problems. The only words in the Democratic platform which bore on military and naval policy dealt with the desirability of retaining naval and coaling stations in the Philippines. This change in administration, therefore, meant the shelving of the Stimson plan. However, the new Secretary of War, Lindley Garrison, informed Wood he would be retained, and the general on his part found many admirable characteristics in the new Secretary.[54]

---

[53] *Ibid.*, p. 125. Stimson felt this was following the military principles of Upton. *Ibid.*, pp. 11-12. Wood also agreed with this view.

[54] Hagedorn, *op. cit.*, Vol. II, pp. 129-130. General Hugh L. Scott who was to serve as a later Chief of Staff, was lavish in his praise of Garrison: "I believe he is the greatest Secretary we have ever had. We certainly have never had one who would keep the politicians out of the War Department the way this one does; they are as scarce around here as hen's teeth. . . ." Scott to Col. H. J. Slocum, November 24, 1914, *Hugh L. Scott Mss. Collection.* Hereafter cited as *Scott Mss.*

Garrison and Wood united in trying to persuade the country to adopt a position of military strength. In the spring and summer of 1913, Wood again and again repeated the need for adequate preparedness. Trained reserves were needed, and he also suggested a year of military training for young men after finishing high school or college. During the summer of 1913 General Wood set up two experimental training camps for students. Only a total of 245 attended the two camps, but the experiment was considered successful enough to be continued.[55] Thus at Monterey and Gettysburg the citizens training camps came into existence four years before our entry into war.[56]

Officially the preparedness forces were led by the Secretary of War. [57] His speeches for preparedness in the summer of 1913 indicated he was in full accord with Wood in opposing a large standing army.[58] The country was faced with a serious depression in 1913 and it would be very difficult to secure support for a large expensive army, although one senator from the Southwest, with his eye on the turbulent Mexican border, insisted upon doubling the size of the Army.[59]

The Secretary of War and the Chief of Staff devoted a large measure of their energy to securing an adequate reserve. They envisaged reducing the seven-year term of enlistment to one year, after which the soldier would become a member of the reserves which would thus grow over the course of years. Garrison recommended attractive inducements such as trade schools in order to encourage enlistments. Those who opposed the Army's reconstruction were accused of favoring a large Regular Army or of being willfully neglectful in providing adequate defenses against reasonably anticipated emergencies.[60] General Wood believed the reserve force should be large enough to put in the field a force of approximately 600,000 men in the opening phases of a war with a first class power. In his opinion, the Regular Army was rapidly approaching efficiency, but the general unpreparedness of the nation provided nothing with which to back it up.

---

[55] Edward H. Brooks: *The National Defense Policy of the Wilson Administration, 1913-1917,* Stanford University Doctoral Mss., 1950, p. 92.

[56] *Annual rpt S/W, 1913,* Vol. I, pp. 19-20.

[57] Edward Brooks Lee, Jr.: *Politics of Our Military National Defense,* Senate Document No. 274, 74th Congress, 3rd Session, (Washington: G.P.O., 1940), p. 18.

[58] Hagedorn, *op. cit.,* Vol. II, pp. 114-115.

[59] Nelson, *op. cit.,* p. 220.

[60] Brooks, *op. cit.,* p. 93.

Powerful opposition to Garrison and Wood was provided by Representative James Hay of Virginia, Chairman of the House Military Affairs Committee, who claimed that the Army was exactly what it was intended to be, "that is a nucleus for the country to rally around in time of war." Neither was there any need for a reserve of the type desired by Garrison and Wood, for the National Guard, of about 120,000, could take up arms in a short-period of time.[61]

With the House Military Affairs Committee in the hands of an "enemy of the War Department" the hopes for the creation of an effective reserve force were indeed dim. Nevertheless, Garrison and Wood kept up their campaign for an adequate reserve system. Their efforts ran up against the Congressional roadblock of opposition and apathy, and ended in failure. The inadequate legislation of 1912 remained in force until the Mexican crisis of 1916.[62]

The War Department Casts Hopeful Eyes at the Volunteers

The only really constructive legislation, although strictly limited in application, was the Volunteer Bill, completed at the height of the Mexican crisis of April, 1914.[63] The Act provided: (1) "The land forces of the United States of America shall consist of the Regular Army, the organized land militia while in the service of the United States, and such volunteer forces as Congress may authorize"; (2) the President when authorized by Congress could call for Volunteers; (3) in case three-fourths of National Guard organizations volunteered their services they were to be accepted before volunteers and placed under federal control.[64]

Even this legislation, recommended since the turn of the century, had difficulty in securing Congressional approval. Only because it cost nothing in peacetime and since it did not interfere with the existing National Guard, and especially since war with Mexico seemed imminent, was the act passed. Because the War Department, in urging passage of the bill, overlooked the probability of total war, and because reliance was placed on the

---

[61] Brooks, *op. cit.*, p. 94.

[62] The Act of August 12, 1912 contemplated a reserve composed of those who had received honorable discharges from the Regular Army who would in case of emergency return to active service. *Annual rpt S/W, 1913*, p. 21. In 1914, Garrison stated the Act had proven utterly useless because only 16 men were in the reserves. *Annual rpt S/W, 1914*, p. 11.

[63] Brooks, *op. cit.*, p. 97.

[64] XXXVIII *Stat* 347-351.

patriotic exuberance of the people, little was accomplished in preparing the nation for war. In fact, the volunteer system was to be discarded in 1917 when America again entered upon war.[65]

The Administration is Lacking in Military Policy

The Administration failed to provide the necessary leadership to prepare the country for possible war. Garrison, in his first annual report, laid the responsibility upon Congress to provide the necessary details for the establishment of an adequate reserve and militia system.[66] Though General Wood was an ardent advocate of preparedness he only recommended the establishment of a trained reserve, improvement in the National Guard, provisions for material and equipment reserves, and the formation of the necessary additional units to complete the organization of the four division force recommended in the Stimson plan of 1912.[67] The Secretary of War did not feel justified in recommending a large appropriation for military aviation, although he admitted that America was far behind in this phase of military power. The Army's aviation program would have to depend upon the results of foreign experimentation.[68]

With so few specific recommendations coming from official sources, and with Representative Hay believing the Army to be adequate, there was but faint hope for constructive legislation or additional appropriations. The War Department's requested budget was slashed about ten million dollars, and the Chairman of the House Military Affairs Committee declared the mobile force of the Army was an ample number to deal with any normal situation that might arise. The 120,000 National Guardsmen "equal to any emergency and ready to respond to any call of duty" obviated the need for any trained reserve. In this climate of official opinion it was idle to expect any significant improvement in the nation's military strength. When it was suggested that the Mexican crisis was reason enough to strengthen the Army, Hay replied that America had enough men and equipment to handle her troublesome neighbor. With no leadership from the White House, Hay's opinion prevailed in the House of Representatives.[69]

---

[65] Brooks, op. cit., pp. 97-98.
[66] Annual rpt S/W, 1913, Vol. I, pp. 1-21.
[67] Report of the Chief of Staff in the Annual rpt S/W, 1913, Vol. I, pp. 192-193.
[68] Annual rpt S/W, 1913, Vol. 1, p. 26.
[69] Brooks, op. cit., pp. 103-104.

The Senate was also not particularly concerned about the seriousness of the Mexican situation and there was no sense of urgency in its consideration of the bill. There was little interest in the suggestion that the Army be expanded to its authorized strength of 100,000, for the appropriation of about $100,000,000 was only enough for an Army of about 85,000 men. The fact that the imminence of war in April could not evoke enthusiasm for preparing the Army indicates that the President was not alone in the lack of interest toward military preparedness.[70]

Sharp criticism emanating from periodicals also failed to convince the Chief Executive and the Congress of the necessity of taking action. Allegations of poor planning and red tape, an incompetent National Guard, and a fatal military weakness in the midst of a dangerous international situation, were ignored just as were the pleas of Theodore Roosevelt, Garrison, and Leonard Wood.[71] Nor was the President influenced by his close friend. Colonel House, who insisted upon an adequate military force to enable the United States to assume the leadership in an international movement to prevent future wars.[72] Although there was pressing need for a strong force, especially after the Vera Cruz operation, the President demonstrated a singular lack of interest in national defense.

The inevitable incident which came as a climax in the tense atmosphere of Mexican-American relations occurred on April 9, 1914, when Mexican authorities arrested at Tampico an American landing party from Admiral Mayo's flagship *Dolphin.* The prisoners were released with "regrets" but the American demand for a 21-gun salute was refused. With Congressional approval, the President ordered the Navy to seize Vera Cruz. On April 21, a force of some 800 Marines and seamen, supported by fire from the *Chester, Prairie,* and *San Francisco,* stormed ashore, and in the subsequent fighting the American forces suffered losses of 15 killed and 56 wounded. This was embarrassingly akin to war, but Wilson was able to avoid further hostilities by accepting the media-

---

[70] Brooks, *op. cit.,* pp. 107-108.

[71] The *Nation,* Vol. XCVIII, April 30, 1914, *The Forum,* Vol. LI, April, 1914, and the *Review of Reviews,* Vol. XIX, January, 1914.

[72] Charles Seymour: *The Intimate Papers of Colonel House* (Boston: Houghton-Mifflin, 1926-1928), Vol. I, p. 297.

tion of Argentina, Brazil, and Chile. However, the American fleet remained off the Mexican coast until November.[73]

Despite the dangers inherent in the Mexican situation and the darkening war clouds over Europe, the President showed no interest in strengthening his own hand, and in fact, became even less responsive to the ever increasing calls for preparedness.

[73] Alden and Westcott, *op. cit.,* p. 336.

CHAPTER 15

America Probes The
Formulas For Preparedness

The President and Preparedness—Secretary of War
Garrison is Somewhat Timid in His Initial Efforts—Gar-
rison Lays the Groundwork For a Military Policy—
Garrison Seeks to Cure the Nation's Military Ills—The
National Defense Act of 1916—A Revolution in Amer-
ican Military Policy—Slow Preparation on the Part of the
Navy

THESE WERE perilous days for America. The smouldering
Mexican pot threatened to boil over, and war in Europe was
already casting ominous shadows over the fair skies of American
peace and neutrality. Also of concern to the Democratic Administration was the domestic scene which once again presented a
sombre picture of unemployment and hunger. Woodrow Wilson
had come to his high office bent upon a wide-spread program of
domestic reform. He was not too well informed on matters of
diplomacy, nor had he seriously considered a military policy. The
New Freedom had little concern or interest in problems of military affairs; nevertheless the question of preparedness was to be
one of the dominant factors in Wilson's first administration. It is
one of the ironies of this President's career that international
affairs and military policy were to play such an important role.

The President and Preparedness

The holocaust in Europe and continuing public agitation over
preparedness led Colonel House once again to discuss military
affairs with the President. But in a meeting on November 4, 1914
he found Wilson still unresponsive to the subject of preparedness.
The President feared that organized labor would interpose serious
objections. Also he could see no immediate need for such a program and he felt that it might shock the country. Furthermore, the
Chief Executive felt reasonably sure that no matter who won the
war, the victor would emerge too exhausted to pose any serious

331

threat to the United States. The subject was brought up again four days later, when Wilson repeated his opposition to any large increase in the Army. He told House that he did not believe that the United States was in any danger of invasion even if the Germans were victorious. To the amazement of House, Wilson further remarked that there would be plenty of time to prepare if and when war came.[1] Some slight shift in the President's attitude came later in the month when he admitted the need for a reserve, but not a large army. This change, however, was not strong enough to prod the Chief Executive into action, though it did indicate some awareness of possible dangers to America.

The question of preparedness was filled with distinct political overtones in December when Representative Augustus P. Gardner, Republican and son-in-law of Senator Henry Cabot Lodge, introduced a resolution to create a National Security Commission to investigate the readiness of the nation. The administration quickly threw its weight against this proposal and the President announced that this was not the time to air the question since he was interested in the possibility that the United States might play an important role in bringing the war to an end.[2] He was not adverse, however, to Senator Chamberlain introducing a bill for the creation of a Council of National Defense to decide the military needs of the country.[3]

The mounting agitation over preparedness was sufficiently strong to induce the President to devote a large portion of his annual message to the subject. In this message of December 8, 1914, Wilson's polished phrases failed to indicate that he was yet ready to face the realities of the problem. He declared that as long as America retained its present political principles it would never be ready for war. America must depend in time of national peril "not upon a standing army, nor yet upon a reserve army, but upon a citizenry trained and accustomed to arms." The Government should provide facilities to accomplish this laudable objective, but the President was not very clear as to how it was to be accomplished. He also advocated the further development of the National Guard "by every means which is not inconsistent with our obliga-

---

[1] Seymour, *op. cit.*, Vol. I, pp. 298-300. For a complete examination see Edward H. Brooks: *The National Defense Policy of the Wilson Administration, 1913-1917*, (Stanford University, Doctoral Mss., 1950).
[2] Brooks, *op. cit.*, pp. 111-112.
[3] New York *Times*, December 8, 1914.

tions to our own people or with the established policy of our Government." The country should not be alarmed nor lose her self possession by a war with which she had nothing to do, whose causes could not touch her. There should be no misconception, Wilson concluded, that the country had been misinformed. "We have not been negligent of national defense. We are not unmindful of the great responsibility resting upon us. We shall learn and profit by the lesson of every experience and every new circumstance; and what is needed will be adequately done." [4]

There was strong criticism of the address both in Democratic and Republican circles. The *Outlook* was unimpressed by the message and demanded a sweeping investigation.[5] Theodore Roosevelt bitterly wrote that Wilson and William Jennings Bryan were the very worst men we ever had in their positions, even worse than Jefferson and Madison.[6] The President's Cabinet also expressed strong disagreement. Garrison did not accept Wilson's policy and David F. Houston believed that the times warranted a change in the traditional policy cited in the President's message.[7]

On the other hand, the Bryan faction in the Democratic party warmly supported the message. Also within the President's own party was an important small-navy group, and it should be remembered that in the last years of the Taft administration, the Democratic House of Representatives had reduced the two-battleship program to one. The indifference of the administration and most Democratic congressmen to all projects of preparedness evidently reflected the drift of opinion in most of the sections and social groups which supported the administration.[8]

In spite of the President's reluctance to deal with the problem, the rising tide of war in Europe and the growing awareness of the public regarding the weak condition of our military establishment

---

[4] Ray S. Baker and William E. Dodd, (ed): The Public Papers of Woodrow Wilson, (New York: Harper and Brothers, 1925-1927, 6 vols.) Vol. III, pp. 223-227. The President's call for a "citizenry trained and accustomed to arms" was really a return to the principles of the Militia Act of 1792. This looked impressive but paper battalions had long been the bane of our military establishment.

[5] *The Outlook*, December 16, 1914.

[6] *Roosevelt-Lodge Correspondence, op. cit.*, Vol. II, p. 450.

[7] New York *Times*, December 9, 1914. David F. Houston: *Eight Years with Wilson's Cabinet*, (New York: Macmillan Co., 1926), 2 Vols., Vol. I, pp. 126-127.

[8] *Brooks, op. cit.*, pp. 115-116. On occasions when Wilson did advocate preparedness he was hardly crystal clear, as when he advocated universal military training "on a voluntary basis." *Current Opinion*, June, 1916.

continued to focus attention on preparedness. The *Army and Navy Journal,* on February 20, 1915, called for one million volunteers as a peace measure. In the following month, with the backing of General Wood, the American Legion, one of the many preparedness groups which arose, was formed for the purpose of enrolling for a reserve force men who had previous military training.[9] This idea was endorsed by Theodore Roosevelt and former Secretaries of War Wright, Dickinson, and Stimson, all of whom became members. The American Legion, however, did not receive the sanction of the War Department. Secretary of War Garrison did not believe that "enlisting a man on a piece of paper is going to make a soldier of him or make him available for the national defense." The Chief of Staff felt that there was danger in the project because it would tend to make thoughtless people rely on it for national defense, and when needed there would be practically nothing there.[10]

Other persons and organizations joined the preparedness campaign. A meeting of the National Security League revealed that it had such prominent and varied speakers as Hudson Maxim, James M. Curley, Judge Alton B. Parker, Bainbridge Colby, and Henry L. Stimson. A clearing house for organizations urging preparedness was provided by the American Defense Society in August, 1915. General Scott was delighted that most of the preparedness struggle was being carried on by civilians for he believed that if a professional soldier advocated an increase in the defenses of the country it would be discounted as merely grinding a personal axe. Scott hoped that the campaign would "produce a sufficient effect on the voters that something may be accomplished next winter." [11]

Numerous volumes appeared on the subject of our military defenses. Civilian authors included Hudson Maxim and Frederic L. Huidekoper while Leonard Wood and William H. Carter among Army officers wrote books pointing out the weak posture of American defenses and urging a prompt alleviation of the deficiencies.[12] A voice not to be disregarded was that of Theodore

[9] New York *Times,* March 3, 1915. This American Legion is not to be confused with the veteran's organization of the same name which was formed after World War I.
[10] Scott to J. M. Dickinson, April 2, 1915, *Scott Mss.*
[11] Scott to C. B. Dougherty, May 26, 1915. *Scott MSS.*
[12] We may cite the following as representative: Leonard Wood: *The Military*

Roosevelt who continued to plead for adequate preparedness. With the Secretary of War now publicizing the need for reorganizing the Army,[13] it was becoming increasingly clear that President Wilson was in an unpopular position.

The Chief Executive's reluctance to enter upon a program of military and naval expansion was based upon a variety of factors. As a pacifist he had developed a profound distrust of the "military mind." In spite of the fact that his foreign policy rendered a clash with Germany a distinct possibility he desired to do nothing that would irritate Germany while negotiations were still pending. He did not want the Kaiser to think that America was preparing for war.[14] It evidently did not occur to Wilson that American military power that could promptly be brought to bear might be the one thing that would make Germany more conciliatory. In the final analysis he was quite understandably more interested in bringing the war to a close than in entering it.

But on the other hand, at least two major considerations were driving Wilson to accept the inevitability of preparedness. The first was the result of continuing turmoil in the world. Japan, Mexico, and Germany all offered threats to the peaceful intentions of the United States.[15] The other major force involved the political implications of the preparedness issue. Unless the President acted decisively the Republicans could make the preparedness question their own and perhaps employ it with devastating effects in the elections of 1916.

Secretary of War Garrison is Somewhat Timid in His Initial Efforts

Similarly to his chief, the Secretary of War sometimes had confused notions concerning the military requirements of the nation. Nevertheless Garrison stood in high regard with the preparedness advocates despite the fact that he rejected the recommendations of his senior generals. In April, 1914, when Leonard Wood retired

---

Obligation of Citizenship, (Princeton University Press, 1915) and *Our Military History, Its Facts and Fallacies,* (Chicago: The Reilly and Britton Co., 1916); Frederic L. Huidepoker: *The Military Unpreparedness of the United States,* (New York: Macmillan Co., 1915).

[13] Lindley M. Garrison: "The Problem of National Defense," *North American Review,* June, 1915, pp. 833-838. As quoted in Brooks, *op. cit.,* p. 125.

[14] John L. Heaton: *Cobb of the World,* (New York: Dodd, Mead & Co., 1924), pp. 219-220. Brooks, *op. cit.,* pp. 125-126.

[15] General Scott considered "the Japanese question more menacing than any other." Scott to Frank West, December 29, 1915. *Scott Mss.*

as Chief of Staff to become the Commanding General of the Department of the East, he urged an increase in enlisted strength, and the creation of new units necessary to fill out the four-division program laid down in 1912. The effect of the World War was clear in the annual report of General Wotherspoon. The new Chief of Staff recommended the creation of a first-line force of 500,000 composed of the Regular Army and its reserve, and a second-line force of 300,000 made up of the National Guard. But Wotherspoon saw no need for haste, he did not regard such an increase as an imperative measure. He concluded by recommending that this program be completed in five years.[16]

The War College Division of the General Staff was unanimous in its opinion that new legislation to increase the efficiency of the Army should proceed along the lines clearly laid down in the "General Staff Report on the Organization of the Land Forces of the United States, 1912." The whole spirit of that report was that real efficiency in the United States Army could not be hoped for until it had been given a permanent tactical organization.[17]

A memorandum of October 17, 1914, entitled "Suggestions for the Annual Report of the Honorable the Secretary of War," and probably written by Scott, made these points: "1. It is believed that one of the greatest needs of the United States today, is a military policy. . . . It should include first a proper reserve. 2. As it requires time to manufacture cannon and ammunition therefore, (sic) a sufficient number of field artillery cannon with ammunition should at once be acquired and kept in stock to properly arm the artillery force agreed upon. 3. A Regular Army, balanced in all its parts, that will after the proper length of service make available at least 500,000 reserves in the shortest possible time. 4. A wise provision therefore for the United States will be to educate a sufficient number of officers to properly train the militia and volunteers."

Garrison rejected most of these recommendations. Strangely enough he did this without drawing down upon himself abuse from the advocates of a strong military establishment. The Secretary escaped this because his remarks on preparedness were merely

---

[16] Brooks, *op. cit.,* p. 123.
[17] Memorandum of Brigadier General W. W. Macomb for the Chief of Staff, December 26, 1914, WCD 8085-3. Records of the General Staff, National *Archives.*

high-sounding platitudes which side-stepped the need for effective measures. In his annual report for 1914 he wrote that those who are thoughtful and have the courage to face the facts of life "take lessons from experience, and strive by wise conduct to attain the desirable things, and by prevision and precaution to protect and defend them when obtained. All governments must therefore have force—physical force—i.e., military force, for these purposes." This was not militarism, he said, but only a necessary, proper, and adequate preparation of the military resources of the nation. The Secretary then listed all the various deficiencies of the Army: officers, reserves, artillery, aviation, motor transport, munitions, and an inadequate mobile force for the protection of the United States. Then he presented recommendations ignoring the wise advice of his military counsellors.

All the organizations, established by law, should be brought up to authorized strength, which would require the addition of about 25,000 enlisted men and 1,000 officers.[18] Other recommendations subsequently submitted for the consideration of Congress included the creation of an Army Transportation Reserve Corps, the provision of a reserve force for the Regular Army, and an increase in the authorized strength of the Coast Artillery Corps.[19] This would do very little to prepare the nation to defend itself, but because Garrison used all the words of the ardent preparationists, his stand was widely praised. Even such die-hard critics of the administration as Senator Henry Cabot Lodge and Roosevelt praised Garrison.[20]

But Congress was not interested in any increase in the Army, and the President again failed to prod Congress into action. An attempt on the part of a Kansas Republican, Representative D. R. Anthony, to implement the four-division plan was unsuccessful. Chairman James Hay of the House Military Affairs Committee opposed any increase, and the White House would not exert pressure upon Congress on behalf of the Army.[21]

Chairman George E. Chamberlain of the Senate Military Affairs Committee was more sympathetic toward preparedness than Hay. However, he objected to the bills as presented by the War

---

[18] Brooks, *op. cit.*, pp. 124-125.
[19] *WCD 8085-3, Records of the General Staff,* National Archives.
[20] Brooks, *op. cit.*, p. 125.
[21] *Army-Navy Journal,* December 12, 19, 1914, January 16, 1915; *New York Times,* February 3, 1915.

Department because they represented "a continuation of what may be called the system of piecemeal legislation heretofore in force looking to the improvement of individual arms and corps rather than the Army as a whole." He suggested to Garrison that the War Department submit a bill for the reorganization of the Army based upon the General Staff Report of 1912. The Senator did not anticipate that any action could be taken at this session of Congress, "but with the beginning of the next session I hope that the subject may be taken up and given that careful consideration which its importance demands."[22] In his reply the Secretary defended his program as exactly in the line of any national consideration of our military needs, also as in conformity with the Report of 1912. "With so vast a subject as this," he continued, "it is practically impossible to settle it all at one time in one measure. Not only questions of cost, but innumerable other questions inject themselves into the discussion, with the result that nothing is done." Garrison felt that the most important immediate objective was to secure the completion of the units we already possessed.[23] Perhaps what he failed to realize was that the legislation of 1901 had set the maximum strength of the Regular Army at 128,653 [24] and this was hardly an adequate force in the dark days of 1915. What was needed was sweeping reorganization. The hesitant steps of the Secretary of War were unlikely to achieve it.

Thus the effort of Senator Chamberlain came to nothing, and it was alleged that by some mysterious or underground route the impression reached the Capitol that the utterances of the President and the Secretary of War were for home consumption. Congress passed the usual one hundred million dollar appropriation bill without recommendation from the White House that a "citizenry trained and accustomed to arms" be provided.[25]

Upon the conclusion of the Sixty-third Congress on March 4, 1915, interest in national defense was intensified by events in Europe which threatened to involve the United States in war. Therefore Garrison directed the War College to make a complete reexamination of military policy with respect to the strength and organization of the armed land forces in peace with a view to the

---

[22] Chamberlain to Garrison, January 26, 1915. *Scott Mss.*
[23] Garrison to Chamberlain, January 30, 1916. *Scott Mss.*
[24] Ganoe, *op. cit.*, p. 458.
[25] Brooks, *op. cit.*, p. 128.

most rapid and efficient development of them to the extent that may be necessary in time of war. The substance of this policy was to be a clearly expressed statement of the recommended strength and organization of ·first, the Regular Army and the Organized Militia; this should be followed by, second, a careful study of the question of a Reserve for both the Regular Army and the Organized Militia and, *if possible to agree upon it,* a plan for the formation of such Reserves; third, the same with respect to the volunteers: their Organized and relation to the Regular Army and the Organized Militia; and fourth, the reserve Material and Supplies which should be available and which could not be promptly obtained if delayed until the outbreak of war.[26]

Garrison Lays the Groundwork for a Military Policy

The spring and summer of 1915 saw the General Staff busily trying to devise some way to reorganize the Army, some way that would accomplish the desired result and still receive the support of Congress.[27] Garrison was anxious that the completed plan have the affirmative and complete approval of the General Staff but he also felt that the most important consideration was to get all of the valuable military legislation from Congress that "we feel it is proper to ask for now and to hope to obtain now." The Secretary also suggested that the overall plan be presented as a broad treatment of the military needs of the nation to be followed up by detailed studies of specific topics so that anyone who wished to intelligently understand the matter could, by referring to this publication or compilation, do so.[28]

While the General Staff was preparing its study, the attitude of Woodrow Wilson took a sharp reversal. On July 21, 1915, the President wrote Garrison and asked him to prepare "a program, with estimates, of what you and the best informed soldiers in your counsels think the country ought to undertake to do." [29] The Chief Executive also tried to pave the way for the administration's future program by holding conferences with congressional leaders.

---

[26] The Adjutant General (H. P. McCain) to Scott, March 22, 1915. *Scott Mss.*
[27] Scott to Colonel H. J. Slocum, April 30, 1915. *Scott Mss.*
[28] Garrison to the General Staff, July 28, 1915. *Scott Mss., Box 17.* When the Report was published in September, 1915, it was followed by thirty studies on specific topics.
[29] Wilson to Garrison, July 21, 1915. *Army and Navy Journal,* September 4, 1915.

As a result of these discussions, Wilson began to incline toward a broad convincing program which was based upon the requirements of the foreign situation and the state of the public finances. However, in the light of his previous attitude and position this hardly meant an all-out attempt to prepare a complete national defense.

Republicans who had previously berated the President for his stand on preparedness were still critical of the Democratic leader. Roosevelt and Lodge felt that the program was designed for political purposes, and the former President was especially vitriolic in his criticisms.[30] The New York *Times* of August 31, 1915 was caustic enough to suggest that Roosevelt was displeased simply because the Republican had lost an election issue. Mr. James Hay, however, was still not convinced that the cry for national defense came from the people. With the opposition of the powerful House Committee still not overcome, any administration measure would be in for hard sledding.[31]

Garrison Seeks to Cure the Nation's Military Ills

When released in September, 1915, the "Statement of a Proper Military Policy for the United States" showed that the labors of the General Staff had resulted in a comprehensive study of the military needs of the country. The War College plan recommended that a mobile force of 500,000 trained and organized troops should be available upon the outbreak of hostilities and that there should be at least 500,000 more available within ninety days thereafter. We should also have a system to raise and train at least 500,000 troops to replace the losses and wastage in personnel incident to war. To meet these needs the plan urged an increase in strength of the Regular Army to 281,000 with a reserve sufficient to build it up to 500,000 in an emergency. More manpower was to come from the proposed Continental Army of 500,000 which was in reality a federalized militia whose members would receive two months training a year for three years. Because of constitutional limitations no provision was made for the National Guard. "No force can be considered a portion of our first line whose control and training is so little subject to Federal authority in peace"

---

[30] Lodge to Roosevelt, August 5, 1915; Roosevelt to Lodge, August 7, 1915. *Roosevelt-Lodge Correspondence, op. cit.,* Vol. II, pp. 461-462.
[31] Scott to John F. McGhee, July 28, 1915. *Scott Mss.*

and, therefore, no legislation affecting the Organized Militia was recommended "beyond the repeal of all provisions of laws now in effect whereby militia or militia organizations may or must be received into the Federal service in advance of any other forces." Attention was also paid to the problem of economic mobilization because the experiences of the war in Europe had shown that prospects of victory were immeasurably lessened by wastage, abuse, and confusion. "Steps should be taken looking forward toward a national organization of our economic and industrial resources as well as our resources in fighting men." The proposed entire force would require eight years to develop.[32]

Seeking to implement the War College study, and following his policy of striving for the obtainable rather than the desirable, Secretary Garrison presented his legislative proposals to Congress. His recommendations, which he considered an irreducible minimum for a reasonably adequate military policy, included an increase in the Regular Army to 141,843 men and the creation of a citizen army of 400,000 men organized, intensively trained for short periods, and equipped with personal accoutrements. The National Guard was to continue in its present status, but with increased federal support and encouragement. As far as reserves were concerned his proposals were not very clear as to how reserves were to be produced by the above forces, and little provision was made for their organization or utilization. The heart of the Secretary's proposal was his citizen or Continental Army plan which proposed the ultimate organization of 400,000 citizen soldiers. They would be raised in annual contingents of 133,000 enlisted for three years with the colors and three years in the reserve. Under the enlistment contract, each man would be liable for a certain fixed period (two months was proposed) of intensive field training in each of his three years with the colors.[33] The proposal, in its essence, was for a nationalized militia force, something which had been advocated by Washington in 1783. But just as Washington's wise proposals had been broken on the unyielding rocks of State rights and prejudice, so too were the recommendations of Garrison to encounter stiff resistance.

[32] *Statement of a Proper Military Policy for the United States* (Washington: Government Printing Office, 1916), pp. 1-21.
[33] Garrison Memorandum of September 17, 1915. *Scott Mss.* Under the Garrison plan the United States would have the following force: Regular Army, 141,843; National Guard, 129,000; Continental Army, 400,000.

The Secretary believed that his plan represented the best that could be accomplished without resort to universal military training. He believed that legal and constitutional obstacles made any other plan out of the question. Replying to criticisms of the plan, the Secretary of War insisted that the Regular Army could not recruit more than 50,000 men in any one year, that there were not sufficient accommodations for more than that, and that anything else would cost too much. If the 133,000 men per year could not be procured for the Continental Army, then the bankruptcy of the volunteer system would be proven. He rejected universal military training on the ground that too many federal officials would be required to administer it.[34]

The plan was opposed by the *Army and Navy Journal* which claimed that the Secretary's proposals would weaken the Regular Army and the National Guard and that it was a political scheme and not a military one.[35] The National Guard Association came to Washington "with blood in their eyes" to fight the Continental Army plan, but the President gave the plan his support and even Mr. Hay agreed to push it through his Committee. The Chief of Staff was of the opinion that the sentiment of the country was such that it would be carried through that winter.[36] Mr. Hay's support, however, was to be of short duration. On November 30 he informed the Secretary that he would not use the bill proposed by the War Department, but intended to formulate a bill in Committee.[37] With the Chairman's attitude toward the Army this was hardly welcome news to the Secretary's ears. Military legislation once again threatened to become a political football. The War Department was somewhat cheered by the President's strong argument for defense in his message to Congress on December 7, 1915, but this was not enough to overcome the gloom caused by

[34] Brooks, *op. cit.*, p. 182.

[35] *Army and Navy Journal*, October 30, November 6, November 13, 1915

[36] Scott to Brigadier General R. K. Evans, November 1, 1915. *Scott Mss., Box 20.* That the National Guard had reason to fear the Continental Army is clear from the sentiments of General Scott: "The Continental Army is nothing more than a federal militia, devised to meet the objections of the Constitution, and it is the Secretary's wish to take such portions of the National Guard as want to come into the Continental Army, rank for rank and grade for grade, provided the States will permit them to do so." Scott to Captain Charles M. de Bremond, December 27, 1915. *Scott Mss.*

[37] Scott to Wood, December 1, 1915. *Scott Mss.* Mr. Hay later stated "that there was but little feeling in Congress for any legislation." Scott to Col. W. S. Scott, December 27, 1915. *Scott Mss.*

Hay's opposition. "Mr. Hay probably dominates his Committee, "wrote General Scott, "and the Committee dominates Congress. That is the way it always has been since Hay has been Chairman, and I expect that is the way it is going to be until somebody else is Chairman. So we will have to wait patiently for results." [38]

General Scott soon received confirmation of his apprehensions concerning the fate of military legislation at the tender hands of Congress. National Guard sentiment was strong, and as the hearings got underway it became evident that the militia was still considered to be our second line of defense, and that there was little support for the Continental Army. Wilson, however, still supported Garrison; as late as mid-January, 1916 he wrote Hay saying that "I wish with all my heart that the Committee could see its ways to a direct and immediate acceptance of the plan for a Continental Army." [39] In the midst of the struggle, the President launched a speaking tour in which preparedness was the main theme.[40] Concluding his tour on February 3, 1916, Wilson returned to Washington to find Congress suspicious and critical of Garrison. The Chief Executive came to the conclusion that his Secretary of War had been peremptory, abrupt, impolitic, and intolerant in his urging of the plan upon Congress. On February 6, the President thought it would be wise to call a conference of congressional leaders in order to iron out differences of opinion on the Army bill. Leaks from the White House to the press indicated that he no longer regarded himself as committed to the Garrison program.[41]

This precipitated a demand on the part of the Secretary that the President make an immediate decision as to whether the White House would support the Continental Army or the militia bill of Hay. Wilson replied on February 10, saying that he would deem it a very serious mistake to shut the door against the attempt of the House Committee to meet the requirements in a way of their own

---

[38] Scott to Col. E. J. Greble, December 8, 1915. *Scott Mss.*
[39] Baker, *op. cit.*, Vol. VI, pp. 34-35.
[40] During the course of his tour Wilson said that he would be "ashamed if I had not learned something in fourteen months . . . We have got the men to waste, but God forbid that we waste them. Men who go as efficient instruments of national honor into the field afford a very handsome spectacle indeed. Men who go in as crude and ignorant boys only indict those in authority for neglect." Frederick Palmer: *Newton D. Baker, America at War*, 2 Vols., (New York: Dodd, Mead & Co., 1931) Vol. I, pp. 41-42.
[41] Brooks, *op. cit.*, pp. 188-189.

choosing, although he himself was not yet convinced that the Hay plan would meet the needs of the Nation. He then rebuked Garrison because he and the officers of the General Staff had testified before Congressional Committees that universal service was the only alternative to the Continental Army. Garrison answered with a letter of resignation on the same day. He stated that it was evident that they hopelessly disagreed on what he conceived to be fundamental principles.[42]

General Scott lamented that "the really good and feasible Continental Army plan" was now dead and he was fearful as to the result on the question of preparedness.[43] The Chief of Staff was extremely critical of the White House for not exerting stronger leadership in Congress. "The policy of the administration has had no champion in either house. Both houses have been in a very chaotic situation." [44] Nevertheless, the President evidently did not feel that Garrison's departure was any loss in the fight for preparedness.[45] In the meantime the War Department was without a head, the Chief of Staff serving as *ad interim* Secretary while the President searched for a successor to Garrison. The leaderless Congress was free to shape its own military policy.

The National Defense Act of 1916

In general terms it may be said that the National Defense Act of June 3, 1916, was the first comprehensive legislation for national defense. It provided for four classes of troops in the United States: First, the Regular Army; second, the National Guard; third, the reserve force; and fourth, the Volunteer Army, which would be raised only in time of war. The strength of the Regular Army would be increased to 175,000 over a period of five years and the strength of the National guard was set at about 457,000 men. Both an officers and enlisted reserve corps was created by the act which also provided for a Reserve Officers Training Corps which would consist of units at the various colleges, academies, and universities throughout the country where military education and training would be given which should give a personnel for the officers' reserve corps that would be better equipped for the duties of an officer than any heretofore available. The Act of 1916 also

[42] New York *Times*, February 11, 1916.
[43] Scott to Major General Frederick Funston, February 11, 1916. *Scott Mss.*
[44] Scott to Lt. Col. G. Hutcheson, February 14, 1916. *Scott Mss., Box 21.*
[45] Brooks, *op. cit.*, p. 192.

affected the General Staff in that the Mobile Army and Coast Artillery Divisions were abolished and the Staff was limited to three general officers and fifty-two junior officers of whom no more than twenty-six could be on duty in the District of Columbia. As the Chief of Staff bitterly commented: "The law limiting the President in the number of General Staff officers he can order to duty in Washington gives us fewer officers here than at any time in the history of the organization and at the most important time of our military development. Just what end of military efficiency it was proposed to serve thereby it is impossible to conjecture."

The Act also attempted to create a federalized National Guard, subject to the call of the President, with the consent of Congress, which was to consist of all able-bodied males between the ages of eighteen and forty-five, "and said Militia shall be divided into three classes, the National Guard, the Naval Militia, and the Unorganized Militia." No program was laid out for the Unorganized Militia, but the National Guardsmen would have to agree to obey the President and defend the Constitution in their enlistment terms of six years of which three were to be in active service and the rest in the reserves. Guardsmen were to be paid with federal funds, which the Secretary of War could curtail or stop if the States did not carry out the necessary provisions of the act.[46]

This act, while containing many salutary and wise provisions, was not geared to the necessities of the times. There was only a small increase in the Regular Army, and in effect the main dependence in time of war was placed upon the National Guard. General Scott had feared that just such a bill would be enacted which would place our military system upon a foundation of sand,

> and we would be worse off than we are now, because we would be saddled with an impossible system. They talk of the States agreeing to do these things, that is, to obey the orders of the national government; but Constitutional jurisdiction can not be given away, or bought or sold, and the first time it came to a legal decision the system would break down.[47]

Critics hurled bitter protests at a bill which was "worse than nothing" and had been passed for petty political reasons, "against the united opposition of our military experts." The Act had been opposed by "faithful public servants" like ex-Secretary of War

---

[46] Annual Report, S/W, 1916, Vol. I, pp. 155-208.
[47] Scott to John F. McGee, January 18, 1916. *Scott Mss.*

Root (Rep.); ex-Secretary of War Wright (Dem.); ex-Secretary of War Garrison (Dem.), who tendered his resignation as a protest against the bill; ex-Secretary of War Stimson (Rep.); ex-Assistant Secretary of War Breckinridge (Dem.), who resigned as a protest against the bill; and Secretary of War Baker (Dem.). There were many others but their voices "have been but faintly heard . . . through the hubub of platitudes which heralded the bill." [48] Former Assistant Secretary of War Henry Breckinridge angrily termed the bill as either a comedy or a tragedy. "A comedy if only a passing ridiculous phase of the progress toward real national defense. A tragedy, if it is an accurate presage of what is to be the final result of the labors of this Congress on the great problem of the national security." [49] Mobilization of the National Guard on the Mexican border and continuing adherence to the shopworn principle of volunteering were to prove that the National Defense Act of 1916 had failed to come to grips with one of the fundamental problems of the American military establishment—manpower—which could be justly and fairly secured through universal military training.

A Revolution in American Military Policy

The year 1917 brought grave diplomatic crises to the United States, but it was thought wise to interfere as little as possible with the National Defense Act of 1916, to the end that it might be given a fair trial.[50] In December, 1916 General Wood said that he believed our condition to be more dangerous than at any time in our national history, except perhaps during the darkest moments of the Civil War.[51] Many in the War Department were highly in favor of discarding the present legislation with its ultimate dependence on volunteering, and substituting the more reliable compulsive system in order to get a suitable supply of manpower.

As early as April, 1915 Wood argued for a system of universal military training based on the Swiss plan. He said that the volunteer system had failed us in the past and would fail us in the future. It was uncertain in operation, prevented organized preparation, and tended to destroy that individual sense of obligation for

---

[48] *Century Magazine*, August, 1916, p. 801.
[49] Henry Breckinridge: *Preparedness* (Pamphlet, New York, 1916), p. 3.
[50] Senator George E. Chamberlain to Newton D. Baker, January 23, 1917. *Scott Mss.*
[51] Wood to William C. Church, December 20, 1916. *Church Mss.*

military service which should be found in every citizen. It costs excessively in life and treasure, he said, and does not permit that condition of preparedness which must exist if we are to wage war successfully with any great power prepared for war.[52]

In the hearings before the House Committee on Military Affairs, January 10, 1916, the Chief of Staff boldly advocated compulsory military service. General Scott believed that universal military training has been the cornerstone upon which has been built every republic in the history of the world, and its abandonment would be the signal for decline and obliteration. He pleaded for training young men so that on the outbreak of war they would be able to render efficient service. "To send men into battle who have not been given this thorough training is not only a useless waste of our resources in men but, to anyone who understands anything of the realities of modern war, convicts the people of the country who are responsible for such proceedings, of criminal neglect."[53] Scott looked for "the sky to fall on me" for talking about universal service, but for some reason his head remained unscathed. The National Security League endorsed the idea, and it began to look as if there might be compulsory service in the United States before a very great length of time.[54]

Wilson, however, regretted that in the testimony Scott's opinion and the opinion of others in favor of compulsory military training should have been made to seem part of the judgment of the Department of War in favor of a continental reserve.[55] Scott respectfully suggested in his reply that the President had been misinformed in thinking that the plan for a Continental Army was urged because it would be a step toward universal service. This would not be any more true of a Continental Army than of one formed from the National Guard or "any other plan which fails to produce the requisite number of men voluntarily—as if the number will not come forward for any plan voluntarily the Nation must resort to the draft or go without."[56]

The basis of a proposed bill for universal service was drawn up by Captain George Van Horn Moseley and printed in the *Army and Navy Journal* on June 17, 1916. This proposal called

[52] Wood, *The Military Obligation of Citizenship*, pp. 33-34.
[53] *Annual Report, S/W, 1916*, pp. 160-163.
[54] Scott to General W. S. Edgerley, January 24, 1916. *Scott Mss.*
[55] Wilson to Scott, February 14, 1916. *Scott Mss.*
[56] Scott to Wilson, February 18, 1916. *Scott Mss.*

for six months service for all able-bodied male citizens, including those who had declared their intention of becoming citizens. In a statement appearing in the Boston *Transcript* of October 31, 1916, Captain Moseley was quoted as saying that his proposal provided a system whereby able-bodied young men are liable to be trained for a period of six months in the calendar year in which they become eighteen years of age, adding: "Each young man takes his training in one dose and is done with it. The course is long enough to make a qualified soldier out of the average young man. The course is so arranged as to interfere to a minimum degree with schooling." The National Security League proposed to put the whole force of its 75,000 members behind the movement to get the matter of universal military training before Congress and the people. "With all these forces working together," the *Army and Navy Journal* happily remarked, "it would seem that the prospects for a speedy and satisfactory outcome of the universal military training question are very bright." [57]

With the increasing seriousness of our relations with Germany, General Scott was able to convince Secretary of War Newton D. Baker of the necessity of universal military training, and Baker in turn was able to persuade the President.[58] The War College Division was ordered, in December, 1916, to draft a plan for universal service in peacetime though many were still very "insistent that nothing shall be done to strengthen our defenses. They seem to think that a special providence watches over the United States as that inasmuch as we have been protected from disaster in times gone by that protection will continue." [59]

The War College plan was submitted to Congress and upon the declaration of war on April 6, 1917, the question became one of urgent necessity. There immediately arose the question of whether or not volunteering should be tried before conscription was resorted to. Sentiment in the House of Representatives seemed to be "overwhelmingly in favor of giving the boys a chance to volunteer first." The White House was warned that if an attempt was made to put through a bill providing for universal service "without affording opportunity to volunteer such an attempt

---

[57] *Army and Navy Journal*, November 4, 1916. General Wood was also quite elated over what he considered to be this favorable climate of opinion.
[58] Morison and Commager, *op. cit.*, Vol. II, p. 478.
[59] Senator Chamberlain to Church, January 22, 1917. *Church Mss.*

would, in my judgment, provoke a bitter fight on the floor with the result in doubt."[60] Secretary Baker, however, continued to press the President to throw his support behind the bill. Baker cited the example of the Civil War as an illustration of the fact that the volunteer system was no answer to the problem of procuring manpower.[61] With the support of the Administration the Selective Service Act was passed on May 18, 1917. It provided that all men between the ages of twenty-one and thirty must register Subsequent modifications embraced all men between eighteen and forty-five, making for a total of 24,234,021 registrants. The wartime Army inducted 2,180,296 while the Regular Army, National Guard, Navy and Marine Corps swelled their ranks by voluntary enlistments.[62] Thus the perennial problem of manpower was solved at the outset of the war in a manner for the wisdom of which our past military history gave ample precedents.

Slow Preparation on the Part of the Navy

The Navy, in the years preceding the outbreak of war, continued to increase its efficiency and strength although at times its pace was not all that could be desired. Certainly there was great need for a strong Navy in view of the fearful struggle that was convulsing Europe. The United States would be the chief neutral carrier of the world and as such could expect to have her commerce hampered by both belligerents. It did not require a crystal ball to see that one of the chief weapons in Britain's arsenal would be a blockade of Germany, and that the German Empire would retaliate by attempting to cut off the flow of supplies and munitions to England which would be coming from America. Thus if there was not to be a repetition of the humiliation of the Napoleonic Wars, America would have to protect her rights as a neutral nation. The surest way of guaranteeing American freedom of the seas was a strong Naval force which could command respect from both belligerents.[63]

---

[60] Edward W. Pou to Joseph P. Tumulty, April 11, 1917. *Wilson Mss., File 2, Box 116.*
[61] Baker to Wilson, April 13, 1917. *Wilson Mss., File 11, Box 117.*
[62] Morison and Commager, *op. cit.,* Vol. II, pp. 478-479.
[63] This, of course, is proceeding on the assumption that America would follow a path of true neutrality. A strong force would be of no avail if our diplomacy did not choose to utilize it. Nevertheless, no matter what course we followed—true neutrality or eventual entrance into the war—a strong Navy was necessary to achieve realization of our national aims.

From 1906 to 1914, regular increases in the Navy provided for twelve first class battleships. In the appropriation bills these ships were uniformly described as carrying as heavy armor and as powerful armament as any vessel of their class, and as having the highest practicable speed and greatest desirable radius of action. Through 1912, the authorized costs, exclusive of armor and armament, was $6,000,000 each, but for 1913 and 1914, $7,420,000 was appropriated.[64]

The construction of four new battleships was urged by President Roosevelt in 1908 but this aroused apprehension in many quarters for fear that it would be interpreted by the world as a signal for a naval race. Considering that the navies of the great powers were considerably stronger than the American this criticism was hardly valid.[65] The House of Representatives, however, defeated the President's proposals and provided for the construction of only two new battleships.[66] The annual two-ship program was curtailed by the Democratic House in 1912 when it provided for the construction of only one ship.[67] Evidently there were those who believed that America should slow up her naval program as evidence that we preferred arbitration to gunpowder as a means of adjusting international differences.[68]

The war in Europe brought about a more sympathetic attitude on the part of Congress to the needs of the naval establishment. In 1915 the Congress returned to the two-ship program and also authorized eight or more submarines. Two additional battleships were authorized contingent upon the sale of two obsolete vessels.[69] The tempo of naval construction was stepped up in 1916 when Congress passed legislation which would provide for ten first class battleships, six cruisers, fifty destroyers, nine fleet submarines, and

[64] By first class ships is meant ships of 10,000 tons or more displacement. XXXIV Stat, pp. 582, 1203; XXXV Stat, p. 777; XXXVI Stat, p. 1287; XXXVII Stat, pp. 354, 911.
[65] The following is a comparison of the principal Naval Powers:

	Battleships	Cruisers	Destroyers	Submarines
Great Britain ..	52	35	144	44
France	18	21	44	44
United States ...	25	12	16	12
Germany	22	8	64	2
Japan	11	11	55	10

Annual Report, S/N, 1908, p. 11.
[66] XXXV Stat, p. 158.
[67] XXXVII Stat, p. 354.
[68] Literary Digest, March 2, 1912.
[69] XXXVIII Stat, pp. 413-415.

fifty-eight coast submarines.[70] This program was to be completed in three years. That the Nation favored this large naval expansion was indicated in a poll taken of newspaper editors by the *Literary Digest* which revealed that 40% favored a Navy second only to Great Britain's, while 60% favored a Navy as large as any in the world.[71]

Much constructive naval legislation was enacted prior to America's entrance into the war. The Naval Militia was strengthened in 1914, and the creation of a National Naval Reserve was authorized.[72] By the Act of August 29, 1916, the strength of the Marine Corps was increased by 3,235 men and the President was further authorized to increase the enlisted strength of the Corps to 17,400.[73] A very important milestone was passed on March 3, 1915, with the creation of the Office of Chief of Naval Operations, which was to have under its control war plans and fleet operations, corresponding to the functions of a General Staff.[74] The Coast Guard was established in 1915 by combining the Revenue Cutter Service and the Life Saving Service into one organization. This new service was to automatically become a part of the Navy in time of war.[75]

The war in Europe gave the United States an unusual opportunity to observe and evaluate the utilization and effectiveness of the airplane, then in its infancy, as a weapon of waging war. Though on a relatively small scale, the Navy enthusiastically pursued various experiments in the use and design of Naval aircraft. Naval officials were quick to grasp the significance of aircraft development and its use in naval warfare. As early as 1913 the Navy was authorized to detail thirty officers to aviation duty. The advent of the air age was further recognized by a $10,000 appro-

---

[70] *Annual Report, S/N, 1916*, p. 1.
[71] *Literary Digest*, March 11, 1916. Also not to be forgotten was the strong group of pacifists and non-militarists who had a strong voice in Senator Robert La Follette. Cf. Walter Mills, *Road to War* (New York, Houghton Mifflin Co., 1935), p. 236.
[72] XXXVIII *Stat*, p. 384. The Naval Reserve was established in 1915. The Reserve had been recommended in the *Annual Report of the S/N, 1912*, pp. 63-64.
[73] XXXIX *Stat*, p. 612. The Strength of the Marine Corps in 1913 was 9,921. *Annual Report, S/N, 1913*, p. 5.
[74] XXXVIII *Stat*, p. 929. "During its first year, however, the office was handicapped by lack of provision for subordinate officers, and by the resignation in April of its first chief, Admiral Bradley A. Fiske, on the issue of more vigorous steps toward preparedness." Alden and Westcott, *op. cit.*, p. 340.
[75] *Annual Report, S/N, 1915*, p. 207.

priation for naval aviation.[76] It is interesting to note that for fiscal year 1916, the amount appropriated for aviation was $1,000,000 and for fiscal year 1917, $3,500,000.[77]

In July of 1915, Secretary Daniels proposed a plan for Navy experimental work on a broader scale than had ever before been attempted. Its adoption by Congress, according to Daniels, would place the United States far above the other countries in the machinery of warfare. At the same time, President Wilson announced that he would call into consultation high officers of the Army and Navy for the purpose of formulating a definite and consistent policy of national defense.[78] These maneuvers appeared to result from the criticisms levelled against the effectiveness of the Navy.

The Navy was certainly far better prepared for war than was the Army. Nevertheless serious charges were hurled at the deficiencies in the Navy's readiness. In 1920, Rear Admiral William S. Sims wrote a letter to the Secretary of the Navy in which among other points, he stressed the delays due to unpreparedness in both material and personnel, at the outbreak of hostilities, and our lack of definite plans for effective, aggressive war. The Congressional investigation that followed largely supported the Admiral Sims' charges in that 66% of the Navy's ships, on April 6, 1917, were in need of repair; that not more than 10% had their full complement of personnel; and "that only after several months of costly delay was our full naval strength thrown into the war." [79] In spite of this, however, it was also asserted that without the excellent work of the United States Navy, the Allies would have been defeated before American help could have arrived.[80]

---

[76] XXXVII *Stat,* pp. 892, 894. "The best scientific and military judgment of the world is that no nation can be said to be fully prepared for war that neglects this new military weapon of offense and defense." *Annual Report, S/N, 1913,* p. 17.

[77] XXXVIII *Stat,* p. 930, 39 *Stat,* p. 559. On April 24, 1915, a board consisting of civilians and Army and Navy officers convened for "the purpose of studying methods to advance the general subject of aeronautics in the Army and Navy."

[78] Richmond *Times-Dispatch,* April 25, 1915; July 17, July 27.

[79] Alden and Westcott, *op. cit.,* p. 339.

[80] Morison and Commager, *op. cit.,* Vol. II, p. 483.

CHAPTER 16

World War I

The Demands Upon American Manpower—Lack of Unity
Invites Disaster—The Enlargement of the Army Presents
Difficulties—The General Staff is Vindicated—Allied
Sideshows Create New Problems—The American Eagle
Spreads His Wings—"We Are Ready Now, Sir"

O N APRIL 6, 1917, Congress declared: "The state of war
between the United States and the Imperial German Government which had been thrust upon the United States is hereby
formally declared." Thus America entered the European War
which had been raging since August, 1914, and it now became
necessary for Congress and the White House to consider the
measures needed for the enlargement of our military forces and
the coordination of the industrial strength of the nation. It was
understood that this great war involved not only larger armies
than the United States had ever assembled, but also far-reaching
modifications of ordinary industrial processes and wider depar-
tures from the peacetime activities of the people. The task of
America was to immediately increase its naval and military forces;
and the agricultural and industrial systems of the nation had to
support these enlarged military establishments, as well as carry
an increasing financial, industrial, and agricultural burden for the
support of the Allied Powers who had borne not only the full fury
of the German military machine, but also the continuing drain
upon their economic resources and their capacity for production
which so titanic and long-continued a struggle necessarily entailed.[1]

The Demands Upon American Manpower

Other wars in which America had participated had clearly
demonstrated the difficulties in securing and retaining a sufficient
body of manpower. This problem was obviated soon after the outbreak of war by the passage of the Selective Service Act on May
18, 1917. The Army, however, would be faced with the problems
of training, organizing, and transporting the vast numbers of men

[1] *Annual Rpt, S/W, 1917,* p. 5.

to be mobilized. Also not to be forgotten were the sometimes hysterical demands of the Allies for American troops, as if the manpower reservoir was inexhaustible.

With the coming of war neither the American Government nor people had any conception of the demands that would be made upon the nation's manpower. Approaching disaster to Allied armies would, however, make American arms an essential factor in Entente success. The spring of 1917 was brightened for the Allies only by America's entrance into the war. The great offensive of the Somme had bogged down in a welter of blood and recriminations which was followed by mutiny in the French army. The overthrow of the Czar in March, while encouraging to the friends of democracy, also shed an ominous portent that Russia might withdraw from the war. The Italian front was discouraging and there was always the menace of the German submarines which threatened the whole war effort of the Allies. Perhaps the calculated gamble of the German High Command would succeed, the gamble that with submarine warfare she could force a decision before American arms could weight the scales in the Allies' favor.

It was not long before frantic cries for American troops were echoing in the corridors of the White House and the War Department. •The French felt that it was vital that the United States should *immediately* send an important army to Europe. Not only was this imperative for Allied success and morale, but it would also have a depressing effect on the Germans who believed that America's land participation in the war would be limited to sending money and supplies to the Allies.[2] The Allies, however, had no agreed-upon plan for the utilization of American manpower. The British and French Missions, which arrived in Washington during the latter part of April, had as their first concern the raising of loans for their depleted war chests. Once this pressing necessity was disposed of, the conferees agreed that the military situation was desperate and that evidence of good faith should be given promptly by the actual presence of American soldiers in France to show our flag.[3] The visiting war missions, however, gave no clear-cut guidance as to America's military role and it was one of the tasks of the newly appointed Chief of the American Ex-

---

[2] Seymour, *op. cit.*, Vol. III, p. 8.
[3] Frederick Palmer, *Bliss, Peacemaker*, (New York, Dodd, Mead and Co., 1934), pp. 145-146.

peditionary Forces to chart the future requirements of the American Army.

General John J. Pershing, with his carefully chosen staff, sailed for Europe on May 28; 1917. After a careful survey of the situation, Pershing cabled, on July 6, his estimate of the situation. He called for a million men in France with provision for expansion to two million. Not only manpower was necessary, but supplies, facilities, and equipment of every description to sustain a large American force in France.[4] This was but one in a long series of cables from Pershing to the War Department in which he very clearly stated the gravity of the situation and the necessity of American troops in France. In September he cabled the Secretary of War that there was considerable talk of the possibility of peace during the winter. The failure to stop the German armies, continued Pershing, and the revolution in Russia had a depressing effect upon the already downcast morale in both the British and French armies.[5] In his *Memoirs,* David Lloyd George wrote that in the autumn of 1917 American troops were arriving with what seemed to be disconcerting and perplexing slowness. "Both the French and ourselves were apprehensive lest, if it were not speeded up, it should arrive too late to save the Allied Front from collapse in face of the formidable German attack. The reservoir of French manpower had almost run dry and ours was approaching exhaustion." [6]

Throughout the bleak fall of 1917 there came these repeated warnings of an Allied catastrophe which could only be prevented by American troops. To Pershing, in November, the situation at best was grave and he urged that the most intense energy should be put into developing America's fighting forces for active service during the coming summer. "There is no telling what might happen if we defer our utmost exertion until 1919." [7] General Bliss agreed with Pershing in a memorandum of December 15, 1917: "A military crisis is to be apprehended culminating not later than the end of the next spring, in which, without great assistance from the

[4] *Ibid.,* p. 164.
[5] John J. Pershing, *My Experiences in the World War* (New York, 1931), Vol. I, p. 173.
[6] *War Memoirs of David Lloyd George,* Vol. V, p. 397.
[7] Pershing, *op. cit.,* Vol. I, pp. 237-238, 249-250.

United States, the advantage will probably lie with the Central Powers." [8]

Although the critical nature of the crisis was well known on both sides of the Atlantic, American troops moved only in small trickles to take their place on the Western Front. Pershing had called for a million men in France by May of 1918, but in April, a full year after our declaration of war, there were only 320,000 in the American Expeditionary Forces.[9] This can be readily explained by a number of factors, chief among which was the immense problem of organizing, training, supplying, and transporting the troops to France. Another difficulty in the way of establishing an army in France was the question as to whether there was to be an integrated or an independent American Army. It was quite apparent that the English were reluctant to divert their precious shipping for the transportation of an American Army unless those troops were fed promptly into their lines as part of their own organizations in order to maintain their manpower at full strength.[10]

Fortunately for the safeguarding of the identity and independence of the American Army the War Department had the foresight to understand the pressures which would be exerted by our Allies. Pershing was instructed to cooperate with the Allies, but in so doing the underlying idea was that the forces of the United States were to be a separate and distinct component of the combined forces, and their identity was to be preserved.[11] The Allies, desperate for manpower, and perhaps also suspicious of the ability and efficiency of the American Army, particularly the command and staff, made determined efforts to integrate American units into their own armies. Their efforts, however, were doomed to failure when they encountered the granite resoluteness of Pershing who was understandingly and unswervingly supported by the War Department.

When General Tasker H. Bliss returned to Europe in January, 1918, as American military representative on the Supreme War Council, he first had a conference in London with General Robertson, British Chief of Staff, and Lord Derby, Minister of War. Bliss found the gentlemen "badly rattled" because the Germans had

---

[8] Ray S. Baker, *Woodrow Wilson: Life and Letters* (Garden City, New York. 1927-1939), Vol. VII, p. 411.
[9] *Annual Rpt, S/W, 1918*, p. 9.
[10] Palmer, *Bliss, op. cit.*, p. 153. Bliss to Baker, May 25, 1917.
[11] Baker to Pershing, May 26, 1917. *Wilson Mss.* File II. Box 119.

superiority in men and munitions. The primary British demand was for 150,000 Americans to go at once on the British line. "They want men and they want them quickly. The proposition is, in a general way, for them to take our men with simply their rifles and the ammunition therefor and their clothing—the British to transport them and supply them in every way." General Robertson stated that the failure to receive the 150 battalions would invite disaster on the British front.[12] A consideration of American manpower and the amalgamation of American troops was taken up by the Supreme War Council on January 30 and 31. Foch, Petain, and Haig were agreed that an independent American Army could not be counted on for effective aid in 1918, and that the only method of rendering them useful at the earliest possible moment would be by amalgamating American regiments or battalions in French and British divisions.[13] Bliss, however, stood firm against the demand of the Allies and he ended the discussion by saying that "permanent amalgamation of our units with British and French units would be intolerable to American sentiment." [14] Bliss did agree to a plan whereby six entire American divisions would be brought to Europe and the infantry and auxiliary troops were to be trained with British divisions by battalions.[15]

American manpower was again the theme of a discussion by the Council on February 1. It adopted a resolution stating that as an absolutely necessary condition for the safety of the Western Front during the year 1918, American troops must arrive at the rate of not less than two complete divisions per month. In the opinion of Bliss there was no time for delay. "If it can be done we will have here 21 divisions by about July. It is of vital importance that this be done. Can you do it?" [16] The answer, to be provided by the combined resources of the British and American merchant fleets, was in the affirmative. With the great tide of American troops thereafter flowing into the fields and trenches of France there was to be less pressure exerted by the Allies for the integration of American troops into their armies.

---

[12] Bliss to Baker, January 22, 1918. Palmer, *Bliss, op. cit.,* pp. 216-217.
[13] Report by A. H. Frazier,· *Foreign Relations of the United States, 1918, Supplement I,* Vol. I, p. 63.
[14] Palmer, *Bliss, op. cit.,* pp. 222-23.
[15] Ray S. Baker, *op. cit.,* Vol. VII, p. 510.
[16] Palmer, Newton D. Baker, *op. cit.,* Vol. II, p. 117.

During the nineteen months of our participation in the war over 2,000,000 American troops were transported to France. Half of these were sent over in the first thirteen menths and the remainder in the last six months. Following the military crisis in April, 1918, the miracle of transportation took place. The number of men in May was more than twice the number for April, and June exceeded May. Before the first of July 1,000,000 men had sailed. The problem of the submarine and deficiencies in shipping had been overcome.[17]

Negotiations over the use of American troops were seemingly successfully concluded in April, 1918, after the great German offensive of March, on the basis of a memorandum drawn up by Secretary Baker. The United States planned to transport infantry and machine gun personnel numbering 120,000 a month from April through July. The troops would be under the command of Pershing and at his discretion could be assigned for training and use with British and French divisions "as the exigencies of the situation from time to time require; it being understood that this program . . . is a concession to the exigencies of the present military situation." It was also clearly understood that temporary service in Allied armies would not prejudice the eventual formation of an independent American Army. Pershing offered "all we have" to meet the immediate danger but he was inflexible in insisting that the independence of the Army be assured.[18] Thus the objective of a separate American Army was postponed but not lost sight of.

On August 16, 1918, General Pershing took command of the American First Army, the first step toward the consolidation of all American troops in France. Two days later he requested the British to return three of the five divisions which had been serving with the British forces; and Haig, though reluctant, agreed.[19] The Allies' desperate need for American troops, the valor those troops had shown under fire, and the rocklike insistence of Pershing, Bliss, and Baker had united to preserve the independence of the Army.

---

[17] Leonard P. Ayres, *The War with Germany: A Statistical Summary*. (Washington: Government Printing Office, 1919), pp. 37-38.
[18] Baker Memorandum, April 19, 1918. Ray S. Baker, *op. cit.*, Vol. VIII, p. 97; Palmer, Bliss, *op. cit.*, p. 252; Pershing, *op. cit.*, Vol. I, p. 365.
[19] Pershing, *op. cit.*, Vol. II, pp. 212, 217-218.

Lack of Unity Invites Disaster

For the first three years of the war, Allied unity and coordination was a myth. Lack of these elements threatened to further prolong the conflict if not to bring disaster. It was only under the impact of the Communist seizure of power in Russia and the tragedy of the Italian defeat at Caporetto in October of 1917 [20] that the policy of close cooperation took hold. Allied statesmen and soldiers met on November 7, 1917, in the small Italian town of Rapallo and formed the Supreme War Council for the coordination of the Allied War effort.

The Supreme War Council was a political body composed of "the Prime Minister and a member of the Government of each of the great Powers whose armies are fighting on that (the Western) Front." No Commander in Chief was authorized but the Council was viewed as an agency for the adoption and maintenance of a general policy for the Allies in the prosecution of the war, consistent with the total resources available and the most effective distribution of those resources among the various theaters of operations. A permanent military representative from each of the powers was to be attached to the Council.[21] The question which the Rapallo Agreement left unanswered and bequeathed as a legacy of bitter debate in the months to come, was whether or not it would achieve unity of military control. Many thoughtful observers were to answer in the negative.[22]

Allied statesmen and soldiers realized the need for cooperative action but it was difficult for them to submerge their nationalistic aims, prejudices, and jealousies. The necessity to do so was admitted by everybody. The difficulty was to determine the method by which such unprecedented coordination could be effected. There was a marked unwillingness on the part of either the British or French to accept another national as commander of their armies. Lloyd George had, early in 1917, put General Haig under the command of the Frenchman Nivelle, but the main result, according to General Bliss, was mutual recrimination and the be-

---

[20] Sydney H. Zebel, *A History of Europe Since 1870,* (New York: J. B. Lippincott and Co., 1948), p. 456.
[21] For the full text of the Rapallo Agreement see Seymour, *op. cit.,* Vol. III, p. 246.
[22] Seymour, *op. cit.,* Vol. III, pp. 254-255.

lief of British troops that they had been sacrificed in a hopeless attempt to secure success for their ally.[23]

The drive to make the Supreme War Council a real instrument of Allied military unity was doomed to failure unless agreement could be reached on a Commander in Chief. Here, however, determined opposition was presented by the British Prime Minister, David Lloyd George. In a speech to the House of Commons on November 19, he said that the appointment of a Commander in Chief would produce real friction, and might really produce not merely friction between the Armies, but friction between the nations and the Government. Lloyd George was to insist, in the face of the proposals of the French for the creation of a unified military control, that the Supreme War Council be under political domination. One reason advanced by the British Prime Minister was that it was impossible to separate problems of general policy from military strategy. He told Colonel House and the French that he would agree to no change in the Rapallo Agreement and that the military representatives were simply to be advisers to the political representatives. As General Bliss bitterly remarked: "In all of the conferences of that time and up to the great disaster of four months later, any suggestions as to a Commander in Chief only developed the belief that it was quite impossible." [24]

To both House and Bliss unity of control in the conduct of military operations in a given theater was essential to success. Therefore they drew up a memorandum for the President in which they urged the creation of a purely military council, "it being assumed that one or more of the principal Allied nations may be unwilling to place their military forces under a single Commander in Chief." They also believed that the Supreme War Council should be composed of the commanders in the field, together with the chiefs of staff of those same national forces or officers designated by these chiefs of staff and representing them. Finally, as a substitute for a commander in chief, there should be a president of the Supreme War Council, having power to execute their will.[25] These were the first recommendations of our observers abroad concerning the Council, and after seeing it in action in the first week

---

[23] *Ibid*, pp. 214, 249-250, 262.
[24] *Ibid*, p. 250.
[25] Memorandum of Bliss and House, November 25, 1917. *Ibid.*, pp. 253-254.

of December they were to be even more determined in their efforts to secure unity of command.

House and Bliss both were convinced that strong action on the part of Wilson could make the Supreme War Council an organic being instead of a facade to veil the quarreling Allies. House was quick to agree with Lloyd George that the United States should have a military representative on the Council, but America should not participate in political decisions.[26] Wilson in a cable of November 16 instructed House to "take the position that we not only approve a continuance of the plan for a war council but insist on it . . . . Baker and I are agreed that Bliss should be our military member."[27] Perhaps if the President had not been so quick in his acceptance of the Supreme War Council he could have exerted enough pressure on the squabbling Allies to force them to accept the principle of a commander in chief.

In his report of December 18, Bliss pointed out that the military crisis was not only due to the Russian collapse, but also largely due to lack of military coordination; lack of unity of control on the part of Allied forces in the field. Securing of this unified control, he continued, "is within the power of the President if it is in anyone's power. The military men of the Allies admit its necessity and are ready for it."[28] House was also convinced that reorganization was necessary, for "the Supreme War Council as at present constituted is almost a farce. It could be the most efficient instrument to win the war. The United States can make it so, and I hope she will exercise her undisputed power to do it."[29] Though this was sound advice from two of his most trusted advisers the President made no significant moves to implement such a policy or to force a decision in the question of a commander in chief.

With no real unity of military purpose there was little that the Supreme War Council could do except make recommendations

---

[26] House to Wilson, November 13, 1917. Ray S. Baker, *op. cit.,* Vol. VII, p. 354.

[27] Seymour, *op. cit.,* Vol. III, p. 220.

[28] Palmer, Bliss, *op. cit.,* pp. 203-206. Bliss concluded by saying "The difficulty will come with the political men. They have a feeling that military men, uncontrolled, may direct military movements counter to ultimate political interests. They do not fully realize that now the only problem is to beat the Central Powers."

[29] House to Wilson, December 14, 1917. Seymour, *op. cit.,* Vol. III, pp. 300-302.

and tender advice to the respective governments. That sound recommendations were made, there is little dispute, but without power and a supreme commander to implement these recommendations, unified command remained a fiction. One very important function of the Council was the centralizing and correlating of information which was to be a very valuable asset to Foch when he did assume supreme command.[30] If military defeat at Caporetto had sown the seeds of military unity it was to take another near tragedy to bring those seeds to bear fruit. On March 21, 1918, the most powerful and fully prepared military offensive in all history broke against the British front and threatened to divide the British and French armies. Not only did frantic appeals for American reinforcements go in a barrage to Washington, but at last the iron compulsion of facts broke down the barriers against unity. On April 3 Foch was given the strategic direction of military operations and his powers were further confirmed and strengthened on April 24, when he was made Commander in Chief of the Allied Armies.[31] Unity had at last come to the Allies, and one of the important tasks for America in the months ahead was to preserve that principle of unified military control.

The Enlargement of the Army Presents Difficulties

The Act of May 18, 1917, entitled "An act to authorize the President to increase temporarily the Military Establishment of the United States" envisaged three sources of manpower:

1. The Regular Army, whose authorized strength was increased to 18,033 officers and 470,185 enlisted men.

2. The National Guard, which on June 30, 1917, had a total of 3,803 officers and 107,320 enlisted men, expected to raise its force to 13,377 officers and 456,800 enlisted men.

3. The National Army, raised by Selective Service under which the President was empowered to summon two units of 500,000 each at such time as he should determine.[32]

These three divisions, needless to say, were very different organizations. The Regular Army was a veteran establishment of professional soldiers; the National Guard a volunteer organization of local origin maintained primarily for the preservation of domestic order in the States, with an emergency duty toward the national

---

[30] *Ibid.*, pp. 271-272.
[31] Palmer, Bliss, *op. cit.*, pp. 251, 252. Italy never accepted this as including the Italian Army.
[32] *Annual Rpt, S/W, 1917*, p. 6.

defense; the National Army an unknown quantity, unorganized, untrained, and existing only on paper.[33] Congress, however, wisely tried to eliminate differences between these three organizations. Enlistments in the Regular Army and the National Guard were authorized to be made for the duration of the war rather than for fixed terms; age requirements in the Regular Army and the Guard were made the same; the rights and privileges of members of the three forces were largely identical. The act created but one Army, selected by three processes.[34]

In the raising of the Army the country and War Department could justifiably be proud of their accomplishment. Upon the outbreak of hostilities there were only 200,000 in the Army, two-thirds of whom were Regulars and the rest National Guardsmen who had been called for duty on the Mexican border. This small force was expanded to twenty times its size and when the war ended 4,000,000 men had served.[35]

The raising, organizing, and training of these vast numbers put a very severe drain upon the Regular Army and the officer corps. It was estimated that about 200,000 officers would be needed, yet there were less than 9,000 in the Army in April, 1917. Of these only 5,791 were Regulars and the rest were officers of the National Guard. The primary source of supply for officers was the officers' training camps which supplied approximately one half of the number required. Of every six officers, one had had previous military training in the Regular Army, the National Guard, or the ranks; three came from the officers' training camps; and the other two came from civilian life into the Army, with little or no previous military training. In this last group the majority were physicians, a few were ministers, and most of the rest were men of special business or technical qualifications who were taken into the supply services or staff corps.[36]

The typical combat unit of the American Army was the in-

---

[33] Ayres, *op. cit.*, p. 17, speaking of Selective Service says: "The willingness with which the American people accepted the universal draft was the most remarkable feature in the history of our preparation for war. It is a noteworthy evidence of the enthusiastic support given by the country to the war program that, despite previous hostility to the principle of universal liability for military service . . . the standing of the drafted soldier was fully as honorable in the estimation of his companions and of the country in general as was that of the man who enlisted voluntarily."
[34] *Annual Rpt, S/W, 1917*, p. 18.
[35] Ayres, *op. cit.*, p. 16.
[36] *Ibid.*, p. 21.

fantry division, which in World War I contained about 1,000 officers and 27,000 men. Training and replacement organizations of about 10,000 men, known as depot brigades, were also used but in most cases recruits were put into the divisions which were the organizations in which they would see action. The average soldier had six months of training in the United States, two months overseas, and one month in a quiet sector before going into battle. Before the end of hostilities there were trained and sent overseas forty-two American divisions. Twelve were well advanced in their training, and four more were being organized. The War Department planned to have eighty divisions overseas by July, 1919, and one hundred by the end of the year.[37]

Tremendous problems in supplying the Army with food, clothing, and equipment were met and solved. Immense purchases were necessary on the part of the War Department to supply the necessities of the rapidly expanding Army. A well defined and adequate supply system had been able to meet the needs of the small Regular Army, and it had also been able to accumulate reserve material as Congress from time to time appropriated the necessary funds. But the mobilization of the National Guard on the Mexican border consumed those reserves, and the maintenance of the Army on the border required an increase which equalled the entire capacity of those industries who ordinarily devoted themselves to the production of military supplies.[38]

In addition to supplying the needs of the Army in the zone of the interior, it became necessary to accumulate in France huge stores of clothing and equipment for the troops enroute to Europe. The stream of supplies going to an army may be compared to the water thrown upon a fire by a bucket brigade. For every bucketful thrown on the fire there must be many that have been taken from the source of supply and are on the way. As the distance from the source increases the quantity in the "pipeline" constantly grows. When an army is 3,000 or 4,000 miles from its sources of supply the amount of supplies in reserve and in transit are enormous as compared with the quantities actually consumed each month.[39] The great appropriations by Congress tell the story from the financial point of view. In 1917 the normal appropriation for the Quarter-

[37] *Ibid.*, p. 25.
[38] *Annual Rpt, S/W, 1917*, p. 38.
[39] Ayres, *op. cit.*, p. 50.

master Department was $186,305,000. Appropriations in 1918 amounted to three billion dollars, a sum greater than the normal annual appropriation for the entire expenses of the Government.[40]

Before our armies could function in the field, numerous and extensive piers, docks, and warehouses had to be built at the French ports, and railroads with the necessary rolling stock had to be constructed. For the distribution of supplies in the American Expeditionary Forces, the Services of Supply was created, an organization to which one fourth of all the troops who went overseas were assigned.[41]

Under Major General W. M. Black, Chief of Engineers, a program of construction was prepared, providing for the movement and supply in France of not less than 4,000,000 men. This meant the development of some sixteen French ports located from the English Channel to the Mediterranean, the solving of an immense railroad problem, and the provision of cars and locomotives to supplement the greatly depleted supply of French rolling stock. The orders placed at home and abroad up to November, 1918 amounted to $700,000,000, a sum five times as great as all the purchases of material, equipment, and supplies made for the Panama Canal.[42]

American engineers constructed in France 1,000 miles of standard-gauge railroad track, and 125 miles of narrow-gauge track while the Signal Corps strung 100,000 miles of telephone and telegraph wire. The test of the efficiency of the supply service, however, lies not in the listing of statistics, impressive though they may be, but rather when the army is engaged in battle. Measured by that test the work of feeding, clothing, and equipping the American Army was well done, for, in the main, the expeditionary forces received what they needed.[43]

While the problems of organizing, transporting, and supplying the Army were being solved, the Army was gaining fresh laurels and glory for itself and America. Some 1,390,000 American troops saw action on the Western Front and at the time of

---

[40] *Annual Rpt, S/W, 1917*, p. 38.
[41] Ayres, *op. cit.*, p. 62.
[42] *Annual Rpt, S/W, 1918*, p. 34.
[43] Ayres, *op. cit.*, pp. 60-61, 84. One deficiency which was not overcome was in artillery. In round numbers we had in France 3,500 pieces of artillery, of which only 500 were made in America, and we used on the firing line 2,250 pieces of which only 100 were made in America. *Ibid.*, p. 84.

their greatest activity in October, 1918, twenty-nine American divisions held 101 miles of the front, or 23 per cent of the entire Allied battle line.[44] American manpower and valor were essential factors in the Allied equation of victory. Such a notable contribution was largely made possible through prior reforms in the War Department, and especially the creation of the General Staff.

The General Staff is Vindicated

The most striking commentary on the activities of the General Staff in World War I may be had by a comparison with the War Department of the Spanish-American War. In that war, with no General Staff, the War Department was hard pressed to land some 20,000 men in Cuba,[45] but in World War I we supplied and trained 4,000,000 and landed 2,000,000 in France. The General Staff faced its supreme test in this war. Its creation and acceptance had touched off years of bitter debate,[46] and if it had failed to realize the promises of its advocates it seems highly likely that the General Staff concept, gained after so many years of arduous struggle, would have been discarded as a factor in American military policy.

Unfortunately, upon the outbreak of war, the General Staff was organized under the provisions of the Act of June 3, 1916. Under this act the strength of the General Staff was limited to fifty-five officers with the proviso that "not more than one-half of all the officers detailed in said Corps shall at any time be stationed, or assigned to, or employed upon, any duty, in or near the District of Columbia." [47]

Section five of the Act seemed to be an attempt on the part of some members of Congress to limit the functions of the staff to "the consideration of more or less abstract questions of military policy" and would have meant in effect a return to the old system of more or less independent bureaus. Secretary of War Baker, however, was a supporter of the General Staff; he came to the conclusion that "the structure erected by the Act of 1903 remains as then created, except for the explicit modifications provided in the Act of 1916." Baker concluded that the Staff was not only to

---

[44] *Ibid.*, p. 101.
[45] *Cf.* Chapter 12 of this volume.
[46] *Cf.* Chapter 13 of this volume.
[47] *Annual Rpt, S/W, 1916*, p. 51.

consider Staff problems, but to act as a coordinating and reconciling agency.[48]

On April 6, 1917, the date of the declaration of war, the General Staff consisted of nineteen officers stationed in Washington and of twenty-two officers stationed elsewhere.[49] The task of preparing the plans for creating, mobilizing, organizing, training, equipping, transporting to Europe, and of maintaining and supplying an Army there, accordingly devolved upon a group of about twenty officers who constituted the General Staff authorized by law to be stationed in Washington.

The Act of May 12, 1917 increased the General Staff to ninety-one officers and removed, for the period of the emergency only, the restrictions of the Act of 1916, relative to the number of officers authorized to be stationed in Washington. Further legislation followed on May 18, 1917, which authorized the President to provide the necessary officers, line and staff, for the forces raised under this act, and removed, for the period of the emergency, the legislative restrictions as to the strength and organization of the General Staff. With legislative limitations now removed the General Staff by November 1, 1918 grew to a total of 1,222 officers.[50]

The complexity of the problems raised by the sheer magnitude of the war dictated a reorganization of the Staff in February, 1918. The Chief of Staff was to be the immediate adviser of the Secretary of War upon all matters relating to the military establishment and was charged by the Secretary of War with the planning and development of the Army program in its entirety. He was given these supervising and coordinating powers in order that the war policies of the Secretary of War might be harmoniously executed by all agencies of the military establishment. With the increased burdens placed upon the General Staff it became necessary to reorganize the Staff into the following divisions: I, Executive Division; II, War Plans Division; III, Purchase and Supply Division; IV, Storage and Traffic Division; V, Army Operations Division.[51]

---

[48] *Annual Rpt, S/W, 1916,* pp. 49-50.

[49] Memorandum, November 16, 1918. Major General James G. Harbord *Mss Collection.* Hereafter cited as *Harbord Mss.*

[50] *Ibid.* During this time the clerical force increased from 107 to 2884, exclusive of 447 enlisted men.

[51] Memorandum for the Adjutant General approved by the Secretary of War, February 7, 1918. *Wilson Mss.* File II, Box 119.

Inevitably there were criticisms of the War Department which of course reflected on the work of the General Staff. Secretary of War Baker was summoned before a Senate investigating committee on January 10, 1918, and required to answer questions from four to six hours a day for three days. Baker admitted certain delays and errors, but he stoutly maintained that the War Department had accomplished a tremendous undertaking in as efficient a manner as possible.[52] The Secretary's position was vehemently attacked by Senator Chamberlain who declared in an address before the National Security League that the military establishment of America had fallen down.

The White House quickly sprang to the defense of Baker and the War Department with the President publicly branding the Senator's statement as "an astonishing and absolutely unjustifiable distortion of the truth." Wilson continued by declaring his confidence in the War Department which "has performed a task of unparalleled magnitude and difficulty with extraordinary promptness and efficiency," and as for his Secretary of War he was regarded "as one of the ablest public officials I have ever known." [53] With this judgment of the President it is difficult to disagree, and it was the General Staff, and its support by the Secretary, that contributed so heavily to ultimate victory.

The staff concept was to gain further renown under the bright banners of the American Expeditionary Forces. The creation of a General Staff for the American Expeditionary Forces occupied the early attention of General Pershing, who believed the first requisite of victory was an organization that could give intelligent direction to effort.[54] No matter how capable our divisions, battalions, and companies, success would have been impossible without a thoroughly coordinated effort. A General Staff, under the Commander in Chief, had to be created to carry out the policy and direct the details of administration, supply, preparation, and operations of the Army as a whole.

Pershing borrowed from British and French concepts and experience in setting up his own General Staff. His staff was divided

---

[52] Ray S. Baker, *op. cit.*, Vol. VII, p. 463. See also Palmer, Newton D. Baker, *op. cit.*, Vol. II, pp. 53-61.

[53] Ray S. Baker, *op. cit.*, Vol. VII, p. 485.

[54] Report of General Pershing, November 20, 1918. *Annual Rpt, S/W, 1918*, p. 67.

into five groups, each with its own chief who was an assistant to the Chief of the General Staff:

> G.1 is in charge of organization and equipment of troops, replacements, tonnage, priority of overseas shipment, the auxiliary welfare association and cognate subjects; G.2 has censorship, enemy intelligence, gathering and disseminating information, preparation of maps, and all similar subjects; G.3 is charged with all strategic subjects and plans, movement of troops, and the supervision of combat operations; G.4 coordinates important questions of supply, construction, transport arrangements for combat, and of the operations of the service of supply, and of hospitalization and the evacuation of the sick and wounded; G.5 supervises the various schools and has general direction and coordination of education and training.[55]

Without an efficient General Staff for the A.E.F. it is difficult to imagine the successful triumphs in the battle of logistics which ultimately witnessed 2,086,000 American troops in France. American manpower was decisive, but the proper utilization of that manpower depended, in the last analysis, upon the General Staff both in Washington and at Pershing's headquarters.

Allied Sideshows Create New Problems

One of the severest strains put upon Allied unity and American participation in the war came with the collapse of Russia. The withdrawal of Russia from the war and the seizure of power by the Bolshevik regime raised not only diplomatic but also military problems which the Allies insisted demanded intervention in Russia.

Two arguments for intervention cited by the Allies again and again were related to the prosecution of the war. First, with Russia out of the war, Germany would be able to mass her forces in the West for a knockout blow; and secondly, she would, in consequence, reap a rich harvest of munitions and foodstuffs from Russia, thus largely mitigating the effects of the Allied blockade.

It was the opinion of the Allies in late November, 1917 that the Russian collapse was so complete that she should be left out of any further consideration as even a passive agent working for the Allies.[56] From that premise it was easy to draw the conclusion

---

[55] *Ibid.*, p. 68.
[56] Bliss to Baker, December 18, 1917. *Robert Lansing Mss.* Hereafter cited as *Lansing Mss.* For a full description of the whole question of intervention see Eugene H. Bacon: *Russian-American Relations, 1917-1921*, (Georgetown University, Doctoral Mss., 1951).

that the Allies should do something about the loss of military pressure on Germany from the East. Secretary of State Robert Lansing was of that opinion, as is indicated in his *Diary* entry for December 31, 1917. He felt that the Russian collapse would mean an increase in the German armies in the West and the Austrians in Italy. He gloomily noted that the prospects for the new year were indeed dark.[57]

General Bliss was inclined to believe that the pressure for intervention came largely from military and psychological reasons. He wrote Baker that at two meetings of the Supreme War Council he found conviction that the situation was desperate and "the feeling here has become somewhat panicky." Bliss suggested the possibility of German consolidation in Russia which would enable her to smash the Western Front before American strength could reach France. "All of these things are a matter of anxious thought here, resulting in a feeling of almost desperation which the Government in Washington must keep in mind as the probable explanation for such propositions as the recent one of Japanese intervention in Siberia."[58] Bliss was less tolerant of Allied fears when Joint Note No. 20 came up for discussion in the Supreme War Council on April 9, 1918. He refused to sign the Note which advocated immediate Allied intervention in Siberia as the only course that would insure any serious military resistance to Germany from that direction.[59]

But support for the Allied view came from Pershing on June 7 in a cable to the War Department in which he expressed the fear that Germany might recruit manpower from Russia. "With Russia once in the conflict on the side of Germany," Pershing cabled, "the manpower of the Central Powers would become relatively inexhaustible. I would earnestly recommend that this side of the question be considered without delay."[60] Such cables must have had a depressing effect on Lansing for even without Russian manpower the Germans outnumbered the Allies, by half a million or more.[61] Perhaps the same view was held in the British War Office

---

[57] Lansing *Diary*, December 31, 1917. *Lansing Mss.*
[58] Bliss to Baker, February 25, 1918. Tasker H. Bliss *Mss Collection*. Hereafter cited as *Bliss Mss.*
[59] Bliss report, February 6, 1920. *Foreign Relations, Lansing Papers*, Vol. II, p. 272.
[60] Palmer, *Newton D. Baker, op. cit.*, Vol. II, pp. 315-316.
[61] Lansing to Edward N. Smith, June 14, 1918. *Lansing Mss*, Vol. 36.

for it cabled Washington shrilly that "unless Allied intervention is undertaken in Siberia forthwith we have no chance of being ultimately victorious, and shall incur serious risk of defeat in the meantime." [62] The French added pressure by a message from Foch to Wilson saying that the Germans were diverting divisions from Russia and that this seemed to be a decisive military argument in favor of an intervention by the Allies, since those divisions were destined for the Western Front.[63]

The psychological effect of intervention was emphasized in a British cable to Colonel House saying that one of the chief advantages "we might expect from intervention would be the very depressing effect which the recreation of an Eastern Front would have on the Central Powers, particularly Austria." [64] This theme was repeated to House by Marcel Delaney, the new French Ambassador to Japan enroute to his post. Delaney carried a personal message from Clemenceau to Wilson, to the effect that the French Prime Minister "considers intervention imperative not only because he believes it will stimulate the morale of the French people more than anything else, and that they need stimulating in this hour of trial." [65]

These were the principal arguments used by the Allies to secure American agreement and participation in intervention. What effect did they have? The constant clamor for intervention kept the Administration constantly on the defense, and as Wilson was to find out later in Paris it is very difficult to always reply with an abrupt negative. Secondly, the Allied drive was carried on so skilfully and persistently that even before the White House fully realized it, intervention seemed to be an accepted fact and the only question was what character it should assume.[66]

Americans were largely unimpressed with the alleged military advantages of intervention. The prospect of unrestricted Japanese intervention, which might enlarge the Japanese sphere of influence in that area, prompted House to inform Wilson that not only would it be a political mistake to send Japanese troops into Siberia

[62] Balfour to Reading, June 20, 1918. Edward M. *House Mss Collection, Yale University Library*. Hereafter cited as *House Mss.*
[63] Ray S. Baker, *op. cit.*, Vol. VIII, p. 235.
[64] Wiseman to House, May 1, 1918. *House Mss.*
[65] Seymour, *op. cit.*, Vol. III, p. 407.
[66] Lansing Notes, October 3, 1921. *Foreign Relations, Lansing Papers,* Vol. II, p. 394.

but "there is no military advantage that I can think of that would offset the harm." [67] General March, equally opposed, influenced Secretary Baker to reach the same decision. [68]

Lansing noted in his *Diary* that there were two chief considerations in the question of Japanese intervention. The first was the moral effect it would have upon the Russian people and the second was the military aspect. He felt that it would be unwise and inexpedient to support the request for Japanese intervention. The most likely result would be to unite the factions in Russia against this country and thereby deliver Russia into the hands of Germany. In addition, there was no great compensating military advantage to be expected. In Lansing's opinion the United States should await further developments. [69]

Six days later Lansing had changed his opinion somewhat in the light of reports received of the activities of German war prisoners in Siberia who threatened to take control. He wrote the President that he did not see how Japan could be expected to refrain from taking military measures and the question now presented was whether Japan alone or the Powers arrayed against Germany acting jointly should constitute the expeditionary force. [70] On March 20, 1918 the Chief Executive informed Lansing that he was not prepared to change the policy adopted, which was against military intervention. "This I think," Lansing later wrote, "was due to the opposition of his military advisers who throughout were hostile to intervention." [71]

Wilson repeated his opposition to military action in Russia at a Cabinet meeting on March 29. Secretaries Lane and Burleson thought that we should go in with the Japanese but the Secretary of State disagreed. Wilson again failed to see any military advantage. [72] General March in a letter to Bliss further amplified the President's views. He wrote that the attitude of Wilson was one of holding to the principle of preservation of Russian territorial integrity and political independence. "Intervention via Vladi-

---

[67] Seymour, *op. cit.*, Vol. III, p. 391.
[68] Peyton C. March, *The Nation at War* (Garden City, New York), Doubleday Doran & Co., 1932, p. 115.
[69] Lansing *Diary*, March 18, 1918. *Lansing Mss.*
[70] Lansing to Wilson, March 24, 1918. *Foreign Relations, Lansing Papers,* Vol. II, pp. 357-358.
[71] Lansing Notes, October 3, 1921. *Ibid.*, p. 394.
[72] Daniels *Diary*, March 29, 1918. Josephus *Daniels Mss. Collection*. Hereafter cited as *Daniels Mss.*

vostok," wrote March, "is deemed impractical because of the vast distance involved, the size of the force necessary to be effective, and financing such an expedition would mean a burden which the United States at this time ought not to assume." Both March and the President were afraid of the reaction of the Russian people to a really effective expedition.

Lansing had much of the same opinion as to the impracticability of intervention. He felt, during the early part of June, that it was a waste of time to discuss it until we could get shipping for an Allied force. He also pointed out that intervention would mean a weakening of the Western Front. The Secretary of State believed that we should wait until we had a preponderance of manpower in France before determining our policy. This *Diary* Memorandum of Lansing's was predicated on the premise that it would be a serious mistake for Japan to go in alone, and he felt that such action should not be permitted if it could be prevented.[73]

Admiral William S. Benson, Chief of Naval Operations, made American military opinion on the question of intervention unanimous in his Memorandum of June 22:

> The conclusion of the whole matter after all seems to be that this war must be won by the successful operations on the Western front by the Allied armies and to undertake any operations that would interfere with this effort would seem to be ill-advised. In order to be successful the general and well recognized principle of concentration of effort should be strictly adhered to.[74]

General March again emphatically espoused the same view to the President two days later. The war was to be won or lost on the Western Front and substantial diversions of troops would be a serious mistake. March later asserted that "President Wilson agreed in toto with this presentation of the matter." [75]

Despite advice of America's military leaders, the United States, bowing to Allied pressure, did consent on July 17, 1918 to the sending of an Allied Force to Siberia. The American contingent under the command of General William S. Graves numbered 9,000 while the Japanese force reached a total of 72,000.[76] The chief result of the expedition was to increase Japanese-American friction

---

[73] Lansing *Diary*, June 12, 1918. *Lansing Mss.*
[74] Benson Memorandum, June 22, 1918. *Daniels Mss.*
[75] March, *op. cit.*, pp. 116-117, 120.
[76] Bacon, *op. cit.*, Chapter V.

and to save the Maritime Provinces for the Soviet Union. It may also have contributed to a stubborn conviction on the part of Soviet leaders that the United States is aggressively hostile to their regime. At any rate they have employed the example of American "invasions" of Russia for propagandistic effect on their own people.

An examination of American motives at this point is not out of place. Wilson was certainly suspicious of Japanese motives and he may have felt that intervention was inevitable, and that more restraint upon Japan could be exercised by participating in the expedition. But that is not the whole story of America's decision to intervene. The continuous pressure of the Allies undoubtedly played a large part. Newton D. Baker on two occasions gave as the compelling reason for Wilson's consent his desire to cooperate with the Allies. Later in an interview with Ray S. Baker he asserted that "troops were sent largely in the hope of restraining Japanese ambitions." Breckinridge Long also spoke of the tremendous pressure of the Allies and Wilson's desire to reconcile the position of America with that of the Allies.

Not only did we consent to intervention in Siberia, but America also sent an expeditionary force to Northern Russia, again upon the urgings of the Supreme War Council. Much the same reasons were advanced as for the Siberian intervention, with the Allies calling for the dispatch of two American battalions.[77] These sideshows contributed little or nothing to the winning of the war, but they did illustrate that American military minds had a better grasp of reality than did their Allied counterparts and also that the Allies and America had different diplomatic objectives. Bliss in a letter to March gave some interesting sidelights from his observations:

> I think that with the British and French, more particularly the latter, the idea of pushing the movement from Murmansk and Archangel grows out of their belief that nothing of material value will result from the movement in Siberia from Vladivostok. In regard to the situation in Siberia we are quite in the dark. As I have said before, if our Allies have any axes to grind in Russia, let them go and do it. I think that the war has got to be ended on the Western Front and I fully agree with you and Pershing that every effort of ours should be concentrated

---

[77] *Cf.* Bacon, *op. cit.,* Chapter VII and Leonid I. Strakhovsky, *The Origins of American Intervention in North Russia,* (Princeton U. Press, 1937).

here. I think that it is easy to see what is at the bottom of the minds of our allies in all of these distant expeditions. They are haunted by a fear that *something* may happen that will bring the war to an end before the allies will be in a position to impose what terms they please on Germany and undo all that the latter has done during the war in various parts of the world.[78]

The American Eagle Spreads His Wings

The first important expenditures for Army aviation were allotted in 1898 when the War Department authorized the appropriation of $50,000 for experiments in aerodynamics to be conducted by Professor Samuel P. Langley under the supervision of the Signal Corps. Langley's attempts to build a flying machine ended in failure in 1903, and in the following year further appropriations were suspended.[79] Though the efforts of the Army were unsuccessful, two pioneers, Orville and Wilbur Wright, made the first airplane flight in December of 1903 and ushered in the air age.

On August 1, 1907, an Aeronautical Division was established in the office of the Chief Signal Officer to assume responsibility for all matters pertaining to military ballooning, air machines, and all similar subjects. The following year, on February 10, the Signal Corps contracted with the Wright brothers for the construction of the Army's initial airplane.[80] On September 3, 1908 the test flight of this machine was conducted by Orville Wright at Fort Myer, Virginia. The first Army passenger carrier in the "Wright Flyer" was Lieutenant Frank P. Lahm, during these trial flights on September 9, 1908. A few days later, Lieutenant Thomas E. Selfridge was killed and Orville Wright injured during further test flights and, therefore, final Army acceptance was postponed until August 2, 1909, by which time improvements had been made and successful flights accomplished.[81]

Further progress in the development of airpower was slow until World War I accelerated the expansion and increased the potency of the United States air arm. Early in 1917 the air program called for 1,850 aviators and 300 balloonists, 16 airplane squadrons, 16 balloons, and 9 aviation schools, at an estimated cost of $54,250,-

[78] Bliss to March, September 3, 1918. *Bliss Mss.*
[79] Chandler and Lahm, *op. cit.*, pp. 93-98.
[80] *The Official Guide to the Army Air Forces,* (New York: Simon & Schuster, 1944), pp. 341-342. Hereafter cited as *Official AAF Guide.*
[81] Chandler and Lahm, *op. cit.*, pp. 152-160.

000.[82] With the declaration of war in April, greater interest and confidence by Congress in airpower was manifested by the passage of legislation and appropriations to enable rapid expansion.[83] On July 24, 1917 Congress appropriated $640,000,000 for air power, and the Aviation Section of the Signal Corps was authorized to expand to 9,989 officers and 87,083 enlisted men.[84]

The American entry of airpower in Europe was marked by the assignment, on June 30, 1917 of Lieutenant Colonel William Mitchell to the American Expeditionary Forces as aviation officer. In 1918 the embryonic United States Air Service, after a baptism of fire, evolved into a potent weapon. On February 18, 1918 the 103rd Pursuit Squadron, A.E.F. composed of members of the LaFayette Escadrille, began operations at the front under the tactical control of the French. The first operations across the enemy's lines were made in mid-March by the 94th Squadron of the First Pursuit Group.[85]

During mid-September one of the largest air armadas of the war was massed to participate in the St. Mihiel drive. A total of 1,481 planes were engaged in the air battle and the air arm of the A.E.F. flew 3,593 hours in artillery direction, observation, bombing, ground strafing, and air combat.

American pilots shot down in the course of the war 755 officially confirmed enemy aircraft and 71 balloons. Our losses were 357 planes and 43 balloons. The Air Service participated in 215 bombing missions, dropped over 255,000 pounds of explosives, flew 35,000 hours over the enemy's lines, and took nearly 18,000 photographs. The 35 balloon companies in France, with 466 officers and 6,365 men, made 1,642 ascensions with 3,111 hours in the air.[86]

Naval aviation also played an important part in the successful prosecution of the war. The chief task of the Navy's air arm was patrolling the long coast lines, watching for submarines, and furnishing aerial escort for the convoy of troops, supply, and merchant ships to and from European ports. Before the war ended the Navy's aviation personnel reached a total of 40,000 equipped with

[82] *Official AAF Guide*, p. 343.
[83] Upon the declaration of war the United States had 55 obsolete airplanes and a total personnel of 1,200. Ayres, *op. cit.*, pp. 99-100.
[84] *Official AAF Guide*, pp. 343-344.
[85] *Official AAF Guide*, p. 344.
[86] *Ibid.*, pp. 344-345.

1,170 flying boats, 695 seaplanes, 262 land planes, 10 free balloons, and 15 dirigibles. The performance of the flying sailors so impressed the Secretary of the Navy that he predicted in his last *Annual Report:* "Naval aviation will, in the not distant future, possess an importance second only to that of ships." [87]

"We Are Ready Now, Sir"

The first flotilla of American destroyers reached the British Isles on May 4, 1917 to be greeted by an English ship flying the international signal, "Welcome to the American colors." These first American vessels were to be under the command of the British Vice Admiral Sir Lewis Bayly whose first question was, "When will you be ready to go to sea?" "We are ready now, sir," was the reply of the American commander. Thus translated into action was "that splendid cooperation between the British and American navies which has hardly a parallel in naval history." [88]

Even before America's entrance into the war close contact had been established with the British Admirality,[89] and Admiral William S. Sims had been chosen to head the American naval mission to London. This liaison was quickly supplemented by full collaboration and cooperation once America declared war.[90] Coordination of naval effort was deemed essential to victory because of the havoc wrought by the German U-boats.

The first two cablegrams from Sims on April 14, emphasized the seriousness of the situation. He reported that the amount of British, Allied, and neutral shipping sunk in February was 536,000 tons, in March 571,000 tons, and in the first ten days of April 205,000. American naval help was badly needed.[91] Ten days later, he again cabled the Navy Department that the situation was critical and recommended that all available destroyers be sent the earliest possible date.[92] To Ambassador Page the submarine threat was the most serious situation that had confronted the Allies since

---

[87] Josephus Daniels, *The Wilson Era: Years of War and After,* 1917-1923, (University of North Carolina Press, 1946), pp. 121-123.
[88] Daniels, *op. cit.,* pp. 73-74, 69.
[89] *Ibid.,* p. 65.
[90] A conference of American, British, and French Admirals was held at Hampton Roads only three days after the American declaration of war. Ray S. Baker, *op. cit.,* Vol. VII, p. 11.
[91] Sims to Secretary of the Navy, April 14, 1917. *Foreign Relations, 1917, Supplement 2,* Vol. I, pp. 23-25.
[92] Ray S. Baker, *op. cit.,* Vol. VII, p. 34. See also *Foreign Relations, 1917, Supplement 2,* Vol. I, pp. 46-47.

battle of the Marne.[93] On the same day, June 20, 1917 Sims sent an urgent cable for "the immediate dispatch to this area of all possible destroyers and anti-submarine craft of any description, if the submarine issue is to be effectively met." [94] Sims was a great believer in the maxim of concentration of forces, so he utilized the Ambassador to back up his pleas. Page was a man who was easily worried and he was not a difficult convert. "Sims sends me . . . the most alarming reports of the submarine situation which are confirmed by the Admirality here. He says that the war will be won or lost in the submarine zone within a few months. Time is the essence of the problem and anti-submarine craft which cannot be assembled in the submarine zone almost immediately may come too late." [95]

Replacement of lost tonnage and protection of shipping was one of the greatest problems confronting America. It would be no use to levy great armies if there were no shipping to transport them, and, what was more important, to supply the wants of the civil populations and the armies of the Allies.[96] America made a heroic effort and did provide the necessary tonnage.[97] but the problem of the U-boat had to be conquered by the Navy.

Thus the American Navy faced a two-fold task in the war, to protect American and Allied shipping and to provide safe transportation for the millions of troops to be sent overseas. The first squadron of American naval vessels was reinforced by others until by July the total number of American destroyers in British waters was thirty-four. At the end of the war we had seventy-nine destroyers in Europe.[98] These destroyers and other American contributions were to be a potent factor in ending the menace of the German submarine.

---

[93] Page to Secretary of State, June 20, 1917. *Ibid.,* pp. 106-107.

[94] Ray S. Baker, *op. cit.,* Vol. VII, pp. 121-122.

[95] Page to Secretary of State, June 27, 1917. *Foreign Relations, 1917, Supplement 2,* Vol. I, pp. 111-112.

[96] Medill McCormick to House. Seymour, *op. cit.,* Vol. III, p. 189.

[97] The magnitude of the building program is illustrated by the fact that, in 1917 the United States had 61 shipyards equipped with 142 ways for steel vessels and 73 for wooden ships. By 1919, there were 341 yards with 1284 ways for steel ships and 816 for wooden boats. On July 4, 1918, 95 ships were launched to celebrate Independence Day. Louis M. Hacker and Helene S. Zahler, *The United States in the 20th Century,* (New York: Appleton-Century-Crofts, 1952), p. 203.

[98] Alden and Westcott, *op. cit.,* p. 345.

Largely due to American insistence, the British instituted the convoy system in May, 1917.[99] Over British technical objections, the American Navy laid down a mine barrage closing the North Sea from Scotland to Norway. Few U-boats were able to penetrate this wall of about 70,000 mines, fifteen to thirty-five miles wide.[100] Ever increasing countermeasures all but paralyzed the submarine. The U-boat was detected and located by the hydrophone. It was assailed by depth charges, 300 lb. bombs dropped by destroyers and motor-chasers to explode far beneath the surface; it was spotted and attacked by aircraft; it was stalked and torpedoed by Allied submarines.[101]

The Navy, which armed, manned, and convoyed the troop transports, assured the safe arrival of the American Expeditionary Forces in France. No American troop transport was lost on its voyage to France. The Navy could well be proud of its role in providing safety for the troops and immense tons of supplies that arrived on the Western Front.[102]

Not only did the Navy assure the safety of "the bridge to France," but some of the brightest chapters in the proud record of the Marine Corps were written in the bloody battles of Chateau Thierry, Belleau Wood, St. Mihiel, and elsewhere. The fighting at Belleau Wood, which saved Paris, saw the heaviest American casualty rate, with the Marines suffering fifty-two percent of their total engaged. Thirty thousand Marines saw overseas service and Pershing fittingly praised their "brilliant exploits in battle." [103]

The Nation was proud of the military exploits of its armed forces. However, we had had time to raise and prepare our fighting forces. Would we again dismantle our military machine in the fond hope that this was the war to end all wars or would we keep our powder dry until the promised millenium of peace was a reality?

---

[99] The convoy system was strongly advocated by Sims (*Ibid.*, p. 346), and according to Daniels early in the war the President said to him: "Daniels, why don't the British convoy their merchant ships and thus protect them from submarines?" Ray S. Baker, *op. cit.*, Vol. VII, p. 44.

[100] Alden and Westcott, *op. cit.*, pp. 355-357.

[101] Morison and Commager, *op. cit.*, Vol. II, p. 480. The view that submarines were probably the most effective weapon was supported by Admiral Sims as quoted in Alden and Westcott, *op. cit.*, p. 354.

[102] Ayres, *op. cit.*, pp. 47-48.

[103] Daniels, *op. cit.*, pp. 150-152. These casualties were even higher than at Iwo Jima which were a little under 39%.

Only the temper of the nation, the leadership of the Chief Executive, and the actions of Congress could determine the answer. The guns were stilled, the military men departed, and once again America was faced with an evaluation of its military policy.

CHAPTER 17

America Seeks Security
Through Disarmament

Rapid Demobilization—The War Department Plans for
its Postwar Role—The Dubious Security of Diplomatic
Agreements—The Air Force: Controversy and Progress
—Public Opinion, Politics, and Veterans

Rapid Demobilization

THE STILLING of the guns on the Western Front was the immediate signal for America to scrap the war machine and restore its parts to the peaceful order in which they had been found. Some of the processes of demobilization had begun even before the signing of the armistice. In late October the Ordnance Department had created an organization for the scrapping of war industries, and on November 1 the War Department had stopped sending combat troops to France.[1] The plan for the demobilization of the Army of the United States had as its general object the transfer of all men, prior to their discharge, to the demobilization camp in or nearest the State of their residence.[2] There was also presented to the War Department the choice of discharging the Army by industrial classes or by military units. The latter course was adopted. One of the most important considerations compelling unit demobilization was the fact that industrial demobilization could at best only be put partially into operation since it could not be used for the troops overseas, where the military situation would not permit the return of men to this country according to occupation.[3]

Returning the American forces to their civilian occupations was accomplished in a remarkably short period of time. On May 25, 1919 General Peyton C. March, the Chief of Staff, was able

---

[1] Benedict Crowell and Robert F. Wilson: *How America Went to War-Demobilization* (Yale University Press, 1921), p, 3.
[2] On August 7, 1918, the three components of the Army, the National Army, Regular Army, and National Guard were designated under the title of Army of the United States. *Annual Report, S/W, 1919*, pp. 13, 56.
[3] *Annual Report, S/W, 1920*, p. 153.

to announce that all American soldiers in France, with the exception of the Regular Army Divisions, would be homeward bound by June 12. On the first anniversary of the signing of the armistice, 3,236,266 troops had been demobilized.[4] The entire process of discharging enlisted personnel was practically completed by April 1, 1920.[5]

Several factors may be ascribed to this rapid dissolution of American armed forces. Logically, now that its military mission had been accomplished, there was no further need for such a large Army and Navy. The nature of the Army, which in its great bulk was drawn from civilian life, must also be kept in mind. Four million American homes demanded their men at once and all other considerations were minor to both the people and the Government.[6] Congress, reflecting the will of the people, put pressure on the War Department to increase the flow of returning soldiers.

The War Department Plans for its Postwar Role

Not all of the attention of the War Department was devoted to demobilizing the Army, for it was realized that this process meant the practical annihilation of all organized forces in the United States. Once again the War Department and the country was faced with the problem of formulating a military policy. America had the benefit of the lessons of the war, but would the nation take advantage of the experience gained through so much expenditure of treasure and blood?

As a stopgap measure, the War Department requested permission from Congress to reopen enlistments in the Regular Army as authorized by the National Defense Act of 1916. Authority was granted by Congress, and volunteers were allowed to choose between one or three year enlistment periods. This, of course, was only temporary relief; the larger question of military policy remained untouched. In January, 1919 the first major legislative proposal was presented by the War Department to Congress for an establishment of an Army of 500,000 men which envisaged a system of universal military training.[7] Another purpose of the bill

---

[4] *Annual Report, S/W, 1919,* p. 17.
[5] *Annual Report, S/W, 1920,* p. 27.
[6] Crowell and Wilson, *op. cit.,* p. 5.
[7] *Annual Report, S/W, 1919,* pp. 58, 64. Under this authorization, tne Army from March 1, 1919, to November 1, 1919, recruited 73,563 for one year service and 63,497 for three years.

was to reorganize the War Department by strengthening the General Staff in its control of the entire military establishment. The arguments for the bill were strongly set forth in the Secretary's *Annual Report* for 1919, but the proposed legislation received little support.[8]

It is interesting to note that one provision of the bill called for the elimination of the Regular Army Reserve.[9] General March cited as the reason for this decision "the distinct disadvantage in the effort to get men to serve in the Regular Army. They will not go in for seven years service, three years in the Regular Army and four years in the reserve."[10] Past experience gave ample precedents as to the truth of the General March's statement, but it did seem shortsighted on the part of the War Department to scrap the reserve concept simply because the old system had been unsatisfactory. It would have been wiser, instead, to have devised a system whereby this important source of military strength could have been an efficient arm of our military establishment.

The *Army and Navy Journal* feared that the War Department's bold proposal would raise the traditional specter of a standing army which might menace American liberties. "The only relief," the editorial lamented, "that both the army and navy can have . . . lies in the hope that our experience in the World War may have educated the American people in military matters to a greater degree than ever before and a reaction to this will be felt in Congress." Unless this happened there was little prospect that there would be any marked improvement in our military policy.[11]

The War Department's attitude toward the National Guard which "has for the most part disappeared and . . . it would be some time before it can be effectively reconstituted," also aroused opposition.[12] The Guard, however, had strong support in Congress,

---

[8] The strength of the Army laid down in this bill would provide a minimum force for one field army of five corps, skeletonized to about 50% of its strength, March, *op. cit.*, p. 336.

[9] *National Defense Hearings Historical Documents Relating to Reorganization Plans of the War Department and to the Present National Defense Act,* (1927), (Washington, G.P.O., 1927), Vol. I, p. 242. Hereafter cited as *National Defense Hearings.*

[10] *National Defense Hearings*, Vol. I, p. 290.

[11] A member of the House Military Affairs Committee told General March that "I do not believe the people of this country will stand for the sized Army which you provide for in this bill in time of peace." *Ibid.*, Vol. I, p. 303.

[12] The National Guard Association convention of 1919 adopted resolutions opposing passage of the bill and addressed letters to the Adjutant General of every State urging that pressure be brought to bear upon Congress. New York *Times*, August 8, 1919.

as testimony in the hearings indicated. With full confidence in the ability of the National Guard to fulfill the needs of the nation in any emergency, its supporters shied away from any plan which might increase the influence of the Regular Army.[13]

This shyness was reflected in the attitude of Congress toward universal military training. The section of the bill dealing with this proposal was quickly scuttled.[14] Even Pershing's strong plea, which laid stress not only upon the military advantages, but also the physical and educational aspects, was rebuffed with the comment: "We are in danger of having many beautiful schemes thrust upon us which, if adopted, would make the Army a college rather than a fighting unit." [15]

Public sentiment was said to be unalterably opposed to a large standing army,[16] and the voice of the people began to be heard in the halls of Congress. The National Grange, representing nearly a million farmers, at its annual convention in 1919 very clearly expressed its opposition to militarism, universal military servce, and a large standing army. The Grange deplored "any effort to develop in America a caste of authority which has its sole excuse in a shoulder strap, and any tendency in thought which would substitute armed force for moral ideals." The convention expressed its faith in the traditional ideal of a citizen army springing from the soil in a moment of danger. This army would be untrained but it would be equipped with Justice and Americanism which presumably was all that any army needed, at least any American army. "We favor the preparedness of right, rather than the preparedness of might." [17]

The National Defense Act of June 4, 1920 emerged from the debate over the military policy of the United States in the form of a series of amendments to the National Defense Act of 1916, but the amendments were so comprehensive that an almost entirely new act was thus written. Specifically it provided that the Army of the United States would consist of the Regular Army, the National Guard while in the service of the United States, and the organized

[13] National Defense Hearings, Vol. I, pp. 276-277.
[14] March, op. cit., pp. 337-340.
[15] National Defense Hearings, Vol. I, p. 386.
[16] Review of Reviews, December, 1919, p. 631.
[17] T. C. Atkeson to Julius Kahn, Chairman of the House Military Affairs Committee, and all members of the Committee, January 20, 1919. F. L. Greene (Rep. from Vermont) Mss Collection.

Reserves, including the Officers' Reserve Corps and the Enlisted Reserve Corps. The old division of the country into territorial or geographical departments was abandoned, and a tactical organization was created for the first time. America was divided into nine corps areas serving three tactical armies with their headquarters at Governors Island, New York; the Presidio, San Francisco; and Fort McPherson, Georgia. Each corps area was to contain one Regular Army division, two National Guard, and three Organized Reserve divisions.[18] Thus constituted the Regular Army was fixed at 280,000 enlisted men, including the Philippine Scouts, and 17,700 Officers.

Among the new agencies created by the law was a War Council, consisting of the Secretary and Assistant Secretary of War, the General of the Army (Pershing), and the Chief of Staff. It was the duty of this Council to meet from time to time to consider policies and procedures regarding the multitude of War Department functions. The Finance Department was another new branch, charged with the disbursement of all of the funds of the War Department. In the Medical Department, a new branch appeared known as the Medical Administrative Corps; and members of the Army Nurse Corps were given relative military rank. The Chemical Warfare Service was created, its personnel fixed, and its duties defined. Similarly the Air Service was established, but no definition of its mission was attempted.

Provisions were made for the training of reserve officers of which the most important was that providing for the establishment of Reserve Officers Training Corps programs in colleges and high schools. These were to contain units of the several arms, corps, and services in such numbers and strength as the President might direct. But no units could be established until a Regular officer had been assigned and until the school had established a two-year course of military training as prescribed by the Secretary of War. The Citizens Military Training Camp was initiated to qualify personnel as commissioned or noncommissioned officers. The candidate would enter the basic course, on a volunteer basis, after

---

[18] Major General William G. Haan, Chief of the War Plans Division, described this plan in September, 1920 as constituting a balanced peacetime force. Frederic L. Paxson: *Postwar Years*, (University of California Press, 1948), p. 142.

which, if qualified, he could attend, in successive years, the advanced courses.

Few changes were made in the provisions of former laws relating to the National Guard. The chief change was the decision to reshape the Militia Bureau in the War Department and put the National Guard in greater control of its own affairs. The Guard was still under State control in peacetime, and it was further recognized as being still part of the militia:

> The militia of the United States shall consist of all able-bodied citizens of the United States and all other able-bodied males who have or who shall have declared their intention of becoming citizens of the United States, who shall be more than eighteen years of age and, except as hereafter provided, not more than forty-five years of age, and said militia shall be divided into three classes, the National Guard, the Naval Militia, and the Unorganized Militia.

The President was authorized to use the National Guard but this could be done only when Congress authorized the use of the armed land forces for any purpose requiring the use of troops in excess of those in the Regular Army.

An important section of the act was devoted to the organization of the General Staff which was to consist of the Chief of Staff, four assistants, and eighty-eight other officers not below the rank of captain. The General Staff was to prepare plans for national defense

> and the use of the military forces for that purpose, both separately and in conjunction with the naval forces, and for the mobilization of the manhood of the Nation and its material resources in an emergency, to investigate and report upon all questions affecting the efficiency of the Army of the United States, and its state of preparation for military operations; and to render professional aid and assistance to the Secretary of War and the Chief of Staff.

The Assistant Secretary of War was charged with the procurement of military supplies and with other business of the War Department pertaining thereto and the assurance of adequate provision for the mobilization of material and industrial organizations essential to war-time needs.[19]

Most of the comments on the National Defense Act agreed

---

[19] XIL *Stat*, 759-812.

with General March's estimate that it was based on the experiences of the war and was sound military policy.[20]

The feeling of the general public, however, was one of apathy and a desire to forget not only the war but military subjects as well. During the war there had been a great deal of discussion with reference to the introduction of military training as a compulsory course in the schools and with reference to building the biggest Navy in the world. But such subjects were not vitally interesting in the 1920's while America was seeking to lead the world in a crusade of moral righteousness. The energy required to keep our military establishment on a sound basis took too much time for the busy nation in the decade after the war. Nor could such proposals be favorably regarded by the new Republican regime which was dedicated to governmental economy as one of the means of combating the postwar depression.

In this atmosphere, successive legislation enacted as rigid economy measures rendered the National Defense Act ineffective. In 1921 the Regular Army was reduced to 150,000 [21] and "the morale of the commissioned personnel of the Army has practically ceased to exist." [22] In 1922, over a thousand "surplus" Regular Army officers were discharged as a part of the reduction of the Army, and thousands of others forced to accept a demotion. From 1922 through 1926, 137,000 men were provided for, and from 1927 to 1935, 118,750 were authorized.[23] It is ironic to note, as General March points out, that an army of 100,000 had been imposed upon Germany in order to render her impotent.[24] As early as 1921, Pershing was casting a very critical eye upon the low state to which the Army had fallen. "If war should come, we should be in almost as much confusion as we were when you and I started out single handed and alone to organize an army to fight the world war." [25] The Army had indeed fallen upon dark days, and when in 1924 it prepared to test its mobilization plans, the National Council for the Prevention of War protested against such

---

[20] March, *op. cit.*, p. 343.

[21] *Annual Report, S/W,* 1921, p. 24.

[22] General James G. Harbord to Pershing, March 20, 1921. *Harbord Mss.* Harbord felt that if the Republican Party did not show substantial economies it would lose the House of Representatives in the following election.

[23] Paxson, *op. cit.*, p. 341.

[24] March, *op. cit.*, p. 341.

[25] Pershing to Harbord, March 12, 1921. *Harbord Mss.*

a military demonstration. Church organizations denounced the proposed test and one of the State Governors refused to permit the National Guard of that State to participate and further rebuked the trial mobilization "at a time when all the people of the civilized nations of the world are demanding reduction of armaments." [26]

Storm signals regarding the state of the nation's defenses were sent up by the Secretaries of War and every Chief of Staff in the period between the two great wars. In July, 1925 Pershing noted that under our very eyes "there have already been serious reductions made by Congress" and that "the politician, himself oftentimes uninformed as to his country's history, frequently appeals to the ignorance and unthinking on the score of economy." [27]

A shortage of manpower was also reflected in scarcities of material and lack of sufficient training. "In many cases," General Douglas MacArthur declared in 1934, "there is but one officer on duty with an entire battalion; this lack of officers (has) brought Regular Army training in the continental United States to a virtual standstill . . . correction is mandatory." [28] Supplies and new weapon development suffered much the same fate. The Congressional attitude toward material was the thrifty view that the huge surpluses of the war should be used before new supplies were purchased. This was a commendable attitude as far as blankets and shoes are concerned, but it did not provide for the necessary technical advances in new weapons. According to General MacArthur, stocks of material were "inadequate even for limited forces . . . and, such as they are, manifestly obolescent." This meant that the Army possessed only a few tanks, of World War I vintage and thoroughly obsolete, while in Germany General Guderian was building the swift and powerful armored vehicles that were to make possible his dazzling successes of 1940. [29]

The factors which account for the Army's rapid deterioration

---

[26] Paxson, op. cit., p. 142.
[27] Watson, op. cit., p. 18.
[28] "Let me give you a specific example of these reductions upon the efficiency of the Army. During this period I commanded a post which had for its garrison a battalion of infantry, the basic fighting unit of every army. It was a battalion only in name, for it could muster barely 200 men, including cooks, clerks and kitchen police, (was) present for the little field training that could be accomplished with available funds. The normal strength of a battalion in most armies of the world varies from 800 to 1,000 men." General George C. Marshall to Rep. Ross A. Collins, June 21, 1940. Ibid., p. 25.
[29] Watson, op. cit., p. 18.

are many and complex. Understandably, there was war weariness and a burning desire on the part of the American people for a return to "normalcy." A well prepared Army was not regarded as normal for the United States, and, in addition, it would be expensive. The United States was again being penny wise and pound foolish. Governmental economy was one of the keynotes of the Harding-Coolidge administration and as usual the armed forces were an inviting target for a reduction in expenditures. This was also a period when American's attention was focused upon business and production and the Army was largely viewed as an anachronism. New delights and wonders dazzled American eyes during the golden twenties which made it extremely difficult for the public to peer into the sad state to which the Army had fallen. The great depression of 1929 accelerated the demands for curtailment of military appropriations.

The public and Congress could also say that "the war to end all wars" made an efficient Army an unnecessary luxury. Certainly the country was convinced that never again would we go to war. Thus the 1920's were well acclimated to the principle that America could gain what security was necessary not through planned defense but by disarmament.

The Dubious Security of Diplomatic Agreements

While America had repudiated the League of Nations her statesmen kept an alert finger on the pulse of the world. In the years following the war the United States assumed many obligations and responsibilities which should have prompted a corres ponding increase in our military establishment. A vigorous American policy in the Far East and ominous overtones from Europe rendered it imperative to at least keep up the authorized strength of the Act of 1920. But the nation was in no mood to remember George Washington's maxim of preparedness and preferred to rely for security upon a false and dangerous principle of disarmament. Disarmament became a strange American obsession.

The Washington Conference of 1921-1922 was not only concerned with the problem of averting a possible naval race among the United States, Great Britain, and Japan, but it was also dealt with the Far Eastern situation. One of the first results of the conference was the Four-Power Treaty wherein the United States, Britain, Japan, and France promised to respect one another's territorial possessions in the Far East and to refer future disputes to joint consultation. It also stated that if the rights of the signatories were threatened by another Power they "shall communicate with one another fully and frankly in order to arrive at an understanding as to the most efficient measures to be taken, jointly or separately, to meet the exigencies of the particular situation." While this article was vague it certainly hinted at cooperative armed effort.[30] The Nine-Power Treaty which promised to respect the sovereignty, the independence, and the territorial and administrative integrity of China and to respect the principles of the Open Door Notes, was a self denying ordinance.[31] Nevertheless, it was to be an important pivot of American Far Eastern Policy which succeeding Secretaries of State would interpret as calling for American enforcement.

The Naval Treaty of February 6, 1922 provided for equality in battleships and aircraft carriers between the United States and Great Britain, with Japan, France, and Italy accepting subordinate positions according to the following ratio: 5:5:3:1 2/3: 1 2/3.[32] No definite arrangements concerning auxiliary naval craft (such as cruisers) were made. The only important reference to auxiliary craft was contained in two articles which had the effect of providing a ceiling of 10,000 tons and eight-inch guns for cruisers. The treaty was to remain in effect until December 31, 1936, unless one of the signatories gave two years prior notice of its intention to terminate the treaty, "whereupon the Treaty shall terminate as regards all the Contracting Powers." [33]

Under this treaty, the United States destroyed nineteen prewar capital ships and thirteen under construction, many of which were almost completed. This country not only destroyed the greatest tonnage in history, but agreed at the same time to refrain from completing the most powerful fleet ever planned by any

---

[30] Bailey, op. cit., p. 695. This Four-Power Treaty was also the vehicle for the abrogation of the Anglo-Japanese Alliance.

[31] Ibid., pp. 696-697.

[32] A means for Japan to accept a lower ratio than the United States and Britain and still preserve "face" was found in the agreement of America not to further fortify her Pacific islands with the exception of Hawaii. Britain accepted a similar prohibition in regard to her Pacific possessions. Since America and Britain would lack adequate bases this would mean that Japan would be supreme in Asiatic waters. Ibid., p. 693.

[33] Foreign Relations, 1922, Vol. I, pp. 251, 265.

nation.[34] Naval experts sharply criticized the treaties as well as the agreement to leave the western Pacific unfortified. Strict observance of these treaties left the United States crippled. Failure to defend American interests coupled with the failure to attain naval parity with Great Britain[35] prompted the General Board of the Navy to adopt as a guiding principle the creation of a Navy which would be in all respects second to none.[36]

While the Washington Conference had obviated the danger of a naval race in capital ships, no such curtailment had been placed upon smaller vessels, and this set in motion a race in the construction of cruisers, submarines, and other vessels. The United States did not keep up with the other countries, and as a matter of fact even failed to build up to the capital ship strength to which she was entitled. In an effort to apply disarmament to smaller craft, President Coolidge called for another Naval Conference on February 10, 1927. This Geneva Conference was an utter failure and helped to reinforce the conviction in many American circles that the only way to bring about disarmament was to construct such a large navy that the other nations to protect their economies would be compelled to agree to limitation.[37]

The next attempt at naval disarmament was the London Naval Conference of 1930. The resulting treaty, which was signed on April 22, 1930, provided for maximums in all types of naval craft. The Japanese retained the same ratio in capital ships, but they received a 10-10-6 ratio in heavy cruisers, and a 10-10-7 ratio in light cruisers and other auxiliary craft.[38] Japan made further gains at the conference by the increased ratios given her. The 5:3 ratio between America and Japan, which in the opinion of the United States Navy gave only a fair chance of victory in the western Pacific, had been reduced to a point where operations in Oriental waters would be extremely perilous.[39]

---

[34] Davis, *op. cit.*, p. 300. The total tonnage destroyed by the Powers is as follows: United States, 842,380; Great Britain, 447,750; Japan, 354,709. *Ibid.*, p. 299.
[35] Harold and Margaret Sprout: *Toward a New Order in Sea Power*, pp. 267-268.
[36] Davis, *op. cit.*, pp. 309-310.
[37] Bailey, *op. cit.*, pp. 706-707.
[38] *Ibid.*, pp. 718-719.
[39] Davis, *op. cit.*, p. 345. The project of naval disarmament ended in utter failure with the signing of the London Treaty of March 25, 1936. It provided for some limitations, but it contained escape clauses, and it was further rendered useless by the nonadherence of Japan. Bailey, *op. cit.*, pp. 742-743.

The relative strength of the American-Japanese fleets was of importance because of the growing friction between the two nations. Since the end of the Russo-Japanese War in 1905, the relationship had become increasingly strained over such questions as immigration, Japan's twenty-one demands upon China, Shantung, and Siberia. Then in the early thirties when Japanese troops marched into Manchuria, Secretary of State Henry L. Stimson attempted unsuccessfully to vitalize the Kellogg-Briand Treaty.[40] The Manchurian crisis of 1931-1932 deeply involved America in the growing Far Eastern crisis and made a clash between Japan and America a distinct possibility.[41]

During this period of naval disarmament and growing international tension, appropriations remained at a relatively low level and the Navy remained below authorized treaty strength. The $1,019,170,000 appropriation for the fiscal year 1921 was slashed to $536,930,000 the following year, and until fiscal year 1936 it averaged around $350,000,000. The total personnel for the Navy, for the same period, hovered slightly over an average of 90,000.[42]

America had entered the postwar period with hopeful visions of a new world order in which reason, logic, and disarmament would pave the way toward world peace. But the unsettled problems and bitterness of the Versailles Peace Conference provided anything but the proper milieu for the entertainment of such thoughts. The world was in ferment, but America slept, trusting in diplomacy and disarmament to protect her from a cruel and implacable fate.

The Air Force: Controversy and Progress

The war record of the Air Service proved conclusively to people like Brigadier General William Mitchell "that the future predominance in commerce and the future economical development of a country lies in the air."[43] Thus was ushered in a period

---

[40] The Kellogg-Briand Treaty, or Pact of Paris, was signed on August 27, 1928 and bound the signatories to renounce war as an instrument of national policy. Secretary Stimson believed that the pact involved consultive obligations and that neutrality was an obsolete American concept. Charles C. Tansill: *Back Door to War*, (Chicago: Henry Regnery Co., 1952), p. 218.

[41] A Cabinet meeting of March 7, 1933, discussed "the possibility of American involvement in war in the Far East . . . ." *Ibid.*, p. 118.

[42] Davis, *op. cit.*, pp. 470, 474.

[43] William Mitchell: *Our Air Force—Keystone of Defense*, (New York, E. P. Dutton and Co., 1921), p. 4.

of controversy, sparked by Mitchell, over the role that airpower was to play in the military establishment of the United States. The controversy hinged over the creation of an independent Air Corps and the question of airpower vs. seapower. Mitchell argued that the airplane had brought with it a new doctrine of war which called for a reassessment of traditional military doctrines. "In the future," he wrote, "no nation can call itself great unless its air power is properly organized and provided for, because air power, both from a military and economic standpoint will not only dominate the land but the sea as well." Mitchell urged the creation of a Department of Aeronautics charged with the complete air defense and development of the country with its personnel entirely apart from the Army and Navy.[44] The advocates of a separate air force argued that airpower had outgrown its function as a servant of the Army and Navy, and it had proved itself effective in independent offensive and defensive operations. "The tactics and strategy demanded for its best use are so different from those of the Army or Navy that the next logical step would seem to be independence of both arms of the service."[45]

An independent Air Force would be charged with distinct functions according to its proponents. First of all, it would occupy the gap between the Army and Navy in the matter of coast defense. Secondly, it would be able to strike at enemy objectives which could not be reached by either of its sister services. Lastly, it would take advantage of opportunities opened up by the new science of aviation.[46]

Mitchell intensified the debate by asserting "The great battleship on the water is as vulnerable to air attack today as was the 'knight in armor' to the footman armed with a musket." He then compared the cost of a battleship to that of an airplane and declared that the cost of capital ships offered a very serious burden on the resources of a country.[47] The Air Service and Mitchell attempted to drive home this point in a series of tests conducted

---

[44] William Mitchell, *Winged Defense*, (New York: G. P. Putnam and Sons, 1935), pp. 1-3. He also advocated the creation of a Department of National Defense with sub-heads for the Air, Army, and Navy.
[45] *Review of Reviews*, Vol. 73, March, 1926, pp. 314-315.
[46] *Ibid*. Rear Admiral William A. Moffett, Chief of the Navy Bureau of Aeronautics, regarded the idea of a separate air force as strategically unsound and also believed that it would add to the cost of the military establishment.
[47] William Mitchell "Air Power vs. Sea Power," *Review of Reviews*, Vol. 63, March, 1921, pp. 273-277.

in 1922 when captured German naval vessels and the U.S.S. *Alabama* were sunk by air action. In the following year, two more American vessels were destroyed in American bombing tests.[48] Despite these tests, the general attitude toward airpower remained one of disinterest or disbelief.

The vigorous stand which Mitchell took against what he called the blind opposition of the regular Army and Navy bureaucracies that had arrogated to themselves the policy of standing squarely in the way of progress culminated in a court martial for utterances alleged to be detrimental to discipline. He resigned from the Army in February, 1926, declaring that the United States was unorganized for modern defense. "Despite the expenditure of nearly $500,-000,000 for aviation since the war and the loss of scores of our airmen," he said, "We have no real military air force for the protection of our great country." [49] This controversial pioneer had indeed charted a course which was to be largely vindicated over the course of years.

The period following the war was one of limited appropriations and of a small number of personnel for the Army's air arm. For the first six years of peace the average annual appropriation was slightly over $16,000,000 while the total number of personnel numbered about 10,000. Even with these limited funds, new techniques, tactics, and equipment were tested at such places as Wright Field, Dayton, Ohio, Langley Field, Virginia, and San Antonio, Texas. Transcontinental flights were made, research in the use of radio, night photography, and instrument flying were all some of the accomplishments of the twenties and early thirties.[50]

Certain organizational changes were also made in the Air Service. During the latter months of the war, the Air Service was set up as a separate branch of the Army, distinct from the Signal Corps, and on July 2, 1926 the Air Corps Act became law. The Air Service was redesignated as the Air Corps and a five-year expansion program was initiated which called for 1,514 officers, 16,000 enlisted men, and 1,800 serviceable planes. While funds were often lacking, the Air Corps did make notable strides and

---

[48] *Official AAF Guide*, pp. 348-350.
[49] According to the figures of the *Official AAF Guide*, the figure was closer to $100,000,000. Pp. 346-351.
[50] *Official AAF Guide*, pp. 346-353. The number of craft was reported in 1922 as being 1681 serviceable airplanes, 55 free balloons, 448 observation balloons, and 13 non-rigid airships.

perhaps one of its outstanding achievements was the formation of a small body of devoted and skilled men who were to later organize the program for training thousands for air duty when war came.

Public Opinion, Politics, and Veterans

The legislation placed upon the statute books since the close of the World War gave no assurance that America would be prepared unless sufficient appropriations and volunteers were forthcoming to recruit the Regular Army, the National Guard, and the Reserves to the strength provided for by the National Defense Act of 1920. This in turn would depend largely upon public opinion and the action taken in response by Congress. Propaganda was coming into full age, and upon no other subject was it so fully exploited as upon national armaments.[51]

The *Nation* attacked the National Defense Act for authorizing too many officers, "enough for a two million man army," and for trying to convert the country to militarism by implanting the Reserve Officers' Training Corps in our schools. The General Staff also came under fire as a body of militarists who probably controlled Presidents and "certainly Secretaries of War and Congress."[52]

Taking the *Nation* as typical of those public information organs who clamored against an adequate military establishment, an analysis of editorials between 1921-1931 indicated that they advocated the reduction of the Armed Forces and urged world disarmament. They indicated also that, although the public objected to increased military budgets, Congress continued to pass high appropriations. The *Nation,* citing specific instances, endeavored to show how some of the naval bases were being maintained solely because of political influence and the greedy desire of "patriotic" groups to maintain local prosperity. Similar pork barrel allegations were made regarding ship contracts. The magazine cited examples of naval complicity in this political log rolling and condemned the Navy's efforts to pad the payroll and increase its strength in men and ships. Although most of the editorials were extremely critical of the Navy, they inferred that the Army and Air Corps were no

[51] William R. Green, "Alarmists and Pacifists," *Saturday Evening Post,* Vol. 197, June 6, 1925, p. 33.
[52] *The Nation,* Vol. 120, February 18, 1925, pp. 183-184.

better. Severe and often extremely bitter criticisms were levelled at prominent individuals who supported the thesis of increased military expenditures.

In support of these allegations, the *Nation* utilized misleading and vague figures and selected a few insignificant foreign criticisms in support. With these arguments it proceeded to indicate great public disapproval of the military budgets and the world armament race. It urged that America lead in disarmament by stripping itself of its defenses in the hope that the world would follow suit. Russia, Japan, Italy, and Britain were presented as being no menace to the United States. The magazine's attitude toward the Armed Forces and increased military expenditures might be summed up by quoting an excerpt from a speech given by the Undersecretary of State, Mr. William Castle, who said: "Every nation needs an army for internal police purposes but beyond this every soldier is a potential offensive force." According to the *Nation,* this was true statesmanship.[53]

In sharp contrast to this point of view was the *Outlook* which noted that American was going through a period of revulsion against war while "pacifism has been revived and in some quarters is almost in fashion." Nevertheless, it was pointed out that one of the lessons we should have learned in the World War was "when war comes the Nation ought to have under its control all its resources—not only its manpower for the battlefield, but also its industrial power." [54]

Such sound advice, however, was ignored. Rigid economy slashed at the very sinews of the National Defense Act and rendered it impotent. Military writers hammered away at this point but they were voices crying in the wilderness of public apathy. Brigadier General Henry J. Reilly, publisher of the *Army and Navy Journal,* very clearly demonstrated the effects of economy on the size, morale, and training of our Army. Writing in January, 1927, he pointed out that only the Organized Officers Reserve had reached its full strength while the other components were greatly undermanned. Living conditions for both officers and men were

---

[53] *The Nation,* Vol. 112, June 15, 1921, p. 836; Vol. 114, May 3, 1922, p. 515; Vol. 118, April 9, 1924, p. 382; Vol. 126, January 4, 1928, p. 9; Vol. 127, November 28, 1928, p. 564; Vol. 133, October 14, 1931, p. 378.

[54] *The Outlook,* Vol. 137, August, 1924, pp. 531-532.

poor, morale was low, as evidenced by 14,000 desertions in 1926, and both training and equipment were woefully inadequate.[55] Certainly, even a cursory examination of the Nation's press of this period would reveal that there was no lack of warning as to the weak posture of our military establishment,[56] but neither the country nor the Administration took heed.

An analysis of the political platforms of the Democratic and Republican Parties reveals that they claimed to favor an adequate military establishment, though they never defined their terms, and at the same time they were pressing for a reduction in expenditures for the military establishment. Also noticeable was a disposition to use the subject for partisan political purposes.

After the war, the Democratic 66th Congress launched an exhaustive investigation of the War Department and its activities which General March was convinced was done solely for political reasons since the inquiry ended once the Harding Administration took office.[57] The committee's reports were extremely critical of the War Department and "if half of what the majority of the subcommittee says in its reports is true, the United States could have played no effective part in the prosecution of the war." [58] Four million young men could look back upon their gallant service and find as their reward that Congress spent a year and a half "criticizing, blaming, and dispraising the Army and its efforts until they had robbed the soldier's profession of its distinction." Secretary Baker believed "that the attitude which Congress has assumed toward the Army and its achievements" had a great deal to do with the difficulty the Army had in procuring recruits.[59]

In the Republican platform of 1920 the Democratic Administration was severely castigated for leading an unprepared nation into war, and for its conduct of the entire war effort. The platform pledged a program of tax reduction, and while it also advocated

---

[55] Henry J. Reilly, "Our Crumbling National Defense," *Century Magazine,* Vol. 113, January, 1927, pp. 273-280.
[56] e. g. Josephus Daniels, "Why the United States Needs a Big Navy," *Saturday Evening Post,* Vol. 193, March 19, 1921; Captain N. H. Goss "The Case for the Navy," *Review of Reviews,* Vol. 77, May, 1928; Albert W. Atwood, "Why a Navy," *Saturday Evening Post,* Vol. 205, January 12, 1933; Anonymous "An Army of Amateurs," *American Mercury,* Vol. 6, October 1925; Major General Fox Connor "The National Defense," *North American Review,* Vol. 225, January, 1928.
[57] March, *op. cit.,* p. 352.
[58] Minority Report of H. D. Flood, March 2, 1921, as cited in *Ibid.,* p. 353.
[59] Baker to Harbord, March 17, 1920, *Harbord Mss.*

an adequate Army, Navy, and Merchant Marine, it proposed to do this with a large reduction in the appropriations for defense purposes.[60] In 1924, the Democrats were in a position to criticize the Administration for having what they claimed was a large military establishment, with special reference to the Army. They demanded a strict and sweeping reduction of armaments in both land and sea forces and international agreements to limit armaments. The Republicans asserted that the Army had been reduced to the absolute minimum consistent with national safety. They urged the appropriation of sufficient funds to provide for the training of all members of the National Guard, the Citizens Military Training Corps, the Reserve Officers' Training Corps, and for all reservists who would volunteer for training.[61]

With succeeding administrations dedicated to economy and with Congress holding the purse strings it is difficult to escape the conclusion that the National Defense Act of 1920 was foredoomed to failure. No military policy could be successful implemented without the necessary financial sinews as General MacArthur forcefully pointed out in regard to our armored forces in 1932, when he said they suffered from one thing "and one thing only—that Congress will not give them enough money to equip them properly with modern tanks." [62]

Two important organizations, the American Legion and the Veterans of Foreign Wars, tried to arouse the country to an awareness of the need for preparedness. The American Legion was supposed to have been organized at a caucus of the American Expeditionary Forces in Paris, March, 1919. Prior to this caucus there was talk about the need for a veterans organization to keep America reminded that she never again must be left unprepared for national defense.[63] This assembled group resolved: "That we favor universal military training and the administration of such a policy should be removed from the complete control of any exclusive military organization or caste." At the St. Louis caucus of May, 1919, the delegates agreed that a system of universal mili-

---

[60] *Republican Party Campaign Textbook—1920*, pp. 3-10.

[61] *Democratic Party Campaign Textbook—1924*, pp. 5-6.

[62] Watson, *op. cit.*, p. 22.

[63] Justin Grey with Victor H. Bernstein: *The Inside Story of the American Legion*, (New York: Boni & Gaer, 1948), p. 58.

tary training was essential to the protection of the United States.[64] A preamble was drawn up at this meeting, organizational work took place rapidly, and by September 16, 1919, the American Legion was chartered by an Act of Congress.

The First National Convention, which took place in Minneapolis in November, 1919, set the tone and pattern for the military policy favored by the Legion. The committee on military policy declared that they favored a national military and naval system based upon a universal military obligation, "to include a small regular army and navy, and a citizen-army and navy capable of rapid expansion sufficient to meet any national emergency." The committee also recommended that military training in high schools and colleges be encouraged along with the continuance of camps for the training and education of officers. The convention also went on record as favoring "a policy of universal military training but ask that such a system be free of military caste." [65]

At its second convention the Legion pointed with pride to the National Defense Act [66] while at its next two conventions increasing attention was paid to the Navy with the demand for "an adequate navy for the maintenance of our country as a world power and the protection of those policies which are distinctly American." [67] Succeeding meetings emphasized the Legion's concern over the Nation's military program and its continued advocacy of necessary measures to develop the strength of our Army, Navy, and Air Corps. In regard to the Air Corps, the Legion believed that we were the most backward of any first class power in the development of airpower. It also advocated the inauguration of a separate department for the Air Corps and a single Department of National Defense consisting of the Land Forces, Sea Forces, an Air Force, and a Munitions Department.[68]

The Veterans of Foreign Wars took up the keynote of preparedness from the American Legion. From the very end of World

---

[64] Robert S. Jones, *A History of the American Legion*, (Indianapolis: Bobbs-Merrill Co., 1946), pp. 85, 90.

[65] *Proceedings of the First National Convention*, (Washington: G.P.O., 1920), p. 57.

[66] *The Legion Calls the Turn*, (Indianapolis, 1947), p. 65. Robert Jones, *op. cit.*, p. 89, infers that the Legion exerted quite an influence in the enactment of the National Defense Act of 1920.

[67] *Proceedings of the Third Annual Convention*, (Washington: G.P.O., 1922), p. 122.

[68] *Proceedings of the Tenth Annual Convention*, (Washington: G.P.O., 1929) pp. 286, 298-300.

War I they valiantly fought any attempt by Congress to cut military appropriations. The V.F.W. directed particular attention toward expanding the various reserve components such as the National Guard and the Organized Reserves.[69]

Down through the years they consistently urged the universal draft of all the nation's resources including finance, manpower, and materials. The organization continually expressed the considered conviction that we should have the most modern and best manned Navy in the world with strategically located bases, and a merchant marine second to none. In 1926 they strongly advocated an efficient Air Corps in both the Army and Navy to include procurement of additional aircraft, improvement of facilities, and sufficient personnel.[70]

In the year 1926, grave concern was felt over the fact that the Defense Act of 1920 was still a paper plan. A complete program was urged to make this plan a reality and to bring our armed forces up to the strength deemed necessary. Strong recommendations were made to provide the Navy with funds to build up to treaty strength, and to increase the size of the Army.[71]

In 1931, although the bite of poverty was felt throughout the nation, a strong and positive call was made for specific forces and programs. The V.F.W. was vehement in its opposition against any reductions in our armed forces. A resolution was passed by the encampment condemning Congress for reducing our national defenses below a safe limit.[72]

These pleas of the veterans' organization made but little impression upon the country. With the onslaught of the depression in 1929 America was increasingly concerned with her financial plight. A new administration would take office in 1933, faced not only with the grim specter of hunger stalking the streets, but also the sound of marching boots in Europe and Asia. The Roosevelt Administration was to fall heir to a depleted military establishment, acute economic distress, and intensified international difficulties.

---

[69] V. O. Key, *Politics, Parties, and Pressure Groups,* (New York: Crowell Co., 1947), p. 129 says "The Veterans of Foreign Wars shouted for nationalistic measures and for national defense, as well as showing a strong awareness of the threat of communism and fascism."
[70] *Proceedings 27th Encampment V.F.W.,* (Washington: G.P.O., 1927), p. 247.
[71] *Ibid.,* p. 181.
[72] *Proceeding 32nd Encampment V.F.W.,* (Washington: G.P.O., 1932), p. 305.

CHAPTER 18

America Rearms on the Eve of War

The Army Grows Slowly—War Intensifies the Need for Rearmament—The Nation is Called to Arms—Aid to the Allies and Defense are Interwoven—"Convoys Mean Shooting and Shooting Means War"—The Navy Expands Under Roosevelt—Airpower Comes Into Its Own—Economic Mobilization Planning

POSTWAR APATHY, disarmament, and the raging fury of the depression had so reduced the effectiveness of the Army that in 1933 the Chief of Staff, General Douglas MacArthur, estimated that the United States stood seventeenth in rank among the world's armies. Plans in 1929 and 1931 to provide for an increase in personnel and for mobilization in time of war ran into the familiar trio of opposition—disarmament, apathy, and economy—and got nowhere. Personnel was not increased at all.[1]

Perhaps even more than in the twenties the decade of the thirties reflected an increasing American aversion to war, with a clearly heard obligato of pacifism. Attention was directed toward the immense profits of the munition makers of World War I, and a school of revisionist historians sought to explode the idea that Germany had been solely responsible for the war. The thesis of Big Business putting pressure upon Wilson for America's entrance into the war was exhaustively examined in 1934 by a special Senate Committee headed by Senator Gerald P. Nye, and while there was no evidence of Wilson's suasion by industrialists the committee's hearings encouraged America in its determination to stay out of future wars.[2]

Legislation aimed at preventing foreign entanglements and assuring American neutrality was enacted beginning with the Johnson Act in 1934 which forbade nations in default on war debts to again borrow from the United States, and with South America's Chaco War looming on the horizon Congress author-

---

[1] Watson, *op. cit.*, p. 24.

[2] It is significant to note that Alger Hiss was chief legal counsel for the Nye Committee.

ized the President to ban the sale of arms to belligerents.[3] In 1935 Congress passed the first of a series of neutrality acts through which America renounced many of her traditional claims to freedom of the seas. The Act of 1935 and subsequent legislation extending through 1937 prohibited the sale or transport of munitions to belligerents, loans to nations at war, and made travel on belligerent vessels unlawful for American citizens. It was believed that the safeguards thus provided would minimize hazards which the United States had encountered from 1914 to 1917.[4] Thus America exhibited more satisfaction and faith in legislation designed to keep us out of war than in providing adequate armament in case war did break down these legislative barriers.

The Army Grows Slowly

The 1931 plan of the War Department for wartime mobilization of manpower and resources was intended to save lives and millions of dollars, but its critics said that it was fraught with grave dangers, because it might imperil the worldwide disarmament movement. "War programs," according to the Federal Council of Churches of Christ in America, would tend to "create suspicion and fear among the nations of the world and diminish rather than increase, the security of the United States." Here again was the old controversy over whether we should prepare for war in time of peace, and while much of the press was agreed upon the wisdom of the plan, many argued that it was still "much better to place emphasis on plans for peace." [5]

In 1933 the strength of the Army was approximately 14,000 officers and 122,000 enlisted men.[6] Basic policies had to be predicated upon these low figures rather than upon the authorized strength of 280,000 as provided in the National Defense Act of 1920. General MacArthur, in June, 1933, drew up plans for mobilization based upon three contingencies: (1) the current strength of the Army; (2) a recommended strength of 165,000; (3) the authorized strength of 280,000. Mobilization with the cur-

---

[3] Dixon Wector: *The Age of the Great Depression, 1929-1941,* (New York: Macmillan Co., 1948), p. 305.
[4] Bailey, *op. cit.,* pp. 741-742. For a full and scholarly description of this legislation see Edwin Borchard and William P. Loge, *Neutrality for the United States,* (New Haven: Yale University Press, 1940).
[5] *Literary Digest,* Vol. 109, May 30, 1931, p. 8.
[6] Watson, *op. cit.,* p. 25.

rent strength of the Army would take at least four to six months; and while the force of 165,000 provided no immediately available Army, it would permit the creation of a more rounded establishment which would provide for efficient expansion. Only the third plan could provide a balanced army corps for immediate action and also a framework for later expansion. But no one had any hope of securing such a force; consequently attention was directed toward building up to the goal of 165,000. War Department planning of the period was conducted with efficiency albeit in an air of unreality because their recommendations were presented not with any hope of obtaining immediate results, but so that those responsible would understand the situation and be able to correct it when possible.

One may understand the attitude of the War Department, for at the very time its plan was under preparation, President Franklin D. Roosevelt urged Congress to cut $144,000,000 from the Army's budget and reduce its personnel by retiring 4,000 officers and dropping 12,000 enlisted men. Editor Oswald Garrison Villard, *of The Nation,* was heartily in favor of further cuts because appropriations had been sliced for much more vital services of the Government, and in addition, he could see no threat to the peace of the United States, hence no need for a large Army.[7] The effort to deflate our military establishment was also welcomed by the Baltimore *Sun* which asserted: "We have been spending larger sums for military and naval preparation than any nation on the face of the earth." The New York *World-Telegram* was confident that economy would mean not only a less expensive but a more efficient Army while the old cry "that the Administration is destroying the Army" could not be taken seriously.

A contrary view was expressed by the Washington *Post.* Criticizing the Administration's program, it observed that "for several years the United States Army has been held down to the status of a national police force and a nucleus for training a defensive machine in case of emergency. Every rule of reason suggests that it not be further curtailed." Reduction was impossible, was also the opinion of the Rochester *Democrat and Chronicle,* "without grave danger to our national defenses"; while the New

---

[7] Oswald Garrison Villard: "Issues and Men—The Army and Navy Forever," *The Nation,* Vol. 136, February 8, 1933, p. 139.

York *American* of the Hearst chain was even more emphatic: "To destroy what is left of our Regular Army, which is the backbone of our defense on land would be to mortgage the defense and independence of the nation, and let a vital part of our national insurance lapse." [8] The proposed slashes were withdrawn, and while it was evident that public opinion was opposed to any further reductions in the Army, it was also clear that there was no mandate from the people for an increase in our armed forces.

The strength of the Army rose slowly from a total of 135,684 in 1933 to 138,569 in 1935, and it was not until 1936 that the goal of a 165,000 man Army was reached.[9] Only under the spur of the dangerous international situation, which posed potential dangers to the peace and security of America, did the Administration take important steps toward rearmament in 1938.

In his message to Congress of January 28, 1938, President Roosevelt spoke about what he called the "beginning of a vast program of rearmament." This rearmament was necessary, the Chief Executive said, because of the breakdown of efforts to secure limitations on armaments, and the seriousness of the world crisis. "Our national defense is, in the light of increasing armaments of other nations, inadequate for purposes of national security and requires increase for that reason." The message was chiefly concerned with increased naval armaments. Only about $17,000,000 was recommended for the Army.[10]

The President's message precipitated a sharp discussion in both houses of Congress. The suggestion of increased armaments caused an immediate reaction on the part of peace societies and their representatives in Congress, while intimations given in the British Parliament that the British and American fleets were acting in concert in the Far East brought prompt and incisive questions concerning the Administration's foreign policy.[11] The Munich Agreement of September 30, 1938 struck a note of added urgency

---

[8] *Literary Digest,* Vol. 115, May 6, 1933, p. 8.

[9] Watson, *op. cit.,* p. 16.

[10] Samuel I. Rosenman (ed.): *The Public Papers and Addresses of Franklin D. Roosevelt,* (New York: Macmillan and Co., 1941), Vol. VII, pp. 68-71. Hereafter cited as *Public Papers of F.D.R.*

[11] *The Congressional Digest,* Vol. 17, No. 3, March, 1938, p. 67. For a discussion of the relationship between diplomacy and rearmament see the testimony of Dr. Charles A. Beard in *Ibid.,* pp. 90-92, and Bruce Bliven: Should Congress Approve the Proposed National Defense Program?" *New Republic,* January 26, 1938 as cited in *Ibid.,* pp. 92-93.

in the debate over rearmament. This gave signal for a White House conference on November 14, and from that occasion stemmed the effective rearming of the nation's ground and air forces. At this conference which included Mr. Roosevelt and his principal military and civilian advisers, the Chief Executive presented his views on the immediate needs of the military establishment. His proposals were concentrated upon the need for airpower and he paid scant attention to the need for bolstering the ground forces.[12]

The tempo of rearmament picked up rapidly after this conference, for now the armed forces had a vocal and powerful advocate to persuade Congress and the people of the necessity for strengthening our military establishments. In a message to Congress on January 12, 1939, the President warned that our existing forces were so utterly inadequate that they must be immediately strengthened, and he called for increased expenditures for materiel, airplanes, and pilot training.[13] This Presidential warning, coupled with the alarming gravity of a world seemingly poised on the precipice of war, induced Congress to increase appropriations to $1,631,181,944 which was almost $600,000,000 more than the sum authorized in 1938.[14]

Though increased appropriations were forthcoming from Congress neither the size nor the efficiency of the Army were materially improved. In July of 1939 the Army had 174,079 enlisted men scattered throughout 130 posts and camps, and in the United States there was no functioning corps or field army.[15]

The War Plans Division of the General Staff predicated its studies upon the strength of the Army which meant that emphasis was placed upon principles of passive defense. Their plans, in the harsh light of reality, were little more than staff studies which looked to a possible future conflict with a single enemy. These so-called "color plans," each possible enemy being designated by a color, usually provided for the waging of an ultimate offensive, but in view of the weakness of our forces this could only be accomplished long after the outbreak of hostilities. The result was that comprehensive planning, which is the only planning of im-

---

[12] Watson, *op. cit.*, p. 126.
[13] *Public Papers of F.D.R.*, Vol. VIII, pp. 71-72.
[14] Charles A. Beard: *American Foreign Policy in the Making, 1932-1940*, (Yale University Press, 1949), p. 38.
[15] Watson, *op. cit.*, pp. 87, 148-149.

portance, had made far less headway in the Army than in the Navy.[16]

Planning received a much needed stimulus from the Joint Army and Navy Board in May of 1939.[17] The Joint Board came to the conclusion that Army and Navy planning had to be actively implemented, and therefore its Joint Planning Commission was instructed to draw up new plans more in accord with the realities of the world situation and the safety of the United States. These new studies, known as the RAINBOW plans, contemplated the possibility of waging war not with one enemy in one theater of operations as had the previous color plans, but envisaged war against several foes in more than one area of the world. Five plans, drawn up with the code names of RAINBOW 1, 2, 3, 4, and 5, are summarized by an official Army historian, Mark S. Watson, as follows:

> 1. To prevent violations of the Monroe Doctrine, and to protect the United States, its possessions, and its sea trade.
> 2. To carry out Plan No. 1, and also to sustain the authority of democratic powers in the Pacific zones.
> 3. To secure control of the western Pacific.
> 4. To afford hemisphere defense, through sending U. S. task forces if needed to South America, and to the Eastern Atlantic.
> 5. To achieve the purposes of Plans 1 and 4, also to provide ultimately for sending forces to Africa or Europe in order to effect the decisive defeat of Germany or Italy or both. This plan assumed U. S. cooperation with Great Britain and France.[18]

RAINBOW No. 1 received primary attention following the President's approval of October 14, 1939, but the other plans were also given study and consideration. Numbers 2 and 3 were cancelled by the Joint Board in August, 1941, and Numbers 1 and 4 were dropped by May of 1942 though many of their recommendations had borne fruit. Following the American-British staff conversations of 1941, RAINBOW 5 was enlarged into War Department Operation Plan, RAINBOW 5 and War Department Concentration Plan, RAINBOW 5. "This grand composite was the basic

---

[16]*Ibid.*, p. 87.

[17] *Cf.* Chapter 13 for the creation of the Joint Board. After its reconstitution in 1919 its members from the Army were the Chief of Staff, Assistant Chief of Staff G-3, and Chief of War Department Planning while the Navy was represented by the Chief of Naval Operations, the Assistant Chief, and the Director of the Navy's War Planning Division.

[18] Watson, *op. cit.*, pp. 103-104.

plan in readiness when war actually came in December, 1941, the program having been continuously restudied and amplified in the light of co-ordination with British plans." [19]

War Intensifies the Need for Rearmament

The coming of the European war in September, 1939 placed in sharp focus the military deficiencies of the United States. However, despite the clear danger that America might be involved, the peaceful inclinations of the people still served as a barrier to effective rearmament. American sympathies were overwhelmingly in favor of the Allied cause,[20] but the nation did not want to participate in the holocaust that was sweeping Europe. The President and the nation advocated a policy of neutrality. Efforts to increase American armaments were relatively modest until the fall of France.

On September 8, 1939, Roosevelt issued his proclamation of a "limited" national emergency and on the same day he authorized increases in the strength of the armed forces. The increase in the Army called for only 17,000 men. Such a minuscule expansion of the Army was due to fear of an unfavorable political reaction, and also because the War Department was somewhat dubious about pouring in vast numbers of untrained men into the skeletonized divisions of the Army for fear that the recruits might unfavorably affect the efficiency of the Army. This initial increase raised the strength of the Regular Army to 227,000 while the National Guard was to be increased from 200,000 to 235,000 men. Only a few emergency expenditures were requested because this was all the President believed the public would be ready to accept without undue excitement.[21]

There was no doubt as to the Administration's attitude toward the belligerent powers. Two weeks after the outbreak of war the President called a special session of Congress to consider repeal of the Neutrality Acts.[22] After six weeks of debate the arms embargo was lifted and the President was authorized to proclaim danger zones in which American shipping would be prohibited.

---

[19] *Ibid.*, pp. 103-104.
[20] According to a Gallup Poll of October 22, 1939, 84% wanted the Allies to win, 2% favored Germany, while 14% expressed no opinion. Bailey, *op. cit.*, p. 755.
[21] Watson, *op. cit.*, pp. 156-157.
[22] An earlier attempt to repeal the Neutrality Acts in the spring and summer of 1939 had failed.

The Allies could now purchase munitions in the United States but only on a cash and carry basis.[23]

The calm on the western front was broken with dramatic suddenness in the spring of 1940; the lightning success of Nazi arms was to usher in a much more vigorous and forthright program of preparedness.

On May 16, 1940, the President appeared before Congress and asked for 50,000 airplanes and an appropriation of $896,-000,000.[24] The following weeks were to be followed by additional requests, and the mood of Country and Congress had so changed following the downfall of France that by October 8, 1940, Congress had appropriated over seventeen billion dollars for defense.[25] The armed forces now had the necessary funds but there still remained the question of manpower.

The Nation is Called to Arms

The National Guard was one source of manpower for the expanding Army, so on May 31, 1940, the President asked authority from Congress to call the Guard into active service.[26] Under the law the Chief Executive could not call the Guard into active service except "when Congress shall have declared a national emergency and shall have authorized the use of armed land forces of the United States in excess of those of the regular army." Though it lacked modern equipment and was at less than forty percent of its authorized strength,[27] the National Guard represented one of the few organized defense assets.

While the Congress was considering the President's request, the Burke-Wadsworth Bill calling for selective service was introduced on June 20, 1940. It is interesting to note that the initiative for the bill came from neither the White House nor the War Department, but from a group of civilians.[28] Only when it was evident that the legislation had a large measure of support both in Congress and in the press did the President throw his weight behind selective service.

---

[23] Bailey, *op. cit.*, pp. 760-761. Restrictions on loans and on travel on belligerent ships were retained.
[24] *Public Papers of F.D.R.*, Vol. IX, p. 201.
[25] Bailey, *op. cit.*, p. 768.
[26] *Public Papers of F.D.R.*, Vol. IX, p. 252.
[27] *Biennial Report of the Chief of Staff, July 1, 1939 to June 30, 1941*, p. 4. Hereafter cited as *Biennial Report, C/S, 1939-1941*.
[28] Watson, *ov. cit.*, p. 192.

Even if the threat of Hitlerism were removed, in the opinion of the Washington *Star*, it would still be most desirable to have compulsory military training. It would give our young men the benefits of disciplined training and physical conditioning and "it would serve to inculcate the spirit of universal service—military and civil—which we must learn if this democracy is to survive in a new world order." [29] The Baltimore *Sun* believed this was the only way the expanding ranks of our military establishment could be filled, and it was "equally obvious that once the necessity for compulsory service is admitted, such service cannot be fairly demanded unless it is universal in its over-all application." [30]

Though there was strong public support for both measures, the authorization for calling the National Guard was not given until August 27, 1940. The first units were inducted on September 16, the same day that the President signed the Selective Service Act. Under this act the Army of the United States was to consist of 1,400,000 men of which 500,000 were to be in the Regular Army, 270,000 in the National Guard, and 630,000 selectees. [31] The pendulum of public opinion had now swung sharply toward an urgent demand for enormous and immediate increases in the armed forces.

Tremendous problems had to be met and solved in this rapid expansion of the Army. Housing, equipment, organization, training, and all the myriad problems which confronted the Army in World War I again burdened the desks of the War Department. Though the Army was just emerging from a period of dark days it was better prepared to solve the problems of a rapid mobilization than in previous years. Better staff planning, a more efficient National Guard, and the backlog of reserve officers—all were assets of great value. The problem of officer procurement was largely solved by the fact that during the postwar years over 100,000 reserve officers had been trained largely through the medium of the Reserve Officers Training Corps. "These Reserve Officers constituted the principle available asset which we possessed at this time. Without their assistance the program could not have been carried out except in a superficial manner." [32]

---

[29] June 9, 1940.
[30] June 20, 1940.
[31] *Biennial Report, C/S, 1939-1941*, pp. 6-7.
[32] *Ibid.*, p. 7.

Aid to the Allies and Defense Are Interwoven

While the mobilization of America was taking place, steps were initiated to provide Great Britain with ever increasing aid in the belief that America's defense and destiny were linked to the success of Allied arms. Under this doctrine of aid to the Allies, the United States abandoned all pretenses of neutrality and drifted ever closer to the brink of war. "By this support," the President told Congress in his message of January 6, 1941, "we express our determination that the democratic cause shall prevail; and we strengthen the defense and security of our own Nation." [33]

On September 2, 1940, Roosevelt announced the famous "Destroyer Deal" with Great Britain in which America acquired the right to naval and air bases in Newfoundland, Bermuda, the Bahamas, Jamaica, St. Lucia, Trinidad, Antigua, and British Guiana. "The right to bases in Newfoundland and Bermuda are gifts—generously given and gladly received. The other bases mentioned have been acquired in exchange for fifty of our over-age destroyers." [34]

Press reaction to the President's message was in the main extremely laudatory not only because it was believed that the destroyers would be of immense help to the British, but also because this was the most effective defense measure in the whole preparedness program.[35] The "Destroyer Deal" meant a marked strengthening in America's strategic position in the Atlantic, and when the bases were established

> the American frontier will be extended to the Amazon River and the Grand Banks off Newfoundland; the United States will exercise virtually unchallengeable domination of the Caribbean area, and our outer bastions of defense will be emplaced in blue water 700 to 1,000 miles to the east of our coastline.[36]

The thesis that the security of America was bound up with the survival and independence of the British Commonwealth of Nations was to receive a severe testing when the British would no longer be able to pay cash for shipping and other supplies.[37] The

G.P.O., 1943), pp. 608-611. Hereafter cited as *Peace and War.*
[33] *Peace and War: United States Foreign Policy, 1931-1941,* (Washington:
[34] *Ibid.,* pp. 564-565.
[35] *Christian Science Monitor,* December 4, 1940. For a roundup of editorial opinion see the New York *Times* of September 3, 1940.
[36] Hanson W. Baldwin, New York *Times,* September 4, 1940.
[37] Tansill, *op. cit.,* p. 603.

Neutrality Act of 1939 specifically prohibited loans to belligerents. While England remained dependent upon American supplies, her resources were not adequate to a cash-and-carry basis. The question of how to get around the Neutrality Act would soon arise. At a press conference on December 8, 1940 Roosevelt signified that he had found the answer; he suggested that we lend munitions.[38] The proposal was further outlined in a radio address to the country on December 29 when the American people were told that aid to Britain was now a question of national security. If England went down "all of us in the Americas would be living at the point of a gun."[39]

The Lend-Lease proposal was presented by the Chief Executive to Congress in his message of January 6, 1941, in which he said this was an unprecedented moment in the history of the Union, "because at no previous time has American security been as seriously threatened from without as it is today." Speaking in a slow pace with ever increasing tones "almost reaching the proportions of a shout," [40] Roosevelt stated: ". . . . our most useful and immediate role is to act as an arsenal for them as well as ourselves." This meant increasing our appropriations and spending to an amount never before visualized in the history of our country. The President also called upon the nation to tell the democracies of the world, and particularly Great Britain,

> we Americans are vitally concerned in your defense of freedom. We are putting forth our energies, our resources and our organizing powers to give you strength to remain and maintain a free world. We shall send you in ever increasing numbers, ships, planes, tanks, guns. This is our purpose and our pledge.[41]

A major portion of public opinion, including the business community, approved the President's plan, although there was marked opposition in some quarters. That America was rushing to the defense of the democratic way of life seemed to satisfy a large faction who believed that the United States should morally enlist on the side of the nations resisting the totalitarian states and the President would have the active support of American public opinion in his contention that we must continue to furnish aid and

---

[38] New York *Times*, December 18, 1940. The President said: "What I am trying to do is to eliminate the dollar sign."
[39] *Peace and War*, pp. 599-601.
[40] New Orleans *Times-Picayune*, January 7, 1941.
[41] *Peace and War*, pp. 608-611.

that we could not stop furnishing supplies when the cash available to the defenders of liberty runs out.[42]

While a few editorials thought Lend-Lease would be a measure of peace insurance, others pointed out that it meant the end of our alleged neutrality, for no nation can openly ally herself with a belligerent and pretend to be neutral. The Detroit *Free Press* could draw only one conclusion: "We will be an actual participant to save England. We are at war without having one declared." [43]

The advocates of aid to the Allies warmly espoused Lend-Lease as a defense measure which would keep the war away from America, while the America First Committee denounced it as a "blank-check bill" and a sure guarantee of war. "Lending war equipment," in the opinion of Senator Robert Taft of Ohio, "is a good deal like lending chewing gum. You don't want it back." Senator Burton K. Wheeler of Montana branded the proposal as the "New Deal's 'triple A' foreign policy—to plow under every fourth American boy." [44] Despite this bitter opposition, public opinion[45] favored Lend-Lease and the bill passed and was signed by the President on March 11, 1941. On the same day he approved a list of articles for immediate shipment, and the following day he asked Congress for an initial appropriation of seven billion dollars to implement the act.[46]

The act authorized the President to secure through government facilities or to buy from private producers any defense article or any other commodity or article for defense. These goods could be sold, exchanged, or leased to the government of any country whose defense the President deemed vital to the defense of the United States in return for "payment in kind or property or any

---

[42] Los Angeles *Times*, January 7, 1941. Other editorials registering approval include: New Orleans *Times-Picayune*, Chicago *Daily News*, Boston *Globe*, Cleveland *Plain-Dealer*, Birmingham *Age-Herald*, Minneapolis *Tribune*, Boston *Post*, Atlanta *Constitution*, Kansas City *Star*, New York *Herald Tribune*, New York *Times*, Baltimore *Sun*, Des Moines *Register*, and the Indianapolis *Star*. The dates for the above are all January 7, 1941 with the exception of the Cleveland *Plain-Dealer* and the New York *Times* which are January 6, 1941.

[43] Detroit *Free Press*, January 7, 1941. The Denver *Post*, of the same date, denounced the President as a dictator and scored what it termed his request for "blank-check authority." The Chicago *Tribune*, January 7, 1941, also scored the proposal.

[44] As quoted in Bailey, *op. cit.*, pp. 773-774. This referred to a previous policy of the Roosevelt Administration for reducing agricultural surpluses.

[45] On March 8, 1941, the count of the Gallup Poll was 56% favorable, 27% opposed, 8% qualified support, and 9% with no opinion. New York *Times*, March 10, 1941.

[46] Chicago *Tribune*, March 12, 1941.

other direct or indirect benefit which the President deems satisfactory." Convoying was forbidden as was also the entry of American ships into combat zones, but otherwise the President was given wide powers notwithstanding the provisions of any other law.[47]

Another important step in acquiring additional naval bases and in securing the safety of the sea lanes to England, came with the American occupation of Greenland and Iceland in the spring of 1941.[48] These and the previously acquired bases were important because of the obvious fact that the weapons and munitions pouring out of American factories would do Britain little good rusting on the bottom of the Atlantic. This brought up the question of convoys and possible incidents in the Atlantic that could lead to war.

"Convoys Mean Shooting and Shooting Means War"

As previously noted, the Neutrality Act of November 4, 1939 prohibited American shipping from entering the waters around the British Isles and the entire European coast from Bergen to the Spanish border. The Lend-Lease Act continued this restriction. The Panama Conference also tried to protect shipping by proclaiming a neutrality zone around the Americas which varied in width from 300 to 1,000 miles, and the belligerents were warned to refrain from naval activity within that area.[49] The Lend-Lease Act also forbade the authorization of convoying vessels by naval vessels of the United States, and thus it seems clear that American legislators were determined to prevent submarine incidents which might involve America in war.

Despite this prohibition and the Administration's pledge during the course of the debate over Lend-Lease that it had not contemplated using convoys, the subject was discussed in the course of staff conversations between Britain and America which eventuated in the ABC-1 Staff Agreement of March 27, 1941. Under this agreement the United States Navy assumed the responsibility for the "organization of a force for escort-of-convoy."[50] The inevitable incidents started as early as April 10, and by September 11 Roosevelt announced that American naval vessels had been issued

[47] *Peace and War,* pp. 627-630.
[48] Bailey, *op. cit.,* pp. 778-782.
[49] Bailey, *op. cit.,* p. 762.
[50] Tansill, *op. cit.,* p. 609.

"shoot on sight" orders. The following month he urged Congress to repeal the "crippling provisions" of the Neutrality Act so that America could better uphold the principle of freedom of the seas. By November 13, 1941, the Neutrality Act was repealed which meant that American shipping could now enter European waters and thus further help Great Britain.[51]

With the passage of Lend-Lease and the use of convoys in the Atlantic, America virtually went to war with Germany. All that was lacking was the formal declaration, but Germany was not obliging enough to take this step, and the Chief Executive hesitated to ask Congress for a declaration of war because of the isolationist strength which was still powerful in America. Admiral Harold R. Stark, Chief of Naval Operations, summed up the picture on November 7, 1941: "The Navy is already in the war of the Atlantic, but the country doesn't seem to realize it. Apathy, to the point of opposition, is evident in a considerable section of the press. Whether the country knows it or not, we are at war."[52] Peace sentiments and apathy were soon to be rudely shaken by the bombs on Pearl Harbor, but until then the country was officially at peace.

The Navy Expands Under Roosevelt

Despite the last-minute frenzy of preparations for our ground forces, the Navy would have been far better prepared for World War II than the Army if it had not suffered the debacle of Pearl Harbor. Under the naval limitation treaties following World War I we had scrapped 928,000 tons of naval shipping.[53] In the twelve years following the Washington Conference, the United States failed to provide a building program even for the replacement of obsolete vessels. Other nations not only failed to follow our policy of unilateral disarmament, but continued to build toward treaty limits by a systematic and orderly annual increase.

It was not until the advent of the Roosevelt Administration in 1933 that the United States awakened from its illusions regarding naval disarmament as a means of attaining national security. In that year Congress authorized the construction of thirty-two new

---

[51] Bailey, *op. cit.*, pp. 785-789.
[52] As quoted in Tansill, *op. cit.*, p. 645. Some naval officers referred to the operations in the Atlantic as "waging neutrality."
[53] Admiral Clark H. Woodward: "The Navy's Mission," *Vital Speeches of the Day*, April 1, 1939, Vol. V, p. 438.

ships. In 1934 the Vinson-Trammel Act gave sanction for building the Navy to its treaty limits and provided for 141 new ships of various types.[54] With the failure of naval disarmament clearly revealed by 1936 and in the light of the menacing world situation, Roosevelt asked Congress in January, 1938, to appropriate a billion dollars for the construction of a two-ocean Navy.[55] A year later, when it was decided to establish a permanent Atlantic Fleet, the United States was fully committed to the concept, if not the reality, of a two-ocean Navy.[56]

The coming of the European war in 1939 meant an increased tempo of activity for the Navy. The promulgation of the President's limited emergency proclamation of September 8, 1939, raised the authorized naval strength from 131,485 to 191,000 and meant the recall to active service of personnel on the retired and reserve lists.[57] Construction was started on new vessels with the view of bringing strength up to that authorized by previous legislation.[58]

Following the fall of France, a tremendous expansion of the Naval establishment was initiated. This consisted of a greatly increased building program; also, the fleet was to be expanded by 70%, the work on ships already under construction was to be accelerated, and there was to be an acquisition and conversion of merchant ships for auxiliary and patrol purposes. The goal of naval aviation was raised to 15,000 planes and the authorized personnel was increased to 232,000 men. This tremendous program meant that whereas in June, 1940 there were only 12 private shipyards building vessels for the Navy, by June, 1941 the number had increased to 108. In June of 1941 there were 697 new vessels under construction. The procurement of 2,059 new airplanes was accomplished in the twelve months following June, 1940, in comparison with 306 for the previous year.[59]

---

[54] *Ibid.*
[55] *The Congressional Digest,* March, 1938, Vol. XVIII, No. 3, pp. 67-97.
[56] Harry J. Carman and Harold C. Syrett: *A History of the American People,* (New York: Alfred A. Knopf, 1952), Vol. II, p. 628.
[57] *United States Navy at War, 1941-1945,* Reports of Fleet Admiral Ernest J. King, (Washington: G.P.O., 1946), p. 9. Hereafter cited as *U.S. Navy at War.*
[58] *Annual Rpt S/N, 1940,* p. 1. Construction of new vessels for fiscal year 1940 included: 2 battleships, 2 cruisers, 8 destroyers, 15 submarines, and 4 smaller auxiliary craft. New construction for fiscal year 1941 was to provide for 2 battleships, 6 submarines, 1 aircraft carrier, 2 cruisers, 8 destroyers, and 5 smaller auxiliary craft.
[59] *Annual Rpt S/N, 1941,* pp. 2, 3, 9, 14.

The personnel strength of the Navy, including the Marine Corps and the Coast Guard, soared from a total of 146,198 on September 8, 1939 to 420,522 by December 7, 1941.[60] This rapid rise put severe strains on the Navy's organizational facilities. Particularly acute was the problem of securing the necessary additional officers. In 1940 it was estimated that 12,200 new officers would be required, but this figure rose to 26,000 under the expanded program of 1941.[61] To meet this pressing need an increased emphasis was put on the Reserve Officers program, and the four year Naval Academy course was condensed to three. However, with the coming of the war, the Navy was able to meet its growing need for officers only by the granting of direct commissions to duly qualified civilians.[62]

Airpower Comes Into Its Own

As for the other services, the early thirties were not conducive to a growth in the power and development of the Air Corps. Crippled appropriations and economies did not give the American eagle much opportunity to spread his wings. In 1933 the United States ranked fourth in airpower, being behind France, Italy, and Great Britain.[63] It should be borne in mind that an air force that is not in existence on the outbreak of war cannot be brought into being quickly enough to exercise its power in the early, yet vital period of hostilities. "Its state of preparedness in the early stages of a war before ground forces have made contact might well be the decisive factor in determining the outcome." [64]

The 1930's saw important technical strides being taken in the advancement of airpower as a potent military weapon. However, in the climate of economy and unpreparedness the expansion of the Air Corps was not looked upon with favor until 1936. In that year Congress authorized an increase in serviceable planes from 1800 to 2320.[65] The appropriations in the period 1936-1938 were

---

[60] *U. S. Navy at War, p. 20.* The increases in the period for the various branches was as follows: Navy: 126,414 to 325,095; Marine Corps: 19,701 to 70,425; Coast Guard: 10,079 to 25,002.
[61] *Annual Rpt S/N, 1940,* p. 6. *Annual Rpt S/N, 1941,* pp. 3-4.
[62] *U. S. Navy at War,* p. 21.
[63] *The Aircraft Yearbook for 1933,* (New York: D. Van Nostrand Co., 1934), p. 61. From 1920 to 1939, the concept of air power was evolved around the airplane as a defensive weapon. The strategic concept of high altitude precision bombing was a thing of the future.
[64] Speech of the Asst S/W for Aeronautics, December 1, 1932 in *Ibid.*
[65] *Official AAF Guide,* p. 354.

doubled over those of 1933-1935, but aircraft procurement was slow and by the fall of 1938 the Air Corps only had 1,600 planes.[66]

After the Munich crisis of 1938 a growing realization came to the United States that airpower would be a significant factor in the war which seemed inevitable in Europe, and that America was lagging behind not only in numerical production but also in technical superiority. The War Department had not been unaware of the problem, and, spurred on by the President, announced on October 16, 1938, a plan which called for the revamping of the air program. This plan called for a great increase in the number of planes. It was felt that these could be procured by standardization and mass production of certain types of aircraft. Attention was also to be devoted to experimental development of new types of speedy planes designed to keep the United States ahead of developments abroad.[67]

Following the White House conference of November 14, 1938 [68] and subsequent modifications in the plans for an expanding Air Corps it was finally decided by January 11, 1939 to concentrate on a yearly production of 6,000 planes.[69] The following day the President asked Congress for $300,000,000 for plane purchases and for authorization to train 20,000 civilian pilots a year.[70] The proposal for the annual training of 20,000 pilots in the colleges and universities had been presented by the Civil Aeronautics Authority in December of 1938, and it had won the Chief Executive's approval. The plan called for giving flight training to college students between the ages of 18 and 25 and required them to meet the physical standards for a commercial pilot's certificate. In this way it was hoped a valuable source of trained pilots could be created to meet any national emergency.[71]

By April 3, 1939 legislation had been passed by Congress and signed by the President which authorized 6,000 planes for the Air Corps with an appropriation of $300,000,000. The bill also provided for calling Air Corps reserve officers to active duty and in-

[66] Watson, *op. cit.,* p. 127.
[67] New York *Herald Tribune,* October 16, 1938.
[68] *Supra,* p. 6.
[69] Watson, *op. cit.,* pp. 136-143.
[70] *Official AAF Guide,* p. 355.
[71] *Pilot Training for University Students,* (Washington: G.P.O., 1938), Pamphlet.

creased the strength of the Air Corps to 3,203 officers and 45,000 enlisted men. Authority for the training of civilian pilots was provided in the Civilian Pilot Training Act of June 27, 1939, with the training to be done under the supervision of the Civil Aeronautics Authority.[72]

The momentous events in Europe in the spring of 1940 gave impetus not only to an increase in the Army and Navy, but also to the Air Corps. In June the War Department announced plans to train 7,000 pilots and 3,600 bombardiers and navigators annually. On June 29 a program calling for 12,835 planes (54 combat groups) by April 1, 1942, was approved as the Army's first aviation objective for training, organization, and procurement. All existing limitations for fiscal year 1941 were suspended as to the number of flying cadets, the number and rank of Reserve Air Corps Officers called to active duty, and the number of serviceable planes which could be procured.[73]

The goal of 7,000 pilots was to be increased to 12,000 by a Presidential directive of August, 1940, and this in turn was superseded by the 30,000 pilot program of December 17, 1940.[74] The gigantic increase in the Air Corps was predicated upon the role that airpower had played in the success of Hitler's armies and an awareness that America must also have an efficient air arm. Colonel E. M. Benitez writing in *Military Review* pointed out that airpower played a predominant part in the campaigns in Poland, Finland, and the Low Countries;[75] while Major General Henry H. (Hap) Arnold asserted that for the proper defense of the United States a strong Army and Navy were needed along with an air force more powerful than any which exists in the world today.[76] From a few hundred planes to 50,000 planes a year, from a few hundred newly trained pilots to 7,000, then 12,000 and finally 30,000 a year, was a dazzling transition for the Air Corps.

In the great build-up of the Air Corps there was again heard the cry for air autonomy.[77] The General Staff, while recognizing

---

[72] *Official AAF Guide*, p. 355.
[73] *Ibid.*, pp. 355-356.
[74] Watson, *op. cit.*, p. 279.
[75] Colonel E. M. Benitez, "Conclusions of the European War," *Military Review*, Vol. XX, June, 1940.
[76] Henry H. Arnold: "Air Power in Modern Wars," *Army and Navy Journal*, November 30, 1940.
[77] For an extensive treatment of the subject see Watson, *op. cit.*, Ch. IX.

the new importance of the air arm, nevertheless opposed the creation of a separate Air Force as a grave error which would "completely disrupt the splendid organization now in process of building" and for this attitude "we are accused of being unprogressive, jealous of prerogatives, and incredibly shortsighted." [78] The question was at least temporarily resolved on June 20, 1941, with the creation of the Army Air Forces which was charged with the consolidation of all Army air activities.[79]

A striking way to evaluate the tremendous expansion of the Air Force is to compare its status in 1938 with what it was on the outbreak of war. In September of 1938 the Air Corps contained 22,000 men, at a time when the German *Luftwaffe* was training a million officers and men. There was one training center at San Antonio, Texas, which graduated three classes a year, usually less than 100 pilots in each class. There were about 1,000 combat type aircraft compared with a total of 2,500 in 1941. Enlisted strength had grown from 20,000 to more than 180,000 while officers had increased from 2,000 to nearly 17,000.

During 1940 and 1941 expansion after expansion occurred, until the Air Force was embarked upon a program which called for the training of 30,000 pilots, 10,000 bombardiers and navigators, and 100,000 mechanics and technicians per year to man 84 groups, which, if these objectives were reached, would give the Air Force a total strength of 41,000 officers and 600,000 enlisted men.[80]

Economic Mobilization Planning

Following our experiences in World War I it was recognized that in the event of a future conflict the economy of the country must be a well directed and organized instrument of the nation's military resources. So great had been the demands of that war upon the economies of the participating nations that it was clearly evident that future wars involving mechanization, great armies, air armadas, and far flung fleets would engulf the entire economies of the belligerents.

The National Defense Act of 1920 had placed the responsibility upon the Assistant Secretary of War for the assurance of ade-

---

[78] "General Marshall's Address," *Army and Navy Journal*, September 20, 1941.
[79] Watson, *op. cit.*, p. 293.
[80] *The Aircraft Yearbook for 1942*, pp. 42-43.

quate provision for the mobilization of material and industrial organizations essential to wartime needs.[81] Following World War I the military services, coordinated by the Army and Navy Munitions Board, undertook a planning program to prepare for future emergencies. This board produced four successive editions of an Industrial Mobilization Plan (1930-31, 1933, 1936, and 1939), which provided for the control, under civilian direction, of the nation's resources in wartime.[82]

However, when the emergency came in 1938, the Industrial Mobilization Plan, in some of its most essential features, was ignored. Once again the nation moved uncertainly. Controls and administration were improvised and many of the same mistakes of World War I were repeated. The great rearmament program put a heavy strain on the industrial machinery of the country and it became evident that direction and planning were sorely needed. The War Department recommended the establishment of a War Resources Administration in 1940, but President Roosevelt countered with the establishment of a National Defense Advisory Commission which was "probably due largely to the Administration's fear that American public opinion was not then prepared for such a drastic step as the establishment of a really powerful central administrative body." [83]

On December 20, 1940 the President established the Office of Production Management, with Mr. William S. Knudsen as director, to speed up and coördinate the output of war material. According to the New York *Times* there was thus created an authority capable of making decisions rather than offering advice; and the announcement by the President ought to help substantially to accelerate a defense program which had admittedly been lagging.[84]

---

[81] *Cf.* Chapter 17.

[82] Harry P. Yoshpe: "Economic Mobilization Planning Between the Two World Wars," *Military Affairs*, Vol. XV, No. 4, Winter, 1951.

[83] Lowell M. Pumphrey: "Planning for Economic Warfare," *Military Affairs*, Vol. V, 1941. Edward R. Stettinius in an article in the *Army and Navy Journal* of October 5, 1940, wrote: "Preparing America for defense is primarily a 'Production Job'; it is a question of turning the full force of our national initiative and energy to the task of changing raw materials into vast numbers of airplanes, tanks, ships, guns and other instruments of war, promptly and with a minimum disturbance to our normal peace-time life."

[84] New York *Times*, December 21, 1940. The editorial concluded by stating: "Hitherto Mr. Knudsen has not had power to buy so much as a tack-hammer for the Army on his own authority. He now becomes an executive, instead of an 'adviser,' with power to make and enforce decisions. This is the type of organization for defense which both the Army and Navy have repeatedly recommended in reports to Congress."

However, this new agency's authority was never clearly defined and the real possibilities of economic warfare were still only very partially exploited in this country. They showed every sign of being left in that state for a considerable time.[85] Shortly after the country went to war, Knudsen's board was replaced by the War Production Board under Donald Nelson who had general authority over the war procurement and production program.[86]

America had gone a long way in rearming since Munich, but the deficiencies, neglect, and apathy of the past decades could not be entirely overcome in three years. Armies, fleets, air armadas, and industrial production require wise foresight and planning, and once again the United States would pay a high price for its peacetime neglect of the military establishment.

---

[85] Pumphrey, *op. cit.*, p. 196.
[86] Carman and Syrett, *op. cit.*, Vol. II, p. 653.

CHAPTER 19

The Road to Victory

Elements of Unpreparedness—The War Department Reorganization of 1942—The Emergence of Combined
Planning—The Mobilization of Manpower—National Objectives and Strategy—The Price of Victory—The Wide
Blue Yonder—Second to None—The Arsenal of Democracy—The Atomic Age

THE BOMBS which brought death and destruction to Pearl
Harbor found the United States frantically rushing preparations for defense. Lend-lease had made a start in gearing the
American economy to war production, and Selective Service was
in the process of providing the nucleus for a well trained Army.
On the whole, however, the country was again unprepared; for
even in the face of rising international tension in the months before
the Japanese attack the American people failed to realize the peril
which involved their country and its vital interests.[1]

Elements of Unpreparedness

The unawareness of the country as to the imminence of war
was vividly reflected in the debate to amend the Selective Service
Act so as to prevent the loss of draftees, Reserve Officers, and
National Guardsmen at the end of their one-year period of duty.
Twelve months had proved too short for proper training, particularly in view of the great shortage of equipment, and if the men
were released it would mean the virtual emasculation of the Army.
The War Department also asked Congress to over-ride legislation
which restricted the service of National Guardsmen and selectees
to the Western Hemisphere and American possessions.[2] To the
New York *Times* it would be an "act of reckless folly to demobilize more than two-thirds of an incompletely trained Army
in the midst of a World War and at one of the great crises of our
history." [3] Despite these forebodings, only with the greatest diffi-

---

[1] For a discussion of peace sentiment and isolationist strength in this period
see Robert E. Sherwood's chapter "The Phony War" in his *Roosevelt and
Hopkins: An Intimate History,* New York, 1948.
[2] For a full discussion of the struggle see Watson, *op. cit.,* pp. 218-231,
[3] July 11, 1941.

culty was a bill squeezed through the House of Representatives by the margin of only one vote on August 12, 1941,[4] thus preventing the dismantling of our Army on the eve of war.

A year after the German juggernaut of men, machines, and planes had crashed through the Low Countries and France there still remained alarming deficiencies in materiel and equipment. It was plain that progress had, in many directions, been slow. There was a glaring lack of guns of all types and their ammunition; of tanks; of military planes, of ships. The New York *Times* in an editorial of July 3, 1941, charged that our four armored divisions had not yet received a single new medium tank, and there was not available a single Army dive-bomber. These deficiencies, it concluded, were largely attributable to lack of proper planning. What was needed was a War Planning Board able to make the over-all strategic and industrial decisions. Until such a board was functioning effectively we might expect continuance of a lopsided and archaic defense program, with many needless gaps and bottlenecks.

Another reason for lack of equipment, in addition to the failure to provide over-all planning and authority, lay in the vast streams of arms being sent to Britain and her allies. This inevitably meant deficiencies in the Army, and the War Department on many occasions protested to the White House, but "the determining power was that of the President . . . and to that superior authority the military services necessarily bowed." [5]

The War Department had failed in the period between the two wars to devote enough attention to the development of new weapons and modern equipment. As late as 1939 only 19.6% of the $646,000,000 budget was devoted to new equipment. In the following year, Chief of Staff George Marshall was still reluctant to replace the 75-mm gun of World War I with the recommended 105-mm howitzer as the principal artillery weapon of the infantry division. Marshall was unwilling to make the change because he believed other equipment was more urgently needed and also because of the large stocks of 75-mm ammunition on hand.[6]

American involvement in global war was to reveal weaknesses in the War Department structure. Only minor revisions had taken

[4] Watson, *op. cit.,* p. 230.
[5] Ibid, p. 330.
[6] Ibid, pp. 31, 39.

place since the National Defense Act of 1920 and the epic proportions of World War II quickly dictated an overhaul in the basic concepts and organizations of both the War Department and the General Staff.

One change which had occurred in 1934 seemed to be a departure from the historic tradition of the Army, for under a War Department order the Chief of Staff was to be the supreme commander of our armies in the field. General Harbord believed "unless it is changed before we have another war it will have to be thrown overboard in the face of the enemy or we shall face a failure," for "no war has ever been run successfully when commanded by a staff officer in a distant capital." [7] Former Secretary of War Newton D. Baker agreed with the conclusions expressed by Harbord and furthermore, in time of emergency, the President's hands should not be tied by giving him "a commander in chief who for any one of a dozen reasons is needed in the War Department while some other officer . . . is the better choice for the field command." If this practice continued it would be necessary to choose the Chief of Staff, not because of his administrative qualifications, but because of his talents for field service. [8] This procedure, it might also be added, did not contemplate more than one theater of operations.

The War Department Reorganization of 1942

The most drastic and fundamental change which the War Department had experienced since the establishment of the General Staff by Elihu Root in 1903 [9] was accomplished by the reorganization of March 9, 1942. Neither the War Department nor the General Staff were geared to global war, and while sweeping changes in time of war are dangerous, the Army planners felt they would be severely handicapped unless specific areas of responsibility and authority were laid down for their guidance. By November 3, 1941, General Marshall was firm in his belief of the necessity for action since the War Department "is the poorest command post in the Army, and we must do something about it, although I do not yet know what we will do." [10]

---

[7] James G. Harbord to Newton D. Baker, October 2, 1934. *Harbord Mss.*
[8] Baker to Harbord, October 4, 1934. *Harbord Mss.*
[9] Nelson, *op. cit.*, p. 335.
[10] As quoted in Frederick S. Haydon: "War Department Reorganization, August, 1941-March, 1942" *Military Affairs*, Vol. XVI, No. 3, Fall, 1952.

A study of the staff-command relationship of the War Department had been undertaken in August, 1941, and by January, 1942, Major General Joseph T. McNarney was appointed to work out the final details. On February 1, 1942 McNarney's recommendations, in a memorandum of model brevity, were presented to the Chief of Staff. McNarney's proposals formed the basis for the subsequent reorganization. As described by the Secretary of War, Henry L Stimson, the reorganization achieved unity and celerity of control, a broad decentralization of detail and a more intimate relationship between air and ground fighting.[11]

Army activities within the continental United States were grouped under three heads: a commander of the Air Forces, a commander of the Ground Forces, and a commander of the Services of Supply.[12] All air activities, including planning, logistics, administration, and strategic air functions were placed under the single direction of the Army Air Forces. The Army Ground Forces would be responsible for training, the combat arms, and for four new commands: the Replacement School Command, the Antiaircraft Command, the Tank Destroyer Command, and the Armored Force. The sharp lines of demarcation which separated the combat arms was thought to be removed with the elimination of the Offices of the Chiefs of Infantry, Cavalry, Field Artillery, and Coast Artillery. Similar to the War Department General Staff, the Ground Forces and the Air Forces would each have their own General Staff.

Remaining in the War Department was a "small, alert, compact air-ground General Staff," to exercise strategic direction, control the field armies, and determine the grand outline of military policy. One of its traditional organs, the War Plans Division, was to be shortly absorbed by the newly created Operations Division. Administrative planning, personnel records, production, procurement, and other pertinent subjects were transferred to the Services of Supply under the command of Lieutenant General Brehon B. Somervell. In this transfer the Offices of the Chiefs of operating technical and supply branches like the Corps of Engineers, Ordnance, and Chemical Warfare were retained as separate bureaus, in contrast with the scrapping of the corresponding heads of the combat arms.[13]

---

[11] *Annual Rpt*, S/W, 1942, p. 15.
[12] Later, March 12, 1943, to be renamed the Army Service Forces.
[13] Haydon, *op. cit.*

The Emergence of Combined Planning

Corresponding with this reorganization of the Army came a series of efforts looking to a close integration of the Army and Navy, and, in addition, with the military forces of our allies. By World War II, advances in the science of warfare had made this imperative. Not only had land and sea forces acquired range and speeds far greater than ever before, but a third major force, airpower, had been introduced. New methods of communication permitted any one of the three forces to work closely with either or both of the others. New amphibious vehicles, at home on land and water, broke former limitations. Parachute and glider operations brought the air and ground forces closer together as did air-ground cooperation in attacking enemy strong points and installations. It was possible to use the combined weight of a nation's armed forces against a single objective or in a coordinated action over a wide area. Germany had employed combined ground-air-sea operations with devastating effects, and if America was to secure victory this blueprint of success had to be followed. This called for teamwork on an unprecedented scale.

The need for a unified command to make the necessary cooperation possible was recognized immediately, and in each theater of operations a single commander was given authority over all armed forces in his area.[14] In their campaigns, theater commanders were able to use not only ground, air, or naval elements singly, but all three together under a single command. General Dwight D. Eisenhower, speaking later of his experiences as Supreme Allied Commander, said: "During those long months in Europe, my associates and I came to understand that in a major conflict there was no such thing as a separate land, sea, or air war. Single purpose and direction and careful balancing of forces were necessary." "We also came to believe," he continued, "that in the broader field of preparation and production of forces, in planning and control of operations, a closely knitted headquarters in Washington would add to material efficiency and economy."[15]

---

[14] Baltimore *Sun*, January 30, 1942. To the *Sun*, no accomplishment since the beginning of the war "exceeds in importance the agreement formally announced today by Secretary of War Stimson, whereby the responsibility for each joint army-navy operation is definitely given to one designated commander, and only to one. It puts an end to the old punctilio whereby the army's responsibilities have traditionally covered the land area, plus exactly so many miles off shore, and the navy's official field of action has been at sea."

[15] Dwight D. Eisenhower: *Crusade in Europe* (Garden City, 1948), p. 58.

This necessity for teamwork in Washington was recognized early in the war. Accordingly, the Joint Chiefs of Staff was created to coordinate the operations of our Armed Forces on a world-wide basis. The United States Joint Chiefs of Staff came into existence as a result of a decision made at the Anglo-American Military Staff Conference in Washington, December 1941-January 1942, to establish the Combined Chiefs of Staff. "Its seven members, four Americans and three Britons, gradually developed an authority and influence exceeded only by the decisive meetings between the President and Prime Minister." [16] The Joint Chiefs of Staff became the American representatives on the Combined Chiefs of Staff and was in a large degree the counterpart of the already existing British Chiefs of Staff Committee.

In addition to its role with the Combined Chiefs of Staffs, the Joint Chiefs of Staff became the principal agency for the coordination of the Army and Navy.[17] Its first meeting as an organized body was held on February 9, 1942. The original members were the Chief of Staff of the Army, the Chief of Naval Operations, the Commander in Chief of the United States Fleet, and the Commanding General of the Army Air Forces. In March, 1942 the duties of the Chief of Naval Operations and the Commander in Chief of the Fleet were combined in one person, but the membership was raised again to four in July when the military adviser of the President was added. From July, 1942 to the conclusion of the war the members of the Joint Chiefs of Staff were General George C. Marshall, Army Chief of Staff, Admiral Ernest King, Chief of Naval Operations, and General Henry H. Arnold, Commander of the Army Air Forces, with Admiral William Leahy, the President's personal representative known as Chief of Staff to the Commander in Chief, as Chairman.[18]

The functions and duties of the Joint Chiefs of Staff were not formally defined during the war. This resulted in great flexibility of organization and the extension of activities to meet the requirements of war. The Joint Chiefs advised the President with regard to military strategy, the requirements, production, and allocations of munitions and shipping, the manpower needs of the Armed

[16] Henry L. Stimson and McGeorge Bundy, *On Active Service in Peace and War*. (New York. Harper Bros., 1948), p. 413.
[17] Watson, *op. cit.*, pp. 280-281.
[18] *U. S. Navy at War*, pp. 89-90.

Forces, and matters of Joint Army-Navy policy. Beside collaborating with the British as part of the Combined Chiefs of Staff, the Joint Chiefs, under the direction of the President, made strategic plans and issued directives to implement them. They were also responsible for the strategic conduct of the war in areas, such as the Pacific, where the United States had primary responsibility.[19]

This agency planned global strategy, coordinated military plans, and doled out available resources so as to maintain each of the military components in a posture of effectiveness. Its unified direction was one of the most important factors enabling the United States, together with the Allies, to defeat first Germany and then Japan. As the Chief Executive's direct military advisers, the Joint Chiefs, in Stimson's opinion, had a most salutary effect on the President's weakness for snap decisions. It certainly "represented a vast improvement over anything that had existed before, and on the whole it was astonishingly successful," said Stimson, but it did contain one fundamental weakness. The Joint Chiefs of Staff "remained incapable of enforcing a decision against the will of any one of its members," and there was always the danger of a bitter conflict which might render its work impotent.[20]

The Mobilization of Manpower

War in Europe and Asia which necessitated the raising of a military establishment of over fifteen million members produced stresses and strains unknown to American history. The vast numbers in uniform added greatly to the demand for war goods and farm products which in turn was reflected by an acute pinch in manpower in both industry and agriculture. Not only did America have to supply its own forces for an unprecedented global war, but the United States also had to serve as an "arsenal of democracy" for the ever growing demands of the Allies.

The United States entered the war years with a population of over 130,000,000. Under the impact of world events legislation was enacted in October, 1940, which established the first peacetime Selective Service System and required registration of all males between the ages of 21 and 35. In August, 1941, four months before Pearl Harbor, deferment was granted to all over 28 years of age, and all those of that age who had been inducted were re-

---

[19] *Ibid.*, Stimson and Bundy, *op. cit.*, pp. 413-414.
[20] Stimson and Bundy, *op. cit.*, pp. 414, 515-516.

leased from service. With the advent of Pearl Harbor there was a direct about-face, and on December 20, 1941 legislation was passed requiring the registration of males between the ages of 18 and 64, with military liability for those from 20 to 44. In November, 1942 registrants between the ages of 18 and 44 were declared liable for military service, but in December of the same year the armed forces set their upper age limit for inductees at 38.[21]

By a Presidential Executive Order on September 29, 1940, Lieutenant Colonel Lewis B. Hershey was named to carry out the provisions of the Selective Service Act. On July 31, 1941 he was named Director of Selective Service and in this position he rose to the rank of Major General. The Selective Service Act was enacted with the primary objective of obtaining men for military service, but it must also be recognized that the act also had the responsibility for the deferment of those necessary to the national economy. It was largely administered (under the rather loose control of the States) from Washington, a majority of the workers being voluntary, unpaid civilians. This decentralized system was deliberately adopted to place the responsibility for selection for military service squarely on the community in which the selectee lived.[22]

Until January, 1943 only the Army made calls for inductees. So many voluntary enlistments were made specifically for the Navy or the Army Air Forces that the only source of manpower for the ground arms were draftees or rejected volunteers. This situation led to the cessation of voluntary enlistments in December, 1942, all service personnel being furnished by the Selective Service from January, 1943 to October, 1945 when voluntary enlistment was renewed.[23]

Depletion of manpower in the lower age brackets became more pronounced as the war progressed and with but 100,000 youths becoming 18 years of age each month, age limits and physical standards were adjusted to make the supply fit the demand. In general, when the military situation was critical the

---

[21] Hacker and Zahler, *op. cit.*, p. 502; Stimson and Bundy, *op. cit.*, pp. 473-474. There was considerable reluctance to permit the drafting of those under 20, but as General Marshall noted in 1945, "men of 18, 19, and 20 make our finest soldiers." *Ibid.*

[22] *Selective Service in Peacetime, First Report of the Director of Selective Service*, (Washington: G.P.O., 1942), pp. 110-115. The principle of Selective Service was first employed in the Confederacy in April, 1862.

[23] Hacker and Zahler, *op. cit.*, p. 502.

armed forces would relent somewhat on both age and physical standards, but when it was estimated that fewer than usual were necessary the age limit would come down and physical standards would go up.

One means of relieving the drain on the nation's manpower was the utilization of women in the armed forces. The Women's Army Auxiliary Corps (WAAC) was established in May, 1942, under Mrs. Oveta Culp Hobby. Its designation was changed to Women's Army Corps (WAC) in 1943 and with Colonel Hobby as its head its total numbers reached 100,000. Women for the Navy were recruited under the banners of the Women Appointed for Voluntary Emergency Service (WAVES), under Lieutenant Commander Mildred McAfee, which had its beginnings in July, 1942.[24] The women entered military service on a voluntary basis restricted to noncombatant activity. More than 200,000 women performed technical, clerical, and mechanical duties which released men for combat.[25] It was a pleasure for Admiral King to report "that in addition to their having earned an excellent reputation as a part of the Navy, they have become an inspiration to all hands in naval uniform." [26]

Accentuating the manpower shortage and alarming to the military establishment, not only because of its wartime needs but also because of its future implications, was the large number of rejections under the operation of the draft. The manpower not used or not usable to the armed forces in World War II was reflected in Class IV-F of the Selective Service System. The total of these through August 1, 1945, was 4,828,000. This total is broken down into four classifications. Those rejected for manifestly disqualifying defects numbered 510,500. Rejections for mental diseases constituted 856,200, a factor which climbed at an increasing rate throughout the war, and 76,300 were rejected for nonmedical causes. The largest number of rejections were for physical defects, these totalling 2,708,700.[27]

---

[24] The use of women in war was not something new. "There had been 'marinettes,' 'yeomanettes,' Army nurses, Navy nurses, Signal Corps telephone operators, Motor Corps drivers, and others in the first World War. None, however, had actually been in the military, and high officials relinquished male monopoly in the second World War only with reluctance and under pressure." James E. Barnes: *Wealth of the American People,* (New York: Prentice-Hall, 1949), p. 815. Women in the Marine Corps were simply called Marines.

[25] Hacker and Zahler, *op. cit.,* p. 502.

[26] *U. S. Navy at War,* p. 30.

[27] *Selective Service and Victory, Fourth Report of the Director of Selective Service,* (Washington: G.P.O., 1948), p. 666.

National Objectives and Strategy

Though America suffered an initial humiliating defeat at the hands of the Japanese, the main force of the American war effort was not directed at the overthrow of the Empire of Nippon, but rather at crushing Hitler's Germany. This policy was consistently followed throughout the war with campaigns in the Pacific being considered holding operations while the main force of Allied effort was directed at Germany.

This grand strategy had been laid down before America's entrance into the war, and it was quite apparent that the major national objectives of the United States related to military policy could be broadly stated as the

> preservation of the territorial, economic and ideological integrity of the United States and the remainder of the Western Hemisphere; prevention of the further extension of Japanese territorial domination; eventual establishment in Europe and Asia of balances of power which will most nearly ensure political stability in those regions and the future security of the United States.[28]

In the eventuality of American participation in war, it had been understood that the United States would in all probability have to fight a war on two fronts. American and British staff planners had engaged in a series of conferences from January 29 to March 27, 1941 to discuss the subject of Anglo-American cooperation should the United States be compelled to resort to war.[29] The underlying assumptions on which the discussions hinged are clearly stated in the report of the conference:

> The Staff Conference assumes that when the United States becomes involved in war with Germany, it will at the same time engage in war with Italy. In those circumstances, the possibility of a state of war arising between Japan, and an association of the United States, the British Commonwealth and its Allies . . . must be taken into account . . . Since Germany is the predominant member of the Axis Powers, the Atlantic and European area is considered to be the decisive theatre. The principal United

---

[28] A memorandum of Stark and Marshall, Sept., 1941, as quoted in Edgar A. Mowrer: *The Nightmare of American Foreign Policy*, (New York: 1949), p. 125. An earlier appraisal of American objectives had been produced by the War Plans Division in July, 1941, which called for the defense of the Monroe Doctrine, aid to Britain, efforts to restrain Japan in the Far East, and freedom of the seas. "The principal theater of operations is Europe, but other possible theaters may later appear desirable. The defeat of our potential enemies is primarily dependent on the defeat of Germany." Watson, *op. cit.*, p. 353.

[29] Charles A. Beard: *President Roosevelt and the Coming of the War, 1941* (Yale University Press, 1948), p. 432.

States military effort will be exerted in that theatre, and operations of United States forces in other theatres will be conducted in such a manner as to facilitate that effort.[30]

With primary attention on the European theater this necessarily meant close ties and cooperation with the Soviet Union, the only nation at the time which had important ground forces opposing Germany. Cooperation with Russia played an ever more important role in shaping the thinking of the Roosevelt Administration to make a determined effort to placate the Russian Bear. The President was convinced of the necessity of assuring Stalin of our fullest cooperation, and of avoiding the slightest cause of offense to the Kremlin.[81]

In the opinion of Thomas A. Bailey, Hitler's fatal attack on "the Mongol halfwits" of Russia effected an overnight revolution in American public opinion. On June 21, 1941, Stalin was a cynical, self-seeking, ruthless aggressor; on June 22 he was an ally —a very welcome ally—of those who were seeking to halt Hitlerism. Sweeping promises of American aid were sent to Russia, loans were made available, and on November 6, 1941, Stalin was pledged the sum of one billion dollars in Lend-Lease.[82]

Despite Russia's plight, President Roosevelt failed to exact any *quid pro quo* for the generous American assistance that was pouring to the relief of the hard pressed Red Armies. The hope of the Chief Executive was that in the end "if we gave Stalin everything he asked for, if we treated him with the greatest possible generosity, if we treated him as if he were a great gentleman, that in the end Stalin would turn out to be a peace loving democrat and all the problems of the world would be solved." [33]

Numerous conferences were held with the Russians during the course of the war at which problems of military strategy and postwar international organizations were discussed, but preoccupation

---

[30] *Joint Congressional Committee Reports on Pearl Harbor,* part 15, pp. 1489 ff. Hereafter cited as *JCCR*. For further elaboration on this point see *JCCR*, part 26, p. 264 f.

[81] Forrest Davis: "What Really Happened at Teheran," *Saturday Evening Post,* May 13, 1944.

[32] Bailey, *op. cit.,* p. 781. According to Bernard Baruch, without Lend-Lease from America the Red Army would not have been able to drive the Germans from Russia. *Saturday Evening Post,* June 12, 1948. See also Sherwood, *op. cit.*

[33] House Committee on Un-American Activities, *Testimony of Hon. William C. Bullitt, March 24, 1947,* p. 10. Forrest Davis, a journalist who had access to the White House during this period, outlined the President's policy in an article in the *Saturday Evening Post,* April 10, 1943, entitled "Roosevelt's World Blueprint."

with the war caused the administration to postpone decision on many fundamental issues on which agreement had not been reached with Russia.[34] One is of course tempted to speculate on what the fate of the postwar world would have been if the Roosevelt administration had not postponed the settling of fundamental questions when Russia was in dire straits and desperately needed American aid.

The Price of Victory

By the end of the war in Europe the Army was over twice the size of the American Expeditionary Forces of World War I. In 1918 the United States had an Army of 4,057,101 of whom 2,086,000 had served overseas.[35] In May, 1945, the comparable figures, including the WAC, were 8,291,336 and 5,472,282.[36] Even with our overwhelming air and firepower, the war had been the most costly of any in which the Nation had been engaged. Army casualties from Pearl Harbor to June 30, 1945 included 570,783 [37] wounded 201,367 killed, 114,205 prisoners, and 56,-867 missing.[38]

In the past wars it had been the practice to organize as many divisions as possible, fight those divisions until casualties reduced them to bare skeletons, then withdraw them from the line and rebuild them in a rear area. The system in World War II involved individual replacements fed from training centers to the divisions to keep them at full strength. Under this plan 89 divisions of ground troops and 273 combat air groups were kept at full strength.[39]

The training of our vast Army, as well as provision of depot facilities for the overseas theaters, required the construction of

---

[34] Vera M. Dean: *The United States and Russia*, (New York: Scribners and Sons, 1949), p. 22.

[35] *Cf.* Chapter 16.

[36] *The War Reports of Marshall, Arnold, King.* (New York: J. B. Lippincott Co., 1947), pp. 264-274. Hereafter cited as *War Reports*.

[37] "The loss of wounded after treatment at dressing stations was only three per cent, half that of World War I. This saving of life was due to the use of blood plasma and whole blood on the battlefield to reduce shock, to the 'miracle' drugs pencillin and sulfanilmide, and to the practice of air evacuation to hospitals." Leland D. Baldwin: *Recent American History*, (New York: American Book Co., 1954), p. 395.

[38] *War Reports*, p. 274.

[39] *Ibid.*, p. 267. The huge size of the Armed Forces and the problems arising from coalition warfare led to the creation of two new ranks, General of the Army and Fleet Admiral. Baldwin, *op. cit.*, p. 395.

about 3700 post or cantonment installations of varying sizes and descriptions in the United States. The Army Service Forces accomplished a prodigious task in the supply of food, clothing, munitions, and transportation which involved the operation of a fleet of 1,537 ships, the handling of 7,370,000 men, and 101,750,000 measurement tons of cargo.[40]

The Nation's weapons upon the outbreak of war were all inferior quantitatively, and in some cases qualitatively, to those of the Axis Powers, but the vastly superior industrial establishment of the United States eventually overcame the initial advantage of the enemy. During the last two years of the war the Army was so well armed and equipped that it was able to mount operations in various corners of the globe with a strategic inferiority in numbers. Air and sea superiority, plus mobility and firepower made possible tactical superiority at the points chosen for attack.[41]

This largest Army in our history made a tremendous contribution to total victory, but a very heavy cost was exacted for its years of neglect. Fresh laurels, from Guadalcanal to the Elbe, had been added to the Army's banners. Nevertheless, the price of these dearly won wreaths of victory was a reflection upon those who had allowed the Army to deteriorate following World War I.

The Wide Blue Yonder

In many respects, airpower played a dominating role in the far flung areas of combat in World War II. Certainly the United States Army Air Forces developed one of the largest and most effective striking forces the world had ever seen. The Army Air Forces dropped 641,201 tons of bombs upon Germany proper and 502,781 tons were sent on their mission of destruction to the Japanese homeland. In the course of its operations the Air Forces flew a total of 2,362,800 combat sorties.[42] The personnel and planes required to carry out the missions of the Army Air Forces were indeed stupendous. At the peak of its strength in March, 1944, it numbered 2,411,294, including 306,889 officers. Between July, 1940 and August, 1945 the Air Force acquired 158,880 aircraft, of which 47,050 were fighters, and the rest bombers and trainers. A total of 65,164 aircraft were lost, both at home and

---

[40] *War Reports,* p. 285.
[41] *War Reports,* p. 255.
[42] The Army Air Forces dropped a total of 2,057,244 tons of bombs. *The Aircraft Yearbook* for 1946, p. 77. A sortie is one flight by one plane.

abroad, and the Army Air Forces suffered 121,867 casualties, 40,061 being fatalities.[43]

Here indeed was vindication of the crucial role and importance of airpower as advanced by such prophets as General Mitchell and the Italian military writer, General Giulio Douhet. Mistakes were made; strategic bombing was a new military weapon, and we had to learn many things as we went along;[44] and indeed, in some instances, interest in strategic bombing led it to neglect tactical support of ground troops. Neither was the Air Force able to "deliver on its promise to drop bombs in pickle-barrels, and before the end of the war it was utilizing 'saturation' bombing." [45]

But German generals, manufacturers, party men, and transportation experts saw our air domination as the root of their disaster, particularly in the incessant bleeding of their industry by strategic bombing, especially the oil campaign and the cumulative dislocation of transportation.[46]

In appraising the part of the Army Air Forces in bringing victory to the Pacific, General Arnold felt "that our air power's part may fairly be called decisive." The collapse of Japan, in the view of the Commanding General of the Air Forces, vindicated the strategic concept of offensive operations in the Far East. This strategy had been to advance airpower to the point where a full scale air attack could be launched upon the homeland of Japan, with the possibility that such attack would bring about the defeat of Japan without invasion, and with the certainty that it would play a vital role in preparation for, and cooperation with, an invasion. No invasion was necessary.[47]

In his report of 1945 General Arnold laid down what he conceived to be some of the lessons of the war as applied to airpower. War was no longer something restricted to battle lines, but it extends to the innermost parts of a nation. Therefore, our population, industrial, and governmental centers were open to surprise, devastating attacks which made air superiority an imperative for

[43] Aircraft Yearbook for 1946, pp. 80, 81. Total overseas strength reached a total of 1,224,006, including 163,886 officers in April, 1945.
[44] *War Reports*, p. 435.
[45] Baldwin, *op. cit.*, pp. 397-398.
[46] *War Reports*, pp. 435-436. "Krupp von Bohlen told interrogating officers that the production capacity of the Krupp plants when the American overran the territory was exactly zero." Lewis H. Brereton: *The Brereton Diaries*, (New York: William Morrow & Co., 1946), p. 426.
[47] *War Reports*, p. 437.

effective defense. The Air Force alone would not be sufficient, but without it there could be no national security.[48]

The General Arnold urged the maintenance of a striking air arm in being, continued scientific research and development, support of commercial air transportation, overseas bases, close co-operation with the Army and Navy, and an expansible Air Force and aviation industry. He also reminded the country of the historical lessons of the past, for the people of the United States, "peace-loving and hoping for world-wide acceptance of our concept of democracy, having never sponsored a strong peace-time military organization. History has demonstrated that we have thereby neither avoided war nor deterred others from going to war."[49]

Second to None

"Japan lost the war because she lost command of the sea, and in doing so lost—to us—the island bases from which her factories and cities could be destroyed by air." Thus Admiral King asserted the traditional importance of naval power and the role of the United States Navy in bringing victory to America in Asia. Sea power was also important in the European theater, because of the necessity of transmitting our entire military effort across the Atlantic and supporting it there. Without command of the sea, this could not have been done.[50]

In accomplishing the far-flung missions of the sea arm of our military establishment, the United States built the greatest Navy in the history of the world, and the rule of Britannia was replaced by Columbia.[51] To man this huge armada the Navy increased its

---

[48] *Ibid.,* pp. 452-53. "Today, Japanese and German cities lie in ruins, but they merely suggest the vast destruction that can be done with the weapons of tomorrow. The first target of a potential aggressor might well be our industrial system or our major centers of population. If the United States is to be secure in the future, we must never relinquish the means of preventing such a blow." *Ibid.,* p. 454.

[49] *War Reports,* pp. 454-456.

[50] *U. S. Navy at War,* p. 167.

[51] The following table shows the growth of the U. S. Navy from December, 1941 to October, 1945:

	1941	Sunk	Built	1945
Battleships	17	2	8	23
Aircraft Carriers	7	5	27	28
Escort Carriers	...	6	110	70
Cruisers	37	10	48	72
Destroyers	172	71	349	373
Destroyer Escorts	...	11	412	365
Submarines	113	52	203	240

personnel from a total of 420,522 in 1941 to 4,063,458 at the end of hostilities.[52] The Navy's air arm was also the scene of great expansion with about 70,000 pilots being trained for the Navy and Marine Corps. At the end of war it had approximately 22,000 combat aircraft.[53]

The outstanding development of this war, in the field of joint undertakings, was the perfection of amphibious operations, the most difficult of all operations in modern warfare.[54] The modern doctrines and techniques of amphibious warfare were developed by the Marine Corps during the period between the two World Wars and perfected by them during World War II.[55] The United States developed during the war more amphibious knowledge, skill, and equipment than any other country in the world. In addition to the doctrine developed by the Marines before the war, the subject was also studied and war-gamed by the Army at its Command and General Staff School. Marine and Army divisions on the Pacific Coast practised embarkations and amphibious assaults during the training period in 1940-42, and very intensive and large-scale amphibious exercises were conducted by Army and Navy elements in the Mediterranean area and in England prior to the invasion of the Continent.[56] Since the war, amphibious instruction has been given in the Armed Forces Staff College at Norfolk and at the Marine Corps Amphibious Training Centers in Virginia and California.

Under the impetus of and during the European War, the Joint Army-Navy Board proposed the formation of two task forces for amphibious training. The First Joint Training Force, later known as Amphibious Force, Atlantic Fleet, consisted of the 1st Marine Division and the Army's 1st Infantry Division under the command of Marine Major General Holland M. Smith. The Second Joint Training Force, later designated as Amphibious Force, Pacific Fleet, was composed of the 2nd Marine Division and the

---

Small craft constructed (mine layers, patrol boats, landing craft, etc.) totalled 109,786. *U. S. Navy at War,* pp. 252-284. Discrepancies in the above table are due to Lend-Lease, change in category, etc.

[53] *Ibid.,* pp. 20, 217, 221, 222. The breakdown in the Navy's strength in 1945 is as follows: Navy—3,408,347; Marine Corps—484,631; Coast Guard—170,480.

[53] *Ibid.,* pp..225-231.

[54] *Ibid.,* p. 171.

[55] Jeter A. Iseley and Philip Crowl: *The United States Marines and Amphibious War,* (Princeton U. Press, 1951), p. 3.

[56] Tansill, *op. cit.,* p. 593.

3rd Infantry Division both, under the command of Marine Major General C. B. Vogel. Unity of command was exercised by the commanders in chief of the respective fleets.[57] The 1st and 2nd Marine Divisions, pioneers in amphibious training, successfully assaulted during the war in the Pacific, the beaches at Guadalcanal, Tarawa, Saipan, Tinian, Peleliu, and Okinawa.

Admiral King was convinced the war had amply vindicated a basic concept of the Navy, conceived some twenty-five years ago, "Naval aviation is and must always be an integral and primary component of the fleet." This necessarily involved the plea for the aircraft carrier as a major and vital element of naval strength. The only weakness of the carrier was its vulnerability which demanded the support of other naval vessels, and thereby placed an additional premium on the flexibility and balance of the fleet. The balanced fleet is the effective fleet.[58]

The reports of General Arnold and Admiral King seemed to lay the groundwork for further controversy over the respective roles of air and sea power. Another element in the argument was to appear on August 6, 1945, when the first atomic bomb was dropped on the city of Hiroshima thus opening the atomic age.

The Arsenal of Democracy

Global war meant an unprecedented demand upon the American industrial machine. Previous efforts to gear the economy to the demands of Lend-Lease and rearmament had not been too successful largely because the nation was still at peace and unwilling to accept the drastic measures necessary for the smooth running of a war economy.[59] Pearl Harbor shook the nation out of its lethargy; effective administrative procedures were now possible.[60]

Under new authority granted by Congress President Roosevelt

---

[57] Greenfield, Palmer, and Wiley, *The Organization of Ground Combat Troops,* (Washington, G.P.O., 1947), pp. 86-87.

[58] *U. S. Navy at War,* p. 170.

[59] *Cf.* Chapter 18.

[60] The War Powers Act of December 18, 1941 authorized the President to redistribute the tasks of the several boards and agencies for a more efficient prosecution of the war. "Existing laws were liberalized to facilitate the governments' procurement of essential supplies, while the Trading-with-the-Enemy Act of 1917 was brought up to date to give the President control over all communications and the right to use property confiscated from the enemy or enemy aliens." Oscar T. Barck and Nelson M. Blake: *Since 1900,* (New York: Macmillan Co., revised edition, 1952), p. 670.

created the War Production Board in January, 1942, with Donald Nelson as its chairman. Nelson was told by the Chief Executive that our fate and that of our Allies—our liberties, our honor and our substance—depended upon American Industry.[61] Nelson's chief task, then, was to increase production and to secure adequate supplies for the demands of the war industries.

Stemming from the War Production Board, a bewildering hierarchy of agencies was set up. On May 28, 1943 these were merged into the Office of War Mobilization headed by James F. Byrnes. This agency was described as the nearest thing to an orderly planning committee for the home front that had yet been devised.[62] The strains of economic mobilization and the clash of personalities[63] seemed at times to indicate failure and mismanagement of American industry,[64] but this was not a true barometer of the tremendous flow of goods from American factories and plants.

American war production in 1940 was small; in 1942 it equalled the production of Germany, Italy, and Japan combined. In 1943 it was one and one-half times as great as total Axis war production, and in 1944 twice as great.[65] Translated into terms of munitions and equipment this meant that the production of 23,228 aircraft in the period July 1, 1940 to December, 1941 rose to 96,359 in 1944, and for the same period tanks soared from a total of 4,258 to 17,565, while machine guns climbed from 126,113 to 798,782.[66] This was a war not only of men, but also of

---

[61] Morison and Commager, *op. cit.*, Vol. II, p. 679. This supplanted the Council of National Defense composed by the President and key Cabinet members.

[62] Among the more important were the Small War Plants Corporation, two hundred Industry Advisory Committees, Rubber Administration, Board of Economic Warfare, Foreign Economic Administration, and Office of Economic Stabilization. Barck and Blake, *op. cit.*, pp. 670-672. Associated with Byrnes, whose powers were so great he was dubbed the "Assistant President," were Stimson, Knox, Hopkins, Nelson, and Fred Vinson.

[63] Among the most spectacular was the clash between the Vice President, Henry A. Wallace, chairman of the Board of Economic Warfare, and Jesse Jones, Secretary of Commerce. As a result of this feud the Board of Economic Warfare was abolished and the Office of Economic Warfare under Leo Crowley was created. Jones later claimed that Wallace's performance cost him his renomination as Vice President in 1944. Jesse H. Jones and Edward Angly: *Fifty Billion Dollars*, (New York: Macmillan Co., 1951), pp. 485-511.

[64] A Senate Committee to investigate the national defense program was established under the chairmanship of Harry S. Truman.

[65] Barck and Blake, *op. cit.*, p. 680.

[66] Morison and Commager, *op. cit.*, Vol. II, p. 680.

machines. American industrial production played a significant role in final victory.

The Atomic Age

The use of atomic energy for military purposes had been the subject of study in the United States since 1939 when President Roosevelt was convinced by the arguments of Alexander Sachs and Albert Einstein that if the United States did not at once embark upon atomic research, Germany might soon rule the world.[67] In December, 1941, the Office of Scientific Research, headed by Dr. Vannevar Bush, decided to make an all-out attempt to develop atomic energy for military purposes. With great secrecy and under the direction of the War Department the construction of the atomic bomb went ahead. "The entire purpose was the production of a military weapon; on no other ground could the wartime expenditure of so much time and money have been justified."[68] Employment of those engaged in atomic research and development reached a peak of 125,000, and two billion dollars were spent on the greatest scientific gamble in history.[69]

The decision to drop the atomic bomb on Japan was a purely military one,[70] and its results were decisive. The first A-bomb was dropped on Hiroshima on August 6, 1945, resulting in the loss of 80,000 lives. Two days later Russia invaded Manchuria, and on the following day the second bomb was dropped on Nagasaki. The Japanese promptly sued for peace.[71]

What would be the impact of this new engine of destruction upon the American military establishment? Certainly changes would have to be made, but technology does not eliminate the need for men in war. The number of men that were involved in the delivery of the atomic bomb on Hiroshima was tremendous. General Marshall also warned America "not to fall victim to over-confidence. This tremendous discovery will not be ours exclusively indefinitely." To General Arnold the influence of atomic energy on airpower could be stated very simply. "It has made Air Power all important. Air Power provides not only the best present means

---

[67] Baldwin, *op. cit.*, pp. 403-404.
[68] Stimson and Bundy, *op. cit.*, pp. 612-613. For a discussion of atomic power see Vannevar Bush: *Modern Arms and Free Men*, (New York: Simon and Schuster, 1949).
[69] Statement of President Truman, New York *Times*, August 6, 1945.
[70] Stimson and Bundy, *op. cit.*, pp. 624-633.
[71] Baldwin, *op. cit.*, p. 497.

of striking an enemy with atomic bombs, but also the best available protection against the misuse of atomic explosives." [72]

World War II very clearly emphasized that hostilities had grown steadily more destructive and more costly. Man's ability to release atomic energy meant also man's ability to destroy himself. The bombs on Hiroshima and Nagasaki ended the war, and they also made it wholly clear, said Mr. Stimson, "that we must never have another war. This is the lesson that men and leaders everywhere must learn, and I believe that when they learn it they will find a way to lasting peace. There is no other choice." [73]

The year 1945 also ushered in the establishment of the United Nations at San Francisco on June 26, 1945. [74] The atomic bomb and the United Nations were to be pivots of American policy in the forthcoming years, but neither could be a substitute for an effective military policy. The war had vanquished the threat of fascism, but in its stead there arose militant communism and a host of postwar problems. Immediate problems of reconversion, unification, occupation forces, and demobilization were to be faced by the nation. America had emerged from her previous wars with an acute revulsion against this savage form of human behavior, and the nation had confused military preparedness with the causes of war. In each case she had then proceeded to drift into another catastrophe. George Washington had cautioned against this error in 1793 when he told Congress: "There is a rank due to the United States among nations, which will be withheld, if not absolutely lost, by the reputation of weakness—if we desire to avoid insult we must be ready to repel it; if we desire to secure peace it must be known that we are at all times ready for war." [75]

---

[72] *War Reports*, pp. 255, 293, 462.
[73] Henry L. Stimson as quoted in Stimson and Bundy, *op. cit.*, p. 633.
[74] Ruhl J. Bartlett (ed.) *The Record of American Diplomacy*, (New York: Alfred A. Knopf, 1947), p. 676.
[75] *War Reports*, pp. 289, 300.

CHAPTER 20

Demobilization and Unification

The Mighty War Machine is Dismantled—Universal Military Training and the Draft—The Case for Unification— The Navy's Case—A Compromise Emerges—Changes Are Found Necessary

CERTAIN differences may be noted in the America emerging from two world wars. In 1918 there was a strong desire for "normalcy," but the participants of World War II had little opportunity to evade the chaos left in the wake of war. While the League of Nations had occasioned a bitter, partisan political debate, the United Nations was enthusiastically accepted by Country and Congress. Both wars left a host of problems on the international and domestic scene, and demobilization was the central theme.

The Mighty War Machine is Dismantled

Seven times since 1775 the United States had begun wars with an inadequate Army, built a fighting force in a race against time, and emerged victorious. After each war, the military establishment was dismantled with as much agility as it was increased, and with as little regard for the obvious lessons learned. At the beginning of 1945 America had a fighting force of over 11,000,-000 spread over the four corners of the world. On May 8, 1945, the Third Reich surrendered and the first phase of demobilization began.[1] The war in Asia was yet to be won and the military might of the United States was to be shifted from the European theater to the Pacific.

The partial demobilization following victory in Europe was based upon the military requirements necessary to defeat Japan. The War Department estimated it would still need a force of 6,968,000 which was a reduction of a little over 1,300,000 men. The troops to be demobilized would be separated from the service

[1] The *Army Navy Journal*, May 12, 1945, printed a War Department announcement to the effect that 1,300,000 officers, men, and members of the WAC would be released in a year.

under a point system which had been developed "to insure that those men who had been overseas longest and have fought hardest and those who have children, get first consideration in demobilization." [2]

Under the War Department plan it was estimated that 400,000 troops would be needed for the occupation of Germany and a total strength of a little less than 7,000,000 would be required for that task and the destruction of the Japanese Empire. In order to discharge as many long service combat troops as possible, and still keep up the strength of the Army, the continuance of Selective Service calls was urged. In the interests of fair play, discharges would be based upon standards applying equally to all theaters of war. The War Department, according to the New York *Herald Tribune,* of May 7, 1945, deserved high praise for its sober, factual and convincing statement of policy concerning redeployment of the Army after victory in Europe.

A more critical attitude, however, was soon to be evident. Even before the defeat of Japan there was some discontent among the troops and public over the demobilization policy despite explanations from the War Department that lack of shipping and the urgency of proceeding with the Pacific war were the actual factors slowing up releases. Sharp criticism came from Capitol Hill where Senator Edwin C. Johnson of Colorado described the Army's policies as being "blind, stupid and criminal." [3]

With the Japanese acceptance of surrender terms on August 14, 1945, the cry to "bring the boys home" reached a deafening volume. The American public, as reflected in the press,[4] agitated for the immediate release of the combat veterans already in the United States and those coming home from Europe bound for the Far East. Bowing to this pressure, President Truman made a

[2] War Department *Press Release,* May 5, 1945. Point totals were computed on the basis of the following four factors: 1. Service—1 point for each month of Army service since September 16, 1940; 2. Overseas service—1 point for each month served overseas since September 16, 1940; 3. Combat credit—5 points for each decoration and combat participation star; 4. Parenthood—12 points for each child under 18 up to a limit of three children. The first total announced as necessary for the discharge of enlisted men was 85 points.
[3] *Army-Naval Journal,* August 11, 1945.
[4] The record of demobilization was "appalling" to the Chicago *Tribune,* September 8, 1945; while the New York *Daily Worker,* September 21, 1945, reported "the American people are properly impatient with the slow progress being made in demobilizing our armed forces"; and the Denver *Post,* September 3, 1945, stated: "The quickest and fullest possible demobilization of the Armed Forces is the nation's number 1 job now."

special broadcast to the nation and the Armed Forces overseas promising most of them would be released as soon as the "ships and planes can get you here." [5]

Some few, however, protested against "the pressures for drastic acceleration in demobilization" which threatened to wreck the military establishment. It was difficult for the New York *Herald Tribune* (September 17) to see how the armed forces could be broken up "by indiscriminate withdrawals without inviting serious dangers and jeopardizing that victory which has been so dearly bought."

The War Department quickly lowered its point discharge level to 80 and announced the discharge of enlisted personnel 35 years of age or over who had two years of service. "The War Department," commented the Denver *Post,* on September 5, "undoubtedly understands that if it doesn't liberalize and speed up its discharge system, drastic congressional action to chop down the size of the armed forces is likely." Continuing agitation finally forced the War Department to abandon "the point system for discharges by late winter and all men with two years service were to be released." [6]

On the 25th of September President Truman asked Congress to slash more than $28,500,000,000 from military appropriations, and he gave assurances that the Army would be reduced to 1,950,000 men by June, 1946. Two days later Robert P. Patterson, who had succeeded Stimson as Secretary of War, warned of the necessity of retaining enough military strength to enforce the surrender of Germany and Japan, but pledged not to keep any more men than were needed in the service. "If future events permit it," the Army would be reduced even lower than the 1,950,000 total presaged by the President. But Congress, as well as the people, insisted upon immediate action. Public pressure forced the frantic Congressional leaders to initiate a series of measures arbitrarily regulating and hastening military discharges. [7]

[5] New York *Times,* September 3, 1945.

[6] Seattle *Daily Times,* September 20, 1945. Additional pressure on the War Department was added by General MacArthur's statement of September 17, that "smooth progress" of the occupation of Japan made possible a "drastic cut" in the number of troops originally estimated. New York *Times,* September 17, 1945.

[7] New Orleans *Times-Picayune,* September 13, 1945. "Members of Congress," in the opinion of the Seattle *Daily Times,* September 24, 1945, "are the principal thorn in the side of the Army and Navy. The public, to be sure, is responsible for the heavy mail which is flowing into Capitol Hill."

Further pressure was provided by a demonstration of 20,000 soldiers on January 6, 1946 in Manila, claiming that the Philippines were capable of handling their own internal problems. This gathering was scored by the Chicago *Tribune* of January 8, 1946 as an inexcusable violation of military discipline and of doubtful merit as a means by which the men could bring their predicament to the attention of the people back home. But the cause of the troops overseas was taken up by Eleanor Roosevelt who, writing from London, viewed their complaints as "very logical." The troops she talked to felt there was some "injustice in the way people are sent home" and also "a great many of them feel that more men are kept in the area than are really needed for the work and that this is done by officers who find their jobs not too unpleasant and like to have a good number of men under them." [8]

On March 13, 1946 the War Department, always sensitive to pressure, announced that the Army's planned strength for July 1, 1947 was 1,070,000 officers and men, of whom 400,000 would be in the Air Force. This would require a reduction of almost 500,000 from the July 1, 1946 figure of 1,550,000, and there was no assurance of meeting the obligations assigned to the Army without a continuation of Selective Service. [9] The same day Secretary of State James Byrnes outlined a pessimistic picture of world conditions before the House Military Affairs Committee, with Secretary of War Patterson and General Eisenhower calling for an extension of the draft to insure the projected Army goal of 1,070,000. [10]

Universal Military Training and the Draft

During the war years there had been considerable sentiment for providing a postwar system of universal military training. The New York *Times* declared "such a law is essential, and the time to adopt it is now." [11] The two wartime Secretaries of the Navy, Knox and Forrestal, urged the adoption of a system of compulsory mili-

---

[8] Eleanor Roosevelt to Dwight D. Eisenhower, January 12, 1946. Appendix X, p. 480 in John C. Sparrow: "History of Personnel Demobilization in the United States Army," (Washington: Office of Chief of Military History, Manuscript, 1951).

[9] War Department *Press Release,* March 13, 1946.

[10] *Facts on File,* March 10-16, 1946.

[11] September 1, 1943. The *Times* of November 17, 1943 reported a Gallup poll survey on the question as showing "what used to be a substantial majority against such a system of service in peacetime has now become a top-heavy majority of more than two to one in favor of it."

tary training as did General Marshall and Secretary Stimson. "We believe there is widespread popular support for it which needs only to be rallied by the President in order to become politically effective." [12]

As the war drew to its conclusion, a group of prominent educators, including the Presidents of Yale, Dartmouth, M.I.T., Amherst, and Lafayette, addressed a letter to President Roosevelt urging immediate consideration of the question rather than postponing the decision until the end of the war. "We know too well the reaction which occurs after a conflict is over; the general desire to forget it." These sentiments found support with the American Legion, which pressed for a full and frank public discussion. [13]

With the end of the war in Europe the tempo of the drive for universal military training picked up. Testifying before the House Military Affairs Committee on June 15, 1945, Secretary Stimson declared the concept of the United Nations contemplated the use of force to restrain aggression. As a prime factor in this world organization, the United States could not neglect to provide the means to implement this blueprint of world peace. General Eisenhower expressed the opinion that in any serious test of military strength "the quicker the maximum potential can be converted into tactical power, the surer the victory and the less the cost." On July 5, the Post War Military Policy Committee of the House of Representatives, endorsed the broad principle of universal military training and recommended the adoption of legislation to put the program into effect. [14]

In his last annual report as Chief of Staff, General Marshall took up the question of our future military policy and in particular the question of universal military training. To General Marshall, military strength depended upon a large number of men trained in the science of war. There were two methods available for the defense of the country. The first was based upon a large professional Army which Marshall opposed as being too expensive and running counter to America's traditions. The alternative was a relatively small, highly mobile, professional Army and a large, well-trained citizen reserve. Past experience, he asserted, with the

---

[12] New York *Times,* January 15, 1944, June 28, 1944, November 18, 1944.
[13] *Ibid.,* February 10 and 18, 1945. For a contemporary wartime discussion of universal military training see Edward A. Fitzpatrick: *Universal Military Training,* (New York: McGraw Hill, Inc., 1945).
[14] New York *Times,* June 16 and July 6, 1945.

National Guard, Citizen's Military Training Camps, and the Reserve Officers Training Corps demonstrated that a suitably large reserve could not be built up by such means. The establishment of universal military training would not mean the abolition of these units. It would, on the contrary, strengthen them. Universal military training would provide the reservoir from which they would draw new strength. "Only by universal military training," Marshall concluded, "can full vigor and life be instilled into the Reserve system." [15]

In a message to Congress on September 6, 1945, President Truman called for a continuance of Selective Service for men between 18 and 25 for a two-year term of service. He also informed Congress of impending messages with respect to a comprehensive and continuous program of national security, including a universal training program, unification of the armed forces, and the use and control of atomic energy.[16]

The President's promise of a program for universal military training was fulfilled on October 23, 1945, when he addressed a joint session of Congress. The Chief Executive asked for the enactment of a one-year program for all males of 18 years, or upon graduation from high school, and this training should be taken before they reach 20 whether physically qualified for actual combat service or not. Upon completion of the year of training, in cluding instruction in the use of weapons and mechanical skills, the youths would become members of the general reserves for six years, after which they would move into the "secondary reserve." This program, emphasized the President, was not conscription, and its objective was to train citizens for duty in a possible national emergency.[17]

To the New York *Herald Tribune* (October 24, 1945) the message "may well stand in the future as one of the fundamental documents in American history." If the nation was to survive it needed strength, and the nation could not afford to do less than adopt universal military training. The New York *Times* heartily agreed and urged Congress to act promptly to adopt the plan for universal military training. The San Francisco *Chronicle*, however, felt that President Truman was trying to "sugarcoat the pill" in

---

[15] *War Reports*, pp. 289-296.
[16] New York *Times*, September 7, 1945.
[17] *Ibid.*, October 24, 1945.

saying this was not conscription. "Universal military training remains just that and a system in which the American mind finds no pleasure." The Salt Lake City *Deseret News* was more outspoken in its opposition to "compulsory military training, whether it be for a year or a decade." [18] The national board of the United Council of Church Women also went on record as being opposed to the proposal which it termed a "Nazi program." [19]

Congress was in no hurry to take up such a controversial issue so soon before a presidential election and no action was taken on either extending Selective Service or Universal Military Training in the remaining months of 1945. In his State of the Union Message to Congress in January, 1946, the President again asked Congress for an extension of the draft beyond May 15, and insisted upon unification as well as universal military training.[20] Congressional response to these proposals was filled with many reservations which prompted the New York *Times* to say on March 11, "Congress appears not only to be out of step with the President but also out of step with the American people."

Extension of Selective Service was hotly debated in Congress, but by May 14, only a few hours before the act would expire, no action had been taken. A temporary stop-gap measure was hastily pushed through both houses which continued the legislation for six weeks, but limited inductions to men between the ages of 20 and 30. On June 25, 1946, Selective Service was again extended until March 31, 1947. This new extension modified the act in several important respects. The age limits for those subject to the draft were set at 19 to 44, and the term of service was fixed at 18 months. Fathers were exempt and those who were then in the service were to be released by August 1. The size of the Army was not to exceed 1,310,000 by January 1, 1947 and it was to be further reduced to 1,070,000 by July 1, 1947.[21]

While Congress remained undecided on the question of universal military training, the War Department on October 2, 1946 issued a new plan on the subject. This provided one year of com-

---

[18] October 24, 1945. As might be expected the Communist organ, the New York *Daily Worker,* October 24, 1945, was bitter in its reaction "because we oppose the foreign policy for which it is to be the instrument."
[19] *Facts on File,* October 24-30, 1945.
[20] *Ibid.,* January 20-26, 1946.
[21] Ibid, May 12-18, 1946; June 23-29, 1946. The strength of the Navy was not to exceed 558,000 men on July 1, 1947 and the Marine Corps figure was set at 108,000.

pulsory training for young men between 18 and 20. The first six months would be spent in special Army training centers. For the second six months the inductees could have intensive and specialized training with the Army, or they could select any one of eight alternative programs. These would include enlistment in the regular services, the National Guard, or the Enlisted Reserve Corps. However, training units would not be part of the armed services; inductees would be subject to a specially drawn "Code of Conduct" instead of the Articles of War; and the nonmilitary phases of their training would be supervised by a civilian advisory board appointed by the White House, and headed by Dr. Karl T. Compton. The plan called for the training of 1,000,000 men annually at an estimated cost of $2,000,000,000. The Navy would receive three of every eleven men, but the trainees would not be employed in combat and would receive a monthly allowance in lieu of pay.[22]

Continuing interest was shown in the project by the President when on December 19, 1947 he appointed a commission of nine members to study the question of universal military training. The commission was charged with the responsibility for formulating plans implementing the system in a manner to give the country the largest measure of protection, provide for the spiritual, mental and physical development of the young men in training and keep cost at the lowest level consistent with national security.[23]

The report, submitted May 29, 1947, strongly advocated the adoption of a universal military training program. Some of the more important recommendations included:

1. All males to be subject to training at 18 years of age or after finishing secondary school.

2. Service to be divided into two parts, the first six months in basic training or on shipboard and the second offering the following options:
   a. Enlistment in one of the services for two years.
   b. A second six months training.
   c. Enrollment in a national service academy.
   d. Enrollment in the National Guard or Organized Reserve.
   e. Enrollment in Reserve Officers' Training Corps or Enlisted Reserve Corps at College.

3. A civil commission to be in over-all charge of the program.

---

[22] *Ibid.*, September 29-October 5, 1946; New York *Times,* October 3, 1946.
[23] *A Program for National Security, Report of the President's Advisory Commission on Universal Training,* (Washington: G.P.O., 1947), p. 1. Hereafter cited as *President's Advisory Commission.*

4. Pay for the trainees to be $25 per month.[24]

The report was hailed by the New York *Times* as required reading for "timid congressmen," for "it is difficult to see any possible ground for criticism either of the Commission or its findings." Congressional reaction to the report of the Compton Commission, however, was not favorable. Fear of "militarism" and the estimated cost of the program, $1,750,000,000 a year, were perhaps the two chief obstacles in its passage. Congress had been avoiding universal military training since the end of the war, and the Republican 80th Congress was in no mood to listen to the Democratic President. Some members of Congress also expressed the belief that if the unification measure was passed and if adequate funds were given to the Armed Forces, the Congress would have done its duty toward national security.[25] The Compton Report was quietly buried, though its subject matter remained very much alive.

The Selective Service Act of 1940, and its subsequent extensions, ended operations of its system which on March 31, 1947, was succeeded by the Office of Selective Service Records with General Hershey continuing as Director. In March of 1948, because of the threatening attitude of the USSR,[26] President Truman reported to Congress the obvious need for increasing the nation's armed forces. After a bitter struggle Congress passed the Selective Service Act of June, 1948, with a life span of two years.[27] Only a few men were actually called under this act, and this situation continued until the Communist aggression in Korea in 1950 made further extension of Selective Service necessary. On June 20, 1950 the law was extended until July 9, 1951, and draft boards were ordered to call inductees to active duty.[28]

After the outbreak of the Korean War, President Truman an-

---

[24] *President's Advisory Commission.* For a good summary see the New York *Times* of June 2, 1947.

[25] New York *Times*, June 2, 3, 18, 1947. Differing with this point of view the editorial stated: "But the Unification Bill and the Army and Navy Budgets cover only the professional services. The reserves also are important. A trained reserve is what UMT would supply. It would supply this essential factor, as the President said, in the most democratic, the most economical and effective way."

[26] Walter Millis (ed.): *The Forrestal Diaries*, (New York: The Viking Press, 1951), pp. 372, 386, 393-394. Hereafter cited as *Forrestal Diaries.*

[27] *National Military Establishment, First Report of the Secretary of Defense, 1948*, p. 61.

[28] *War Department Press Release*, June 21, 1950.

nounced on August 11, 1950 his decision not to press for enactment of Universal Military Training at that session of Congress for fear it might delay more pressing programs needed in the Korean crisis.[29] This decision was followed by a request to Congress on August 29 not to pass such legislation until 1951. The more immediate demands of the Korean War, President Truman insisted, would make it impossible at that time or in the immediate foreseeable future to take military installations and training personnel away from the Army for assignment to the universal military training program. The Senate Armed Service Committee shelved the bill on August 30.[30]

Early in the 82nd Congress a bill was introduced bearing the title Universal Military Training and Service Act. The bill covered the extension of Selective Service and provided for a system of UMT to become operative at some undetermined future date. The act was passed by a heavy bi-partisan majority in June, 1951, with a convenient rider to the effect that the UMT provisions of the bill remained subject to further debate by Congress before the program could be implemented.[31]

What the passage of the law really amounted to was an extension of the draft law to 1955 and the appointment of a civilian commission to draft a plan for universal military training to be considered at some future date. No positive action was taken to implement the UMT provision until, under the prodding of the military, Carl Vinson, Chairman of the House Armed Services Committee, introduced a bill in March, 1952. Again Congress reacted unfavorably[32] in spite of two amendments proposed by Vinson that the start of a UMT program be postponed until the present draft was over and an automatic expiration date for the program be set for July 1, 1958.[33] These amendments, if incorporated into the bill, would have destroyed its original purpose. Consequently, the vote sending it back to the House for further study was perhaps not as unfortunate as was believed by the Armed Forces.

After March, 1952 no important action was taken on the sub-

---

[29] New York *Times,* August 11, 1950.
[30] New York *Times,* September 1, 1950.
[31] *Department of Defense, Semiannual Report of the Secretary of Defense, January 1 to June 30, 1951,* pp. 14-16.
[32] *Time,* March 17, 1952.
[33] *Newsweek,* March 17, 1952.

ject and it remained suspended by a general acceptance of current Selective Service procedures. Writing in *U. S. News and World Report*, March 14, 1952, David Lawrence stated: "What defeated the UMT bill was the decision to set up a plan that parallels but does not really substitute for or supplement the Selective Service operation."

The Case for Unification

Proponents of unification of the Armed Forces put forward the thesis that in the light of our past military experience and especially the recent lessons of World War II, a degree of coordination among our land, sea, and air forces, never before required, was now necessary. "We must have a close correlation between our foreign policy and our military policy," [34] and an armed service merger was the real hope of conserving much manpower, material and energy. [35]

Hearings on the proposal to establish a single department of the armed forces were held before a Select Committee of the House on Postwar Military Policy from April 24 to May 19, 1944. Spokesmen for the War Department testified in favor of the program with Lieutenant General McNarney, Deputy Chief of Staff, presenting a plan for unification. Representatives of the Navy were generally noncommittal and suggested further study. The committee reported on June 15, 1944 that the time was inopportune for such legislation, and strongly urged the War and Navy Departments to make further studies of the subject. [36]

Though the hearings helped to highlight the question of unification, the proposal did not represent the sudden emergence of a new and original concept. It was only one in a series of a long continuing effort which had been expressed through the years by a constant procession of legislative proposals and hearings. [37]

With the end of hostilities in Europe more attention could be

[34] Lieutenant General (later General) J. Lawton Collins: "National Security-The Military Viewpoint," *Vital Speeches of the Day*, Vol. 13, May, 1947. General Johnson Hagood: "Unify our Fighting Forces," *Colliers*, March 14, 1942, emphasized that as many as six agencies were charged with the defense of Pearl Harbor, each receiving orders from a different source.

[35] Testimony of Assistant Secretary of War, John J. McCloy, before Senate Committee, November 23, 1945. *Facts on File*, November 21-27, 1945.

[36] *Hearings before the Select Committee on Postwar Military Policy*, House Report No. 1645, 78th Congress, 2d Session.

[37] *Cf.* Legare, *op. cit.*, for a discussion of previous legislative hearings and proposals on unification.

devoted to the subject, and President Truman told the Secretary
of the Navy, James F. Forrestal, he intended to wrap up the entire
question of unification into one package and present it to Congress.[38] Before the Chief Executive's package was presented, the
Senate Judiciary Committee opened hearings on September 8 on a
Government reorganization bill, the terms of which would permit
the formation of a single department of defense.[39]

Testimony on the part of representatives of the War Department before Congress strongly advocated a merger of the armed
forces. Secretary of War Robert P. Patterson urged the creation
of a single Department of National Defense headed by a cabinet
officer, with control over ground, air, and naval components as a
necessary step for adequate defense in the atomic age. General
Henry H. Arnold was convinced of the necessity for a single national defense unit, in which airpower would be co-equal in
strength and influence with the Army and Navy.[40] General
Marshall also threw his weight behind the proposal in telling a
Senate committee of the imperative need for a single defense establishment "to maintain through the years a military posture that
will secure us a lasting peace." The coordination between the
Army and Navy during the war, he contended, did not prevent
expensive duplication and waste of facilities and lost motion.[41]

Distinguished field commanders also endorsed unification, with
General MacArthur urging "one family instead of three." On
November 16, 1945 General Eisenhower told a Senate committee
that a single defense command was essential in time of peace in
order to avoid another Pearl Harbor and to effect a possible
twenty-five per cent saving in personnel and expenses.[42]

The White House proposal for unification was submitted to
the Congress on December 19, 1945. The President asked for
unification of the armed services under a single cabinet officer in
order to realize the following objectives: (1) Integrated strategic
plans and a unified military program and budget; (2) the econ-

[38] At Potsdam, July, 1945. *Forrestal Diaries*, p. 115.
[39] *Army and Navy Journal*, September 8, 1945.
[40] *Facts on File*, October 17-23, 1945.
[41] *Ibid.* On May 9, 1945 Marshall said "that he was unshakably committed
to the thesis of a single civiliañ Secretary with a single military Chief of Staff."
Forrestal Diaries, p. 60.
[42] *Facts on File*, October 31-November 6, 1945. Nov. 14-20, 1945. Army-
Navy "competition," according to General Brehon B. Somervell, in procurement and other activities would be eliminated by "a consolidation of these
complex services." *Ibid.*, December 16, 22, 1945.

omies achieved through unified control of supply and service functions; (3) coordination between the military and the rest of the government; (4) the strongest means for civilian control of the military; (5) unified training and scientific research; (6) unity of command in outlying bases; and (7) consistent and equitable personnel policies.

The proposal was accompanied by a recommendation for the following organization:

1. The Secretary of National Defense (a civilian)
   A. Civilian organization: (1) Undersecretary of National Defense; (2) Assistant Secretaries for Army, Navy, and Air; (3) Other Assistant Secretaries for whatever duties the President and Secretary may determine.
   B. Military Organization: (1) Chief of Staff of National Defense (to be rotated among the services); (2) a commander for each of the three component branches; (3) An Advisory Council to the President and Secretary to be made up of the Chief of Staff of National Defense and the three service commanders.[43]

The Navy's Case

The Navy put up a vigorous battle against some of the concepts of unification, but it was by no means a blind opposition to any change in the *status quo*. Questions of command authority and fear of a possible submergence of the Marine Corps and loss of this arm were at the root of the Navy's disapproval. Admiral William D. Leahy believed unification of administration "held promises of usefulness in economy . . . but I did not approve of unification of command of the military services under anybody except the President." He also feared that the Navy would suffer from the expansion of one of the other services.[44] Secretary Forrestal while also suspicious of some of the proposals for unification was convinced "the Navy Department cannot be in the position of merely taking the negative in this discussion, but it must come up with positive and constructive recommendations." [45]

---

[43] New York *Times*, December 20, 1945. The President's message "represented a defeat for Forrestal's and the Navy's and the Navy's point of view." *Forrestal Diaries*, p. 119.

[44] William D. Leahy: *I Was There*, (New York: Whittlessey House, 1950), p. 371.

[45] *Forrestal Diaries*, p. 61. Earlier the Secretary had written: "I have been telling King, Nimitz and Company it is my judgment that as of today the Navy has lost its case, and that either in Congress or in public poll the Army's point of view would prevail." Forrestal to Palmer Hoyt, September 2, 1944. *Ibid.*, p. 60.

In order to come up with such recommendations Forrestal commissioned Ferdinand Eberstadt to make a thorough study of the question. Forrestal's directive of June 19, 1945 asked for consideration of the following questions:

1. Would unification of the War and Navy Departments under a single head improve our national security?
2. If not, what changes in the present relationships of the military services and departments has our war experience indicated as desirable to improve our national security?
`3. What form of postwar organization should be established and maintained to enable the military services and other government department and agencies to provide for and ·protect our national security? [46]

With reference to the specific questions asked by the Secretary, Mr. Eberstadt reported that existing conditions did not warrant unification of the Army and Navy and it would not improve the national security. Furthermore, neither a unified nor a coordinate form of reorganization would advance all desirable objectives of postwar military policy. The coordinate form, however, would be better adapted to achieve those policies which seemed to be more important. Mr. Eberstadt further felt a desirable goal was to bind the military services and other governmental departments and agencies together in such a way as to achieve the most productive and harmonious whole. This would involve close organizational ties between the State Department and the armed forces, the military departments in strategy and logistics, and the military services and agencies responsible for planning and carrying out scientific research and the mobilization of industrial and manpower resources. The coordinate form of military organization, it was added, was more in line with the principles of our Constitution, our customs, and our traditions. In lieu of the proposed Army-Navy merger, the creation of the air arm as a third defense establishment with cabinet status was recommended.[47] One observer believed "its analysis and recommendations became in fact the principal basis for the unification act finally adopted two years later." [48]

Criticism from the Navy over proposals to unify the armed

---

[46] *Forrestal Diaries*, p. 63.
[47] Ferdinand Eberstadt: *Unification of War and Navy Departments and Postwar Organization for National Security. A Report to Hon. James Forrestal.* (Washington: G.P.O., 1945).
[48] Walter Millis in *Forrestal Diaries*, pp. 64-65.

forces were sharp and at times bitter.[49] In testifying upon a Senate bill for unification Forrestal assailed it for its "many defects" and because it "concentrates power in one hand beyond the capacity of any one man." On the following day, October 23, 1945, Fleet Admiral Ernest J. King called such measures for unification "revolutionary, dangerous and unnecessary" and said each organization was too large and complex to be handled efficiently as a single unit.[50] The attack was continued by General Alexander A. Vandegrift, commandant of the Marine Corps, who said the proposed merger might bring about absolute control by a "highly organized and politically astute group" with "only one shade of opinion." Furthermore, the "proposed economies will imperil the country's safety by stifling free development" of the military profession.[51] There was no doubt that the Navy presented a united front in opposition to the consolidation of the War and Navy Departments.

The struggle over unification dragged through the fall of 1945 marked by sharp clashes between the Army and Navy. The controversy turned into such a bitter free-for-all "that Washington began to call it 'The Battle of the Potomac'. From the white Navy building east of the river and the Pentagon to the west came a commotion the like of which hadn't been heard since the Confederates stormed the Potomac." [52]

A Compromise Emerges

The President's proposal of December 19, 1945 formed the basis for a bill reported out by the Senate Military Affairs Committee in April, 1946. The Navy continued its active opposition to the plan until finally the Chief Executive ordered active Navy officers to stop publicly discussing the plan except before Congressional committees.[53] The controversy was so sharp that the President felt compelled to call the Secretaries of War and Navy to the White House for a conference on May 13 to bring together their

---

[49] Admiral William V. Pratt: "A Case Against Merging the Army and Navy," *Newsweek*, September 17, 1945. Concluding his attack the Admiral wrote: "Might it not be well to think a bit before we start an experiment, which after all that can be said in its favor, does have some of the earmarks of what was done in Germany and Japan"?

[50] *Facts on File,* October 17-23, 1945.

[51] Ibid, October 24-30, 1945.

[52] *Newsweek,* November 19, 1945.

[53] *Facts on File,* April 14-20, 1946. On April 20, the *Army and Navy Journal* reported: "President Truman became more specific as to his charges that Navy personnel were lobbying and propagandizing against his recommendations."

point of agreement on the proposed unification in a compromise plan acceptable to both services. The Chief Executive issued no ultimatum but expressed the hope the Secretaries would get together in an effort to have all differences ironed out by 31 May.[54]

This meeting represented a decisive victory for Forrestal, largely reversing the effects of the defeat he had suffered in December with the President's initial message on unification. The conferees found a large area of agreement. The Army had no objections to the creation of a Council of Common Defense (later named the National Security Council), a National Security Resources Board, a Central Intelligence Agency, or to a Military Munitions Board. Secretary of War Patterson was no longer pressing for a single Chief of Staff and he also yielded on the basic organization to be composed of three autonomous Departments, each headed by a Secretary with cabinet rank, and a military commander. Only one major point of difference remained, and that was over the powers to be given to the single over-all Secretary of Defense.[55]

After studying the reports and recommendations submitted to him by Patterson and Forrestal, Truman laid down, on June 15, 1946, a twelve-point program on which he believed unification should be established. Of the twelve points, eight had been agreed upon by the Army and Navy, while the remaining four were settled by the President.[56] The Chief Executive's plan called for: (1) a single Department of National Defense with a civilian Secretary with cabinet rank; (2) three coordinated services—Army, Navy, Air—each headed by a Secretary not of cabinet rank, but they would sit in the proposed Council of National Defense; (3) a unified air force, with the Navy to operate its own craft except for land-based planes for reconnaissance, anti-submarine warfare, and protection of shipping;[57] (4) continuance of the present Marine Corps; (5) a Council of National Defense to integrate our foreign and military policies; (6) a National Security Resources Board;

---

[54] *Army and Navy Journal*, May 18, 1946.
[55] *Forrestal Diaries*, pp. 162-163.
[56] The Army demanded unification, three coordinated services, a unified air force, and a single Chief of Staff; the Navy opposed these and asked for continuance of the Marine Corps.
[57] "Forrestal was well aware of the disastrous nature of this last decision. The history of the war was full of examples to prove the vital need for naval control over land-based aviation used in support of naval operations." *Forrestal Diaries*, pp. 167-168.

(7) Joint Chiefs of Staff; (8) no single Chief of Staff; (9) a Central Intelligence Agency; (10) a single procurement and supply agency; (11) a single research agency; (12) a single agency on military training and education.[58]

Though Forrestal believed the President's program was a substantial defeat for his own and the Navy's views[59] he pledged his support to the objectives of the plan[60] and continued to work for revisions. Not until January 16, 1947 did the Army and Navy finally resolve their differences[61] and agree to jointly recommend a plan for unification of the armed forces under a Secretary of National Defense so as to place the Army, the Navy (to include Marine Corps and Naval Aviation), and the Air Forces, each with a military chief, under the Departments of the Army, the Navy, and the Air Force respectively.[62]

The majority of editorial comment hailed the plan for unification as promoting both efficiency and security.[63] Many papers, however, criticized it as not going far enough toward a merger. The elevation of the Air Force to a position of parity with the Army and Navy was generally welcomed. But it was feared that operation of the three units as independent entities with three Secretaries having access to the President, although under a Secretary of National Defense, would have a tendency to create confusion of authority.

Further legislative hearings were held, and not until July 26 was approval given to the National Security Act of 1947, in which, with the Army, Navy, and Air Force as co-equals, the Armed Forces of the United States were unified under a single civilian Secretary of Defense. The act was implemented by an executive order stating the functions of each service, and on the same day James Forrestal was nominated as the nation's first Secretary of Defense.[64] The act went into effect on September 17, 1947 with Forrestal taking oath of office in a brief ceremony at the Pentagon.

The National Security Act was organized under three head-

---

[58] *Facts on File,* June 9-15, 1946.
[59] *Forrestal Diaries,* p. 167.
[60] *Facts on File,* June 23-29, 1946.
[61] *Forrestal Diaries,* pp. 228-231.
[62] *Army and Navy Journal,* January 18, 1947.
[63] This editorial opinion is from a survey in *U. S. News and World Report,* January 31, 1947.
[64] *Forrestal Diaries,* pp. 295-296. LXI *Stat.* pt. I, 495-510.

ings: Title I, Coordination for National Security; Title II, The National Military Establishment; Title III, Miscellaneous Provisions. Under Title I three agencies were created:

1. *The National Security Council* composed of the President, the Secretary of Defense, the secretaries of the three services, the chairman of the National Security Board, and others appointed at the discretion of the President including the secretaries of other executive departments, the chairman of the Munitions Board, and the chairman of the Research and Development Board.

2. *The Central Intelligence Agency* which was to make its reports and recommendations to the National Security Council. Its duties were to coordinate the intelligence activities of the several government departments, to correlate and evaluate intelligence material gathered, and to provide for its distribution within the government.

3. *The National Security Resources Board* whose duty it was to keep the President informed concerning the coordination of military and civilian mobilization in the event of war.

The National Military Establishment consisted of the three military departments, Army, Navy, Air, headed by the Secretary of Defense who was designated as the Chief Executive's principal assistant in all matters relating to national security. It also included the following agencies authorized or created under the National Security Act:

1. *The War Council* composed of the Secretary of Defense (ch.), the secretaries of the Army, Navy, and Air Force, the Army Chief of Staff, Chief of Naval Operations, the Air Chief of Staff.

2. *The Joint Chiefs of Staff* consisting of the Army Chief of Staff, Chief of Naval Operations, Air Chief of Staff, and the Chief of Staff to the President when there is one. The Joint Chiefs were authorized to have a staff of not more than 100 officers, made up approximately of an equal number from each of the services. The chairmanship would rotate among the services.

3. *A Munitions Board* with a chairman appointed by the President and an undersecretary, or assistant secretary, from each of the military departments.

4. *The Research and Development Board* composed of a chairman appointed by the President and two representatives from each of the three armed services.[65]

Changes Are Found Necessary

After the enactment of the National Security Act of 1947, the operation of the law was observed with critical scrutiny and it

---

[65] LXI *Stat.* 495-510.

soon became apparent that the road to unification was at times extremely rocky. The Hoover Commission found, in 1948-1949, continued disharmony, lack of unified planning, extravagance in military budgets, waste in expenditures, which indicated a serious lack of understanding of the effect of military costs and spending upon the economy of the nation.[66] Guiding principles for an efficient organization, as reported by the Hoover Commission, were centralization of authority in the Executive, the establishment of clear lines of command and accountability, and direct supervision of operations. It appeared, however, that these principles had not been followed in the passage of the National Security Act of 1947:

> 1. The authority of the President had been curtailed by Statutory stipulation of the membership and duties of both the National Security Council and the National Security Resources Board.
> 2. The authority of the Secretary of Defense and hence the control of the President, was weak and qualified by the provisions of the Act of 1947 which set up a rigid structure of federation, rather than unification.
> 3. In direct proportion to the limitations and confusions of authority among their civilian superiors, the military were left without civilian control.[67]

On March 5, 1949 the President recommended the amendment of the act to accomplish two basic purposes: first, to convert the National Military Establishment into an Executive Department of the government, to be known as the Department of Defense; second, to provide the Secretary of Defense with appropriate responsibility and authority. The Chief Executive further recommended that, within the new Department of Defense, the Department of the Army, and the Navy, and the Air Force be designated as military departments. The responsibility of the Secretary of Defense for exercising direction, authority, and control over the affairs of the Department of Defense was to be made clear.[68]

After extensive hearings the National Security Act of 1947 was amended by Public Law 216, 81st Congress, on August 10, 1949. The act converted the National Military Establishment into an executive department of the government, and changed its name to Department of Defense. The Departments of the Army, Navy,

---

[66] Herbert Hoover: *The National Security Organization. A Report to the Congress by the Commission of the Executive Branch of the Government, February, 1949.* (Washington: G.P.O., 1949).
[67] *Ibid.*
[68] New York *Times,* March 6, 1949.

and Air Force were designated as military departments instead of executive branches. By deletions and amendments, the law provided the Secretary of Defense with appropriate responsibility and authority to carry out his new obligations. The act prohibited the establishment of a single Chief of Staff over the armed forces, or the establishment of an armed forces general staff. This, of course, did not apply to the Joint Chiefs of Staff or to the Joint Staff. Congress also again announced its intent not to merge the military departments, but only to provide for their coordination and unified direction under the civilian control of the Secretary of Defense.[69]

New agencies subsequently established in the Department of Defense included the Defense Supply Management Agency, a Reserve Forces Policy Board, and a Director of Installations. Under the reorganization which became effective June 30, 1953 the Research and Development Board, the Munitions Board, the Defense Supply Management Agency, and the Director of Installations were abolished and their functions transferred to the Secretary of Defense who was provided with six additional Assistant Secretaries and a General Council.[70]

Radical changes had taken place in the military establishment of the American people who throughout the period were keenly interested and concerned with the shaping of our military policy. Also of vital importance was the shaping of our foreign policy under the wintry blasts of the "Cold War" and the grim reality of atomic weapons.

---

[69] LXIII *Stat.* pt. I, 578-592. Truman praised the act but called one provision a "backward step"—the section placing "new and cumbersome restrictions" on the National Security Council. This provision made the Vice President a member of the Council, but dropped the Army, Navy, and Air Force Secretaries. New York *Times*, August 11, 1949.

[70] *U. S. Government Organization Manual,* (Washington: G.P.O., 1953-1954), pp. 119-120.

CHAPTER 21

Problems of Peace

The Atom and Soviet Intransigence—The Cold War and
American Diplomacy—The Postwar Navy—The Rocky
Road of Unification—The Budget and Preparedness—
The Reserves

THE ATOMIC BOMB which destroyed Hiroshima also
changed many of our concepts regarding the waging of war
and opened a fresh page in military history. Atomic energy
coupled with rocket propulsion provides the world with the most
terrible weapon ever known. So far as one can see into the future,
atomic weapons appear to provide the ultimate in man-made
destructiveness, and to represent the final triumph of the offense
over the defense.[1] The development of the hydrogen bomb under-
scores the validity of the thesis of there being no defense against
the terrible new weapons of our generation. The problem of controlling atomic weapons was perhaps the most crucial facing the
nation following World War II. If there could be no effective
agreement reached on atomic energy the hopes for a peaceful future would be dim and international amity and cooperation would
be a mockery. "Let us not deceive ourselves: We must elect World
Peace or World Destruction." [2]

The Atom and Soviet Intransigence

Two main ideas were proposed as to the solution of atomic
warfare. One was for the United States to retain its monopoly and
thus ensure its military safety, while others advocated the sharing
of America's atomic secrets with the rest of the world. Following
the first line of thought was former President Herbert Hoover who
urged the country to retain its atomic knowledge in order to gain
time in which to devise effective methods for its control.[3] Secretary

---

[1] Hanson Baldwin in *Life*, August 20, 1945. Also sharing this view was Major
General Thomas F. Farrell, deputy director of the Manhattan project, who
wrote: "There is no 'conceivable defense' at present against the atomic bomb,
except to have more of them than your enemy or to stop him from using them
against you by hitting him first." New York *Times*, September 21, 1945.
[2] Address of Bernard M. Baruch before the United Nations, June 14, 1946,
as quoted in Bartlett, *op. cit.*, p. 699.
[3] *Facts on File*, September 26-October 2, 1945.

of Commerce Henry A. Wallace, on the other hand, was "completely, everlastingly and wholeheartedly in favor of giving it to the Russians." [4]

The atomic bomb, which lay at the core of the whole problem of postwar military policy, was the entire subject of a Cabinet meeting on September 21, 1945. This discussion at the White House laid the foundation for future American policy as reflected in the President's message to Congress of October 3, and the Baruch plan. [5]

In his message to Congress of October 3, 1945 President Truman warned that atomic force in ignorant or evil hands could inflict untold disaster upon the nation and the world. He urged immediate legislation to create an atomic energy commission and the fixing of a national policy whose objectives should be promotion of the national welfare, securing the national defense, safeguarding world peace, and the acquisition of further knowledge. On the question of international control the President said discussion could not be safely delayed until the United Nations was functioning. The Chief Executive therefore proposed to start discussions at once with Britain and Canada. "The hope of civilization," he concluded, "lies in renunciation of the use and development of the atomic bomb," and directing the use of atomic energy toward peaceful and humanitarian ends. [6]

Many scientists who had contributed to the making of the bomb criticized the American policy of secrecy as leading to an unending war more savage than the last. The Association of Los Alamos Scientists argued that other nations would be producing atomic power before many years and that the use of atomic energy must be controlled by a world authority. [7] Dr. J. R. Oppenheimer also felt only international control could prevent the development of a situation in which the peoples of the world would be at the mercy of destructive forces the like of which they could not even imagine. "Temporarily the advantage is ours," he said, "but actually the advent of atomic power has weakened the military position of the United States." [8] The solution proposed by Albert Einstein was the formation of a world government com-

---

[4] *Forrestal Diaries,* p. 95.
[5] *Ibid.,* pp. 94, 96.
[6] New York *Times,* October 4, 1945.
[7] *Facts on File,* October 10-16, 1945.
[8] New York *Times,* October 18, 1945.

posed of the United States, Great Britain, and Russia with the three nations giving this government all their military strength.[9]

A more pedestrian proposal came from Senator Tom Connally who suggested that the United States furnish a flying task force of atomic bombers to the United Nations Security Council, but retain the secret of their awful power. Senator James Meade of New York urged the formulation of an international agreement to outlaw the use of atomic bombs in warfare.[10]

While these suggestions were filling the air the President of the United States, the Prime Minister of Great Britain, and the Prime Minister of Canada agreed on November 15, 1945 to have the United Nations take up the subject of control of atomic energy. As a result of this conference and agreement, the Secretary of State, the Foreign Minister of the Soviet Union, and the Foreign Minister of Great Britain met in Moscow on December 27, 1945 to draw up proposals to be presented. A further development was the passage of a resolution on January 24, 1946 establishing the Atomic Energy Commission of the United Nations.[11]

Bernard M. Baruch, representing the United States, presented to the United Nations meeting at Hunter College, New York, on June 14, 1946 the American plan for the control of atomic energy.[12] The proposal was divided into fourteen parts covering all phases of the development and use of atomic energy. The essential parts of the plan were well summarized by the New York *Times:*

> As soon as a satisfactory international agency can be set up; as soon as other powers have joined with us to guarantee that agency and give it the scope and authority it needs; as soon as we are assured that no other nation will or can use atomic bombs against us, the United States will cease the manufacture of atomic weapons, will destroy the bombs now in its possession, will give to the new agency, by stages as required, all pertinent information, and finally will turn over to this agency control of its own uranium and thorium deposits, its own primary production plants and the output of these plants.[13]

---

[9] Baltimore *Sun,* October 27, 1945. Thirty prominent Americans, headed by Justice Owen J. Roberts, advocated the scrapping of the United Nations and the creation of a World Federal Government to insure against an atomic war which would destroy civilization and possibly mankind itself. *Facts on File,* October 10-16, 1945.
[10] Baltimore *Sun,* September 9, 1945.
[11] New York *Times,* June 15, 1946.
[12] Bartlett, *op. cit.,* pp. 699-704.
[13] June 15, 1946.

In its essence the plan presented three conditions which made its rejection inevitable, the surrender of the veto power on all questions referring to atomic power, an inspection and control system, and the subjugation of sovereignty. The Soviet Union would surely reject all three conditions, and it was highly doubtful if the United States would permit an international agency to exercise complete control and authority over territory and facilities within her boundaries. The plan had weaknesses, but at least it was a start on the path toward control of atomic power. However, the start was no more than that, and efforts to achieve international control of atomic power ran against the roadblock of Soviet intransigence.

The proposal was doomed to an early death from the date of its presentation to the Commission. With regard to surrendering the veto power the Soviet delegate said, "the Security Council should retain full control of the subject, with each of the Big Four retaining its veto power." [14] This position on the part of Russia was forecast by the Washington *Times Herald:* "Most of the debate seems to center around the proposed renunciation of the veto power as to atomic energy by the Big Five nations. This power is especially dear . . . and if Russia consents to give up an iota of it a semi-miracle will have been performed." Even if all the nations of the world consented to a renunciation of their veto power, in the opinion of the Philadelphia *Inquirer,* it would have to be done by a pledge, international agreement, or treaty. Such a pledge would not be enough.[15] An international agreement or treaty was not sufficient either since history is "salted and peppered with evidence that treaties are not necessarily binding." [16] Looking at the question again the *Inquirer,* June 16, 1946, raised the point of "what if Russia would initially accept the U. S. conditions only to throw them aside once we have surrendered the atomic secrets? What would be the sequel to such treachery? War? With Russia in possession of the atomic bomb?"

With respect to a surrender of national sovereignty the Baruch plan "must surely rank among the most revolutionary documents in history." Though the Cleveland *Plain Dealer* believed "Amer-

---

[14] New York *Times,* June 20, 1946. For the official Russian rejection of the Baruch plan see the speech of Andrei A. Gromyko, March 5, 1947, as quoted in Bartlett, *op. cit.,* pp. 704-707.

[15] June 15, 1946.

[16] Baltimore *Sun,* June 15, 1946.

ican reluctance to surrender a portion of national sovereignty is no longer a problem," the Baltimore *Sun* felt the important question to be answered was: "Has the United Nations organization yet attained such an authoritative position in world affairs that we can begin thinking of intrusting to it our A-bomb know how?" [17]

Discussion on the control of atomic energy continued until May, 1948, when the Atomic Energy Commission of the United Nations adjourned *sine die*. Upon the request of the smaller member nations, the Commission resumed hearings on February 19, 1949, but in July these were again dropped for the major powers were no closer to an agreement. What was already a dangerous situation assumed the proportions of a crisis with the announcement in 1949 of Russian development of atomic weapons.[18] Americans were shocked when they realized Russia's rapid mastery of atomic secrets was partially due to espionage involving Canadian,[19] American, and British citizens.[20]

There was no hope of reaching an understanding with the Soviet Union on the use of atomic energy or even in stopping the atomic armament race, so in 1951 President Truman ordered work begun on the development of the hydrogen bomb. The successful creation of this new horror weapon added a new note of urgency to the quest for world peace, and security against the march of Soviet imperialism.

The Cold War and American Diplomacy

The "Grand Alliance" which had held together in the face of a common danger was not long in breaking up. America became increasingly worried over the spread of Russian power in Europe as well as the Communist attempt to seize control in China. In an effort to halt the spread of Red imperialism and to recreate a balance of power, the United States embarked on a series of far

---

[17] Kansas City *Star*, June 15, 1946. "This not only was an unprecedented surrender of sovereignty by the United States but showed an unusual hospitality to socialization." Baldwin, *op. cit.*, p. 689.

[18] Hacker and Zahler, *op. cit.*, p. 594.

[19] The disclosure of the Canadian spy ring in February, 1946, led Joseph E. Davies, former Ambassador to Russia, to remark: "Russia, in self-defense, has every moral right to seek atomic bomb secrets through military espionage if excluded from such information by her former fighting allies." *Facts on File*, February 17-23, 1946.

[20] The arrest of Dr. Klaus Fuchs, February, 1950, by the British, led to the arrest of a group of American agents. Julius and Ethel Rosenberg were sentenced to die in April, 1951, while Morton Sobell and David Greenglass were given long sentences. Barck and Blake, *op. cit.*, p. 816.

reaching steps which included the Truman Doctrine, the European Recovery Program, the North Atlantic Treaty Organization, the Mutual Defense Assistance Act, the Point Four Program, and the Mutual Security Program.[21]

The chaos and destruction of World War II produced a realization of the necessity for reconstruction even before the guns were stilled, but it was believed that international agencies could meet the needs more appropriately than individual governments. The first agency established was the United Nations Relief and Rehabilitation Administration in 1943 with the United States contributing 2.66 billion dollars before operations were ended in 1947. Emerging from the Bretton Woods Conference of 1944 were the International Bank for Reconstruction and Development and the International Monetary Fund which were created in 1945. America subscribed 5.9 billion dollars as its share in these agencies.[22]

However, with the termination of Lend-Lease and the precarious financial situation of Great Britain new arrangements were found necessary. A financial agreement was negotiated with England in September, 1945, under which a loan of 3.75 billion dollars was made available the following year. The British loan and the termination of UNRRA[23] were followed in 1947 by an interim foreign aid program.[24]

Even with American assistance, Great Britain's economic position was so shaky that her statesmen reluctantly came to the conclusion England could no longer continue her program of assist-

---

[21] Selected readings on the subject include: *Documents on American Foreign Relations,* (Princeton University Press, 1947-1952), vols. VII-XII; Halford L. Hoskins: *The Atlantic Pact,* (Washington: Public Affairs Press, 1949); *Strengthening the Forces of Freedom: Selected Speeches and Statements of Secretary of State Acheson, February 1949-April 1950,* (Washington: G.P.O., 1950); Seymour E. Harris: *European Recovery Program,* (Harvard University Press, 1948).

[22] United States Department of Commerce: *Supplement and Foreign Transactions of the United States Government, Major Legislation 1940-1950,* (Washington: G.P.O., 1951); Brookings Institute: *Administration of Foreign Affairs and Overseas Operations,* (Washington: The Brookings Institute, 1951), p. 28; W. A. Brown and R. Opie: *American Foreign Assistance,* (Washington: The Brookings Institute, 1953).

[23] "UNRRA performed an essential function during its existence, but by 1946 some of its field operations had fallen into the hands of communists and were being used as a means of political pressure. Congress therefore refused to support it after the close of that year, and each government became responsible for relief within its own jurisdiction." Baldwin, *op cit,* p. 540.

[24] *Statistical Abstract of the United States, 1952,* (Washington: G.P.O., 1952), pp. 831-839.

ance to Greece. With Great Britain withdrawing this would mean Communistic domination of the Hellenic peninsula and possible Red control of the Mediterranean. This was extremely disturbing to America and the general consensus of the Cabinet was that we should support Greece to the extent that we could persuade Congress and the country of the necessity. The President was in agreement and he promised to make a very explicit statement on Turkey and Greece.[25]

In his message to Congress on March 12, 1947, President Truman asked for a $400,000,000 program of military and economic aid for Greece and Turkey. The message also had far reaching implications for it was American policy to help democratic peoples work out a life free from coercion, but the United States could not realize its objectives "unless we are willing to help free people to maintain their free institutions and their national integrity against aggressive movements that seek to impose upon them totalitarian regimes." This was simply recognizing Communist imperialism as undermining "the foundations of international peace and hence the security of the United States."[26]

Not since Pearl Harbor had there been such widespread controversy over an issue of American foreign policy as the Truman Doctrine provoked.[27] After a bitter debate the program was approved by Congress on May 15, 1947. American assistance brought the bloody civil war in Greece to an end by October, 1949, but this was only the first step in a sweeping program of foreign aid initiated under the impact of the Cold War.

Soon after the Greek crisis it became apparent that the problem of aid to Europe should be considered on a broader basis. On June 5, 1947 Secretary of State Marshall laid down a new approach to the problem in saying our policy

> is not directed against any country or doctrine, but against hunger, poverty, desperation and chaos. Its purpose should be the revival of a working economy in the world so as to permit the emergence of political and social conditions in which free institutions can exist. Such assistance I am convinced must not be on a piecemeal basis as various crises develop . . . The initiative I think must come from Europe . . . The program should be a joint one agreed to by a number, if not all, the European nations.[28]

[25] *Forrestal Diaries*, pp. 251-252.
[26] Bartlett, *op. cit.*, pp. 725-729.
[27] Barck and Blake, *op. cit.*, p. 780.
[28] New York *Times*, June 6, 1947.

The Marshall Plan was enthusiastically received in Western Europe (the Soviet Union and her satellite states refused to cooperate), where sixteen nations drew up a four-year program which would require some sixteen billion dollars from America.[29] The European Recovery Program not only offered American financial aid but it also envisaged shipments of machinery and raw materials, and the sending of American industrial experts to enable European industries to increase their efficiency and get back on their feet.[30]

Public response to the proposal was in general favorable, and the New York *Times,* January 2, 1948, looked hopefully toward the Marshall Plan as "a fundamental restoration of European economy as an essential condition for the restoration of peace and the survival of Western civilization." Supporters of the plan, such as Secretary of Defense Forrestal, argued that if the program was not adopted there would be an enormous increase in military expenditures. "We would have to appropriate as much for defense in a single year as for the entire Marshall Plan." [31]

In December, 1947, President Truman asked Congress to approve a four-year program of European aid at a total cost of about seventeen billion dollars. Congressional opposition lessened after the Communist seizure of power in Czechoslovakia in February, 1948, and on April 3, the Chief Executive signed the Foreign Assistance Act of 1948 which provided $5,300,000,000 for the first year.[32] The Marshall Plan was ended in 1951 after having poured about twelve billion dollars into Europe, but aid was continued in other forms.

By far the largest amount of military aid authorized and appropriated was in conjunction with the Mutual Defense Assistance Program of October, 1949.[33] This act was designed to implement

---

[29] Barck and Blake, *op. cit.,* p. 781.

[30] Baldwin, *op. cit.,* pp. 745-746.

[31] New York *Times,* January 18, 1948. Agreeing with Forrestal the editorial concluded: "But it remains true that what we spend to build up peaceful democratic nations will reduce the cost of protecting ourselves against unpeaceful and undemocratic nations. Specifically, $17,000,000,000 effectively invested in restoring full productivity to sixteen European countries with a total population of 270,000,000 will buy more protection than the same amount invested in weapons of war."

[32] Barck and Blake, *op. cit.,* p. 782. Aid on a much smaller scale was also instituted under the Point Four Program of June, 1950.

[33] *Administration of Foreign Affairs and Overseas Operations,* p. 174.

the North Atlantic Treaty, drawn up in August, 1949 as an alliance between the United States, Canada, Denmark, Iceland, Italy, Norway, the United Kingdom, France, Belgium, the Netherlands, and Luxembourg. The signatories declared that an armed attack against one or more of them in Europe or North America would be considered an attack against them all, and therefore they agreed to take such action as each member state deemed necessary. Secretary of State Dean Acheson assured the Senate that the pact did not commit American troops to the permanent defense of Europe, but he did not deny that in case of war the United States had the moral obligation to give as much assistance as though it had been assailed directly.[34]

Following on the heels of the above legislation was the Mutual Security Program authorized by the Mutual Security Act of October 10, 1951. This act brought the component parts of American foreign aid under the unified direction and supervision of the Director for Mutual Security. The Director also became head of the Mutual Security Agency which had taken over the functions of the Economic Cooperation Administration on December 30, 1950.[35]

The Postwar Navy

The United States emerged from the second World War with the most powerful naval force in the history of the world. Demobilization and economy, however, quickly whittled down the size and effectiveness of the fleets which had dominated the sea lanes of the world during the war. Upon the end of hostilities Secretary James Forrestal pleaded for the preservation of our naval power as the key to our security,[36] but few heeded him.

In the interest of national economy, it became necessary to demobilize, to a large measure, the largest fleet ever built. A program was quickly initiated to lay up in the so-called "mothball fleets" approximately 6,800 vessels which were declared surplus to the needs of the postwar Navy.[37] It was the policy of the Navy to maintain these Reserve Fleets in the highest practicable state of

---

[34] Baldwin, *op. cit.*, pp. 751-752.
[35] New York *Times*, October 11, 1951.
[36] *Annual Report, S/N, 1945,* p. 1.
[37] *Annual Report, S/N, 1946,* p. 35.

material readiness,[38] but economy measures made deterioration almost unavoidable.[39]

Demobilization also meant a sharp decline in the personnel of the Navy. From a total of almost three and one half million in September, 1945, the Navy was striving for a goal of 45,400 officers and 350,000 enlisted men on the eve of the Korean war.[40] Fortunately, the Navy had instituted a Reserve program following the war and by 1947 the Reserves had a total strength of 133,510 which was sixty percent of its planned strength.[41]

Symptomatic of the Navy's difficulties in the postwar years was the supercarrier controversy of 1949. On April 23, 1949 Secretary of Defense Louis Johnson[42] ordered construction to be halted on the 65,000 ton supercarrier *United States* which the Navy had intended to use for the launching of atomic bombs. The keel had only been laid five days previously, and abandonment of the project represented a victory for the Air Force which demanded sole responsibility for strategic bombing.[43]

Secretary of the Navy John L. Sullivan, in office since September, 1947, resigned April 26 in protest against Johnson's action. In his letter of resignation he accused the Secretary of overruling a project which had been approved by the President, Congress, and top naval strategists. Johnson's action was described as a blow against national defense which would result in a renewed effort to abolish the Marine Corps and to transfer all Naval and Marine aviation elsewhere. Even of greater significance, Sullivan continued, "is the unprecedented action in so drastically and arbitrarily restricting the plans of an armed service without consultation with the service. The consequences are far-reaching and can be tragic." [44]

[38] *Department of Defense Semiannual Report, Report of S/N, July 1, to December 31, 1949*, p. 173.
[39] *Department of Defense Annual Report, Report of S/N, 1949*, pp. 205-207. It is also to be noted that another matter of some concern to the Navy was the decline in private shipbuilding. The number of private plants engaged in naval shipbuilding was reduced from a wartime peak of 228 to 5 by 1947, "and with the modest program now in sight, no material increase in the number of plants engaged in naval shipbuilding is anticipated." *Annual Report, S/N, 1947*, p. 41.
[40] *Department of Defense Annual Report, Report of S/N, 1949*, pp. 216-217.
[41] *Annual Report, S/N, 1947*, p. 32.
[42] Forrestal had resigned on March 3, 1949.
[43] *New York Times*, April 24, 1949.
[44] *Ibid.*, April 27, 1949.

The cancellation of the supercarrier was a surface manifestation of the interservice rivalries and feuds that were soon to flare up in the bitter "Admiral's revolt" in which unification was to receive its most serious testing. "The process of unification," Forrestal wrote, "proceeds, but not always at an even pace—three steps forward and about one backward, I would say." [45]

The Rocky Road of Unification

Unification involved not merely interservice relations, but far larger questions revolving around the roles and missions of the services, lack of agreement on strategic weapons, and the allocations of funds. [46] The "first really serious attempt to grapple with the paralyzing divisions between the Services and to re-form the Military Establishment as a whole into a genuinely integrated team," [47] took place at the Key West Conference from the 11th to the 14th of March, 1948. The Conference was attended by the Joint Chiefs (Leahy, Bradley, Denfeld, and Spaatz), their aides, and Secretary Forrestal.

Not all of the difficulties were resolved, but certain broad, basic decisions were reached by the Joint Chiefs which included:

1. For planning purposes, Marine Corps to be limited to four divisions with the inclusion of a sentence in the final document that the Marines are not to create another land army.

2. Air Force recognizes right of Navy to proceed with the development of weapons the Navy considers essential to its function but with the proviso the Navy will not develop a separate strategic air force, this function being reserved to the Air Force.

3. Air Force recognizes the right and need for the Navy to participate in an all-out air campaign. [48]

In August of 1948 another conference between the Joint Chiefs and Forrestal was held at the Naval War College, Newport, Rhode Island, to wrestle once more with the problems which the Key West Conference had failed to settle. Another stumbling block to an agreement was over control of atomic bombs. The Conference agreed as an interim measure, that the Chief, Armed Forces Special Weapons Project would report to the Chief of Staff, U. S.

---

[45] Forrestal to Admiral Sherman, February 14, 1948. *Forrestal Diaries*, p. 373
[46] *Ibid.*, p. 478.
[47] *Ibid.*, p. 390.
[48] *Ibid.*, pp. 392-393. According to Forrestal, additional points included: "Navy not to be denied use of A-bomb;" "Navy to proceed with development of 80,000 ton carrier and development of HA (high altitude) aircraft to carry missiles therefrom."

Air Force. Since the Special Weapons Project controlled the atomic bomb, this gave temporary operational control to the Air Force. The Air Force, however, was obligated to utilize any strategic bombing capabilities the Navy might develop.[49]

In addition to these questions, the status of airpower was to provide the spark which ignited the bitter controversy among the services. In 1947 President Truman had appointed Thomas K. Finletter as chairman of the Air Policy Committee to review the whole question of air policy, while at the same time a Joint Congressional Aviation Policy Board was studying the same issue. Both the Finletter Report of January 13, 1948 and the Congressional Committee recommended the establishment of seventy regular air groups which was considerably higher than the fifty-five groups set up under the President's budget.[50]

When Louis Johnson was sworn in as Secretary of Defense in March, 1949 he made several very important decisions which set the stage for the "revolt of the Admirals." Sensing public sentiment, Johnson advocated a reduction in military expenditures. He also decided to support strategic air power. B-36's carrying atom bombs and using them in retaliation for an initial attack would be America's force in being. In addition, his decision to wield the axe on the Navy's supercarrier set in motion one of the most acrimonious quarrels in American military history.[51]

The contest was drawn when the Air Force cancelled orders for 470 advanced type planes in order to buy seventy-five B-36's. Representative James E. Van Zandt of Pennsylvania demanded a probe, May 26, 1949, and noted that there were disturbing reports involving fraud and favoritism. An investigation by the House Armed Services Committee cleared all those concerned in the B-36 bomber procurement program after it was revealed that a civilian Navy employee had made the anonymous charges without any evidence to support his allegations.[52]

Captain John G. Crommelin, a Navy flyer, charged on September 10, 1949 that senior officers of the Army and Air Force

---

[49] *Ibid.*, pp. 476-477.
[50] *Ibid.*, pp. 373-374.
[51] For several interesting articles on Johnson see: "Task of Louis Johnson," *US News and World Report*, March 11, 1949; "New Secretary," *Newsweek*, March 21, 1949; "Secretary Johnson," *New Republic*, March 21, 1949; "Talking Man," *Life*, May 9, 1949.
[52] New York *Times*, May 27 and August 26, 1949.

wanted to destroy naval aviation in order to strengthen their control over the Department of Defense. He claimed that the future of the Navy and the country were at stake and he decided to violate official orders against public discussion of the feud over airpower among the armed forces because he hoped "this will blow the whole thing open and bring on another Congressional investigation." [53]

On October 3, Crommelin released confidential letters from three admirals criticizing the defense establishment. The letters to Navy Secretary Matthews were from Vice Admiral Gerald P. Bogan, Commander, First Task Force in the Pacific with two indorsements by Admiral Arthur W. Radford, Commander-in-Chief of the Pacific Fleet, and Admiral Louis Denfeld, Chief of Naval Operations. To Admiral Bogan "it would be sheer balderdash to assume that there has been anything approaching [unity] among the Secretariat, the Joint Staff or the high command of the three services. Bickering is still the rule. Unanimity is non-existent. We are fearful that the country is being sold a false bill of goods" concerning the success of unification. A majority of the officers in the Pacific Fleet, wrote Radford, were in agreement with the views of Bogan and Crommelin, and in the view of Louis Denfeld "a Navy stripped of its offensive power means a nation stripped of its offensive power." [54]

The House Armed Services Committee immediately decided to investigate the entire status of the nation's defenses. One of the first witnesses was Admiral Radford who in public testimony on October 7 bitterly denounced the B-36 as a billion dollar blunder. He then proceeded to term the atomic blitz theory of warfare a fallacious concept and warned that the Air Force's concentration on heavy bombers to the neglect of fighters and tactical planes might be disastrous if war came. The Defense Department was criticized for making decisions concerning the Navy "without proper information" and Johnson's cancellation of the supercarrier was considered unsound. [55]

Other prominent naval figures who expressed their thoughts during the dispute included Admiral William F. Halsey, Admiral

---

[53] *Ibid.*, September 11, 1949.
[54] New York *Times*, October 4, 1949.
[55] New York *Times*, October 8, 1949. See also for further material on the dispute: "Complete Text of Statement in Defense Dispute," *US News and World Report*, October 28, 1949.

Thomas C. Kinkaid, and Fleet Admiral Ernest J. King, who stoutly maintained that the Air Force's policy of waging war by long distance was unsound and dangerously deceptive to the American people. Tactical airpower, they asserted, had been demonstrated in World War II as being superior to strategic bombing.[56]

The Navy's case was summed up by Admiral Denfeld who claimed the Navy was being dangerously weakened by uninformed and arbitrary decisions. Secretary Johnson was sharply criticized not only for his cancellation of the carrier, but also because he violated the spirit and concept of unification.[57]

Biting rebuttal of the Navy's charges were delivered by General Omar Bradley, the chairman of the Joint Chiefs of Staff. The Navy's admirals were charged with open rebellion against civil authority and with having done infinite harm to the United States. They were further accused of misrepresentations and false insinuation. Bradley asked for a public withdrawal of their charges against the Joint Chiefs and Secretary Johnson.[58]

Bradley continued his attack the next day, giving his support to the Air Force on every point. The Navy, he said, had opposed unification from the beginning and had not accepted it completely to date. The reason for the Navy being outvoted so often by the Joint Chiefs was because Naval officers were still preoccupied with their island hopping campaigns and sometimes failed to realize the kind of continental operations that war with Russia would involve.[59]

General Eisenhower hurried down from Columbia University to pour some oil on the troubled waters. He cautioned against expecting perfection too quickly, took no side in the dispute, and said the conflict was basically over how the defense dollar was to be divided. The last witnesses were Secretary Johnson, Herbert

---

[56] New York *Times,* October 13, 1949. Other naval officers who were sharply critical in their testimony included: Admiral William H. P. Blandy, Rear Admiral Ralph A. Ofstie, Brigadier General Vernon A. Magee of the Marine Corps, Admiral Chester W. Nimitz, and Admiral Raymond A. Spruance.

[57] New York *Times,* October 14, 1949.

[58] *Ibid.,* October 20, 1949. The admirals were called "Fancy Dans who won't hit the line with all they have on every play unless they can call the signals."

[59] *Ibid.,* October 21, 1949. The Air Force, represented by Secretary Stuart Symington and General Hoyt S. Vandenberg, Air Force Chief of Staff, put up a vigorous defense of the military capabilities of the B-36. *Ibid.,* October 19, 20, 1949.

Hoover, and General George C. Marshall who all pleaded for unity.[60]

The public display of interservice rivalries may have served to clear the air. The consensus was that the "revolt of the admirals" had failed to better the Navy's position.[61] On October 27, President Truman removed Admiral Denfeld as Chief of Naval Operations[62] and appointed in his place Admiral Forrest P. Sherman who actually managed to retrieve some of the Navy's prestige and to resume work on the supercarrier.[63]

The Budget and Preparedness

Budget and manpower fluctuations during Johnson's tenure of office reflected a drive for economy. Following a war this was nothing new in American history, but the economy drive this time was spearheaded by the Secretary of Defense. Prior to the establishment of the Department of Defense the National Military Establishment, according to Johnson, "was still suffering from costly war-born spending habits. It was like a fat man—and like a fat man, was in poor condition to run a race until the fat could be transformed into muscle." [64]

In choosing between butter and guns the Secretary of Defense left no doubt as to where his choice lay. He chose butter. The cost of national security, with appropriations totalling approximately 15 billion dollars a year, was too heavy a burden on the nation's taxpayers, he claimed. It could not go on indefinitely without depressing our standard of living.[65] Therefore, by his order, reductions were made in personnel, equipment, and facilities.[66]

President Truman's budget request of January 9, 1950, served to cut further "fat" from the military establishment. The Chief Executive asked for an appropriation of 13.5 billion dollars for the military and contemplated reducing the personnel of the armed forces by 190,628. The sum requested would be enough to maintain a ten-division Army, a Navy of 238 major combat vessels

[60] New York *Times,* October 21, 22, 1949.
[61] Baldwin, *op. cit.,* p. 710.
[62] New York *Times,* October 28, 1949.
[63] Baldwin, *op. cit.,* p. 710.
[64] *Department of Defense Semiannual Report of the Secretary of Defense, July 1 to December 1, 1949,* p. 42.
[65] *Ibid.,* p. 9.
[66] The total of our armed forces dropped 64,073 in the last half of 1949. *Ibid.,* p. 254.

(a 50-ship cut from 1950's original authorization), and a 48-group Air Force.[67]

In testimony released by a Senate Appropriations subcommittee on June 9, 1949, General Bradley was quoted as saying the armed forces were not in shape to fight a major war and would not be ready for another year, although they were being built up to a point where they would be able to ward off an enemy attack. The National Press Club of Washington was told by General J. Lawton Collins on November 4 that the Army was getting back in shape and in four or five months "will be ready to fight anyone and whip them, any time, anywhere." Speaking in December of 1949, Secretary Johnson assured his audience the United States was making certain that no enemy could defeat it by a sudden "4 o'clock in the morning attack" and America could "launch a successful counterattack spearheaded by the Air Force." [68]

On March 3, 1950, Johnson advised the Overseas Press Club of New York that the American defense situation was more encouraging than at any time since V-J Day.[69] This did not go entirely unchallenged; Stewart Alsop, a bitter critic of the Secretary, charged in his column in the New York *Herald Tribune* of March 6 that Johnson was deceiving the American people with his speeches; and that his economies had so whittled down American air strength we were headed straight for disaster.

After the outbreak of the Korean War, Johnson and the Congress frantically tried to rebuild the shattered war machine, but his feud with Secretary of State Acheson[70] and the inadequacies of our defenses forced his resignation on September 12, 1950. A Pentagon witticism perhaps summarizes his career as Secretary: "Louis said we could lick the Russians—he didn't mean the North Koreans." [71]

---

[67] New York *Times,* January 10, 1950.

[68] *Ibid.,* June 10, November 5, and December 8, 1949. In an article of February 23, 1950, *Life* reported the Soviet Union was spending 25% of its 65 billion a year national income on their armed forces while only 6% of America's 222 billion income was going for defense. Other comparisons included: combat planes—Russia, 9,000, U. S.—3,300; annual plane production—Russia, 7,000, U. S.—1,200; army—Russia, 2,600,000, U. S., 640,000.

[69] New York *Times,* March 4, 1950.

[70] See "Johnson vs. Acheson," *Newsweek,* April 10, 1950; "Johnson or Acheson," *Life,* June 24, 1950.

[71] Baldwin, *op. cit.,* p. 711.

The Reserves

In order to make a comprehensive study for the laying of the groundwork for an adequate and efficient Reserve Force, Secretary of Defense Forrestal appointed a Committee on Civilian Components which came to be called the Gray Board, after its chairman, Assistant Secretary of the Army Gordon Gray.[72] The Committee's report was released on June 30, 1948, containing many valuable recommendations and suggestions which were later to be implemented. Some of its major points were:

1. Interservice unity must be attained.
2. National security requires all services to have a Reserve Force.
3. Organization, training, administration, and supply of the Reserves should be completely integrated with those of the regular establishment.
4. The structure of the Reserve Forces should be simplified and made common to the three services.
5. The over-all mission of the Reserves of each service should be to provide trained units and qualified officer personnel to meet the requirements for the reinforcement and expansion of each service in time of national emergency or war.
6. National Guard and Officer Reserve Corps units were not capable of participating effectively in major combat operations on M-Day.[73]
7. Members of the Reserve Forces should be organized into tactical or training units, planned on the same general training lines as that proposed for the Army.
8. Specialist personnel should be organized into units designed to utilize their professional skills.[74]

Another recommendation was for the establishment of a Joint Inter-Service Committee to consider, recommend, and report to the Secretary of Defense on Reserve Force policies and procedures of joint or common interest to the Reserve Forces of all the Services. In June of 1949, Louis Johnson created the Civil Components Policy Board which was reconstituted as the Reserve Forces Policy

---

[72] I. M. McQuiston: "History of the Reserves Since the Second World War," *Military Affairs,* Vol. XVII, No. 1, Spring, 1953, p. 23. This entire volume is an historical symposium on the reserves of the armed forces.

[73] The Gray Board's attitude toward the National Guard brought this retort: "Kidnapping of the National Guard by the Federal Government has been proposed by Secretary Forrestal's Gray Board. They've asked for a fight, and they'll get it." *The National Guardsman,* September, 1948.

[74] *Department of Defense—Report of Committee on Civilian Components* (Washington: G.P.O., 1948), pp. 9-46

Board by Secretary Marshall and has been established by law, the Armed Forces Act, effective January 1, 1953.[75]

Membership in the Reserves has traditionally been voluntary, but the Universal Military Training and Service Act of 1951 imposed a reserve obligation on all persons who entered the services after 24 June 1948. The legislation, however, failed to make continued training mandatory. The armed services were subjected to a great deal of criticism in their disposition of the reserves in the Korean War and if such mistakes are to be avoided in the future it seems evident that the Reserve must be kept strong by a regulated input of trained personnel of proper age groups who will not be subject to deferment upon call to active duty.[76]

The Communist North Korean aggression of June, 1950 once again involved the United States in war. Some familiar aspects were again present: grave unpreparedness and a frantic rush to provide men and material. But this was to be a different war for America. There was to be no all-out drive for victory, but rather the striving for limited objectives under the banners of the United Nations. It was a costly and highly unpopular war with its full importance yet to be weighed upon the scales of history. The armed services were subjected to considerable criticism in their disposition of Reserve personnel in the Korean war.

The Reserve Forces

In addition to our experience in the Korean war there were other reasons why the problem of military manpower was reviewed by the 84th Congress. The Universal Military Training and Service Act (65 Stat 75) was due to expire on June 30, 1955, thus affecting the existing authority for the induction of men by the Selective Service System. At the same time there appeared to be no diminution of the international threat of aggression and of the need of the United States to be prepared in the event of sudden nuclear warfare. It was necessary to re-examine the military strength needed by the Armed Forces on a steady, long-term basis and to relate this factor to the numbers of trained reserves that would be essential to augment the regular units during a national emergency. Above all it was important to examine the Reserve structure in the light of the objectives we had hoped to achieve when the then existing laws were passed.

Several studies by executive and legislative groups in prior years revealed that the Reserve forces were suffering from a complication of difficulties.

On January 13, 1955, President Eisenhower sent to the Congress his message on "The Military Security of the United States."[77] He pointed out that our security depended upon having active forces ready for instant action and trained Reserve forces that were ready for mobilization. "Never in peacetime," said the President, "have we achieved this proper military posture. The penalties of our unreadiness have been manifold—in treasure, in blood, in the heartbreak of a mighty nation buying time with the lives of men." The President referred to the fact that his recommendations were based upon exhaustive studies that had been made of military manpower. He recommended that the then existing authority for inducting young men by the Selective Service System be extended for four years—from July 1, 1955 to July 1, 1959; that the special legislation authorizing induction of doctors and dentists be extended from July 1, 1955 to July 1, 1957; and that the Congress enact legislation to strengthen the Reserve forces so that they could meet the requirements for essential mobilization.

With regard to the Reserve forces the Congress enacted the Reserve Forces Act of 1955 (Public Law 305, 84th Congress). The new bill consisted of amendments to existing basic laws: The Universal Military Training and Service Act and the Armed Services Reserve Act. One of the most significant changes was the reduction of total military obligation covering active and Reserve service from 8 to 6 years.

The Ready Reserve would be strengthened by increasing its membership from 1.5 to 2.9 million and by emphasizing a training program that would insure military preparedness. Continuous screening of units and members of the Ready Reserve would be carried out according to regulations prescribed by the President, and it would be possible for the Secretary of a military department to transfer men from the Ready into the Standby Reserve. The criteria for the screening process were designed to insure that combat veterans were transferred out of the Ready

---

[77] Message from the President of the United States Relative to the Military Security of the United States. H. DOC. NO. 68, 84th Cong., 1st Session.

Reserve so that they would not be called to active duty a second or third time; that attrition would be avoided among the members or units; that there would be a proper balance of military skills; that essential civilian skills would be protected; and that notice would be taken of individual cases involving extreme personal or community hardship.

The Ready Reserve was to be composed of persons who had entered the active forces after July 27, 1953, the Korean cease-fire date, and those who entered prior to that time would not be required to participate in Ready Reserve training unless they agreed to do so. In a national emergency declared by the President, he could order up to 1,000,000 Ready Reservists without further authority from the Congress.

The recall to active duty of members of the Standby Reserve, however, could only be made during a war or a national emergency declared by the Congress, and then only after the Director of Selective Service had determined whether or not the persons were available.

Two new means whereby men could become members of the Ready Reserve Forces were made available by the provisions of this bill: (1). A six-year enlistment directly into the Reserves with the understanding that two years would be spent in active service; and (2) an eight-year enlistment in a new program authorized for four years, combining six months basic training with 7½ years of participation in Ready Reserve training.

(1) The six-year enlistment directly into a Reserve component (except the National Guard and the Air National Guard) carried with it an agreement for the enlistee that he would accept active duty for two years. Thereafter he was to become a member of the Ready Reserve for a period of time which would add up to five years of active and Reserve service. Thus there was an inducement for a man to reduce his total military obligation of six years to five if he participated satisfactorily in the Ready Reserve program.

(2) The eight-year enlistment in one of the Reserve components (except the National Guard and the Air National Guard) would be open to a quota of young men who had not yet reached 18½ years of age and had not received a notice to report for induction. This program would be available only until July 1,

1959 and could be started whenever the President found that the authorized strength of the Ready Reserve of the various components was not being maintained. Under such circumstances the President could authorize the acceptance of volunteers, but the quota could not exceed 250,000 each year. The regulations were to be prescribed by the Secretary of Defense. Young men who volunteered for this program were to be deferred from induction as long as they performed satisfactorily in the Reserve component, but they remained liable for induction until they were 28 years old. The program was also available to persons with critical skills who were working in essential industries and research pertaining to defense, regardless of their age when they were ordered to report for induction.

The men in this program were to be paid $50.00 a month during the six months they were on active duty for training, and to have other benefits such as hospitalization, and subsistence and travel allowances, but not certain benefits provided by the National Service Life Insurance Act of 1940. These reservists were also eligible for re-employment rights for 60 days after they had completed their six months' training. The National Security Training Commission was to advise the President and the Secretary of Defense regarding the welfare of those who took the six-months training.

To insure that the members and units of the Ready Reserve were militarily prepared in a national emergency, the training provisions were specifically set forth in H.R. 7000. The minimum training for any one year was to consist of 48 assemblies for drill (or the equivalent periods when authorized by the appropriate Secretary of a military department) plus active duty for training for no more than 17 days. If a reservist elected not to participate in this type of training, he had the alternative of active duty for training for no more than 30 days each year. If, however, a Ready Reservist refused to follow either one of the training alternatives, he could be ordered involuntarily for a period of duty not to exceed 45 days each year. (Hardly enough of an "insurance" to insure satisfactory participation by any large group of reservists.)

A special provision had been written into the bill with regard to qualified graduates of the Army and Air Force ROTC and the Marine Corps platoon leader's class. They were to receive commissions when they graduated, and if they were not needed for active duty for service, they were to be ordered to active duty as officers for six months' training. Thereafter they were expected to participate in the training programs of the Ready Reserve. Failure to do so would result in revoking their commissions.

Another amendment to existing law concerned ordained ministers and theological students. Ministers could request a discharge, and students of the ministry were not required to serve on active duty or training while they were attending recognized divinity schools.

In order that Congress should be able to keep in touch with the administration and regulation of the various Reserve programs, the bill provided that the Secretary of Defense should keep records of those on active duty training and in a drill pay status. Furthermore, the Secretary of Defense was required to make an annual January report to the President and the Congress on the progress that was being made in strengthening the Reserve Forces.

CHAPTER 22

Korea and the New Look

"Blood, Sweat, and Tears"—Building For Limited and Cold Wars—The Problems of Peripheral Warfare—The New Look

IN THE LATE hours of June 24, 1950, Washington received word of the invasion of the Republic of Korea by the Red Army of North Korea. The Administration immediately called for a meeting of the United Nations Security Council which was held on the afternoon of June 25 with the Soviet representative not in attendance. The Security Council named the Republic of Korea "a lawfully established government" and termed the attack "a breach of the peace." The North Korean authorities were called upon to cease their attack and withdraw to the thirty-eighth parallel. Two days later the Security Council called upon the members of the United Nations to furnish such assistance to the Republic of Korea "as may be necessary to repel the armed attack and to restore international peace and security in the area." [1]

On the same day President Truman announced: (1) the ordering of American naval and air forces to the aid of South Korea; (2) the dispatch of the Seventh Fleet to protect Formosa from attack by China, and also to prevent Chiang Kai-Shek from raiding the mainland; (3) the stepping up of military aid to the Philippines and French Indo-China. Communism, the President remarked, had passed from the use of subversion for seizing independent nations to armed invasion and war. The Chief Executive concluded his momentous announcement by saying, " a return to the rule of force in international affairs would have far-reaching effects. The United States will continue to uphold the rule of law." [2]

It quickly became apparent that greater aid would have to be rushed to prevent the speedy collapse of South Korea, which was

---

[1] *In Quest of Peace and Security: Selected Documents on American Foreign Policy, 1941-1951,* Department of State Publication 4245, (Washington: G.P.O., 1951), pp. 74-75.
[2] New York *Times,* June 28, 1950.

vainly trying to halt the well trained and equipped invaders. On June 29, President Truman authorized General MacArthur to send supporting ground units to Korea and to begin air strikes against North Korean targets.[3] The Security Council of the United Nations on July 7 called upon its members to make their military forces available to a unified command under the United States, and requested America to designate the commander.[4]

"Blood, Sweat, and Tears"

It would be difficult to exaggerate the problems which confronted the U. N. troops.[5] The Korean rainy season had just started and the nearest American troops were the understrength occupation forces in Japan. Furthermore, the troops in Japan had been mainly engaged in their occupation duties and there were few seasoned veterans to aid the green troops in their initial baptism of fire.[6] The situation was not much better at home, for the United States was not prepared for war in 1950.

As noted in the preceding chapters, the armed forces had suffered drastic reductions upon the conclusion of World War II. Few trained units were available for immediate commitment to Korea, and these, owing to rapid personnel turnover, were inadequately trained. There were in existence only twelve American combat divisions, and all, with the exception of the 1st Infantry Division, were considerably understrength. To compound the difficulties it was held inadvisable to send all available troops to Korea, for fear of a Communist thrust elsewhere.[7]

In June of 1950 the Navy was putting more ships and planes into mothballs, its personnel was being sharply reduced, and the Shore Establishment was being cut to the barest essentials. The bulk of the Navy's funds and efforts were being devoted to main-

---

[3] *Ibid.*, June 30, 1950.

[4] *In Quest of Peace and Security*, p. 76.

[5] Office of the Chief of Military History: *Korea—1950*. (Washington: G.P.O., 1952), p. 11. Hereafter cited as *Korea—1950*.

[6] *Korea—1950*, pp. 11, 14. There were four divisions in the Eighth Army in Japan.

[7] *Ibid.*, p. 14. The Army was 38,500 under its authorized strength of 630,000 men, and "since World War II there have been serious deficits in all major types of Army equipment. *Department of Defense Semiannual Report, Report of S/A, January 1, June 30, 1950*, p. 68. The Air Force was in better shape though lacking the recommended strength in air groups. It numbered approximately 564,000 men which was 3,700 below authorized and required levels, p. 172. Two of the twelve divisions cited above were in the Marine Corps.

taining the combat readiness of its Active Fleet which numbered 672 vessels. Its personnel was nearing the objective of a reduced strength of 375,042 officers and men which would have permitted an average manning level of 65% of wartime complements for all of the ships in the Active Fleet. The Navy was not ready for sustained combat operations over a long period of time. Additional personnel, ships, and planes were needed quickly.[8]

The first weeks of the war witnessed gallant attempts on the part of the Army to trade space for time. By early August, the American Eighth Army under the command of General Walton H. Walker had its back to the sea in the southeast corner of the peninsula in an area about the size of Connecticut. The next six weeks unfolded one of the most brilliant defenses in modern warfare as the crucial Battle of the Pusan Beachhead was fought.[9]

The battle was brought to a dramatic conclusion by MacArthur's brilliant amphibious attack at Inchon, the seaport of Seoul, on September 15. Seoul fell to the Marines on September 27th and the Korean Reds, cut off from their bases, began to retreat from the Pusan Perimeter. By the end of the month they had given up nearly all territory south of the thirty-seventh parallel. The retreat of the North Korean Army degenerated gradually into a rout. The question of whether or not to pursue the fleeing aggressors across the thirty-eighth parallel was given a rather vague sanction by a United Nations resolution of October 7, 1950, which authorized the taking of all appropriate steps to ensure conditions of stability throughout Korea.[10]

The victory-flushed Eighth Army routed the demoralized North Koreans whose capital, Pyongyang, fell on October 19. By the last week in October the Red Army of North Korea was utterly crushed with its remnants fleeing toward the mountainous borderlands adjacent to Manchuria and the Soviet Union. The United Nations army moved forward virtually at will. The victorious march came to an end, however, with the appearance of Chinese Communist "Volunteers" which created an entirely new war.

The participation of Chinese troops had been noted during the

---

[8] *Department of Defense Semiannual Report, Report of S/N, January 1 to June 30, 1951*, pp. 145, 147, 181.
[9] Baldwin, *op. cit.*, pp. 774-775; *Korea—1950*, pp. 14-20, 77-84.
[10] *In Quest of Peace and Security*, p. 77.

last week of October, but the full fury of the Chinese counter-offensive did not take place until November 25, when they halted the advance of the United Nations forces toward the Yalu River. Disaster once again loomed on the horizon. The Allied forces, fighting a stubborn rear guard action which prevented a complete catastrophe, were forced out of North Korea and were not able to set up new defensive positions south of Seoul until mid-January of 1951.

From this point on, the war developed into a stalemate broken by cease-fire agreements and efforts to achieve a truce. American commanders in the field were restrained by the Administration from initiating an all-out offensive and from attacking the "privileged sanctuary" of the Chinese in Manchuria. Fears were expressed that if Manchuria was subjected to bombings it would be the prelude to World War III. General MacArthur took violent exception to this point of view. He could see no substitute for victory. Policy disagreements between MacArthur and Washington led to his recall on April 11, 1951, and the "great debate" over American foreign policy was set off.

MacArthur's thesis was presented in an address before a joint session of Congress on April 19. The Korean War must be won, he said, and not end in a stalemate; the bombing of Chinese bases in Manchuria, blockading the Chinese coast, and using Chinese Nationalist forces would not necessarily bring the Soviet Union into the war.[11]

The decision, however, was to be made not on purely military considerations, but within the broad framework of American diplomacy. From the standpoint of the Administration the United Nations' objectives in Korea were to end aggression, to safeguard against its renewal, and to restore peace. This involved the waging of limited warfare designed to preserve the coalition of United Nations Allies in Korea, and to prevent the possible enlargement of the conflict into World War III.[12] The Joint Chiefs held that their overriding concern was the safety of the United States, and

---

[11] New York *Times*, April 20, 1951.

[12] *Hearings Before the Committee on Armed Services and the Committee on Foreign Relations to Conduct an Inquiry into the Military Situation in the Far East and the Facts Surrounding the Relief of General of the Army Douglas MacArthur from His Assignments in that Area,* (Washington: G.P.O., 1951), Part 3, pp. 1667-2291. Needless to say there were many who disagreed with the Secretary of State.

"we felt the action urged by General MacArthur would hazard this safety without promising any certain proportionate gain." [13]

MacArthur's advice was disregarded, and the bitter, inconclusive war was ended by a truce signed on July 27, 1953. Though America's allies had insisted on the sharing of military decisions in Korea, they offered no objections to the United States supplying all but a small percentage of the military force of the United Nations. The cost in casualties to America was extremely high with over 26,000 killed, 100,000 wounded, and 11,000 missing or captured. The Republic of Korea suffered a toll of approximately 257,000 killed, wounded, or missing, whereas the combined total for the other United Nations forces was only about 13,000.[14]

The Korean War witnessed a rapid build-up of American forces. The aggression had made it clear that Russia and her satellites were willing to hazard a general war by aggression in various parts of the world, unless opposed by deterrent military strength.[15] General George C. Marshall was appointed Secretary of Defense after the resignation of Louis Johnson on September 12, 1950, to direct the rebuilding of America's military forces.

The military program initiated had two major objectives. The first was a rapid increase in the Army, Navy, and Air Force to a combined strength of 3,600,000 by July, 1952, adequately trained and supplied with the best weapons and equipment available. The second aim was the establishment of an orderly procedure for the maintenance of the new military strength over an indefinite number of years and at greatly increasing the readiness of American industry and manpower for full mobilization.[16]

Building for Limited and Cold Wars

One of the paradoxes of the crisis was the Army mobilizing, demobilizing, and fighting a war at the same time. The ten divisions available at the outbreak of war increased to eighteen in the

---

[13] General Omar N. Bradley: "A Soldier's Farewell," *Saturday Evening Post,* August 22, 1953, p. 63. "We may have been wrong. As of today I still believe that we were right, because at the particular time we did not have the necessary armed might to risk such a course of action, as well as the safety of Europe."

[14] Baldwin, *op. cit.,* p. 781.

[15] *Semiannual Report of the Secretary of Defense, January 1 to June 30, 1951,* p. 2.

[16] *Semiannual Report of the Secretary of Defense, January 1 to June 30, 1951,* p. 2.

next year with two more being added by June of 1952. The largest increase in personnel, slightly over a million men,[17] occurred during the first year of the war, but the release of men kept the size of the Army fairly constant after June, 1951, when the total strength reached 1,531,596. In fiscal year 1952 the net increase was only 65,000 and at one point during the year we were considerably overstrength and were forced to adjust the separation rate accordingly.[18]

In the following year, the Army's strength decreased by 62,600 men, but despite the reduction in net strength and the large turnover in personnel, a force of 20 combat divisions, 18 separate regiments and regimental combat teams, over 100 antiaircraft battalions, and more than 150 other combat battalions, was maintained.[19]

The first important source of manpower to be tapped was the trained soldier with 310,000 reservists and National Guardsmen called to active duty. By July of 1951, reservists were being gradually released,[20] but the following year saw approximately 120,000 members of the National Guard still on active duty.[21] By the end of the war the total size of the National Guard was 215,341 with approximately one fourth on active duty.[22]

Although the total strength of the Army Reserve was 798,026 on July 1, 1953, the number of organized units, and the assigned strength of these units, showed an alarming decrease. One of the important tasks faced by the Army was to induce reservists who had a statutory reserve obligation to join units and take an active part in the reserve program. The Universal Military Training and Service Act of 1951 permitted the mandatory assignment of reservists to organized units, but it was questionable whether actual active participation in group training could be enforced under

---

[17] *Ibid., Report of S/A*, p. 81.

[18] *Semiannual Report of the Secretary of Defense, Report of S/A, January 1 to June 30, 1952*, p. 112. The enlisted strength was made up of 45% Regular Army, 40% selectees, and 15% reserves and National Guard.

[19] *Semiannual Report of the Secretary of Defense, Report of S/A, January 1 to June 30, 1953*, p. 99.

[20] *Semiannual Report of the Secretary of Defense, Report of S/A, January 1 to June 30, 1951*, p. 81.

[21] *Semiannual Report of the Secretary of Defense, Report of S/A, January 1 to June 30, 1952*, p. 116.

[22] *Semiannual Report of the Secretary of Defense, Report of S/A, January 1 to June 30, 1953*, p. 106.

present statutes.[23] The Washington *News*, April 7, 1954, published an article asserting there were over 1,500,000 in the reserves, but of these only 185,000 were in active training units. High military officials such as the chairman of the Joint Chiefs, Admiral Radford, were reported to be gravely concerned over the situation.

The Army's combat replacement system, the largest systematic rotation of troops from combat in any nation's military history, added greatly to training and logistical problems. The rotation plan was first established in April, 1951, with the first shipload of returnees docking at Seattle on May 5, 1951. By June 1952 about 350,000 officers and enlisted men from the Far East Command had been returned to the United States. The plan was "one of the major reflections of the Army's respect for the individual soldier," and because of it "the burden of combat is being widely distributed, instead of being allowed to rest indefinitely upon the shoulders of a comparatively few." [24]

The personnel strength of the Navy in June of 1950 was 375,042. This increased almost 95% in the following year, reaching a total of 732,152 on June 30, 1951. An increase of 64% in the Active Fleet was accomplished in the same period with the number of ships rising from 672 to 1,102.[25] Just prior to the signing of the truce, there were 794,440 Navy personnel and 249,206 Marines on active duty.[26] The bulk of the operating forces were about equally divided between the Atlantic and Pacific Oceans. The Navy was organized into four fleets with the First Fleet operating in the Eastern Pacific and the Seventh Fleet being deployed in Korean and Chinese waters. The Second Fleet was based on the east coast of the United States and the Sixth Fleet was in the Mediterranean. These were organized around attack aircraft carriers operating in carrier task forces.[27]

From a starting position of 48 regular wings and an authorized

---

[23] *Semiannual Report of the Department of Defense, Report of S/A, January 1 to June 30, 1953*, pp. 103-105.

[24] *Semiannual Report of the Secretary of Defense, Report of S/A, January 1 to 30, 1952*, pp. 107-108.

[25] *Semiannual Report of the Department of Defense, Report of S/N, January 1 to June 30, 1951*, pp. 147, 181.

[26] *Semiannual Report of the Department of Defense, Report of S/N, January 1 to June 30, 1953*, p. 170. There were 134,375 Navy and 19,775 Marine Reserves on drill pay status.

[27] *Ibid.*, p. 180. In millions of dollars the appropriations for the Navy in the following fiscal years were as follows: 1950, 12,481; 1952, 16,098; 1953, 12,628; 1954, 9,358. *Ibid.*, p. 230.

strength of 416,314, the Air Force was authorized by a series of decisions reached between July 1950 and January 1951, to expand to a total of 95 wings and 1,061,000 military personnel, not later than June 30, 1952. By June 30, 1951, 87 wings were brought into being and a personnel strength of 788,381 was reached. The greater part of the increase from 48 to 87 wings was provided by the 31 wings called to active service, 21 from the Air National Guard and 10 from the Organized Reserve. The Air Force then raised its goal to 95 wings to be reached by June 30, 1952.[28]

While the Air Force committed a considerable portion of its strength in Korea, at home it proceeded with the establishment of a firm base for any necessary future expansion. Emphasis was placed on providing a powerful air defense for the United States, and positive measures were taken to increase tactical air power. The ability of the Strategic Air Command to strike powerful retaliatory blows in response to any attacks against this Nation were increased as a matter of urgent necessity and to lessen the possibility that a major war might be forced upon us.[29]

The decision to further increase the planned size of the Air Force to 126 combat wings plus supporting elements was announced by President Truman in December, 1951.[30] In the early months of the following year, the goal was again increased to 143 wings thus giving the Air Force a large share of the fiscal year 1953 defense budget.[31] Then the signing of the Korean truce, increased developments in firepower, and the financial burden of the over-all military program emphasized the necessity for a complete "new look" at the nation's military requirements. While the Joint Chiefs were studying the problem, the 1954 budget of the Air Force was based on an interim program which continued the expansion of U. S. airpower.[32]

In addition to carrying out an ambitious construction program

---

[28] *Semiannual Report of the Department of Defense, Report of the Secretary of the A/F, January 1 to June 30, 1951*, pp. 198, 200.
[29] *Semiannual Report of the Department of Defense, Report of the Secretary of the A/F, July 1 to December 31, 1950*, p. 29.
[30] *Semiannual Report of the Department of Defense, Report of the Secretary of the A/F, July 1 to December 31, 1951*, p. 35.
[31] *Semiannual Report of the Department of Defense, Report of the Secretary of the A/F, January 1 to June 30, 1952*, p. 203.
[32] *Semiannual Report of the Department of Defense, Report of the Secretary of the A/F, January 1 to June 30, 1953*, p. 247.

of overseas bases, another important step of the period was laying the groundwork for the establishment of an Air Force Academy. The Air Force was confident it would be able to utilize the experiences of West Point and Annapolis to create the best possible institution in which to train junior officers for a career of leadership in the USAF.[33]

Industrial mobilization planning was not geared to an all-out or "crash" program. Rather, George Marshall and Robert A. Lovett, who succeeded Marshall as Secretary of Defense, held out for a less violent, steadier, more orderly increase which the United States could support and sustain for the long pull.[34] Orders were broadly distributed among the factories of America to assure manufacturers of sufficient production orders to warrant the maintenance of large plant capacity. Some have recently advocated the narrowing of this broad production base in the interests of efficiency and economy. This would be desirable, General Bradley thought, "if we don't have a general war." [35]

The Problems of Peripheral Warfare

The present policy of world Communism seeks to advance its power through a variety of means including propaganda, espionage, internal subversion, and peripheral warfare.[36] Local and limited wars at a time and place of Soviet choosing and the use of other nationals instead of their own troops are characteristics of peripheral warfare. Greece, Indo-China, and Korea are all outstanding examples of this Soviet technique to drain the wealth and power away from the free world. Such a policy would tend to overextend the commitments of the United States and would place an intolerable burden upon our economy and military resources. Wars that were not wars and peace without victory were something novel to America, but the future of the nation depended upon finding some solution or relief.

Secretary of State John Foster Dulles believed that America must give up the idea of a "house-by-house defense" as contained in peripheral warfare. Instead, primary reliance for our defense and

[33] *Ibid.*, p. 259.
[34] Bradley, *op. cit.*, p. 62.
[35] *Ibid.*
[36] For an informative and scholarly discussion of peripheral warfare see James D. Atkinson: "The Communist Revolution in Warfare," *United States Naval Institute Proceedings*, March, 1953.

world peace should be "placed upon the combining of two concepts, namely, the creation of power on a community basis and the use of that power so as to deter aggression by making it costly to an aggressor."[37] The creation of power on a community basis meant renewed emphasis on the doctrine of collective security, while the second idea was to make sure that a potential aggressor would know in advance that he could and would be made to suffer for his aggression more than he could possibly gain by it.[38]

It remains to be seen whether this is the answer to peripheral warfare. Certainly there is nothing new in the ideas of Secretary Dulles and it would be perhaps pedantic to point out that these concepts have been tried in the past and failed. It also seems doubtful if the doctrines of Dulles could be applied to nationalist uprisings even if they were clearly sponsored by Soviet conspiracy. Massive retaliation may also be questioned in the light of whether there would be available and suitable targets, unless, of course, the blow was delivered directly against the Soviet Union. Massive retaliation, it should also be kept in mind, is not a one-way street. At any event, strong deterrent power seems to be a part of the "New Look."

The New Look

"New phrases are often introduced into the language to highlight an idea or to confuse the human mind." [39] In the 20th Century America has had the Square Deal, New Freedom, New Deal, Fair Deal, and now the New Look. The New Look has been applied to many things such as new styles in clothing, new approaches by the State Department to the world situation, and to a revised concept of emphasizing new military weapons. As an example of the confusion surrounding the term, news reporters in asking Secretary of Defense Charles Wilson what the New Look was, said, "In other words you keep the enemy guessing and you keep us guessing." "Well," answered the Secretary, "you are paid to guess, aren't you?" [40]

One new element in America's 1954 military posture was the

---

[37] John Foster Dulles: "Policy for Peace and Security" *The Department of State bulletin,* March 29, 1954.
[38] *Ibid.*
[39] George E. Sokolsky: "The 'New Look'," *Washington Post and Times Herald,* March 26, 1954.
[40] *Life:* "Deconfusing the 'New Look,," March 29, 1954.

degree of preparedness as reflected in the budget. After the other wars in which the United States had participated there had been a frantic rush to beat the swords into ploughshares. America had been chronically unprepared for the wars of the past and certainly the example of America's leaning toward small military forces was not followed by the rest of the world nor did devotion to pacifism help to prevent the outbreak of war.

President Eisenhower has given the definition of the New Look in military affairs. "It is," he said, "simply an attempt by intelligent people to keep abreast of the times." The President used as an analogy the D-Day invasion of the Normandy beaches which he commanded. "What," he asked, "would two atomic bombs have done to the whole thing?" [41]

The military budget for fiscal year 1955 (37.6 billion dollars) represents an attempt to maintain American military power during the unforeseeable fluctuations and threats of the Cold War. "We have never before," said Admiral Radford, "attempted to keep forces of this size over such an extended period of time." [42] The proposed military establishment will include an Army of over a million men, an Air Force of almost another million, and the largest Navy in the world.

Renewed emphasis on military alliances was also a part of the New Look. In the world of today, according to Secretary Dulles, no nation could develop for itself "defensive power of adequate scope and flexibility. In seeking to do so, each would become a garrison state and none would achieve security." Starting with the Inter-American Treaty of Reciprocal Assistance in 1947 and followed by NATO in 1949 the principle was established that an armed attack against one would be considered as an attack against all. The same concept was evolving in other areas such as the Western Pacific and the Middle East which "show the growing acceptance of the collective security concept we describe." [43]

The increasing importance of atomic weapons as a part of our military strategy is also new. The NATO defensive plan for Europe envisages the use of ground troops to force a concentration of the invader's forces into targets against which it would be profit-

---

[41] *Washington Post and Times Herald,* March 20, 1954.
[42] *Life,* March 29, 1954.
[43] Dulles, *op. cit.,* p. 460.

able to employ atomic weapons.[44] Because of the increased emphasis on atomic weapons and in light of their cost, cuts were made in other areas of the military budget. General Matthew Ridgeway, Army Chief of Staff, told Congress he was not entirely in accord with the reduction, for "we are steadily reducing Army forces—a reduction through which our capabilities will be lowered while our responsibilities for meeting the continuing enemy threat has yet to be correspondingly lessened." [45]

Whether the New Look is a more realistic appraisal of the military establishment or whether it is to be a prelude for sweeping economies and reductions in force is yet to be determined. Many observers were skeptical of economy moves which purportedly strengthened America's defense. "If a cut of five billion dollars in the Air Force makes us stronger," asked Senator Richard B. Russell, "why not cut off ten billion and make ourselves twice as strong?" [46]

In 1961 the "New Frontier" of President Kennedy's administration gave promise of more muscle and a better balance of forces in our defensive posture, with a greater capability for immediate action against a "brush fire war" as well as massive power to deter a would be aggressor.

---

[44] General Thomas T. Handy, who in 1954 was General Alfred M. Gruenther's deputy commander of American units in Europe, said our forces there have grown to 400,000 men, "but our defense picture is not wholly satisfactory by any means." *Washington Post and Times Herald,* March 26, 1954.
[45] *Washington Post and Times Herald,* March 16, 1954.
[46] *Reader's Digest,* February, 1954, p. 22.

CHAPTER 23

Policy In a Changing World

The Need for Mutual Security—The Regional Alliances—
Military and Economic Assistance—The Tally Sheet—
Civil Defense—To Make the Security Program More
Effective—The Pentagon Puzzle; Reorganization—Total
or Limited Wars?—Definition of Total and Limited War
—Disarmament and Nuclear Blackmail—Missiles and the
Strategic Air Command—"In Time of. Peace Prepare
for War"

As the decade of the 1950's drew to a close it required no seer to say the United States had weathered severe storms, yet if there was a lightening of the horizon it was very difficult to discern. Our paramount problem was, and continues to be, the question of national security, indeed survival, in the face of the threat posed by the Soviet Union. Thus our military establishment continues to occupy center stage in national affairs. Recent years have witnessed important changes in our defense structure dealing with alliance and aid programs, reorganization of the Department of Defense, missiles, space explorations, and the ever present danger of war. It has been a time of controversy both within and without the Department of Defense. Such discussions are not to be construed as a sign of weakness, but rather that there are different approaches and opinions to problems which affect us all. Indeed, it is encouraging to note the greater public awareness and interest in these questions. President Kennedy faces many of the difficult decisions that also crossed the desk of former President Eisenhower, and from time to time will doubtless institute policy changes with various shifts of emphasis and degree. The problems, however, will remain essentially the same, and the President will need the continuing support of Congress and of a public which will not be satisfied with a second best defense policy.

The Need for Mutual Security

Even before the last shot was fired in the holocaust of World War II, it had become increasingly clear that the United States would fall heir to the responsibilities of world leadership. This leadership, which heretofore had been shared by the great powers of the world, was fraught with many problems and danger areas, the like of which Americans had never before experienced because of their geographic isolation from Europe.[1] The serious implications of these problems manifested themselves everywhere in the devastated areas of war-torn Europe where people were now looking for immediate relief and a rebirth of freedom.

But the United States was not to be permitted to play this new role alone. On the stage of power politics was now spread the shadow of the Soviet Union which had cast itself in an opposing role of leadership without sanction from the rest of the world. The Soviets began in earnest to serve notice that they would challenge the American position and supported those intentions with acts and deeds which threatened the envelopment of the entire European continent. The error of unconditional surrender had now begun to plague the allies. The political vacuum, following in the wake of annihilation, was being filled by the Soviets in accord with preconceived plans.

Accommodation with western ideologies was not the intention of the Soviet rulers. On the contrary, the time was propitious for carrying out the basic principles of the Bolshevik Revolution of November, 1917—world domination through the establishment of dictatorships of the proletariat. There were no public pronouncements to bear this out. But Europe in 1945 was fertile ground for sowing the seeds of communism. Starvation, disease, economic stagnation, and political prostration stalked the world.

If these were the signals for marshaling the forces of communism they served also as signals for the free nations of the world to mobilize their resources to rescue the people. The European Recovery Program (Marshall Plan) quickly went into effect, together with other aid programs and the first dikes were put into place by the United States to stem the rising tide of communism. Economic aid, and later military assistance, complementary to each other, comprised one barrel of a double-barreled ef-

---

[1] This new role was a novel experience in the United States where Americans had lived under the comparative security of two oceans. See William T. R. Fox, "Civilians, Soldiers, and American Military Policy," *World Politics*, Vol. VII, April, 1955, p. 404. See also "International Security: The Military Aspect," *The Rockefeller Report on the Problems of U.S. Defense*, New York, Doubleday and Co. Inc. 1958, pp. 8, 11. Hereafter cited as *"International Security."*

fort to thwart Soviet ambitions. The other was outlined in a system of collective defense on a regional basis to serve emphatic notice that the free world had every intention of defending itself against the aggressive designs of the Sino-Soviet bloc.

The Regional Alliances

By 1947, few Americans remained to be convinced that the United States would lose the peace if some positive action was not taken to halt immediately the spread of communism. Fewer still were those who did not perceive in the new Russian policies the seriousness of the Communist threat to the peace of the world.

As one by one the smaller nations of Eastern Europe were forced into a satellite status under Russia, the United States assumed the major responsibility for countering the Communist challenge.[2] A beginning had already been made when the United States championed the United Nations organization. But this was not enough. With the full realization that the world was weary of war, American leadership began to lay the foundations for a system of international agreements which could be made strong enough to guarantee peace and progress for all. Toward this end, a defensive shield was created in the establishment of the North Atlantic Treaty Organization (NATO).[3] But this organization was only one of several to be developed along these lines.[4]

The idea of a system of collective defense grew out of the experiences of the western hemisphere where, for over a century, the foreign policy of the United States was aimed at maintaining the freedom and independence of the Latin-American republics. This fundamental concept was strengthened during World War II by the initiation of a policy of co-operative effort for hemisphere defense in 1942,[5] and followed in 1947 by the negotiation of the

---

[2] Despite this early warning, by 1961, approximately one-third of the people of the world lived under Communist domination.

[3] The original signatories were the United States, United Kingdom, Canada, France, Belgium, the Netherlands, Luxembourg, Norway, Denmark, Iceland, Italy, and Portugal. Greece and Turkey joined in 1951, and West Germany in 1955.

[4] By 1957, the United States was party to eight defensive treaties involving 42 other sovereign states. It also had bilateral defense assistance agreements with some 50 countries. See U.S. Defense Policies in 1957, *House Doc. No. 436,* January 10, 1958.

[5] Leo Stanton Rowe, *The Third Meeting of the Ministers of Foreign Affairs of the American Republics,* Pan American Union, Washington, D. C., 1942, p. 3.

Inter-American Treaty of Reciprocal Assistance.[6] Two years later the Ninth International Conference of American States further emphasized the purposes of collective defense by the creation of the Organization of American States.[7] Thus, by 1950, when the mutual security program was first enunciated, the United States had extended the shield of security over South America as well as over western Europe.

Communist aggression in Korea, coming on the heels of the Soviet Union's first successful explosion of an atom bomb, spurred the free world to increased activity to avoid the dangers of further aggression. Before the end of the year 1950, the emphasis in the American plan of mutual security shifted from economic assistance to rearmament. Moreover, the United States began to cast worried glances toward Asia and Australia lest these areas also fall prey to the influence of Sino-Soviet aspirations.[8]

On September 1, 1951, Australia, New Zealand, and the United States affirmed their intentions for collective defense under the ANZUS Treaty. Three years later, on September 8, 1954, the Southeast Asia Treaty Organization (SEATO) was announced to the world. Although this treaty did not include Cambodia, Laos, and Viet-Nam, the protocol of the treaty reaffirmed the determination of member nations to support these states in their endeavor to maintain their freedom and independence.[9]

Other collective security agreements include the Central Treaty Organization (CENTO), successor to the Baghdad Pact. This treaty was concluded between Turkey and Iran in February 1955 and subsequently enlarged to include the United Kingdom, Paki-

[6] See "Inter American Conference for the Maintenance of Continental Peace and Security," *Report of the Delegation of the United States,* Department of State Publication 3016, Conference Series II, American Republics, Washington, D. C., 1948, p. 11. This is known as the Rio Pact and includes the United States and 21 Latin-American republics.

[7] Decisions reached by the Council of Foreign Ministers were binding upon all signatories to the Rio Pact with the reservation that no country was required to use armed force against aggression without its consent. Articles 7, 17 of the Rio Pact. A motion to create a permanent military organization within the framework of the Pact was turned down on the grounds that such an organization might violate the sovereignty of the signatory powers. See Josef L. Kunz, "The Bogata Charter of the Organization of American States," *American Journal of International Law,* July, 1948, p. 576.

[8] In 1951 the Sino-Soviet bloc gained control of Tibet and in 1954 north Viet-Nam came into this orbit. See *The Mutual Security Program* 1959, p. 5.

[9] The regional alliances were strengthened by a series of bilateral treaties between the United States and Japan, U.S. and the Philippines, U.S. and Korea, and U.S. and Taiwan. See U.S. Defense Policies in 1957, *House Doc. No. 436,* pp. 123-124.

stan, and Iraq.[10] Although the United States is not a member of
CENTO, this country joined CENTO's Economic, Military, and
Countersubversive committees. For all practical purposes the
Treaty was an interlocking alliance between NATO and SEATO.[11]

In 1948, when Marshal Tito declared his independence of
Moscow, the United States was quick to enter into a bilateral
agreement with Yugoslavia to provide assistance "in furtherance
of the purposes of the Charter of the United Nations and to
strengthen the defenses of the Federal People's Republic of Yugoslavia against aggression." [12] And finally, the strategic location of
Spain, especially for air and naval bases, was worked into the defensive perimeter of the free world by a bilateral agreement between the United States and that country in 1953.[13]

Military and Economic Assistance

Security and the preservation of liberty and freedom by means
of mutual assistance are the foundation stones of the regional
alliances. This system of collective defense is in conformity with
the charter of the United Nations which strives to make collective
security work on a broader basis than regionalism. Membership in
the United Nations of itself is small assurance of security because
of the many devious ways the Sino-Soviet bloc seeks to undermine
and destroy free institutions, even the United Nations organization
itself. The exercise of the veto by the Soviets in the deliberations
of the United Nations is menacingly dangerous to the peace of the
world.

Adherence to a collective defense pact of itself is small assurance of security. For this reason, the Congress of the United
States put teeth into the North Atlantic Treaty Organization by
the adoption of the Mutual Defense Assistance Act of 1949. After
reaffirming the intention of the United States to achieve international peace and security through the instrumentality of the
United Nations, Congress declared:

> The efforts of the United States and other countries to promote
> peace and security in furtherance of the purposes of the Charter

---

[10] The name of the organization was changed to Central Treaty Organization
on August 9, 1959.
[11] Pakistan is also a member of SEATO. Greece, Turkey, Iran, Thailand and
the Philippines are members of one or more of the Alliances.
[12] *Department of State Publication 4230,* Washington, Govt. Printing Office,
1951.
[13] U.S. Defense Policies Since WW II, *House Doc. No. 100,* p. 33.

of the United Nations require additional measures . . . These measures include the furnishing of military assistance . . . [14]

On October 10, 1951, Congress combined the economic development, defense assistance, and technical assistance programs into one law—the Mutual Security Act of 1951.[15]

Henceforth all forms of assistance to bolster the efforts of allies, in consonance with their abilities to support the effort at collective defense, would be worked out within the broad reference of the Mutual Security Program. Military assistance ranging from material, Military Assistance Advisory Groups,[16] and the training of personnel of recipient countries in the United States, could be more effectively programmed to accomplish its objectives.

The creation of local forces was made more effective by the application of these forms of assistance, especially in those areas where the economy of the country was unable to support the requirements for a standing military force to act as a deterrent against aggression. This form of assistance was termed Defense Support and was extended to twelve nations with the result that a force of some three million trained men was placed on the perimeter of the Iron Curtain.

In consequence of the consolidation of the assistance programs, the mutual security program became one of the major instruments of American foreign policy. It was designed to streamline this policy in terms of American commitments over the world. It was furthermore, the response of the United States to the challenges which arose from three interrelated currents of change: the increasing danger of:

> Communist imperialism, the revolution of rising expectations in less developed nations, and the greatly increased interdependence of nations resulting from the onward rush of modern science and technology.[17]

Even more than that, the program became the instrument for meeting the very urgent need to help the free world so that it might help itself.

[14] U.S. Defense Policies Since WW II, *House Doc. No. 100,* p. 31.

[15] *Ibid.* See also *The Mutual Security Program 1958,* A Summary Presentation, June 1957, Dept. of State, Dept. of Defense, International Cooperation Administration, p. 25.

[16] These included American military personnel selected because of technical and administrative ability to serve on the staff of the American Ambassador in those countries requiring assistance. In 1958 a school was established in Arlington, Virginia, to train American personnel in the duties required of them in such assignments.

[17] *The Mutual Security Program 1960,* p. 3.

This free world orientation was also noted by the rulers in Moscow and Peiping. In a bold change of front, the Communist thrust turned toward the less developed countries in order to avoid a head-on clash with those who were prepared to defend themselves. It was not a military thrust, but rather the more insidious economic penetration which placed the Communist partnership in the apparent position of friend and benefactor. They played the pied piper in the critical areas of the world which embraced the Middle East, Latin America, Asia, and Africa with a population of some two billion souls, most of whom were living in poverty and illiteracy.

During the decade following 1950, the problem of maintaining the security of these areas grew increasingly more acute, especially among the newly established nations. This problem grew out of the legislation governing military and economic assistance. Sections 141 and 142 (a) of the Mutual Security Act of 1954 prescribed that such assistance would be furnished only upon agreement by the recipient nation to ten specific undertakings. Legal niceties, acceptable to more sophisticated nations, were viewed with suspicion and alarm in less developed countries. Since most of the new states were recently under some form of colonial rule, they were extremely sensitive to any suggestion of outside interference, and they were reluctant to enter into agreements which could be interpreted as "impairment of their independence to determine their own national policies." [18]

Such a lack of understanding of American policies, in these unsophisticated areas, was plausible. The United States could ill afford to neglect these attitudes. Failure to take positive action to correct these misapprehensions could plunge the free world into the abyss of their own ignorance whence there might be no return. As of this writing, this problem is under the careful scrutiny of the American government and there is little doubt that corrective action is one of the fundamental aims of the new administration.

In assessing the Soviet threat in these critical areas, Lieutenant General Arthur G. Trudeau called attention to the consequences that would follow from the possible loss of Middle East oil. "Who-

---

[18] *The President's Committee to Study the United States Military Assistance Program, Final Report,* August 17, 1959, p. 38. Hereafter cited as *Draper Report.* On the surface Soviet foreign aid appears to have no strings attached and hence is more appealing to these new states.

ever controls the oil of the Middle East," he said, "controls the economy and hence the industrial and political complex of Western Europe." More important than this perhaps, from the American viewpoint, was his statement that "whoever controls the area within a thousand-mile radius of Cairo today can control most of the eastern hemisphere and vitally affect the future of the western hemisphere." [19] A primary objective in these areas then, was to keep them free and friendly. This could be accomplished by the extension of the economic aid necessary to do so.[20]

The Tally Sheet

The development of the Mutual Security Program since 1950 was an indication of the mutuality of interests that had grown between the United States and other nations in previously remote continents. Modern technology had forged this chain of interdependence which grew more pronounced year by year. America had become dependent upon far-flung allies for a large part of the raw materials used by industry. Aside from this economic and industrial cohesion, the United States also needed the missile and air bases made available by these same allies. This combination of facts posed the greatest single deterrent to Communist military aggression.[21]

Potentially, the free world possessed the capacity to contain communism. This potential was developed by the United States as the moral leader of the world. While the Government made its resources available to make this possible, other nations have contributed to the program of mutual security in proportion to their own strength and capacity. It was this close partnership which gave strength and tone to the program. In addition to the contributions enumerated above, the United States has sought, since 1945, to encourage trade among the free nations of the world,[22] to make needed capital available to those nations,[23] and to promote friendly understanding.[24]

[19] Lt. Gen. Arthur G. Trudeau, "Soviet Economic Threat," *Military Review,* January, 1961, p. 34.
[20] *Ibid.*, p. 43.
[21] *The Mutual Security Program 1960*, p. 9.
[22] By reciprocal trade legislation and by participation in the General Agreement on Tariffs and Trade (GATT).
[23] By contribution to the International Bank for Reconstruction and Development and by establishing the Development Loan Fund.
[24] By campaigns of truth including broadcasts behind the Iron Curtain.

Firmly resolute in the determination to protect security and freedom, the free world partnership has served abundant notice that Communist aggression would not be tolerated in any part of the free world. The strong deterrent resulting from this partnership has gone far to prove to the Sino-Soviet bloc that any aggressive move on their part would prove too risky and too costly. The returns which the Communist bloc could hope to expect from open aggression were reduced to a bare minimum because of the ability of the free world to retaliate quickly and effectively. Furthermore, in the danger areas of the world the shield of security has demonstrated the will to resist.

It would be difficult to estimate the number of times the Korean episode would have been re-enacted in the absence of the strong deterrent nourished by the Mutual Security Program. But no assessment of its true value in maintaining the peace could be made without taking into account the willing sacrifices made by the American people who have repeatedly shown "they are prepared to make whatever sacrifices are really necessary to insure our national safety." [25]

Since 1950, the United States has expended over fifty billions of dollars to support this program. The returns on this huge investment have been invaluable. It has been a kind of peace insurance whose premiums, considering the American gross national product, the population, the resources, the cultural and social as well as political values, were relatively small. Furthermore, while the program has improved the economic conditions of the free world, it has also rendered the American economy viable.

Any alternative to the Mutual Security Program would necessarily involve a negation of the basic principles of American foreign policy. Such an abdication of position would result, among other things, in:

> . . . successive losses of free nations to international communism, weakening of those allies who remain, loss of many of our overseas bases, abandoning of our position of leadership in the world, massive increases in our own defense budgets, and heavy inductions of American youth into our own armed forces. Ultimately, the alternative to the Mutual Security Program would be a beleaguered America whose freedom and economy would be severely

---

[25] John Foster Dulles, "Policy for Security and Peace," *Department of State Bulletin,* March 29, 1954, p. 463.

limited, surrounded by a world in which the mass of peoples and nations are controlled by international communism.[26]

Civil Defense

Interwoven with the Mutual Security Program is the whole broad field of civil defense. As the attacking vehicles become speedier and the weapons more destructive, a broad plan of effective defense becomes ever more necessary. The United States could well look to the measures taken by England during World War II for guidance. Passive defense or civil defense can be accomplished efficiently by the fabrication of shelter areas for the population and by insistence upon the dispersal of industry and air defense stations as well as air bases. The known ability of a nation to withstand attack by a strong passive defense "will become an increasingly important deterrent." [27]

Toward this end, the Office of Civil and Defense Mobilization was created on the national level. Steps were taken to instruct the civil population on all phases of an emergency to include the period of attack and post attack for protection against the hazards of all out war. Much progress has been made in this field since the end of the war, but much more remains to be accomplished.

While engaging in civil defense activities to protect the American population, the Government must be prepared to assist:

> . . . our allies in similar efforts. Nothing would demonstrate better our basic concern for the security of our allies than a readiness to co-operate in the protection of their populations.
>
> The main feature to note with respect to civil defense is that it is overdue. It does not make sense for the free world to engage in a major military effort without at the same time protecting its most important resource: its civilian population.[28]

To Make the Security Program More Effective

In 1959, the President's Committee to Study the United States Military Assistance Program (the Draper Committee), made its report to the Chief Executive with many specific recommendations for improving the efficiency of operations in this field. Among these recommendations were those for the better supervision and

---

[26] *The Mutual Security Program 1960*, p. 23.
[27] *International Security*, p. 21.
[28] *Ibid.*, p. 48.

administration of the assistance programs. Attention was drawn toward the need for clarifying the lines of responsibility shared by the Department of State and the Department of Defense. Along these lines the recommendations called for the following:

1.   The functioning of the Department of State to provide foreign policy direction for, and to coordinate, the military and economic assistance programs, should be strengthened.

2.   Clear responsibility for military assistance operations should be focused on the Department of Defense . . .[29]

Because of the close relationship between these departments, few could deny the necessity for closer coordination between them in the administration and supervision of the Military Assistance Program. This fact was well recognized in both departments.

The Pentagon Puzzle; Reorganization

World War II emphasized the need for a more rigid integration of all phases of a national effort to fight and win a war. This imperative need had been learned during the Civil War and again during World War I. Now the nation and the people could no longer flirt with the specious notion that plans for the conduct of a war could be delayed until the outbreak of hostilities and that the necessary teamwork between industry and the military would follow as a natural consequence of a national emergency. Such things as industrial mobilization, procurement of material and personnel, transportation, and research and development, along with a host of associated activities would have to be integrated and coordinated in times of peace if a national catastrophe was to be avoided. This involved a re-evaluation of the entire structure of national security, encompassing the integration of foreign and military policy; the coordination of military, industrial, and civilian mobilization; and the coordination, under one head, of the armed forces for efficiency and economy of operations and administration.[30]

Structurally, the organization for national security in 1947 was basically sound, but much remained to be accomplished to streamline the organization for greater efficiency as well as economy.

---

[29] *Draper Report*, Final Report, p. 11.
[30] See pp. 452-460. Although this subject has been treated above in connection with unification of the armed forces, mention is made here because it also properly belongs in a discussion of national security.

It could no longer be doubted that military and foreign policies were inseparable and closely interwoven in the overall policy of national security. The need for flexibility in the structure was clearly recognized. But it was still to be recognized from the focus of the nuclear bomb and the fearful implications of the new family of weapons the bomb had given birth to. Clearly then, steps were necessary to gear the security organization to the challenge of this new weaponry which was capable within a matter of hours of dispatching missiles on their errands of destruction. This challenge had to be met not only to preserve American liberties, but also to assure the free world that the United States of America would continue to be the bulwark of freedom.

But development by giant steps in the field of military science is not in the repertoire of a democracy. To ensure compliance with the will of the people, it is necessary to make haste slowly. This is not only sound democratic principle, it is also good common sense. Step-by-step development, though slower and perhaps more aggravating, is usually more precise and less painful.

The defense structure established by the National Security Act of 1947 was not correct and precise in every detail. Nor were the authors of the Act so vain as to think they had modeled a permanent organization. They did, however, recognize that a beginning had to be made and that once underway, changes would become apparent and necessary. In this spirit, the step was taken.

On the top level, the structure remained fairly constant through the years under discussion. The National Security Council together with the Central Intelligence Agency (C. I. A.) structurally remain today as they were in 1947. The National Security Resources Board (NSRB) went through several changes and is today known as the Office of Civil and Defense Mobilization (OCDM). The position of the Secretary of Defense has been re-defined in several laws aimed at improving his control and responsibility over the armed services.

In effect, the position of the Secretary of Defense with reference to the National Military Establishment of 1947 was not very clearly defined *vis a vis* the principles of civilian control. At best, the Secretary was "stuck" with an organization over which he had inadequate control.[31] The Armed Forces Policy Council, the Joint

---

[31] See "The President's Plan of Organization," *Army,* Association of the U.S. Army, Washington, D. C., May 1958 v. 33.

Chiefs of Staff, the Munitions Board, and the Research and Development Board as well as the three military departments (Army, Navy, Air Force) were all statutory agencies; that is, they existed by law. The Secretary of Defense could only exercise general direction, authority, and control over the departments and agencies of the National Military Establishment.[32] Clear lines of command responsibility, accountability, and authority for the direction of the armed forces were not clearly visible.[33]

As noted above, the Act of 1947 was amended in 1949 in order to clearly establish the line of command and accountability. To assist the Secretary of Defense, a Deputy Secretary of Defense and three assistant secretaryships were provided for. Although the creation of a single Chief of Staff over the armed forces was prohibited in the new law, it did establish a Chairman of the Joint Chiefs of Staff and the Joint Staff was increased from 100 to 210 officers.[34] With this organization the United States moved into the Korean War and began the build-up of American forces in Europe to contain the relentless surge of militant communism throughout the world.

Meanwhile, as American commitments throughout the world grew to enormous proportions, dictating even the need for a series of regional alliances, the responsibilities of the Secretary of Defense grew apace. But the organization he directed was not flexible enough to enable him to properly carry out his duties. Added to this, the episode of the Korean conflict underscored the limitations and inefficiency of the statutory board structure. The Secretary's staff lacked the flexibility to adjust readily and efficiently to constantly changing conditions and ever increasing requirements for material, for men, and for research and development in aeronautics.

With these facts indelibly imprinted in his mind, together with a strong desire to avoid the fatal error of lagging behind the Soviet Union, whose designs against the free world by now were an open secret, President Eisenhower, on April 30, 1953, submitted to Congress his Reorganization Plan No. 6.[35]

---

[32] *First Report of the Secretary of Defense,* Washington, Govt. Printing Office, 1948, p. 3. See also pp. 459-460 above.
[33] See Eugene Duffield, "Organizing for Defense," *Harvard Business Review,* October, 1953, p. 29.
[34] Public Law 216, 81st Cong. 1st Sess., Ch. 412, August 10, 1949.
[35] House of Representatives, *Document No. 136,* Report of Committee on Government Operations, 83d Cong. 1st Sess. June 22, 1953.

Congress was reminded by the President of the failure to give proper thought to the problems of reorganization and adequacy of the armed forces. Past periods of international stress, he continued, found us poorly prepared and on such occasions:

> We have had to commit to battle insufficient and improperly organized military forces to hold the foe until our citizenry could be more fully mobilized and our resources marshaled. We know that we cannot permit a repetition of those conditions.[36]

But in preparing the country against such errors, care was necessary to avoid peril to the very things Americans were seeking to defend. "We must not," Congress was admonished by the President, "create a nation mighty in arms that is lacking in liberty and bankrupt in resources." [37]

Now was the time to strengthen the ground work of the national defense apparatus if we were to preserve the liberties of the people. Six years of experience with the basic law revealed that the military establishment was not securely founded on basic constitutional principles and traditions. Toward this end, it was urgently necessary to draw a clear line of unchallenged civilian responsibility in the Defense Establishment. There was little doubt that as currently constituted the Department of Defense lacked these "clear" lines of responsibility and authority. Orders going through successive layers of control from the President, through the Secretary of Defense and the secretaries of the military departments, over the operations of all branches of the Department of Defense were a constant and ever present danger to the security of the nation.

On June 30, 1953 Plan No. 6 became effective. The secretaries of the military departments were shorn of their independent status and became, in addition to heading up their respective departments, "operating managers" for the Secretary of Defense.[38] The directive attempted also to lay the quietus upon the con-

---

[36] *Ibid*, p. 2.
[37] *Ibid*.
[38] See Armed Forces Management, November, 1959, p. 24. Congress also approved Reorganization Plan No. 3 of 1953. See 67 Stat 634. The Office of Defense Mobilization was created to expedite the mobilization requirements necessary to meet the threat of the entrance of Communist China into the Korean War. This plan transferred the functions of the National Security Resources Board and the Office of Defense Mobilization to a new Office of Defense Mobilization. It also had responsibility for supervision over stockpiling strategic and critical materials. This eliminated the Munitions Board and the Department of Interior responsibilities in these areas.

fusion and misunderstanding growing out of the controversy concerning roles and missions. The provisions of the Key West Agreement of 1948, designed to smooth out these differences of opinion, were rescinded. Now, instead of the Joint Chiefs of Staff designating one of their own members as executive agent for a unified command,[39] the Secretary of Defense would designate in each case a military department to serve in the capacity of executive agent. This new arrangement, it was felt, would definitely fix the channel of responsibility and authority from the President to a commander of a unified command through the Secretary of Defense and the designated Secretary of a military department. By taking this action, responsibility would be fixed along "a definite channel of accountable civilian officials as intended by the National Security Act."[40]

Flexibility within the Department of Defense to meet changing requirements was to be provided by the abolition of the statutory boards and positions in the office of the Secretary of Defense. These functions were transferred to the Secretary of Defense and six additional assistant secretaries or a total of nine such officers were authorized. According to the Chief Executive, these provisions would be the key to the attainment of increased effectiveness at low cost. Furthermore, the assistant secretaries of defense would provide the Secretary with a continuing review of the programs of the Defense Establishment and help him institute major improvements in their execution.[41] And this the assistant secretaries would undertake to accomplish without interfering in the direct lines of responsibility and authority between the Secretary of Defense and the secretaries of the three military departments.[42]

While the Reorganization Plan was being considered by Congress, the portion of the plan relating to the Joint Chiefs of Staff encountered opposition.[43] Exception was taken to the Presidential proposals to give the Chairman authority to select membership

[39] A unified command is a joint force, under a single commander, which is composed of significant elements of two or more services, and which is constituted and so designated by the Joint Chiefs of Staff or by a commander of an existing unified command which was established by the Joint Chiefs of Staff. See *Dictionary of United States Military Terms for Joint Usage*, p. 111.
[40] *House Doc. No. 136*, p. 4.
[41] *Ibid*, p. 5.
[42] *Ibid*.
[43] See *House Report No. 633*, Committee on Government Operations, 83d Congress, 1st Session, *Passim*.

and determine tenure on the Joint Staff and to place the Joint Staff under the "management" of the Chairman.

There were those who saw in these proposals an attempt to force upon the nation a kind of Prussian General Staff which would ultimately destroy the liberties of the people. For example Brigadier General Robert W. Johnson, a man of experience in the industrial area and a top official of the War Production Board, thought it was only necessary to review the history of the Army General Staff to determine that the proposal to enlarge the responsibilities of the Chairman of the Joint Chiefs of Staff was in fact a carefully conceived plan to create a Prussian type of staff system. Such a system, he claimed, would take a stranglehold on the American economy. Few indeed are those, continued Johnson, who realize:

> . . . the extent of the direct and indirect power of the military in our nation today. Few are those who realize how determined, dangerous, and nearly successful was the military's effort to gain control of key areas of our economy in World War II.[44]

No one doubts the tremendous influence exerted by the military services over the economy of the nation, especially today when the Department of Defense expends more than 40 billions of dollars annually. Few are those indeed who can say that defense spending is not closely connected with every facet of American life. Procurement policies of the Department of Defense are such that it is necessary to keep a sensitive finger on the pulse of industry. To do otherwise would be to commit national as well as international suicide. Labor relations, industrial relations, public relations, etc., are influenced by the Department of Defense not to control and strangle the nation, but rather to maintain a balanced and harmonious relationship in these fields thereby creating the healthy economy the nation demands and deserves.

Arguments to support the position of the President are not wanting. And it must always be remembered that devotion to the nation, service to the people, protection of civil and individual liberties, and the solid support of the constitution are not monopolies of certain individuals outside the military services.

To relegate to the senior citizens in the military services the role of "usurper" does not serve the best interests of the people, and demonstrates a peculiar ignorance of American history. To ad-

---

[44] *Ibid,* p. 4. See also Ferdinard Eberstadt's Views *Ibid,* p. 5.

mit the premise that military leaders are to be looked upon with a special kind of suspicion negates the basic principles of the Bill of Rights and even would make it impossible for a general to be elected President of the United States.

An organization is nothing more than a framework of responsibilities, authority, and accountablility. Everyone is responsible to someone for his actions or for his failure to act. A Chairman of the Joint Chiefs of Staff is responsible to someone and this legal restraint is real, and hard, and difficult to break down. Any criticism of the staff organization of the armed services would have to be viewed in the light of these principles of organization. Criticism is a healthy thing. There are those who welcome it. But a fair appraisal would be to look at the American staff system through the lens of America and her traditions and not through the lens of Prussia or some other autocracy in the world.

Nonetheless, the conjectural debate on the merits or demerits of the staff system in the defense organization continued. There were many who looked beyond the Joint Chiefs of Staff organization in their desire to streamline direction and control of the nation's armed forces in order to be better prepared to wage successful war if war was forced upon the United States. Today the arguments no longer concern the Chairman of the Joint Chiefs of Staff but rather the creation of a "super" chief of staff over all the armed forces responsible to the President through the Secretary of Defense.[45] Proponents of this plan point with great accuracy to the reduction in time in the early warning system. Destructive missiles can be launched not in a matter of hours but rather in a matter of minutes. Consequently, they say, it behooves the country to be ready to place control of operations in the hands of a professional soldier[46] with broad experience in the military service.

However, even this claim to broad military experience was subject to questioning when, despite the relentless surge of Communism throughout the world and the reportedly strengthened military position of Soviet Russia, steps were taken to reduce the armed forces of the United States. This began to take place al-

---

[45] Cf. *United States Defense Policies in 1957*, Library of Congress Legislative Reference Service, January 10, 1958 *House Document No. 436*, 85th Congress 2d Sess., pp. 57-58 hereafter cited as U.S. Def Policies 1957.

[46] The term soldier is used here in the generic sense to mean General or Admiral.

most immediately after the Korean Truce. It was in the midst of the Reduction in Force program (RIF) that a halt was called, not from the initiative of an American awareness to the dangers of reduction in force, but rather from the startling news on October 4, 1957, that the Soviets had put a celestial satellite in outer space.[47] Recovering from the initial shock of this concrete evidence that the Russians meant business, the American people began to take a good look into the "new look."

Acutely aware of the need of popular approbation of his policies, President Eisenhower in his January, 1958 State of the Union message, indicated that he would make some changes in the Department of Defense structure where they were urgently needed. Security of the nation demanded as much and American prestige, seriously shaken by the advent of "Sputnik," had to be preserved or the entire system of collective security bolstered by the United States might collapse.[48] Despite the good intentions of the President and even of the officials of the Department of Defense, it was evident that regardless of the purpose of the plan to bring about efficiency of operation, no plan could work with maximum efficiency unless the people concerned with it sought to make it work. It was not difficult to find reasons why, in spite of the elaborate modifications that had been made in the structure of the Department of Defense, the United States was not ahead of the Soviet Union in the missiles field.

One could look for answers in the relationship that existed between the Assistant Secretary of Research and Development, and the Assistant Secretary of Applications Engineering. These officials held differing views on where the emphasis of the defense effort should be placed. On March 18, 1957, Secretary of Defense Charles Wilson tried to solve the problem by merging the two offices into that of Research and Engineering. Wilson was inlined to place the emphasis upon applied research and engineering rather than upon basic research. The result was the scientific lag in American missile and outer space research.[49]

On November 15, 1957 the new Secretary of Defense, Neil H.

---

[47] This came on the heels of a successful firing by the Soviets of an ICBM on August 26 and in November another satellite was launched into space.

[48] This is merely another example, and there are many to be found throughout the whole course of American history, of reacting rather than acting. It cannot be said that this country has a positive military policy if it is geared only to react.

[49] See U. S. Def Policies 1957, p. 54.

McElroy, in an attempt to close this gap established the Office of Director of Guided Missiles, reporting directly to the Secretary of Defense.[50] But this was merely a stopgap rather than a closing of the gap. President Eisenhower preferred to re-examine the entire organization of the Department of Defense. He could now go before Congress with sufficient evidence of the fact that legislative limitations were curtailing the efficiency he was endeavoring to secure from the Department of Defense.[51] The time was at hand for a bold move toward greater unification of the armed services in the interest of national security.[52]

Many doubts still existed, which had to be overcome, about the advisability of further unification. Former Secretary Wilson gave wide circulation to these misgivings in his opposition to the idea of a centralized procurement agency for common suppliers. Such a concentration of effort he considered "dangerous to our national security." A wiser course, it was Wilson's contention, dictated a clarification of policy at Department of Defense level and then decentralized purchasing in order to promote efficiency and to "avoid the concentration of stupidity."[53]

But by now very serious doubts had been raised in the minds of many members of Congress with reference to the adequacy of the existing organization for national defense to meet its responsibilities. This appeared to be an indication that they favored further unification. Division of opinion among this group appeared to be whether further unification should be sought within the framework of existing legislation or whether sweeping changes should be made[54] in order to clear the air of the confusion which was breeding indecision.

Taking his cue from this latter group, President Eisenhower on April 3, 1958, delivered a message to Congress in which he outlined his principles for streamlining the Department of Defense in order to better meet its responsibilities.[55]

In carefully selected phrases the Chief Executive traced the

---

[50] Department of Defense *News Release No. 1110-57,* November 15, 1957.
[51] Lack of efficiency could also be attributed to the large number of civilian officials in the Department of Defense created by his Plan No. 6. Now there was too much civilian control, which hampered efficiency of operation. See U. S. Def Policies 1957, p. 60.
[52] President Eisenhower appointed the Rockefeller Committee to study the organization and functions of the Department of Defense.
[53] Quoted in U.S. Def Policies 1957, p. 61.
[54] *Ibid.,* p. 60.
[55] See *Army,* May 1958, pp. 30-38.

evolution in organization since World War II. These various steps, he insisted, were necessary, sound, and in the direction pointed by the lessons of modern warfare. But by the caution displayed in the past to re-assure ourselves against the possibility of a dangerous concentration of power in the hands of one person:

> . . . we have impaired civilian authority and denied ourselves a fully effective defense. We must cling no longer to statutory barriers that weaken executive action and civilian authority. We must free ourselves of emotional attachments to service systems of an era that is no more.
>
> I therefore propose, for America's safety, that we now modernize our defense establishment and make it efficient enough and flexible enough to enable it to meet the fateful challenge of continuing revolutionary change.[56]

Congressional attention was drawn by the President toward the vital necessity of the following: (1) The need for complete unity in strategic planning and operational direction; (2) preservation of the separation of the three services; (3) the abolition of the system of executive agents for the unified commands; (4) the addition of an integrated operations division in the Joint Staff; (5) delineation of the responsibilities of the service secretaries; and (6) increase the authority of the Secretary of Defense (a) in the field of Research and Development, (b) over defense funds, and (c) over distribution of the functions of the Department of Defense. Proposed changes also were recommended in the area of legislative liaison and public affairs as well as in the important area of promotion and assignment of top-ranking officers.

Complete unification of the armed forces at department level was not the intention of these proposals. As an effective and practical working arrangement the President emphasized unification at the point of contact—the operational forces—where lack of effective unity could spell the difference between success and failure in any war, limited or all out. Separate ground, sea, or air battles, in Presidential estimation, were a thing of the past. Future contingencies would demand organizational units such as the unified commands which the President called ". . . the cutting edge of our military machine." The entire defense organization had to be streamlined in such a manner as to make these commands truly effective.

---

[56] *Ibid.,* p. 33.

To accomplish this, unquestioned command authority would have to be definitely fixed. Forces assigned to the unified commands would be by authority of the Secretary of Defense, and removed therefrom only by authority of the Secretary of Defense or the Commander-in-Chief. Commands of this type, lamented the President, "we do not have today." And, to the extent that the existing legislation prohibits their creation, "to that extent we cannot fully marshal our armed strength."[57]

It was not the intention of this plan to cast into the discard the traditional concept of separate forces. But it was the settled determination of the President to clear the channels of command to permit transmission of orders directly to unified commands from the Commander-in-Chief and the Secretary of Defense. The number of headquarters between the Commander-in-Chief and the commander of a unified command "must be kept at a very minimum." An increase of the levels between them would court delay, confusion of authority, and diffusion of responsibility. "When military responsibility is unclear, civilian authority is uncertain." [58]

Under existing laws, the military department with major responsibility for a unified command (appoints the commander, etc.) was designated by the Secretary of Defense as "executive agent" for that command.[59] This naturally placed two other individuals in the chain of command, *i.e.*, the Secretary of that Department and his Chief of Staff. In times of great national emergencies this cumbersome and time-consuming device could prove fatal. For this reason, even before the President delivered his plan to Congress, he had issued orders abolishing the system of executive agents. Now, however, he was asking for legislation to repeal the statutory authority of the Chief of Staff of the Air Force to command major units of the Air Force, as well as the repeal of the statutory authority of the Chief of Naval Operations to command naval operating forces.

In keeping with this shift of responsibilities and authority, the Joint Chiefs of Staff were directed to serve as a staff assisting the Secretary of Defense in his exercise of direction over unified commands. Orders issued to the commands by the Joint Chiefs of Staff would be under the authority and in the name of the Secre-

---

[57] *Ibid.*, p. 34.
[58] *Ibid.*
[59] Designation of executive agents was made by administrative order rather than by law.

tary of Defense. The primary duties of the Joint Chiefs were to be concerned with advising and assisting the Secretary of Defense "in respect to their duties and not to perform any of their duties independently of the Secretary's direction." [60]

In furtherance of the unification process at the operating levels, the President abolished the committee system[61] within the Joint Staff and directed the addition, in that staff, of an integrated operations division. Congress was asked to remove the statutory limitations on the size of the Joint Staff and to authorize the Chairman of the Joint Chiefs to assign duties to the Joint Staff and, with the approval of the Secretary of Defense, to appoint its director.

Serving in two capacities had increased the burdens of the members of the Joint Chiefs and made it difficult for each to devote adequate time to his duties as a member of the Joint Chiefs of Staff as well as chief of his military Service. Attempts to solve this problem only increased the difficulty. Solution seemed to be only in additional legislation which would clearly enable each chief of a military Service to "delegate major portions of his Service responsibilities to his Vice Chief."

Under these recommended procedures, the secretaries of the military departments would be relieved of direct responsibility for military operations. This would enable them, under the supervision of the Secretary of Defense, to better perform the primary function of managing the vast administrative, training, and logistic functions of the Department of Defense.

Little could be hoped for in any attempt at reorganization without strengthening the position of the Secretary of Defense. The Chief Executive called attention to what he termed "inconsistency and confusion" in the National Security Act with reference to the degree of direction, authority, and control the Secretary of Defense could exercise over the military departments separately administered by their respective secretaries. The President did not deny the necessity for the Secretary of Defense to decentralize the administration of a vast defense establishment. However, he held little brief for the apparent contradiction that

---

[60] *Army*, May, 1958, p. 35.

[61] Under this system officers representing each of the military departments acted on documents prepared by the staff groups before they were forwarded to the Joint Chiefs of Staff. This was looked upon as cumbersome. However, there was merit in the committee system if only for the preservation of doctrine.

the three military departments could be administered separately and yet directed by one administrator who was supposed to establish integrated policies and procedures. Specifically, attention was drawn toward the need for removing all doubts concerning the Secretary's authority to transfer, reassign, abolish, or consolidate the functions of the Department.[62]

Meanwhile, draft legislation to carry out these recommendations was being developed by the Department of Defense. Because of the urgency of the situation, Congress was asked to consider them promptly and to co-operate fully in making these essential improvements in our defense establishment. In this country, under the Constitution,

> . . . effective military defense requires a full partnership of the Congress and the Executive. Thus, acting in accord with our respective duties and our highest traditions, we shall achieve an efficient defense organization capable of safeguarding our freedom and serving us in our quest for an enduring peace.[63]

Between the time the bill was introduced in Congress and the final enactment of the Reorganization Act of 1958, many issues were raised not only by the military services but also by the general public, and a great national debate ensued.[64] A large chorus of opposition was heard from a host of self-styled experts on the staff concept, who viewed any increase in the joint staff as symptomatic of a Prussian device to be used to destroy the liberties of the people. Some were even fearful of concentrating too much power in the hands of the Secretary of Defense. With reference to the military services three major areas of dispute seemed apparent: (1) depriving a Service Secretary and his military chief of the right of appeal to Congress; (2) the transfer and reassignment of functions; and (3) preservation of the prerogatives of each service.

In the halls of Congress the issues were squarely joined but by a little give and take the President's program was adopted. Changes were made in the draft legislation covering the three areas at issue. The Secretary of a military department or his Chief of Staff was authorized to present to Congress, on his own initia-

---

[62] *Army,* May, 1958, p. 37.
[63] *Ibid.;* p. 38.
[64] See Oscar N. Hibler "A New Wineskin: An Analysis of the Reorganization Act of 1958," *The JAG Journal,* Office of the Judge Advocate of the Navy, December 1958-January, 1959 p. 3. See also *Army,* May, 1958, pp. 21-22.

tive, any recommendations relating to the Department of Defense.[65] The new law was very specific with reference to keeping the three services separate and replaced the phrase "separately administered" with "separately organized." To avoid the possibility that an Assistant Secretary of Defense might bypass the chain of command in the issuance of orders, an Assistant Secretary could be authorized to issue orders to a military department only when the authorization was in writing and covering a specific subject area.

On the subject of transfer of functions, Congress refused to go as far as the President desired and a compromise was developed. The Chief Executive, upon the imminence of hostilities, was empowered to transfer, reassign, or consolidate, but not abolish, any function assigned by law to the armed services. This would remain in effect until the termination of such an emergency and no longer. Transfer of any function by the Secretary of Defense, other than major combat functions, could be made only after careful Congressional review. However, if the Secretary of Defense desired, he could exercise this authority of transfer in the field of new weapons systems and in carrying out any supply activity common to more than one military department.

Generally, the Defense Reorganization Act of 1958 increased the authority of the Secretary of Defense in the operational direction of the Armed Forces and also in the field of research and development. The number of assistant secretaries was reduced from nine to seven but a new position of Director of Defense Research and Engineering was created.[66] The statutory command status of the Chief of Naval Operations and the Chief of Staff of the Air Force was abolished and hereafter they would merely supervise members of their respective organizations in a manner consistent with the full operational command vested in the unified and specified combatant commands. Forces once assigned to a unified command would remain until removed by authority of the Secretary of Defense. On the other hand, all forces not assigned to a unified or specified command would remain in their respective departments. The Act also provided that administrative responsibility over the forces assigned to those commands would

---

[65] The President called this legalized insubordination. See *Armed Forces Management,* November 1959, p. 25.
[66] The position of Director of Guided Missiles established by Secretary McElroy in November. 1957 was merged in with the R and E Directorate.

remain with the parent military Service. Logistical support for those forces could be vested, as directed by the Secretary of Defense, in one or more of the services.

The organizational concepts encompassed by the Act were summarized by *Armed Forces Management* [67] to define: (1) the Office of the Secretary of Defense, including his civilian advisors in specialized fields; (2) the Joint Chiefs of Staff, his military advisors; (3) the military departments each with their civilian and military staffs responsible for training and equipping effective and efficient armed forces; (4) the unified and specified 'commands each with full command over the operational forces assigned to them for the conduct of a defense wide military mission; and (5) such other agencies as the Secretary of Defense establishes from time to time, as for example the National Security Agency and the Advanced Research Projects Agency.

As it now stands, the current organization for national security was intended to meet the requirements for efficient integration of the military services in Washington and in the field. Indeed it was also intended to meet the requirements for close integration of foreign, domestic, and military policies as success in a shooting war as well as in a cold war became more dependent on the effective coordination of all our national policies.[68] This means also effective and close coordination between the Department of State and the Department of Defense. Toward this end, the reorganization of 1958 has established trends which if carefully analyzed and wisely adopted will-provide the kind of national security the nation seeks.

In a recent issue of *Armed Forces Management* the whole fabric of national security as provided in existing legislation and by government agencies, was seriously questioned. Inquiring into the possibility of a failure of the nation's defense mission, the author of one of the lead articles summed up his premise by saying, "Today we face defeat in a grim "trilemma":

1. Continuation of the arms race, to handle the temporary necessity of deterrence, cannot solve the problem of the future security of the United States . . .

2. Disarmament, either unilaterally, or through some negotiated disposable agreement, guarantees nothing except making the U. S. weak against some unforeseen future threat.

---

[67] November, 1959, p. 25.
[68] *Armed Forces Management*, November, 1960, p. 28.

3. Delay . . . the paralysis of not knowing what to do . . . [will] destroy the future security of the United States . . .

The way to national security is not in any of these three directions, but in a break-through to a whole new kind of goal . . . the goal of security for the world. Are we of sufficient stature to commit ourselves . . . to the idea of coveting safety for our neighbors, as we do for ourselves? If we are not capable of this level of motivation, as a nation, do we deserve to survive? [69]

According to this author there is need of a new organization for National Security Research to explore the fields of Public Anxiety, Military Safety Technology, and Political Science.[70] However, these fields are currently being intensively studied by the Department of Defense.

The endeavor in the United States to lead the peoples of the world toward the ultimate goal of freedom, peace, and security is rather new. It must be remembered that the United States rose to the challenge only after World War II and the legislation of 1958 is indicative of an increased awareness on the part of American leadership, civilian and military, and the people as well, of the larger role this country must play to guarantee the security of the world as much as it becomes humanly possible to do so. The organization to carry out these large responsibilities now exists. The extent to which it succeeds depends upon the manner in which officials of the Department of Defense and Department of State coordinate and cooperate in the fulfillment of their duties and missions.

Total or Limited Wars?

The United States, leader of the free Western world, and the Union of Soviet Socialist Republics (U.S.S.R.), leader of the Communist world, are approaching a new phase in history in which neither can guarantee their own survival from nuclear attack. The U.S.S.R. have nuclear weapons and they have an inter-continental delivery capability. The so-called "missile gap" is of marginal importance. The very fact that the Soviets do have

---

[69] Howard G. Kurtz, "Is Defense Failing its Mission?" *Armed Forces Management*, October, 1960, p. 21.

[70] The author maintains that the effort of the Defense Department in these fields is disjointed and "ineptly programmed." See *Ibid.*, p. 21. These needs were recognized as early as 1947 during the hearings on unification. See U.S. Cong. *Senate and House Hearings,* on Unification, on HR 2312, May 2, 1947, 80th Cong.

the weapons and the capability to deliver them gives the Communists nuclear parity with the United States.

The implications of this shift in the balance of power to a state of nuclear equilibrium are of great significance and confront the United States with its gravest challenge in history. Many hold the opinion that an awareness of the colossal and total destruction of nuclear weapons serves as a reasonable safeguard against total war. The reasons being that such a war involving nuclear weapons in mass would result in no decision, for the havoc that would be delivered would most certainly render even the victor the vanquished. For this reason alone, it is argued, total war is not likely to result from any normal series of incidents. It is obvious that if this nuclear equilibrium swings heavily in favor of the Soviet Union, the possibility of total war increases proportionately. Even if the balance of nuclear power should favor the U.S.S.R., and granting them the advantage of striking the first blow, it is conceivable that each side would suffer such terrible destruction that neither side could obtain a reasonable degree of victory. In the words of Sir Winston Churchill:

> . . . it may be—that when the advance of destructive weapons enables everyone to kill everybody else, no one will want to kill anyone at all. At any rate, it seems pretty safe to say that a war which begins by both sides suffering what they dread most . . . is less likely to occur than one which dangles the lurid prize of former days before ambitious eyes.[71]

American national policy has been based in part on the belief that the greatest single deterrent to total war is the threat of, and the in-being capability of, a devastating, mass, air counterattack on the U.S.S.R. This policy has proved reasonably effective to date, and the United States must continue to place heavy emphasis upon it. Recent events, however, have shown that this policy by itself will not completely deter Soviet Russia in its avowed objective of world domination. The pattern of Communist expansion through limited local aggression, such as that in Korea, Indochina, Laos, etc., strongly indicates that the Soviets believe they are in a position, as a result of nuclear equilibrium, to risk local wars in peripheral areas. Certainly this danger is one which the United States must be prepared to meet. Otherwise, the Free World may be nibbled away until it has lost the total war without

---

[71] Quoted by Sir John Slessor, *Strategy for the West,* (New York: William Morrow Co., 1954), p. 1.

ever fighting. Thus the problems posed by limited wars are of the gravest consequence to the military planners and the people of the United States.[72]

Definition of Total and Limited War

Total war is generally interpreted to mean that the entire resources of a nation are mobilized and used against an enemy in support of the nation's policies for national survival, and both soldiers and civilians are subject to enemy attack. But the totality of any war varies among the belligerents. Thus the Korean war was total for the North and South Koreans, but limited for the United States. It is probable that total war for the United States would be signaled by a nuclear attack on its homeland, followed by a massive retaliatory nuclear attack on the Soviet Union. Total war is thus defined as a war in which the United States uses nuclear weapons, without restraint, against an enemy.

The alternative to total war is limited war. In contrast to total war, limited war does not utilize the full resources of a belligerent. Limited war is not something new. Prior to 1914 many wars were limited as to the degree of national mobilization of resources, and also as to the geographical areas of combat. However, under the system of alliances which exist today, there is the ever present and great danger that an attack on one nation will automatically spread to others.

Application of the term limited war is of recent vintage. It has been applied to the Berlin airlift, the guerrilla war in Greece, the Korean war, and the civil war in Indochina. Other popular terms which are often used in referring to limited war are "police action," "local wars," "small wars," and "peripheral wars." In addition, Mr. Finletter classifies "limited wars" as "local wars" and "part-way wars." The difference in the latter is:

> . . . that air power would be used beyond the immediate fighting areas and include strategic bombing as well as close support and battlefield interdictions . . . but not attacking targets of such importance or with such violence as to provoke total war . . . but possibly with atomic bombs.[73]

It is thus readily apparent that the term "limited war" is used

---

[72] Brig. Gen. C. N. Barclay, *The New Warfare* (London: Wm. Clowes and Sons, Ltd., 1953), p. 33.
[73] Thomas K. Finletter, *Power and Policy*, (New York: Harcourt Brace and Co., 1954), p. 324.

very loosely to cover any type of military activity in which there is a significant limitation as to forces, weapons, objectives, geographical areas of combat, or any combination thereof. The question of limited war is further complicated by the problem of preventing limited wars from spreading into total war and by the concept of disengagement in Western Europe which was advanced by George Kennan in 1957.[74]

Disarmament and Nuclear Blackmail

Considerable thought and many millions of words have been devoted to world disarmament as a suggested initial step toward peace. But this is fraught with danger. World disarmament stands little chance of success so long as there is a total lack of a moral and spiritual basis for international agreements between the West and the Communist Empire. Actually, world disarmament could be an invitation to war.[75] For example, abolition of nuclear weapons only, would give communism an overwhelming advantage in manpower, which could very well precipitate World War III. Even if substantial agreement on the limitation of both nuclear and conventional arms could be attained, it is extremely doubtful that communism could be trusted to abide by its commitment for any longer than it served the Communist purpose.

Until a practical formula for disarmament can be discovered, nuclear equilibrium confronts both the U.S.S.R. and the United States with the dire possibility that the present "cold war" may explode any second into total or limited war. The problem is further complicated by the fact that these are not the only two nations with nuclear capabilities. The admission of Red China into the "Nuclear Club" is not a cheerful prospect. Disarmament, while alluring to the frightened and heavily burdened taxpayer,

---

[74] Other pertinent volumes dealing with varying aspects of the subject under consideration include: James D. Atkinson, *The Edge of War*, Chicago: Henry Regnery Co. 1960), Hanson W. Baldwin, *The Great Arms Race*, (New York: Frederick A. Praeger, 1958), Bernard Brodie, *Strategy in the Missile Age*, (Princeton: Princeton U. Press, 1959), Raymond L. Garthoff, *Soviet Strategy in the Nuclear Age*, (New York: Frederick A. Praeger, 1958), James M. Gavin, *War and Peace in the Space Age*, (New York: Harper and Brothers, 1958), George F. Kennan, *Russia, the Atom and the West*, (New York: Harper and Brothers, 1958), John F. Kennedy, *The Strategy of Peace*, (New York: Harper and Bros., 1960), Henry A. Kissinger, *Nuclear Weapons and Foreign Policy* (New York: Harper Bros., 1957), Maxwell D. Taylor, *The Uncertain Trumpet*, (New York: Harper & Bros., 1959).

[75] X. A. Voight, a British political analyst. Letter in *Time Magazine*, January 17, 1955, p. 29.

must not blind us to the realities of the world we live in. As Admiral Joy says,

> We are in a world conflict with communism, one presently being fought with threats of force, with ideologies, diplomatic maneuverings, and economic pressure. It is a fight to the finish. In it there will be no substitute for victory; either the darkness of communism will engulf the world, or the banner of freedom will fly over all lands.[76]

Disarmament also brings into focus the problem of nuclear blackmail. Indochina revealed the difficulty of implementing the policy of massive retaliation. In the future, it seems quite likely that the U.S.S.R. or Red China will see a greater opportunity, at less risk, to nibble away at the under developed nations along their periphery. These moves can take many forms, from subversion and infiltration to open attack. In general, subversion and infiltration must be fought by other than military means. Overt attack, on the other hand, must be met by military effort. The threat of the use of nuclear weapons would probably be made, and therefore we must be prepared to meet this question as a form of nuclear blackmail.

Missiles and the Strategic Air Command

The guided missile captured the imagination of the public and has been sometimes regarded as a panacea for all the complex problems of defense. It cannot fit that bill. Versatility is required for an effective defense organization. While the foremost concern in creating missile systems was understandably their potential in safeguarding national security, their usefulness in the peaceful purposes of science was also foreseen. Most of the space projects which have been undertaken, or are now underway, made use of the propulsion, guidance, and structural techniques developed under the ballistic missile program.

While Sputnik I startled the world, it also created a sense of urgency in our missile and space programs, giving rise to a number of reorganizations. These reorganizations did not prevent rivalry and program delays. According to Dr. Wernher von Braun "the country is wasting time and energy in ponderous reappraisals

---

[76] C. Turner Joy, *How Communists Negotiate,* (New York: The MacMillan Co., 1955), p. 51.

and re-examinations." [77] Since our missile program began to accelerate sharply in 1954, the United States has come a long way. There are an impressive number of prime contractors and subcontractors who are not only tooled up to handle current orders, but are also striving to anticipate, by research, the needs of the future. In general, we have a well conceived and broad base for missile development, testing, and production. In carrying out such a program there has evolved a unique science-industry-military team.[78]

Roles, weapon systems, and missions in our missile program have not been fully defined, but one constant in our recent policy has been the Strategic Air Command which is a combination of aircraft and missiles. Thus, starting with S.A.C. the following is designed as a brief summary of our missile program.

The mission assigned the Commander-in-Chief, Strategic Air Command, directs that he:

1. Organize, train, equip, administer, and prepare strategic air forces for combat, including strategic reconnaissance, bombardment, missiles, and special mission and support units in accordance with directives and policies issued by Headquarters USAF.

2. Exercise command over all forces allocated to him by the Joint Chiefs of Staff or other appropriate authority.

3. With assigned forces and with other forces as may be made available by the Joint Chiefs of Staff, conduct strategic air operations as defined in the functions of the Armed Forces.

4. Conduct such other air operations as the Joint Chiefs of Staff direct.

5. Support other commanders under the Joint Chiefs of Staff in their missions.

6. Prepare plans to accomplish these missions in a general emergency.[79]

The Strategic Air Command is organized into four numbered air forces—three located in the Zone of the Interior (ZI) and one overseas—plus two air divisions located overseas not integral to any numbered air force, a missile division, and other special mission and support units. The three ZI numbered air forces comprise

---

[77] Jack Raymond, "U.S. Tries New Approach to Space," *New York Times,* October 24, 1959.
[78] Bernard A. Schriever, "Taming of the Blue and Beyond," *AFP* No. 1-1-1, July, 1959, Department of the Air Force.
[79] Department of the Air Force, Air Force Reg. 23-12, *Department of the Air Force, Organization—Field, Strategic Air Command,* May 5, 1958, p. 1.

approximately fifty wings of heavy and medium bombardment and reconnaissance aircraft. The one missile division is organized into four strategic missile wings. The overseas numbered air force and the overseas air divisions contain special support units not organic to ZI based forces.[80]

The backbone of SAC's delivery capability is currently the B-52 medium bomber with an ever increasing number of B-47 heavy bombers phasing into the inventory. The supersonic B-58 medium bomber, the Intercontinental Ballistic Missiles—*Atlas* and *Titan*—and the Intermediate Range Ballistic Missiles—*Thor* and *Jupiter*—assigned to SAC are in varying stages of operational readiness. An ICBM unit operating the air breathing *Snark* has been operational for some time. SAC has air-to-surface capability utilizing the *Rascal* and the improved replacement vehicle *Hound Dog.* Weapons under development in 1961 of direct interest to SAC included the *WS (Weapons System) 110A* supersonic long range bomber with borane fuel jet engines, the *WS 125A* atomic powered long range bomber, the recently successfully tested *Minuteman* ICBM utilizing solid state propellants, and the *Quail,* an air launched decoy designed to confuse enemy defenses.[81] Strategic fighter units previously assigned SAC have been transferred to other commands or inactivated. All B-36 aircraft have been replaced by modern jet bombers.

SAC's nuclear carriers are supported in their global mission by KC-97 and KC-135 aerial tankers, the former being replaced by the latter as fast as production permits. SAC's personnel strength in 1961 was approximately 198,000 officers and airmen of whom 98% are in flying units or in direct support thereof. Some 3,000 combat crews are currently assigned to SAC's mission: "To safeguard peace by deterring a potential aggressor through the threat of *atomic* reprisals which could be carried out at any time at any point on the *globe;* in the event of war to destroy the enemy's air power (phase 1) and the enemy's war potential (phase 2)." [82]

The Army's missile complex includes the *Lacrosse,* a surface-to-surface missile which was assigned to units in the summer of 1959. A tactical weapon with a range of 20 miles, it is designed

---

[80] Department of the Air Force, *Handbook of USAF Command, Organization and Functions,* April 1958, Chart No. 17.
[81] "America's Weapons for Tomorrow," *Interavis,* November, 1957.
[82] "Sword, Shield, and Mailed Fist," *Ibid.*

to give close ground support. *Little John,* a solid fuel free flight rocket with a range of about ten miles, is intended to complement the *Honest John,* which has a longer range and has been based in Europe and the Far East for several years. The Army also places high priority on the *Pershing,* to replace the *Redstone,* and the *Sergeant* as a successor to the *Corporal.* The Army's air defense weapons include the liquid propellant *Nike-Ajax* now (1961) in the process of replacement by the solid fuel *Nike-Hercules* which has a range of about eighty miles. Adding to the *Nike* defensive system is the low altitude *Hawk.* In Research and Development is the *Nike-Zeus* designed as the anti-missile-missile system.

The Navy has not been remiss in its missile program, with the development of the *Terrier, Tartar, Zuni, Corvus,* and the *Super Bullpup.* However, the Navy's chief pride and joy is the *Polaris* aboard atomic submarines. This has indeed added a new dimension of warfare. Our atomic powered subs armed with the Polaris and on station, are "a prime factor in the U.S. deterrent to all-out war." [83] Further, the submarine has extended its range of operation. The *Nautilus* and *Skate* by their trips under the polar ice caps revealed the possibility of operations in the Barents Sea to the east of Spitsbergen and north of the Bering Strait around Wrangel.

"In Time of Peace Prepare for War"

In some respects the period in which America is now entering will be one of the most difficult in the nation's history. There is an uneasy truce in the Far East, but certainly the ferment in Asia has not been stilled. There is no effective military weight in Europe to match the might of Soviet arms, and equally disturbing are growing indications of serious rifts between the United States and her European allies. The doctrine of "co-existence" holds out glittering promises, but there seems to be no abatement in the steady pressures of the Cold War.

Dangling like the sword of Damocles over world civilization is the terrifying threat of atomic warfare. Thoughts of total war and extermination fill the thoughts of men with dread of the present and forebodings of the future. Unhappily, America must

---

[83] Leland C. Allen, "The Role of Undersea Warfare in U.S. Strategic Doctrine," *Military Affairs,* Fall, 1959.

learn to live with the horror weapons, and with extreme caution plan for their use in the event of war. Perhaps the future or mutual forebearance will bar the use of atomic warfare, but until then America must be on guard.

The experiences of the United States in the 20th century emphasize and reiterate the need for preparedness and an adequate military establishment. Living under the constant shadow of war forbids a return to earlier periods of complacency and unpreparedness. The burden of maintaining an adequate military establishment falls primarily upon the Chief Executive and the Congress, but in our Republic the people must also assume a large measure of responsibility.

Many people have long opposed a strong military force for fear "the military" would exert a dangerous and baneful influence upon our institutions. The specter of militarism has been one of the most potent influences in blocking the strength and development of our armed forces. Actually, our military chieftains have never disputed their subordination to civil authority and have been zealous guardians of our most cherished beliefs. The military also have been accused of possessing a "caste system" of which West Point and Annapolis are cited as glaring examples. Presumably under a "caste system" only West Point graduates could hope for rank and preferment in the Army, but neither Leonard Wood nor George Marshall were graduates of that famed institution. It is also interesting to point out that those military leaders who became President were most conscious of the demarcation between civil and military authority, and scrupulously adhered to this line of policy.

Perhaps the factors which are really objected to are the military concepts of responsibility and authority without which no military organization would be worthy of the name. The military services have been pointed out as undemocratic, but what other institutions have gone so far and so fast in the problem of racial integration? Far from being antagonistic or a threat to democracy, the nation's armed forces are one of its principal bulwarks and inspirations.

The tremendous cost of our military establishment is indeed a severe drain on the country's economy and in the course of years the cries of the purse conscious will fill the air. Economy is desirable and laudable, but not at the expense of our national security. The country is faced with a unique situation in the Cold War, a position that calls for patience, fortitude, and the long view. Victories perhaps may be few, sacrifices many, but the rewards great if America retains her strength, courage, and determination. The nation cannot afford to do less.

Today the United States has a far-flung defensive system.[84] Never before has diplomacy given America so many serious commitments, and it must be kept in mind that military policy, and its strategic planning, is not separate and distinct from foreign policy. Both the State and Defense Departments must work closely together and the military cannot be weakened without correspondingly lessening the effects of our diplomacy.

From Valley Forge to Antietam to Pusan, Americans have fought and died gallantly for their hearths and homes. In many instances their sacrifices and efforts have been needlessly compounded by the failure of the Nation to provide an adequate military establishment. The United States has traditionally entered war unprepared and emerged victorious. If America is again forced to take up arms unprepared she may well lose the heritage for which so many have fought and died.

---

[84] *Semiannual Report of the Department of Defense, Report of S/A, January 1, to June 30, 1953, pp. 95-96.*

Bibliography

I. Manuscript Sources

Records of the War Department:
Records of the Adjutant General's Office, National Archives.
Letterbooks of the Secretary of War, Letters Sent and Received.
Records of the War Department General Staff, National Archives.
Private Papers (In Mss. Division, Library of Congress, unless otherwise noted)
Baker, Newton D.
Bliss, Tasker H.
Calhoun, John C.
Church, William C.
Corbin, Henry C.
Daniels, Josephus
Garrison, Lindley (Princeton University Library)
Harbord, James G.
House, Edward M. (Yale University Library)
Lamont, Daniel S.
Lansing, Robert
Lincoln, Abraham
Roosevelt, Theodore
Root, Elihu
Scott, Hugh L.
Taft, William H.
Taylor, Zachary
Washington, George
Wilson, Woodrow

II. Printed Sources

Official Documents

American State Papers: Military Affairs, Naval Affairs, Foreign Affairs, American Archives
Annual Reports of the S/A
Annual Reports of the S/N
Annual Reports of the S/W
Ayrse, Leonard P. *The War with Germany: A Statistical Summary,* Washington, 1919
Congressional Globe
Department of Defense Semiannual and Annual Reports
Department of State, Papers Relating to the Foreign Relations of the United States
Journals of the Continental Congress
Maryland, House of Delegates, *Votes and Proceedings*
Massachusetts, *Journal of the House of Representatives*
New Hampshire, *Journal of the Proceedings of the Honorable House of Representatives*
New Jersey, *Votes and Proceedings of the General Assembly*
Journal of the Proceedings of the Legislative Council
Minutes and Proceedings of the Joint Meeting

531

New York, *Votes and Proceedings of the Senate*
Votes and Proceedings of the Assembly
Pennsylvania, *Minutes of the Third Session of the Eighth General Assembly of the Commonwealth*
The President's Committee to Study the United States Military Assistance Program, Final Report, 1959 ("Draper Report")
Rhode Island, *Journal of the House of Delegates*
Congress: Special Reports, Hearings and Investigations relating to the Military Establishment
United States Statutes at Large
War of the Rebellion. A Compilation of Official Records of the Union and the Confederacy, Washington, 1880-1901
Virginia, *Journal of the House of Delegates*

Unofficial Collections of Documents, Writings, Miscellaneous

Alvord, Clarence W. & Greene, E. B. (eds.) *Governors Letter Books, 1818-1834*, Collections of the Illinois State Historical Library, 1909
Baker, Ray S. & Dodd, William E. (eds.) *The Public Papers of Woodrow Wilson*, New York, 1925-1927
Bassett, J. S. *Correspondence on Andrew Jackson*, Washington, 1927
Burnett, Edmond C. (ed.), *Letters of Members of the Continental Congress*, Washington, 1931
Commager, Henry S., *Documents of American History*, New York, 1947
Documents on American Foreign Relations, Trenton, 1947-1952
Farrand, Max. *The Records of the National Convention of 1787*, New Haven, 1911
Fitzpatrick, John C. (ed.), *The Writings of George Washington*, Washington, 1934
Ford, Paul L. *The Writings of Thomas Jefferson*, New York, 1904
Hamilton, S. M. (ed.) *The Writings of James Monroe*, New York, 1901
Hunt, Gailard (ed.), *The Writings of James Madison*, New York, 1901
Lipscomb, A. A. & Bergh, Albert (eds.) *The Writings of Thomas Jefferson*, Washington, 1903
Morison, Elting E. (ed.) *Letters of Theodore Roosevelt*, Cambridge, 1951
Official Guide to the Army Air Forces, New York, 1944
Richardson, James D. *A Compilation of the Messages and Papers of the Presidents*, Washington, 1896
Rosenman, Samuel I. (ed.) *The Public Papers and Addresses of Franklin D. Roosevelt*, New York, 1941
Wirt, William (ed.) *Letters and Writings of James Madison*, Philadelphia, 1865
Thorndike, Rachel S. *Sherman Letters*, New York, 1894

III. Newspapers and Periodicals

Newspapers

Birmingham, Alabama
Age-Herald

Los Angeles, California
Times

San Francisco, California
Daily Bulletin

Denver, Colorado
Post
Rocky Mountain Herald
Hartford, Connecticut
Courant
New Haven, Connecticut
Journal

Washington, D. C.
  Daily Morning Chronicle
  National Intelligencer
  Post
  Post and Times-Herald
  Star
  Times-Herald

Atlanta, Georgia
  Constitution

Savannah, Georgia
  Republican and Evening Ledger

Chicago, Illinois
  Daily News
  Journal of Commerce
  Tribune

Indianapolis, Indiana
  Star

Des Moines, Iowa
  Register

Kansas City, Kansas
  Star

Lexington, Kentucky
  Reporter

New Orleans, Louisiana
  Picayune
  Times-Democrat
  Times-Picayune

Baltimore, Maryland
  Niles Weekly Register
  Sun

Boston, Massachusetts
  Advertiser
  Christian Science Monitor
  Courier
  Evening Transcript
  Gazette and Country Journal
  Globe
  Independent Chronicle
  New England Palladium
  Patriot
  Post
  Repertory and General Advertiser
  North American and Mercantile Advertiser

Detroit, Michigan
  Free Press

Minneapolis, Minnesota
  Tribune

St. Paul, Minnesota
  Pioneer Press

Omaha, Nebraska
  Herald

Concord, New Hampshire
  Patriot

Albany, New York
  Register

Buffalo, New York
  Commercial Advertiser

New York, New York
  Daily Worker
  Evening Post
  Herald
  Herald-Tribune
  Journal and Patriotic Register
  National Advocate
  Republican Watch-Tower
  Sun
  Times
  World

Cleveland, Ohio
  Plain-Dealer

Portland, Oregon
  Oregonian

Philadelphia, Pennsylvania
  Aurora
  Gazette of the United States
  Independent Gazette
  Inquirer
  North American
  Public Ledger

Newport, Rhode Island
  Mercury

Providence, Rhode Island
  Gazette and Country Journal

Charleston, South Carolina
  Courier

Nashville, Tennessee
  American

Galveston, Texas
  Daily News

Norfolk, Virginia
  Gazette and Public Ledger

Richmond, Virginia
  Enquirer
  Times-Dispatch

Seattle, Washington
  Daily News

Periodicals

American Historical Review
American Journal of International
  Law
American Mercury
Armed Forces Management
Army
Army and Navy Journal
Atlantic Monthly
Century Magazine
Colliers
Congressional Digest
Current Opinion
Everybody's Magazine
Facts on File
Forum
Harvard Business Review
Harvard Law Review
Infantry Journal
Interavis
Iowa Historical Record
J. A. G. Journal
Journal of American History
Life
Literary Digest

Maryland Historical Magazine
Massachusetts Magazine
Military Affairs
Military Review
National Guardsman
Nation
New Republic
Newsweek
North American Review
Philadelphia Ladies Magazine
Outlook
Proceedings of the U. S. Naval
  Institute
Public Affairs Bulletin
Review of Reviews
Saturday Evening Post
Thought
Time
United Service
U. S. News and World Report
Vital Speeches of the Day
World Politics
Yale Law Review

IV. Diaries, Memoirs, Miscellaneous

Alger, Russel A. *The Spanish-American War*, New York, 1901
Brereton, Lewis H. *The Brereton Diaries*, New York, 1946
Bush, Vannevar. *Modern Arms and Free Men*, New York, 1949
Crowell, Benedict & Wilson, Robert F. *How America Went to War—Demobilization*, New Haven, 1921
Daniels, Josephus. The Wilson Era: *Years of War and After, 1917-1923*, Chapel Hill, 1946
Eisenhower, Dwight D. *Crusade in Europe*, Garden City, 1948
Grant, U. S. *Personal Memoirs of U. S. Grant*, New York, 1885
Hamilton, J. C. (ed.) *The Federalist*, New York, 1937
Houston, David F. *Eight Years with Wilson's Cabinet*, New York, 1926
Jones, Jesse & Angley, Edward. *Fifty Billion Dollars*, New York, 1951
Knox, Henry. "A Plan for the General Arrangement of the Militia of the United States," 1786, Rare Book Room, Library of Congress.
Leahy, William D. *I Was There*, New York, 1950.
McClellan, George B. *McClellan's Own Story*, New York, 1887
March, Peyton C. *The Nation at War*, Garden City, 1932
Miles, Nelson S. *Personal Recollections and Observations of General Nelson A. Miles*, Chicago, 1896
Millis, Walter & Duffield, E. S. *The Forrestal Diaries*, New York, 1951
Mitchell, William. *Our Air Force*, New York, 1921; *Winged Defense*, New York, 1935
Schoolcraft, Henry R. *Personal Memoirs of a Residence of Thirty Years With the Indian Tribes on the American Frontiers*, Phiadelphia, 1851
Scott, Winfield. *Memoirs*, New York, 1864
Sherman, William T. *Memoirs*, New York, 1931

Stimson, Henry L. & Bundy, McGeorge. *On Active Service in Peace and War,* New York, 1948

Von Steuben, Baron. "A Letter on the Subject of an Established Militia and Military Arrangements Addressed to the Inhabitants of the United States," New York, 1754

V. Biographies, Histories, Special Studies

Adams, Henry. *History of the United States of America,* New York, 1889

Adams, James T. *New England in the Republic, 1778-1850,* Boston, 1927

Ahern, George P. *A Chronicle of the Army War College, 1899-1919,* Washington, 1919

Alden, Carroll S. & Westcott, Allen. *The United States Navy,* New York, 1943

Bacon, Eugene H. *Russian-American Relations, 1917-1921,* Georgetown University Doctoral Mss, 1951

Baker, Ray S. *Woodrow Wilson Life and Letters,* Garden City, 1927-1938

Baldwin, Leland D. *Recent American History,* New York, 1954

Ballard, Colin. *The Military Genius of Abraham Lincoln,* Cleveland, 1952

Barck, Oscar T. & Blake, Nelson, M. *Since 1900,* New York, 1952

Barclay, Brig. Gen. C. N. *The New Warfare,* London, 1953

Barnes, James E. *The Wealth of the American People,* New York, 1949

Bartlett, Ruhl J. (ed.) *The Record of American Diplomacy,* New York, 1947

Bailey, Thomas A. *A Diplomatic History of the American People,* New York, 1950

Beard, Charles A. *President Roosevelt and the Coming of War 1941,* New Haven, 1948; *American Foreign Policy in the Making, 1932-1940,* New Haven, 1949

Bemis, Samuel F. *John Quincy Adams and the Foundations of American Foreign Policy,* New York, 1949; *The Diplomacy of the American Revolution,* New York, 1935

Bierne, Francis. *The War of 1812,* New York, 1949

Borchard, Edwin, & Loge, William P. *Neutrality for the United States,* New Haven, 1940

Brant, Irving. *James Madison, The Nationalist, 1780-1787,* New York, 1948; *James Madison, Father of the Constitution, 1787-1800,* New York, 1950

Brooks, Edward H. *The National Defense Policy of the Wilson Administration 1913-1917,* Stanford University Doctoral Mss., 1950

Brooks, Van Wyck. *Henry Knox: Soldier of the Revolution,* New York, 1900

Boyton, Charles B. *History of the Navy,* New York, 1867

Carman, Harry J. & Syrett, Harold C. *A History of the American People,* New York, 1952

Carter, William H. *Creation of the American General Staff,* Washington, 1924

Catton, Bruce. *US. Grant and the American Military Tradition,* Boston, 1954

Chandler, Charles de Forest & Lahm, Frank. *How Our Army Grew Wings,* New York, 1943 .

Coulter, E. Merton. *The Confederate States of America, 1861-1865,* Baton Rouge, 1950

Curti, Merle. *The Growth of American Thought,* New York, 1943.

Davis, George T. *A Navy Second to None,* New York, 1940

Dean, Vera M. *The United States and Russia,* New York, 1949.

DeVoto, Bernard. *The Year of Decision,* Boston, 1943.

Dickinson, John. *The Building of an Army,* New York, 1922

Dowley, Clifford. *Experiment in Rebellion,* New York, 1946

Eliot, George F. *The Ramparts We Watch,* New York, 1938

Finletter, Thomas K. *Power and Policy,* New York, 1954

Fiske, John. *The Critical Period of American History, 1783-1789,* Boston, 1916
Freeman, Douglas S. *George Washington,* New York, 1950-1952
French, Allen. *The First Year of the American Revolution,* Boston, 1934
Fuess, Charles M. *Daniel Webster,* Boston, 1930
Ganoe, William A. *The History of the United States Army,* New York, 1942
Greenfield, Kent, *et al. The Organization of Ground Combat Troops,* Washington, 1947.
Hacker, Louis M. & Zahler, Helene. *The United States in the 20th Century,* New York, 1948
Hagedorn, Hermann. *Leonard Wood: A Biography,* New York, 1931
Hamilton, Holman. *Zachary Taylor, Soldier in the White House,* New York, 1951
Harris, Seymour E. *European Recovery Program,* Cambridge, 1948
Heaton, John L. *Cobb of the World,* New York, 1924
Hirsch, Mark D. *William C. Whitney, Modern Warwick,* New York, 1948
Henry, Robert S. *Story of the Confederacy,* Indianapolis, 1931
Hendrick, Burton J. *Lincoln's War Cabinet,* Boston, 1946
Holley, I. B. *Ideas and Weapons,* New York, 1953
Hoskins, Halford L. *The Atlantic Pact,* Washington, 1949
Huidekoper, Frederic L. *The Military Unpreparedness of the United States,* New York, 1915
Ingersoll, Charles J. *Historical Sketch of the Second War Between the United States and Great Britain,* Philadelphia, 1849
Ingersoll, L. D. *A History of the War Department of the United States,* Washington, 1880
Iseley, Jeter A. and Crowl, Philip. *The United States Marines and Amphibious War,* Princeton, 1951.
Jacobs, James R. *Tarnished Warrior,* New York, 1938
James, Marquis. *Andrew Jackson, The Border Captain,* Indianapolis, 1933.
Jessup, Phillip C. *Elihu Root,* New York, 1938.
Johnson, Robert U. & Buel, Clarence (eds.). *Battles and Leaders of the Civil War,* New York, 1884-1887
Jones, Robert S. *A History of the American Legion,* Indianapolis, 1946
Josephson, Matthew. *The Politicoes, 1865-1896,* New York, 1938
Joy, C. Turner. *How Communists Negotiate,* New York, 1955
Kinnaird, Lawrence (ed.) "Spain in the Mississippi Valley, 1765-1794," *Annual Report of the American Historical Society, 1945,* Washington, 1945.
Knox, Dudley. *A History of the United States Navy,* New York, 1948
Lee, Edward B. Jr., *Politics of Our Military National Defense,* Washington, 1940
Legare, Lawrence J. *Unification of the Armed Forces,* Harvard University Doctoral Mss., 1951
Leech, Margaret. *Reveille in Washington,* New York, 1945
Lewis, Lloyd. *Sherman, Fighting Prophet,* New York, 1932
Livesey, William P. *Mahan on Sea Power,* Norman, Oklahoma, 1946
Lodge, Henry C. *The War With Spain,* New York, 1899
Lossing, Benson J. *Pictorial Fieldbook of the War of 1822,* New York, 1868; *Pictorial History of the Civil War,* Philadelphia, 1866
McMaster, John B. *History of the People of the United States,* New York, 1908
Mahan, Alfred T. *From Sail to Steam,* New York, 1907; *The Major Objectives of the Navies in the War of Independence,* London, 1913
Malone, Dumas, *Jefferson, the Virginian,* Boston, 1948
Meneely, A. Howard. *The War Department, 1861,* New York, 1928
Michie, Peter S. *General McClellan,* New York, 1901
Miller, John C. *Origins of the American Revolution,* Boston, 1943; *The Triumph of Freedom,* Boston, 1948

Millis, Walter. *The Martial Spirit,* New York, 1931; *Road to War,* New York, 1935

Milton, George F. *Conflict: The American Civil War,* New York, 1946; *Abraham Lincoln and the Fifth Column,* New York, 1942

Morison, Samuel E. & Commager, Henry S. *The Growth of the American Republic,* New York, 1950

Moore, A. B. *Conscription and Conflict in the Confederacy,* **New York, 1924**

Moore, Frank. *The Civil War in Song and Story, 1860-1865,* Philadelphia, 1889

Nelson, Otto L. *National Security and the General Staff,* Washington, 1946

Nevins, Allen. *Grover Cleveland, A Study in Courage,* New York, 1947

O'Connor, Richard. *Sheridan the Inevitable,* Indianapolis, 1953

Owsley, Frank. *King Cotton Diplomacy,* Chicago, 1931

Palmer, Frederick. *Newton D. Baker,* New York, 1931; *Bliss, Peacemaker,* New York, 1934; *John J. Pershing, General of the Armies,* Harrisburg, 1948

Palmer, John McAuley. *Washington, Lincoln, Wilson. Three War Statesmen,* New York, 1930; *America in Arms,* Washington, 1943

Paxson, Frederic L. *Postwar Years,* Berkeley, California, 1948

Poore, Ben Perley. *Perley's Reminiscences,* Philadelphia, 1886.

Pratt, Fletcher. *Stanton, Lincoln's War Secretary.* New York, 1953

Pratt, Julius W. *America's Colonial Experiment,* New York, 1951

Pringle, Henry. *Theodore Roosevelt,* New York, 1931.

Randall, James G. *Constitutional Problems under Lincoln,* New York, 1926; *Civil War and Reconstruction,* New York, 1938; *Lincoln the President,* New York, 1945

Reeves, Ira L. *Military Education in the United States,* New York, 1914.

Richardson, Leon B. *William E. Chandler,* New York, 1940

Rockefeller Report on the Problems of U. S. Defense, New York, 1958

Rowe, Leo Stanton. *The Third Meeting of the Ministers of Foreign Affairs of the American Republics,* Washington, 1942

Scott, James B. *The Militia,* Washington, 1917.

Seymour, Charles. *The Intimate Papers of Colonel House,* Boston, 1926-28

Shannon, Fred A. *The Organization and Administration of the Union Army, 1861-1865,* Cleveland, 1928

Sherwood, Robert. *Roosevelt and Hopkins: An Intimate History,* New York, 1948

Shindler, Henry. *History of the Army Service Schools,* Fort Leavenworth, 1908.

Shrene, Royal O. *The Finished Scoundrel,* Indianapolis, 1933

Slessor, Sir John. *Strategy for the West,* New York, 1954

Smith, Justin. *The War With Mexico,* New York, 1919

Spaulding, Oliver A. *United States Army in War and Peace,* New York, 1937; *General von Steuben,* New Haven, 1937

Sprague, John Y. *The Origin, Progress and Conclusion of the Florida War,* New York, 1848

Sprout, Harold and Margaret. *The Rise of American Naval Power, 1776-1918,* Trenton, 1942

Strong, Josiah. *Our Country,* New York, 1885.

Swisher, Carl B. *American Constitutional Development,* New York, 1943

Tansill, Charles C. *Back Door to War,* Chicago, 1952

Tarbell, Ida M. *The Nationalization of Business,* New York, 1946

Tate, Allan. *Jefferson Davis, His Rise and Fall,* New York, 1929

Thwaites, Rueben G. *The Story of the Black Hawk War,* State Historical Society of Wisconsin, 1892

Upton, Emory. *The Military Policy of the United States,* Washington, 1916

Van Deusen, Glydon G. *The Life of Henry Clay,* Boston, 1937

Watson, Mark S. *The War Department: Chief of Staff; Prewar Plans and Preparations,* Washington, 1950

Wector, Dixon. *The Age of the Great Depression, 1929-1941,* New York, 1948

Weissberger, Bernard A. *Reporters for the Union,* Boston, 1953

Wieand, Harold T. *The History of the Development of the United States Naval Reserves,* Pittsburg University Doctoral Mss., 1951

Winsor, Justin. *Narrative and Critical History of America,* Boston, 1888

Wiltse, Charles M. *John Calhoun, Nationalist, 1782-1828,* Indianapolis, 1944

Wood, Walter B. & Edmonds, J. E. *The Civil War in the United States,* London, 1905

Wilkerson, Marcus. *Public Opinion of the Spanish-American War,* Baton Rouge, 1932

INDEX

539